# THE IMPERIAL GUPTAS

*A Political History*

# THE IMPERIAL GUPTAS

## A Political History

Kiran Kumar Thaplyal

Aryan Books International
New Delhi

The Imperial Guptas: A Political History

ISBN: 978-81-7305-432-7



Published in **2012** by

**Aryan Books International**

Pooja Apartments, 4B, Ansari Road, New Delhi-110 002 (India)
Tel.: 23287589, 23255799; Fax: 91-11-23270385
E-mail: aryanbooks@gmail.com
**www.aryanbooks.co.in**

Printed in India at Mudrak, Delhi-110091

For

Saumya, Aditya,
Shreya and Shaurya

# Preface

The pesent work is a project of the University Grants Commission. The history of the Imperial Guptas has been a favourite subject of a number of historians dealing with the history of ancient India. The Gupta dynasty is known for kings who were great conquerors, capable administrators, and some of them also had keen interest in literature and music. The Gupta age is characterised by all round development in the field of sculpture, painting, literature, science and mathematics. As an individual king, more works have been authored on the Maurya ruler Aśoka than on any other king of ancient India; but as a dynasty, the works on the Imperial Guptas outnumber those of any ancient Indian dynasty. Despite this, on many points the evidence relating to the history of this dynasty remains inadequate, or dubious, and at times it is interpreted by different scholars in a way which is mutually conflicting, and the chronological position of some kings still remains highly controversial. Fresh pieces of evidence are being brought to light by the discovery of new inscriptions, coins, and literary references, and a considerable number of them, it can be presumed, are still waiting to be discovered. New readings of the text of inscriptions, is at times, facilitated by the availability of better facsimiles, and the find of new evidence may lead to confirmation or rejection of the old readings, or provide an altogether new information regarding some aspects of history. In the present work, an attempt has been made to include the latest available source material, and various interpretations offered by different scholars.

In the case of some kings, because of the paucity of evidence, not much information is available regarding the events of their reigns; and there has been much discussion on such aspects as their historicity, or their status, or their place in the genealogy and chronology of the Gupta dynasty. In case of Kācha (Chapter 4), whose status as king is known only from his coins, which are the only source of his existence, the bulk of the matter is devoted to the discussion of various views regarding determining his position in the genealogy and chronology. In the case of Rāmagupta (Chapter 6), the information about his career that can be garnered from literary sources is that he agreed to surrender his queen to the Śaka invader and that his younger brother, Chandragupta, disguising himself as the queen killed the Śaka king, and later also Rāmagupta, and married the latter's widow. Most of the space regarding him in this work is devoted to the reappraisal of the evidence—literary, epigraphic and numismatic, with a view to ascertaining whether or not a king named Rāmagupta existed in the Gupta dynasty, and if he did exist, what was his chronological position. In the case of Govindagupta (Chapter 8), about whose status, date, and chronological position there is a lot of controversy, most of the discussion is related with such matters as to whether he was the elder or younger brother of Kumāragupta I; whether he held the office of *yuvarāja*; whether he served as governor of Vaiśālī; whether the Mandasor inscription refers to his status as a king or as a prince serving as governor; and if he did become king whether he attained that position in natural course or by the use of force, and whether he succeeded Chandragupta II, or Kumāragupta I, or Skandagupta—the three views expressed by different scholars.

The sources of the Gupta history have been discussed by several scholars, and in some cases in great details. P L Gupta, for example, in his *Imperial Guptas*, has devoted as many as 166 pages to the sources. In this work only the salient features of the more important ones have been briefly discussed in Chapter 1. Sources, particularly epigraphic and numismatic, pertaining to each Gupta king, have been briefly enumerated before detailing his history. K P Jayaswal and some other scholars relied much on literary evidence, some of which, in the light of more trustworthy epigraphic and numismatic evidence, appears dubious in nature, and a few literary works which were used for the reconstruction of history by some scholars have proved as modern forgeries. However, such information from literary sources which is not mythical in nature, and is not contradicted by epigraphic and numismatic evidence, has been utilized in the present work. Some references to literary texts are based on secondary sources.

It has been my endeavour to mention the views of different scholars on different problems, highlighting their main points, and indicate concurrence or otherwise in regard to them, and if possible, suggest new interpretations. In cases where the evidence was meagre or indecisive, I have merely mentioned the views of different scholars, leaving it to the readers to draw their own conclusions. The evidence relating to the history of the Gupta kings who ruled after Skandagupta is rather meagre and in some cases conflicting, and the Hūṇa invasions and the conquests of Yaśodharman loom large. There could very well be a separate chapter on some important dynasties contemporary to the Guptas, such as the Vākāṭakas, the Maukharis, the Later Guptas, the Aulikaras and the Hūṇas, giving a connected account of their history. But I have refrained from doing so as I wanted to be focused on the history of the Imperial Guptas. The history of these dynasties is very briefly touched upon in relation to the Gupta history, either in the text or in the footnotes. As the work deals with the political history of the Imperial Guptas, matters relating to society, religion, economy, art, etc., of the Gupta period have not been discussed.

In the Bibliography, under subheading A, is given a list of all the inscriptions of the kings of the Gupta dynasty and the important ones of contemporary dynasties, with bibliographical details, and in the text, by way of reference the serial number of the inscription in question from the list is cited within brackets. This has been done with a view to minimizing the number of footnotes. The work contains six Appendices dealing with certain aspects relating to Gupta history which needed some detailed discusion. In the case of Appendix III, since the views (together with the references) of different scholars, past and present, have been incorporated in *King Chandra and the Mehrauli Pillar,* edited by M C Joshi and S K Gupta, the references have been cited from that work. I have not given a detailed Bibliography as the same is available in *The Imperial Guptas—A Bibliography* by Jagdish S Yadava and Nirmala Yadava and published by the American Institute of Indian Studies, New Delhi in 1997.

When several scholars have expressed the same view, generally reference has been made to only one or to a few of them. In case the same scholar has contributed a number of articles on the same subject, I have mentioned either a few or only one of them in the Bibliography. If a scholar authored a book in which he incorporated his views expressed in his articles published earlier (e.g., A S Altekar in the *Coinage of the Gupta Empire,* and D R Bhandarkar, in *Corpus Inscriptionum Indicarum,* Vol. III), I have mostly cited the book. The enumeration of all articles relating to history of Imperial Guptas authored by me has been done with a view to acknowledging the gratefulness to the editors and publishers of the journals or volumes in which they have been published. It would also give an idea to the readers that I have been dabbling with the history of the dynasty intermittently since long. The material contained in them has been incorporated in the present work with or without modification. The diacritical marks used in this work are those followed in the publications of the Archaeological Survey of India and have been shown in a separate page.

My debt to the earlier scholars who contributed to the Gupta history is immense, as will be evident from references to their books and articles in the text and footnotes. Prof S P Shukla and Dr Prashant Srivastava went through the entire manuscript and offered valuable suggestions. The latter also helped in meticulously preparing the manuscript press-ready and in several other ways. I sincerely thank the two scholars, who are my former students. The Gupta gold coins-types in black and white have been reproduced from the *Catalogue of the Gupta Gold Coins in the Bayana Hoard,* by A S Altekar. When the book was about to be sent to Press, I could get coloured photographs of some of the Gupta gold coins in the State Museum, Lucknow, and also the permission of its authorities to publish them. Shri Vikas Arya deserves my thanks for bringing out this work nicely and promptly.

**Kiran Kumar Thaplyal**

# Contents

# List of Illustrations

COLOUR PLATES

BLACK-AND-WHITE PLATES

# Roman Equivalents of Nāgarī Letters

| | | | | | | | |
|---|---|---|---|---|---|---|---|
| अ | a | क् | k | ठ् | ṭh | ब् | b |
| आ | ā | ख् | kh | ड् | ḍ | भ् | bh |
| इ | i | ग् | g | ढ् | ḍh | म् | m |
| ई | ī | घ् | gh | ण् | ṇ | य् | y |
| उ | u | ङ् | ṅ | त् | t | र् | r |
| ऊ | ū | च् | ch | थ् | th | ल् | l |
| ए | e | छ् | chh | द् | d | व् | v |
| ऐ | ai | ज् | j | ध् | dh | श् | ś |
| ओ | o | झ् | jh | न् | n | ष् | sh |
| औ | au | ञ | ñ | प् | p | स् | s |
| ऋ | ṛi | ट् | ṭ | फ् | ph | ह् | h |

| | |
|---|---|
| *Anusvāra* | ṁ |
| *Visarga* | ḥ |

# 1
# Sources

## I

The sources of the political history of the Imperial Guptas are epigraphs, seals, coins, and literary works. The inscriptions, on rocks, walls of caves, stone pillars, slabs of stone, pedestals of stone statues, copperplates, and on an iron pillar at Mehrauli—the only one of its kind in the Gupta period—are the most important sources for the reconstruction of the history of this dynasty. The significance of the epigraphs for the Gupta history can be understood by the fact that before the decipherment, interpretation and publication of the epigraphs of the Gupta dynasty not a single king of the dynasty was known to history. J F Fleet's *Corpus Inscriptionum Indicarum*, III, published in 1888, comprising epigraphs of the Guptas and their contemporary dynasties known till then, forms a landmark in the study of the Gupta history, and still remains a standard work. Thereafter, a number of new epigraphs have been discovered and published, and new interpretations of the old ones have been attempted. Such epigraphs have been included in the *Corpus Inscriptionum Indicarum*, III, authored by D R Bhandarkar and edited by B Ch Chhabra and G S Gai. Bhandarkar submitted the manuscript of the work to Chhabra, the then Government Epigraphist, in 1950 for preparing press-copy, but it was published after 31 years, in 1981.[1] In between the submission and publication of the work, a few inscriptions bearing on the Gupta history came to light and were incorporated in it by the editors,

Chhabra and Gai. These include the three inscriptions of Rāmagupta, in Gupta script, from village Durjanpur, near Vidiśā (No. 5), the site from where a number of coins of Rāmagupta have been found. The inscriptions refer to the installation of Jaina images by Rāmagupta, who significantly is referred to as *mahārājādhirāja,* a title borne by almost all the kings of the Imperial Gupta dynasty from Chandragupta I onwards. They provide the most significant evidence in favour of the view that Rāmagupta was a king of that dynasty.

One of the most important inscriptions that came to light recently is the Risthal inscription of Prakāśadharman of the Aulikara dynasty (No.78). The similarity in the name-ending suggests that he belonged to the family to which Yaśodharman belonged. In the Risthal inscription, the date for Prakāśadharman is AD 515, while the date known for Yaśodharman, from one of the two Mandasor inscriptions (No. 79) of that king is AD 532. Since Prakāśadharman's rule might have continued for a few more years after AD 515, and Yaśodharman might have become king a few years earlier than AD 532, the former may be taken as the immediate predecessor of the latter, and also his father. The epigraph gives the lineage of Prakāśadharman, and thus for the first time the ancestry of Yaśodharman also comes to light. Till the find of this epigraph, Yaśodharman's position was like that of a meteor, which suddenly appears on the horizon, and after showing its dazzling brilliance, disappears. The epigraph also provides information, not known from any other source, viz., that Prakāśadharman defeated the Hūṇa king, Toramāṇa.

Another newly discovered important inscription, a fragmentary one, is the Ramtek inscription of the Vākāṭaka dynasty belonging to the reign of Pravarasena II (No. 85). It throws new light on Gupta-Vākāṭaka history and their mutual relationship. The reading and interpretation of the inscription is not quite certain as the inscription is damaged at several places, and I have mainly followed A M Shastri's reading and interpretation. From this inscription it is known, for the first time, that Ghaṭotkachagupta was a son of Chandragupta II. It gives him the status of a king, as he has been referred to as *rājarāja*. It seems that he rebelled against his brother Kumāragupta I, declared himself king, and issued coins (of which only two specimens are known) in his name, but was soon overthrown by Kumāragupta I. Curiously, and contrary to the custom relating to marriage in north India, the epigraph, according to the reading and interpretation of some scholars, mentions his marriage with the daughter of his sister (or stepsister)—the Vākāṭaka queen Prabhāvatīguptā (with whom is identified the female bearing the name ending in *muṇḍā* of the inscription) who is said to have been born after three brothers. The epigraph refers to Chandragupta II as *deva-deva*, i.e. 'king of kings' (rather than 'god of gods'), 'lord of three seas' and one who bore the entire burden of the administration of the Vākāṭaka kingdom. It informs that on Ghaṭotkachagupta's demise, his wife was forcibly brought by her brother, the Vākāṭaka ruler, to her paternal house, which suggests that the relationship between the Guptas and the Vākāṭakas had become quite strained.

Some epigraphs of the Gupta period are official, and others, private. Of the former, the most significant ones are the *praśastis*, which were generally composed by court officials or court poets who had the advantage of having first-hand knowledge about the kings and their achievements. But at times, the royal protégés, with a view to pleasing their patrons, and thereby gaining their favour, exaggerated their good qualities and achievements, or ascribed to them achievements, which were never attained and qualities which they did not possess. The eulogistic descriptions at times overshadow historical facts, and as such, the information supplied by the *praśastis* regarding the patron kings has to be taken with a certain amount of reservation.

Such expressions as the glory of Samudragupta was caused by his conquest of the whole world *(sarva-pṛithvī-vijaya-janita)* in the Allahabad pillar inscription (No. 1), or that the king was intent on conquering the whole world *(kṛitsna-pṛithvī)* for Chandragupta II in the Udaigiri inscription (No. 7), and a similar expression (*jitvā pṛithvīṁ samagrām*) for Skandagupta in the Junagarh inscription of that ruler (No. 30), seem to be inspired by the ideal of *chakravartī*, who is supposed to rule an extensive area, at least extending from the Himalayas to the sea.

The Allahabad pillar inscription of Samudragupta is engraved on the Aśokan pillar which bears three types of Aśokan inscriptions, of which one is addressed to the *mahāmātras* at Kauśāmbī, and in all probability was originally erected in that ancient city which had been the meeting point of the important routes running from east to west, and from north to south. The inscription is partly in prose and partly in verse, and comprises 32 lines and a half. It is damaged at certain places, particularly in the beginning. It was composed by Harisheṇa, a high-ranking officer of Samudragupta, who has been referred to as a *mahāsāndhivigrahika*, a *kumārāmātya* and a *mahādaṇḍanāyaka*, and a son of *mahādaṇḍanāyaka* Dhruvabhūti;[2] it was engraved under the supervision of *Mahādaṇḍanāyaka* Tilabhaṭaka. The language and style of the epigraph shows that Harisheṇa was a poet and a scholar of high order. The inscription throws significant light on the personality and achievements of Samudragupta. It refers to his conquests in northern India (Āryāvarta) and southern India (Dakshiṇāpatha), mentioning the names of the kings defeated by him, and in the latter case also the territories ruled by them, which makes its statement more trustworthy in comparison to the vague statements of conquests of many kings met with in most of the ancient epigraphs. It throws light on Samudragupta's carefully thought out and aptly executed policy towards the various powers—the defeated kings of the north and those of the south, the frontier kings, the republican tribes and the foreign powers, and also highlights his great poetic skill and musical talent. The proper identification of the areas occupied by the various political powers, indigenous and foreign, monarchical and republican, mentioned in this epigraph, throws welcome light on the political geography of that time. From this inscription we 'know more of this great king than perhaps any other ruler in ancient India, with the solitary exception of Aśoka'.[3]

The posthumous Mehrauli pillar inscription (No. 12) details the achievements of King Chandra—his defeating of a confederacy of kings in Bengal and his successful campaign as far as the region occupied by the Vāhlīkas, and also refers to his Vaishṇava leanings. The identification of this king has been a matter of great controversy and kings of the Maurya, Nāga, Kushāṇa, Hūṇa, Gupta, Khaḍga and other dynasties, have been proposed by different scholars, but the view that seeks to identify him with Chandragupta II appears the most acceptable (Appendix III).

The Bhitari pillar inscription of Skandagupta (No. 33) refers to the invasion of the Pushyamitras and the Hūṇas, and the victory of that Gupta prince over them, and also to his establishing the family fortune (*vaṁśa-Lakshmī*), which had become shaky *(vichalita)* and had almost convulged (*vipluta*). The non-mention of Skandagupta's mother in the genealogical portion of the inscription has led to much speculation regarding her status (Chapter 10). The Junagarh rock inscription of the same ruler (No. 30) provides the earliest date (AD 455) for his reign and throws light on his victory over 'snake-like kings' and *mlechchhas* (i.e. the Hūṇas). It informs about the bursting of the artificially created lake, Sudarśana, due to excessive rain and its repair by Chakrapālita, in charge of Girnar city. He served under his father, Parṇadatta, who, it is stated, had been selected by Skandagupta, after deep deliberation, as the most competent official for governing Surāshṭra region.

The Mandasor inscription of the silk-weavers' guild (No. 38) bears two dates—529 and 493 in the Mālava era, the initial year of which is 57 BC, and which later came to be known as the Vikrama era (Appendix IV). The inscription throws light on the migration of the guild from Lāṭa to Daśapura (Mandasor), and the building of a Sun temple at the place of their settling in AD 436, when Bandhuvarman was administering the Malwa region under his Gupta overlord, Kumāragupta I. The guild repaired the same in AD 472, after it had suffered immense damage. The name of the king who was ruling in AD 472 is not mentioned, but probably it was Kumāragupta II, known from the Sarnath inscription of AD 473 (No. 37).

One of the two Mandasor inscriptions of Yaśodharman, the undated one (No. 80), records his defeating the mighty Hūṇa king, Mihirakula, and his holding sway over the territories, which even the Guptas had not brought under their rule. The mention of the victories recalls the conventional *digvijaya* of a *chakravartī*, and there may be some exaggeration in his claims. The other inscription of that king from the same site (No. 79) bears the date in Mālava era, which corresponds to AD 532.

At one time the Eran pillar inscription of Budhagupta (No. 44) was the only epigraph known for that king, and it was believed that he was a local ruler of the Malwa region. But gradually, with the discovery of new inscriptions of the king from various sites in UP, Bihar and Bengal (Chapter 11), some of which refer to him as *mahārājādhirāja*, a title of a paramount sovereign, it became clear that he held sway over almost the whole area that had been under Skandagupta, except perhaps the Gujarat region.

A review of the earlier published epigraphic material has, at times, modified the readings and led to new interpretations, in some cases quite different from the previous ones. Fleet,[4] following Prinsep, considered Samudragupta's Allahabad pillar inscription as posthumous. Later, scholars[5] showed that the expression going to heaven in the inscription relates to Samudragupta's fame, and not to his person, and also that references to that king in that inscription as *eshāṁ* (of this) and not *teshāṁ* (of that), and *asya* and not *tasya*, show that he was alive at the time of its composition. The name of Purugupta's queen on the Bhitari seal was read by Hoernle[6] and Fleet[7] as Vatsadevī, but on the Nālandā sealing, discovered later, it was read by H N Sastri as Vainyadevī[8] which was corrected by N P Chakravarti as Chandradevī,[9] and the name of the queen of Narasiṁhagupta on the Bhitari seal was read by Hoernle[10] as Śrīmatīdevī, and by Fleet[11] as Mahālakshmīdevī, but on a Nālandā sealing, the name is clearly Śrīmitradevī.[12] The sealing of Vainyagupta from Nālandā (No. 51), mentioning him as son of Purugupta, leaves no doubt regarding his being a king of the Gupta dynasty; and to him have been ascribed the coins with the title *Dvādaśāditya*, which, because of the wrong reading of the name of the king as *Chandra* (now corrected as *Vainya*), had earlier been taken as issued by Chandragupta III. Perhaps the Nālandā sealings, bearing the genealogy of the Gupta rulers up to the owner of the seal, had been affixed to the correspondence of the Gupta rulers addressed to the authorities of the Buddhist monastic establishment at Nālandā.

A few epigraphs give information, which is different from that known from other inscriptions, or mention kings in a different way. Thus, the Supia inscription (No. 32) and two Vākāṭaka records (Nos. 82, 84), mention Ghaṭotkacha, and not Gupta, as the founder of the Gupta dynasty, and the former refers to Chandragupta II and Kumāragupta I, not by name but by their *virudas*—*Vikramāditya* and *Mahendrāditya*, respectively.

In a few cases, the inscriptions were correctly deciphered, but were interpreted in a way that is historically impossible. A case in point[13] is the interpretation of the figure 529 in the Mandasor inscription of the silk-weavers' guild (No. 38) by one scholar, not as referring to the date in the Mālava era which gives the date AD 472, but as indicating the time lag between the construction and repair of the Sun temple. This would place the act of repair sometime in the tenth century AD, which is impossible as the date, arrived at on the basis of the palaeographic evidence as well as the internal evidence of the inscription, is fifth century AD, and hence the view was not accepted by any scholar.

The epigraphic evidence relating the marriage of Chandragupta II's daughter, Prabhāvatīguptā, to Rudrasena II Vākāṭaka, which was solemnized some time before Chandragupta II's conquest of the Śakas, provides an important datum for Vākāṭaka chronology, since the Vākāṭaka inscriptions are dated in regnal years, and not with reference to any era. It is from Prabhāvatīguptā's Chammak copperplate inscription (No. 83) that we know that Chandragupta II had another name, Devagupta, another form of which is Devarāja known from an inscription of an officer of that king from Sanchi (No. 9).

The inscriptions of Toramāṇa (Nos. 75 and 76) and Mihirakula (No. 77) throw light on the Hūṇa conquest in India during the rule of the Gupta dynasty. Of the three Sanjeli plates, the first (No. 76), of *Mahārāja* Bhūta, is dated year 3 of his lord Toramāṇa. Another plate of the same *mahārāja*, dated year 6, mentions him as meditating on the feet of *paramabhaṭṭāraka*, whose name has not been mentioned and hence there is a good deal of speculation about his identity. The third plate was issued by *Mahārāja* Mātṛidāsa, son of *Mahārāja* Bhūta, and records the grant of land to God Nārāyaṇa. Kings of the Parivrājaka and some other dynasties date their inscriptions in the Gupta era, which is generally taken to suggest that they acknowledged the suzerainty of the Imperial Guptas.

The copperplate inscriptions dealing with the grant of land or village by kings to brāhmaṇas or to Buddhist establishments generally detail genealogy of the family of the donor king, often excluding collaterals. They also mention important offices and officials related to the grant in their various capacities. Some of them record the donation of land by private individuals after purchasing it from the government, and throw light on the mode of purchasing land and on the administrative setup. The Damodarpur copperplates (Nos. 22, 24, 43 and 45), for example, mention the name of the king, the *uparika* (governor) of the *bhukti* (province), the *vishaya-pati* (head of the district), and the District Board comprising the representatives of the *śreshṭhis* (merchant–cum-bankers), the *sārthavāhas*, (caravan merchants), the *kulikas* (artisans) and the *kāyasthas* (scribes and record-keepers). The members of the Board examined the application for the purchase of the land, and finding it in order, recommended the sale of land. The applicant for the purchase of land was instructed to deposit the then prevailing price of the land in the royal treasury. On his compliance, the boundaries of the land donated were demarcated. The details of the deed were recorded on one copperplate or more than one copperplate, which was/were handed over to the donee to be kept by him as a proof of his ownership of the land.

Some copperplate inscriptions, like those on the Nālandā plate of year 5 (No. 3) and Gayā plate of year 9 (No. 4) of Samudragupta, are not original. Fleet,[14] in the case of the Gayā plate, pointed out that the palaeographic feature, the use of Prākrit *uchchhanna* for Sanskrit *utsanna*, the opening expression *mahā-nau-hastyaśva*, etc., which finds mention on records of much lates date, and the indiscriminate use of *v* and *b* indicate *circa* eighth century as its date. D C Sircar,[15] however, dates it to the sixth or seventh century AD. But even the latter date is much later than the time of Samudragupta (fourth century AD). In both the plates, Samudragupta is mentioned as a performer of horse-sacrifice (*aśvamedha*), which he could hardly have performed before the fifth year of his reign. The sacrifice has not been mentioned in the Allahabad pillar inscription which belongs to the late phase of his career, after he had made extensive conquests, which have been recorded in that inscription. Both the plates refer to him as *parama-bhāgavata,* which epithet has not been used for him in any other epigraph belonging to his reign.[16] S R Goyal[17] opines that this epithet must have been used for him in the records of his successors from which a part of the text was copied to replace the damaged part of the original plate; it may, however, be mentioned that in the genealogies met with in the records of the Gupta kings the epithet has been used practically for all the successors of Samudragupta, but never for him or for any of his predecessors, though the non-mention does not rule out that he was a Vaishṇava; in fact the representation of the *garuḍa*, the vehicle of Lord Vishṇu, on his coins and seals would favour it. Both the plates contain the expression *mahā-nau-hasty-aśva* etc. When Fleet wrote his *Corpus*, the first occurrence of this expression was seen in the Deo Barnark inscription of Jīvitagupta II (first half of the eighth century AD);[18] but with new discoveries, it is met with in the Banskhera copperplate inscription (AD 628) and the Madhuban copperplate inscription (AD 631) of Hársha[19] and in the Gunaighar copperplate of Vainyagupta of AD 507 (No. 50), the last-mentioned one being its earliest example known so far. In both Nālandā and Gayā plates of Samudragupta, the epithets used for him from *uchchhettuḥ* to *dauhitrasya,* have been given in genitive, and thereafter from *utpannaḥ* to *Samudraguptaḥ* in nominative, which is grammatically wrong. The use of *v* and *b* indiscriminately, as D C Sircar points out, shows "that the grant was fabricated not earlier than the 5th-6th century, when, in North India, the sign for *ba* began to be replaced by *va* gradually".[20] Though the text of the Nālandā plate shows many features similar to the Gayā plate, its script is of *circa* fifth century AD.[21] Some similarity of 'language, style and content', and the fact that one Gopasvāmī is mentioned as the executing officer in both of them suggesting that he was an historical figure, indicate that the original plates in partly damaged form were available to the engraver of the extant plates to copy from.[22] The genealogy in particular, it appears, was badly mutilated on the original plates of Samudragupta and was copied from that met with on the grants of his successors, without correcting the adjectives applied to his name in genitive (which was appropriate in the epigraphs of his successors as in them the genealogy continued after him, but not in his own epigraphs in which the genealogy ended with him) to nominative, which should be the proper form in his own grant. On palaeographic grounds it can be said that there was a gap of more than a century in between the engraving of the two plates. Since the copiers copied the text, partly from the damaged plates of Samudragupta and partly from those of the successors of that king, some letters resemble those of his time and some those of the period in which the extant plates were inscribed to replace the original ones. In the case of the Gaya copperplate, the seal, which had been affixed to the original plate but later got separated from it or was separated from it deliberately, was not damaged, and was fused to the new plate, with a view to imparting sanctity to the grant. It is because of this that there is variation in the metal of the plate and that of the seal, and also in the script of the letters on the seal which are of the time of Samudragupta (fourth century AD), and those on the plate, which are of a later date. It is difficult to agree with the view of T P Verma[23] that the two plates are "neither replacement of the original ones nor certified copy of the lost records", and that the writing on them perfectly matches with other inscriptions of the Gupta period.

A number of epigraphs of the Gupta period are undated. The ascription of such ones to the Gupta period is done on the basis of palaeography or the mention in the epigraph of a king or some other personage whose date is known from other sources. But fixing date on the basis of palaeography alone is not always safe and at times there is much difference of opinion amongst scholars regarding the date arrived at on its basis. In case of dated epigraphs, the dates are either in regnal years or with reference to some era. But in some of the latter cases, the era, is not specified. In the absence of the mention of the name of the era, it has to be guessed on the basis of palaeography and contents of the inscription, and in some cases scholars hold different views. The Mathura pillar inscription of Chandragupta II (No. 6) is the earliest Gupta record to bear a date which can definitely be ascribed to the Gupta era. From the epigraph it is known that year 61 of the [Gupta] Era was the fifth regnal year of Chandragupta II.[24]

II

The seals of the Imperial Gupta kings provide most important information regarding the genealogy, and to some extent also the chronology of the kings of the dynasty, though the chronological order of some of the kings still remains controversial. The Vaiśālī sealing of Dhruvasvāminī (No. 13) mentions her as wife of *Mahārājādhirāja* Chandragupta II and mother of *Mahārāja* Govindagupta. This led scholars to speculate about her role and also about the status of Govindagupta in the Gupta history (Chapter 8). Ghaṭotkachagupta of a sealing from the same site (No. 29) is to be identified with the homonym known from coins and from the Tumain inscription (No. 19), and not with the second Gupta ruler, Ghaṭotkacha, for reasons given below (Chapter 9). Till the time the Bhitari seal of Kumāragupta (No. 55) came to light in 1889, Skandagupta was the last known ruler of the Gupta dynasty; with the find of the seal, were added Purugupta, his son Narasiṁhagupta, and the latter's son Kumāragupta [III], the issuer of the seal. The Nālandā sealing of Budhagupta (No. 47) contains complete genealogy from the first ruler of the dynasty, viz., Gupta, to the owner of the seal, who is mentioned as the grandson of Kumāragupta I and the son of Purugupta. With this evidence, the view held by some scholars that he was a son of Skandagupta has been given up. The Nālandā sealing of Vainyagupta (No. 51), of which the lowest one-third part bearing four lines only is preserved, gives the genealogy (as partly restored): Chandragupta II, Kumāragupta I, Purugupta (as restored) and Vainyagupta. Of the two fragmentary Nālandā sealings of Narasiṁhagupta (No. 53), the better preserved one provides the genealogy from Gupta to him, and refers to him as a son of Purugupta and grandson of Kumāragupta [I]. The fragmentary Nālandā sealing of Vishṇugupta (No. 58) mentions four names in the following genealogical order—Purugupta (as restored), Narasiṁhagupta, Kumāragupta [III], and Vishṇugupta. The last-mentioned king is to be identified with King Vishṇu known from the coins in the Kalighat hoard, found in AD 1783,[25] which leave no doubt about Vishṇu being a king of the Imperial Gupta dynasty. He is to be identified with the Gupta ruler who was the author of the fifth Damodarpur copperplate inscription. It is now known that Budhagupta, Vainyagupta and Narasiṁhagupta were all sons of Purugupta. In none of these genealogies on seals King Skandagupta finds mention. This seems to be because he was a collateral, while the seals give only father-to-son successions, or, less probably, because of his strained relations with his brother Purugupta, to whose progenies the seals recording the genealogies belong.

III

The Gupta coins (Plates at the end) have been discovered in hoards, over 60 in number,[26] or as stray finds. They have been manufactured by the die-struck method. A few *repousse* gold coins, found in Orissa and Chhattisgarh, bear the legends *Mahendrāditya* or *Śrī Kramāditya*, and *garuḍa* device. The legend and the device are in relief, made by the *repousse* technique, i.e. producing the device and the legend by striking from the back. Some[27] consider them as issued by Gupta kings Kumāragupta (whose title was *Mahendrāditya*) and Skandagupta (whose title was *Kramāditya*). Others hold that as the coins are different from the normal Gupta coins, as none of them has been found in Gupta coin-hoards, and as they all have been found only in the areas that were under the rule of the kings of the Śarabhapurīya and Nala dynasties, they should be taken as issued by kings of either of the two dynasties. S R Goyal[28] opines that these coins were issued by the Nala kings in the name of the two Gupta rulers Kumāragupta I and Skandagupta respectively, of whom they were subordinate allies.

The gold coins of the Guptas have been referred to in their inscriptions as *dīnāras,* after the Roman *dinarius* which were brought to India in large numbers due to trade, are of 21 types.[29] Generally, there has been a gradual Indianization of devices on the Gupta coins.[30] The long coat and trousers of the Kushāṇa type met with in the Standard type of Samudragupta, is replaced by the *dhotī* in the Tiger-slayer and waist-cloth in the Lyrist type of that king. In place of the peaked Kushāṇa cap of the Standard type, it is turban in the Tiger-slayer type. Instead of Ardochsho on the Kushāṇa coins, Lakshmī with a flower in her hand is depicted on the reverse of the Battle-axe type of the same Gupta ruler. Goddess Gaṅgā riding a *makara* on the Tiger-slayer type, queen and horse on the *Aśvamedha* type, and dwarf in the *Chhatra* type, are based not on Kushāṇa coins, but on indigenous tradition. Even in the Standard type of Samudragupta, which is very close to the Kushāṇa type, the *garuḍa* standard replaces the *triśūla,* and the king is shown wearing a close-fitting cap instead of the peaked Kushāṇa headdress. The figures are shown wearing Indian jewellery—ear-rings, necklace, armlets, anklets, etc. The coins of the early kings—Samudragupta, Chandragupta II, and Kumāragupta I, are more artistic than those of Skandagupta and his successors. The Gupta kings were the first to introduce metrical legends on coins.

The coins bear *virudas* of the Imperial Gupta kings. Samudragupta's *viruda* is *parākrama* (or *parākramāṅka*), Chandragupta II's, *Vikrama* (or *Vikramāditya*), Kumāragupta I's, *Mahendrāditya*, Skandagupta's, *Kramāditya* (and on one type of silver coins, *Vikramāditya*), and *Kramāditya* is also the *viruda* of Kumāragupta II, Ghaṭotkachagupta and Kumāragupta III (in the case of the last, with *śrī* prefixed to it). The title of Budhagupta is *Vikrama*, of Vainyagupta, *Dvādaśāditya*, of Narasiṁhagupta, *Bālāditya*, and of Vishṇugupta, *Chandrāditya*. On the basis of certain numismatic features, particularly higher weight, some scholars suggested the possibility of the existence of kings Samudragupta II and Chandragupta III as ruling in the last years of the fifth or the early years of the sixth century AD. Others consider them as higher weight coins issued by Samudragupta and Chandragupta II, respectively.

Chandragupta II issued silver coins in imitation of the Śaka coins after conquering the Śaka territories (Chapter 7). A few silver coins bearing the names of Gupta kings have been found which are different from Gupta gold coins in weight, but in device and legend are copies of their counterparts in gold. A silver coin of Chandragupta I-Kumāradevī type has been reported by A L Srivastava,[31] three coins of this type by Y B Singh[32], and one each has been published by B R Mani[33] and O P Singh.[34] In silver, one coin of Standard type and one of the Lyrist type of Samudragupta were published by Upendra Thakur,[35] a Lyrist type of coin of that ruler by A S Altekar,[36] a Standard type of that ruler by Y B Singh,[37] and one of the same type of his coins and a *Chhatra* type of coin of Chandragupta II by B R Mani.[38] Two dozen silver coins of Gupta kings were seen by Ashvini Agrawal with an antique dealer in Patna.[39] These silver coins are much lighter in weight than their gold counterparts. Some scholars consider these as modern forgeries.[40] A silver coin showing on one side the obverse device of the coin of Kanishka and on another side the obverse of the *Apratigha* type of coin of Kumāragupta I has been reported, which is clearly a case of forgery.[41] Taking these silver coins as genuine, as some scholars have done would mean that silver currency had been introduced earlier than the reign of Chandragupta II who is definitely known to have issued silver coins for his newly conquered Śaka territories of Gujarat and adjoining regions. His silver coins were not modelled after his gold coins but were imitation of silver coins of the Śaka kings. This was done for the convenience of the people of that region as they had been in circulation there for about three centuries. He, however, introduced the *garuḍa* device in place of the hill symbol met with on the Śaka coins, and the date in Gupta era in place of the Śaka era to show that the Śakas had been supplanted by the Guptas. Only two more kings—Kumāragupta and Skandagupta—are known to have issued silver coins with these features for that region, from which it can be inferred that Skandagupta was the last Gupta king to retain hold over the erstwhile Śaka territories. Kumāragupta I introduced a new type of silver coins bearing the device of a fan-tailed peacock, for circulation in the Madhyadeśa, which was continued by Skandagupta and Budhagupta.

Copper coins of the Gupta kings Samudragupta,[42] Rāmagupta, Chandragupta II and Kumāragupta I are known. Rāmagupta issued coins only in this metal and in fairly large numbers; the copper coins of other Gupta rulers are quite rare. This was mainly because Kushāṇa copper coins were in circulation in abundance, and so the Gupta kings did not feel the necessity of issuing a large number of coins in that metal.

The gold coins were used for costly transactions such as purchase of land and in long distance trade. Copper and silver coins were generally meant to cater to the local needs and continued to be issued in a region in imitation of an earlier type, even after change of kings and dynasties. The provenance of such coins are more helpful in determining the extent of the territory of the issuing authority, than the gold coins which often travel to more distant places. As seen above, the Gupta kings issued silver coins for the newly conquered territories of the Śakas in imitation of the coins of the Śaka rulers, and they are mostly confined to that area. Rāmagupta's copper coins, found in eastern Malwa, show some closeness to the Nāga coins and some other coins of that region.

The Chandragupta I-Kumāradevī coin-type suggests the great importance attached to the Gupta-Lichchhavi matrimonial alliance, which is also reflected in the phrase *Lichchhavi-dauhitra,* 'daughter's son of the Lichchhavi (chief)',used for Samudragupta in the Gupta epigraphs. The figure of the king, as shown on the coins of Samudragupta, throws welcome light on his personality, and some scholars,[43] taking the figure of the king as portraying truly his physical features and the legend as based on reality, have drawn a rather lively picture of Samudragupta's personality. The *Aśvamedha* type of coins of Samudragupta reflects the might of that ruler as a great conqueror, who has been referred to as *chi=rotsann=āśvamedh=*

*āharttā* (Appendix II), a phrase used for him in the epigraphs of the dynasty, and his Lyrist type provides a numismatic corroboration of the great musical talent of that king, as mentioned in the Allahabad pillar inscription (No. 1), which refers to him as more talented than the great mythical musicians Nārada and Tumburu. Some Gupta coins were intended to show the king's love for, and skill in hunting— tiger, lion or rhinoceros. The most common type, the Archer type, was meant to convey that the king was a skilled archer. Some scholars opine that the Tiger-slayer type of coins of Samudragupta suggests his conquest of the Ganga valley, the region where tigers thrive; the Lion-slayer type of Chandragupta II, his conquest of Kathiawar—a well-known habitat of lions; and the Rhinoceros-slayer type of Kumāragupta I, of his conquest of Assam, where rhinoceroses are found. Others opine that such depictions on coins are meant to show that the king was a skilled hunter, and need not be taken as an evidence of his conquest of a particular region. Some silver coins of Kumāragupta I depict a *triśūla*-like device similar to that found on Valabhī coins. It is supposed by a few scholars that the Gupta king issued these coins on conquering Valabhī territories, as the Valabhī coins bearing such devices are earlier in date than Gupta coins bearing the same.[44] The dates on the coins help in fixing their relative chronology.

On the coins of some later kings of the Imperial Gupta dynasty, individual letters are seen in between the legs of king[45] – *re* on the coins of Vainyagupta, *ru, u,* or *ma* on the coins of *Prakāśāditya, gre* or *gu* on those of Narasiṁhagupta, *go, jo* or *ja* on those of Kumāragupta III, and *ru* on those of Vishṇugupta. These letters are not seen on the coins of Budhagupta or his predecessors. The presence of such letters on coins bearing the legend *Prakāśāditya,* without the king's name, would favour placing the issuer of the coin-type later than Budhagupta[46] and on this ground, his identification with Purugupta suggested by some scholars[47] becomes unacceptable. The identification of Bhānugupta with *Prakāśāditya* once suggested by P L Gupta[48] appears to be reinforced by K S Shukla's reading the name Bhānugupta on a coin bearing the device of a king on horse and the legend *Prakāśāditya.*[49]

The weight of the gold coins of the kings of the Imperial Gupta dynasty, lacks uniformity and is as below[50]: coins of Chandragupta I, Kācha and Samudragupta weigh 118-120 grains; of Chandragupta II, about 121 grains, but some heavy ones, 128 grains; of Kumāragupta I, majority of coins, 124-128 grains, and a few, 130 grains; of Skandagupta, the earlier ones, 130-132 grains, and later ones, 142-144 grains; of Kumāragupta II, 139-143 grains; of Budhagupta, 141.4-144.5 grains; of Vainyagupta and Narasiṁhagupta, 144.5-148 grains; of Kumāragupta III, 147-148 and those of Vishṇugupta, 149-151 grains.

While the weight of the Gupta gold coins generally increased with successive generations of kings, the percentage of gold generally decreased. The following information for the percentage of gold in the coins is after P L Gupta.[51] The presence of gold in coins of the Gupta kings up to Chandragupta II is above 80%; in the coins of Kumāragupta I, 70 to 78%; in the coins of Skandagupta, 67 to 79%; and in those of Kumāragupta II, 79%. In the coins of Budhagupta, the gold content is 70 to 78%, in those of Prakāśāditya, 77%, and in those of Vainyagupta, 73%. The gold content in type I coins of Narasiṁhagupta is 71 %, and in his Type II coins and in those of Kumāragupta III, 54 %. In the coins of Vishṇugupta, the percentage of gold is as low as 43%. It may be stated that in the case of Skandagupta's heavy weight coins, though the percentage of gold is less than in the coins of his predecessors, yet because of increase in weight of the coins, the gold content per coin is almost the same as that in the coins of the earlier kings, and the lighter variety of his own coins. The coins of Vishṇugupta, with extremely poor percentage of gold, though higher in weight, reflect poor economic condition.

The Guptas began issuing gold coins on the weight-standard of 122-123 grains, which was earlier followed by the Kushāṇas. P L Gupta[52] shows disagreement with the view of Altekar[53] that the Kushāṇas themselves issued their coins in imitation of the weight-standard of Roman coins, and also with another view of that scholar that the Gupta kings increased the weight of their gold coins in successive generations in order to attain the *suvarṇa* standard. As to the first view of Altekar, Gupta points out that while the Kushāṇas issued coins on 122-123 grains, the majority of Roman kings immediately preceding the Kushāṇas, issued coins of much lesser weight, about 112-113 grains. As to the second view of Altekar, Gupta states that the weight of the coins of Skandagupta reaches about 144 grains, very near the *suvarṇa* standard, but it did not stop at that point as it should have if the aim had been to attain the *suvarṇa* standard, but continued to increase and reached as high as 151 grains during the reign of Vishṇugupta. S R Goyal[54] opines that if the intention was to achieve *suvarṇa* standard, then it would have been achieved at one stroke, rather than gradually.

As regards the catalogues dealing with Gupta coins, those by V A Smith (1906), John Allan (1914), A S Altekar (1954), B Ch Chhabra (1986), and by P L Gupta and Sarojini Srivastava (1986) may be mentioned (which have been detailed in the Biliography). The *Coinage of the Gupta Empire*, in the *Corpus of Indian Coins* series, by Altekar (1957), deals with all the important aspects of the Gupta coins meticulously and in historical perspective.

IV

Literary evidence for the Gupta history is not as direct and reliable as the epigraphic or numismatic. K P Jayaswal and some other scholars have liberally used literary sources for the reconstruction of the Gupta history. Most of the works referring to the Gupta dynasty or Gupta kings, directly or indirectly, belong to the post-Gupta period, and the date of some of them cannot be ascertained with certainty. Further, the information met with in some of them is contradicted by the known facts of history and a few of them have proved to be forgeries of modern times.

In Kālidāsa's *Raghuvaṁśam*[55] is mentioned the handing over of the throne by the ruling king to Prince Raghu, happiness of the people over the decision, jealousy of the feudatory rulers, Raghu's subduing of the enemies and his making fresh conquests. These pieces of information relating to Raghu, resemble with what has been stated in the case of Samudragupta's being nominated as successor by his father in the Allahabad pillar inscription (No. 1).[56] S R Goyal[57] states that Raghu's conquests described by Kālidāsa, whom, like some other scholars, he considers as a contemporary of Samudragupta and Chandragupta II, may be used for the reconstruction of the Gupta conquests, as his conquests of Pārasīkas and the Hūṇas are similar to the Gupta conquest of the Vāhlīkas. The fact that in the same text the king of Magadha is the first to be introduced in the *svayaṁvara* of Indumatī, is taken to suggest the importance of the Gupta king.[58] The epic *Setubandha*, now not available, according to its commentary, was either composed by Kālidāsa, or by Pravarasena (identified by some scholars with Pravarasena II Vākāṭaka) and edited by Kālidāsa.[59] This would indicate Gupta influence on the Vākāṭakas, as Kālidāsa is considered by many scholars as a court poet of Chandragupta II Vikramāditya.

In the *Harsha-charita*,[60] there is a significant reference to Chandragupta in the guise of a fair lady, killing the Śaka king, who coveted the wife of another person. It corroborates the evidence of the *Devī-Chandraguptam,* as quoted by later writers, relating to Chandragupta II's killing the Śaka king who had forced his elder brother Rāmagupta to agree to surrender his queen. It suggests that the story relating to Rāmagupta was known to Bāṇa (first half of the seventh century AD). The commentary of Śaṅkara (*c.* twelfth century AD or may be later) on the *Harsha-charita* elaborates that the queen in question was Dhruvadevī, the wife of the brother of Chandragupta II.[61]

Quite significant is the evidence of Viśākhadatta's Sanskrit drama *Devī-Chandraguptam,* not found in original but passages from it have been preserved in the form of quotations in later works, which have been discussed in the context of Rāmagupta (Chapter 6), and are mentioned here very briefly. Some fragments of the drama are met with in the *Nāṭya-darpaṇa* of Rāmachandra and Guṇachandra (12th century AD), and three extracts of it are found in the *Śṛiṅgāra-prakāśa* of Bhoja. Passages of this drama have also been found in *Nāṭaka-lakshaṇa-ratna-kośa* of Sāgaranandī. R D Banerji[62] was the first scholar to utilize these extracts for the reconstruction of the history. According to the story, drawn on the basis of the various quotes from the drama of Viśākhadatta, Rāmagupta, with the consent of his ministers, agreed to surrender his queen to the invading Śaka king. His brave younger brother resorted to *vetāla-sādhanā,* and later in the guise of the queen entered the Śaka camp, along with some soldiers in the guise of females, and killed the Śaka king. This made Rāmagupta jealous of him. In order to save himself, Chandragupta feigned madness. The events thereafter are not mentioned in the available fragments of the drama, but other sources (Chapter 6, below) indicate that Chandragupta in that condition entered the palace, killed the unguarded Rāmagupta, and thereafter, married Dhruvadevī.

K P Jayaswal[63] considered *Kaumudī-mahotsava* as an historical drama, which according to him was written in *c* AD 350, and is based on events contemporary to Chandragupta I. But though the *Bharata-vākya* of the play states that it depicts contemporary events, it is difficult to believe that it actually does so. As P L Gupta[64] points out, some dramatists put anachronous words into the mouth of the *sūtradhāra* of the play, and also that the influence of Bāṇa, Bhavabhūti and Daṇḍin, who all belonged to the post-Gupta period, can be seen on this work. Vijjikā, the authoress of this work, has been identified by some scholars with Vijayabhaṭṭārikā, daughter-in-law of the Chālukya king, Pulakeśin II.[65] The work, as will be shown below (Chapter 3), is hardly of any value for the reconstruction of the Gupta history.

Jinasena's *Hari-vaṁśa*[66] (completed in 705 Śaka = AD 783), assigns a total period of 231 years for the Gupta rule. From it, it is known that the Gupta rule began 241 years after the commencement of the Śaka era, that is, in (78+241 =) AD 319. The *Kuvalaya-mālā* of Udyotanasūrī (completed in AD 779) mentions Hūṇa king, Toramāṇa and his *guru* Harigupta of the Gupta family, whose disciple was Devagupta.[67] The position of Devagupta and Harigupta in the Gupta history cannot be ascertained with certainty. Devagupta is also known as another name of Chandragupta II, but he ruled much earlier than Toramāṇa. The work, *Tiloya-paṇṇati* of Jadavāsaha (Yativṛishabha), at one place, gives the total period of reign for the Guptas as 231 years, and at another, 255 years, which has been interpreted by some scholars as referring to the end of the Gupta rule in Magadha-cum-Bengal and the Orissan regions respectively, the latter marking its final phase.[68]

In the *Auchitya-vichāra-charchā* of Kshemendra are quoted two verses from *Kuntaleśvara-dautya* (now lost), attributed to Kālidāsa.[69] According to it, Vikramāditya (i.e. Chandragupta II) deputed Kālidāsa to the court of the Kuntala king. From a passage quoted from that work by Bhoja and Rājaśekhara, Kālidāsa reported to Vikramāditya that the Kuntala king was deeply interested in wine and women. Vikramāditya's response was that the Kuntala king may enjoy life the way he liked, as he (Vikramāditya) would take care of the administration of the kingdom of that ruler.[70] Some scholars identify Kuntaleśvara with Vākāṭaka king Pravarasena II.

According to the *Rāja-taraṅgiṇī*,[71] Vikramāditya of Ujjayinī appointed Mātṛigupta as the king of Kashmir, who after his patron's death, abdicated in favour of Pravarasena. Some scholars identify Vikramāditya with Chandragupta II, Mātṛigupta with Kālidāsa, and Pravarasena with the Vākāṭaka king Pravarasena II;[72] others rightly reject these identifications.

The *Kāvya-mīmāṁsā* of Rājaśekhara quotes a verse,[73] which says that King Śarmagupta, when attacked by a Khaśa king of the Himalayan region, agreed to the surrendering of his queen Dhruvasvāminī. This has been cited as an example of an historical event. It lends some support to the story of *Devī-Chandraguptam*, referred to above. The work refers to Kārttikeya who is identified by Mirashi[74] with Rājaśekhara's patron, King Mahīpāla of the Gurjara-Pratīhāra dynasty. Some identify Kārttikeya of the verse with Kumāragupta I who was named after that deity.[75] But others raise objection to it, stating that the court poet would not have dared writing such a derogatory thing relating to the mother of the reigning king.[76] D R Bhandarkar takes Kārttikeya-nagara as one compound and identifies the town with Baijnath in Almora district and states that the king whose praises were sung should be identified with Chandragupta II.[77]

In the *Kathā-saritsāgara* of Somadeva[78] (11th century AD), it is said that Mahendrāditya, a very powerful king of charitable disposition, anointing his son Vikramāditya as king, went to Vārāṇasī with his queen, Saumyadarśanā.[79] Vikramāditya conquered regions in the south, west and central India, Gangetic plain and Kashmir, and destroyed the Kambojas, Yavanas, the Hūṇas, the Tokharians and the Persians. *Mahendrāditya* is a title of Kumāragupta I, and though *Vikramāditya* is known as the popular title of Chandragupta II, it is also met with on a coin-type of Skandagupta whose usual title was *Kramāditya*, which means almost the same as *Vikramāditya*. It has been suggested that Kumāragupta I abdicated in favour of Skandagupta. However, the only foreign people definitely defeated by Skandagupta are the Hūṇas, and the defeat of the Yavanas, the Tokharians and Persians does not fit in the context of the reign of that Gupta king. It is extremely doubtful that Kumāragupta I abdicated (Chapter 9).

The *Ubhayasārikā* of Vararuchi and the *Pādatāḍitakam* of Śyāmilaka forming part of the *Chaturbhāṇī*, refer to Kumāragupta I and Skandagupta, respectively.[80] The *Āyurvedadīpikā* commentary of Chakrapāṇidatta (twelfth century) mentions Chandragupta II disguising himself as a lunatic with a view to killing his brother,[81] which corroborates similar evidence of the *Devī-Chandraguptam*.

The *Ārya-Mañjuśrī-mūlakalpa*,[82] a Mahāyānist work of pre-eleventh century, generally gives the title of the king or the first letter of his name, or the first letter of the name of the tribe, rather than the full name of the king or tribe. In verses 646-47, it refers to kings Samudra, Vikrama, Mahendra and Sa-initialled, whose another name was Devarāja and who was succeeded by Bāla.[83] These kings have been identified with Samudragupta, Chandragupta II Vikramāditya, Kumāragupta I Mahendrāditya, Skandagupta, and Narasiṁhagupta Bālāditya, respectively. It mentions Kumāra in verse 674, Ukāra in verse 675, Deva in verse 676, Chandra in verse 677, Dvādaśa in verse 678, Bhakārākhya in verse 760 and Pakārākhya in verse 761.[84] Kumāra has been identified with Kumāragupta II by some, and Kumāragupta III by others. Ukāra is taken to stand for Upendra which is one of the names of Vishṇu and is identified with Vishṇugupta. Deva is identified by some with Budhagupta (=Buddhagupta; Buddha is a *deva,* i.e. god, for the Buddhists) or it may be a name of a king not known from any other source. Chandra is taken by some scholars as Chandragupta III, to whom some scholars ascribe the heavyweight coins bearing the name Chandra. Dvādaśa is identified with Vainyagupta *Dvādaśāditya*, Bhakāra with Bhānugupta and Pakāra with Prakaṭāditya of the Sarnath inscription, or with Prakāśāditya of coins. There is, however, no unanimity amongst scholars regarding these identifications. It appears that the author of the *Ārya-Mañjuśrī-mūlakalpa* was acquainted with the names of the kings of the Imperial Gupta dynasty, but he did not possess proper knowledge about their chronological position and their activities. It is also possible that in the work the verses are not arranged in proper sequence. K P Jayaswal[85] considers the *Ārya-Mañjuśrī-mūlakalpa,* as 'a true history' for the Gupta period. S R Goyal[86] is of the view that the work 'helps us in giving a coherent picture to the data supplied by the epigraphic and numismatic sources.' Majumdar,[87] and many other scholars, however, do not consider it as a reliable source of history.

According to the *Chandragarbha-pariprichchhā,* a Mahāyānist Sanskrit Buddhist text, Duḥprasahahasta, son of King Mahendrasena of Kauśāmbī, defeated the invaders—the Yavanas, the Pahlikas and the Śakunas.[88] Mahendrasena is identified by K P Jayaswal with Kumāragupta I, and his son with Skandagupta, and the Yavanas with the Hūṇas, Pahlikas with Sassanians, and Śakunas with the Kushāṇas. However, Kauśāmbī does not seem to have been the capital of the Imperial Guptas, at least during the time of Kumāragupta I, though it would have been an important city within the kingdom. The reason for Kumāragupta I's special association with Kauśāmbī, has been discussed below (Appendix VI). There does not seem the possibility of the Yavanas and the Pahlavas attacking the Gupta empire. In view of this, its evidence regarding abdication of the king mentioned in the work also becomes doubtful.[89]

The *Vasubandhu-charita* mentions a King Vikramāditya who sent his queen and Prince Bālāditya to Vasubandhu for learning the tenets of Buddhism, and that after becoming king, Bālāditya patronized that Buddhist scholar. Takakusu fixed the date of Vasubandhu between AD 420 and 500. The king and the prince, however, have been identified by different scholars variously as Chandragupta I and Samudragupta,

Chandragupta II and Kumāragupta I, Chandragupta II and Govindagupta, Skandagupta and Narasiṁhagupta Bālāditya, and Purugupta and Narasiṁhagupta Bālāditya respectively. It may, however be stated that while of the Gupta kings Chandragupta II and Skandagupta are known as *Vikramāditya*, Narasiṁhagupta alone is known as *Bālāditya*.

In the *Kāvyālaṅkāra-sūtra-vṛitti* of Vāmana,[90] is quoted a verse, of which neither the source nor the author is known, mentioning one Chandraprakāśa, son of Chandragupta. In it there is a reference to *sāchivya* (ministership) of either Subandhu, author of the *Vāsavadattā*, or of Vasubandhu, a Buddhist scholar, in relation to the king. Some scholars consider Chandraprakāśa as name of the king, while others take it as an epithet meaning 'who was like the light of the moon'. Since Chandraprakāśa has been referred to as *tanaya* (son) of Chandragupta, the father and son have generally been identified as either Chandragupta I and Samudragupta or Chandragupta II and Kumāragupta I.

Very little has been preserved of the work *Kṛishṇa-charitam*, and that too only from the two cantos. At the end of the both, it is stated that *Mahārājādhirāja Parama-bhāgavata* Samudragupta was its author, and in the first one, Samudragupta is called *Vikramāṅka*, and in the second, as *Parākramāṅka*, which (latter) is his typical title. Majority of the scholars consider the work is a modern forgery,[91] and only a few take it as genuine.[92]

Of the purāṇas, only *Vishṇu*, *Vāyu* and *Bhāgavata* refer very briefly to the Guptas, and their evidence is mostly used in determining their original home and the extent of their kingdom before Samudragupta. B Bhattacharya published some verses from the Kaliyuga-rājavṛittānta of the *Bhavishyottara-purāṇa* and emphasized its significance as a source of history, particularly of the Gupta history.[93] The text refers to Chandragupta as of Parvatīya caste who served under Chandraśrī, an Andhra king of Magadha. He married Kumāradevī, a Lichchhavi princess of Nepal, murdered Chandraśrī and became regent of the prince. Later, he killed the prince and anointed himself as king of Magadha, and associated his son, Kācha, in administration. He was murdered by his son, Samudragupta, who became king and took the title Aśokāditya. The new king was skilled in the art of music and literature, and ruled for 51 years. He was followed by his son Chandragupta *Vikramāditya*, and the latter by his son *Mahendrāditya*, who performed a horse-sacrifice. The son of the last-mentioned was Skandagupta, who defeated the Hūṇas and Pushyasheṇa. Skandagupta's nephew was Narasiṁhagupta *Bālāditya*, son of Sthiragupta *Prakāśāditya*, and the latter's son was Kumāragupta *Kramāditya* who defeated the Hūṇas and Īśānavarman. Much of the evidence of this text is opposed to the known facts of history. There is no evidence to show that the caste of the Guptas was Parvatīya. Samudragupta did not murder his father, nor was his title *Aśokāditya.* Skandagupta defeated the Pushyamitras, and not Pushyasheṇa, and Kumāragupta, who defeated Īśānavarman, was a king of that name belonging to the Later Gupta dynasty, and not the homonym of the Imperial Gupta dynasty. On the Bhitari seal of Kumāragupta, discovered in 1893, Bühler suggested the possibility of reading the name of the grandfather of Kumāragupta [III] and father of Narasiṁhagupta as *Sthiragupta.*[94] which in 1903 was corrected as *Purugupta.*[95] The fact that the author of the Kaliyuga-rājavṛittānta of the *Bhavishyottara-purāṇa* had access to Bühler's reading, *Sthiragupta*, shows that the work is 'a palpable modern forgery',[96] which obviously was committed in or shortly after 1893, and probably before 1903, as the forger had no knowledge of its corrected form, *Purugupta.*[97] Thus, the work is not reliable for reconstructing Gupta history.[98]

The Chinese pilgrim Fa-hien (stay in India *c.* 400-410) gives details about the religious and social conditions of the time, but hardly furnishes any information about the political history, so much so, that he does not mention the name of the then ruling Gupta king, Chandragupta II. Another Chinese pilgrim, Hiuen-tsang, who stayed in India from AD 629 to 644, refers to a few earlier kings, some of whom can be taken as Gupta rulers. He refers to Bālāditya, as a tributary of Mihirakula, who later on defeated that Hūṇa king. Still another Chinese pilgrim, I-tsing, refers to the statement in the itinerary of the Korean monk, Hwui-lun, that Che-li-ki-to (Śrīgupta) constructed a temple at *Mi-li-kia-si-kia-po-no,* (taken by some for Mṛigaśikhāvana, and by others, for Mṛigasthāpana), and mentions the distance and direction in which it was situated with reference to Bodhgaya, which has a bearing on the original home of the Guptas (Chapter 2, below)

The name of Samudragupta occurs in the *Fa-yan-chu-lin*, a Chinese work which preserves the memories of Wang-Hiuen-tse who visited India in the seventh century AD.[99] Significantly, the Javanese text *Tantrikāmandaka* refers to Aiśvaryapāla, king of Java, as a scion of the Ikshvāku dynasty who traced his genealogy from Samudragupta.[100]

Alberuni, in his work, *Kitab-ul-Hind* (11th century), gives the significant information that the Gupta era began 241 years after the Śaka era which became the main plank for fixing the initial year of the Gupta era (Appendix IV). The *Mujmal-ut-Tawarikh*, written by Abu Hasan Ali in 13th century, is a translation of an Arabic work, which itself was based on an Indian work.[101] According to this text, Rawwal and Barkamaris were brothers. The latter was chosen as husband by a princess, but the former forcibly took her and made her his queen. On being invaded by a Śaka king, Rawwal, along with his brother, queen and some officials and people, took shelter in a fort on a hill. The invader captured the fort and asked Rawwal to send his queen for him and the wives of his officers for his own officers as condition for peace. Rawwal, with his ministers consenting, agreed to the condition, but Barkamaris, disguised as the queen, and other officers as females, hiding weapons on their persons, entered Śaka king's camp and killed him and his men. This enhanced the prestige of Barkamaris and Rawwal became jealous of him. Barkamaris, to save himself from the wrath of Rawwal, feigned madness, reached in that condition in his brother's palace, killed him and married his queen.

## NOTES AND REFERENCES

1. *Vide* D R Bhandarkar, *Corpus Inscriptionum Indicarum*, III, 'Preface'.
2. Dhruvabhūti has been referred to as *Khādyaṭapākika,* which has been taken by some scholars as the officer-in-charge of the royal kitchen. D C Sircar (*Select Inscriptions*, I, p. 268) suggests that perhaps *khādyaṭakūṭa pākika* is meant, and some scholars (e.g. D R Bhandarkar, *Corpus Inscriptionum Indicarum*, III, pp. 11-12) take him as a native of Khādyaṭapāka. A locality called Khādyaṭapāra is referred to in the Dhanaidaha copperplate inscription (No. 18).
3. R C Majumdar, in *Comprehensive History of India,* III(i), p. 17.
4. *Corpus Inscriptionum Indicarum*, III, No. 16. He gives the title of the inscription as 'Allahabad Posthumous Pillar Inscription of Samudragupta.'
5. B Ch Chhabra, *Indian Historical Quarterly*, XXIV, pp. 104ff.
6. *Journal of the Asiatic Society of Bengal*, LVIII, p. 89.
7. *Indian Antiquary,* XIX, 1890, p. 225.
8. *Memoirs of the Archaeological Survey of India,* No. 66, p. 64.
9. *Ibid.*, p. 65, n. 2.
10. *Journal of the Asiatic Society of Bengal*, LVIII, 1889, p. 89.
11. *Indian Antiquary,* XIX, 1890, p. 227.
12. *Memoirs of the Archaeological Survey of India,* No. 66, p. 66.
13. K Rama Pishoriti, *Indian Historical Quarterly*, IV, pp. 10-11.
14. *Corpus Inscriptionum Indicarum*, III, pp. 255-56.

15. *Select Inscriptions*, I, p. 272.
16. D C Sircar,in *Epigraphia Indica,* XXVI, p. 136.
17. S R Goyal, *The Imperial Guptas*, p. 133.
18. K K Thaplyal, *Inscriptions of the Maukharis, Later Guptas, Puṣpabhūtis, and Yaśovarman of Kanauj*, pp. 71ff.
19. For Banskhera plates, *ibid*., pp. 177ff, and for Madhuban plates, *ibid*., pp. 182ff.
20. D C Sircar, *Select Inscriptions*, I, p. 271.
21. *Ibid*., p. 271, n 6.
22. R C Majumdar, *Indian Culture*, XI, 227.
23. T P Verma, *Prāgdhārā*, No. 17, pp. 117-18.
24. Based on the reading in the damaged part of the inscription as *pañchame* by D C Sircar; Bhandarkar read it as *prathame*, and took it to refer tothe first regnal year.
25. Allan, *Catalogue of the Coins of the Gupta Dynasties, and of Śaśāṅka, the King of Gauḍa, in the British Museum, London*, pp. cxxiv-cxxvi.
26. P L Gupta (*Imperial Guptas*, pp. 32-33, 79-85) lists 63 hoards.
27. For example, P L Gupta, *Imperial Guptas*, p. 96.
28. S R Goyal, *Imperial Guptas*, p. 319.
29. Some of the types are common to more than one king while others are exclusive to a particular king. The Chandragupta I-Kumāradevī type is taken variously as issued by Chandragupta I, Samudragupta and the Lichchhavis, and we agree with the last-mentioned view, for reasons stated in the Appendix I. Samudragupta issued Standard, Archer, Battle-axe, Tiger-slayer, Lyrist and *Aśvamedha* types of coins. Of Chandragupta II, seven types are known, namely, Archer, Horseman, Lion-slayer, *Chhatra*, Couch, King-and-Queen, and *Chakravikrama*. The largest number of coin-types were issued by Kumāragupta I. They are:–Archer, Swordsman, Horseman, Tiger-slayer, Lion—slayer, Elephant-rider, Elephant-rider-lion-slayer, Rhinoceros-slayer, Kārttikeya, *Chhatra*, Lyrist, *Aśvamedha*, *Apratigha* and King-and-Queen. Skandagupta's coins are merely of four types–Archer, *Chhatra* (only one specimen), Horseman (only one specimen) and King-and-Queen (or King–and-Lakshmī). Ghaṭotkachagupta issued Archer type only, Prakāśāditya (in all probability identical with Bhānugupta) Horse-rider-lion-slayer type, while Kumāragupta II, Budhagupta, Vainyagupta, Narasiṁhagupta, Kumāragupta III and Vishṇugupta issued Archer type only.
30. See A S Altekar, *Coinage of the Gupta Empire*, pp. 15ff.
31. *Journal of the Numismatic Society of India*, XXXVII, pp. 83-83.
32. Y B Singh, *Journal of the Numismatic Society of India*, XLI, pp. 46-47.
33. B R Mani, *Journal of the Numismatic Society of India*, XLIII, pp. 56-57.
34. *Ibid*., XLIV, pp. 48-51.
35. *East and West*, XXIV, pp. 121ff.
36. *Journal of the Numismatic Society of India*, XXI, pp. 191-92.
37. *Journal of the Numismatic Society of India*, XLI, pp. 47-50.
38. *Journal of the Numismatic Society of India*, XLIII, p. 58.

39. *Rise and Fall of the Imperial Guptas*, p. 19.
40. A S Altekar, *Journal of the Numismatic Society of India*, XXI, pp. 191-92; Ashvini Agrawal, *Rise and Fall of the Imperial Guptas*, p. 19.
41. Ashvini Agrawal, *Rise and Fall of the Imperial Guptas*, p. 19.
42. For references to copper coins which have been attributed to Samudragupta, see S R Goyal, *The Imperial Guptas*, p. 146.
43. R K Mookerji, *Indian Culture*, IX, p. 177; and R C Majumdar, in *Comprehensive History of India*, III(i), p. 31.
44. P L Gupta, *Gupta Sāmrājya*, pp. 88-89. Allan, however, identifies the device as *garuḍa*, which occurs on other silver coins of Kumāragupta I (*Catalogue of the Coins of the Gupta Dynasties, and of Śaśāṅka, the King of Gauḍa, in the British Museum, London*, Intro, xcvi).
45. P L Gupta, *The Imperial Guptas*, p. 88.
46. For example, P L Gupta, *ibid*., pp. 193-94.
47. For example, Allan, *Catalogue of the Coins of the Gupta Dynasties, and of Śaśāṅka, the King of Gauḍa, in the British Museum, London*, Intro, pp. l-li.
48. *Journal of the Numismatic Society of India*, XII, pp. 34-35; J W Curtis, *Journal of the Numismatic Society of India*, XX, pp. 73-76.
49. *Journal of the Numismatic Society of India*, XLII, pp. 21ff.
50. P L Gupta, *The Imperial Guptas*, p. 70.
51. P L Gupta, *ibid*., p. 70.
52. *Ibid*., p. 69.
53. *The Coinage of the Gupta Empire*, p. 295.
54. S R Goyal, *The Imperial Guptas*, p. 54.
55. Canto IV.
56. It has been opined that the *Raghuvaṁśam* gives clue to the Lyrist type of coins of Samudragupta, and the Rhinoceros-slayer type of Kumaragupta. See Ashvini Agrawal, *Rise and Fall of the Imperial Guptas*, p. 35.
57. S R Goyal, *The Imperial Guptas*, p. 149.
58. D R Bhandarkar, *Corpus Inscriptionum Indicarum*, III, p. 70.
59. P L Gupta, *Gupta Sāmrājya*, pp. 131-32.
60. *Harsha-charita*, ed. by P V Kane, 2nd ed., Delhi, 1965, Chapter VI, p. 51.
61. It reads—*Chandragupta-bhrātṛi-jāyāṁ Dhruvadevīṁ....*
62. *The Age of the Imperial Guptas*, 26ff.
63. *Journal of the Bihar and Orissa Research Society*, XIX, pp. 113-14.
64. *Imperial Guptas*, 134, and n. 37 on p. 137.
65. Shakuntala Rao Sastri, *Kaumudīmahotsava*, p. 12.
66. The relevant passages have been cited by P L Gupta, *The Imperial Guptas*, pp. 129ff.
67. P L Gupta, *Gupta Sāmrājya*, p. 140; he quotes original verses.
68. P L Gupta, *ibid*., p. 120; he quotes original verses.
69. P L Gupta, *Imperial Guptas*, p. 143.
70. As quoted in *ibid*., p. 144.

71. D R Bhandarkar, *Corpus Inscriptionum Indicarum*, III, pp. 68-69.
72. *Ibid.*
73. *Kāvyamīmaṁsā* (Gaekwad Oriental Series, No.1), p. 47.
74. *Indian Antiquary*, LXII, p. 201.
75. A S Altekar, *Journal of the Bihar and Orissa Research Society*, XIV, p. 242.
76. V V Mirashi, *Indian Antiquary*, LXII, 1983, p. 203.
77. D R Bhandarkar, *Corpus Inscriptionum Indicarum*, III, pp. 48-49.
78. The relevant passages have been translated by P L Gupta, *Gupta Sāmrājya*, pp. 51-53.
79. Incidentally, there is a great controversy about the name of the mother of Skandagupta. B P Sinha (*Decline of the Kingdom of Magadha*, p. 3, n.2) accepts this as her name.
80. J Agrawala, *Journal of Oriental Institute*, XV, pp. 375-78.
81. P L Gupta, *The Imperial Guptas*, p. 150.
82. The relevant verses have been quoted by P L Gupta, *The Imperial Guptas*, pp. 122ff.
83. P L Gupta, *ibid.*, pp. 122-123.
84. P L Gupta, *ibid.*, pp. 123ff.
85. K P Jayaswal, *Imperial History of India*, p. 34.
86. S R Goyal, *The Imperial Guptas*, p. 446
87. R C Majumdar, in *Comprehensive History of India*, III (i), p. 100, n 49.
88. Translation of the relevant verse, in P L Gupta, *Imperial Guptas*, p. 154.
89. *Vide* Ashvini Agrawal, *Rise and Fall of the Imperial Guptas*, p. 200..
90. S R Goyal, *The Imperial Guptas*, p. 251.
91. D C Sircar, *Journal of the Numismatic Society of India*, VI, p. 35.
92. B Bhattacharya, *Journal of the Ganganath Jha Research Institute*, I, pp. 287ff; T P Verma, *Pragdhārā*, No. 17, pp. 117-18.
93. *Journal of the Ganganath Jha Research Institute*, I, p. 287; *Journal of the Bihar Rersearch Society*, XXX, 1ff. These had been quoted earlier by T S Narayan Sastri in his *Age of Śaṅkara* (1916) and by M Krishnamachariar in his *Classical Sanskrit Literature* (1937). P L Gupta earlier (*Journal of the Numismatic Society of India*, V, pp. 33, 36) considered it as a source of the Gupta history, but later (*The Imperial Guptas*, p. 121), did not take it as such.
94. *Journal of the Royal Asiatic Society of Great Britain and Ireland*, 1893, p. 83, n 2.
95. See also U N Roy, *Gupta Rājavaṁśa tathā Usakā Yuga*, pp. 44- 45.
96. R C Majumdar, in *The Vākāṭaka-Gupta Age*, p. 133n.
97. See B P Sinha, *Decline of the Kingdom of Magadha*, p. 16; and R C Majumdar, in *Comprehensive History of India*, III(i), pp. 14-15.
98. R C Majumdar, *Indian Historical Quarterly*, XX, pp. 345ff; See also D C Sircar, *Journal of the Numismatic Society of India*, VI, pp. 34-36.
99. *Vide* S R Goyal, *The Imperial Guptas*, p. 147.
100. *Indian Historical Quarterly*, 1933, pp. 930ff.
101. *Vide* P L Gupta, *The Imperial Guptas*, pp. 155-56; he quotes translation of the relevant passages.

# 2
# Caste and Original Home of the Imperial Guptas

## A. THE CASTE OF THE GUPTAS

'The origins of the Imperial Guptas is wrapped in obscurity'.[1] Members of the Gupta families find mention in early Brāhmī inscriptions.[2] Upagupta was a Buddhist monk whose father was Gupta.[3] Vishṇugupta was another name of Kauṭilya, and Brahmagupta was a great astrologer. The name Gupta, in fact, is known among 'saints, monks, warriors, royal scribes, and goldsmiths',[4] but none of these is known as connected with the Imperial Gupta family. *Guptānvaya*, i.e. 'of the Gupta family', is comparable to *Pālānvaya*, 'of the Pāla family';[5] but, whereas in the case of the Gupta dynasty, the name of the first king, Gupta, itself was chosen as a name-ending for other kings from the time of Chandragupta I onwards, in the case of the Pāla dynasty, the first ruler's name was not Pāla but Gopāla, and like him all other kings have *pāla* name-ending. *Gupta* could be a contraction of a bigger name, and the full name of Ghaṭotkacha could very well have been Ghaṭotkachagupta, as per the rule of Sanskrit grammar, Satyabhāmā could be contracted either as Satya or Bhāmā.[6] However, it is unlikely, as the first king of the Gupta dynasty has invariably been referred to as Gupta, and the second, as Ghaṭotkacha.

There is no clear mention of the *varṇa* or *gotra* of the kings of the Gupta dynasty, either in literature or in inscriptions. Inferences have been drawn from certain literary and epigraphic references by different scholars, who variously consider them as belonging to different *varṇas*, and a few even place them outside the pale of the *varṇas*. There is a suggestion that a coin with legend *Śrīgupta* showing affiliation with the Nāga coins may belong to the homonym Gupta ruler, and so he should be taken as of Nāga origin.[7] But the coin should not be ascribed to that Gupta ruler as he was a feudatory, and feudatory rulers are not known issuing coins. According to D R Bhandarkar,[8] the Guptas seem to have been originally a foreign tribe like the Ābhīras and the Gurjaras, and were 'merged into the Hindu population leaving a trace of its name in the various castes, into which it was lost'. The view, however, lacks evidence and hence does not seem convincing. The same scholar, at another place in the same work,[9] considers the Imperial Guptas as of solar race. R C Majumdar[10] does not rule out the possibility of the existence of a 'clan or family which ramified in course of time and spread in different parts of India'. But, as he himself admits, there is hardly any evidence to substantiate it. Below we discuss the various views relating to the caste of the Guptas.

### Vaiśyas

Some scholars, such as A S Altekar,[11] S K Aiyangar,[12] and V V Mirashi,[13] basing mainly on the fact that the kings of the dynasty bore *gupta*-ending names, which the smṛitis[14] prescribe for the names of the vaiśyas, consider the Guptas as belonging to that *varṇa*. Satyaketu Vidyalankar[15] points out that Dhāraṇa is a well known *gotra* of Agrawal vaiśyas and therefore takes the Guptas, whose *gotra*, as inferred from the Vākāṭaka inscriptions (Nos. 82, 84), was the same, as belonging to the vaiśya *varṇa*. P L Gupta holds the same view and opines that though the Guptas were vaiśyas they had been given the status of kshatriyas by the brāhmaṇas[16] However, there are examples of *gupta*-ending names for brāhmaṇas too and also the kshatriyas. It is quite possible that *gupta*-ending in the names of the kings of the Gupta dynasty has nothing to do with the above-mentioned smṛiti injunction, but was added to the names of the Gupta kings from the time of Chandragupta I, after the name of the first ruler of that dynasty, a supposition supported by the fact that the second Gupta king Ghaṭotkacha does not bear a *gupta*-ending name.

## JATS

K P Jayaswal[17] and a few other scholars consider the Guptas as Jats, who originally lived in the Punjab. The evidence on which the view is based is briefly be summarized here: (i) In the *Kaumudī-mahotsava,* Chaṇḍasena (whom Jayaswal identifies with Chandragupta I) is referred to as a kāraskara, unworthy of becoming a ruler;[18] (ii) Baudhāyana calls kāraskara as *araṭṭa* with a lower position in the society; (iii) Kāraskaras were a branch of the Madra people who were also Jartikas (=Jāṭs); (iv) In Chandragomin's *Chāndra-vyākaraṇa, Jarto* (= Jāṭ) in the expression *ajayajjarto-Hūṇān,* stands for Gupta king Skandagupta who was the conqueror of the Hūṇas;[19] (v) The Gupta family of kings in Nepal are mentioned as milkmen (Ahīras) and the Jats, too, are similarly known;[20] (vi) Prabhāvatīguptā mentions her *gotra* as Dhāraṇa (Nos. 82, 84), which is taken to be her paternal *gotra,* since her husband's *gotra* was Vishṇuvṛiddha, and a branch of Jāṭas are known as Dhārī;[21] (vii) *Jāta* in the expression *Madhurāyāṁ jāta-vaṁśāḍhyaḥ* in the *Ārya-Mañjuśrī-mūlakalpa,* has been taken for Jāṭa.[22]

The view that the Guptas were Jats has some drawbacks. The *Kaumudī-mahotsava* is not an authentic source of history (Chapter 1). A Madra princess Mādrī is known as married to Pāṇḍu, who is known as a kshatriya, and it may be inferred that the Madra people were of the same *varṇa.* As regards the evidence of *jarto* being the conqueror of the Hūṇas in the *Chāndra-vyākaraṇa,* Hoernle[23] suggested that the reference may be to Yaśodharman who also defeated the Hūṇas, and not necessarily for Skandagupta. Dhāraṇa, as will be seen below, is also known as a *gotra* of the brāhmaṇas.

## KSHATRIYAS

Some scholars consider the Guptas as kshatriyas. Even the evidence of the *Kaumudī-mahotsava,* which most scholars do not consider as a trustworthy source of history, is not solely in favour of taking the Guptas as of low caste. It may be stated that Sundaravarmā is mentioned as a kshatriya, his adopted son Chaṇḍasena, who has been identified with Chandragupta I by Jayaswal,[24] would also have been a kshatriya. Chandragupta I married the Lichchhavi princess, Kumāradevī. The Lichchhavis in the early Buddhist literature have been praised much among the kshatriyas. They were admired for their features and gait by the Buddha.[25] They claimed and obtained a share in the relics of the Buddha, on the ground that like him they were kshatriyas.[26] The kshatriya king, Bimbisāra, had a Lichchhavi princess as his queen and the mother of the kshatriya Mahāvīra, the Jaina Tīrthaṅkara, too, was a Lichchhavi princess. In the Nepalese inscriptions, the Lichchhavis are mentioned as Sūryavaṁśī kshatriyas, and Hiuen-tsang,[27] the Chinese pilgrim, also refers to them as such. Manu[28] calls them as *vrātya* (fallen) kshatriyas, but this he probably does because most of the Lichchhavis were followers of heterodox sects—Buddhism and Jainism, on account of which they were not liked by him, as he was a great champion of Brahmanism. Some scholars believe that Kālidāsa was a contemporary of Chandragupta II and he considerably modelled his account of Raghu in his *Raghuvaṁśam* on the achievements of the Gupta kings. The mention of Raghu in that work as Sūryavaṁśī (*Sūryavaṁśa-prabhavaḥ*) is taken by some as indicative of the kshatriya origin of the Gupta kings, who adopted *āditya* titles which, it is suggested, they would have done because they considered themselves as of solar race.[29] There are examples of *gupta*-ending names of kshatriya kings. In a Sirpur inscription,[30] Mahāśivagupta calls himself as Chandravaṁśī kshatriya, and refers to Vikramāditya Chandraguptarāja (=Chandragupta II) as progenitor of his family. In the Panchobha (Darbhanga district, Bihar) copperplate inscription,[31] six kings with *gupta*-ending names have been mentioned as belonging to the Gupta dynasty, and also as descendants of Arjuna. Since Arjuna of the *Mahābhārata* fame was a kshatriya, the Guptas may also be taken as belonging to that *varṇa*. The Guttas (Guptas) of Dharwar call themselves as Somavaṁśī kshatriyas and descendants of Vikramāditya, lord of Pāṭaliputra,[32] who should be identified with Chandragupta II. In the *Tantri-Kāmandaka*, a Javanese text, Aiśvaryapāla, an Ikshvāku kshatriya, traces his origin to Samudragupta.[33] The Vākaṭākas were brāhmaṇas, and prince Rudrasena II of this dynasty was married to Prabhāvatīguptā, daughter of the Gupta king, Chandragupta II. The brāhmaṇa prince could marry a kshatriya princess as it would be an *anuloma* form of marriage, which is permissible according to the dharmaśāstra works. The depiction of *chandradhvaja* on the Chandragupta I-Kumāradevī type of coins, according to Chhabra, may have been intended to indicate that the king was a Chandravaṁśī kshatriya.[34] Chandragupta II has been referred to as *rājarshi* in an Udaigiri inscription (No. 11), a term which has been used for saintly kshatriyas like Janaka and Viśvāmitra, while saintly brāhmaṇas have been referred to as *viprarshi* (No. 75).

It has been argued that if the Guptas would have been brāhmaṇas, as some scholars suggest, they should have mentioned it in their inscriptions.[35] As they belonged to the kshatriya *varṇa*, they did not deem it necessary to mention themselves as such, since kings were generally supposed to be of kshatriya *varṇa*. Further, even a kshatriya could take the *gotra* of his brāhmaṇa priest, and so the Dhāraṇa *gotra* of the Guptas need not necessarily be interpreted to indicate that they were brāhmaṇas.[36]

## Brāhmaṇas

Some scholars consider Guptas as brāhmaṇas. A few brāhmaṇas are known with *gupta*-ending names, for example, Vishṇugupta, better known as Kauṭilya, the author of the *Arthaśāstra* and Brahmagupta, the great astrologer. The Guptas had matrimonial alliance with the royal brāhmaṇa families of the Vākāṭakas and Kadambas. Prabhāvatī, the daughter of Chandragupta II, was married to Rudrasena II Vākāṭaka (Poona plate, No. 82, and Rithpur plate, No. 84) and a Kadamba princess, daughter of King Kākusthavarman was married to a Gupta prince as per the evidence of the Talgunda inscription (No. 91). The marriage of a Gupta princess with a Vākāṭaka prince would be an *anuloma* marriage, and would be a *praśasta* (acceptable) form even if the a Guptas were not brāhmaṇas. But marriage of a brāhmaṇa Kadamba princess to a Gupta prince belonging to a *varṇa* other than brāhmaṇa would be a *pratiloma* marriage, which is not only not allowed but also condemned by the dharmaśāstra works; therefore, it is argued that the Guptas should be taken as belonging to the brāhmaṇa *varṇa*. Though against this, it can be said that the founder of the Kadamba dynasty, Mayūraśarman, gave up brāhmaṇa *vṛitti* and adopted the *vṛitti* of kshariya *varṇa* and his successors bear names ending in *varman* which is the name-ending the smṛitis prescribe for the kshatriyas, and not *śarman*-ending ones which is prescribed for the brāhmaṇas, and hence a marriage of a Kadamba princess with a Gupta prince would be of *praśasta* form, even if the Guptas were kshatriyas.

Prabhāvatīguptā, the Vākāṭaka queen, calls herself as of Dhāraṇa *gotra*, which is different from Vishṇuvṛiddha, the *gotra* of her husband. It is inferred that Dhāraṇa was the *gotra* of her parental family, the Guptas. Dasharatha Sharma points out that the *Skanda-purāṇa*[37] refers to the brāhmaṇas of Dhāraṇa *gotra* living in Dharmāraṇya which stands for a region within Mirzapur district, and the Guptas were either kshatriyas or vaiśyas who had adopted the *gotra* of their brahmanical priests.[38] S R Goyal who, is of the view that the original kingdom of the Guptas was in eastern Uttar Pradesh, finds this reference in the *Skanda-purāṇa* as supportive evidence for it and also for his view that the Guptas were brāhmaṇas. A brāhmaṇa donee of Dhāraṇa *gotra*, it may be mentioned in passing, is known from Kurud plates of Narendra.[39] Dhāriṇī is one of the subdivisions of the Agastya *gaṇa* of brāhmaṇas of the Agastya clan.[40]

H C Raychaudhuri[41] connects the Dhāraṇa *gotra* of the Guptas with Dhāriṇī, chief-queen of Agnimitra, who was a brāhmaṇa. The time lag between the Śuṅgas and the Guptas and the fact that Dhāriṇī is the name of the āuṅga queen whereas Dhāraṇa is the name of the *gotra*, makes the view rather of doubtful validity.[42] According to the dharmaśāstra works, after marriage a woman is supposed to take the *gotra* of her husband.[43] The *Garuḍa-purāṇa*[44] says that normally the married woman should perform rituals according to the *gotra* of her husband, but in the case of *apraśasta* form of marriage (like *āsura* and *rākshasa*) it should be done in accordance with the paternal *gotra*. From this it has been inferred that the marriage of Prabhāvatīguptā with Rudrasena II was of the *apraśasta* type. In the absence of definite evidence, this does not seem likely. It seems more convincing that Prabhāvatīguptā took pride in her Gupta lineage, and on that account in her inscriptions gave the genealogy and *gotra* of the Gupta kings, and not that of the Vākāṭakas. There is, however, a view that in the expression in the Vākāṭaka inscriptions: *dhāraṇa-gotra-Nāgakul=otpannā Kuberanāgādevyām=utpannā*, Dhāraṇa *gotra* is mentioned in the context of the Nāgas rather than that of Prabhāvatīguptā,[45] and that in the Kuruspal inscription of Someśvaradeva[46] of Nāga family, the name of a queen is mentioned as Dhāraṇa-*mahādevī*, in which, like Kautsī and Vātsī, Dhāraṇa is derived from the *gotra*.[47]

Paramārtha, who, according to some scholars, should be placed in the sixth century AD, states that the sister of Bālāditya, generally identified with Narasiṁhagupta Bālāditya of the Gupta dynasty, was married to Vasurāta, a brāhmaṇa.[48] The minister of Yaśodharman, Dharmadosha by name, was a brāhmaṇa, and his grandfather Ravikīrti was married to Bhānuguptā who perhaps was a sister of the Gupta king, Bhānugupta.[49]

Thus, different scholars, basing their interpretations on different pieces of evidence, have expressed different views regarding the *varṇa* of the

Guptas. With the evidence at hand regarding the *varṇa* or caste of the Guptas, nothing can be said with certainty.

## B. ORIGINAL HOME

Like the *varṇa* of the Guptas, there is much controversy regarding their original home. In none of their inscriptions is there any reference to their capital. The name Pāṭaliputra occurs but it is not stated that it was their capital. As such one has to depend on the meagre information available from Chinese source and the purāṇas, as also the findspots of the inscriptions and coins of early kings of that dynasty. Most scholars have tried to settle the issue of the original home of the Guptas mainly on the basis of I-tsing's account which itself is based on the account of the Korean monk Hwui-lun. D C Ganguly[50] following the revised translation of the Chinese account by Beal, and also by E Chavannes,[51] states that the distance between the Mahābodhi temple (at Gaya) and *Mi-li-kia-si-kia-po-no*, near which a temple erected by Śrīgupta was situated more than 40 stages i.e., about 228 miles (taking one stage equal to 5. 5/7 miles)[52] to the east of Nālandā, and therefore the latter should be located in Murshidabad. A Cambridge illustrated manuscript, dated 1015, shows a *stūpa* with the label inscription meaning 'Mṛigasthāpana *stūpa* of Vārendra'.[52] Taking *Mi-li-kia-si-kia-po-no* as identical with Mṛigasthāpana, it has been suggested that the said temple near it could be either in Murshidabad,[54] or in Vārendra itself. Some scholars[55] opine that the inclusion of Vārendra in Śrī-Gupta's territory does not necessarily mean that it was the original home of the Guptas. R C Majumdar[56] is of the view that since the Chinese pilgrim speaks of the donation of 24 villages to the temple by him, it should have been situated within his territory. In his view, Magadha, either partly or wholly, also formed part of the early Gupta kingdom; he, however, is undecided as to whether that region was the original home of the Guptas, who later extended their power to Bengal, or it was vice-versa.[57]

Some scholars do not agree with the above identification. J Agrawal,[58] following the earlier translation of Chinese account by Beal, identifies the place of the temple erected by Śrī-Gupta differently, as below. In the account of I-tsing, after the mention of Ādityasena's temple at Mahābodhi, Nālandā is abruptly introduced and *Mi-li-kia-si-kia-po-no*, which, according to him and a few other scholars, should be rendered as Mṛigaśikhāvana (and not Mṛigasthāpana as done by some scholars), where the temple built by Śrī-Gupta was located. The Mahābodhi temple is mentioned as situated more than 40 *yojanas* to its east. Seven *yojanas* to the north-east of Mahābodhi temple is placed the Nālandā temple. Agrawal argues that the account relating to a place to the east of Nālandā should have followed, and not preceded, the description of Nālandā, and hence, the placing of *Mi-li-kia-si-kia-po-no* 40 *yojanas* to the east of Nālandā appears curious. It is argued that when I-tsing made this statement, he had not reached Nālandā, but was at some place to its west, and that it would seem to indicate that he first arrived at Rājagṛiha, where Gṛidhrakūṭa and Kukkuṭārāma were situated, then to Śrāvastī where Jetavana Park was located, and then to the Deer Park in Sarnath, and from there he went to Nālandā. It is further argued that it is difficult to believe that the Chinese pilgrim would have omitted a visit to Sarnath, an extremely sacred site to the Buddhists and a centre of Buddhist pilgrimage as Buddha delivered his First Sermon there, and instead would have chosen to visit some little known spot in Vārendra. It therefore appears reasonable, he says, that Śrīgupta got constructed a temple at Sarnath, and this would favour the location of the original home of the Guptas in eastern Uttar Pradesh. R C Majumdar,[59] however, considers J Agrawal's attempt to locate the temple at Sarnath as vitiated by his reliance upon an old and obsolete translation of Beal in preference to the revised translation by the same scholar and also by Chavannes.

An inscription in the Gupta characters on the pedestal of an image at Sarnath states that the image was installed by Śrī-Gupta the lord (*svāmī*).[60] It is difficult to say if the person is identical with the homonym Gupta king; and even if the identification is accepted it would not in itself necessarily prove that Sarnath formed a part of his kingdom, as an outsider could also install image at that great centre of pilgrimage.[61]

Goyal[62] forcefully argues that the original home of the Imperial Guptas was in the eastern Uttar Pradesh. His view is mainly based on numismatic and epigraphic evidence, particularly the find-spots of the coins, singly or in hoards, and those of the inscriptions, and may be summarized in the present paragraph. Chandragupta-Kumāradevī type of coins, as stated by Altekar,[63] have been found at Ayodhyā, Lucknow, Sitapur, Tanda, Ghazipur and Vārāṇasī, all in eastern Uttar Pradesh, and outside that region, only Mathura, Bayana (Rajasthan) and Hajipur (Bihar) are their findspots. Of the hoards of Gupta coins, 15 are from eastern Uttar Pradesh, while Bengal and Bihar have yielded five each only. The hoards from eastern Uttar Pradesh mostly contain the coins of the early kings of the Imperial Gupta dynasty, most of those from the last two regions contain coins of the later kings of that dynasty.[64] Of the early Gupta inscriptions from the time of Samudragupta to Skandagupta, eight come from eastern Uttar Pradesh, two (three, if, as per the view of Goyal, Bihar pillar is taken as bearing, not one but two inscriptions) from Magadha and six from Bengal. The Gaya copperplate, though found in Bihar, was issued, as its text says, from Ayodhyā. Whereas all the eight inscriptions from eastern Uttar Pradesh are on stone and the earliest one belongs to Samudragupta, those from Bengal are copperplate grants, and the earliest ones belong to the time of Kumāragupta I. The choice of Prayāga for Samudragupta's *praśasti,* the earliest and the most important of the Gupta inscriptions, must have been guided by the consideration that it was very important site in the Gupta kingdom, in all probability, its capital. The Kauśāmbī style of Brāhmī, first seen in this epigraph, appears to have been patronized by the Gupta administration, and became popular in other regions later on. A good number of Gupta antiquities have been found at such sites as Kauśāmbī, Bhita, Gadhwa and Jhusi, all in Allahabad district. The introduction of Ganga-Yamuna motif in Gupta sculpture was guided by the fact that it symbolized Prayāga region which should have been the original home of the Guptas.[65] The *Vāyu-purāṇa* places Gupta territory, most probably during the reign of Chandragupta I, in Prayāga, Sāketa and Magadha, and the first two are located in eastern Uttar Pradesh. The *Vishṇu-purāṇa* has *Anu-Gaṅgā-Prayāgaṁ Māgadhā Guptāścha bhokshyanti,*[66] i.e. 'the Māgadhas and the Guptas will enjoy, i.e. rule over, the area on Gaṅgā up to Prayāga'.[67] S R Goyal[68] is of the view that by the Māgadhas, the Lichchhavis are meant, and that after the marriage of Chandragupta I with Kumāradevī, they jointly ruled the Gupta territory in eastern Uttar Pradesh, and the Lichchhavi territory in Magadha. It has been suggested by D C Sircar[69] that the installation of a Vishṇu image at Bhitari (Ghazipur district) by Skandagupta for the merit of his father, Kumāragupta, was done on the occasion of the latter's annual *śrāddha,* and T P Verma[70] opines that this would have been done in the original home of the Guptas, since according to the *śāstras* that ritual should be performed either at Gayā, or Vārāṇasī, or at one's ancestral home. The *Chandragarbha-paripṛichchhā* mentions the birth of Mahendrasena, identified with Kumāragupta I, at Kauśāmbī.[71] Goyal[72] is of the view that the Guptas were Dhāraṇa *gotrīya* brāhmaṇas of Mirzapur, the

Dharmāraṇya of the purāṇas, and before coming to power, served the Maghas, whom they later supplanted. According to him, the find-spots of early Gupta inscriptions, coins and coin–hoards, and other archaeological and literary evidence taken together suggest that the original home of the Guptas was in eastern Uttar Pradesh, and the centre of their power was located at Prayāga.[73] As regards the purāṇic evidence, it is not uniform. While the *Vāyu-purāṇa* mentions Sāketa forming part of the Gupta territory, the *Vishṇu-purāṇa* does not do so. Some scholars infer from this that the latter refers to the earlier phase of the Gupta kingdom, and the former, to a later one. While some prefer the version *anu Gaṅgā Prayāgaṁ cha* meaning 'the territories along the Gaṅgā and Prayāga', others prefer *anu Gaṅgaṁ Prayāgam* as meaning 'Prayāga on the Gaṅgā'. Further it is not known for certain as to which king's territories the purāṇic evidence refers to.

Scholars who disagree with the view that eastern Uttar Pradesh was the original home of the Guptas, put forth following arguments against it.[74] The earliest Gupta coins, the Chandragupta-Kumāradevī type, are generally found in association with the coins of kings Samudragupta, Chandragupta II, and others. The coins would not have been buried earlier than the latest king represented in the hoard, and therefore the bearing of the hoards on the extent of kingdom should be in the context of the latest king known from them. The find–spot of the inscriptions is not a foolproof criterion for determining the original home. The Mauryan homeland was Bihar, but with the exception of a few, all the Mauryan inscriptions have been found outside that region. Similarly, Vārendra region was the original home of the Pālas, but it has yielded only a few of the large number of their inscriptions. Most scholars hold that as one of the inscriptions of Aśoka, viz., the Queen's Edict,on the pillar at Allahabad, was addressed to the *mahāmātras* of Kauśāmbī, the pillar was installed by Aśoka at that city from where it was brought to Prayāga by a Moghul emperor, either by Akbar, or by Jahangir whose inscription has been engraved on it. The choice of engraving of the Samudragupta's inscription would have been guided by the administrative importance of Kauśāmbī. Even if the pillar stood at the present location since the time of Aśoka, it is not in itself a strong evidence in favour of its being the capital of the Guptas. As regards the evidence of the Kauśāmbī style of writing used for the Allahabad pillar inscription, the choice would have much depended on the liking and dexterity of the scribe which could be influenced by the tools used and the training received by him. Allahabad, Kauśāmbī, Bhita, Gadhwa and Jhusi, where this script has been commonly used, are no doubt within Allahabad district in eastern Uttar Pradesh, but that style of script has also been found in early Gupta inscriptions at Sanchi and Udaigiri both in Madhya Pradesh. As to Skandagupta's installing an image in memory of his father Kumāragupta at Bhitari, it could have been done because of some special affiliation of the latter monarch with that site; he might have breathed his last at that place, rather than it being the original home of the Guptas. It is not certain that the Gaṅgā-Yamunā motif represents the heartland of the Gupta empire; and if it was a regional motif the Guptas would hardly have used it for monuments located in different parts of their empire. The Buddhist scholar, Paramārtha, mentions Ayodhyā as the capital of Vikramāditya who is identified by some with Chandragupta II and by others with some other king of the Gupta dynasty. There is no evidence of Ayodhyā being an important political centre in the beginning of the Gupta rule. While only two Gupta coin-hoards and a few stray Gupta coins have been found in Bihar, a number of Gupta sealings have come to light from that region, from Nālandā and Vaiśālī and a copperplate from Gayā (though issued from Ayodhyā). Coins and sealings travel from one region to another, and therefore no definite conclusion can be drawn regarding the extent of the empire of kings solely on the basis of their find-spots, yet the finding of a large number of Gupta sealings from Nālandā and Vaiśālī is not without significance. It has been suggested that Samudragupta extended his territories by conquering regions located to the west of Allahabad, and in the east of it the only kingdom was that of Chandra of the Susunia inscription in west Bengal, and therefore the area in between already formed part of the Gupta kingdom. Some part of it would have been the kingdom inherited by Chandragupta I, and some extended during his time.[75] It has been pointed out[76] that Mirzapur should not be considered as the original home of the Guptas, merely because it was the original home of the brāhmaṇas of Dhāraṇa *gotra*. The original home of the Vākāṭakas was in Bundelkhand, but their kingdom was founded in the Deccan. Prayāga has been an important place of pilgrimage, though it does not find place in the seven cities which are stated as *moksha-dāyikā*. U N Roy[77] doubts even its status as a city in ancient times, which was then enjoyed by Kauśāmbī, situated nearby. According to him, Prayāga attained the status of a city during the time of Akbar when it was named Allahabad. Ashvini Agrawal[78] opines that the region around Prayāga formed part of the territories of the Maghas, and therefore it would not have been the capital of the early Gupta kings.

B P Sinha[79] considers Mathura-Ayodhyā region as the original home of the Guptas. He believes that the Guptas were of the Dhāraṇa *gotra, w*hich is the *gotra* of the Jats of Mathura. This view has not found favour with scholars. The relevant text has also been read as *Mathurāyāṁ jāto vaṁśāḍhya* and taken as referring to the birth (of Samudragupta) and not to his jat lineage. Besides, Mathura had not become part of the Gupta empire before Samudragupta defeated its ruler, Gaṇapatināga (Chapter 5). B P Sinha would include Sāketa as part of early Gupta kingdom on the ground that it has been mentioned in the purāṇas prominently; but it does not find mention in some of the purāṇas mentioning the territories ruled by the Guptas. No reliance can be laid on the view, drawn on the basis of he physical features of kings based on the depiction of their figures of four Gupta kings on twenty silver coins that the original home of the Imperial Guptas should be located in the region covering Northern Uttar Pradesh, Haryana and Punjab.[80]

There is a view that Pāṭaliputra, which finds mention in the Gupta inscriptions, was the capital of the Guptas almost from the beginning of the rule of that dynasty.[81] The Allahabad pillar inscription (No. 1) refers to it as Pushpāhvaya. A Gadhwa inscription (No. 28) mentions Pāṭaliputra. In the Udaigiri inscription (No. 11), Vīrasena Śāba, a high official of Chandragupta II, says he hailed from Pāṭaliputra and had come (to Vidiśā) along with the king. S R Goyal[82] argues that if Pāṭaliputra had been the capital from the beginning of the Gupta rule, then Vīrasena, who was a central government officer, would not have needed to state that he belonged to Pāṭaliputra, and the city was mentioned because it was his birth place. We, however, are of the opinion that Vīrasena felt that on the basis of the location of his inscription, some people might take him as an inhabitant of a place in the neighbourhood of Udaigiri, and therefore he made it a point to mention in the inscription that he had come there from Pātaliputra, situated far away. He states that he came there accompanying king Chandragupta II in course of his military expedition. It can be presumed, that Chandraguta II hailed from the same city, which would have been his capital. Vīrasena would have been proud of hailing from the renowned capital city, and made such statement as he wanted that people should know it. Fleet considers the mention of Pushpāhva, i.e. Pāṭaliputra, in the Allahabad pillar inscription of Samudragupta as good ground for taking that city as his capital.[83] But from the evidence cited above, it can be presumed, but cannot be said with certainty, that Pāṭaliputra was the capital of the Guptas from the very beginning of their rule. All said, the original home of the Guptas still remains uncertain, and the safest statement in this regard wouild be that it should have been located somewhere in the area extending from eastern Uttar Pradesh to Western Bengal.[84]

## NOTES AND REFERENCES

1. H C Raychaudhuri, *Political History of Ancient India*, p. 467n.
2. Gauptī is mentioned as grandmother of Śuṅga king, Dhanabhūti (D C Sircar, *Select Inscriptions*, I, p. 87). For other epigraphic references, see R C Majumdar, in *The Vākāṭaka-Gupta Age*, p, 126; S R Goyal, *Gupta Sāmrājya kā Itihāsa*, pp. 18-19.
3. *Divyāvadāna*, ed. by Cowell and Neil, (reprint) Vārāṇasī; 1987, p. 348.
4. R C Majumdar, in *Comprehensive History of India*, III (i), p. 4.
5. R C Majumdar, in *ibid.*, p. 5.
6. See *ibid.*, p. 5; he cites the example of such contraction from the *Mahābhāshya.*
7. R K Sethi, *Journal of the Numismatic Society of India*, XLIII, pp. 62ff.
8. D R Bhandarkar, *Corpus Inscriptionum Indicarum*, III, p. 4.
9. *Ibid.*, pp. 69-70.
10. R C Majumdar, in *Comprehensive History of India*, III(i), p. 5.
11. A S Altekar in *The Vākāṭaka-Gupta Age*, pp. 342, 344.
12. *Ancient India and South Indian History and Culture*, I, p. 180.
13. *Vākāṭaka Rājavaṁśa kā Itihāsa tathā Abhilekha*, p. 56.
14. For example, *Manu*, II, 32.
15. *Agrawala Jāti kā Prāchīna Itihāsa*, as referred to by P L Gupta, in *Imperial Guptas*, p. 241, n 14.
16. P L Gupta (*The Imperial Guptas*, p. 234) also states that since the *gotra* of the Guptas can be inferred and since the śūdras do not have *gotras*, they could not have been śūdras.
17. *Imperial History of India*, pp. 114-16. For details regarding the theory of jat origin of the Guptas, see P L Gupta, *The Imperial Guptas*, pp. 232-33.
18. R K Mookerji (*Gupta Empire*, p. 14), too, considers them as kāraskaras.
19. K P Jayaswal, *Imperial History of India*, p. 115. According to him, it refers to Skandagupta. In one manuscript of the work, it is *japto*, which he suggests may be a mistake for *gupto* (P L Gupta, *Gupta Sāmrājya*, p. 223, n. 2), in which case there is no reference to the Jats.
20. *Journal of the Bihar and Orissa Research Society*, XIX, p. 7.
21. *Journal of the Bihar and Orissa Research Society*, XIX, p. 45.
22. K P Jayaswal, *Imperial History of India*, p. 53, verse 759.
23. A F R Hoernle, *Journal of the Royal Asiatic Society of Great Britain and Ireland*, 1909, pp. 89 ff.

24. *Imperial History of India,* pp. 113-14.
25. Buddha is said to have likened the Lichchhavis, for their features, to gods. For reference see H C Raychaudhuri, *Political History of Ancient India,* p. 111
26. *Mahāparinibbānasutta,* VI. 51-61; *Buddhist Suttas,* Sacred Books of the East, XI, pp. 131-34.
27. T Watters, *On Yuang Chwang's Travels in India,* II, p. 84.
28. *Manu (The Laws of Manu, Sacred Books of the East, vol. 25),* X, 20, 22.
29. For example, D R Bhandarkar, *Corpus Inscriptionum Indicarum,* III, pp. 69-70.
30. *Epigraphia Indica,* XI, pp.184ff.
31. *Journal of the Bihar and Orissa Research Society,* V, pp. 582.
32. D R Bhandarkar, *Corpus Inscriptionum Indicarum,* III, pp. 61-62, and references cited in footnote 2 on p. 61.
33. *Indian Historical Quarterly,* IX, 1933, pp. 930ff.
34. B Ch Chhabra, *Catalogue of the Gupta Gold Coins in the Bayana Hoard in the National Museum,* p. xxii.
35. T R Sharma, *Personal and Geographical Names in the Gupta Inscriptions,* p. 18.
36. For references to scholars who believe that the Guptas were kshatriyas, see S R Goyal, *Gupta Sāmrājya kā Itihāsa,* p. 24, n. 1.
37. *Skanda-purāṇa,* Brahma-khaṇḍa, 35-37; Dharmāraṇya-khaṇḍa 21 Chapter IX, verses 27-31, *vide* S R Goyal, *The Imperial Guptas,* p. 82, fn 2.
38. *Purāṇa,* VII, p. 185.
39. *Epigraphia Indica,* XXXI, p. 265.
40. John Borough, *The Early brahmanical System of the Gotras and Pravaras,* p. 189, *vide* D K Ganguly, *Imperial Guptas and Their Times,* p. 24, n. 72.
41. H C Raychaudhuri, *Political History of Ancient India,* p. 367, n. 43.
42. U N Roy, *Gupta Rājavaṁśa tathā Usakā Yuga,* p. 48.
43. *Vivāhānantaraṁ nārī patigotreṇa gotriṇī, Mahānirvāṇatantra,* XII. 75, *vide* D C Sircar, *Select Inscriptions,* I, p. 436, n. 9.
44. *Vide* U N Roy, *Gupta Rājavaṁśa tathā Usakā Yuga,* pp. 45, 427n.
45. Ashvini Agrawal, *Rise and Fall of the Imperial Guptas,* p. 83,
46. *Epigraphia Indica,* X, pp. 31f.
47. Ashvini Agrawal, *Rise and Fall of the Imperial Guptas,* p. 83.
48. J Takakusu, *Journal of the Royal Asiatic Society of Great Britain and Ireland,* 1905, pp. 33ff.
49. J F Fleet, *Corpus Inscriptionum Indicarum,* III, p. 152.
50. D C Ganguly, *Indian Historical Quarterly,* XIV, pp. 532-35
51. *Vide* D K Ganguly, *The Imperial Guptas and Their Times,* p. 11. He points out that the Teisho edition of *Kau-fa-kau-sang-Chien* also gives the same information.
52. As Nālandā, situated 40 miles away from Bodhgayā, is stated by I-tsing as 7 stages, so one stage would be equal to 5. 5/7 miles.
53. R C Majumdar, in *Comprehensive History of India,* III (i), p. 8. The Chinese form reads *Mi-li-kia-si-kia-po-no; vide* B N Mukherjee's comment in H C Raychaudhuri, *Political History of Ancient India,* p. 764.

54. *Vide* D C Ganguly, *Indian Historical Quarterly*, XIV, p. 534.
55. For example, B N Mukherjee's comments in H C Raychaudhuri, *Political History of Ancient India*, p. 765.
56. In *Comprehensive History of India*, III(i), p. 8.
57. According to S K Maity, the early Gupta chieftains ruled somewhere in Bengal under the Lichchhavis who ruled in Magadha and adjoining area (*The Imperial Guptas and Their Times*, 15).
58. J Agrawal, *Indian Historical Quarterly*, XXII, p. 28.
59. *Comprehensive History of India*, III(i), p. 8, n. 15.
60. B N Mukherjee, Comments, in H C Raychaudhuri's, *Political History of Ancient India*, p. 765.
61. *Ibid.*
62. S R Goyal, *The Imperial Guptas*, pp. 66 ff. He opines that the original kingdom of the Guptas cannot be decided only on the assumption that Chi-li-ki-to and Śrīgupta are identical (*The Imperial Guptas*, p. 68).
63. *Coinage of the Gupta Empire*, p. 26.
64. S R Goyal, *The Imperial Guptas*, pp. 69-70.
65. H C Raychaudhuri (*Political History of Ancient India*, pp. 486-87) also had hinted that the motif may symbolize connection with Gangetic Doab.
66. Pargiter, *The Dynasties of the Kali Age*, pp. 73-74.
67. See also R C Majumdar, in *The Vākāṭaka-Gupta Age*, p. 134.
68. *The Imperial Guptas*, pp. 74-75.
69. D C Sircar, *Select Inscriptions*, I, p. 324, n. 3.
70. T P Verma, in B Ch Chhabra, *et al.* (ed.), *Reappraising Gupta History for S R Goyal*, p. 102.
71. R C Majumdar, *The Classical Age*, p. 26, n. 3.
72. S R Goyal, *The Imperial Guptas*, pp. 69ff.
73. S R Goyal, *ibid.*
74. Based mainly on D K Ganguly, *The Imperial Guptas and Their Times*, pp. 14-17; see also U N Roy in *K P Jayaswal Commemoration Volume*, pp. 361ff.
75. See also D K Ganguly, *The Imperial Guptas and their Times*, pp. 16-17.
76. U N Roy, *Gupta Rājavaṁśa tathā Usakā Yuga*, pp. 59-60.
77. U N Roy, *ibid.*, p. 6o.
78. Ashvini Agrawal, *Rise and Fall of the Imperial Guptas*, p. 82.
79. B P Sinha, *Journal of the Bihar Research Society*, XXXVII (iii-iv), pp. 142ff. He opines that probably the Imperial Guptas came from the west, "and with the help of the Lichchhavis conquered Magadha and made it a centre of their activities".
80. B Chakravarty, *Journal of the Numismatic Society of India*, LI, pp. 60-61.
81. For example, V A Smith, *Journal of the Royal Asiatic Society of Great Britain and Ireland*, 1889, p. 55.
82. *The Imperial Guptas*, pp. 41-42.
83. J F Fleet, *Corpus Inscriptionum Indicarum*, III, p. 5.
84. See also R C Majumdar, in *Comprehensive History of India*, III(i), pp. 8-9.

# 3

# *Mahārāja* Gupta to *Mahārājādhirāja* Chandragupta I

## POLITICAL CONDITION

The political condition of northern India from the end of the Kushāṇa rule to the beginning of that of the Guptas is not clearly known, and the period was even dubbed by some scholars as 'dark age'. The region was divided into a number of large or small, monarchical or republican states. There is a lot of controversy as to who ruled in Magadha in the last quarter of the third and the first quarter of the fourth century AD. According to R D Banerji,[1] Kushāṇas still had their hold over that region and were driven out from there by Chandragupta I. But most of the scholars rightly do not agree with this view and hold that the Kushāṇas as a political power in this period were confined to north-western India. The evidence of the Allahabad pillar inscription mentioning a number of kings ruling in the Ganga valley shows that the area had become free from the Kushāṇa yoke much earlier.

In different parts of the Punjab, Haryana and Rajasthan resided the Yaudheyas, the Ārjunāyanas, the Madrakas and the Mālavas (Chapter 5), while in the Kullu valley were the Kuṇindas. Altekar[2] is of the opinion that there was a confederation of the tribal republics of the Yaudheyas, Kuṇindas and the Ārjunāyanas under the leadership of the first mentioned one, who were the most prominent among them, and that it was responsible for driving out the Kushāṇas from the hinterland before the Guptas came to power. The headship of the republican tribes had become hereditary. A Yaudheya chief has been referred to as *mahārāja* and *mahāsenāpati*,[3] and another one as *mahārāja-mahāsenāpati-mahākshatrapa*, the last title indicating Śaka influence on them.[4] The head of the Sanakānīka family, known from an inscription from Udaigiri (No. 7), bore the title *mahārāja*. The Yaudheyas and the Kuṇindas as their coin-legends indicate had dedicated their kingdoms to their patron-deities Kārttikeya and Śiva, respectively.[5] Pires is of the view that Magadha was then under the Maukharis.[6] But there is no evidence to show that the Maukharis were a political power at that time; their rule in Magadha cannot be traced earlier than the fifth century AD. Jayaswal is of the opinion that Pāṭaliputra was the capital of Kotakula, which finds mention in the Allahabad pillar inscription.[7] But the inscription only mentions the presence of a king of Kota family as Samudragupta's captive at a city named Pushpa, and that does not necessarily mean that it was his capital or that his rule was in and around that city. Further, Pushpapura generally stands for Pāṭaliputra, but in some cases also connotes Kānyakubja.

P L Gupta[8] opines that at the time of the rise of the Guptas, Magadha was under the Sātavāhanas, which, as shown below, is not in the least possible. Some scholars[9] believe that Magadha with its capital at Pāṭaliputra was occupied in this period by the Muruṇḍas, and they were the overlords of the early Guptas. It is stated in a Chinese text that the Chinese embassy in Fu-nan learnt from that country's ambassador returning from India that Meou-loun was the title of the then (i.e. the third century AD) ruling king of India, and also that the Indian king sent Yueh-chih horses to the king of Fu-nan.[10] Meou-loun is taken to stand for Muruṇḍa. The Muruṇḍas have also been identified with the Maroundai of Ptolemy (second century AD),[11] who locates them 'on the left bank of the Ganges, south of the Gogra, down to the top of the delta'. D R Bhandarkar[12] considers the Muruṇḍas as of foreign origin ruling over the greater part of the Ganga valley in the early centuries of the Christian era. But as neither coins, nor inscriptions belonging to the Muruṇḍas are known, and as the area mentioned under their rule is almost the same as is known to have been under the Kushāṇas, he suggests that the two may be taken as identical. Some references pertaining to the geographical location of the Muruṇḍas do not favour their rule in Magadha with Pāṭaliputra as their capital. Viśvasphāṇi, referred to in the purāṇas, which mention thirteen Muruṇḍa kings, as a king of Magadha before the beginning of the Gupta rule, is taken by some scholars as a Muruṇḍa ruler, though according to another view[13] the name of the king is Indian, meaning 'conqueror of the world'. It has been suggested that Dharmadamadhara, known from a coin from Shisupalgarh,[14] may have been a Muruṇḍa ruler.[15] King Rudradāmaśrī, known from a fragmentary inscription from Mirzapur,[16] palaeographically datable to the third or the fourth century AD, is considered by some scholars as a Muruṇḍa.[17] A Vaiśālī seal-inscription refers to Queen Prabhudamā as a daughter of *Mahākshatrapa* Rudrasiṁha and sister of *Mahākshatrapa* Rudrasena[18] but makes no mention of her husband. D C Sircar[19] and some other scholars take her as a daughter of Western Kshatrapa ruler Rudrasiṁha I (181-88 and AD 191-97) and a sister of Rudrasena I (*c*. AD 199-222). S Chattopadhyaya suggests that she would have been a queen of a Muruṇḍa king, then ruling in the region around Vaiśālī.[20] It may be stated that while some scholars[21] believe that the Muruṇḍas were quite significant in mid-second-mid-third century AD, others are opposed to assigning any significant political role to them in the Ganga valley.[22] The Jaina *Prabhāvakacharita* of Prabhāchandrasūri[23] mentions an *āchārya* Pādalipta's converting a Muruṇḍa king to Jainism at Pāṭaliputra while on his visit there.[24] According to the *Āvaśyaka Bṛihadvṛitti*, a Muruṇḍa king of Pāṭaliputra sent an ambassador to the king of Peshawar.[25] Some terracotta figures from Patna, Vaiśālī and other sites in Bihar, datable between *c* AD 100 and 300 show some non-Indian features, which are considered by some scholars as suggestive of the presence of the Muruṇḍas in that area.[26] The queen of Uchchakalpa king Jayanātha (fifth century AD) has been mentioned as Muruṇḍasvāminī.[27] But neither the region where her parental family was located, nor the status of her family is known. In eastern India were the states of Samataṭa, Ḍavāka and Kāmarūpa, which find mention as border states of Samudragupta in the Allahabad pillar inscription (No. 1); their geographical position will be discussed later, in Chapter 5.

The purāṇas mention some Nāga ruling families. The *Vishṇu-purāṇa*[28] ascribes nine Nāga kings to three states, viz. Padmāvatī, Kāntipurī and Mathurā. The *Vāyu -purāṇa* and the *Brahmāṇḍa -purāṇa* refer to nine Nāga kings of Champāvatī and seven of Mathurā[29] According to Jayaswal, Kantīpurī was the seat of the Bhāraśivas, who are generally taken to be of Nāga lineage,[30] though nowhere are they mentioned as such. In fact, only one king of their family, namely Bhavanāga, is known and that too only from the Vākāṭaka records, and his nāga–ending name suggests that he belonged to the Nāga tribe. The Bhāraśivas are said to have performed ten sacrifices and this is taken to be the genesis of the name Daśāśvamedha for a *ghāṭ* at Vārāṇasī, and it is believed by some scholars, that the city was within their kingdom.[31] Some scholars consider Padmāvatī as their seat.[32] K P Jayaswal[33] gives the credit to the Bhāraśivas for defeating the Kushāṇas. Ahichchhatrā also seems to have been an important seat of Nāga power. During the time of Samudragupta its king was Achyuta, whose coins bearing legend *Achyu*, have been found in and around that ancient city, and who as per the evidence of the Allahabad pillar inscription (No. 1) was supplanted by Samudragupta.

Over the Deccan and some parts north of the Vindhyas, was the rule of the Vākāṭakas. K P Jayaswal[34] was of the opinion that there was an extensive Vākāṭaka empire established by King Pravarasena I, the performer of four horse-sacrifices, and that the Gupta ruler Chandragupta I and even Samudragupta in the earlier phase of his career, accepted his suzerainty. This, however, is unlikely. There was a matrimonial alliance between the Nāgas and the Vākāṭakas; Rudrasena I, the grandson of Pravarasena—the performer of four *aśvamedha* sacrifices, and son of Gautamīputra, has been referred to as Bhavanāga-*dauhitra*, 'daughter's son of Bhavanāga', which shows that the Vākāṭakas deemed matrimonial alliance with the Bhāraśivas as of great significance.

In Baghelkhand and the region around Kauśāmbī ruled the Maghas, known mainly from a fairly large number of their coins, many of them from Kauśāmbī. A hoard of their coins has been found at Fatehpur.[35] Some inscriptions of this dynasty have been found at Bandhogarh and Kauśāmbī,[36] and some seals, from sites like Bhita and Rajghat.[37] Most of the kings, as the evidence of epigraphs, seals and coins shows, have *magha* as the name-ending. Coins of King Magha have been found,[38] who should have been the founder of the dynasty which was named after him. Therefore, Magha, and not Megha as mentioned in the purāṇas,[39] is the correct form of the name of the dynasty.

Western India was under the Kārddamaka Śakas who had been ruling there for a couple of centuries. Epigraphic evidence shows that Śaka Śrīdharavarman was ruling in the region around Sanchi.[40] Shāka tribe was ruling in the western Punjab, and in the central Punjab were the Shīlada and the Gaḍahara tribes known from coins.[41] In the north were the kingdoms of Kartṛipura and Nepal, which find mention in

Samudragupta's Allahabad pillar inscription as 'border' states of his kingdom. In the north-west was the kingdom of Kashmir. The Sassanians, during Bahman II's reign, had conquered Sindh.[42] In an inscription of Shapur (AD 309-79) from Persepolis, the brother of that king has been referred to as an officer in charge of Sindh, Sakastan and Turkistan.[43] Thus at the time of the beginning of the rule of the Imperial Guptas, northern India was fragmented into several states, large and small, monarchical and tribal. Below, we discuss the history of the first three Gupta kings.

## *MAHĀRĀJA* GUPTA

The Gupta epigraphs detailing genealogy mention the first king of the dynasty as Śrī-Gupta. It appears that the name of the king was Gupta and *śrī* was added as an honorific prefix,[44] and did not form part of the name. If the name would have been Śrīgupta then normally it would have been prefixed by *śrī* and inscribed as *Śrī*-Śrīgupta, as seen in *Śrī*-Śrīmatī—the name of a queen of the Later Gupta dynasty.[45] I-tsing, who travelled in India between AD 671 and 695, in his memoir, composed in AD 691-92, refers to the account of the Korean monk, Hwui-lun (also called Prajñāvarmā), which states that 500 years or so before, as per the 'tradition handed down from ancient times by old men', *Mahārāja* Che-li-ki-to built a temple for the use of the Chinese priests and endowed 24 large villages for its maintenance.[46] The name of the king may be rendered as Śrīgupta.[47] Fleet[48] points out that 500 years later from AD 691-92 when I-tsing wrote his memoir, would mean end of the second century AD, which is too early a date for the grandfather of Chandragupta I whose accession took place in AD 319, and that the founder of the Gupta dynasty was Gupta, and not Śrīgupta as met with in the Chinese account, and hence the two should not be taken as identical, unless it is believed that I-tsing mistook the prefix Śrī as part of the name. S K Aiyangar,[49] too, taking them as two separate individuals opines that probably the king mentioned by I-tsing was the grandfather of Gupta. It is, however, difficult to believe that the grandfather of *Mahārāja* Gupta, whose existence is not known from any source, would have been so eminent as to grant 24 villages. Allan,[50] however, opines that the figure 500 should not be taken literally and could refer to any date between 400 and 500 years, and by this reckoning, the king can be placed in the middle of the third century AD. It may be noted that another Chinese pilgrim, Hiuen-tsang, who stayed in India from AD 629 to AD 644, also records the date of some happenings incorrectly as, for example, can be seen in his placing Mihirakula 'some centuries' before his own time whereas the Hūṇa king lived only about a century earlier.[51] Therefore, the date given by I-tsing should not be deemed as exact, but as approximate. He considers it unlikely that two kings of the name Śrīgupta (or Gupta) ruled in the area of Magadha within such a brief period. Raychaudhuri,[52] however, points out that two kings of the name Chandragupta and two of the name of Kumāragupta, in the Gupta dynasty itself are known to have ruled within a short period. Like a few other scholars, he believes that I-tsing's record refers to king 'Śrīgupta' while the name in the Gupta epigraphs should be taken as 'Gupta', *Śrī* in the latter case being an honorific prefix and not part of the name. The legend *Śrīr-Guptasya* on some seals, discussed below, and not *Śrīguptasya*, supports the view that the name of the owner of the seal was Gupta, which is one of Vishṇu's thousand names.[53] However, it cannot be stated with certainty that the seal belonged to the Gupta king of the same name. The mention of the kings of the Gupta dynasty as *Gupta-vaṁśajāḥ* in the purāṇas may be taken to mean as born in the family of Gupta, which would favour the view that Gupta was the name of the founder of the dynasty.

A seal bearing the legend *Gutasya*,[54] in a mixture of Sanskrit and Prakrit, is taken by some as belonging to the first Gupta king. However, the Prakrit form of the name does not favour the identification as the epigraphs and coin-legends of the Guptas are all in Sanskrit. A sealing of unknown provenance with the Sanskrit legend *Śrīr-Guptasya*, has been reported from the collection of Hoernle.[55] Some sealings from Sunet bear identical legend of which we published two from the collection of the Indian Museum, Calcutta.[56] One such sealing has been published by J Agrawal,[57] and a few such sealings were seen by me in the collection of G B Sharma. Sunet lies in north-west India whereas the kingdom of the early Guptas lay in eastern Uttar Pradesh and Magadha. It is possible for a sealing to travel to a place away from the location of the owner of the seal. However, it is less likely that Śrī-Gupta made frequent correspondence with some person or office located at Sunet, situated far away from his kingdom. These sealings should better be taken as issued by someone of the same name residing in Sunet or its neighbourhood. A sealing with the name Śrī-gupta in the fourth century script has been found at Rajghat (Vārāṇasī).[58] However, in the absence of the title *mahārāja*, the identity of the issuer of this seal, like the other seals referred to above, with the first Gupta ruler would remain doubtful. The Kaliyuga-rājavṛittānta of the *Bhavishyottara-purāṇa* mentions Gupta king Śrī-Gupta as lord of Śrī-parvata, but the evidence has to be ignored since the work has been proved as a forgery (Chapter 1).

If Chandragupta I's accession is placed in AD 319, then the combined reign period of his two predecessors could be about 50 years,which may be placed from AD 269 to 319. But if AD 319 is taken as the date of accession of Samudragupta, suggested as one of the possibilities by some scholars (Appendix IV), taking the year 5 in his Nālandā copperplate inscription as pertaining to the Gupta era, then Chandragupta I would have become king earlier than that, and the first Gupta ruler would very well have begun his rule in *c* AD 250, which would bring him closer to 500 years before I-tsing. R K Mookerji[59] considers 319 as the date of coronation of Chandragupta I and suggests long reigns for his two predecessors—from AD 240 to AD 280 for the first Gupta ruler and 280 to 319 for his son, which brings Śrīgupta nearer to the date arrived at as per the memoirs of I-tsing. If Śrīgupta is taken as the grandfather of Gupta, then the genealogy of the Gupta dynasty met with in the Gupta epigraphs should normally have been traced from him, which is not the case. Smith argued that 'Gupta', which means 'protected', does not go well as a proper name, while Śrīgupta, 'protected by Śrī', is an appropriate name and this should be the rendering of the Chinese Che-li-ki-to also.[60] D R Bhandarkar is also doubtful about 'Gupta' being a proper name.[61] The names Chandra, Samudra, Kumāra, etc., he says, are genuine proper names, and joining these with the dynastic name, gupta, forms a complete name, viz. Chandragupta, Samudragupta, Kumāragupta, etc.; and if Gupta was his first name, then the addition of the family name would make it Gupta-gupta, which sounds strange. But as stated above, Gupta is one of the names of Vishṇu, and hence a complete name by itself, therefore there would be no need of adding *gupta* to it. According to Bhandarkar,[62] Gupta, even though a non-entity, was mentioned, and as 'it served no useful purpose to reveal his name, and so he has been mentioned by his family name Gupta, and the title *mahārāja* was appended to it, it seems by way of courtesy' by the officials of Samudragupta and the practice was followed by the other Gupta rulers.[63] But *gupta* as a name-ending was for the first time introduced by Chandragupta I, whose father has been referred to as Ghaṭotkacha, and not Ghaṭotkachagupta, and therefore it is better to take

Gupta, and not Śrīgupta, as the name of the grandfather of Chandragupta I. B Ch Chhabra[64] states that Chandragupta I, by adding Gupta to his name, showed respect to his grandfather, the founder of the Gupta dynasty, and at the same time, as a Vaishṇava, showed respect to Vishṇu, one of whose names is Gupta.

D R Bhandarkar is of the view that in the Imperial Gupta genealogy, the name 'Gupta' has been mentioned because Chandragupta I was the first independent king of the Gupta family, and the names of his father and grandfather had to be specified, as 'it is customary to introduce an illustrious personage by specifying details at least two generations preceding him'.[65] R D Banerji is of the opinion that in the fourth century AD, the title *mahārāja* had ceased to denote an imperial rank or even that of an independent prince and had come to be used for the feudatories and governors. The imperial rank came to be denoted by *mahārājādhirāja*, which is the title of practically all the Gupta kings except the first two rulers,[66] and therefore the first two rulers should be taken as petty princes. This conclusion finds support from the fact that, of the kings mentioned in the epigraphs detailing Gupta genealogy as met with in several inscriptions, the names of the queens of only these two rulers do not find mention. It may, however be stated that the title *mahārāja* [67] has also been used by some Vākāṭaka and Nāga rulers, who were contemporaries of the Gupta kings, though in all probability they were independent kings, and some scholars therefore suggest that it is not necessary to conclude from the *mahāraja* title of the first two Gupta rulers that they were feudatories. S R Goyal[68] states that the title *rājā* has been used even for the mighty king Samudragupta in his Tiger-slayer type of coins,[69] and as such, the two *mahārājas* could have been independent kings. But that is an exceptional case; in other coins and epigraphs he has invariably been referred to as *mahārājādhirāja*. In the Gupta seals detailing genealogy, the first two kings of the Gupta dynasty are invariably referred to as *mahārajas*, and the rest as *mahārājādhirājas*. The statement of Ashvini Agrawal[70] that even the mighty king Aśoka has been referred to as *rājā*, is not relevant in this context, as in the time of that ruler, *rājā* was the only title used for sovereigns, great and small; the titles *mahārāja* and *mahārājādhirāja* had not been introduced till then. J S Negi does not rule out the possibility (though he does not favour it) that Gupta may not have been an historical personage at all but an eponymous ancestor invented for explaining the derivation of the dynastic name *Guptavaṁśa* or *Guptakula*.[71] In his view, "it is not wholly impossible that the word *prapautra* denotes the relationship of Gupta with Samudragupta in the epigraphs is in the general sense of 'descendant'."

According to V A Smith, the first two Gupta rulers were feudatories of some Indo-Scythian sovereign.[72] R D Banerji[73] takes them as feudatories of the Kushāṇas. Majumdar[74] considers that unlikely, as according to him, during this period, Kushāṇa rule was confined to north-western India and as such there is no question of driving them out from Magadha. Allan considers King Gupta to have ruled over Pāṭaliputra and the neighbouring region.[75] Some scholars hold that the Guptas were subservient to the Lichchhavis. D C Ganguly[76] locates the capital of the first Gupta king in Bengal. S R Goyal[77] who believes that the original kingdom of the Guptas was in eastern UP, holds that the first ruler of the dynasty was a high official or a feudatory in the service of the Maghas who ruled over the Baghelkhand region. The number of kings of Magha dynasty is fairly large and a number of their coins seals and inscriptions are known, indicating the long reign of that dynasty. It may be that the Maghas became subordinate to Chandragupta I, whose rule, as inferred from the purāṇic evidence, included Prayāga and its adjoining regions.

There is not evidence for the religious leanings of King Gupta. If he, like the other Gupta kings, was a Vaishṇava, then his erecting a Buddhist temple and endowing villages to it reflects his liberal religious outlook, which is also seen in the case of his great-grandson, Samudragupta, in all probability a Vaishṇava, granting permission to the Sri Lankan monks for erecting a Buddhist monastery at Bodhgaya (Chapter 5). A few scholars give Gupta the credit of founding the Gupta era with initial year AD 319. But it does not seem likely that he would have done so as he was a feudatory, and besides, placing the beginning of his reign in AD 319 would mean quite short periods for the rules of Chandragupta I and Samudragupta, which is unlikely.

## GHAṬOTKACHA

Gupta was succeeded by his son Ghaṭotkacha.[78] In the Gupta epigraphs detailing genealogy, Ghaṭotkacha, like his father, Gupta, has been referred to as *mahārāja*, in contradistinction to his son, Chandragupta I and the latter's successors, who have been mentioned as *mahārājādhirāja*. Most scholars believe that his status was that of a feudatory. In only one Gupta inscription, viz. the Supia (Rewa district) inscription of the time of

Skandagupta (No. 32), the genealogy of the Gupta kings begins with this ruler, and not with his father, as is the case with the genealogy met with in the official Gupta records. This, however, is also the case with the two records of Vākāṭaka queen, Prabhāvatīguptā, daughter of Chandragupta II, namely, the Rithpur (No. 84) and Poona (No. 82) copperplates. R C Majumdar,[79] considering the fact that the above-mentioned epigraphs referring to Ghaṭotkacha as the first Gupta king are not official Gupta records, opines that 'we cannot attach much importance to the omission of Gupta, the name of the first ruler'. He considers it as a slip, probably not due to 'ignorance' but due to 'inadvertence' on the part of the composers of these records.[80] However, if the omission is deliberate, then Ghaṭotkacha was regarded as a more important figure than his father. In the Rithpur plate the genealogy begins with *Guptānāmādirājo* and in the Poona plates with *Guptādirāja*, and in both cases it is followed by the name of Ghaṭotkacha.[81] Both these expressions have been translated by the editors of the epigraphs as 'Ghaṭotkacha who had Gupta as the first king'. This interpretation cannot be entirely ruled out, though the view that they mean that Ghaṭotkacha was the first king of the Gupta dynasty seems more convincing and is generally accepted.[82] The Supia inscription mentions the Gupta dynasty as Ghaṭotkacha-*vaṁśa*, and after Ghaṭotkacha, it mentions Samudragupta, leaving Chandragupta I, and calls Samudragupta as *mahārāja*, and not *mahārājādhirāja*. D R Bhandarkar[83] suggests that Ghaṭotkacha was the first king of the dynasty, and the name Gupta was added to give a two generation pedigree to Chandragupta I. The Gupta-Lichchhavi matrimonial alliance in the form of Chandragupta I-Kumāradevī marriage was probably negotiated by Ghaṭotkacha.[84] It has been suggested that the marriage took place in about AD 308, some years before the accession of Chandragupta I in AD 319. Goyal[85] opines that it was the marriage of a Bhāraśiva princess to a Vākāṭaka prince that motivated the Guptas and the Lichchhavis to enter into a matrimonial alliance.

The Gupta epigraphs invariably mention the second Gupta ruler as Ghaṭotkacha, and not Ghaṭotkachagupta. No inscription or coin of this ruler is known. Coins bearing the name Kācha cannot be ascribed to him (Chapter 4); he should not to be identified with Ghaṭotkachagupta known from two coins—one in the St Petersburg collection[86] and another in the Ajit Ghose's collection.[87] Nor should he be identified with the homonym of a Vaiśālī sealing, though T Bloch,[88] V A Smith[89] and R G Basak[90] identified him with that ruler. Ghaṭotkachagupta of coins and the sealing should better be identified with the homonym mentioned in the Tumain inscription of the time of King Kumāragupta I (No. 19) dated Gupta era 116 (= AD 435), and in a recently discovered Vākāṭaka inscription (No. 85) which in clear terms mentions him as a son of Chandragupta II, rather than with Ghaṭotkacha, the second Gupta ruler. It is difficult to agree with the view that the formidable physical strength of Ghaṭotkacha elicited the praise of his neighbours and induced them to enter into matrimonial alliance with him,[91] or that possibly the name Ghaṭotkacha was given to him after he proved himself a young man of martial vigour and adventurous spirit.[92] Most probably, the name Ghaṭotkacha was given after the homonym *Mahābhārata* hero in the name-giving (*nāmakaraṇa)* ceremony, which must have been performed a few days after his birth; and there is hardly any possibility of the development of such physical features in an infant. There is no evidence in support of the view that it was adopted as a second name by the Gupta prince because of his achievements in his adulthood. H C Raychaudhuri[93] suggests that some stories in the *Mahābhārata*, describing the sins and inequities of Ghaṭotkacha, the son of Bhīma begotten on Hiḍimbā, were omitted in the final redaction of that epic during the Gupta age 'out of deference' to the Gupta ruler Ghaṭotkacha. His reign period may be placed between *c.* 299 and *c.* 319 though, as stated above, R K Mookerji would assign him a reign period of 40 years.

## CHANDRAGUPTA I

### I

Chandragupta I was the first *mahārājādhirāja* of the Gupta dynasty, which indicates his independent sovereign status in contradistinction to his father Ghaṭotkacha and grandfather Gupta, who were *mahārājas*, i.e. feudatories. As seen above, some scholars point out that in that age even some independent kings bore the title *mahārāja*. K P Jayaswal[94] holds that Chandragupta I (and even Samudragupta in the early phase of his reign) accepted the suzerainty of Pravarasena Vākāṭaka, the performer of four horse sacrifices. T P Verma,[95] also opines that not only the two *mahārājas,* Gupta and Ghaṭotkacha, were feudatories, but even the first *mahārājādhirāja*, Chandragupta I, had the same status. In support of his view he refers to the evidence of the Supia inscription of Skandagupta

(No. 32), in which the genealogy begins with Samudragupta born in the family of Ghaṭotkacha and does not mention Chandragupta I. But this is an exception; and since in all the inscriptions of the Gupta dynasty detailing genealogy, the order of succession is—*Mahārāja* Gupta, his son *Mahārāja* Ghaṭotkacha, and the latter's son *Mahārājādhirāja* Chandragupta, it would be unfair to discard the overwhelming evidence, and base conclusion on the evidence of merely one inscription which is a private and not an official one. Verma's view that the title *mahārājādhirāja* was ascribed to Chandragupta I as it was not deemed proper to portray Samudragupta's father as a feudatory, does not seem convincing; for if the intention would have been to glorify the ancestors of Samudragupta in this way, then the title *mahārājādhirāja* would very well have been ascribed also to the first two kings—Gupta and Ghaṭotkacha. Nor can one agree with his view that since the earliest Gupta inscriptions belong to Samudragupta, he should have been the first independent king of the Gupta dynasty. Of the Mauryan dynasty, the earliest inscriptions belong to Aśoka, although Chandragupta, his illustrious grandfather, and Bindusāra, his father, had ruled before him as paramount sovereigns. As will be seen below, the extent of the kingdom of Chandragupta I, which was much augmented by the amalgamation of the Lichchhavi territories in it as a result of his marriage with the Lichchhavi princess, was worthy of a *mahārādhirāja.* It is rather curious that whereas scholars like Fleet,[96] Aiyangar[97] and Basak[98] identify Chandragupta I with King Chandra of the Mehrauli inscription (a view to which we do not subscribe, as will be seen in Appendix III) and ascribe to him extensive conquests as far as Bactria, and defeating in Vaṅga the enemies who had united against him, and states that the water of the southern sea was scented by the air of his prowess, Jayaswal and Verma are not ready to concede to him even the status of an independent king. Both the views represent two extremes, one much overrating the achievements of Chandragupta I, and the other considerably underrating them.

Chandragupta I was the first king of the dynasty in whose name and the name of his queen Kumāradevī were issued a type of gold coins, designated by the numismatists as 'Chandragupta I-Kumāradevī' type, showing on the obverse standing figures of Chandragupta and Kumāradevī with their names inscribed, and on the reverse, a goddess riding a lion and the legend *Lichchhavayaḥ.* The authorship of the coin-type has variously been ascribed to Chandragupta I, Samudragupta, and the Lichchhavis by different scholars on various grounds which have been discussed in detail in Appendix I, below. Some scholars have ascribed a few other coin-types to this ruler[99] but their ascription remains doubtful.

It is generally believed that the Gupta era, commencing in AD 319, was founded by Chandragupta I, most probably on the occasion of his coronation (Appendix IV, below). His marriage must have been solemnized some years earlier than that date, probably in about AD 308, as suggested by some scholars. If the Nālandā copperplate inscription of Samudragupta, dated year 5 (No. 3), is a copy of the partly damaged genuine plate of that ruler and if the date is to be referred to the Gupta Era, it would mean that Chandragupta I ruled for five years, or even less, and that Samudragupta had become king in or before AD 324. There is a view that it is possible that the later kings continued to give date counting from Samudragupta's accession, and thus an era—the Gupta era—came to be founded.[100] However, it seems more convincing that the plate gives the regnal year of Samudragupta. S R Goyal[101] suggests that Chandragupta II, in whose Mathura inscription is met with for the first time the use of the date in the Gupta Era (though without naming the era as 'Gupta era') founded that era, but counted the years from the date of the accession of Chandragupta I, the first *mahārājādhirāja* of the Gupta dynasty (Appendix IV) as its beginning.

K P Jayaswal reconstructed the history of Chandragupta I on the basis of the evidence of the *Kaumudī-mahotsava*, which he considered as a fairly reliable source of history.[102] While a few other scholars[103] also hold that the work contains some historical material, most scholars[104] reject it as a source of history. According to the text, Chaṇḍasena was an adopted son of King Sundaravarman of Magadha and also his commander. After Sundaravarman's own son, Kalyāṇavarman[105] was born, relation between him and Chaṇḍasena became strained, and the latter, allying himself with the 'barbarous' Lichchhavis, killed Sundaravarman and became king. Later, Kalyāṇavarman, with the help of his father's minister, Mantragupta, uprooted Chaṇḍasena and his progeny. Jayaswal identifies Chaṇḍasena with Chandragupta I, and Kalyāṇavarman with the Kotakulaja (scion of the Kota family) of the Allahabad pillar inscription who was captured by the army of Samudragupta. This reconstruction of the Gupta history, however, does not fit in with the known facts about it. The Gupta epigraphs detailing genealogy, mention Chandragupta I's father as Ghaṭotkacha, and not Sundaravarman. Chandragupta I is not known to have become king after killing his father, and he had a fairly long reign. His progeny was not uprooted but succeeded him.[106] Chandra in Prakrit should normally be Chanda rather than Chaṇḍa, and while Chandragupta I has a *gupta*-ending name which is the name–ending of all his successors, Chaṇḍasena has a *sena*-ending name, which is not the name-ending of any Gupta ruler. The *Kaumudī-mahotsava* calls Chaṇḍasena a kāraskara, which it is doubtful that Chandragupta I was.[107] It refers to the Lichchhavis (which is the only significant link between this work and the epigraphic and numismatic evidence) as *mlechchhas*, which is incorrect.[108]

P L Gupta[109] suggested that as in the *Kaumudī-mahotsava*, Kalyāṇavarman has been referred to as Karṇiputra, so his father Sundavarman was Karṇi, which should be taken as a short form of Sātakarṇi. He identified Magadha-kula of the *Kaumudī-mahotsava* with the Sātavāhana-kula, and supported it with the evidence of Kaliyuga-rājavṛittānta of the *Bhavishyottara-purāṇa*, which, according to him, mentions the Andhra king Chandraśrī as a king of Magadha. But as against this, it has been pointed out that no king with a *varman*-ending name is known in the Sātavāhana dynasty, that the Sātavāhana family has never been called Magadha-kula, and that Karṇiputra is not an abbreviation of Sātakarṇi, but is a mistake for *karṇipatra*, i.e., the leaf of the *karṇikā* plant.[110] No Sātavāhana king, not even the greatest of them—Gautamīputra—had effective control on any part of northern India, and even in the inscription of his son he has been merely mentioned as 'lord of the Dakshiṇāpatha'. There was no Āndhra rule in the fourth century AD, and the evidence of the Kaliyuga-rājavṛittānta cannot be relied upon as it has proved to be a modern forgery (Chapter 1), and even P L Gupta,[111] in his later writings expresses doubt about the historical value of its evidence. The view of R D Banerji[112] that at the time of the beginning of the rise of the Gupta power, the later Kushāṇas, whose copper coins in large number and also some gold coins have been found in the Magadha region,[113] had hold over it, and that Chandragupta I was the leader of a band of heroes, who imbued with national spirit successfully fought 'war of independence' against them, and also the reason why the view cannot be sustained, have been stated above.

## II

The marriage of Chandragupta I with the Lichchhavi princess Kumāradevī, was an event of considerable significance in the history of that period and particularly in that of the Gupta dynasty. Significantly, of all the Gupta queens, it is only Kumāradevī whose paternal family finds mention in epigraphs and coins. It is generally believed that the extension of power and prestige of Chandragupta I, and his rise from a *mahārāja*, a local ruler, to that of a *mahārājādhirāja*, an independent sovereign, were the result of this matrimonial alliance.[114] The alliance was also an important factor in Chandragupta's selecting Samudragupta as his successor, which proved to be of great significance in shaping the course of history. Matrimonial alliances for political gain were not uncommon in ancient India.[115]

There is however, difference of opinion amongst scholars regarding the status of Kumāradevī, her nativity and the importance of her marriage with Chandragupta I. Allan[116] suggests that the alliance was the result of the conquest of the Lichchhavis of Vaiśālī by Chandragupta I, one of his earliest conquests, and the treaty between the two that followed. Basak[117] and Sohoni,[118] too, are of the same view. This, however, does not seem to be convincing. If the maternal grandfather of Samudragupta was defeated by his father Chandragupta I, then he would not have taken pride in calling himself as *Lichchhavi-dauhitra* (daughter's son of the Lichchhavi [chief]).[119] In the list of the territories mentioned in the *Vāyu-purāṇa* which as will be seen below, seems to refer to Chandragupta I's reign, Vaiśālī, which was the capital of the Lichchhavis during the time of the Buddha, does not find mention among the early territories of the Guptas. On the Chandragupta-Kumāradevī type of coins, Kumāradevī is shown along with her husband, and some scholars[120] interpret it as indicative of her status as joint sovereign with him, which status she would not have been given, had she been the daughter of the vanquished Lichchhavi chief. Nor in that case importance would have been shown to the Lichchhhavis by referring to Samudragupta as *Lichchhavi-dauhitra* in his own and in his successors' epigraphs. There is a view[121] that *Lichchhavi-dauhitra* for Samudragupta and also other known examples of kings referring themselves as *dauhitra* of their maternal grandfather, are meant only to show that the kings took pride in mentioning such relationship and nothing more, and it is not necessary to infer that the Lichchhavis contributed greatly to the rise of the Guptas. However, from the representation of the Lichchhavi princess Kumāradevī on coins with her name either prefixed or suffixed with *śrī*, and also the name of her tribe—the Lichchhavis—which has no parallel in the whole of the Gupta history, it is reasonable to infer that the Guptas owed much to them.[122]

The location of the Lichchhavi territories during the first quarter of the fourth century AD is a matter of controversy, and variously Pāṭaliputra,[123] Vaiśālī[124] and Nepal[125] have been suggested in that connection. In fact, after the Lichchhavis were conquered by Ajātaśatru, till the time of Kumāradevī's marriage with Chandragupta I, we hear nothing of them as a political power. The view that Chandragupta I's matrimonial alliance was with the Lichchhavis of Nepal, is not convincing as it does not seem that Kumāradevī would have been given so much of importance in the records of Samudragupta and his successors if she had been the daughter of the chief of Nepal, as Nepal is mentioned as a subordinate border state (*pratyanta*) of Samudragupta in the Allahabad pillar inscription (No. 1). The use of the plural *Lichchhavayaḥ* clearly shows that the tribe as a unit is meant, and not a single Lichchhavi person or a family, and the reference could not be to the Lichchhavis of Nepal who had a monarchical form of government. S Chattopadhyaya[126] opines that Kumāradevī might not have been a princess but a commoner belonging to a Lichchhavi family But Chandragupta I as a prince or king would normally have married a princess (who was to become his chief queen), rather than a commoner. If she would have been a commoner, the Lichchhavis would not have found a place in the legend on the Chandragupta I-Kumāradevī type of coins, nor would Samudragupta have taken pride in calling himself *Lichchhavi-dauhitra*. Smith, who earlier located Lichchhavis in Nepal,[127] later, changed his opinion in favour of Pāṭaliputra as their capital.[128] The Allahabad pillar inscription refers to Samudragupta as amusing himself in a city called Pushpa, which is generally taken to indicate Pāṭaliputra which would have been located within the Gupta territory.[129] Allan[130] believes that the temple referred to by I-tsing as built by Śrīgupta was in Magadha, and not in Murshidabad or Vārendra, or eastern Uttar Pradesh as some scholars variously hold, and Pāṭaliputra was within his territory. And if so, it could have formed part of the kingdom of his son Ghaṭotkacha, and grandson, Chandragupta I.

The Lichchhavis were quite prominent and the marriage of Chandragupta I with their princess was of great significance and help in the rise of the Gupta power. It is generally believed that Kumāradevī's father was the last male chief of the Lichchhavis, and she was his only child. Some scholars hold that being a female child, as per smṛiti rules, she could not have succeeded her father. V S Pathak[131] points out that *putrikāputra* (son of a daughter) is one of the twelve types of sons who, as *dvyāmushyāyaṇa*, could inherit his father's and also his maternal grandfather's property, and, therefore, it would have been Samudragupta, and not Chandragupta I, who would have inherited the Lichchhavi territory. As per the smṛiti rule, Samudragupta could be an inheritor of his paternal kingdom only if he had no brothers.[132] But this condition would not apply in the case of Samudragupta, as he was selected by his father, King Chandragupta I, as his successor to the Gupta throne. Trautmann[133] is of the view that the smṛiti rules relating to inheritance are meant for general property, and should not be applied for the kingdom. D R Bhandarkar[134] opines that by this marriage alliance, Chandragupta became a joint ruler of the Lichchhavi territory.

It is known that Vākāṭaka king Pravarasena I entered into a matrimonial alliance with the Bhāraśivas by getting his son, crown-prince Gautamīputra, married with the daughter of the Bhāraśiva ruler Bhavanāga. S R Goyal[135] is of the view that it took place in about AD 300, and that it was with a view to countering the danger posed by this Vākāṭaka-Bhāraśiva alliance that the Guptas and the Lichchhavis entered into matrimonial alliance. It appears that Pravarasena I Vākāṭaka took the title of *samrāṭ* after matrimonial alliance with the Bhāraśivas, and Chandragupta I, after his marriage with the Lichchhavi princess, designated himself as *mahārājādhirāja*, both titles being suggestive of the rank of independent sovereign. But as D K Ganguly points out, in the case of the Vākāṭaka-Bhāraśiva alliance, there is no evidence to show that the Vākāṭakas offered any help to the Nāgas when Samudragupta invaded them and conquered them and amalgamated their kingdom in his own.[136]

The help of the Lichchhavis to the Guptas in their rise as a great political power is beyond doubt.[137] H C Raychaudhuri[138] opines that on the Chandragupta-Kumāradevī type of coins, the representation of Chandragupta I and Kumāradevī and their names on the obverse and the deity identified by some as Lakshmī together with the legend *Lichchhavayaḥ* on the reverse suggests that the prosperity that Chandragupta I enjoyed was the result of the matrimonial alliance with the Lichchhavis. Allan[139] is of the view that the advantage of the alliance was in relating Chandragupta I with the 'ancient heritage of the Lichchhavis' rather than in bringing some material gain to him. But some scholars, basing on Manu's statement[140] that the Lichchhavis were *vrātya* (unorthodox and impure) kshatriyas, rate them low socially, which goes against the view of Allan. Others, however, point out that Manu was a champion of Brahmanical religion and calls Lichchhavis as *vrātyas* as they patronized the heterodox sects, Buddhism and Jainism, and therefore his view need not be taken as reflecting their actual status.

The matrimonial alliance of the Guptas with the Lichchhavis led to the amalgamation of the Lichchhavi territories with the Gupta kingdom. Scholars differ regarding the circumstances under which it happened. Smith is of the opinion that Chandragupta I got Pāṭaliputra as the result of his marriage with the Lichchhavi princess. S K Aiyangar,[141] however, disagrees with him and points out that the purāṇic evidence tends to show that Magadha, within which Pāṭaliputra is located, was part of his kingdom. Some scholars[142] hold that legally the amalgamation of the two kingdoms took place on the accession of Samudragupta; others opine that it took place immediately after Chandragupta I's marriage with the Lichchhavi princess. D K Ganguly[143] opines that Vaiśālī was gifted by the Lichchhavis to Chandragupta I in dowry and was amalgamated in the Gupta empire. Others point out that the portrait of Kumāradevī along with that of Chandragupta I and the mention of the clan of the Lichchhavis in the coin-legend suggest that the queen was a sovereign in 'her own right.'[144] Altekar[145] believes that there was joint rule of Chandragupta I and Kumāradevī like that of William and Mary in the history of England. In the Allahabad pillar inscription, however, Samudragupta alone was nominated as successor to the throne by Chandragupta I, and not along with Kumāradevī. D K Ganguly[146] argues that in the King-and-Queen type of coins Kumāragupta I, the king and his queen are similarly disposed, but no scholar has ever suggested the possibility of a joint rule in that case, and therefore joint rule need not be inferred in the case of Chandragupta-Kumāradevī type of coins. But the comparison is not quite apt, as on the coins of Kumāragupta I neither the name of the queen is mentioned nor that of her family, nor do the epigraphs of his own or that of his successors mention the family of his queen. Besides, Kumāragupta I issued the coin type in question in imitation of the Chandragupta-Kumaradevī type, and so no such inference need be drawn in his case.

S R Goyal[147] speculates that at the time of his maternal grandfather's death, Samudragupta, the legal heir of the Lichchhavi territory, was a minor, and Chandragupta I acted as the regent for administering the Lichchhavi territory. This, he suggests, would explain the joint rule of the Guptas and the Māgadhas (who are identified by him with the Lichchhavis), as stated in the *Vishṇu-purāṇa*. According to this view legally the amalgamation of the Lichchhavi territory with Gupta kingdom would have taken place only with the accession of Samudragupta. Whatever be the case, the marriage alliance was a master stroke with which the Guptas got the Lichchhavi territory. It may be stated that about 800 years earlier, the Magadhan king, Ajātaśatru, could get hold over the Lichchhavi territories after sixteen years of war waged against them, and that too by resorting to dubious means.[148] The amalgamation of the Lichchhavi territories with that of the Guptas would have given the latter control over the iron and copper mines,[149] and considerably augmented their political and economic resources, which would have been of great help in enabling Chandragupta's son Samudragupta to launch successful offensive against the kings of the north and south India.

## III

Some idea about the extent of Chandragupta I's empire can be formed from the conquests of Samudragupta in northern and southern India, dealt with in Chapter 5. It can be said that the territories conquered by him were outside the kingdom of Chandragupta I. The evidence of the purāṇas, which refer to the territories ruled by the Guptas is also helpful in this regard. The *Vāyu-purāṇa* states –

*Anu-Gaṅgā Prayāgaṁ cha Sāketaṁ Magadhāṁs=tathā*
*Etān janapadān sarvān bhokshyante Gupta-vaṁśajāḥ.*

*Gupta-vaṁśajāḥ*[150] stands for the Imperial Guptas whose progenitor was Gupta. Bhandarkar[151] points out that the above verse is faulty, because Prayāga and Sāketa are not *janapadas*, but cities, and literally the text would mean Prayāga and Sāketa on the Gaṅgā, though Sāketa is not on that river but on the Sarayū. Moreover, it does not mention Kāśī, which lies in between Prayāga and Magadha. The verse, however, is generally taken to mean 'Kings born of the Gupta family will enjoy all these territories, viz., Prayāga (Allahabad) on the Ganges, Sāketa (Oudh) and Magadha (South Bihar)'.[152] Ashvini Agrawal[153] suggests that *anu-Gaṅgaṁ*[154] (and not *anu-Gaṅgā*), which form is met with in one of the *Vāyu-purāṇa* manuscripts, should be considered as the correct version, as it goes well with *anu-Gaṅgaṁ Hastināpuram* and such other examples cited by Kaiyaṭa while commenting on the *Mahābhāshya*[155] and obviates the placing of Sāketa on the Gaṅgā. Allan[156] and some other scholars consider this purāṇic evidence as indicative of the extent of the empire of Chandragupta I.

Pargiter[157] is also of the view that as the purāṇic account does not refer to Samudragupta's empire or his conquests, it must be referring to the reign of Chandragupta I. A few scholars suggest that the purāṇic evidence regarding the extent of the Gupta territory may conform to the kingdom of one of the predecessors of Chandragupta I.[158] There is also a suggestion that it may refer to the decadent phase of the Gupta empire in the first half of the sixth century AD. But both the views are not acceptable. In the first case, the kingdom that included Prayāga, Sāketa and Magadha was large enough to be worthy of a *mahārājādhirāja*, rather than of a *mahārāja*, which was the rank of the two predecessors of Chandragupta I. And as to the second, in its last phase, the Gupta empire seems to have been considerably reduced, and confined to Magadha and Bengal, whereas the purāṇic evidence cited above mentions Prayāga and Sāketa under the Gupta rule, but does not mention Bengal.[159] As stated above, like most scholars, this author does not agree with the view[160] that Chandra of the Mehrauli pillar inscription, who was a great conqueror and the master of an extensive empire, should be identified with Chandragupta I, and hence do not ascribe to him the large-scale conquests mentioned in that inscription, as has been done by a few scholars (Appendix III, below).

The *Vishṇu-purāṇa* has the following—*Anu-Gaṅgā Prayāgaṁ Māgadhā Guptāścha bhokshyanti.* The text omits Sāketa, and makes Māgadhā as a separate people ruling jointly with the Guptas.[161] There is a view that Māgadhas need not be taken as separate people but as qualifying the Guptas and the translation should be 'Guptas of Magadha'.[162] S R Goyal identifies Māgadhas with the Lichchhavis and suggests that it points to the joint rule of the Guptas and the Lichchhavis.[163] There is a view that the Lichchhavis were at Vaiśālī and since Chandragupta I as a result of his marriage with Kumāradevī became only a *de facto*, and not *de jure*, ruler of that region, it has not been referred to in the Purāṇas amongst the territories under the Guptas, though they should be referring to the extent of the Gupta kingdom during the reign of Chandragupta I. The *Bhāgavata-purāṇa* has *anu-Gāṅgaṁ=ā-Prayāgaṁ Guptāṁ bhokshyanti medinīṁ*, meaning '[They] will enjoy the protected earth along the Gaṅgā up to Prayāga', which is faulty as it 'leaves the sentence without a subject'.[164] There is merit in the view that of the different versions of the purāṇas, *anu-Gaṅgaṁ Prayāgañcha Sāketaṁ*, etc., met with in one of the manuscripts of the *Vāyu-purāṇa*, should be accepted.[165] As per the evidence of the Allahabad pillar inscription, Samudragupta uprooted the Nāga kings, who, according to the purāṇic evidence, ruled over Vidiśā, Mathurā and Padmāvatī. He conquered King Chandravarman who is to be identified with the homonym of the Susunia (Bankura district) inscription (No. 59). He conquered Mahākosala region, and Samataṭa (south-eastern Bengal) was a border state of that king. This shows that these territories were outside the kingdom of Chandragupta I. It is difficult to agree with the view of Ashvini Agrawal that Chandragupta I had conquered the Nāgas, but after his death they rebelled and were conquered by Samudragupta.[166] On the basis of the evidence of the Mehrauli pillar inscription, some scholars suggest that Bengal was first conquered by Chandragupta II, whom they identify with King Chandra of that inscription. From the purāṇic verses cited above, it is generally inferred that Chandragupta I's kingdom included Oudh, Prayāga and southern Bihar; and on the basis of one interpretation of the evidence of I-tsing's account mentioned above, it may have also included some parts of Bengal. The kingdom was large enough to earn him the title of *mahārājādhirāja*. The end of the rule of Chandragupta may be placed in *c* AD 344 (Appendix V). He declared in the Assembly his son Samudragupta as his successor, and, according to some scholars, perhaps abdicated in his favour. However, it appears that after him, another of his son named Kācha, usurped the throne and ruled for a short period.

## NOTES AND REFERENCES

1. R D Banerji, *The Age of the Imperial Guptas*, p. 2ff.
2. In *The Vākāṭaka-Gupta Age*, pp. 28ff.
3. J F Fleet, *Corpus Inscriptionum Indicarum*, III, p. 252.
4. A M Shastri, *Journal of the Andhra Historical Research Society*, XXXVIII, 1983-84, pp. 151ff.
5. J N Banerjea, *Development of the Hindu Iconography*, second ed., p. 142.
6. Pires, *The Maukharis*, p. 9.
7. K P Jayaswal, *Journal of the Bihar and Orissa Research Society*, XIX, p. 33.
8. P L Gupta, *The Imperial Guptas*, pp. 244-45.
9. Allan (*Catalogue of the Coins of the Gupta Dynasties, and of Śaśāṅka, the King of Gauḍa, in the British Museum, London*, p. xxx) opines that it was perhaps 'the decline of he Muruṇḍa power that gave the Gupta dynasty the opportunity for expansion.'
10. K P Jayaswal, *Imperial History of India*, p. 94.
11. *Geography*, VII, 2.14.
12. D R Bhandarkar, *Corpus Inscriptionum Indicarum*, III, p. 28.
13. U N Roy, *Gupta Rājavaṁśa tathā Usakā Yuga*, p. 72.

14. Illustrated in *Ancient India,* Bulletin of the Archaeological Survey of India, no. 5, pl. XLVIIIa.
15. See note by A S Altekar, in *ibid.*, p. 100.
16. *Indian Archaeology: A Review*, 1959-60, p. 61 (and not p. 65, as given in S R Goyal, *The Imperial Guptas*, p. 93, n.1.
17. S R Goyal, *The Imperial Guptas*, pp. 92-93. On the basis of date he has been taken as related to Western Śaka family (*Indian Archaeology: A Review*, 1959-60, p. 61).
18. *Archaeological Survey of India—Annual Report*, 1913-14, p. 13, No. 248, pl. XLVII.
19. In *The Age of Imperial Unity*, p. 187.
20. *Early History of North India*, p. 154. For the view of Dasharatha Sharma that she was a queen of Samudragupta, see Chapter V, below.
21. S R Goyal, *The Imperial Guptas*, pp. 90ff.
22. Ashvini Agrawal, *Rise and Fall of the Imperial Guptas*, pp. 71ff. He is of the opinion that the Chinese sources are based on second hand information and the location of the capital of Meou-loun 7000 *li* from the mouth of the Gaṅgā cannot be placed in Pāṭaliputra and would rather be Lampak in Afghanistan to which area they are ascribed by Hemachandrāchārya (*ibid.*).
23. *Vide* Ashvini Agrawal, *Rise and Fall of the Imperial Guptas*, pp. 72-73.
24. But according to this text the same person saw a king named Kṛishṇa ruling at Mānyakheṭa when he visited that city. Kṛishṇa should be identified with the homonym Rāshṭrakūṭa ruler who ruled in the second half of the eighth century AD. The placing of the two kings much removed from each other in time, as contemporaries, makes the evidence of the work unreliable (Ashvini Agrawal, *Rise and Fall of the Imperial Guptas*, pp. 72-73). The evidence of the *Tiloyapaṇṇati* places the Muruṇḍas in 246 BC (*ibid.* p. 73).
25. *Malaviya Commemoration Volume*, p. 284 (*vide* S R Goyal, *The Imperial Guptas*, p. 91).
26. S R Goyal, *The Imperial Guptas*, p. 92, n. 4.
27. For Muruṇḍasvāminī, see Fleet, *Corpus Inscriptionum Indicarum*, III, p. 136, and for Muruṇḍadevī, *ibid.*, p. 137.
28. *Dynasties of the Kali Age*, p. 53n.
29. *Ibid.*, p. 53.
30. *Journal of the Bihar and Orissa Research Society*, XIX, p. 29.
31. *Ibid.*
32. D R Bhandarkar, *Corpus Inscriptionum Indicarum*, III, pp. 10-11.
33. *Journal of the Bihar and Orissa Research Society*, XIX, p. 5.
34. *Journal of the Bihar and Orissa Research Society*, XIX, pp. 4-5.
35. A M Sastri, *Kauśāmbī Hoard of Magha Coins*, Nagpur, 1979, p. 5.
36. *Ibid.*, pp. 21-22.
37. For seals from Bhita, see *Archaeological Survey of India—Annual Report*, 1911-12, p. 51, nos. 26-28. For Rajghat seals, see K K Thaplyal, *Studies in Ancient Indian Seals*, pp. 36ff.
38. A M Sastri, *Kauśāmbī Hoard of Magha Coins*, p. 10.
39. A M Sastri, *ibid.*, p. 5.
40. D C Sircar, *Select Inscriptions*, I, pp. 186-87.

41. For coins, see Altekar, *The Coinage of the Gupta Empire*, p. 52.
42. S R Goyal, *Gupta Sāmrājya kā Itihāsa*, p. 40.
43. *Ibid.*
44. J F Fleet, *Corpus Inscriptionum Indicarum*, III, p. 8, n. 3; J Allan, *Catalogue of the Coins of the Gupta Dynasties, and of Śaśāṅka, the King of Gauḍa, in the British Museum, London*, p. xiv.
45. Line 2 of the Deo Barnark Inscription of Jīvitagupta, K K Thaplyal, *Inscriptions of the Maukharis, Later Guptas, Puṣpabhūtis, and Yaśovarman of Kanauj*, pp. 171, 173.
46. *Vide* S Beal, *The Life of Hiuen-tsang*, pp. xxxvi-xxxvii.
47. J S Negi (*Some Indological Studies*, I, p. 168) suggests that Chi-li-ki-to may simply mean an illustrious king of the Gupta dynasty.
48. J F Fleet, *Corpus Inscriptionum Indicarum*, III, p. 8, n. 2.
49. S K Aiyangar, *Journal of Indian History*, VI, p. 3.
50. *Catalogue of the Coins of the Gupta Dynasties, and of Śaśāṅka, the King of Gauḍa, in the British Museum, London*, intro. p. xv.
51. T Watters, *On Yuan Chwang's Travels in India*, I, p. 288. For other examples, see D K Ganguly, *The Imperial Guptas and Their Times*, pp. 8-9.
52. *Political History of Ancient India*, p. 468.
53. *Journal of the Numismatic Society of India*, IX, pp. 137-45.
54. E J Rapson, *Journal of the Royal Asiatic Society of Great Britain and Ireland*, 1905, p. 81.
55. *Vide Catalogue of the Coins of the Gupta Dynasties, and of Śaśāṅka, the King of Gauḍa, in the British Museum, London*, Intro, p. xiv. See also R J Rapson, *Journal of the Royal Asiatic Society of Great Britain and Ireland*, 1901, p. 99.
56. Nos. 4681-A-12865 and 4671-A-12859; see K K Thaplyal, *Studies in Ancient Indian Seals*, p. 65.
57. *Journal of the Numismatic Society of India*, XXVII, pp. 98-99.
58. S R Goyal, *The Imperial Guptas*, p. 105.
59. *Gupta Empire*, p. 11.
60. V A Smith, *Journal of the Asiatic Society of Bengal*, LIII(i), p. 119.
61. D R Bhandarkar, *Corpus Inscriptionum Indicarum*, III, p. 3.
62. *Ibid.*
63. *Ibid.*
64. B Ch Chhabra, *Catalogue of the Gupta Gold Coins of the Bayana Hoard in the National Museum*, p. xvi.
65. D R Bhandarkar, *Corpus Inscriptionum Indicarum*, III, p. 3.
66. R D Banerji, *The Age of the Imperial Guptas*, p. 3.
67. Among Indian kings, Khāravela (*c* first century BC) is perhaps the first to have used the title *mahārāja* (instead of *rājā*) and in his case, it undoubtedly stands for a paramount sovereign. Roughly, about the same time, some Kuṇinda and other tribal chiefs also used this title.
68. S R Goyal, *The Imperial Guptas*, p. 108, n. 1.
69. A S Altekar, *The Coinage of the Gupta Empire*, p. 71f.
70. Ashvini Agrawal, *Rise and Fall of the Imperial Guptas*, p. 85.
71. J S Negi, *Some Indological Studies*, I, p. 168.

72. V A Smith, *Journal of the Royal Asiatic Society of Great Britain and Ireland*, 1889, p. 55.
73. R D Banerji, *The Age of the Imperial Guptas*, p. 2.
74. R C Majumdar, in *Comprehensive History of India*, III(i), p. 1.
75. J Allan, *Catalogue of the Coins of the Gupta Dynasties, and of Śaśāṅka, the King of Gauḍa, in the British Museum, London*, p. xiv.
76. *Indian Historical Quarterly*, XIV, 532ff; *ibid.*, XXVIII, pp. 386-91.
77. S R Goyal, *The Imperial Guptas*, p. 107, n. 3.
78. Ghaṭotkacha which is the name of a hero in the *Mahābhārata*, need not be taken as a Sanskrtized form of a foreign name, as is suggested by some scholars.
79. In *Comprehensive History of India*, III(i), pp. 9-10.
80. *Ibid.*
81. *Ibid.*, p. 9, n. 21.
82. *Ibid.*, p. 9.
83. D R Bhandarkar, *Corpus Inscriptionum Indicarum*, III, p. 3.
84. S R Goyal, *The Imperial Guptas*, p. 107n. R G Basak (*History of North-Eastern India*, p. 8) is of the opinion that Ghaṭotkacha was a local ruler ruling from Pāṭaliputra; he might have conquered Vaiśalī with the help of his son Chandragupta and compelled the Lichchhavi chief to marry his daughter to the latter. However, he does not rule out the possibility of Chandagupta I himself conquering that territory.
85. S R Goyal, *The Imperial Guptas*, pp. 415-16.
86. A S Altekar, *The Coinage of the Gupta Empire*, p. 264.
87. *Journal of the Numismatic Society of India*, XXII, pp. 260-61.
88. *Archaeological Survey of India—Annual Report*, 1903-04, p. 102.
89. *Journal of the Royal Asiatic Society of Great Britain and Ireland*, 1905, p. 153.
90. *The History of North-Eastern India*, p. 7.
91. Ashvini Agrawal, *Rise and Fall of the Imperial Guptas*, p. 87.
92. *Ibid*. We are not told as to what was his original name. One may as well suggest that he like Ghaṭotkacha of the *Mahābhārata* was born of pre-marital relationship, though this seems unlikely, as his father, the king, would not have liked people to come to know such a relationship.
93. H C Raychaudhuri, *Calcutta Review*, 1934, p. 213.
94. K P Jayaswal, *Journal of the Bihar and Orissa Research Society*, XIX, pp. 4-5.
95. *Journal of the Numismatic Society of India*, LIII, pp. 115 ff.; also B Ch Chhabra, *et al.*, (ed.), *Reappraising Gupta History for S R Goyal*, p. 92. Nisar Ahmad (*Journal of the Numismatic Society of India*, LIII, p.107) has expressed similar view regarding the status of Chandragupta I.
96. J F Fleet, *Corpus Inscriptionum Indicarum*, III, p. 190, n. 1.
97. S K Aiyangar, *Journal of Indian History*, VI, pp. 22ff.
98. R G Basak, *History of North-Eastern India*, pp. 14ff.
99. Krishnaswami Aiyangar, (*Ancient India and South Indian History and Culture*, I, pp. 182ff; *Journal of Indian History*, VI, University Supplement, p. 9) opines that on Class I of the *Chhatra* type of coins, the royal figure is shown in a form different from those of Chandragupta II met with on other classes of this coins -

type, and therefore should be attributed not to him but to Chandragupta I. This is also the view of D R Bhandarkar (*Corpus Inscriptionum Indicarum*, III, p. 7-8) He says, "If any king of the Imperial Gupta dynasty had the first claim to issue this coinage, it was Chandragupta I', the first *mahārājādhirāja* of the family, more particularly as the type was not issued by other Gupta kings. He (*ibid.*) also opines that all the kings of the Gupta dynasty issued Archer type of coins and therefore it seems reasonable to suppose that Chandragupta I also would have done so. In our view, it is not issuing a coin-type but for the first time issuing it, that is relevant. Bhandarkar is of the view that some of the large varieties of Archer type of coins attributed to Chandragupta II may infact belong to Chandragupta I. But the coins under consideration bear the title *Vikramāditya*, and while it is the most common *āditya* title of Chandragupta II, there is no evidence to show that Chandragupta I also bore that title. Bhandarkar, however, does not consider this as a hurdle in the identification as the titles *vikrama* and *kramāditya* were borne by Skandagupta and a few other rulers of the Gupta dynasty, and might also have been the title of Chandragupta I. B Ch Chhabra (*Journal of the Numismatic Society of India*, XI, pp. 15ff) attributes to Chandragupta I a unique Standard type of coin, usually attributed to Chandragupta II by other scholars, mainly on the grounds that it does not bear the title *Vikramāditya*. But it has been pointed out (S R Goyal, *The Imperial Guptas*, p. 117n) that the title also does not occur on one variety of Archer type of Chandragupta II. Further, the coin-type bears the epithet *parama-bhāgavata*, and there is no evidence of the epithet being applied to Chandragupta I.

100. R C Majumdar, in *The Vākāṭaka-Gupta Age*, p. 32; in *Comprehensive History of India*, III(i), p. 15, n. 44.
101. S R Goyal, *The Imperial Guptas*, pp. 124 ff.
102. *Journal of the Bihar and Orissa Research Society*, XIX, pp. 113-14.
103. Dasharatha Sharma, *Journal of the Bihar and Orissa Research Society*, XXI 77; *ibid.*, XXII, pp. 275 ff.
104. For example, F W Thomas, *Indian Culture*, IX, p. 100; R C Majumdar, in *The Vākāṭaka-Gupta Age*, p. 133n.
105. E A Pires (*The Maukharis*, pp. 17and 28) considers Sundaravarman and Kalyāṇavarman as belonging to the Maukhari dynasty. But except for the similarity of *varman* name-ending, there is nothing to identify the two. The existence of the Maukhari dynasty in the first quarter of the fourth century AD is not known from any source.
106. Though he selected Samudragupta as his successor, the latter became king only after supplanting Kācha who had usurped the throne (Chapter 4, below).
107. For the caste of the Guptas, see Chapter 2, above.
108. R C Majumdar, in *Comprehensive History of India*, III(i) p, 14.
109. P L Gupta, *The Imperial Guptas*, p. 244.
110. J Agrawala, *Proceedings of the Indian History Congress*, 1948, pp. 94-9.
111. P L Gupta, *The Imperial Guptas*, p. 121.
112. R D Banerji, *The Age of the Imperial Guptas*, pp. 2-5.

113. According to R D Banerji (*ibid.*, p. 2) gold and copper coins of the later Kushāṇas were in abundance in the markets of Patna and Gaya.
114. For example, R G Basak, *The History of North-Eastern India*, p. 11.
115. For references to such marriages, see R G Basak, *The History of North-Eastern India*, pp. 9-10.
116. *Catalogue of the Coins of the Gupta Dynasties, and of āaśāṅka, the King of Gauḍa, in the British Museum, London*, p. xix.
117. R G Basak, *The History of North-Eastern India*, p. 8.
118. S V Sohoni, *Journal of the Numismatic Society of India*, V, p. 41.
119. In ancient India, mother's *gotra* (e.g. *Vātsī-putra, Kautsī-putra)* has been used for distinguishing princes born of different mothers, and one may presume that in *Lichchhavi-dauhitra* the clan name is meant to serve the same purpose. But no other Gupta king has been referred to with relation to mother's family. Further, the term has been used not only by Samudragupta for himself, but also by his successors for him, and in their time, it would not have been of any relevance to differentiate him from the sons of other queens of Chandragupta I. The term *Lichchhavi-dauhitra* for Samudragupta can be compared with *Bhavanāga-dauhitra* for the Vākāṭaka prince, Rudrasena I, and 'son of a Vākāṭaka princess' for Vishṇukuṇḍin Mādhavasena, and undoubtedly reflects the great regard in which the Lichchhavis were held by the Guptas.
120. For example, Altekar, *The Coinage of the Gupta Empire*, pp. 30-31.
121. T P Verma, *Journal of the Numismatic Society of India*, LIII, p. 120.
122. However, in some other cases the reference to someone as *dauhitra* of some one may be in the sense in which Verma takes it. A case in view is the mention of Goparāja in the Eran pillar inscription of Bhānugupta (No. 52), as *dauhitra* of Śarabharāja, who in all probability, is the same as Śarabha the founder of the Śarabhapurīya dynasty, for it is known that the latter was succeeded by his son Narendra.
123. V A Smith, *Early History of India*, p. 279.
124. A S Altekar, *The Coinage of the Gupta Empire*, p. 2.
125. *Journal of the Royal Asiatic Society of Great Britain and Ireland*, 1889, p. 55.
126. *Early History of North India*, pp. 173-74.
127. *Journal of the Royal Asiatic Society of Great Britain and Ireland*, 1889, p. 55.
128. *Early History of India*, p. 279.
129. Pushpapura (the same as Kusumapura), besides being used for Pāṭaliputra, has also been used for Kānyakubja (below).
130. *Catalogue of the Coins of the Gupta Dynasties, and of Śaśāṅka, the King of Gauḍa, in the British Museum, London*, pp. xv-xvi.
131. *Journal of the Numismatic Society of India*, XIX, pp. 140-41.
132. D R Bhandarkar, *Corpus Inscriptionum Indicarum*, III, p. 4.
133. T R Trautmann, *Journal of the Royal Asiatic Society of Great Britain and Ireland*, 1972 (i), pp. 5-6.
134. *Corpus Inscriptionum Indicarum*, III, p. 4
135. S R Goyal, *The Imperial Guptas*, p. 111.

136. D K Ganguly, *The Imperial Guptas and their Times*, p. 31.
137. R C Majumdar, in *The Vākāṭaka-Gupta Age*, pp. 127ff; *Comprehensive History of India*, III(i), pp. 10-12. 236; A S Altekar, *The Coinage of the Gupta Empire*, pp. 2, 30.
138. H C Raychaudhuri, *Political History of Ancient India*, pp. 468-69.
139. *Catalogue of the Coins of the Gupta Dynasties, and of Śaśāṅka, the King of Gauḍa, in the British Museum, London*, p. xix.
140. *Manu* (*The Laws of Manu*, The Sacred Books of the East, XXV), X. 20, 22.
141. *Ancient India and South Indian History and Culture*, I, p. 181.
142. For example, V S Pathak, *Journal of the Numismatic Society of India*, XIX, p. 141; S R Goyal, *The Imperial Guptas*, p. 119.
143. *The Imperial Guptas and Their Times*, p. 35.
144. R C Majumdar, in *Comprehensive History of India*, III(i), p. 11.
145. A S Altekar, *The Coinage of the Gupta Empire*, pp. 30-31.
146. D K Ganguli, *The Imperial Guptas and their Times*, p. 84.
147. S R Goyal, *Gupta Sāmrājya kā Itihāsa*, p. 61.
148. H C Raychaudhuri, *Political History of Ancient India*, p. 189.
149. According to Buddhaghosha's *Sumaṅgala-vilāsinī* one of the reasons of Ajātaśatru's attack on the Lichchhavis (in *c* 500 BC) was the breach of trust by the latter regarding the ownership of mines. See H C Raychaudhuri, *Political History of Ancient India*, p. 187.
150. *Dynasties of the Kali Age*, p. 73. In some copies of the *Vāyu-purāṇa*, instead of *Gupta-vaṁśajāḥ*, Gupta, Guhya, Sapta and Maṇidhānyājāḥ have been mentioned (F E Pargiter, *The Dynasties of the Kali Age*, p. 53, n 8).
151. D R Bhandarkar, *Corpus Inscriptionum Indicarum*, III, p. 6.
152. H C Raychaudhuri, *Political History of Ancient India*, p. 469.
153. Ashvini Agrawal, *Rise and Fall of the Imperial Guptas*, pp. 95-96.
154. F E Pargiter, *Dynasties of the Kali Age*, p. 53, n. 1.
155. *Mahābhāshya*, II. 1. 2.
156. *Catalogue of the Coins of the Gupta Dynasties, and of Śaśāṅka, the King of Gauḍa, in the British Museum, London*, p. xix.
157. *Dynasties of the Kali Age*, Intro., p. xii.
158. *Journal of Indian History*, VI, pp. 7-8.
159. Some scholars, who identify the place of the construction of the Chinese temple by Śrīgupta, the first Gupta king, in Northern Bengal, believe that the region was within the Gupta empire since his time.
160. J F Fleet, *Corpus Inscriptionum Indicarum*, III, p. 12; Basak, *The History of North-Eastern India*, pp.14ff. See Appendix III below.
161. R C Majumdar, in *The Vākāṭaka-Gupta Age*, p. 134.
162. P L Gupta, *The Imperial Guptas*, p. 115.
163. S R Goyal, *The Imperial Guptas*, pp. 74-75.
164. Ashvini Agrawal, *Rise and Fall of the Imperial Guptas*, p. 96.
165. *Ibid*.
166. *Ibid*., p. 106.

# 4

# Kācha: Identification and Chronological Position

## I

There is a lot of controversy regarding the identification and placing of Kācha in the Gupta history. The name Kācha neither finds mention in the genealogy of the Gupta kings detailed in their inscriptions, nor is it met with in literature.[1] He is known only from some coins, of just one type with two classes, at present located in different museums.[2] The Bayana hoard contained as many as sixteen such coins. They have also been found in coin-hoards from Jaunpur, Tanda (Faizabad district), Kasarva (Ballia district), Kumarkhan (Ahmedabad district) and Sakori (Damoh district).[3]

Barring one, all coins of Kācha show on the obverse, the king, haloed, standing, wearing an Indian cap and a Kushāṇa coat and trousers, holding a *chakradhvaja*, and offering oblations on the altar by the right hand. Below the left arm, occurs the legend *Kācha*, The circular legend reads *Kācho gām= avajitya divaṁ karmabhir=uttamair=jayati* ('Kācha after conquering the earth, conquers heaven by his noble deeds'). The reverse shows a goddess holding a flower in her right hand and a *cornucopiae* in the left, and the legend *sarva-rāj=ochchhettā*, 'exterminator of all kings'. On only one coin, labelled as 'Variety B' by Altekar,[4] the obverse shows a *garuḍa-dhvaja* in front of the king as an additional feature, and the goddess holds a *pāśa* instead of a flower. In the absence of any tangible evidence, the problem of situating Kācha properly in history, despite many attempts by several scholars, has not been solved to the satisfaction of all.

None of the coins in the Bayana hoard belongs to kings other than those of the Gupta dynasty. With the exception of one coin bearing the legend *Kramāditya*, identified by Altekar[5] with Skandagupta and by P L Gupta[6] with Ghaṭotkachagupta, since both the kings are known to have borne that title, only coins of Kācha, Chandragupta I, Samudragupta, Chandragupta II and Kumāragupta I have been found in that coin-hoard. Except two coins of Chandragupta I, all the coins of the Tanda hoard belong either to Samudragupta or to Kācha.[7] The Ballia hoard contained coins of Samudragupta and Kācha only.[8] The statement of P L Gupta that Kācha coins have been 'found only in those hoards which include the coins of Chandragupta I',[9] is not correct; in fact he himself has mentioned that the Ballia hoard comprises in all 17 coins, of which 16 belong to Samudragupta and one to Kācha. The weight of the Kācha coins ranges between 111 and 118 grains.[10] In shape, size, device, legend, purity of metal, weight and the palaeography of letters, Kācha coins are closely related to Samudragupta,[11] and, as such, some scholars consider him as an immediate predecessor of Samudragupta, others, an immediate successor of that king, and still others as identical with him. In other words, he should be placed after Chandragupta I and before Chandragupta II. The obverse and reverse legends mentioned above, should also be taken into account in determining his chronological position. The following possibilities have been suggested by different scholars. He was either (i) an elder brother of Samudragupta, or (ii) a younger brother of Samudragupta, identified by some with Bhasma mentioned in the *Ārya-Mañjuśrī-mūlakalpa*, or (iii) Kācha of an Ajanta inscription, or (iv) a high official of Samudragupta who usurped the throne during the absence of that Gupta king from the capital in connection with his south Indian campaigns, or (v) Rāmagupta of the *Devī-Chandraguptam* and other texts, or (vi) Ghaṭotkacha, the second Gupta ruler (either as issuer of the coins, or as one who is commemorated in them), or (vii) Samudragupta.

Altekar has in the same work, published in 1957, placed Kācha before Samudragupta while dealing with the history of the Guptas,[12] and as his successor, while describing his coin-type.[13] He, however, till then favoured the view that Kācha was a successor of Samudragupta, though he did not rule out other possibilities.[14] Smith earlier considered Kācha as identical with Samudragupta. [15] Later, he changed his view in favour of taking the two as separate persons,[16] and still later reverted to his old view.[17] J F Fleet,[18] John Allan,[19] R K Mookerji,[20] H C Raychaudhuri,[21] R G Basak,[22] T P Verma[23] and some other scholars take Kācha and Samudragupta as identical. T P Verma is too categorical when he states: 'the fabric, metallurgy, general resemblance, legend, etc., indicate that the Kācha coins *cannot* be separated from those of Samudragupta'[24], and that 'he can be put *neither before nor after him*'.[25] (Italics mine). But the evidence at hand is not so strong as to lead to such a definite conclusion, and, on the other hand, there is quite a weighty evidence in favour of taking Kācha and Samudragupta as two separate persons.

The evidence of typology, though not conclusive, is used as one of the criteria in determining chronology.[26] As pointed out by scholars, the reverse device of goddess on the Kācha coins resembles that on the Tiger-slayer type of the coins of Samudragupta, though there are some significant differences also. In Kācha coins, the goddess holds *cornucopiae* and stands on a mat, while on Samudragupta's Tiger-slayer type, she holds a lotus and rides a *makara*, which device is more Indianized than that met with on the Kācha coins.[27] As pointed out by scholars, the legend on the Kācha coins *Kācho gām=avajitya karmabhir=uttamair-divaṁ jayati* resembles the legend on Samudragupta's Archer type: *Apratiratho vijitya kshitiṁ sucharitair=divaṁ jayati,*[28] that on the *Chhatra* type of Chandragupta II's coins: *Kshitim=avajitya sucharitair=divaṁ jayati Vikramādityaḥ,*[29] and that on the Swordsman type of Kumāragupta I: *Gām=avajitya sucharitaiḥ Kumāragupto divaṁ jayati.*[30] If similarity of the legend in itself could be a fully reliable criterion for dating, then Kācha, Samudragupta, Chandragupta II and Kumāragupta I should be taken either as identical, or as contemporary rulers, which is historically impossible.

## II

The circular legend on the obverse, meaning as one who has won the heaven by his excellent deeds after having conquered the earth, is similar in meaning to the legend on Samudragupta's Standard type. Ashvini Agrawal,[31] who takes Kācha as identical with Samudragupta, suggests that 'excellent deeds' may be taken to refer to the performance of *aśvamedha*, to commemorate which he issued the *Aśvamedha* type of coins, and offering of cows and gold in charity as mentioned in the Allahabad pillar inscription. In his view, it does not go well in case of a rebel, as Kācha has been taken to be by some scholars who suppose that he occupied the kingdom by force, after King Chandragupta I declared Samudragupta as his successor. But as pointed out above, similarity in the meaning of legend itself cannot be considered as a definite proof of the identity of two kings, and there are certain significant points, discussed below, which do not favour the identification of Kācha with Samudragupta. The obverse legend on Kācha coins conveying that Kācha wins heaven by means of noble deeds after conquering the earth, according to some scholars, may suggest that his rule would not have been short as one is likely to infer from the coins, which are of only one type and not large in number, and also from the absence of his epigraphs. In favour of the view that Kācha was different from Samudragupta, it may be stated that not unoften in epigraphs and coin-legends, the achievements of kings have been highly exaggerated; and also that there is a possibility that the statement in the legend may not be a vain boast, and King Kācha might have made some conquests.[32]

As regards the legend *sarva-rāj=ochchhettā* on the reverse, H C Raychaudhuri[33] says: 'To us, it is unthinkable that the style "uprooter of all kings" could have been assumed by a Gupta monarch other than the one who is actually credited with that achievement by a contemporary inscription, before the events presupposed by the expression had actually happened'. In no official epigraph of the Gupta dynasty is the grandiloquent epithet applied to a king other than Samudragupta.[34] It has been argued that if Kācha preceded Samudragupta, and conquered many kings, then how so many kings were left to be conquered by Samudragupta, and if he succeeded Samudragupta, how can he be called *sarva-rāj=ochchhettā*, as per the testimony of the Allahabad pillar inscription (No. 1), the latter—had already conquered a number of kings both in north India (nine kings) and south India (12 kings); and therefore, Kācha should be identified with Samudragupta.[35] Further, it has been suggested[36] that the persons tormented by the valour of Samudragupta as mentioned in verses 5 and 6 of the Allahabad pillar inscription should better be taken to refer to hostile kings who were conquered and pardoned by Samudragupta. The use of the plural for the enemy would favour the reference to many hostile kings rather than to a single rival prince who rebelled against him. But it is also possible that a few princes rebelled either under the banner of Kācha or independently. Ashvini Agrawal[37] opines that the princes of equal birth who, as per the evidence of the Allahabad pillar inscription, became pale-faced, when Chandragupta I declared Samudragupta as his successor, might have 'resigned themselves to the inevitable fate with heavy heart', and that there is not even the slightest hint that they or any one of them rebelled. But against this, it can be stated that it is possible that they kept quiet at that time, but rebelled afterwards.

T P Verma states that in the language of the Incas, *kācha* means 'ocean', i.e. *samudra*, and it is possible that such meaning has been preserved in that language, though it is lost in Sanskrit,[38] and that this would support the theory that Kācha and Samudragupta are names of one and the same ruler. However, this linguistic evidence needs critical and deeper investigation, as the similarity of meaning may be accidental. On the face of it, it would appear curious that the meaning of *kācha* as ocean was known in the Gupta period but this meaning was later completely forgotten, more so as the word *kācha* finds place in the Sanskrit lexicons, which mention its different meanings (below). Moreover, if the Inca language has retained the Sanskrit word, *kācha*, it must have retained many more Sanskrit words, particularly those in common use, of which there is no definite knowledge.

It may be stated that the epithet *sarva-rāj=ochchhettā* for Samudragupta, barring the Nālandā (No. 3) and Gayā (No. 4) copperplate inscriptions, which are not original (Chapter 5), occurs only in the epigraphs of his successors, and not in his own inscriptions and coins and, as such, it is possible that he did not adopt it, but was ascribed to him by his successors. The Vākāṭaka records—the Poona (No. 82) and the Rithpur (No. 84) plates, of Prabhāvatīguptā—ascribe this title to Chandragupta II, instead of Samudragupta, which may be either inadvertent, or a deliberate attempt to glorify him, as he was the father of that Vākāṭaka queen. But, as pointed out by some scholars, the fact that the two plates are separated by at least 20 years, and yet the 'mistake' was not corrected, favours the view that it was done deliberately. One may infer that *sarva-rāj=ochchhettā* was not a title exclusively of Samudragupta. It is likely that Kācha was one of the rebel princes who captured the throne for a short period, despite the nomination of Samudragupta by Chandragupta I as his successor (No. 1) and to impress upon the people that he was a powerful ruler, he took the title *sarva-rāj=ochchhettā.* Later, the successors of Samudragupta ascribed this title exclusively to that great conqueror,[39] as it befitted him the most. The intention might have been to convey that while Kācha was *sarva-rāj=ochchhettā* in name, Samudragupta was truly so by his deeds. Although, like P L Gupta[40] this author is in favour of the view that Kācha and Samudragupta were two different persons, it is difficult to agree with one of the arguments put forth by him in its support. He argues that since in the Allahabad pillar inscription, Samudragupta has been mentioned as *aneka-bhrashṭa-rāj=otsanna-rājavaṁśa-pratishṭhāpaka* (restorer of many royal families fallen and deprived of sovereignty), he would not have adopted the title *sarva-rāj=ohchhettā*, 'exterminator of all kings', for himself, and therefore Kācha coins should not be taken as issued by Samudragupta. In my view, there is no anomaly in the use of both these epithets for the same king in two different contexts. He was an uprooter of such kings as were inimical to him or from whom, he thought, there was danger for his kingdom, and re-established such kings as had accepted his suzerainty and from whom he did not expect hostile behaviour in future. In fact the use of *prasabh=oddharaṇa*, 'forcefully uprooting', in the Allahabad pillar inscription (No. 1) in the context of Samudragupta's conquest of the nine Āryāvarta kings has a similar connotation as *sarva-rāj=ochchhettā*.

The greatest hurdle in taking Kācha and Samudragupta as identical, as also pointed out by other scholars,[41] is the difficulty in explaining as to why on one type of coins only the name occurs as *Kācha*, and on all other types, six in all, it is Samudragupta, and also that why in the inscriptions of the Gupta dynasty detailing genealogy, the name given is invariably Samudragupta, and never Kācha. It is rather unbelievable that the same king issued coins in two different names. As stated above, in most cases, the coins with the name Kācha and also those with the name of Samudragupta have been found in the same coin-hoard. Those who identify Kācha with Samudragupta have tried to explain as to how the same king was known by two different names. Fleet[42] suggested that Kācha was a less formal and personal name, and Samudragupta, an official one. Allan[43] opined that the original name of the king was Kācha, but after conquering the regions up to *samudra* (sea), he took the name Samudragupta. He is of the view that the name he took was Samudra, and *gupta* was added as a name-ending, following the practice that was introduced by Chandragupta I and followed by all the successive Gupta kings thereafter, and that this combined name suitably conveyed that his territories were protected, i.e. bounded, by the sea.[44] But this does not explain as to why the original name has been used only on coins, and also if it was deemed fit to be used on them, then why it has been used only on a single type of coins, while the official name has been used on all other coin-types. Chandragupta II is known to have borne another name, Devarāja (No. 11) or Devagupta (No. 83) but on coins, the name met with is invariably Chandragupta, and never Devarāja or Devagupta.

In favour of the identity of Kācha with Samudragupta, it has been suggested by some scholars that Kācha was a *viruda* of Samudragupta. The Gupta kings are known to have adopted *virudas*, most of which occur on their coins. But the *virudas* convey some sensible meaning or throw light on some aspects of the history of the kings. Since Kācha, as a *viruda*, does not make any sense, the view is not acceptable. As has been pointed out by R D Banerji[45] and A S Altekar,[46] on Gupta coins bearing *virudas*, it is the name of the king and not his *viruda*, that is invariably written in a vertical line near the foot of the royal figure, below his left arm. Since in the case of Kācha coins, too, it is at this place that *Kācha* is written, it should be taken as a name of the king, and not as his *viruda*. There is no reason to believe that, of all the Gupta coins, only in this case the *viruda* has been given the place meant for the name.[47] There is a view[48] that Samudragupta's original name was Kācha and by that name he issued coins for the Lichchhavi territory which he inherited as a Lichchhavi-*dauhitra* (son of the daughter of the Lichchhavi chief), but as king of the Gupta family, he was known by the name of Samudragupta and issued coins with that name. It has been suggested that it was somewhat parallel to the case of the Chālukya prince, a son of the daughter of the Chola king, who was known as Rājendra II in Chālukya history, but on succeeding to the Chola throne, came to be known by the name of Kulottuṅga. *Chakra* in *chakra-dhvaja* on Kācha coins may stand for the Buddhist *dharma-chakra*, and it has been argued that such coins might have been issued for the territories of the Lichchhavis, considerable number of whose population was Buddhist. But against this view, it may be stated that with a few exceptions, all Kācha type of coins have been found in the Gupta territory as it existed before the Lichchhavi territories were amalgamated in it.

## III

Taking Kācha and Samudragupta as two different kings does not create any numismatic problem.[49] In favour of a separate identity of the two, it may be stated that while *chakra-dhvaja* occurs on the coins of Kācha, it does not occur on the coins issued in the name of Samudragupta, for that matter on the coins of any other Gupta king.[50] Further, on a single coin of Kācha, as an additional device *garuḍa-dhvaja* is depicted, which device is not met with on the coins of Chandragupta I-Kumāradevī type, but is quite common on those of Samudragupta and his successors. From this it may be inferred, as has been done by P L Gupta, that the device was introduced by Kācha at the fag end of his reign and that Samudragupta borrowed the device from his coins, which would mean that Kācha succeeded Chandragupta I, and was in turn succeeded by Samudragupta.[51] An alternate suggestion[52] that Kācha followed Samudragupta and in the beginning of his career introduced the *garuḍa-dhvaja* device on his coins in imitation of Samudragupta's coins, but discontinued the practice, having realized that *chakra-dhvaja* in the king's right hand rendered a second *dhvaja* superfluous, though possible, is less convincing, particularly as the device occurs on the coins of the successors of Samudragupta.

Some scholars hold the view that Kācha was a younger brother of Samudragupta. It has been pointed out that in the *Ārya-Mañjuśrī-mūlakalpa* at one place Samudra is followed by Bhasma. K P Jayaswal[53] suggested that Kācha should be identified with Bhasma, and the suggestion was accepted by some scholars.[54] One of the main arguments in its favour is that Kācha and Bhasma are more or less synonymous, and that the *Ārya-Mañjuśrī-mūlakalpa* at times gives synonyms instead of the names of rulers. The relevant verses have been translated by J Agrawal,[55] and also by P L Gupta, [56] and the latter has also cited the original verses. According to this text, Samudragupta was a local king of Gauḍa, who ruled for three days (or three years). However, from epigraphic evidence, we know that Samudragupta was a paramount sovereign, lord of an extensive empire carved out largely by his own conquests, which must have taken a fairly long time. Bhasma, according to the *Ārya-Mañjuśrī-mūlakalpa*, undertook extensive campaigns, in course of which, he reached up to Kashmir and ruled for 12 years and 15 days. One scholar[57] takes the achievement ascribed to Kācha as an historical fact. But the conquest of Kashmir could have been possible after the conquest of Punjab, which, the evidence at hand suggests, did not take place before the reign of Chandragupta II.[58] No inscription of Bhasma is known, and there is no mention in the *Ārya-Mañjuśrī-mūlakalpa* that he rebelled against Samudragupta. The coin-legend extols Kācha for his noble deeds, while the Buddhist text calls Bhasma as wicked, heartless and of low intelligence. However, the evidence of the *Ārya-Mañjuśrī-mūlakalpa* is not a reliable source for the reconstruction of history.

One could as well suggest that Kācha was one of the sons of Samudragupta, presuming that when Chandragupta II came to the throne after killing his brother Rāmagupta, and married his widow, some high officials, disapproving his act, backed another son of Samudragupta, Kācha, who declared himself as king and issued coins in his own name. He had a very short reign and was ousted by Chandragupta II. This goes well with the numismatic evidence that Kācha coins are very close to the coins of Samudragupta. However, there is no evidence to support this hypothesis.

D R Bhandarkar[59] suggests that the name Rāmagupta in the *Devī-Chandraguptam* should be taken as a scribal error for Kāchagupta (and not that Kācha was a scribal error for Rāma as P L Gupta[60] inadvertently ascribes to that scholar). Bhandarkar's view was accepted by some scholars, and of them Altekar[61] pointed out that in the script of the Gupta period the letters *r* and *k*, and *m* and *ch*, are quite close to each other in shape, and a careless scribe could copy *Rāma* for *Kācha*. The coins of Kācha are not many, and from this it can be inferred that his reign was a short one. The evidence at hand suggests that Rāmagupta, too, had a relatively short reign. But the name of the king on the coins is merely Kācha, both in the circular legend as well as below the left arm of the king, and not Kāchagupta, just as the name of the second ruler of the Gupta dynasty is invariably given in the Gupta genealogy as Ghaṭotkacha, and not Ghaṭotkachagupta. Three epigraphs of the Gupta period from Durjanpur near Vidiśā belong to *Mahārājādhirāja* Rāmagupta (Chapter 6), while no epigraph mentioning the name Kācha has come to light. Further, copper coins bearing the name Rāmagupta and datable to the Gupta period on the basis of paleography of the inscriptions on them, have been found in Vidiśā, Eran, and their neighbourhood, and ascribed to the Gupta king of that name. This shows that the form of the name of the king current in the fourth century AD was Rāmagupta. It is difficult, almost impossible to believe that the same king issued gold coins by the name of Kācha, and copper coins by the name of Rāmagupta.[62] The two, therefore, should better be taken as two different kings. However, it may be stated that at the time when Bhandarkar suggested the identification of Kācha(gupta) with Rāmagupta, neither the coins nor the epigraphs bearing the name Rāmagupta had come to light

Some scholars are of the view that the Kācha coins were issued by *Mahārāja* Ghaṭotkacha, the second Gupta ruler.[63] There are, however, difficulties in accepting the view. There is difference between the two names. There is no similarity of meaning of Kācha which means 'glass', 'crystal', 'alkaline', etc. and *utkacha* in Ghaṭotkacha means 'a person with hairs standing erect (through pleasure)', and Ghaṭotkacha means a person making sounds similar to those arising out of a pitcher, or an astounding intelligent man.[64] Also, Ghaṭotkacha was only a *mahārāja*, a title which in that period generally denoted a feudal lord, and feudal lords in ancient India are not known to have issued any coins in their name, leave alone gold coins. The epithet *sarva-rāj=ochchhettā* does not befit Ghaṭotkacha who was merely a *mahārāja*. Further, if they were the coins of Ghaṭotkacha, then they should be the earliest Gupta coins, and it is rather difficult to believe that the earliest Gupta coin-type issued by a *mahārāja* could be so artistic and evolved as are the Kācha type of coins, and not closest to the Kushāṇa coins as they should normally have been. It can be argued that *Mahārāja* Ghaṭotkacha could as well have been the real founder of the Gupta dynasty and also an independent king, who has been referred to as *ādirāja* (first king) of the Gupta dynasty in the Vākāṭaka records (Nos. 82, 84) and in an inscription, viz. the Supia inscription of the reign of Skandagupta (No. 32). However, the Gupta epigraphs detailing genealogy invariably make a clear-cut distinction between Ghaṭotkacha's title *mahārāja* and his son and successor Chandragupta I's title *mahārājādhirāja*, and it would be reasonable to infer that the former was a feudal lord, and the latter an independent sovereign. Further, if Ghaṭotkacha would have issued coins then it seems reasonable to think that Chandragupta I would have issued at least a few coin-types during his fairly long reign.

## IV

According to R D Banerji,[65] Kācha coins should either be taken as issues of a king of that name, or as commemorative issues of Samudragupta for an elder brother or some other near relative of that name, who died fighting a battle of liberation against the Kushāṇas, who held sway over the region of Magadha and to whom the Guptas till then owed allegiance. The high quality of art in these coins, he suggests, is because they were issued by Samudragupta late in his reign.[66] But, contrary to this view, neither there was Kushāṇa rule in Magadha in the first half of the fourth century AD, nor is there any evidence of the Guptas owing allegiance to them. As against the view that they could be commemorative coins, it may be stated that there is no other evidence of issuing commemorative coins in the Gupta dynasty; in fact no native dynasty in ancient Indian history is known to have issued coins of that category.

Buddha Prakash[67] and M J Sharma[68] identified Kācha of the obverse legend with first of the two persons of this name of an Ajanta inscription.[69] The latter suggests that for him these coins were issued by Samudragupta, who is to be identified with the *sarvā-rājo=chchhettā* of the legend, Sharma opines that it is better to identify Kācha as a loyal high officer of Samudragupta rather than a rebel feudatory.[70] He surmises that Kācha extended wholehearted support to Samudragupta in his struggle against his rivals who challenged his claims to throne despite the fact that his father had nominated him as his successor, and Samudragupta issued these coins in his name as a token of gratitude towards him. He speculates that Kācha was related to Samudragupta through his queen Dattadevī, perhaps as her brother,[71] and also that Samudragupta offered a high office to him. As per genealogical table with dates given by Sharma on the basis of the Ajanta epigraph, Kācha I is placed in *c.* AD 350 which falls within the rule of Samudragupta. Sharma says that of all the theories relating to the identification of Kācha this alone identifies him with a homonym about whose existence and also contemporaneity with Samudragupta there is no doubt.

There is, however, no evidence whatsoever of Kācha of the Ajanta inscription being related to Samudragupta, or to his helping the Gupta king in his struggle for the throne, or to his holding high office under the latter.[72] Verse 5 in the Eran Pillar inscription (No. 2), according to most scholars, seems to refer to the queen of Samudragupta, and not to that of Kācha, and in fact, there is no mention of Kācha in that inscription. There is no example in ancient Indian history of a king of indigenous dynasty issuing coins for his subordinate, howsoever important or helpful he might have been to the ruling king. In fact there was no tradition of issuing coins to commemorate any person of any category.

Aparna Chattopadhyay is of the view[73] that the Kācha coins were issued by Samudragupta, the *sarva-rāj=ochchhettā* of the coin-legend, in the name of Kācha who was his rival, with a view to winning his goodwill. She, too, like some other scholars, surmises that it is likely that Bhasma, who is mentioned as the younger brother, and perhaps a step-brother of

Samudragupta, bore Kācha as a second name. But her view that Samudragupta issued coins for his rival is not at all convincing.

B S Sitholey[74] suggested that Kācha was neither Samudragupta's brother, nor Samudragupta himself, nor his son Rāmagupta. In his opinion, he could not have been a Gupta prince, for he argues, if he had been one such, his name would have been Kāchagupta, as other kings, from the time of Chandragupta I bear *gupta*-ending names. In his opinion, he was a high official of Samudragupta who forcibly occupied the Gupta throne when the latter was engaged in the south Indian campaign. He, however, was ousted by the Gupta ruler on his return from that expedition. It was during his short rule that Kācha issued coins. As the mint masters were the same who had manufactured coin–types of Samudragupta, which he had issued before his south Indian expedition, the coins of Kācha closely resemble them in metal, metrology, shape, size and legend. Since Kācha did not belong to the Gupta family, Sitholey argues, there is no question of his name being mentioned in the genealogies detailed in the Gupta inscriptions. It may be stated that though Altekar favoured the view that Kācha was a Gupta prince, he did not rule out the possibility of his being an upstart who usurped the throne and ruled for a short period.[75] But in those days, while it would not have been very difficult for an ambitious and bold rival prince to raise the banner of revolt and declare himself king during long absence of the ruling king, it would have been quite difficult for an official, not belonging to the Gupta family, to garner the support of the ministers, army officials and other high officials, in fulfilling his ambition of capturing the throne by turning a rebel against the ruling king, particularly a dynamic and powerful king like Samudragupta.

B Ch Chhabra[76] earlier believed that Chandragupta not only declared Samudragupta as his successor but abdicated in his favour. But later[77] he opined that in between his rule and that of Samudragupta, Kācha ruled for a short period. He observes: 'The word Kācha has no familiar ring about it for its adoption as a personal name....' However, as seen above, at least two chieftains bearing the name Kācha are known from an Ajanta inscription. Chhabra derived *Kācha* from *Kacha*, the second part of the name Ghaṭotkacha, which makes Kācha as the son of Ghaṭotkacha, and a brother of Chandragupta I.[78] Chhabra envisages political turmoil in Chandragupta I's old age in which his younger brother Kācha wrested the throne from him for a short period and issued coins in his own name. As Ashvini Agrawal[79] points out, Chhabra's rendering shows Kācha as an appellation rather than a name, and there is no example in the Gupta history of a king naming himself after the name of his father with a view to indicating his relationship. As seen above, the legend Kācha on coins occurs at the place which is exclusively meant for the name of the issuer of the coin and so Kācha should be a personal name and not a derivative one.[80] It should also be noted that in the Gupta coins, the first and not the second part of the name of the king is given; for example, on the coins of Ghaṭotkachagupta, a son of Chandragupta II, as evidenced from a Vākāṭaka inscription from Rāmatek (No. 85), it is *Ghaṭo*, and not *Kācha*.

While R D Banerji takes Kācha coins as issued by Samudragupta in memory of his brother or a near relation, in the circumstances stated above, S C Bhattacharya[81] takes such coins as issued by Samudragupta to commemorate his grandfather, Ghaṭotkacha. Aware of the fact that there is no indigenous tradition of issuing commemorative coins, he states that the Gupta king would have borrowed this practice, like some other elements of the Gupta numismatics, from Graeco-Kushāṇa numismatic tradition, since some Indo-Greek kings, such as Agathocles and Antimachus, are known to have issued commemorative coins.[82] But the Kushāṇas did not issue commemorative coins, and it is the coins of the Kushāṇas, rather than of the Indo–Greeks whose rule had ended some centuries before the beginning of the rule of the Guptas, that were the models before the Guptas when they started manufacturing coins.

Ghaṭotkacha was a mere *mahārāja*, and is not known for any such achievements as would have made him worthy of commemoration, although, as stated above, he, and not Gupta, is mentioned as the first king of the Gupta dynasty in the Vākāṭaka records (Nos. 82, 84) and in the Supia stone inscription of Skandagupta (No. 32). Moreover, if Samudragupta would have introduced the practice of commemorating an ancestor, the later kings of the Gupta dynasty, it may be presumed, should also have followed this practice, particularly when there were such illustrious kings as *Mahārājādhirāja* Samudragupta and *Mahārājādhirāja* Chandragupta II, much more worthy of commemoration. Further, the obverse legend on Kācha coins is in the present tense (*jayati*), which indicates that Kācha was alive, and not dead, at the time when those coins were issued.

In support of the view that Kācha is identical with Ghaṭotkacha, Bhattacharya has put forth some additional arguments. He takes *Kācha* as a modified form of *Kacha*, and latter itself as a truncated form of

*Ghaṭotkacha*,[83] who, in his opinion, is commemorated by *sarva-rāj=ochchhetā* of the legend on the reverse.[84] Like some other scholars, he identifies *sarva-rājo=chchhettā* with Samudragupta who has been given this epithet in the epigraph of his successors. He argues that since some Gupta kings are known as named after their grandfather, such as Chandragupta II after Chandragupta I, and Kumāragupta II after Kumāragupta I, Samudragupta might have been named after his grandfather, Ghaṭotkacha,[85] and the kings name in abbreviated form *Kacha* (*Kācha*) is engraved at the place which is meant for the king's name. It would be the case of one Ghaṭotkacha being commemorated by another Ghaṭotkacha. However, Samudragupta would have commemorated Ghaṭotkacha, his grandfather, if he so desired, irrespective of his being named after him or not. Mere identity of name, which itself is only a speculation, not supported by any evidence, would not have been a strong incentive for Samudragupta to choose Ghaṭotkacha for commemoration. Moreover, if Samudragupta was named Ghaṭotkacha, after his grandfather, then he would have avoided issuing the coins in this form, as it would have created confusion as to whether the name Kācha (= Ghaṭotkacha) on coins refers to the second Gupta king or to his illustrious grandson, and generally people would have inferred that the coins give the name and the title of the same king, viz. Samudragupta, and the purpose of commemorative coins, viz. Samudragupta's commemorating his grandfather, would be defeated.

Bhattacharya rightly points out that *Ghaṭotkacha*, as per grammatical rule, can be abbreviated to Kacha,[86] and in support of his view refers to the abbreviation *ku* for king Kumāragupta on some coins. But on the coins bearing the letter *ku* the full name of the king and his typical *viruda* also find mention, but such is not the case with the Kācha coins. He further states that the abbreviated form would have been *Kacha* but the full legend on coins being in metrical form, it was made *Kācha* to suit the metre. But even in the case of metrical legends, one would normally not make such a change as would create doubt about the name of the king. It may be noted that for avoiding any confusion in the spelling of the king's name, even grammatical rules relating to *sandhi* were bypassed; for example, the form *Śrī-Īśānavarmmā* has been given instead of *Śrīśānavarmmā* in the case of the fourth Maukhari king.[87] One may argue that the scribe committed the error of writing *Kācha* for *Kacha*. However, while there is some possibility of the engraver engraving Kacha for Kācha and thus committing the error of inadvertently omitting a stroke for *ā mātrā*, there is little possibility of his committing the error of adding wrongly a stroke (*ā mātrā*) and thus making *Kacha* as *Kācha*, particularly as *Kācha* is not a word of common use that it could have come offhand to the scribe. Moreover, the name Kācha occurs not only in the metrical legend, but also independently and more prominently at the place where, on Gupta coins king's name is generally engraved, i.e. below his left arm and near his feet. Therefore, the change from *Kacha* to *Kācha* should not be taken as done because of metrical consideration.[88] Bhattacharya points out that on one of the coins in Smith's *Catalogue*, the reading is *Kacha* and infers that 'it cannot therefore really be claimed indubitably that the name of the king was Kācha and not Kacha'.[89] However, it would be reasonable to suppose that in such case the legend being in relief, the stroke for *ā mātrā* on the letter *k*, has got rubbed off as a result of circulation of the coin for a long period. Moreover Kācha, though not a common name, as seen above, in about the same period two rulers of a family bearing that name and ruling as Vākāṭaka feudatories are known from an inscription from Ajanta.

Bhattacharya[90] puts forth one more argument in favour of identifying Kācha with Ghaṭotkacha. He refers to a unique Kācha coin in the Bayana hoard (lebelled as variety 'b' by A S Altekar),[91] which shows the king wearing *dhotī* instead of the Kushāṇa trousers, and bears a *chakra-dhvaja* instead of the ordinary standard in his left hand. The goddess on the reverse holds a noose instead of a flower, and there is a *garuḍa-dhvaja*, which is absent in variety 'a' of his coins, which has been described above. According to Bhattacharya, the presence of both the *garuḍa-dhvaja* and the *chakra-dhvaja* on one and the same coin assumes significance when it is recalled that in the *Mahābhārata*, Ghaṭotkacha, son of the Pāṇḍava hero Bhīma and Hiḍimbā, had these two devices portrayed on his standard. It is undoubtedly an ingenious suggestion and also a forceful evidence put forth by Bhattacharya in favour of identifying Kācha with Ghaṭotkacha. But the device can also be explained in a different way. Ghaṭotkacha might have chosen *chakra-dhvaja* and *garuḍa-dhvaja* because of his Vaishṇava leanings, *chakra* being an *āyudha* of Vishṇu, and *garuḍa*, his *vāhana*, and the latter came to be a popular device on the Gupta coins and seals. It is also possible that *garuḍa*, which is anti-nāgas (serpents) was chosen to symbolize the victory of the Gupta king over some Nāga king or kings. Moreover, the two devices are found together on only one coin, and on all other coins it is only one device, viz., the *chakra-dhvaja*. If the intention was to depict the device for the coin commemorating Gupta king

Ghaṭotkacha, after the device used by Ghaṭotkacha, the *Mahābhārata* hero, then on all his coins, both *chakra-dhvaja* and *garuḍa-dhvaja* would have been shown; but both the devices occur on only one coin, and the rest bear only the *chakra-dhvaja*.

V

S R Goyal[92] considers Kācha as a rival brother of Samudragupta. According to him, the union of the Gupta and Lichchhavi kingdoms as a result of the marriage of Chandragupta I with the Lichchhavi princess, Kumāradevī would have created political and administrative problems. The Guptas had a monarchical form of government, while the Lichchhavis, though their heads practically became hereditary, maintained republican traditions, as is indicated by the coin-legend in plural, *Lichchhavayaḥ*. The Guptas followed Brahmanical religion, while most of the Lichchhavis were followers of the heterodox sects, Buddhism and Jainism. The members of the combined Gupta-Lichchhavi Assembly would have been considerably divided on these lines. While the Lichchhavis would have been happy with Chandragupta I's announcement of Samudragupta, the Lichchhavi-*dauhitra*, as his successor, some Gupta members of the Assembly would not have liked the influence of the *vrātya* Lichchhavis on the Gupta administration. Samudragupta, though a follower of Brahmanical faith, was liberal in his religious outlook, as is seen from his granting permission to Sri Lankan king to build a Buddhist monastery at Bodhgaya, and some scholars believe that Samudragupta was the patron of the Buddhist scholar Vasubandhu. In the *Ārya-Mañjuśrī-mūlakalpa*, disparaging words have been used for Bhasma, a brother of Samudragupta, who, according to Goyal and some other scholars, may be identified with Kācha. This could be because Samudragupta was liberal to Buddhists, while Bhasma was a champion of Brahmanical religion.[93] S R Goyal[94] further points out that Hiuen-tsang[95] informs that the king who ruled before the one who was the patron of Vasubandhu was anti-Buddhist, He suggests that the patron king may be identified with Samudragupta, and the king preceding him, with Kācha.[96] It may also be stated that Hiuen-tsang refers to the immediate predecessor of the patron of Vasubandhu as king with his capital at Śrāvastī and the coins of Kācha have been mostly found in eastern U P.

There is greater possibility that Kācha was a ruler of the Gupta dynasty than of his being an outsider. The views seeking to take Kācha coins as issues of Samudragupta commemorating his brother or relative as R D Banerji suggested, or commemorating the second Gupta ruler Ghaṭotkacha as Bhattacharya has suggested, may be excluded for reasons given above. The identification with Samudragupta has much in its favour, but fails to explain as to why the name Kācha occurs on only one coin-type, whereas in all other coin-types and in all inscriptions the name is invariably Samudragupta. The identification of Kācha with Bhasma of the *Ārya-Mañjuśrī-mūlakalpa* cannot be accepted as the information about Samudragupta, whose brother is mentioned as Bhasma, is much contrary to what we know about him. The theory of identifying Kācha with Rāma(gupta), presuming that Rāma is a scribal error for Kācha is belied by the find of the coins, as well as inscriptions clearly bearing the name as Rāmagupta, and the latter ascribe him the title of *mahārājādhirāja*. Of the different views referred to above, the most likely seems to be the one according to which Kācha was a brother, perhaps an elder one, of Samudragupta. He was one of those princes, who were claimants to the Gupta throne and whose faces, according to the Allahabad pillar inscription (No. 1), became pale when Chandragupta I announced in the Assembly the nomination of Samudragupta as his successor. It seems, Kācha rebelled and occupied the throne for a short period after Chandragupta I, but probably, was overthrown by Samudragupta. The Allahabad pillar inscription, after mentioning the selection of Samudragupta, refers to his defeating some wrong-doers, and of them Kācha would have been the most prominent. The non-occurrence of his name in the Gupta genealogies could be because they do not mention collaterals.

## NOTES AND REFERENCES

1. His name occurs in the Kaliyuga-rāja-vṛittānta of the *Bhavishyottara-purāṇa*; but the work is a modern forgery. See R C Majumdar, *Indian Historical Quarterly*, XX, 345ff; D C Sircar, *Journal of the Numismatic Society of India*, VI, pp. 34-36.
2. Altekar states that seven Kācha coins are there in the British Museum, three in the Indian Museum and five in the State Museum, Lucknow. See *The Coinage of the Gupta Empire*, p. 78.
3. *Ibid.*, pp. 307ff.
4. *Ibid.*, p. 89; *Catalogue of the Gupta Gold Coins in the Bayana Hoard*, p. 66.

5. A S Altekar, *The Coinage of the Gupta Empire*, p. 248.
6. P L Gupta, *The Imperial Guptas*, p. 93.
7. A S Altekar, *The Coinage of the Gupta Empire*, p. 78.
8. *Ibid.*
9. P L Gupta, *The Imperial Guptas*, p. 132.
10. AS Altekar, *The Coinage of the Gupta Empire*, p. 78.
11. *Ibid.*, pp. 79-80.
12. *Ibid.*, p. 3.
13. *Ibid.*, p. 84.
14. *Ibid.*, pp. 77-78.
15. *Journal of the Royal Asiatic Society of Great Britain and Ireland*. 1889, pp. 74-76.
16. *Journal of the Royal Asiatic Society of Great Britain and Ireland*, 1893, p. 95.
17. *Indian Antiquary*, 1902, p. 259.
18. J F Fleet, *Corpus Inscriptionum Indicarum*, III, p. 27, n. 4.
19. John Allan, *Catalogue of the Coins of the Gupta Dynasties, and of Śaśāṅka, the King of Gauḍa, in the British Museum, London*, Introduction, p. xxxiii.
20. R K Mookerji, *The Gupta Empire*, 1947, p. 17.
21. H C Raychaudhuri, *Political History of Ancient India*, p. 533.
22. R G Basak, *The History of North-Eastern India*, pp. 38-39.
23. T P Verma, in B Ch Chhabra *et al.* (ed.), *Reappraising Gupta History for S R Goyal*, pp. 102ff.
24. *Ibid.*, p. 106.
25. *Ibid.*
26. A S Altekar, *The Coinage of the Gupta Empire*, pp. 81-82.
27. *Ibid.*, pp. 69ff.
28. *Ibid.*, p. 55.
29. *Ibid.*, p. 128.
30. *Ibid.*, p. 184.
31. *Journal of the Numismatic Society of India*, XLIII, p. 73.
32. A S Altekar, *The Coinage of the Gupta Empire*, p. 85.
33. *Political History of Ancient India*, p. 470n (continued on p. 471).
34. The Poona (No. 82) and Rithpur (No. 84) copperplates of the Vākāṭaka dynasty apply it, along with other designations of Samudragupta, to Chandragupta II, probably because of carelessness, as it also applies the title *mahārāja* instead of *mahārājādhirāja* to Chandragupta I.
35. See also Ashvini Agrawal, *Rise and Fall of the Imperial Guptas*, p. 105.
36. *Ibid.*, p. 138.
37. Ashvini Agrawal, *Rise and Fall of the Imperial Guptas*, p. 138.
38. T P Verma, in B Ch Chhabra *et al.* (ed.), *Reappraising Gupta History for S R Goyal*, pp. 108-09.
39. P L Gupta, *The Imperial Guptas*, p. 254.
40. *Ibid.*, p. 255.
41. A S Altekar, *The Coinage of the Gupta Empire*, p. 82.

42. J F Fleet, *Corpus Inscriptionum Indicarum*, III, p. 27.
43. *Catalogue of the Coins of the Gupta Dynasties, and of Śaśāṅka, the King of Gauḍa, in the British Museum, London*, pp. xxxii-xxxiv.
44. For similar view, see also R K Mookerji, *Gupta Empire*, p. 17.
45. R D Banerji, *The Age of the Imperial Guptas*, pp. 8-9.
46. A S Altekar, *The Coinage of the Gupta Empire*, p. 81.
47. See also B N Mukherjee's note in H C Raychaudhuri,*Political History of Ancient India*, p. 766.
48. R B Singh, *Gupta Sāmrājya*, pp. 359-60.
49. P L Gupta, *The Imperial Guptas*, p. 255.
50. In *The Coinage of the Gupta Empire* (p. 82) A S Altekar describes *Garuḍadhvaja* type of coin, but does not discuss its chronological positioin.
51. P L Gupta, *The Imperial Guptas*, p. 255.
52. A S Altekar,*The Coinage of the Gupta Empire*, p. 89.
53. *Imperial History of India*, text, p. 52.
54. P L Gupta, *The Imperial Guptas*, p. 256; S R Goyal, *Imperial Guptas*, p. 186; L P Pandey, *Kāśī Nagari Pracharini Patrika*, Saṁvat 2034, parts 3-4, pp. 61-62.
55. Cited by Ashvini Agrawal, *Rise and Fall of the Imperial Guptas*, p. 136.
56. P L Gupta, *The Imperial Guptas*, pp. 122ff.
57. L P Pandey, *Kāśī Nāgarī Prachāriṇī Patrikā*, Saṁvat 2034, parts 3-4, pp. 61-62.
58. See also Ashvini Agrawal, *Rise and Fall of the Imperial Guptas*, p. 138.
59. D R Bhandarkar, *Malaviya Commemoration Volume*, p. 189; *Corpus Inscriptionum Indicarum*, III, p. 51.
60. P L Gupta, *The Imperial Guptas*, p. 183.
61. A S Altekar, *The Coinage of the Gupta Empire*, pp. 84-85.
62. *Ibid.*, pp. 86-87.
63. J Prinsep, *Journal of the Asiatic Society of Bengal*, LIII, p. 2, n. 4, *vide* D R Bhandarkar, *Corpus Inscriptionum Indicarum*, III, p. 51, n. 1; F W Thomas, *vide* A S Altekar, *The Coinage of the Gupta Empire*, p. 79.
64. J F Fleet, *Corpus Inscriptionum Indicarum*, III, p. 27n. It also means a full blown lotus. M Monier-Williams, *Sanskrit-English Dictionary*, p. 175.
65. R D Banerji, *The Age of the Imperial Guptas*, p. 9.
66. *Ibid.*
67. Buddha Prakash, *Aspects of Indian History and Civilization*, pp. 80ff.
68. *Journal of the Epigraphical Society of India*, I, pp. 75ff.
69. *Archaeological Survey of Western India*, IV, p. 129.
70. Sharma, *Journal of the Epigraphical Society of India*, I, p. 79.
71. *Ibid.*, p. 83, n. 25.
72. Sharma (*ibid.*, p. 79) refers to the view of R N Dandekar (*A History of the Guptas*, p. 64) that the Eran inscription suggests that Samudragupta conferred the title *mahārāja* and *rājan* on a feudatory, and opines that he may be identical with Kācha.
73. *Journal of the Oriental Institute, (Baroda)*, XXII, pp. 64ff.

74. *Journal of the Numismatic Society of India*, XII, pp. 38-40.
75. A S Altekar, *The Coinage of the Gupta Empire*, p. 79.
76. B Ch Chhabra, *Indian Culture*, XIV, pp. 141f.
77. B Ch Chhabra, *Catalogue of the Gold Coins of the Bayana Hoard, in the National Museum*, p. xvii.
78. *Ibid.*
79. *Journal of the Numismatic Society of India*, L, pp. 79-80.
80. *Ibid.*, p. 80.
81. S C Bhattacharya, in B Ch Chhabra, *et al.* (ed.), *Reappraising Gupta History for S R Goyal*, pp. 77-82.
82. *Ibid.*
83. *Ibid.*, p. 81.
84. *Ibid.*, p. 79.
85. *Ibid.*, p. 81.
86. *Ibid.*, pp. 80-81.
87. *Vide* K K Thaplyal, *Inscriptions of the Maukharis, Later Guptas, Pushpabhūtis and Yaśovarman of Kanauj*, p. 147.
88. See also S K Jaiswal, *Journal of the Numismatic Society of India*, LV, pp. 114ff.
89. S C Bhattacharya, in B Ch Chhabra, *et al.* (ed.), *Reappraising Gupta History for S R Goyal*, pp. 80-81.
90. *Ibid.*, p. 80.
91. A S Altekar, *Catalogue of the Gupta Gold Coins in the Bayana Hoard*, p. 62.
92. S R Goyal, *Imperial Guptas*, pp. 182-83.
93. S R Goyal, *Gupta Sāmrājya kā Itihāsa*, pp. 84-85.
94. S R Goyal, *ibid.*, p. 85.
95. T Watters, *On Yuan Chwang's Travels in India*, I, pp. 211-12.
96. S R Goyal, *Gupta Sāmrājya kā Itihāsa*, pp. 85-86.

# 5
# Samudragupta: Expansion of the Empire

## I

Samudragupta came to the throne after Kācha, his rebel brother, perhaps overthrowing him. His Allahabad pillar inscription (No. 1),[1] a fairly long *praśasti* composed by his high official, Harisheṇa, throws light on him as a conqueror, a statesman, a poet and a musician. Another epigraph of his reign is the Eran pillar inscription (No. 2). Its location shows that eastern Malwa had come under the Gupta rule during his reign. There are two copperplate inscriptions of this king—the Nālandā copperplate inscription of year 5 (No. 3) and the Gaya copperplate inscription of year 9 (No. 4). The former mentions a land grant to a brāhmaṇa, and refers to Prince Chandragupta, in all probability, in the capacity of a *dūtaka*. The second copperplate inscription refers to the grant of land by the king from royal camp at Ayodhyā. As seen above (Chapter 1), the plates are not original ones as (i) the text has grammatical errors in the use of adjectives for Samudragupta in sixth case-ending, and his name, in the first. (ii) Samudragupta is referred to as *parama-bhāgavata* which epithet is not mentioned for him in any of his epigraphs or coins.[2] (iii) He is mentioned as a performer of *aśvamedha* which, it seems, he could not have performed within the fifth year of his reign; and which does not find mention in his Allahabad pillar inscription, that belonged to the late phase of his reign, as suggested by the mention of his large scale conquests in it. (iv) The text at the beginning of the plates has *mahānau* etc., the earliest example of which occurs in the grant of Vainyagupta, datable to AD 507. (v) It has Prakrit *uchchhanna* for Sanskrit *utsanna*. (vi) It shows indiscriminate use of *v* and *b*, which feature is met with in inscriptions from 5th-6th century AD. (vi) The palaeography of the letters shows features later than the time of Samudragupta.

He issued six types of gold coins[3]—the Standard type, which is his most popular coin-type, the Archer and the Battle-axe types—both showing him as a warrior, the *Aśvamedha* type, providing a testimony of his performing that sacrifice after making conquests, the Tiger–slayer type indicating his love for hunting, and the Lyrist type reflecting his deep interest in music. Some silver coins of the king, modelled after the gold coins, have been found, but there is a controversy regarding their genuineness (Chapter 1). R D Banerji reported two copper coins of this ruler from the Burdwan district of Bengal.[4] K D Bajpai published an Archer type copper coin from R K Sethi's collection,[5] and Ajit Ghose[6] published a bronze coin with a *garuḍa* figure and traces of letters pertaining to Samudragupta's name.

A sealing from Sunet,[7] bears the legend *parākramaḥ* and shows the device of a horse in front of a *yūpa*. *Parākrama* is a typical *viruda* of Samudragupta, and the device, like that met with on his *Aśvamedha* type of coins, relates to his performing horse-sacrifice, which has been prominently mentioned in the epigraphs of his successors. R K Choudhary published a clay lump from Naulagarh (Monghyr district)[8] bearing two impressions from the same seal, showing the device of a trident-battleaxe on a pedestal, and the legend *Samudra* in Gupta characters. He considers the impressions as taken from the seal of the Imperial Gupta ruler, Samudragupta. But the fact that the name on the lump is *Samudra* and not *Samudragupta*, that there is absence of any royal title, and that the seal depicts Śaiva and not Vaishṇava device which is expected on a seal of the Gupta king, who most probably was a Vaishṇava, do not favour attribution of the sealing to that Gupta king.

Samudragupta finds brief mention in the *Ārya-Mañjuśrī-mūlakalpa*.[9] According to a Chinese work which preserves the memoirs of Wang Hiuen-tse, the Chinese envoy who visited India in the seventh century, makes a mention of Samudragupta.[10] Curiously enough, in a Javanese book of fables, *Tantri-Kāmandaka*,[11] King Aiśvaryapāla, who belonged to the

Ikshvāku family, is mentioned as born in the family of Samudragupta. The Kaliyuga-rājavṛittānta of the *Bhavishyottara-purāṇa* refers to Samudragupta and some other Gupta kings but, as seen in Chapter 1, the work is a modern forgery, and hence its evidence cannot be relied upon for the reconstruction of history. The *Matsya-purāṇa*[12] mentions king Pramati and gives the name of his father together with his *gotra* Chandramas, and assigns him a reign of 42 years, of which 30 years were spent by him in military expeditions, conquering regions like Gandhāra, south India and people like the Śakas. V S Agrawala[13] identified him with Chandragupta II, and S R Goyal[14] with Samudragupta. In three leaves published from the *Kṛishṇa-charitam* by J R Kalidasa Shastri in 1941,[15] it is mentioned that the work was of *Mahārājādhirāja-parama-bhāgavata Śrī-*Samudragupta. However, the mention in this work of the authors and literary works belonging to a period later than Samudragupta, shows that it is a forgery.[16]

The date of accession of Samudragupta is not known for certain. If the Nālandā plate of year 5 (No. 3) is taken as dated in the Gupta era, which was founded in AD 319, then he was ruling in AD 324. If Chandragupta I was the founder of the Gupta era, as is believed by most of the scholars, then that ruler had a very short reign of less than five years, which seems unlikely. But if the era was founded by Samudragupta, as a few scholars suggest, then the date of Chandragupta I has to be pushed back from AD 319, which is usually considered as the date of the beginning of the reign of that king (Appendix IV). There is a view that the era was founded by Chandragupta II, who counted its first year from the date of accession of Chandragupta I. Allan[17] places Chandragupta I's accession in AD 320, which he takes as the date for the founding of the Gupta era, and his marriage thereafter, and Samudragupta's accession in AD 335.[18] But the Allahabad pillar inscription mentions that Samudragupta was selected on merit as successor by his father, and there is little possibility of such a selection if these dates are accepted, as at that time the prince would have been a mere lad. The view according to which the beginning of the rule of Samudragupta is placed in about AD 345 seems nearer the truth.

From the Eran inscription of Samudragupta (No. 2), which according to most scholars mentions that the king had acquired Dattadevī by his own *parākrama,* it has been inferred that Samudragupta had won her in a *svayaṁvara.* This may be so, although such an expression as a maiden was acquired by the price of the valour of the man, is a conventional one. It is difficult to accept P L Gupta's view[19] that Dattadevī was the daughter of the Kadamba king, Kākusthavarman, who, as per the evidence of the Talgunda inscription (No. 91), is known to have got his daughter married to a Gupta prince, as the two kings were not contemporaries. The date 80, known for Kākusthavarman is taken in the Gupta era which corresponds to AD 399, and falls within the reign of Chandragupta II. The Eran pillar inscription (No. 2), according to the generally accepted view, refers to Dattadevī[20] as *bahuputravatī* and *bahupautravatī*, i.e. blessed with many sons and grandsons.[21] Since Chandragupta II married Dhruvadevī, the widow of Rāmagupta, in about AD 376, and Samudragupta's rule had come to an end a couple of years earlier, there cannot be any possibility of children born of this union during Samudragupta's reign. But Chandragupta II had married Kuberanāgā some years before he married Dhruvadevī, and the evidence of the Ramtek Prabhāvatī memorial inscription (No. 85), as deciphered and interpreted by some scholars, suggests that at least three sons were born of this union, beside a daughter, whose name ends in *muṇḍā*, and who is probably identical with Prabhāvatīguptā, who was married to Vākāṭaka prince Rudrasena II. Dasharatha Sharma[22] is of the view that Prabhudamā, known from a Vaiśālī sealing,[23] was perhaps a queen of Samudragupta. The seal-legend gives the name of her father, *Mahākshatrapa* Rudrasiṁha – identified by him with Rudrasiṁha II who ruled between AD 305 and 316, and that of her brother—*Mahāksatrapa* Rudrasena, but not of her husband. Sharma suggests that its mention was not deemed necessary as her husband (Samudragupta) was well known. We feel that if she would have been married to Samudragupta, who was a mighty king, she would have mentioned her relatioship with him with great pride.

## II

James Prinsep[24] wrongly read *āchakshāṇaḥ babhūvo* in line 30 of the Allahabad pillar inscription, and took it to mean that Samudragupta was dead at the time of the composition of the inscription. Fleet correctly read the last part of it as *āchakshāṇa iva bhuvo*,[25] but probably being under the influence of Prinsep's translation, took it in the same sense.[26] But, as opined by some scholars, it means that the fame of Samudragupta, and not he himself (as thought by Fleet), had gone to heaven. Bühler pointed out the fallacy of Fleet's translation, but his original paper which was published in German, was out of the reach of most of the scholars, and Fleet's translation prevailed. But afterwards Bühler conveyed his view in a letter to Smith, which was published.[27] Later B Ch Chhabra brought forth unmistakable evidences to show that the inscription was not posthumous.[28] Had Samudragupta been dead before the composition of the inscription, it should have been categorically stated by Harisheṇa, and he must have also mentioned the name of the then ruling king, specially as he speaks of his mind being expanded in consequence of his staying near the *bhaṭṭāraka* (No 1), who must stand for the ruling monarch.[29] Chhabra points out that Harisheṇa's use of *eshāmeva* (of this) with reference to the person described in the immediately preceding passage, viz. Samudragupta, clearly shows that he was alive; for if he were not alive at that time, then the expression should have been *teshāmeva* (of him).[30] Fleet took *eshāmeva* as referring to Chandragupta II,[31] which is uncalled for, as he is not mentioned anywhere in the whole epigraph. Chhabra[32] points out that in *ko nu syād=yo='sya na syād* (No. 1, line 16), the word *asya* clearly refers to Samudragupta, who was then alive. Further, the performance of *aśvamedha* by Samudragupta, so well attested by epigraphic and numismatic evidence, does not find mention in the Allahabad pillar inscription, which shows that it was performed by that king after the composition of the epigraph, and, therefore, it could not be posthumous.

## III

The Allahabad pillar inscription (No. 1) vividly describes the scene of the selection of Samudragupta by Chandragupta I. According to it, an 'emotionally charged' Chandragupta I, after screening all the princes in the royal Assembly, embraced Samudragupta, and said 'You are worthy' (according to Fleet's reading, *āryohi*)[33] or 'come, come' (according to the reading *ehyehi*, suggested by B Ch Chhabra),[34] 'rule the earth'. It is difficult to agree with Chhabra's view[35] that Fleet's reading necessarily gives the impression as if the other sons were *anāryas*. Nor is the opinion of V C Pandey[36] acceptable that because of his *vrātya* Lichchhavi mother, Samudragupta was not regarded as an *ārya* by his rivals, and therefore the king purposely addressed him as *ārya*, which otherwise is not the usual address by a father to his son. The fact that Samudragupta has been proudly referred to as *Lichchhavi-dauhitra* in the Gupta epigraphs goes against this view.

This act of the king made the members of the Assembly happy, and princes of equal birth,[37] who were claimants to the throne, sad. The dramatic way Harisheṇa has recorded the memorable event several years after it took place 'invests it with an unusual degree of importance'.[38] It appears that the action of Chandragupta I was motivated by his apprehension of a war of succession after his death, which would have been much detrimental to the family and empire of the Guptas, and therefore he wanted the issue of the succession to be settled in his life time. He announced Samudragupta as his successor in the Assembly to give the succession some sort of legal validity. The view that the announcement of successor was made in the Assembly because that body had the authority to make the final decision in the matter of succession[39] does not seem to be convincing. In our view, the king might have consulted the members of the Assembly, but the right of making the final decision was vested with him.

Verse 5, which mentions Samudragupta's nomination, also refers to some who were attracted towards him because of his noble qualities, and others who were subdued by his prowess. In the next verse, it is stated that some of the wrongdoers (*ucchchāpakārāḥ*) were defeated by Samudragupta himself in battle *(saṅgrāmeshu sva-bhuja-vijitā)* and that after showing repentance for their wrong doings, they became his friends. As seen above (Chapter 4), S R Goyal[40] opines that in the Gupta-Lichchhavi alliance, the Guptas had monarchical form of government, and the Lichchhavis, largely republican; the former were followers of brahmanical traditions and the latter were largely Buddhists and Jainas. As such, in the amalgamated Gupta-Lichchhavi territories, there would have been some Lichchhavi members of the Assembly, who would have favoured Samudragupta to succeed his father, and the Gupta members, at least some of them, detested the upper hand of the Lichchhavis in administration, and opposed him, and favoured another prince, Kācha, who rebelled and captured the throne and ruled for a very short period.[41] S R Goyal[42] identifies Kācha (who is taken as identical with Bhasma of the *Ārya-Mañjuśrī-mūlakalpa*), with a king of Śrāvastī who was anti-Buddhist and got defeated Buddhist scholar, Manoratha, by foul means. Jayaswal[43] is of the view that Chandragupta I's words to Samudragupta conveying his selection should, on the basis of the *Kaumudī-mahotsava*, be taken as spoken by Chaṇḍasena (whom he identifies with Chandragupta I) to his son, Samudragupta, when he (the former) was lying on his death bed after being defeated at the hands of Kalyāṇavarman. But if Chandragupta

I was a vanquished king, he could not have been in a position to offer to his son the succession to the throne, and would have merely exhorted him to restore the fallen fortunes of his family. The mention in the Allahabad pillar inscription that on hearing the words of Chandragupta I declaring Samudragupta as successor, the members of the Assembly became happy, clearly shows that the event took place in the Assembly, and not in the battlefield.[44]

The fact that the King Chandragupta with tears of happiness in his eyes told Samudragupta to protect the earth is taken by some scholars to indicate that he abdicated in his favour,[45] as the sovereign was old and conscious of his approaching end. Several important ancient works, like the *Rāmāyaṇa* and the *Raghuvaṁśa*, refer to kings abdicating in favour of their sons, and turning *vānaprasthīs.*[46] Basak,[47] however, finds nothing in the inscription to show that Chandragupta I abdicated, and says that it merely refers to the selection of Samudragupta by him—the reigning king. Trautmann, likewise opines that " the event described no more than the designation of an heir apparent...".[48] It may also be stated that the expression *tāten bhakti-naya-vikkrama-toshitena [yo]rājaśabda-vibhavair=abhishechan=ādyaih* in the Eran inscription of Samudragupta (No. 2) has also been taken by some scholars to indicate that Samudragupta was anointed king by Chandragupta I, who was pleased by his devotion, justness and prowess.[49] As will be seen below, Samudragupta abundantly justified his father's preference for him.

## IV

In ancient India, conquest was deemed as a legitimate right of a king, and the ideal of *chakravartī* was an inspiration for a king to bring under his empire the *chakravartī kshetra* – the land from the Himalayas to the sea. The Vedic ideal of a *chakravartī* envisages performance of such *yajñas* as the *aśvamedha* and *vājapeya.* S R Goyal[50] is of the view that Samudragupta was inspired by the Vaishṇava ideal of *chakravartī*, almost in the same way as Aśoka was by the Buddhist ideals of *chakravartī*. The worship of *chakra*, a symbol of *chakravartī*, according to the *Ahirbudhnya–saṁhitā,* a Vaishṇava text, would make a king a universal ruler.[51] In the Allahabad pillar inscription, the fame of the Gupta king is stated as 'caused by the conquest of the whole world' (*sarvva-pṛithivī-vijaya-janita*), and he is referred to as 'binding the earth by the amplitude of the vigour of his arms' (*bāhu-vīrya-prasara-dharaṇi-bandha*). The Gupta kingdom, on the eve of Samudragupta's accession, was located in the fertile Ganga valley rich in wealth of minerals and manpower, and had the potentiality for further expansion in different directions.[52] Samudragupta fought several battles for expanding the kingdom he inherited, and may be a few for safeguarding it, and Harisheṇa, his general and foreign minister and the author of the Allahabad pillar inscription, might have taken active part in some of the campaigns, and also commanded the army in the absence of the king.

## Uprooting of the Āryāvarta Kings

Samudragupta's conquests have been recorded on the pillar of Aśoka who eschewed wars and used pillars and rocks for recording the message of peace and harmony. The inscription, in enumerating the kings defeated by Samudragupta, first mentions the three kings of northern India (Āryāvarta), viz., Achyuta, Nāgasena and a prince whose name is mutilated but begins with *Ga*. Since the first two rulers and one Gaṇapatināga are mentioned again with the other Āryāvarta kings, the name of the third king can be restored as Gaṇapatināga. The view of Aiyangar[53] that these three kings attacked Samudragupta at Pāṭaliputra, is not supported by any evidence. The three kings are followed by the twelve kings of southern India and then nine kings of the Āryāvarta (which, the latter, also include the above-mentioned three kings). But it is generally believed that first he should have conquered the kings of the Āryāvarta which were nearer to his kingdom and made his position strong before launching an expedition in the Dakshiṇāpatha. The Āryāvarta kings conquered by him are detailed below:

### *Rudradeva*

According to K N Dikshit,[54] he should be identified with Rudrasena I Vākāṭaka whose territory, in his view, included Bundelkhand and central and western Deccan, and being a powerful sovereign, his name has been mentioned first among the kings of Āryāvarta defeated by Samudragupta. R C Majumdar also suggests that Samudragupta might have conquered the central Indian territories of the Vākāṭakas.[55] R K Mookerji[56] is of the view that the Gupta king would have acquired Eran in Saugar district by defeating Rudradeva. Goyal opines that Samudragupta would not have penetrated 'deep in the South without bringing the Vākāṭakas within the sphere of his influence'.[57] Some scholars opine that the title of *mahārāja* for that ruler in the Vākāṭaka inscriptions should not be taken as indicative of his feudatory status, as all the Vākāṭaka kings bear that title, except Pravarasena I who, on account of his performing the *vājapeya* sacrifice, was designated *samrāṭ*. A S Altekar[58] is of the view that Rudrasena I Vākāṭaka was an important king and if he had been defeated, it would have been mentioned prominently and in detail. But Goyal points out that in the Allahabad pillar inscription, all the Āryāvarta kings are mentioned only by their names, and no other detail is provided about them[59] Some scholars[60] are of the view that Samudragupta and the Vākāṭaka kings avoided clash with each other, as they knew that it would have been to the advantage of the Śakas, their common enemy. H C Raychaudhuri opines that the identification of Rudradeva with the Vākāṭaka king cannot be accepted as the Vākāṭakas 'were far from being uprooted during the time of Samudragupta'.[61] D C Sircar[62] identifies the king with *Kshatrapa* Rudrasena II or III, but the Śaka territory is not located within Āryāvarta. M M Nagar,[63] S Chattopadhyaya[64] and P L Gupta[65] identify Rudradeva with Rudra, whose coins have been found at Kauśāmbī. It fulfils the condition of the region being within Āryāvarta and the name Rudradeva could very well be abbreviated as Rudra. However, since the territories mentioned in the purāṇas (Chapters 1 and 3) under the Guptas include Prayāga, most probably pertain to the reign of Chandragupta I, Kauśāmbī would have formed a part of his kingdom, and hence there would not have been any need for Samudragupta to conquer it.

### *Matila*

This king has been identified by some scholars with Mattila of a sealing found in Bulandshahar (UP).[66] Allan[67] rejects the idenfication on grounds of absence of any honorific title on the seal, while H C Raychaudhuri[68] accepts it, as he says instances of princes mentioned without title are known. If the two are identical, then Mattila, which is the form met with on his own seal should be the correct form of the name, and not Matila as mentioned in the Allahabad pillar inscription. But besides the absence of a title and difference of spellings in the name, it has been pointed out that there is some difference in the palaeography of the letters of the seal and the epigraph. J Agrawal[69] places the seal in the sixth century AD, whereas the Allahabad pillar inscription belongs to the fourth century AD. The view of S R Goyal that for consideration of metre, Matila has been referred to as Kotakulaja in the Allahabad pillar inscription does not seem convincing.

*Nāgadatta*

Rapson[70] considered Nāgadatta mentioned in the Allahabad pillar inscription as a Nāga king. He has been identified with Nāgabhaṭṭa, son of Maheśvara Nāga of a seal from Lahore.[71] D C Sircar[72] takes him to be a king of northern Bengal and an ancestor of the Gupta viceroys of Puṇḍravardhana *bhukti*, whose names ended in *datta*, as seen in the inscriptions on the Damodarpur copperplates (Nos. 22, 24 and 43). S R Goyal[73] opines that if Sircar's identification is correct, economic considerations would have been an important motivating force behind the conquest of this king.

*Gaṇapatināga*

He was probably a king of Mathurā[74] where a large number of coins bearing the name Gaṇapati have been found and where a Nāga family is known to have ruled according to the purāṇas,[75] rather than a ruler of Vidiśā (Madhya Pradesh) as suggested by Smith[76] and D R Bhandarkar[77], since his coins found in Vidiśā and in its neighbourhood (Narwar, Gohad, Besṇagar, etc.)[78] are relatively fewer in number.[79] The *nāga*-ending in the name is not met with in the legend on the coins, and the identification of the king who issued these coins with Gaṇapatināga is on the basis of the identical first part of the name, the resemblance of the coins with the Nāga coins, and the palaeographic consideration.[80] This would mean that Mathurā was conquered by Samudragupta, and not by Chandragupta II as suggested by D R Bhandarkar.[81] R C Majumdar, though prefers to identify Gaṇapatināga as a king of Mathurā,[82] yet states that Mathurā was conquered either by Chandragupta II or by his father.[83]

*Nāgasena*

According to the *Harsha-charita*,[84] a Nāga ruler named Nāgasena met his doom at Padmāvatī, as a *sārikā* bird divulged his secrets (*Nāga-kula-janmanaḥ sārikā-śrāvit-mantrasya āsīdnāśo Nāgasenasya*). K P Jayaswal[85] opines that Nāgasena of the Allahabad pillar inscription, who was uprooted by Samudragupta, was perhaps different from the homonym mentioned in the *Harsha-charita*, who met his death in different circumstances. In D R Bhandarkar's opinion,[86] there is nothing in Bāṇa's statement that Nāgasena was killed in the palace and the battle might have been fought at Padmāvatī where Nāgasena's minister, as per evidence of the commentary on *Harsha-charita*, would have joined Samudragupta.

Rapson[87] suggests that the *nava*-Nāgas of the *Vishṇu-purāṇa* should be taken to refer to the nine kings of Āryāvarta who belonged to the Nāga race and had formed a confederacy. But since the purāṇa mentions *nava*-Nāgas ruling in three cities – Kāntipurī, Padmāvatī and Mathurā, and not in nine cities, it is better to take the expression in the sense of 'new Nāgas', in contradistinction to the old Nāgas mentioned in the purāṇas in connection with Vidiśā.[88] As referred to above, Ashvini Agrawal[89] is of the view that the Nāgas owed allegiance to Chandragupta I, but later on rebelled and were conquered by Samudragupta. S R Goyal[90] suggests that there was a struggle for succession for the Gupta throne after Chandragupta I, and the Nāgas seem to have sided with Kācha, a rival brother of Samudragupta, which act antagonized the latter immensely, and, he, after becoming king, with a view to taking revenge, vehemently attacked and uprooted them. This may be true, though the campaigns against the Nāgas could as well have been carried even without any provocation from their side, with a view to expanding the Gupta territories at the cost of the neighbouring kings. According to A S Altekar,[91] the Bhāraśiva king Bhavanāga was a ruler of Padmāvatī, and his rule ended in AD 340. Since during Samudragupta's victorious campaign, the king of Padmāvatī was Nāgasena, it would mean that the battle against him was fought after AD 340. The representation of a *garuḍa*, the *vāhana* of Vishṇu, on the coins of Samudragupta may be indicative of his Vaishṇava affiliations, as also of his conquest of the Nāga rulers, as that bird is an arch-enemy of the *nāgas* (serpents).

### *Achyuta*

Some scholars[92] consider Achyutanandin in line 21 of the Allahabad pillar inscription as the name of one king, like Bhūtinandin, Śiśunandin and Yaśonandin referred to in the purāṇas as ruling in the Vidiśā region after the Śuṅgas. But in line 13 of the same inscription the name is simply Achyuta, and there is no evidence of any portion of the epigraph immediately before or after it being damaged. The view that in line 13, Achyutanandin has been abbreviated to Achyuta for the metrical considerations, is not convincing. The ruler has been identified with the king whose coins bearing the legend *Achyu* in Gupta characters have been found at Ahichchhatrā (Ramnagar district) and its neighbouring regions[93] over which area he would have ruled. D R Bhandarkar says at one place[94] that this king probably ruled in Mathurā, which region, as seen above, according to most scholars was under the rule of Gaṇapatināga. At another place in the same work,[95] the learned scholar identifies him with king Achyu, who as per the evidence of the find-spots of his coins ruled around Ahichchhatrā. The legend on different coins occurs as *a*, or *chyu*, or *achyu*, but the letter *ta* is not met with either singly or in combination with other letters on such coins. If Achyu and Achyuta (=Kṛishṇa) are to be taken as identical, then the form *Achyuta* in the Allahabad pillar inscription, which is written in chaste Sanskrit, should be taken as the Sanskritized form of the name, Achyu, as coins of the king should be taken as giving the correct form of his own name in comparison to the epigraph belonging to a king of another dynasty. But if it is presumed that the letter *ta* is invariably out of flan, then the name on the coins would be the same as in the inscription. The identification of the two is accepted by almost all scholars, and would favour the view that Achyu[ta] is a complete name, and Nandin should be taken as another name. Achyuta perhaps was a Nāga king.[96] As stated above, Ashvini Agrawal[97] is of the opinion that Chandragupta I had asserted some suzerainty over the Nāga kings, and on his death, some of them, particularly, Achyu(ta) of Ahichchhatrā and Nāgasena of Mathurā rebelled and were defeated by Samudragupta. There is, however, nothing to substantiate this, and Ahichchhatrā and Mathurā do not seem to have formed part of Chandragupta I's kingdom, which, as stated above (Chapter 3), most probably was confined to the territories around Allahabad, Avadha and Magadha.

*Chandravarman*

Most scholars identify this king with the homonym mentioned in an inscription from Susunia hill, 19 km from Bankura. Therein, he is referred to as the ruler of Pushkaraṇa, which is identified with village Pokharan on the Damodar river in the Bankura district, 40 km from Susunia.[98] H P Sastri identified Pushkaraṇa with Pokharna in Marwar and equated Siṁhavarman, the father of Chandravarman with the homonym of a family of kings in Mandasor.[99] Bhandarkar[100] rightly pointed out the flaws in Sastri's view: '...Sastri maintains that Siṁhavarman was a mere chieftain and Chandravarman a supreme ruler, though both of them have been styled *mahārājas'*. Sastri identified the ruler with King Chandra of the Mehrauli pillar inscription. The identification of this 'local ruler who bore the modest title *mahārāja'* with that mighty emperor is not acceptable.[101]

### *Balavarman*

This king has not been satisfactorily identified. It is difficult to accept K N Dikshit's[102] identification of this king with Balavarman, an ancestor of Bhāskaravarman, king of Kāmarūpa, because in the Allahabad pillar inscription Balavarman is mentioned as an Āryāvarta ruler, and Kāmarūpa does not come within that region, and also because Kāmarūpa finds mention in the same inscription as a border (*pratyanta*) state of Samudragupta.[103] Moreover, the Kāmarūpa king, Balavarman, flourished eight generations before Bhāskaravarman, who ruled in the first half of the seventh century AD. Taking an average of 20 years for one generation, Balavarman should be placed in the latter half of the fifth century AD, whereas the Allahabad pillar inscription mentioning the conquest of Balavarman belongs to *c* AD 350. Mirashi[104] considers Balavarman as a scion of the Magha dynasty. But this does not seem to be the case, for, as stated above (Chapter 3) the Magha territory, which included Kauśāmbī, would have formed part of the Gupta kingdom even during the time of Chandragupta I.[105] Ashvini Agrawal[106] suggests that Balavarman was a successor of the Śaka ruler *Rājan Mahākshatrpa* Śrīdharavarman, who ruled over Eran-Sanchi region.[107] U N Roy[108] suggests that Balavarman was a Maukhari ruler. But there is no evidence of Maukharis as a political power in that period.

The expression *ādy=anek=Āryyāvarta-rāja* in the Allahabad pillar inscription would mean that Samudragupta also conquered a few other kings of northern India, but they being minor ones, have not been individually mentioned by name. But it is also possible that the author of the inscription added this expression merely to glorify his patron.

As stated above, it is open to debate whether Samudragupta first extirpated all the nine Āryāvarta kings, and then carried campaign in the south, or first defeated only three kings of Āryāvarta and thereafter undertook campaign in the south, defeating the twelve kings there, and then conquered the rest of Āryāvarta kings mentioned in the epigraph. D R Bhandarkar[109] is of the opinion that Achyuta, Nāgasena and Gaṇapatināga, and also the prince of the Kota clan formed a strong confederacy, and its destruction by Samudragupta was deemed as a great achievement to be mentioned again while enumerating other Āryāvarta kings. In his opinion, the fact that Samudragupta is said to have singly (*ekena*) and in one movement (*kshaṇāt*) uprooted them, shows that their coalition was defeated at one and the same place.[110] Father Heras[111] is of the view that Samudragupta undertook two campaigns in the Āryāvarta. He assumes that Achyuta, Nandin, Nāgasena and Gaṇapatināga were 'violently exterminated' in the second campaign, in the first, they had been merely 'uprooted', which he takes to mean defeated. R K Mookerji[112] thinks that the inscription mentions the campaigns in the order they were undertaken, and opines that these Āryāvarta kings seem to have joined hands with Samudragupta's rivals in the war of succession and so became the first victim of his attack. N N Ghosh[113] opines that Samudragupta defeated Achyuta, Nāgasena and Gaṇapatināga, but when he was busy in the southern campaign, the Āryāvarta kings made a confederacy, and congregated at Kauśāmbī, located at the junction of high roads, and Samudragupta had to fight a second war in Āryāvarta. Otherwise, he says, there is no point in referring to the above-mentioned three kings a second time after the southern campaign, along with the names of other Āryāvarta kings.

Most scholars are of the opinion that Samudragupta could not have been in a position to lead a campaign in Dakshiṇāpatha, which would take a long time, without establishing and consolidating his suzerainty in Āryāvarta. Therefore, though the Dakshiṇāpatha conquests, because of their importance, are mentioned earlier than the Āryāvarta ones, yet the sequence would have been just the other way round. S R Goyal[114] points out that strictly speaking, the order in which these political powers are mentioned in the Allahabad pillar inscription is 'neither geographical...nor chronological' but based on the policies adopted by Samudragupta towards other powers.

The Allahabad pillar inscription does not mention whether he fought each of the Āryāvarta kings singly, or a few of them provided a combined resistance.[115] However, it does mention that in Āryāvarta, Samudragupta resorted to the type of conquest which has been termed by Kauṭilya as *asura-vijaya* (demon conquest).[116] These kings were violently exterminated (*prasabh=oddharaṇa*).[117] This was done with a view to consolidating his authority in that region, keeping the conquered kingdoms directly under his rule by incorporating them in the empire. It was deemed necessary to do so for the safety and stability of his empire, as he knew that leading a campaign in Dakshiṇāpatha would keep him away from Āryāvarta for a long period. It is because of this that while the kings of Dakshiṇāpatha, who, as will be seen below, after conquest were reinstated, are mentioned along with their territories (or capitals), while the kings of Āryāvarta have been referred to without mentioning the territories they ruled over, as their territories had been incorporated in the Gupta kingdom. The geographical position of Āryāvarta and its resources in men and wealth were helpful in further expansion of the Gupta empire.

## KOTAKULAJA

It is stated in the Allahabad pillar inscription that Samudragupta caused the scion of the Kota family to be captured and regaled thereafter at Pushpāhvaya, the same as Pushpapura, another name of Pāṭaliputra (and also of Kānyakubja). It can be inferred that Samudragupta personally led the campaign against Achyuta, Nāgasena and Gaṇapatināga, but the Kotakulaja was conquered by his army under someone else's commandment.[118] Kota coins have been found in eastern Punjab, Delhi and western Uttar Pradesh, which suggests that the Kota territories were located in the Upper Ganga valley. It is difficult to accept Aiyangar's view[119] that Achyuta, Nāgasena, Gaṇapatināga, and Kotakulaja jointly attacked the Gupta ruler at Pāṭaliputra, and Sohoni's view[120] that the inscription refers not to the capture but to the liberation of Kotakulaja, for lack of evidence in their favour. There is a view that the expression *krīḍitā* in this context is meant to convey not 'regaled' but that Samudragupta defeated the enemy as in sport (i.e. easily).[121] Jayaswal takes Kotakula as the same as Magadhakula of the *Kaumudī-mahotsava*, and Kotakulaja as the lord of Pāṭaliputra who was conquered by Samudragupta.[122] He identifies Kotakulaja with Kalyāṇavarman of the *Kaumudī-mahotsava*[123] and Balavarman of the Allahabad pillar inscription.[124] S R Goyal[125] identifies Kotakulaja with Matila of the same inscription. However, Jayaswal's view seems farfetched, and that of Goyal lacks satisfactory evidence in its support.

## THE *ĀṬAVIKA* KINGS

The Allahabad pillar inscription states that Samudragupta made all the *Āṭavika* kings serve him *(parichārikīkṛita-sarvv=āṭavika-rāja)*. Epigraphs of the Parivrājaka kings (e.g. No. 68) refer to them as lords of the ancestral kingdom Ḍabhāla and 18 *aṭavī* kingdoms. Ḍabhāla is the region around Jabalpur (M P) and the area of the *Āṭavika* kingdoms would have extended upto Chhota Nagpur. Raychaudhuri[126] is of the view that *Āṭavika-rājyas* also included Ghazipur in Uttar Pradesh, but some scholars believe that this part was within the Gupta kingdom even during the reign of Chandragupta I. Samudragupta must have left the *Āṭavika* kingdoms to be administered by their rulers, after receiving the forest produce as tribute and promise of help in course of 'military movement and espionage'.[127] U N Roy[128] suggests that the Tiger-slayer type of coins of Samudragupta marks his victory over the *Āṭavikas*. As '...the ethnic composition, socio-political traditions and economic systems' of tribal states were different from those of the people of the Ganga valley, the merger of their territories with the Gupta kingdom was not deemed worthwhile by Samudragupta.[129]

V

## Dakshiṇāpatha Campaign

As a *vijigīshu* (desirous of making conquests), a king could make conquests in different directions; but normally the choice of areas for conquest depended on various considerations. Samudragupta's conquest of south India might have been motivated considerably by his desire of having a hold over the ports of the eastern coast with a view to receiving the share in the profits from the prosperous overseas trade through them. A number of Roman coins found in the eastern coast, suggest great prosperity of the region due to profitable trade with the Roman Empire which had been more brisk in the pre-Gupta period than in the Gupta period. Trade through these ports was carried on with Sri Lanka and other south-east-Asian countries too which had increased considerably by that time. Samudragupta would also have been keen to acquire wealth from south India by way of tribute from the conquered kings and also as booty. According to Goyal,[130] the expression in the Allahabad pillar inscription that the fortunes (i.e. wealth) of Samudragupta increased because of his policy of *grahaṇa, moksha* and *anugraha* followed in the context of the south Indian kings, reflects the economic gains from his south Indian conquests.[131] K P Jayaswal's view[132] that the Pallavas were a branch of the Vākāṭakas, and that Samudragupta's south Indian conquests were aimed at crushing the power of the Pallavas as he was apprehensive of their invading the Gupta territories jointly with the Vākāṭakas, is not based on any reliable evidence, and has rightly not been accepted by scholars.

Samudragupta, in his Dakshiṇāpatha campaign, carried his arms at least up to Kāñchī, and according to some, even beyond. It is not known whether all or only a few battles of the campaign were commanded by the king himself who has been referred to as conqueror of a 'hundred battles' (*samara-śata*) and also one whose body bore scars caused by different kinds of weapons (No. 1). The undertaking of the arduous south Indian campaign reflects great skill in the planning of transportation, communication and in the management of troops in and outside the battlefield. The following twelve kings of Dakshiṇāpatha, with their territories, or, in a few cases, capitals (e.g. Kañchī and Veṅgī), are mentioned as defeated by Samudragupta:

*Mahendra of Kosala*

In the Allahabad Pillar inscription,'Kosala denotes Mahākosala or Dakshiṇa Kosala comprising Raipur, Durg, Bilaspur and Sambhalpur districts.'[133] Mahendra has been identified by some with Mahendrāditya of the Nala dynasty.[134] D R Bhandarkar[135] is of the view that the scions of the Ikshvāku family settled in certain areas of Dakshiṇāpatha, that southern Kosala is named after Kosala (Avadh) region in the north and that King Mahendra was a scion of that family. In the time of the Pāṇḍuvaṁśī ruler Tīvaradeva (*circa* sixth century AD), the capital of Kosala was Śrīpura, 64 km from Raipur, and possibly it was also the case during the time of Samudragupta's campaign. Some scholars identify Mahendra with the homonym of a seal from Malhar in the Bilaspur district.[136]

*Vyāghrarāja of Mahākāntāra*

D R Bhandarkar[137] states that on the basis of the evidence of the *Mahābhārata,* Mahākāntāra mentioned in the Allahabad pillar inscription has to be distinguished from *sarvv=āṭavika-rājya* referred to in the same epigraph, which denotes forests spread from Bundelkhand to Baghelkhand; and should refer to forests spanning between Kosala and Kaliṅga, i.e., the area of Vishakhapatnam and Ganjam. He suggested the possibility of identifying Vyāghrarāja with Vyāghradeva mentioned in the Nachana-ki-Talai (No. 81) and Ganj (No. 88) inscriptions as a feudatory of the Vākāṭaka king, Pṛthivīsheṇa (*Mahārāja-Śrī-Pṛithivīsheṇa-pādānudhyāta-Vyāghradevo*). However, there is no definite evidence of any conflict between the Guptas and the Vākāṭakas, and Vyāghradeva ruled in Jaso and adjacent territories, which should better be regarded as part of Āryāvarta, rather than of Dakshiṇāpatha. Some scholars opine that Vyāghrarāja ruled in the Jeypore region of Orissa, which finds reference in the inscriptions as Mahāvana, meaning the same as Mahākāntāra (great forest) of the inscription (No. 1). Jayaswal[138] identifies Mahākāntāra with Kankar and Bastar regions, and Ramdas[139] with the Agency tract of Ganjam. There is a view that the legend *Vyāghra-parākramaḥ* on Samudragupta's Tiger-slayer type of coins is suggestive of his victory over Vyāghrarāja.[140]

### *Maṇṭarāja of Kurāla*

Fleet's emendation[141] of Kaurāḷaka into Kairaḷaka, which involves correction of two syllables of the name, has been considered by D R Bhandarkar[142] as 'too egregious to carry conviction.' It is also not acceptable because Krala is in the extreme south—a region to which the Gupta king does not seem to have marched. [143] S R Goyal,[144] however, accepts Fleet's identification, and states that its mention in the epigraph before the kingdoms to its north conquered by Samudragupta is because the political powers have not been mentioned in a geographical order. R Sathianathaier,[145] identifies it with Cherla in Nugur *taluk,* Eastern Godavari district. Keilhorn[146] locates it in the region around Kolleru lake, which he considers the same as Kuṇāla lake referred in the Aihoḷe inscription of Pulakeśin II, located between the Godavari and Krishna. This, however, is not acceptable, as the area falls under Vengi, which is mentioned in the epigraph as a separate kingdom. Barnett is of the view that Kurāla should be identified with one of the villages called Korāḍa in south India. This leaves the choice wide open.[147] Ramdas locates Kurāla in the plain country to the north-east of the Mahendra hill,[148] and Aiyangar with Khurda (district).[149] A recently discovered copperplate grant of King Narendra of Śarabhapurīya dynasty mentions a Maṇṭarāja-*bhukti,* which may be a province named after King Maṇṭarāja. Kurala in that case should be located in the vicinity of south Kosala.[150]

### *Mahendragiri of Pishṭapura*

There is no doubt that Pishṭapura is the same as Pithapuram in the Eastern Godavari district of Andhra Pradesh As will be seen below, the passage *Paishṭapuraka-Mahendragiri Kauṭṭūraka-Svāmidatta* has been interpreted differently by different scholars. The view of Fleet[151] that the name of the king is Mahendra, and *giri* is part of the following Kauṭṭūraka, is not acceptable, as in that case, the text should have been *Gairikūṭaka* and not *Girikūṭaka*. His objection in considering Mahendragiri as a name was mainly based on his belief that *giri*-ending names are mostly used for saints and not for kings.[152] This, however, stands refuted, as such names of kings as Kumāragiri, Kamtagiri, etc., are known.[153] D R Bhandarkar[154] opines that if Sheshadri, which is the name of a mountain, can be a name of a person in ancient and modern times, then Mahendragiri could also be so.

*Svāmidatta of Koṭṭūra*

Fleet's identification[155] of Koṭṭūra with Kottur-pollachi in the Coimbatore district, though followed by Smith,[156] S R Goyal[157] and a few other scholars, is difficult to accept as it is located too far south to be a likely identification.[158] Fleet's alternative identification of it is with Kailasakottak.[159] Jouveau-Dubreuil[160] identified it with Kothoor in the Ganjam district, R Sathianathaier[161] with Koṭṭūr near Tuni in Godavari district, and Saletore[162] with Koṭṭūra in the Bellary district. Ramdas[163] joins *Mahendragiri* with *Koṭṭūraka*, and take the expression as *Paishṭapuraka Māhendragirik=Auṭṭūraka-Svāmidatta*, too mean 'Svāmidatta of Pishṭapura and Auṭṭūra near Mahendragiri'. But the actual reading is *Mahendragiri*— and not *Māhendragiri*—,[164] and such a meaning cannot be derived from it. Besides, the inscription mentions one king and one territory in all other cases, and the same should have been followed in this case as well.[165]

*Damana of Eraṇḍapalla*

As pointed out by Jouveau-Dubreuil,[166] Eraṇḍapalla is Eraṇḍapali, mentioned in Gaṅga king Devendravarman's Siddhantam plates issued from Kaliṅganagara.[167] which probably was near Chicacole. Ramdas[168] identified it with Yendipalli in Golkunda taluq or Endipilli in Ellore taluk, both located in the Vizagapatam district, while R Sathianathaier identified it with Erranguntapalli in Chintalpudi *taluk* of the Western Godavari district.[169] S R Goyal[170] identifies king Damana with the founder of the dynasty to which Śatrudamana belonged, and whose charter in Gupta script has been found in Siṁhapur in Kaliṅga. Fleet's identification of it[171] with Erandol in the eastern Khandesh district of Maharashtra is not acceptable to most of scholars as it would mean Samudragupta in his return journey passed through the western coast, which would not have been the case, as that would have been extremely time consuming and arduous.

### *Vishṇugopa of Kāñchī*

The city of Kāñchī (Conjeeveram) is located in the south-west of Chennai in Chingleput district and was the Pallava capital. D R Bhandarkar[172] identifies Vishṇugopa with the 'earliest Pallava king of that name for whom Jouveau-Dubreuil has assigned the period AD 325-50'.[173]

### *Nīlarāja of Avamukta*

Jayaswal[174] is of the view that Ava country or people who had their capital at Pithuṇḍa, near Godavari, which is based on his reading and interpretation of the Hathigumpha inscription of Khāravela.[175] Pithuṇḍa identified with Ptolemy's Pitundra or Pitunda.[176] H C Raychaudhuri points out that the *Brahma-purāṇa* refers to Avamukta-*kshetra* on the banks of the Godavari and Nīlarāja reminds of Nīlapalli, a sea-port in the Godavari district.[177]

### *Hastivarman of Veṅgī*

The capital of Veṅgī kingdom is now represented by Vegi or Peddavegi, seven miles north of Ellora, between the Krishna and Godavari rivers.[178] Hultzsch identified King Hastivarman with Attivarman of the Ānanda family, but he should be better identified with the homonym of the Śālaṅkāyana dynasty, as suggested by H C Raychaudhuri[179] and R C Majumdar.[180]

### *Ugrasena of Pālaka*

Smith[181] once identified Pālaka with Palaghat or Palakkaddu, south of the Malabar district. It is better identified with Palakkada, a provincial capital mentioned in the Pallava records, and probably located in Nellore district. Ramdas identifies it with Pākkai in that district.[182]

### *Kubera of Devarāshṭra*

Smith's identification[183] of Devarāshṭra with Maharashtra, though supported by some scholars, is not acceptable for the same reason as his identification of Eraṇḍapalla with Erandol, namely it being located in western India, which does not seem to have been conquered by Samudragupta. A copperplate from the Vizagapatam district mentions a village Elamañchi-Kaliṅgadeśa in Devarāshṭra-*vishaya*, which should correspond to the region around Yellamanchili in that district.[184] S K Aiyangar[185] identifies it with Kaliṅganagara. It has been pointed out that the *Mahāvaṁsa* mentions a princess of Kaliṅga, who in the wake of an invasion there, fled to Sri Lanka in the ninth regnal year of King Meghavarṇa of Ceylon, i.e. in AD 361, and since that date falls during Samudragupta's reign, it has been suggested that he was the invader.[186]

### *Dhanañjaya of Kusthalapura*

The identification of Kusthalapura by Smith[187] with Dvārakā in Gujarat, is to be rejected as that would mean Samudragupta returned from his southern Indian campaigns via the western coast, which is unlikely. R Sathianathaier's identification[188] of it with Kuśāvatī or Kuśasthalī corresponding to Ramnagar on the south bank of Narmada near Mandala (MP) is also not acceptable for the same reason. Barnett identifies it with Kuttalur near Polur in North Arcot.[189] Aiyangar points out that a river Kuśasthalī, south of Krishna, is mentioned in the *Kaliṅgattuparṇi* poem.[190] B V Krishna Rao[191] identifies it with the modern town of Kolarupak or Kolipak situated on river Aleru, a tributary of Musi. It was the capital of the territory between Rivers Godavari and Krishna. The chieftains of the Koṭa family in this region, he says, trace their descent from one Dhanañjaya who should be identified with the homonym of the Allahabad pillar inscription.

## Route Followed in the South Indian Campaign

Samudragupta's southern campaign, involving long distances, often passing through unfamiliar, difficult and inhospitable terrains, and territories of hostile rulers, reflect his great statesmanship, shrewd planning, quick mobility, and proper deployment of combative troops. He was one of the few north Indian kings in ancient history who made substantial conquests in south India. The route of Samudragupta's southern campaign is to be determined on the basis of the identification of the southern kingdoms mentioned in the Allahabad pillar inscription. However, of these the identification of only four, namely Kosala, Pishṭapura, Kāñchī and Veṅgī can be taken as certain. There is a lot of difference of opinion among scholars regarding the identification of the others. D R Bhandarkar states that according to the Allahabad pillar inscription, Samudragupta uprooted many (*aneka*), and not all kings of Āryāvarta, while he conquered and freed all (*sarva*) kings of Dakshiṇāpatha[192] The conquered south Indian kings and their territories, it appears, have not been mentioned in strictly chronological sequence of the campaigns or the geographical location of their territories,[193] notwithstanding the views of some scholars to the contrary. One undisputed instance of not following the geographical order is the mention of Vengi, the capital of Hastivarman, 11 km from Ellore, after Kañchī, the capital of Vishṇugopa, though the former is situated to the north of the latter.

As seen above, Fleet, Smith and a few other scholars suggest that Samudragupta's conquests also included territories located in the far south and in the western coast, as they identified Kaurāla with Kerala, Koṭṭūra with Kottura-pollachi in Coimbatore district, Pālaka with Palghat on the Malabar coast, Eraṇḍpalla with Erandol in Khandesh, and Devarāshṭra with Maharashtra. According to Smith,[194] Samudragupta moved from Pāṭaliputra through Chhota Nagpur, attacked and defeated the king of South Kosala, and moving forward, he subdued the kings of the forest country. Continuing his southern advance via the east coast, he vanquished the rulers of Pishṭapura, Kolleru lake, Veṅgī and Kāñchī near Madras. Thereafter, turning westwards, he defeated the king of Palakka in Nellore district, and returned through the western part of the Deccan, subduing the kingdoms of Devarāshṭra (identified by him with Maharashtra) and Eraṇḍapalla (identified by him with Erandol in Khandesh).[195] However, marching through the eastern coast and returning via western India would be an extremely arduous and time-consuming task, which Samudragupta would have avoided. Further, western Deccan was ruled by the Vākāṭakas, and there is no tangible evidence to show that Samudragupta came in conflict with them, and they seem to have continued to rule in an independent capacity during his reign. Devarāshṭra and Erṇḍapalla, as seen above, have been satisfactorily identified in Orissa.

S R Goyal[196] is of the view that Samudragupta's battles in south India were not in continuity and that all kings of that region might not have been defeated in a single, but in more than one expedition. In his opinion, as the Gupta king might have taken different routes for different campaigns, it would be almost impossible to determine the routes followed by him in his campaigns. However, since marching to distant places in the inhospitable terrain of south India would have been quite a tedious and time consuming task, he might have preferred to conqueror as many territories as possible in a single, even though a long-lasting, campaign. Goyal suggests that in a few cases, for example in the case of Kāñchī, the possibility of carrying a naval expedition cannot be ruled out. However, if he had proceeded up to Veṅgī by land then it would have been far more convenient to reach Kāñchī by land route than by launching a naval attack, in addition to it. It seems almost certain, as pointed out by R C Majumdar,[197] that Samudragupta proceeded from Pāṭaliputra through Bilaspur and Sambhalpur districts, but regarding the route followed thereafter, there are two views, both equally plausible. Some scholars believe that he 'passed through the Mahanadi valley to Orissa coast and then proceeded south through the Ganjam and Vizagapatam districts'. The other view regarding the route, as suggested by R Sathianathaier, is that he "passed through [former] Bastar state and East Godavari district to the coastal regions near Pithapuram", and did not visit Vizagapatam or Ganjam.[198] He certainly reached as far south as Kañchī.[199]

It has been suggested[200] that Samudragupta was keen to make further conquests in south India, but because of the troubles created for him by his enemies in the north, had to return, leaving the mission of extensive conquests in south India unfinished. This is possible, though even without trouble in the north, he might have opted to return, as his men in arms (and may be he himself too), being away from their homes for long period of time, would have been exhausted and keen to return home. Any further stay could have created some such situation as in the second half of the fourth century BC, Alexander had faced from his soldiers who, being away from their homes for a long time, were extremely homesick.

According to B V Krishna Rao,[201] the fact that names of the south Indian kings have not been given in order of their geographical position, but in a haphazard manner, suggests that they fought Samudragupta in coalition somewhere in the Deccan. He believes that they were successful in repulsing him, and he abandoned the idea of further conquests, and returned, leaving the kingdoms unconquered. Jouveau-Dubreuil[202] states that Samudragupta, in the course of his south Indian campaign, after conquering south Kosala, reached the coast of Orissa. He defeated Maṇṭarāja of Korāla, Mahendra of Pishṭapura, Svāmidatta of Koṭṭūra, and Damana of Eraṇḍapalla. Thereafter, a confederacy of kings ruling near the mouth of the Godavari and the Krishna—Vishṇugopa of Kāñchī (the most important of them), Nīlarāja of Avamukta, Hastivarman of Veṅgī,

Ugrasena of Pālakka, Kubera of Devarāshṭra, and Dhanañjaya of Kusthalapura, with superior forces, opposed and repulsed the marching army of Samudragupta forcing him to abandon the campaign and return.[203]

Both Krishna Rao and Jouveau-Dubreuil take the expression *sarvva-Dakshiṇāpatha-rāja-grahaṇa-moksh=ānugraha-janita-pratāp=onmiśra-mahābhāgya...* ('whose magnanimity was mingled with his glory produced by his kind favour of setting at liberty after capturing all the kings of Dakshiṇāpatha') in the Allahabad pillar inscription as an attempt to cover up Samudragupta's inability to conquer some of them, and failing to retain hold over some after conquering them. But the epigraph makes no 'invidious distinction between the kings of Orissa and those of Eastern Deccan'.[204] It mentions kings of Dakshiṇāpatha as captured and later released and reinstated, and not to any confederation of kings, or to Samudragupta's defeat.[205] On the statement of Jouveau-Dubreuil, Bhandarkar[206] remarks: 'our amazement knows no bounds'. He points out that if Joveau-Dubreuil takes kings of Kosala, Mahākāntāra, and also of countries on the coast of Orissa, as defeated by the Gupta ruler, then it is not understandable why he does not consider the kings of eastern Deccan headed by Vishṇugopa as defeated by him.[207] It is amazing, he says, that instead of taking the natural meaning of the text that Samudragupta defeated these states, Jouveau-Dubreuil deduces just the opposite conclusion, viz. that Samudragupta could not conquer them, and instead was himself conquered by them.[208] R C Majumdar, dubs Jouveau-Dubreuil's assumption as 'gratuitous'[209] and 'pure imagination'[210] without any evidence to its support, and rejects it outright. There is nothing to warrant that Samudragupta's south Indian campaign was an 'ignominious failure', and that he suffered defeat. On the contrary, all evidences are in favour of his having been successful throughout his campaign.

D R Bhandarkar[211] believes that the south Indian kings confederated in two different groups against Samudragupta, and the rulers in each coalition have been mentioned in the Allahabad pillar inscription in order of their position in the political hierarchy. He says, 'It seems that Vishṇugopa was the overlord and that the rulers of Avamukta, Veṅgī, Pālakka, Devarāshṭra and Kusthalapura were his feudatories in this descending order'; Kāñchī, though situated to the south of Veṅgī, is mentioned first because of its importance.[212] According to him, the other confederation comprised 'Kosala as lord paramount and Mahākāntāra,

Kurāla, Pishṭapura, Koṭṭūra, and Eraṇḍapalla as subsidiaries in this descending order',[213] and the defeat of the king of Kāñchī, he says, presupposes the defeat of the other members of the confederacy. The possibility of some south Indian kings confederating against Samudragupta cannot be ruled out, though there is not the slightest hint about it in the inscription. In works of ancient polity, the neighbouring kingdoms are considered as enemies, and forming confederacies by them for facing invading enemy is rather a rare phenomenon in ancient Indian history. One could suggest the possibility of some kings submitting to Samudragupta without giving a fight, but the general term used in the context of all the south Indian kings is *grahaṇa* (capture), which does not favour such a postulate.

Samudragupta realized that it would be an arduous task to maintain an efficient control over the conquered regions in the south, some of them quite distant from his capital, Pāṭaliputra, located in the north-eastern part of his kingdom. He therefore followed the policy of reconciliation and remained content with the homage offered and tributes paid by the conquered kings, as a mark of their accepting his suzerainty, and did not make an attempt at incorporating the conquered kingdoms in his territory permanently. This policy based on 'enlightened self-interest' would have served his aim to acquire trade facilities with south-eastern Asia through harbours on the south-eastern coast. R D Banerji[214] suggests that Samudragupta's south Indian campaign was in fact a *digvijaya* related to his performing *aśvamedha*, and as such, there was hardly any attempt to incorporate the conquered kingdoms into his empire. He links the performance of *aśvamedha* only with his south Indian conquests, ignoring the north Indian ones, in the course of which he uprooted nine kings. Even if *aśvamedha* would have been related with his southern conquests then, on its accomplishment, it should have found mention in the Allahabad pillar inscription, which, however, is not the case.

The epigraph refers to his relationship with the conquered south Indian kings as capturing (*grahaṇa*), liberating (*moksha*), and favouring (*anugraha*). Favour would have been shown by him by re-instating them in their territories, allowing them autonomy in administering their territories after they acknowledged his sovereignty and agreed to pay periodical tributes to him. This is the type of conquest, which in the *Arthaśāstra*[215] and some other ancient texts is called *dharma-vijaya* in contradistinction to *lobha-vijaya*, in which assets of the defeated enemy are appropriated but life is spared, and to *asura-vijaya* in which enemies are destroyed and their territories annexed. The concept of *dharma-vijayī* is well-illustrated in an oft-quoted verse from the *Raghuvaṁśam* of Kālidāsa, which says that Raghu 'took away the glory, but not the territories of the lord of Mahendra [mountains], who was made captive and then released.'[216] In passing, it may be mentioned that there is a suggestion[217] that the epithet *dharmavijayī* was ascribed to the Vākāṭaka king Prithvīsheṇa I because of his participation as an ally of Samudragupta in the latter's south Indian conquests which were in the nature of *dharmavijaya*.[218] But if in this context anybody deserved the title *dharmavijayī*, it was the victorious emperor, Samudragupta, rather than his subordinate ally.

Ramdas[219] is of the view that *grahaṇa, moksha* and *anugraha* in the context of the south Indian kings should mean capturing some, liberating some, and reinstating some. But the expression *sarvva-dakshiṇāpatha-rāja* shows that the same policy was meant for all south Indian kings. S R Goyal[220] opines that only two policies were followed: those who were captured were liberated (*grahaṇa-moksha*), and those who voluntarily submitted were obliged (*anugraha*) in different ways. But this does not seem to be the case as while in the first case, *grahaṇa* has been used in the context of *moksha*, no expression has been used in the context of *anugraha*. Further, he might have realized that if the defeated king is liberated but not reinstated then he was likely to turn hostile and would try his best to regain his lost kingdom. The policy was not guided so much by Samudragupta's generosity as by his realization of the difficulties he would face in directly administering these distantly located territories.

## VI

### The Frontier States and the Tribal Republics

The remarkable victories of Samudragupta increased his power and prestige, and must have created an impact on the frontier states (*pratyantas*)[22]—the monarchical states located in the northern, north-western and north-eastern India, and the tribal republican states located in the western and north-western India. These two types of *pratyanta* states, tried to propitiate him by offering allegiance to him with a view to securing his friendship and goodwill so that they may be spared of the invasion from his side. The epigraph (No. 1) mentions that these two categories of powers, gratified his imperial command (*paritoshita-prachaṇḍa-śāsana*) by paying taxes (*kara-dāna*), obeying his orders (*ājñā-karaṇa*) and by offering obeisance personally (*praṇām=āgamana*).[222] The view that propitiating command (*paritoshita śāsana*) is a category in itself, is not acceptable. S R Goyal[223] is of the opinion that all the three kinds of policies mentioned in the inscription would not have been applied to all the frontier kings and the tribal republics, and for some one policy would have been applied, and for some, another. He also believes that all the border states and the tribal states would not have entered into subordinate alliance with the Gupta emperor at one and the same time, but at different times, according to their geographical situation and other considerations. The frontier states and the republican states seem to have taken recourse to the acts mentioned above voluntarily, though the possibility of the Gupta emperor using his diplomatic skills in bringing some of them to his fold cannot be ruled out. They seem to have continued to enjoy autonomy in administering their own territories, and also served as buffer states in the context of the Gupta empire *vis-à-vis* other powers. He therefore preferred not to attempt at conquering the territories of the border states—tribal or monarchical—as that would have meant a great strain on state resources. Also, their incorporation in the Gupta empire would have added to the administrative burden of an already extensive kingdom, and it would not be an easy task to maintain an effective hold over them. It is difficult to agree with the view of S R Goyal[224] that since according to the *Amarakośa*, *pratyanta* means *mlechchha* country, the Gupta king would not have liked to incorporate a *mlechchha* territory within his empire. Some of the kingdoms, before Samudragupta conquered them, were his *pratyantas*, yet he did not hesitate to conquer them. It may be mentioned that his son Chandragupta II is known to have conquered the bordering state of the Śakas, who were *mlechchhas* not only according to the definition of *pratyanta* in the *Amarakośa*, but could be termed so also because they were of foreign origin. The monarchical border states were as following.

### *Samataṭa*

Samataṭa comprised Tippera, Noakhali and Chittagaon districts. It has been referred to by Hiuen-tsang.[225] During the seventh century, Samataṭa was ruled by kings of the Khaḍga dynasty, and had as its capital Karmānta, which has been identified with Badkamta, 19 km west of Komilla.[226]

*Ḍavāka*

According to D R Bhandarkar,[227] its identification with 'Kachar district, including the north Kachar hills and the Kopili valley', as suggested by Barua,[228] is more convincing than with Dhaka or certain districts of Bengal as opined by Fleet,[229] or districts of Bogra, Dinajpur and Rajshahi in Bengal as suggested by Smith.[230]

*Kāmarūpa*

D R Bhandarkar[231] identifies Kāmarūpa with the western half of Assam. Samudragupta's contemporary ruler of Kāmarūpa was Pushyavarman, whose position as a subordinate ally can be inferred from the fact that his son and daughter-in-law, Samudravarvman and Dattadevī, were named after the Gupta king and his queen respectively. By this alliance, commodities like sandal, *agaru* and textile of that region would have become more easily available; and besides it would have facilitated trade between the Gupta kingdom and China by road as it passed through Kāmarūpa.

*Nepāla*

It comprised a large part of modern Nepal, particularly the region between Gandaki and Kosi and the valley of Kathmandu.

*Kartṛipura*

Its identification with Kartarpur in Jalandhar district is to be rejected on the grounds that it was founded by the Sikh *guru* Arjunadeva, and there is no evidence of its existence before that.[232] Dasharatha Sharma identifies it with Karor in the Multan district, of Pakistan,[233] at which place, according to Alberuni, Vikramāditya defeated the Śakas. Most scholars[234] identify it with the Katuria kingdom comprising Kumaon, Garhwal and Rohilkhand. According to D R Bhandarkar,[235] its capital was Kārttikeyapura, which he identifies with modern Baijnath in Almora district of Uttarakhand.

Tribal states had been an important feature of ancient Indian history. In course of time, the heads of the tribal republics became hereditary, though the administrative council representing people continued in some form. They generally did not follow an expansionist policy against the monarchical kingdoms, and were in danger of being attacked by them, and on being conquered, became part of their territories The tribal states who entered into alliance with Samudragupta as mentioned in the Allahabad pillar inscription are as below:

*The Mālavas*

They resided in the Punjab during the invasion of Alexander, and in south-east Rajasthan when they were defeated by the Śaka king Nahapāna in the first quarter of the second century AD.[236] In Samudragupta's time they seem to have occupied Mewar and Kota in Rajasthan and parts of Madhya Pradesh adjoining its border. Their capital was Karkoṭanagara, modern Nagar, 8 km to the east of Karkot hills in the south-east of Jaipur, where a large number of their coins have been found.[237] Later, they inhabited the region that came to be named Mālava (Malwa) after them.[238] Their chiefs used the Mālava era, of which the initial year is 57 BC and which was 'handed down traditionally by the Mālavagaṇa'.[239]

*The Ārjunāyanas*

They seem to be named after Arjuna, the Pāṇḍava hero of the *Mahābhārata*, and may be connected with the Pandouoi (Pāṇḍavas) of the Punjab region mentioned by Ptolemy.[240] If the order of mention—Mālavas, Ārjunāyanas and the Yaudheyas in the Allahabad pillar inscription is in accordance to their geographical location, then the Ārjunāyanas may be located somewhere between the Mālavas in the south and the Yaudheyas in the north.[241] In the *Bṛihatsaṁhitā*, they are placed in the northern division.[242] According to Smith,[243] their territory comprised former Bharatpur and Alwar states.

*The Yaudheyas*

Yaudheya coins have been found in various places of Rajasthan, Punjab and Haryana and in Saharanpur district of Uttar Pradesh and Dehradun district of Uttarakhand. A large number of their coin-moulds have been found at Rohtak, Sunet and Sanghol in Ludhiana district. An inscription of the Yaudheyas has been found in Vijaygarh, a hill fort in erstwhile Bharatpur state of Rajasthan.[244] The present–day Johiyas are considered as their descendants. R C Majumdar[245] places them between Bahawalpur and Bharatpur states, and Allan[246] within the Delhi-Jaipur-Agra triangle. They formed a *gaṇa* or tribal oligarchy, but in course of time their chiefs came to be designated as kings, and became hereditary. A sealing refers to the head of the Yaudheyas as *mahārāja, mahākshatrapa* and *mahāsenāpati,* who succeeded the one who too bore the same title.[247]

*The Madrakas*

They are the same as Madras, and were located between the Ravi and Chenab, with their capital at Śākala (Sialkot) in the Punjab.[248]

*The Ābhīras*

An early reference to them occurs in the *Mahābhāshya* of Patañjali.[249] Earlier, they occupied the tract in the lower Indus valley, and the western Rajasthan with the district mentioned as Abiria in the *Periplus,*[250] and in the *Geography* of Ptolemy.[251] An Ābhīra chief supplanted the Sātavāhana power before the middle of the third century AD.[252] Most scholars believe that during Samudragupta's reign, they inhabited Ahirwar located between Jhansi and Vidiśā.[253] A few scholars, however, opine that still they were in the Punjab.[254]

*The Prārjunas*

They are believed to be the same as the Pājjuṇakas (i.e. Prārjunakas) of the *Arthaśāstra,*[255] wherein they are mentioned along with the Gāndhāras. Smith[256] located them in Narsinghpur district (MP), and D R Bhandarkar[257] in Narsinghgarh (MP), as they appear to be associated with the Sanakānīkas, who are mentioned in the Allahabad pillar inscription immediately after them, and whom many scholars place near Vidiśā, because an epigraph (No. 7) of their chief has been found at Udaigiri, located close to it.

*The Sanakānīkas*

The find of an inscription of a Gupta feudatory (*Mahārāja*) of Sanakānīka tribe, from Udaigiri (Vidiśā district) of the reign of Chandragupta II (No. 7), is taken as an evidence of the tribe inhabiting the nearby area. P L Gupta,[258] however, is of the view that if Gaṇapatināga, mentioned as an Āryāvarta king in the Allahabad pillar inscription of Samudragupta, is to be identified as the king of Vidiśā, then the Sanakānīka *Mahārāja* cannot be considered as ruling in that area. According to him, he, like Vīrasena, who as per the testimony of another Udaigiri inscription (No. 11) came there from Pāṭaliputra, and Āmrakārddava, a general of Chandragupta

II, known from a Sanchi inscription (No. 9), who too came from outside, could have come to Vidiśā from elsewhere, perhaps from north-western India, and stayed there for some time on his way to the Vākāṭaka capital. However, as stated above, Gaṇapatināga seems to have been a ruler of Mathurā region. Though Sanakānīkas formed a tribal republic, the office of their chief had become hereditary, as in the Udaigiri epigraph, not only the person whose pious act it records, but also his father and grandfather have been referred to as *mahārājas*.

### *The Kākas*

They find mention in the *Mahābhārata*.[259] P L Gupta[260] locates them in the north-western India, and R D Banerji[261] relates them to the Kākas of Kashmir. But an inscription from Sanchi hill refers to the place (Sanchi) as Kākanādaboṭa, which name seems to have been given after the Kākas. K P Jayaswal[262] identifies Kakpur, a village 32 km from Vidiśā, as their seat.

### *The Kharaparikas*

Hiralal, on the basis of the mention of Kharapara army in a Battisgarh inscription of VS 1385 from Damoh district (MP),[263] places the Kharaparikas in that district. Dasharatha Sharma,[264] considers them identical with the Kharaparas mentioned in the *Nabhi-nandan–Jinoddhāra* and identifies them with the Mongols. P L Gupta[265] opines that the Kharaparas of the Battisgarh inscription were Mongols, but they were different from the indigenous Kharaparikas of the Allahabad pillar inscription. U N Roy[266] suggests that the tribe was so named as its members bore skulls (*kharapara*).

P L Gupta[267] opines that to the south of Samudragupta's territories was the Vākāṭaka kingdom, in the Vidiśā region were the Nāgas, and beyond that were the Western Kshatrapas, and thus, there is hardly any place for the Ābhīras, Prārjunas, Sanakānīkas, Kākas and Kharaparikas in Vidiśā and its neighbourhood, and as such, they must be located in north-western India. However, his view has not found favour with scholars.

In the Allahabad pillar inscription, after mentioning these tribes, is added the word *ādibhiḥ*, which would mean that a few more tribes entered into an alliance with Samudragupta. Some of the tribes, like the Kākas and the Kharaparikas, mentioned in the epigraph, were of little political importance, either they should not have been mentioned, or else all others, of howsoever little significance, should also have been mentioned, and as such the addition of *ādibhiḥ* does not seem to have any historical significance. The tribal republics tribes seem to have been gradually absorbed in the mighty Gupta empire, as after their reference in the Allahabad pillar inscription, they do not find mention as political powers either in literature or in epigraphs. In passing, it may be stated that K P Jayaswal admires Samudragupta for his marshal vigour and qualities of head and heart, but is critical of him for destroying the power of tribal states as he had great admiration for their functioning as republics.

VII

## Foreign Powers

Samudragupta's fame as a great conqueror spread to distant countries, and his military powers must have overawed their rulers, and made them realize that their interest would be best served by propitiating him. The Allahabad pillar inscription mentions certain principalities on the borders of his empire or beyond it, even across the sea, entering into friendly diplomatic alliance with him. With a view to strengthening friendly ties, their chiefs came in person in his attendance (*ātma-nivedana*),[268] and made offerings of maidens in marriage (*kanyopāyana-dāna*).[269] They requested the king for issuing a royal charter (*śāsana*) stamped with a seal bearing *garuḍa* device (*garutmad=aṅka*) allowing them to govern their own principalities. The term used in this context is *sva-vishaya-bhukti*, which literally means 'own districts and provinces', and, as suggested by some, might have been used with the intention of conveying the idea as if their territories formed part of Samudragupta's empire, as its *vishayas* and *bhuktis*.[270] According to another interpretation,[271] these powers requested the Gupta king to grant them charters allowing them the use of Gupta coins bearing the *garuḍa* device (*garutmad=aṅka*), as also to govern their kingdoms. These terms signifying the relationship suggest that the status of these rulers was like that of feudal vassals states. Some Late Kushāṇa type of coins bearing the names Samudra, and a few bearing the name Chandra, are taken to suggest the recognition of the suzerainty of these two kings by the rulers of foreign origin. The 'payment of tribute, the nominal acknowledgement of sovereignty and periodical trips to the imperial court to offer homage' are also the characteristics of vassals in medieval Europe.[272] S R Goyal[273] is of the view that all the powers in this category did not maintain all the three types of relationship mentioned in the epigraph, as it is impossible that all the kings married their daughters to Samudragupta, or all of them attended his court personally, and that, as such, even one of the three policies mentioned in the inscription would have met the requirement of pleasing the Gupta king. The foreign powers mentioned are as below:

### *Daivaputra-shāhi-shāhānushāhi*

The expression has been variously taken as denoting three different powers—*Daivaputra, Shāhi* and *Shāhānishāhi,*[274] or two powers—*Daivaputrashāhi* and *Shāhānishāhi,*[275] or as one power only.[276] D R Bhandarkar[277] points out that since it is not *Devaputra,*[278] but the *taddhita* form *Daivaputra,* which as per grammatical rule cannot stand by itself, and therefore should not be taken for an individual ruler, but as conjoined with *shāhi* and *shāhānushāhi,* and since all the three titles were borne by the Kushāṇa rulers they seem to refer to a Kushāṇa king, who ruled in the Punjab and Afghanistan. Buddha Prakash[279] is of the view that *Daivaputrashāhi-shāhānushāhi* stands for a Later Kushāṇa king, who needed Gupta help as he was at war with the Sassanian emperor, Shapur II, between AD 350 and 356, which would suggest that the Allahabad pillar inscription was composed between these two dates. S R Goyal[280] opines that at that time there was no Kushāṇa king mighty enough to adopt the grandiloquent title *Daivaputra-shāhi-shāhānushāhi,* and identifies *Daivaputrashāhi* with the Kushāṇa king Kidāra, who is referred to as *Kidāra Kushān-sha* on his coins, and who, in his opinion, with the help of Samudragupta, defeated the Sassanian king, Shāpur II, whom he identifies with the *Shāhānushāhi* of the inscription.

### *The Śakas*

They are generally taken to stand for the Western Kshatrapas. Allan[281] opines that the term may have also included the Śakas of the north-western India, who struck coins of the Kushāṇa type bearing the name of Shāka, some of which bear also the letters *Sayatha, Sita,* and *Sana* under the arm of the royal figure on the obverse, which according to some scholars should be the names of the individual rulers.[282] Some coins bear the clan name Shālada and the individual names Bhadra and Pāsaka.[283] D R Bhandarkar[284] says, "...Shāka looks like a *taddhita* form of Śaka or Shaka, and means 'descendant of Śakas'." R D Banerji[285] points out that the type of Gaḍahara coins with the legend *Samudra* so closely resembles the coins of Samudragupta that 'it is possible to say that the Gaḍahara tribe acknowledged Samudragupta's suzerainty'. K P Jayaswal[286] states that a Shālada coin bears the figure resembling that of Chandragupta II as shown on his coins, and the legend, *Chandra*. On such coins the king is shown wearing earrings, which are never seen on the royal figures on Kushāṇa coins.[287] Some of these coins bear the *garuḍa* figure, reminding one of the *garutmad=aṅka* of the Allahabad pillar inscription.

Some Śaka states surrounded by the Kushāṇa and the Sassanian kingdoms, would have tried to placate the friendship of the Gupta king.[288] The subservience of these foreign states does not seem to be the result of their military defeat, though that cannot be entirely ruled out. It is possible that the Gupta emperor exerted diplomatic pressure on at least some of them to enter into alliance with him. However, it appears more likely that the treaty was the result of their own initiative with a view to saving themselves from the wrath of that mighty emperor in the form of an invasion, in which case their defeat was almost a foregone conclusion. Two inscriptions, one from Kankhera near Sanchi, year 13,[289] and another from Eran, year 27,[290] mention King Śrīdharavarman belonging to the Śaka family, who ruled in the first half of the fourth century AD. King Siṁhaśrīsena, son of Īśvaramitra,[291] known from a seal from Eran, datable to the fourth century AD and bearing the hill symbol characteristic of Śaka coins, was a Śaka ruler; however, his relationship with the other Śaka rulers is not known.[292]

*The Muruṇḍas*

If *Daivaputra-shāhi-shāhānushāhi* of the Allahabad pillar inscription is taken as one compound, then it should refer to the Kushāṇas, and the Muruṇḍas should be different from them. H C Raychaudhuri[293] is of the view that Śaka-Muruṇḍas must have included the northern chiefs of Scythian nationality. S R Goyal,[294] also holds a similar view and includes in the Śaka-Muruṇḍa, the Shīladas and the Gaḍaharas of the central Punjab and the Shākas of the Western Punjab.

Some scholars[295] believe that Pāṭaliputra was the Muruṇḍa capital. This, however, does not go well with the Chinese account, which places their capital at a distance of 7000 *li* (about 1600 km) from the mouth of the great river, i.e. Ganga;[296] Pāṭaliputra is much nearer than that.[297] It is suggested that[298] its location was in the north-western India. This is also favoured by the evidence of the purāṇas, which mention the Muruṇḍas ruling for 200 years, as of foreign origin, and associate them with the Yavanas, Śakas and Tushāras.[299] The reference to Muruṇḍa king's sending the Yueh-chih horses for the king of Fu-nan, too would favour locating his territories in the north west.

Sten Konow[300] points out that Muruṇḍa means 'lord', and Śaka-Muruṇḍa should be taken to mean not the 'Śakas and the Muruṇḍas', but 'Śaka lord' (*svāmī*, i.e. 'lord' is a common name-ending of the Śaka kings of western India). Kanishka, in his Zeda inscription,[301] is mentioned as *muroḍa*, which appears to be a form of *muruṇḍa*. S R Goyal[302] is of the view that Muruṇḍas were originally viceroys of the Kushāṇas but continued to rule independently after Kushāṇa rule became confined to the north-western India. The purāṇas state that thirteen Muruṇḍa kings ruled after the Tukhāras (i.e. the Kushāṇas). D R Bhandarkar[303] suggests that Muruṇḍa originally was a title, but afterwards, it also became a family name, like Peshwa of Poona and Nizam of Hyderabad, and as such Śaka-Muruṇḍa may be taken as the Śakas and the Muruṇḍas, and not merely as the Śaka lords. Muruṇḍa-svāminī, the queen of Jayanātha of the Uchchakalpa dynasty[304] was obviously a lady belonging to the Muruṇḍa family, otherwise both the components of the name would mean the same (*svāminī*), which would be curious. Similar is the case with the name Muruṇḍanātha met with on a copperplate found in Bangladesh.[305]

### *Siṁhala and Other Islands*

In the Allahabad pillar inscription, Siṁhala (Sri Lanka) and other islands are mentioned in the same category as the *Daivaputra-shāhi-shāhānushāhi*, the Śakas and the Muruṇḍas, who sought friendly relationship with that powerful Gupta ruler. According to the Chinese account of Wang Hiuen-tse,[306] King Meghavarṇa of Sri Lanka[307] sent an embassy to Samudragupta with rich presents, requesting him to permit building of a monastery at Bodhgaya for Sri Lankan pilgrims, who faced hardships because of lack of proper accommodation there. The permission was granted, and a much spacious and imposing monastery, as Hiuen-tsang's account[308] makes us believe, was built. The same Chinese pilgrim informs that for securing permission, the Sri Lankan king 'gave in tribute to the king of India, all the jewels of his country'. It is presumed that Harisheṇa, the composer of the Allahabad pillar inscription, regarded the presents as tribute and construed the visit of the embassy as *ātma-nivedana* (presenting oneself), and granting land in Bodhgaya by Samudragupta as allowing 'enjoyment of territories by the royal charter', mentioned in that epigraph, as the terms and condition of the alliance of Sri Lanka and other foreign powers with Samudragupta. S R Goyal suggests that some kings might have come on pilgrimage to the holy site within the Gupta territory and visited Samudragupta at his court and this might have been taken by Harisheṇa as *ātmanivedana* (propitiating in person).[309] As stated above, the *Mahāvaṁsa* states that during the ninth year of the reign of Meghavarṇa, which falls in AD 361, because of an invasion on Kaliṅga, its princess, Hemalatā, for the safety of the tooth relic of the Buddha, migrated along with it from Dantapura, capital of Kaliṅga, to Sri Lanka. The date of the event falls within the reign of Samudragupta who conducted a successful campaign in south India, and therefore he might have been the invader. The name of the invader given in the Buddhist work is Yavana Rakta Bāhu. S K Aiyangar opines: 'If Samudragupta's invasion... proved of a destructive character from the point of the view of the Buddhists and the Buddha relics', the name of the invader as Rakta Bāhu and his being of Yavana stock, 'need not be particularly surprising'.[310] S R Goyal, too, suggests that the name in question could have been used for Samudragupta because his invasion led to much bloodshed, but he also includes the possibility of its being the name of the commander of Samudragupta.[311]

The Allahabad pillar inscription adds after Siṁhala, *sarvva-dvīpa-vāsibhiḥ*, 'people of all islands'. This may be an exaggeration on the part of the composer of the *praśasti*. But it is also not unlikely that like the king of Siṁhala, rulers of a few other islands might have entered into an alliance with Samudragupta. According to some scholars, the islands should be identified as Laccadive and Maladive, while others also include Malaysia and Indo-China with which countries India had active communication and trade relations and on which there is a considerable impact of Indian culture and art. It may be mentioned in passing that a gold coin of Chandragupta II has been found in Java.[312] Ancient inscriptions of Java, Sumatra and Borneo are in Sanskrit, which was the result of close cultural relation of the people of these lands with the Indians. King Aiśvaryapāla of Java traces his genealogy to the family of Samudragupta (Chapter 2). It has been pointed out that in the third quarter of the fourth century the king of Champā was at war with China and as such he might have been keen to have friendly relations with Samudragupta, the mighty Gupta king.[313] The archipelago was famous for certain metals, minerals and spices which Indian traders brought from there and earned much profit from their sale, and a good deal of the trade between India and China was through that region.[314] Maritime activities played a vital role in trade and commerce of the Gupta period, and the trans-oceanic orientation of the period may be seen in the name Samudragupta (protected by the ocean), and in the frequently used epithet for him conveying that his 'fame tasted the waters of the four oceans'.[315] The reference in the Allahabad pillar inscription to Samudragupta as equal to Varuṇa, lord of seas, is taken to suggest his political influence over some of the islands.[316] However, these islands, despite sending presents and paying respects by their rulers, seem to have retained their independent political status.[317]

The foreign powers and tribal republics are not referred to in geographical sequence, or in chronological order in their entering into alliance with Samudragupta, but are put together in one group to differentiate from other powers mentioned under other groups, according to the policy adopted by that Gupta king towards them, and by them towards him.[318] *Prima facie*, it seems that the tribal states of Rajasthan, Punjab and western MP, located to the north-west and west of the Gupta empire would have entered into alliance with Samudragupta when he conquered the Nāgas on the western boundary of the Gupta empire, and Samataṭa, Ḍavāka and Kāmarūpa, all located in the eastern direction, when he conquered a part of Bengal.[319] In general, the border states and the tribal republics—all located in northern India, would have entered into alliance with him when he conquered the Āryāvarta kings. The south Indian campaign would have been undertaken by him after uprooting north Indian kings; and, that Sri Lanka and other islands in the Indian ocean, who are mentioned under separate group of powers, would have entered into a treaty with him after his conquest of Dakshiṇāpatha.[320]

## VIII

### Extent of the Empire

The core of Samudragupta's empire comprised the directly ruled area in northern India, partly inherited by him and partly acquired by uprooting the nine Āryāvarta kings and merging their kingdoms into his empire. It included Eastern Malwa, Uttar Pradesh, Bihar, and parts of Bengal. R C Majumdar, at one place, says it probably also included the eastern districts between Lahore and Karnal,[321] but at another, he is uncertain whether it was Samudragupta or his son Chandragupta II, who conquered Mathurā;[322] and still at another place, in the same work, he states Gaṇapatināga, who was conquered by Samudragupta, was a king of Mathurā.[323]

The directly administered area was surrounded by the tributary political entities—five border states in its north, west, and east, and nine tribal states in its west and north-west. Beyond these in the north-west were the territories of the Kushāṇas and the Shākas, and in the west, those of the Śakas —the 'last remnants' of rulers of foreign origin. Thus, the territories of kings and tribal republics owing allegiance to him formed a ring round the core of the Gupta kingdom.[324] In the south (*Dakshiṇāpatha*), were the twelve kings who had been conquered but reinstated after they agreed to pay tributes. In the south and south-east, beyond sea, were Siṁhala (Sri Lanka) and some countries of south-east Asia. The tribal states, the border states, and more so the foreign powers, though subordinate allies, yet were allowed to enjoy autonomy in their internal affairs. As seen above, the terms of alliance in case of the border states (*pratyanta*s) and the tribal states were identical, which varied from those of the foreign powers—both inland and across the sea. The *Āṭavika*s or the forest people were made 'attendants' (*parichāraka*s) by him, perhaps after ensuring the regular supply of forest products by them; however, their internal autonomy seems to have been maintained. There would have been difference in the socio-economic and political set-up of the people of different states, and hence a flexible policy was followed in dealing with different political powers. It was not 'a unified empire under a single ruler.... but as something like a federation of states grouped together in subordinate alliance....'[325] Samudragupta had to face the challenge of 'consolidation of...diversified and unequal units' and of 'adopting and legitimizing a new feudal set-up of relationship in imperial organization'.[326] In practice, Samudragupta's relationship with different powers would have also depended on the distance of their territories in relation to the core Gupta kingdom in the Ganga valley, particularly in relation to Pāṭaliputra, the Gupta capital, the political power and status of the states, the economic condition of their territories, and administrative considerations.

Samudragupta, with a view to emphasizing his imperial position, and aiming at the status of the *chakravartī* performed the time honoured horse-sacrifice (*aśvamedha*). His successors refer to him as one who performed the horse-sacrifice in fullest details, which had not been done by other performers since long. Perhaps no king in Indian history had a greater justification in performing horse-sacrifice than him. Some scholars hold that possibly some of the conquests achieved by him were related to the horse-sacrifice. But the fact that there is no mention of this great event in the Allahabad pillar inscription, indicates that it was performed sometime after the record mentioning the large scale conquests had been engraved.[327] So important was the sacrifice deemed that the king issued a coin-type in gold—the *Aśvamedha* type, to commemorate it. The coin-type shows on one side the sacrificial horse and the circular legend eulogizing Samudragupta for his conquests and on the other side his chief-queen holding *chaurie* and the legend *aśvamedha-parākramaḥ*. The nature, significance and other allied aspects of the horse-sacrifice of the Gupta king have been dealt with separately in Appendix II.

## IX

### Titles and Epithets

The most common royal title of Samudragupta is *mahārājādhirāja*. However, *rājādhirāja* occurs on *Aśvamedha* type of coins,[328] and, curiously, the much less dignified title *rājā* on those of the Tiger-slayer type.[329] Smith[330] suggests that the latter coin-type bearing the title *rājā* is the earliest coin-type and was issued by him during the lifetime of his father Chandragupta I, while K P Jayaswal[331] opines that the use of the title was because the Gupta king had been reduced to the status of a feudatory by the Vākāṭaka ruler Rudrasena I. Both the views are not accepted by scholars, and it probably was due to the carelessness on the part of the mint-master. The other titles or epithets used for the king are *achintya-purusha* ('one beyond comprehension'), which is also a name of Vishṇu,[332] in the Allahabad inscription; *ajita* (unconquered); *ajita-rāja-jetā* (conqueror of unconquered kings); *apratiratha* (matchless chariot-warrior), which is also a name of Vishṇu in the *Vishṇu-sahasranāma,*[333] in the Archer type of coins and which is also seen in the expression *pṛithivyām=apratiratha*, in the Allahabad pillar inscription.[334] *Parākrama*,'valour incarnate', met with on the Standard type, and its combinations, are peculiar to Samudragupta, as *vikrama* and its combinations are to Chandragupta II. *Parākramāṅka*, 'whose appellation (*aṅka*) is *parākrama*', is met with in the Allahabad pillar inscription; and *Aśvamedha-parākrama*, 'whose might was demonstrated by the performance of the horse-sacrifice', occurs on the *Aśvamedha* type of coins. He has been referred to as *chir=otsann=āśvamedh=āharttā*, 'performer of horse sacrifice, which was *utsanna* for long',[335] in the Gupta epigraphs. *Kṛitānta-paraśu*, 'axe of Death' (i.e., Yama)' occurs on the Battle-axe type of coins, and *sarva-rāj=ochchhettā*, 'uprooter of all kings' for him in the inscriptions of his successors.[336] *Samara-śata-vitata-vijaya*, 'eminently victorious in hundreds of battles' is seen as part of the legend on his Standard type of coins. Quite significant is the epithet *Dhanada-Varuṇ=Endr=Āntaka-sama* ('equal to Dhanada, Varuṇa, Indra and Antaka') in the Allahabad pillar inscription. The comparison with these four deities, who are guardians of the four Quarters may have been done with a view to suggesting his conquests in all the four directions, or conveying that in possession of riches, he was equal to Dhanada (Kubera); in extension of suzerainty to the sea, or in imparting justice, to Varuṇa; in power and grandeur, to Indra; and in extirpation of enemies, to Antaka (Yama).[337] The comparison may be intended to indicate divinity of the Gupta emperor, which is also suggested by *parama-daivata*, 'the supreme deity'; *loka-dhāmno deva*, 'a god dwelling on earth', echoing Manu's view regarding the divinity of king.[338] S R Goyal[339] points out that in the *Vishṇu-sahasranāma*, Draviṇa-prada (Kubera), Varuṇa, Mahendra (Indra), and Antaka are names of Vishṇu, and are four of the eight elements which, according to Manu,[340] go in the making of a king. Samudragupta has been referred to as *sva-bhuja-parākram=aika-bandhu*, 'who had friend only in the prowess of his own arms', and *nyāy=āgat=āneka-go-hiraṇya-koṭi-sahasra-pradaḥ*, who in charity 'gave thousands of crores of cows and gold acquired lawfully', in the Allahabad pillar inscription. *Chatur=udadhi-salil=āsvādita-yaśaḥ*, 'whose fame has tasted the water of the four oceans',[341] occurs in the epigraphs of the successors of Samudragupta for him.[342] Interestingly, the epithets *prithivyām=apratiratha*, *chatur=udadhi-salil=āsvadita-yaśa* and *Dhanada-Varuṇ=Endr=Āntaka-sama* are applied to Chandragupta II in the Poona copperplate of Prabhāvatīguptā (No. 82), and at a later period, to a Chālukya chief of Gujarat.[343]

X

## Estimate

Samudragupta combined in himself 'physical vigour and intellectual fervour' and artistic and literary taste. His coins portray him as engaged in peaceful and martial activities. They are extremely artistic and show the aesthetic quality that is so characteristic of the Gupta sculpture, which provides the best examples of Indian art and contributes much to the Gupta age being termed as 'Classical Age'. His effigy on coins shows him a man of good height, with muscular arms and a well developed chest.[344] He is shown variously as holding a bow and an arrow, or shooting a tiger (perhaps in the Ganga valley as indicated by the representation of the river Gaṅgā on the coin-type), or armed with an axe. These depictions give us some idea of his martial activities. The Allahabad pillar inscription states in poetic hyperbole, that Samudragupta surpassed in musical skill, the mythical musicians Nārada and Tumburu. His love for and skill in music find corroboration in his Lyrist type of coins which shows him in scanty dress, sitting cross-legged in a leisurely and relaxed mood, playing on the *vīṇā*, that rests on his knees.[345] He would not have portrayed himself in such a manner if he were not well-versed in that art. King Khāravela (*c* first century BC), in the Hathigumpha inscription,[346] has been referred to as 'versed in the science of music' (*gaṁdhava-veda-budho*), and Śaka king Rudradāman (second century AD), in his Junagarh rock inscription[347] has been credited similarly; but it is only in the case of Samudragupta that it is corroborated by any other source, viz. coins.

In the Allahabad pillar inscription, Samudragupta is mentioned not merely as conquering many kings, as is the case with many ancient Indian monarchs in their *praśastis*. In it the names of the conquered kings of north India, the names of the kings and the territories they ruled over in the case of south Indian kings, and the names of the tribal states, border states and foreign powers who entered into alliance with this Gupta king have been categorically mentioned, as also the different policies he adopted towards each of these categories. This makes its evidence quite reliable.

Samudragupta has been mentioned as one who restored many kingdoms which had been destroyed, and dynasties that had been exterminated (*aneka-bhrashṭa-rājy=otsanna-rājavaṁśa-pratishṭhāpana*), which reminds of the expression *bhrashṭa–rāja-pratishṭhāpaka* used for the Śaka king Rudradāman in his Junagarh inscription.[348] It is difficult to identify with certainty the kings reinstated by him. D R Bhandarkar[349] is of the opinion that after Pravarasena I the Vākāṭakas lost their political power and remained destitute of power for three generations, till Rudrasena I, in the fourth generation, was installed as king by Samudragupta and he remained subordinate to that Gupta ruler.

According to him,[350] the Gupta king did not like to mention the name of the Vākāṭaka king and also of other kings in this category, as he did not like reminding them of their 'unfortunate past' and 'subordinate present'. S R Goyal[351] is of the view that Samudragupta in his own interest established several dynasties, such as the Varmans of Kāmarūpa, Varmans of Mandasor belonging to the family of Bandhuvarman, the Parivrājaka dynasty, the Uchchakalpa dynasty, the Pāṇḍuvaṁśī dynasty, and the dynasty to which Harivarman of the Shankarpur inscription belonged.[352] It is, however, difficult to be sure whether they rose to power of their own or owed their rise to the Gupta emperor.

The Allahabad pillar inscription shows that Samudragupta was a man of learning. It states that in sharpness of intellect he surpassed Bṛihaspati, the *guru* of gods. D R Bhandarkar[353] suggests that as Bṛihaspati is considered to be the founder of a school of *daṇḍa-nīti*, the intention is to convey that Samudragupta was a great expert in diplomacy and statecraft, which is amply reflected in his policy towards various powers, conquered and unconquered. Verse 8 of the epigraph tells that he earned the title of 'prince among poets' (*kavi-rāja*) through his great poetic works 'which could very well be a source of living for the learned' (*vidvaj=jan=opajīvya*). Rājaśekhara in his *Kāvya-mīmāṁsā* states that *kavi-rāja* is one step higher than *mahā-kavi*,[354] and uses *upajīvya* for such works which provide new ideas to the poets and are followed by them.[355] Samudragupta is mentioned as one who mitigated the rivalry between the wealth, whose presiding deity is Lakshmī, and learning, which is the domain of Sarasvatī.[356] No literary work of this king is available. Some portions of a work *Kṛishṇa-chritam*, are known, whose author is mentioned as *Vikramāṅka-mahārājādhirāja-parama-bhāgavata-Śrī*-Samudragupta. But the work has been proved to be a modern forgery.[357] Some scholars identify Samudragupta with Chandraprakāśa, son of Chandragupta (identified with Chandragupta I), who, as per the evidence of the *Kāvy=ālaṅkāra-sūtra-vṛitti* of Vāmana, appointed the Buddhist scholar Vasubandhu as his minister. While some scholars place Vasubandhu in the first half of the fourth century AD, others place him between AD 420 and 500,[358] and as such the identification is by no means certain.

Samudragupta was a brave general and a capable statesman. He possessed great quality of leadership and organizing talent. The epithet *sarva-rāj=ochchhettā*, 'exterminator of all kings' used for him is similar to *sarva-kshatr=āntaka* known for Mahāpadmananda. He has been referred to as 'winner of a hundred battles', possessor of 'tiger's prowess' and of 'irresistible vigour'. It has been stated (No. 1) that his body was marked with several battle scars, which (instead of disfiguring) beautified it, and is meant to convey that he led the army from the front. He had a great passion for war, and by his large-scale conquests, he "made the Gupta eagle fly triumphantly, in its imperial glory, over a major portion of India'.[359] Because of his bravery and great military skill and leadership, Smith[360] called him 'Indian Napoleon'. He is said (No. 1) to have unified politically fragmented land and bound 'the whole earth by the amplitude of the vigour of his own arms' (*bāhu-vīryya-prasara-dharaṇi-bandha*).[361] His policy was an ideal combination of aggression and reconciliation. He has been mentioned as cause for 'the prosperity of good men and destruction of the wicked ones' *(sādhv=asādh=ūdaya-pralaya-hetu)*, which looks like ascribing *avatāra*-like qualities to him.[362] It is said (No. 1) that though irresistible, he was generous and was full of compassion, when sincere devotion was shown to him, and he was committed 'to raise the miserable, the humble, the forlorn and the distressed.' The Allahabad pillar inscription, the most important, almost the sole source of information for the achievements of the king, is a *praśasti* couched in poetic language and composed by a high official of the king, and as such it can be assumed that it contains some exaggerations, yet it may safely be concluded that Samudragupta was a great warrior, a shrewd statesman, a good planner, a talented musician and a man of literary taste.

## NOTES AND REFERENCES

1. Since the inscription is engraved on an Aśokan pillar, which bears the Maurya king's address to the ministers stationed at Kauśāmbī, it is generally believed that the pillar was originally erected in that city and was later transferred to Prayāga, perhaps by Akbar or Jahangir. Some scholars, however, opine that Aśoka got the pillar erected at the present location as Prayāga was a great religious centre.
2. Though there is every possibility that he was a Vaishṇava.
3. A S Altekar, *The Coinage of the Gupta Empire*, 39ff.
4. *The Age of the Imperial Guptas*, p. 214.
5. *Journal of Indian History*, XLII (ii), p. 397.
6. *Journal of the Numismatic Society of India*, XXXIV (ii), p. 223.
7. E J Rapson, *Journal of the Royal Asiatic Society of Great Britain and Ireland*, 1901, p. 102, n 3.
8. *Proceedings of the Indian History Congress*, 1964, pp. 137-40, and figure.

9. K P Jayaswal, *Imperial History of India*, pp. 48-49.
10. S Levi, *Journal.Asiatique*, 1900, pp. 316ff, 401ff, as referred to in W Geiger's translation of the *Mahāvaṁsa*, p. xxxix.
11. *Indian Historical Quarterly*, IX, p. 93.
12. See S R Goyal, *The Imperial Guptas*, p. 148. He is also referred to in the *Vāyu*, *Brahmāṇḍa* and *Liṅga* purāṇas.
13. *Matsya Purāṇa—A Study*,Vārāṇasī, 1963, pp. 228ff and 388.
14. S R Goyal, *The Imperial Guptas*, p. 148.
15. *Vide* Ashvini Agrawal, *Rise and Fall of the Imperial Guptas*, p. 143.
16. D C Sircar, *Journal of the Numismatic Society of India*, V, p. 35.
17. *Catalogue of the Coins of the Gupta Dynasties, and of Śaśāṅka, the King of Gauḍa, in the British Museum, London*, pp. xix-xx).
18. *Ibid.*, xxxii.
19. P L Gupta, *The Imperial Guptas*, p. 283.
20. J Agrawala (*Proceedings of the Indian History Congress*, 1951, pp. 62-63) does not believe that there is a reference to the chief queen of the king, and from the use of the word *babhūva* in the epigaph, he considers that the inscription was posthumous. D C Sircar (*Select Inscriptions*, I, p. 269, n. 2) points out that in Sanskrit past imperfect and past tenses are at times used in the sense of present tense.
21. H C Raychaudhuri, *Political History of Ancient India*, p. 500, n.3. Dandekar (*A History of the Guptas*, p. 64) opines that the reference is to the wife of a feudatory of Samudragupta.
22. *Proceedings of the Indian History Congress*, 1956, pp. 146-48. The marriage, according to him, was in accordance with *kanyopāyana–dāna* mentioned in the Allahabad inscription as terms of alliance of Śakas and other powers with that Gupta ruler. This, however, is not acceptable as Rudrasiṁha's son was Yaśodāman, and not Rudrasena.
23. *Archaeological Survey of India—Annual Report*, 1913-14, on p. 123.
24. *Journal of the Asiatic Society of Bengal*, 1834, pp. 114ff, on p. 123.
25. J F Fleet, *Corpus Inscriptionum Indicarum*, III, p. 9.
26. *Ibid.*, p. 10.
27. *Journal of the Royal Asiatic Society of Great Britain and Ireland*, 1898, pp. 386-87.
28. See B Ch Chhabra, *Indian Historical Quarterly*, XXIV, pp. 104ff.
29. D R Bhandarkar *Corpus Inscriptionum Indicarum*, III, p. 12.
30. B Ch Chhabra, *Indian Historical Quarterly*, XXIV, pp. 112-13.
31. *Corpus inscriptionum Indicarum*, III, p. 17n.
32. B Ch Chhabra, *Indian Historical Quarterly*, XXIV, p. 112.
33. *Corpus Inscriptionum Indicarum*, III, p. 6.
34. *Indian Culture*, XIV, p. 143. S R Goyal (*The Imperial Guptas*, p. 185, n. 6) suggests the reading as *arhyo* ('deserving'), which would mean that Samudragupta was selected on merit.
35. B Ch Chhabra, *Indian Culture*, XIV, p. 142.

36. V C Pandey, *Vishveshvaranand Indological Journal*, XVI,p. 78. The Rithpur plate (No. 84) of Prabhāvatīguptā mentions Samudragupta in relation to his father as *tatpādaparigṛhīta* which term is taken by some scholars to suggest that he was selected by his father as his successor.
37. K C Ojha (*Journal of the Numismatic Society of India*, XII, p. 17) opines that the expression used is *tulya-kulaja*, in the inscription (No. 1) need not necessarily be taken only for brothers, but could include other members of the family.
38. R C Majumdar, in *Comprehensive History of India*, III(i), p. 19.
39. VC Pandey and Anup Pandey, *New History of the Indian People*, p. 259.
40. S R Goyal, *The Imperial Guptas*, p. 183.
41. It may be mentioned that Kācha has been identified with Bhasma of the *Ārya-Mañjuśrī-mūlakalpa* (above), which says that vile brāhmaṇas dominated his government (K P Jayaswal, *Imperial History of India*, p. 48). Some scholars, however, identify Kācha with Samudragupta (Chapter 4).
42. S R Goyal, *The Imperial Guptas*, p. 189.
43. *History of India*, p. 113.
44. See also J Agrawala, in *Festschrift F W Thomas*, 115ff.
45. D R Bhandarkar, *Corpus Inscriptionum Indicarum*, III, p. 8, n. 8; R C Majumdar, in *The Vākāṭaka-Gupta Age*, 1986, p. 137; B Ch Chhabra, *Indian Culture*, XIV, pp. 149-50.
46. According to B Ch Chhabra (*Indian Culture*, XIV, pp. 144ff) the way Chandragupta I went out to hug Samudragupta shows that he was in the evening of his life, a right time for turning a *vānaprasthī*. He cites examples from ancient texts of kings abdicating, anointing son as king. In passing, it may be stated that in the Hathigumpha inscription of Khāravela, he is said to have been anointed king when he entered his 25th year, which might suggest that his father, after anointing him turned *vānaprasthī* (D C Sircar, *Select Inscriptions*, I, p. 213ff). In the Pāla dynasty king Vigrahapāla abdicated in favour of his son Nārāyaṇapāla, and took to religious life.
47. R G Basak, *The History of North-Eastern India*, p. 38.
48. T R Trautmann, *Journal of the Royal Asiatic Society of Great Britain and Ireland*, 1972, p. 3.
49. J Agrawal, *Researches in Indian Epigraphy and Numismatics*, p. 5. Dasharatha Sharma (*Journal of Indian History*, XIV, pp. 27-29) takes it as a reference to the anointing of a *sāmanta* by Samudragupta. T P Verma (*Journal of the Numismatic Society of India*, LIII, p. 129) is of the view that Chandragupta I's choice for Samudragupta must have been already known to the people, including other princes and so there was hardly any reason of the other princes to be upset when the declarаration was made in the Asssembly.
50. S R Goyal, *The Imperial Guptas*, p. 166.
51. V S Agrawala, *Journal of the Numismatic Society of India*, XVI (I), 97ff.
52. For details, see S R Goyal, *Gupta Sāmrājya kā Itihāsa*, pp. 97-98

53. S K Aiyangar believes that Achyuta, Nāgasena and the ruler of the Kota family attacked Samudragupta at Pāṭāliputra (*Ancient India and South Indian History and Culture*, I, p. 218).
54. *Proceedings and Transactions of the First Oriental Conference, Poona*, 1920, p. cxxiv.
55. In *Comprehensive History of India*, III(i), pp. 41-42.
56. R K Mookerji, *Gupta Empire*, 23. This is also the view of S R Goyal (*The Imperial Guptas*, p. 197).
57. S R Goyal, *The Imperial Guptas*, p. 196.
58. In *The Vākāṭaka-Gupta Age*, p. 104.
59. See S R Goyal, *The Imperial Guptas*, p. 196.
60. For example, Ashvini Agrawal, *Rise and Fall of the Imperial Guptas*, p. 132.
61. H C Raychaudhuri, *Political History of Ancient India*, pp. 47f.
62. D C Sircar, *Select Inscriptions*, I, p. 265, n. 2.
63. *Journal of the Numismatic Society of India*, IX, p. 137.
64. *Early History of North India*, p. 189, n. 42.
65. P L Gupta, *The Imperial Guptas*, p. 267.
66. E S Growse, *Indian Antiquary*, XVIII, p. 289. V C Pandey and Anup Pandey (*New History of the Indian People*, p. 365) state that as the seal of Mattila shows Nāga figure and hence he should be taken as a Nāga king.
67. *Catalogue of the Coins of the Gupta Dynasties, and of Śaśāṅka, the King of Gauḍa, in the British Museum, London*, p. xxxiii.
68. H C Raychaudhuri, *Political History of Ancient India*, p. 472.
69. As cited by Ashvini Agrawal, *Rise and Fall of the Imperial Guptas*, pp. 115-16.
70. *Journal of the Royal Asiatic Society of Great Britain and Ireland* 1897, p. 421.
71. See R N Dandekar, *A History of the Guptas*, p. 57.
72. D C Sircar, *Select Inscriptions*, I, p. 65, n. 2.
73. S R Goyal, *The Imperial Guptas*, p. 200.
74. R C Majumdar, in *The Vākāṭaka-Gupta Age*, p. 141; A S Altekar, in *ibid.*, p. 37.
75. A S Altekar, in *The Vākāṭaka-Gupta Age*, p. 37; R C Majumdar, in *ibid.*, p. 14, n. 2.
76. *Early History of India*, 283.
77. D R Bhandarkar, *Corpus Inscriptionum Indicarum* III, p. 9. For references, *ibid.*, n. 1.
78. *Vide* D R Bhandarkar, *ibid*.
79. R C Majumdar, in *Comprehensive History of India*, III(i), p. 23. One may argue that the find of a large number of his coins at Mathura may be because it was a centre of religion, trade and art.
80. V A Smith, *Journal of the Royal Asiatic Society of Great Britain and Ireland*, 1897, pp. 876-77.
81. *Epigraphia Indica*, XXI, p. 3.
82. In *The Vākāṭaka-Gupta Age*, p. 141.
83. R C Majumdar, in *The Vākāṭaka-Gupta Age*, p. 166. This has been also poined out by S R Goyal.
84. *Harsha-charita*, translation by E B Cowell and and F W Thomas, p. 192.

85. *Journal of the Bihar and Orissa Research Society*, XIX, p. 133, n. 1.
86. D R Bhandarkar, *Corpus Inscriptionum Indicarum*, III, p. 10.
87. *Journal of the Royal Asiatic Society of Great Britain and Ireland*, 1897, p. 421.
88. F E Pargiter, *Dynasties of the Kali Age*, p. 73.
89. Ashvini Agrawal, *Rise and Fall of the Imperial Guptas*, p. 106.
90. S R Goyal, *The Imperial Guptas*, p. 191.
91. A S Altekar, in *The Vākāṭaka-Gupta Age*, p. 38
92. For example, D R Bhandarkar, *Corpus Inscriptionum Indicarum*, III, p. 10; S R Goyal, *The Imperial Guptas*, p. 152.
93. J Allan, *Catalogue of the Coins of the Gupta Dynasties, and of Śaśāṅka, the King of Gauḍa, in the British Museum, London*, xxii-xxiii.
94. D R Bhandarkar, *Corpus Inscriptionum Indicarum*, III, p. 21.
95. *Ibid.*, p. 10.
96. R C Majumdar, in *The Vākāṭaka-Gupta Age*, pp. 39-40.
97. Ashvini Agrawal, *Rise and Fall of the Imperial Guptas*, p. 107.
98. K N Dikshit, *Archaeological Survey of India—Annual Report*, 1927-28, p. 188.
99. *Indian Antiquary*, XLII, pp. 217ff.
100. D R Bhandarkar, *Corpus Inscriptionum Indicarum*, III, p. 2.
101. See H C Raychaudhuri, *Political History of Ancient India*, p. 472, n. 2.
102. *Proceedings and Transactions of First Oriental Conference, Poona*, 1920, p. cxxiv.
103. R G Basak, *The History of North-Eastern India*, p. 33.
104. *Epigraphia Indica*, XXVI, p. 304.
105. *Vide* purāṇic evidence—*Anu-Gaṅgā-Prayāgaṁ*, etc., cited above in Chapter 3.
106. Ashvini Agrawal, *Rise and Fall of the Imperial Guptas*, p. 117.
107. *Vide* Kanakhera inscription, *Epigraphia Indica*, XVI, p. 232.
108. U N Roy, *Gupta Rājavaṁśa tathā Usakā Yuga*, p. 119.
109. D R Bhandarkar, *Corpus Inscriptionum Indicarum* III, p. 11.
110. D R Bhandarkar, *ibid.*, p. 9.
111. *Annals of the Bhandarkar Oriental Research Institute*, IX, p. 88.
112. *Gupta Empire*, p. 19.
113. N N Ghosh, *Early History of India*, p. 251.
114. S R Goyal, *The Imperial Guptas*, p. 157.
115. Āryāvarta has been defined variously. According to Manu's (II, 22) definition, it extended from eastern to western sea and from Himalayas to the Vindhyas. It was north of Dakshiṇāpatha, and denoted almost the same region as Uttarāpatha (*cf sakal=ottarāpath=eśvara* for Harsha in Aihole inscription of Pulakeśin II. *Epigraphia Indica*, VI, p. 1ff). According to the *Vasishṭha-dharma-sūtra*, *Baudhāyana-dharma-sūtra* and the *Mahābhāshya* of Patañjali, it was bounded in the west by Adarśana (near modern Hisar), in the east by Kālakavana (near Prayāga), in the north by the Himalayas and in the south, by Pariyātra. Rājaśekhara considers Narmadā as demarcating boundary between Āryāvarta and Dakshiṇāpatha. For different definitions of Āryāvarta, see S R Goyal, *Gupta Sāmrājya kā Itihāsa*, pp. 115-16.

116. In all probability after the Assyrians who are known for their ruthless warfare.
117. D R Bhandarkar (*Corpus Inscriptionum Indicarum*, III, p. 33.) points out that the expression *aneka* used in connection with the Āryāvarta kings shows that only some, and not all, Āryāvarta kings were uprooted.
118. D R Bhandarkar, *Corpus Inscriptionum Indicarum* III, p. 9; R C Majumdar, *Comprehensive History of India*, III(i), p. 21.
119. *Ancient India and South Indian History and Culture*, I, p. 218.
120. *Journal of the Oriental Institute*, XXXIX, p. 41.
121. V C Pandey and Anup Pandey, *A New History of Ancient India*, p. 362.
122. *Journal of the Bihar and Orissa Research Society*, XIX, p. 133.
123. *Ibid*., p. 113.
124. *Ibid*., p. 142.
125. S R Goyal, *Gupta Sāmrājya kā Itihāsa*, pp. 102-03.
126. H C Raychaudhuri, *Political History of Ancient India*, pp. 474-75.
127. M G S Narayanan, in B N Mukherjee *et al.* (ed.), *Śrī Dineśa Chandrikā, Studies in Indology*, D C Sircar Festschrift, p. 286. He suggests that *aṭavi* probably meant the forest areas 'within Āryāvarta, or in the adjoining territories on the slope of the Himalayan ranges' (*ibid*.)
128. U N Roy, *Gupta Rājavaṁśa tathā Usakā Yuga*, p. 133.
129. S R Goyal, *The Imperial Guptas*, p. 202.
130. S R Goyal, *ibid*., p. 214.
131. The Hathigumpha inscription of Khāravela datable to *c*. first century BC (D C Sircar, *Select Inscriptions*, I, pp. 213ff) and the *Raghuvaṁśam* (IV.50) of Kālidāsa (Gupta period) mention Khāravela and Raghu, respectively, as obtaining pearls and other precious things from south India, and in the fourteenth century, Malik Kafur, general of Allauddin Khalji, is known to have acquired fabulous wealth in course of his successful campaign in south India.
132. *Journal of the Bihar and Orissa Research Society*, XIX, p. 136.
133. R C Majumdar, in *Comprehensive History of India*, III(i), p. 38; H C Raychaudhuri, *Political History of Ancient India*, p. 475.
134. R C Majumdar, in *Comprehensive History of India*, III(i), p. 38.
135. D R Bhandarkar, *Corpus Inscriptionum Indicarum*, III, p. 13.
136. B N Mukherjee's Commentary on H C Raychaudhari, *Political History of Ancient India*, p. 766.
137. D R Bhandarkar, *Corpus Inscriptionum Indicarum*, III, p. 14.
138. K P Jayaswal, *Journal of the Bihar and Orissa Research Society*, XIX, p. 137.
139. *Indian Historical Quarterly*, I, p. 684.
140. H C Raychaudhuri, *Political History of Ancient India*, p. 486.
141. J F Fleet, *Corpus Inscriptionum Indicarum*, III, p. 7, n 1.
142. D R Bhandarkar, *Corpus Inscriptionum Indicarum*, III, p. 15.
143. R C Majumdar, in *Comprehensive History of India*, III(i), p. 39.
144. S R Goyal, *The Imperial Guptas*, pp. 151-52.
145. *Studies in Ancient History of Toṇḍamaṇḍalam*, p. 15, as referred to by R C Majumdar, in *Comprehensive History of India*, III(i), p. 39.

146. F Kielhorn, *Epigraphia Indica*, VI, p. 3.
147. L D Barnett, *Bulletin of the School of Oriental and African Studies*, II, p. 570.
148. G Ramdas, *Indian Historical Quarterly*, I, p. 685.
149. *Ancient India and South Indian History and Culture*, I, p. 220; *Journal of Indian History*, VI, pp. 37-39.
150. *Vide* Ashvini Agrawal, *Rise and Fall of the Imperial Guptas*, 108. A M Shastri, in his review of Ashvini Agrawal's book, however, expresses his reservations regarding the correctness of this view.
151. J F Fleet, *Corpus Inscriptionum Indicarum*, III, p. 7, n. 2. The same is the view of G Jouveau-Dubeuil, *Ancient History of Dekhan*, pp. 58-61.
152. J F Fleet, *Corpus Inscriptionum Indicarum*, III, p. 7, n. 2.
153. H C Raychaudhuri, *Political History of Ancient India*, p. 475, n. 2.
154. D R Bhandarkar, *Corpus Inscriptionum Indicarum*, III, pp. 15-16.
155. J F Fleet, *Corpus Inscriptionum Indicarum*, III, p. 7n (continued on p. 8).
156. *Journal of the Royal Asiatic Society of Great Britain and Ireland*, 1897, p. 29.
157. S R Goyal, *The Imperial Guptas*, p. 152; R N Dandekar, *A History of the Guptas*, p. 50.
158. D R Bhandarkar, *Corpus Inscriptionum Indicarum*, III, p. 16.
159. J F Fleet, *Corpus Inscriptionum Indicarum*, III, p. 7, n. 1.
160. *Ancient History of Dekhan*, p. 58.
161. *Studies in Ancient History of Toṇḍamaṇḍalam*, p. 15, as referred to by R C Majumdar, in *Comprehensive History of India*, III(i), p. 40.
162. *Annals of the Bhandarkar Oriental Research Institute*, XXVI, p. 123.
163. *Indian Historical Quarterly*, I, p. 680.
164. D R Bhandarkar, *Corpus Inscriptionum Indicarum*, III, p. 16.
165. *Ibid*. See also R N Dandekar, *A History of the Guptas*, p. 50.
166. *Ancient History of Dekhan*, pp. 59-60.
167. *Epigraphia Indica*, XIII, p. 214.
168. *Indian Historical Quarterly*, I (iv), p. 683.
169. *Studies in Ancient History of Toṇḍamaṇḍalam*, As referred to in R C Majumdar, *Comprehensive History of India*, III(i), p. 40.
170. S R Goyal, *Gupta Sāmrājya kā Itihāsa*, p. 130.
171. *Journal of the Royal Asiatic Society of Great Britain and Ireland*, 1898, p. 369.
172. D R Bhandarkar, *Corpus Inscriptionum Indicarum*, III, p. 16.
173. *Ancient History of Dekhan*, p. 70.
174. As referred to by R C Majumdar, in *Comprehensive History of India*, III(i), p. 40.
175. *Vide* D C Sircar, *Select Inscriptions*, I, pp. 213ff, at p. 217.
176. *Ibid*., p. 220, n. 2.
177. H C Raychaudhuri, *Political History of Ancient India*, p. 176, text, and n. 5.
178. R C Majumdar, in *Comprehensive History of India*, III(i), p. 40.
179. H C Raychaudhuri, *Political History of Ancient India*, pp. 476-77.
180. In *Comprehensive History of India*, III(i), p. 40.
181. *Journal of the Royal Asiatic Society of Great Britain and Ireland*, 1897, p. 873.
182. G Ramdas, *Indian Historical Quarterly*, I, p. 686.

183. *Journal of the Royal Asiatic Society of Great Britain and Ireland*, 1897, p. 874. He suggests the identification of Devarāshṭra with Devagiri (Daulatabad).
184. Krishna Sastri, in *Archaeological Survey of India—Annual Report*, 1908-09, p. 123.
185. S K Aiyangar, *Ancient India and South Indian History and Culture*, I, p. 219, n 1.
186. S K Aiyangar, *ibid.*, I, pp. 231ff. See also S R Goyal, *The Imperial Guptas*, p. 210.
187. *Journal of the Royal Asiatic Society of Great Britain and Ireland*, 1897, p. 874.
188. R. Sathinathair, *Studies in Ancient History of Toṇḍamaṇḍalam*, as referred to by R C Majumdar, in *Comprehensive History of India*, III(i), p. 41.
189. *Calcutta Review*, 1924, p. 253n.
190. *Ancient India and South Indian History and Culture*, I, p. 219n; *Journal of Indian History*, VI, p. 27, n 1.
191. *History of Early Dynasties of Āndhradeśa*, pp. 369-70.
192. D R Bhandarkar, *Corpus Inscriptionum Indicarum*, III, p. 33.
193. J Allan (*Catalogue of the Coins of the Gupta Dynasties, and of Śaśāṅka, the King of Gauḍa, in the British Museum, London*, p. xxi) considers Allahabad pillar inscription 'not professedly chronological nor accurately geographical'. See also S R Goyal, *The Imperial Guptas*, p. 153.
194. V A Smith, *Journal of the Royal Asiatic Society of Great Britain and Ireland*, 1897, p. 875.
195. It has been pointed out that if Devarāshṭra is identical with Maharashtra, and Eraṇḍapalla with Erandol, then, in geographical order, these two territories, together with their kings, should normally have been mentioned last in the list of the rulers, which is not the case (D R Bhandarkar, *Corpus Inscriptionum Indicarum*, III, p. 19). But, as stated above, the territories are not mentioned in strictly geograpical or chronological order.
196. S R Goyal, *The Imperial Guptas*, p. 215.
197. R C Majumdar, in *Comprehensive History of India*, III(i), p. 41.
198. R Sathanathaier, *Studies in the Ancient History of Toṇḍamaṇḍalam*; *vide* R C Majumdar, *Comprehensive History of India*, III(i), p. 41.
199. According to N N Ghosh (*Early History of India*, p. 250), Samudragupta may or may not have advanced as far as Kāñchī, but it seems certain that he never advanced beyond it.
200. Ashvini Agrawal, *Rise and Fall of the Imperial Guptas*, p. 114.
201. *History of Early Dynasties of Andhradeśa*, pp. 364-65, and 372-73.
202. G Jouveau-Dubreil, *Ancient History of Dekhan*, pp. 60-61, *vide* D R Bhandarkar, *Corpus Inscriptionum Indicarum*, III, pp. 17-18.
203. For observations on Jouveau-Dubreil's view, see D R Bhandarkar, *Corpus Inscriptionum Indicarum*, III, pp. 17-18.
204. D R Bhandarkar, *Corpus Inscriptionum Indicarum*, III, p. 18.
205. D R Bhandarkar, *ibid.*, p. 18. However, the inscriptions composed by persons patronised by the kings do not record the defeat or their patrons.
206. *Ibid.*, p. 18.
207. *Ibid.*
208. *Ibid.*

209. R C Majumdar in *The Vākāṭaka-Gupta Age*, p. 147.
210. R C Majumdar, *ibid.*, p. 146, n. 4.
211. *Corpus Inscriptionum Indicarum*, III, p. 19.
212. *Ibid.*, p. 19.
213. *Ibid.*
214. *The Age of the Imperial Guptas*, p. 18.
215. *Arthaśāstra* (Kangle's ed.), 12.1.10-16.
216. *Raghu-vaṁśam*, IV, 43.
*Gṛihīta-pratimuktasya sa- dharmavijayī nṛipaḥ,*
*Śriyaṁ Mahendranāthasya jahāra na tu medinīm.*
217. D C Sircar, *Select Inscriptions*, I, p. 444.
218. S R Goyal, *The Imperial Guptas*, p. 274.
219. *Indian Historical Quarterly*, I, p. 688.
220. S R Goyal, *Gupta Sāmrājya kā Itihāsa*, p. 131.
221. S R Goyal (*The Imperial Guptas*, p. 201, n 4)points out that *pratyanta* is here used in a sense of 'frontier province of a kingdom' as also in the *Raghuvaṁśam* (iv, 26), while in the Aśokan inscriptions it stands for a frontier state.
222. R C Majumdar (in *Comprehensive History of India*, III(i), p. 26) opines that *praṇāma* here does not mean ordinary salutation 'but some official kind of salutation'.
223. S R Goyal, *The Imperial Guptas*, p. 153.
224. *Ibid.*, p. 202
225. T Watters, *On Yuan Chwang's Travels in India*, II, pp. 187-89.
226. R C Majumdar, in *Comprehensive History of India*, III(i), p. 43.
227. D R Bhandarkar, *Corpus Inscriptionum Indicarum*, III, p. 22.
228. *Early History of Kāmarūpa*, p. 42, as referred in D R Bhandarkar, *Corpus Inscriptionum Indicarum*, III, p. 22.
229. J F Fleet, *Corpus Inscriptionum Indicarum*, III, Intro, p. 9, n 3.
230. *Journal of the Royal Asiatic Society of Great Britain and Ireland*, 1897, p. 879.
231. D R Bhandarkar, *Corpus Inscriptionum Indicarum*, III, p. 22.
232. Ashvini Agrawal, *Rise and Fall of the Imperial Guptas*, p. 118. He cites references to its identification with Kartarpur (*ibid.*, p. 149, n. 79).
233. *Journal of Indian History*, 1935, pp. 30ff.
234. For example, Smith, *Journal of the Royal Asiatic Society of Great Britain and Ireland*, 1897, p. 885; Oldham, *ibid.*, 1898, p. 198; D R Bhandarkar, *Corpus Inscriptionum Indicarum*, III, pp. 22-23; R C Majumdar, in *Comprehensive History of India*, III(i), p. 43. Ashvini Agrawal (*Rise and Fall of the Imperial Guptas*, p. 118) says it should be identified with Almora, Garhwal and Kumaon; but Almora is a part of Kumaon. S R Goyal (*The Imperial Guptas*, p. 153, n 3) suggests that Kartṛipura may have been the capital of the Buddhist dynasty of Kṛitya kings of Kashmir, referred to by Hiuen-tsang, which does not seem convincing.
235. D R Bhandarkar, *Corpus Inscriptionum Indicarum*, III, pp. 22-23.
236. D C Sircar, *Select Inscriptions*, I, p. 169.
237. D R Bhandarkar, *Corpus Inscriptionum Indicarum*, III, p. 23.

238. D R Bhandarkar, *ibid.*, p. 23.
239. D C Sircar, *Select Inscriptions*, I, p. 305.
240. *Vide* H C Raychaudhuri, *Political History of Ancient India*, p. 481.
241. R C Majumdar, in *Comprehensive History of India*, III(i), p. 43.
242. *Vide* H C Raychaudhuri, *Political History of Ancient India*, p. 481.
243. *Journal of the Royal Asiatic Society of Great Britain and Ireland*, 1897, p. 886.
244. D R Bhandarkar, *Corpus Inscriptionum Indicarum*, III, p. 24.
245. *Comprehensive History of India*, III(i), p. 23.
246. J Allan, *Catalogue of the Coins of the Gupta Dynasties, and of Śaśāṅka, the King of Gauḍa, in the British Museum, London*, p. lxxxiii.
247. Devendra Handa, *Nidhi*, II, 2007, pp. 35ff.
248. H C Raychaudhuri, *Political History of Ancient India*, p. 481.
249. *Mahābhāshya*, 1. 2. 72.
250. *Vide* H C Raychaudhuri, *Political History of Ancient India*, p. 481.
251. *Ibid*.
252. *Epigraphia Indica*, VIII, p. 88-89.
253. V A Smith, *Journal of the Royal Asiatic Society of Great Britain and Ireland*, 1897, pp. 890-92.
254. Ashvini Agrawal, *Rise and Fall of the Imperial Guptas*, p. 121.
255. *Arthaśāstra*, ed. by R Shamasastry, 8th ed., p. 231.
256. *Journal of the Royal Asiatic Society of Great Britain and Ireland*, 1897, p. 892.
257. D R Bhandarkar, *Corpus Inscriptionum Indicarum*, III, p. 25.
258. P L Gupta, *The Imperial Guptas*, pp. 272-73
259. *Vide* H C Raychaudhuri, *Political History of Ancient India*, p. 482, n. 3.
260. P L Gupta, *The Imperial Guptas*, p. 273.
261. R D Banerji, *The Age of the Imperial Guptas*, p. 23.
262. K P Jayaswal, *Journal of the Bihar and Orissa Research Society*, XVIII, pp. 212-13.
263. *Epigraphia Indica*, XII, p. 46.
264. *Indian Historical Quarterly*, XXXII, p. 98; *ibid.*, XXXVIII, pp. 327ff.
265. P L Gupta, *The Imperial Guptas*, p. 273.
266. U N Roy, *Gupta Rājavaṁśa tathā Usakā Yuga*, p. 152.
267. P L Gupta, *The Imperial Guptas*, p. 274.
268. R G Basak (*Early History of North India*, p. 27) takes *ātma-nivedana* to mean 'self-surrender'. V C Pandey and A C Pandey (*New History of Ancient India*, p. 368) consider it as the same as *ātmopadhāna* of the *Arthaśāstra* of Kauṭilya which conveys, 'I am what you are. My wealth is yours. You may take it in your undertakings.'
269. M G S Narayanan, in B N Mukherjee, *et al.* (ed.), *Śrī Dineśacandrikā*, (D C Sircar Festschrift), p. 287. R G Basak (*The History of North-Eastern India*, p. 27) takes this term as 'presents of maiden princesses (*kanyopāyana*) and payment of tribute of gifts (*dāna*). V C Pandey and Anup Pandey (*New History of Ancient India*, p. 369) point out that Kauṭilya brings the significance of *dāna* under the technical term *upapradāna* in the sense of financial favours; under which 'the foreign kings paid tributes, taxes and gifts to their overlord'. Dikshitar (*Gupta Polity*, p. 342)

translates as 'bringing presents of maidens'. S R Goyal (*Gupta Sāmrājya kā Itihāsa*, p. 137) points out that the *Nābhinandana-jinoddhāra-prabandha* refers to kings marrying the maidens brought as gifts by tributary kings. R C Majumdar (in the *Comprehensive History of India*, III(i), p. 26) thinks that *kanyopāyana—dāna* means 'presenting (*upāyana*) girls of easy virtue and giving (*dāna*) of others (daughters of kings or their relations) in marriage', and in support of the first, refers to Periplus (*Periplus*, Section 49) which says that beautiufl maidens were imported into Barygaza for kings' harem (*ibid.*, fn 23). J Agrawal says it means either *kanyāścha upāyanāni cha teshāṁ dānaṁ*, i.e. 'maidens and presents – the offering of these', or *kanyā eva upāyanāni teshāṁ dānaṁ*, i.e. 'the maidens as presents—offering of these' (as cited by Ashvini Agrawal, *Rise and Fall of the Imperial Guptas*, p. 125). Sohoni (*Annals of the Bhandarkar Oriental Research Institute*, LXII, p. 173) interprets *kanyopāyana* to mean that 'marriage in the feudatory family contracted after obtaining the sanction of the sovereign,' which appears far-fetched.

270. J Allan, *Catalogue of the Coins of the Gupta Dynasties, and of Śaśāṅka, the King of Gauḍa, in the British Museum, London*, pp. xxiv- xxv; D C Sircar, *Select Inscriptions*, I, p. 266, n 2; R C Majumdar, in *Comprehensive History of India*, III(i), p. 26.
271. R C Majumdar, in *Comprehensive History of India*, III(i), p. 26.
272. M G S Narayanan, in B N Mukherjee *et al.* (ed.), *Śrī Dineśacandrikā*, D C Sircar Festshrift, p. 286.
273. S R Goyal, *The Imperial Guptas*, p. 237.
274. J Allan, *Catalogue of the Coins of the Gupta Dynasties, and of Śaśāṅka, the King of Gauḍa, in the British Museum, London*, p. xxv; Fleet, *Corpus Inscriptionum Indicarum*, III, p. 14.
275. S R Goyal, *The Imperial Guptas*, p. 224.
276. D R Bhandarkar, *Corpus Inscriptionum Indicarum*, III, p. 27; R D Banerji, *The Age of the Imperial Guptas*, p. 24; R C Majumdar, in *The Vākāṭaka-Gupta Age*, p. 147; H C Raychaudhuri, *Political History of Ancient India*, pp. 482-83.
277. D R Bhandarkar, *Corpus Inscriptionum Indicarum*, III, p. 27.
278. *Devaputra* is the title inspired by the Chinese title *tien-tzu* which means 'son of gods'.
279. *Indian Historical Quarterly*, XXXII, p. 128.
280. S R Goyal, *The Imperial Guptas*, p. 224.
281. *Catalogue of the Coins of the Gupta Dynasties, and of Śaśāṅka, the King of Gauḍa, in the British Museum, London*, p. xxviii.
282. D R Bhandarkar, *Corpus Inscriptionum Indicarum*, III, p. 29.
283. D R Bhandarkar, *ibid*.
284. D R Bhandarkar, *ibid*., pp. 29-30.
285. *Vide* D R Bhandarkar, *ibid*., III, p. 30.
286. K P Jayaswal, *Journal of the Bihar and Orissa Research Society*, XVIII, p. 209.
287. K P Jayaswal, *Journal of the Bihar and Orissa Research Society*, XIX, p. 146.
288. D R Bhandarkar, *Corpus Inscriptionum Indicarum*, III, p. 30.
289. *Corpus Inscriptionum Indicarum*, IV (i), pp. 15ff.

290. *Ibid.*, p. 53, n.1.
291. Legend, *Rājño Īśvaramitra-putrasya rājño Siṁha-śrī-senasya.* See K D Bajpai, *Journal of the Numismatic Society of India*, XXVIII (i), p. 28.
292. K D Bajpai, *ibid.*, p. 49.
293. H C Raychaudhuri, *Political History of Ancient India*, p. 483.
294. S R Goyal, *The Imperial Guptas*, p. 223.
295. For example, J Allan, *Catalogue of the Coins of the Gupta Dynasties, and of Śaśāṅka, the King of Gauḍa, in the British Museum, London*, p. xxix; Raychaudhuri, *Political History of Ancient India*, p. 483. The view is based mainly on the researches of Sylvain Levi.
296. R C Majumdar, in *The Vākāṭaka-Gupta Age*, p. 147, n 3.
297. Ashvini Agrawal, *Rise and Fall of the Imperial Guptas*, p. 82.
298. P L Gupta, *The Imperial Guptas*, p. 277; Ashvini Agrawal, *Rise and Fall of the Imperial Guptas*, p. 72.
299. R C Majumdar, in *Comprehensive History of India*, III(i), p. 45.
300. Sten Konow, *Epigraphia Indica*, XIV, pp. 292-93.
301. *Ibid.*
302. S R Goyal, *The Imperial Guptas*, p. 92.
303. D R Bhandarkar, *Corpus Inscriptionum Indicarum*, III, p. 29.
304. J F Fleet, *Corpus Inscriptionum Indicarum*, III, p. 136.
305. As referred to in S R Goyal, *The Imperial Guptas*, p. 92.
306. *Vide* W Geiger, (ed.) *Mahāvaṁsa*, p. xxix n. 3.
307. Meghavarṇa, according to Geiger (*The Mahāvaṁśa*, trans, Intro, p. xxxix) ruled from *c* AD 352 to AD 379. According to the traditional reckoning adopted for the *parinirvāṇa* of the Buddha Meghavarṇa's rule is placed between 325 and 352 AD. See also D R Bhandarkar, *Corpus Inscriptionum Indicarum*, III, p. 31, n. 2.
308. T Watters, *On Yuan Chwang's Travels in India*, II, p. 136.
309. S R Goyal, *The Imperial Guptas*, p. 238.
310. S K Aiyanger, *Ancient India and South Indian History and Culture*, I, p. 231ff.
311. S R Goyal, *The Imperial Guptas*, p. 210.
312. P L Gupta, *The Imperial Guptas*, p. 95.
313. S R Goyal, *The Imperial Guptas*, p. 238.
314. S R Goyal (*The Imperial Guptas*, p. 236) is of the view that Samudragupta conquered areas in Bengal perhaps motivated by his desire to bring the port of Tāmralipti under his control because of its importance in trade with south-east Asia.
315. S R Goyal, *ibid.*, p. 38.
316. H C Raychaudhuri, *Political History of Ancient India*, p. 483, n. 1; P L Gupta, *Gupta Sāmrājya*, p. 272.
317. R C Majumdar, in *Comprehensive History of India*, III(i), pp. 28-29.
318. S R Goyal, *The Imperial Guptas*, p. 158.
319. *Ibid.*
320. *Ibid.*, p. 153.
321. R C Majumdar, in *The Classical Age*, p. 9.

322. In *The Vākāṭaka-Gupta Age*, p. 166.
323. In *The Vākāṭaka-Gupta Age*, p. 141. The anomaly in R C Majumdar's writing has been pointed out by S R Goyal, *Imperial Guptas*, p. 293.
324. R C Majumdar, in *Comprehensive History of India*, III(i), p. 29.
325. S K Aiyanger, *Ancient India and South Indian History and Culture*, I, pp. 261-62.
326. M G S Narayanan, in B N Muhherjee, *et al.* (ed.), *Śrī Dineśacandrikā*, D C Sircar Festschrift, p. 288.
327. Unless it is assumed that it was mentioned in that part, which is now mutilated.
328. A S Altekar, *The Coinage of the Gupta Empire*, p. 67ff.
329. *Ibid.*, pp. 71ff.
330. *Journal of the Royal Asiatic Society of Great Britain and Ireland*, 1889, p. 66.
331. *Journal of the Bihar and Orissa Research Society*, XIX, pp. 80-81.
332. B Ch Chhabra, *Catalogue of the Gold Coins of the Bayana Hoard in the National Museum*, p. xxix.
333. B Ch Chhabra, *ibid.*, p. xxiv.
334. This epithet has been applied to Chandragupta II in the Poona copperplate of Prabhāvatīguptā (No. 82).
335. For the meaning of *utsanna*, see Appendix II, below.
336. It also occurs on the coins of Kācha (Chapter 4, above).
337. *Indian Culture*, IX, p. 178.
338. *Manu*, V, 96; VII, 4.
339. S R Goyal, *Gupta Sāmrājya kā Itihāsa*, p. 164.
340. *Manu*,VII. 4. 7.
341. This is applied to Chandragupta II in the Poona copperplate inscription of Prabhāvatīguptā (No. 82).
342. This and a few other epithets of Samudragupta find mention in the Bilsad inscription (No. 14), a fragmentary Mathura inscription of Kumāragupta I (No. 17) and in the Bihar inscription (No. 61) of Purugupta (or one of his sons).
343. *Vide* D R Bhandarkar, *Corpus Inscriptionum Indicarum*, III, p. 43.
344. R C Majumdar, in *The Classical Age*, p. 15. R K Mookerji's reconstruction (*Indian Culture*, IX, p. 77) of the history of Samudragupta on the basis of the device and legends on his coins by taking them at their face-value, which, as pointed out by R C Majumdar (*The Vākāṭaka-Gupta Age*, p. 154 ff), presents a somewhat exaggerated picture of the ruler; Majumdar's own reconstruction of the same, based on coins (*ibid.*, pp. 156ff), is relatively sober.
345. A S Altekar, *The Coinage of the Gupta Empire*, pp. 75ff, pl. III, 15-17.
346. D C Sircar, *Select Inscriptions*, I, pp. 213ff.
347. *Ibid.*, pp. 175ff.
348. D C Sircar, *ibid.*, pp. 175ff.
349. D R Bhandarkar, *Corpus Inscriptionum Indicarum*, III, p. 32.
350. *Ibid.*, p. 33.
351. S R Goyal, *Gupta Sāmrājya kā Itihāsa*, pp. 123-25.
352. In Malwa a dynasty begins with Jayavarman who was followed by Siṁhavarman, Naravarman, Viśvavarman and Bandhuvarman who, the last-

mentioned, is referred to as a feudatory of Kumāragupta [I] in AD 436, in a Mandasor inscription (No. 38). The rule of Jayavarman would have begun in the middle of the fourth century AD. The known dates of the Hastin, the fifth king of the Parivrājaka dynasty, ruling in the erstwhile Nagod and Jasor states, are 156 and 198 (= AD 475 and 517), so Suśarmā the first king of the dynasty may be placed in *c.* AD 360-80. Of the six kings known in the Uchchhakalpa dynasty, the dates for the fifth king, Jayanātha, are GE 174 and 177(= AD 493 and 496) and the first king may have begun his reign near about the last days of Samudragupta's rule. An inscription of the fifth Pāṇḍuvaṁśī king, Śūrabala, datable to the fifth century AD (B Ch Chhabra, *Epigraphia Indica,* VII, p. 132f), mentions his four predecessors. A M Shastrri (in B Ch Chhabra *et al.* (ed.), *Reappraising Gupta History for S R Goyal*, p. 7) dates the beginning of the political career of the Paṇḍuvaṁśī dynasty in *circa* AD 500. According to Goyal, the first king of this dynasty would have flourished in the middle of the fourth century AD. Most of the scholars identify Harivarman of the Shankarpur inscription with the homonym *mahārāja* from whom the Maukhari kings of Kanauj, who may or may not have been related to the Maukharis of the Barabar inscriptions, trace their genealogy in their epigraphs. The Shankarpur epigraph, however, mentions three ancestors of Harivarman—Sālaṇa, *Mahārāja* Vijayavarmā and *Mahārāja* Gītavarmā, not met with in any of the Maukhari epigraphs detailing genealogy. There is great possibility of the migration of the Maukharis from Baghelkhand regioṇ to Kanauj. Allowing 20 years to each generation, the accession of Gītavarman can be placed in *c* AD 435. There is no mention of father-and-son relation between Sālaṇa and Gītavarman, and Goyal suggests that a gap between them can be envisaged and the first king might have been a contemporary of Samudragupta. Goyal gives credit to Samudragupta for creating the above mentioned dynasties. However, other factors must have played role in the rise of these dynasties, at least of some of them.

353. D R Bhandarkar, *Corpus Inscriptionum Indicarum*, III, p. 44.
354. H C Raychaudhuri, *Political History of Ancient India,* p. 485n.
355. D R Bhandarkar, *Corpus Inscriptionum Indicarum,* III, p. 44; S R Goyal, *Gupta Sāmrājya kā Itihāsa*, p. 166.
356. The idea of king's removing such a rivalry between the two is referred to in an inscription of Madanavarman (*Epigraphia Indica,* I, p. 209) and also in Kālidāsa's *Vikramorvaśīyam* (V. 24, *vide* S R Goyal, *Gupta Sāmrājya kā Itihāsa*, p. 166).
357. J Agrawala, *Annals of the Bhandarkar Oriental Research Institute,* XXVI, pp. 313-18.
358. R C Majumdar, in *The Vākāṭaka-Gupta Age*, p. 155, n. 2.
359. R N Dandekar, *The Age of the Guptas and Other Essays*, p. 3.
360. *Early History of India*, p. 183.
361. The statement of R K Mookerji (*Gupta Empire*, p. 38): ' He worked for an international system of brotherhood and peace replacing that of violence, war and aggression' goes well with Aśoka rather than with Samudragupta.
362. According to the *Bhagavadgītā* (IV. 8, *paritrāṇāya sādhūnāṁ vināśāya cha dushkṛitāṁ*), the god incarnates himself for this very purpose.

# 6

# Rāmagupta: From Legend to History

## I

Rāmagupta does not find place in the Gupta epigraphs detailing genealogy. The first source that came to light relating to Rāmagupta are the fragments quoted by later authors from the dramatic work *Devī-Chandraguptam* by Viśākhadatta,[1] which itself is now not available. Sylvan Levi in 1923[2] brought to the notice of scholars six fragments of this work as preserved in the *Nāṭya-darpaṇa* of Rāmachandra and Guṇachandra (12th century AD). Three fragments of Viśākhadatta's work, quoted in the eleventh century texts *Śriṅgāra-prakāśa* and *Sarasvatī-kaṇṭhābharaṇa* of Bhoja, were brought to light by Ramakrishna Kavi and A Rangaswami Sarasvati.[3] R D Banerji, in his Manindra Chandra Nandi Lectures delivered in 1924,[4] was the first scholar to utilize information in Bāṇa's *Harsha-charita* that Chandragupta, in the guise of a woman, killed the Śaka king, and remarks about a Gupta king in the Sanjan copperplate inscription (No. 92), discussed below, for the reconstruction of history. A few years later V Raghvan[5] published two more extracts from the *Devī-Chandraguptam* as quoted in the *Nāṭaka-lakshaṇa-ratna-kośa* of Sāgaranandī. A quotation from the drama also occurs in the *Abhinava-bhāratī* of Abhinavagupta.[6]

Shorn of details, the story of Rāmagupta, as culled from these fragments of the *Devī-Chandraguptam*, may be stated as below. King

Rāmagupta was besieged by a Śaka king, and was forced to agree to the humiliating demand of surrendering his queen, Dhruvadevī, to him. It is stated that Rāmagupta agreed to it with a view to appeasing the *prakṛitis*, which, it has been suggested, should better be taken as ministers rather than as subjects. His younger brother, Chandragupta, unable to bear this dishonour, thought of propitiating *vetāla* (vampire), and later disguised himself as Dhruvadevī, and other officials as female attendants, all equipped with arms hidden within their clothes, entered the Śaka king's camp, and killed him and his men. Thereafter Chandragupta feigned madness, in order to save himself from the wrath of Rāmagupta, who had become jealous of him because of his chivalrous act. Further details are not available from the extant fragments of the drama, but, it is surmised, can to some extent be reconstructed with the help of the *Mujmal-ut-Tawarikh*. The various pieces of evidence relating to Rāmagupta are given below.

In the *Harsha-charita* of Bāṇa, a contemporary of the Pushpabhūti king Harsha (first half of the seventh century AD), it is stated that Chandragupta, in the guise of a female, killed at Aripura (either a city of that name or 'city of enemy'), a Śaka king, who coveted the wife of another man.[7] The commentary of Śaṅkarārya (twelfth century or later)[8] on the *Harsha-charita* adds that Chandragupta killed the Śaka king as he had demanded Dhruvadevī, the wife of his brother.

The *Nāṭaka-lakshaṇa-ratna-kośa* of Sāgaranandī (tenth or eleventh century AD) has a reference to *unmatta* (mad) Chandragupta. It has been assumed[9] that such information would have been also contained in that part of the *Devī-Chandraguptam*, which has been lost. The *Āyurveda-dīpikā* (twelfth century AD), a commentary on the *Charaka-saṁhitā* by Chakrapāṇi, refers to Chandragupta's feigning madness as one of the examples of pretence, and also to killing his own brother.[10]

In the *Kāvya-mīmāṁsā* of Rājaśekhara, according to one interpretation, it is said that the praises of the king were sung in the Himalayan region, by the women of Kārttikeya-nagara, where Senagupta (or Śarmagupta, according to one manuscript), with broken valour (*khaṇḍita-sāhasa*), surrendered his wife to the Khaśa chief.[11] D R Bhandarkar identified Kārttikeya-nagara with Baijnath or Vaidyanath in Almora district, which was in the kingdom of Kartṛipura, (the area comprising Kumaon, Garhwal and Rohilkhand). Kārttikeya-pura as a name of a town is mentioned in the Taleshwar charter of Dyutivarman (sixth century AD), Pandukeshwar plate of Lalitaśūradeva (ninth century AD), and also in the *Devī-purāṇa*.[12] Bhandarkar opines that Kārttikeya-pura was also known as Alipura or Aripura, another form met with in most of the manuscripts of the *Harsha-charita*.[13] The *Rājāvalī* of Mṛityuñjaya Paṇḍita (AD 1808)[14] mentions a king, Rājapāla (or Rakshapāla) of Mayūra family ruling in Indraprastha, who was weak and coward, and was defeated by the Śaka ruler (Śakāditya or Śakadatta) of Kumaon. The aggressor was defeated by Vikramāditya. Rājapāla reminds of Rāmagupta, and Vikramāditya, of Chandragupta II. The work is full of anomalies,[15] yet there is a possibility that it may vaguely be echoing the Rāmagupta episode.

Altekar takes Kārttikeya and Nagara, mentioned in the *Kāvya-mīmāṁsā*, separately, and identifies Kārttikeya with Kumāragupta I as Kumāra is another name of Kārttikeya, and as the figure of Kārttikeya occurs on the coins of that Gupta ruler.[16] D R Bhandarkar,[17] disagreeing with Altekar's view (which has been accepted by some scholars) of taking Kārttikeya as a personal name and also its identification, and states that if it is to be taken as a name, one could as well identify him with Skandagupta, as Skanda is also a name of Kārttikeya. He is of the view that in the verses in question, it is Chandragupta II who is lauded for his achievements by the ladies of Kārttikeyapura. Mirashi[18] also does not agree with Altekar's identification of Karttikeya with Kumāragupta, as in his view, a poet would not have addressed a Gupta king in the context of such a derogatory act relating to his predecessor, nor he would have made the mistakes of giving the name as Śarmagupta (or Senagupta) instead of Rāmagupta, and also of mentioning the invading king as *Khaśādhipati* instead of *Śakādhipati*. He identifies Kārttikeya with the Gurjara-Pratīhāra king, Mahīpāla, who was a patron of Rājaśekhara and who has been referred to by his another court poet, Kshemeśvara in his *Chaṇḍakauśika* as Kārttikeya and as one who conquered Kulūta area, located on the bank of the Satluj. According to him, the verse conveys that the place where Rāmagupta had agreed to surrender Dhruvadevī and Chandragupta II had killed the Śaka ruler, was conquered by the Pratīhāra king, Mahīpāla.[19] He suggests that the incident which forced Rāmagupta to surrender his queen took place near Jalandhar *doab* or Jalalabad,[20] that the name of the capital would have been Nalinapura, which would have been situated near the ancient city of Kulūta, and that the Śaka enemy should be taken as a Kushāṇa king.[21] Jagannath[22] points out that if Kārttikeya and *nagara* are separated then it would mean that the king was praised only by the women of the city, and that too in the Himalayan region where the cities worth their name would have been a few only. He is of the view that the Khaśa overlord taking advantage of the natural defences of mountain fortresses was able to defeat Rāmagupta.[23]

Altekar[24] drew the attention of the scholars to the story of Rawwal and Barkamaris,[25] as narrated in a Persian work, *Mujmal-ut-Tawarikh* (available in manuscript form) by Abul Hasan Ali (AD 1126-93),[26] which was a translation from Arabic work of AD 1026, and the latter itself was a translation of an earlier Sanskrit work. The story resembles to some extent, the plot of the *Devī-Chandraguptam* and some information not met with in the extracts available from the Sanskrit work, it has been suggested,[27] may be reconstructed with the help of this Persian work. According to this work, Barkamaris had won a princess in a *svayaṁvara*, but his elder brother, King Rawwal took her away. Thereafter, Barkamaris devoted himself to study. A former rebel of King Rawwal's father attacked him. Fleeing with his brother Barkamaris, and other members of his family and ministers, he took shelter in a fortress on the top of a mountain. The enemy besieged the fortress and, under pressure and with the advice of his ministers, Rawwal agreed to Śaka king's demand of sending his queen, Dhruvadevī, to him, and other women to his officers. But Barkamaris disapproved of this, and disguising himself as a queen, and some soldiers, as women, and hiding weapon and bugle, entered enemy's camp. He killed the unguarded Śaka king, and on his blowing bugle, his men killed the enemy soldiers. Rawwal's act alienated Dhruvadevī from him and he became low in the eyes of his subjects, while Barkamaris came to be held high for his exemplary chivalry, and the queen was grateful to him for what he had done for her cause. This led to strained relation between the two brothers. Rawwal's *wazir*, Safar, excited king's suspicion against Barkamaris, and the king wanted to kill him. To save himself, Barkamaris feigned madness, which incidentally finds confirmation from the *Devī-Chandraguptam*. Wandering as a mendicant, he came to the palace, where the king and the queen were sucking sugarcane. The king offered a bit of sugarcane to him, and for peeling it, the queen, on king's bidding, gave him a knife. Barkamaris killed the king with the knife, when he was off the guard. It is significant that both the *Devī-Chandraguptam* and the *Mujmal-ut-Tawarikh* refer to the king agreeing to surrender his queen to the invader, to his younger brother disguising himself as female and killing the Śaka king, and to the latter's feigning madness

Barkamaris told Rawwal's minister, Safar, to continue in the office he held, which offer the latter declined. However, on Barkmaris' request, Safar wrote a treatise on a king's duties. Some scholars, taking Safar to be the Persian form of Śikhara, identify him with Śikharasvāmī, a high official of Chandragupta II mentioned in the Karamdanda inscription of the time of Kumāragupta I (No. 20) and who is taken by some as identical with Kāmandaka, the author of the *Kāmandakīya Nītisāra*—an important work on polity. But Kāmandaka and Śikharasvāmī cannot be identical, as Kāmandaka is a *gotra* name of a branch of Viśvāmitra *gotra,* while the *gotra* of Śikharasvāmī, as mentioned in the Karamdanda inscription, is Aśvavājī.[28]

## II

Long back, in Bhandarkar's excavations at Besnagar, was found a coin bearing the device of a lion on one side and crescent and the legend giving some letters of the name Rāmagupta on the other side.[29] But neither the device was properly identified, nor was the legend correctly deciphered, and therefore numismatic evidence about the existence of a king Rāmagupta remained unknown for a long period. A number of coins of Rāmagupta have been found thereafter,[30] mostly in eastern Malwa. They are all in copper, and exhibit several varieties, in so far as the fabric, size and weight are concerned, and may be broadly classified as: (i) lion standing with raised tail, (ii) lion seated to left with tail upraised, (iii) *garuḍa* with expanded feathers, (iv) *kalaśa* with foliage, (v) *kalaśa* without foliage, (vi) *garuḍa-dhvaja*, and (vii) border-line legend.[31]

The legend on these coins gives the name Rāmagupta, mostly in incomplete form, in Gupta characters,[32] and some of these have been found in Gupta layers in archaeological excavations at Eran in Sagar district. *Garuḍa* is the insignia of the Vaishṇava Imperial Guptas, which is met with on their gold and silver coins. Interestingly, lion is also seen on the sealing of Dhruvasvāminī from Vaiśālī (No. 13), which in all probability was her paternal insignia, different from the *garuḍa*, which was the insignia of the Guptas (Appendix VI, below). Dhruvadevī seems to be a dominating figure, as in the entire Gupta history, she is the only queen whose personal seal has been found, and as such, it is not unlikely that Rāmagupta used lion insignia under her influence. Of a few thousand coins of Rāmagupta, those with *garuḍa* device outnumber those with lion device.[33] The weight of these coins ranges from 2.5 grains to 31.3 grains.[34] A H Dani is of the view that copper coins were issued by Rāmagupta as a prince with the concurrence of his father, whom he predeceased. [35] But in ancient India there was no practice of a prince issuing coins, and the view that he died as a prince does not fit in with what is known about him from other sources, which, as will be seen below, clearly refer to his status as king.

R C Majumdar[36] argues that kings of the Gupta dynasty are known for their gold coins, and since no gold coins of Rāmagupta have been found, the homonym of the copper coins should not be taken as a king of that dynasty. D C Sircar[37] also holds the same view for the same reason, as also because Rāmagupta does not find a place in the Gupta epigraphs detailing genealogy. He opines that kings Harigupta and Indragupta are known to have issued *garuḍa* type of copper coins at the end of the fifth or beginning of the sixth century AD, when the Gupta empire was on its decline, and the coins bearing the name Rāmagupta may also be placed in the same period.[38] Goyal,[39] after examining the views of Sircar, concludes that there is no valid reason to deny Rāmagupta a place in the Imperial Gupta dynasty. His observations may briefly be summarized. He points out that while all the coins of Rāmagupta have been found in eastern Malwa, no coins of Harigupta or Indragupta have been found in that region or in its neighbourhood. Sircar prefers to take Rāmagupta of the coins as a king related to the Later Gupta dynasty.[40] In his view, Malwa was under the Hūṇas and thereafter under Yaśodharman and so Rāmagupta would have ruled only after the latter.[41] But contrary to this view, there is no less possibility of dating Rāmagupta's coins as also his three inscriptions discussed below, in the second half of the fourth century AD. Goyal points out that Sircar does not put the conditions of non-availability of gold coins and non-mention of name in the genealogy, when he ascribes Rāmagupta to the Later Gupta dynasty,[42] as he puts for taking him as a king of the Imperial Gupta dynasty. No king of the Later Gupta dynasty is known to have issued coins, and the name of Rāmagupta does not find place in the Later Gupta genealogy. Goyal argues that if Sircar can take Bhānugupta, neither whose coins have been found nor whose name occurs in Gupta genealogy, as an Imperial Gupta king, then why should he deny Rāmagupta the status of a king of the same dynasty.

The coins of Rāmagupta to some extent resemble in fabric and type those of the Mālava and more so with those the Nāga rulers, issued prior to the Gupta conquest of that region.[43] Lion figure is also met with on some coins of the Nāgas. Like them the coins of Rāmagupta are circular or oval in shape and seem to follow the same weight system.[44] Significantly, some of the copper coins of Rāmagupta are quite similar to the coins of the Gupta rulers in the same metal. His *kalaśa* type of coins resemble the coins of Chandragupta II bearing the same device, in style, fabric and weight,[45] and his *garuḍa* type of coins are close to those of the same type of Gupta rulers.[46] This similarity of his coins with the Gupta coins is a significant evidence in favour of taking him as a Gupta ruler. K D Bajpai,[47] who takes Rāmagupta as an Imperial Gupta ruler, explains the circumstance of the absence of his gold coins as below: "...it may be observed that the royal gold mint in the beginning of the Gupta supremacy was probably located at Pāṭaliputra', whereas Rāmagupta seems to have ruled in eastern Malwa and adjoining regions, where he seems to have been appointed as governor, earlier. Since he had no control over Magadha, which was under Chandragupta II, he could not issue gold coins". It may, however, be stated that the gold coins, for that matter coins in any metal of a few kings who are definitely known as belonging to the Imperial Gupta dynasty, are not known, for example, Purugupta (the coins earlier ascribed to him, are taken as issued by Budhagupta) and Govindagupta. So, the absence of gold coins for Rāmagupta need not be considered as an insurmountable hurdle in taking him as a Gupta king. The reason for his coins, all in copper, being confined to Malwa may be because his rule was confined to that region only. P L Gupta[48] is of the view that political condition of the period does not favour the view of R C Majumdar that Rāmagupta was not a Gupta, but a local ruler. He points out that eastern Malwa had been under the Guptas since the reign of Samudragupta, as evidenced by his inscription from Eran. The area around Vidiśā which had been under the Nāgas, after Samudragupta comquered them came under the Guptas. Beyond that area was the region ruled by the Western Kshatrapas, and hence, according to Gupta, there is hardly any space for local rulers, and even if it is conceded that there was some local ruler, he would hardly have been powerful enough to issue coins.[49]

K C Jain[50] considers Rāmagupta of the coins and inscriptions as a king of some collateral branch of the Gupta dynasty ruling in the fourth or fifth century with his capital at Vidiśā, who bore the title *mahārājādhirāja*, as evidenced from his inscriptions. He places Rāmagupta after Chandragupta II, as he believes that Vidiśā region came under 'the Gupta rule for the first time during the reign of of the latter. But there is no evidence of the rule of a collateral branch of the Gupta dynasty in that period. And since an inscription of Samudragupta found at Eran (No. 2), mentions the town of Erakiṇa (Eran) as his personal fief (*sva-bhoga-nagara*), it seems reasonable to infer that Vidiśā region also formed part of his kingdom. The title *mahārājādhirāja* for Rāmagupta in the Vidiśā epigraph is significant as it was borne by all the Imperial Gupta kings, Chandragupta I onwards. K D Bajpai observes, '...the coins of Rāmagupta do not seem to be issues of local chief... From literary and other evidences so far available, we do not know of any other Rāmagupta in the third-fourth centuries AD, except of the Gupta dynasty'.[51]

D R Bhandarkar[52] suggested that the name Rāmagupta in the *Devī-Chandraguptam* should be taken as a scribal error for Kāchagupta because of 'the hurried cursive hand of the scribe'; the letters *ra* and *ka*, and *ma* and *cha*, of the Gupta alphabet being quite near in shape. Altekar[53] agreeing with this view further elucidated: "A little carelessness resulting in the dropping of horizontal stroke of *ka*, which is just like crossing a *t* in the English script, would convert *ka* into *ra*; *cha* can become *ma* if the pen slips to the left just beyond the loop of *cha*.' K P Jayaswal[54] opines that Rāmagupta and Kāchagupta are the names of the same person, the latter being a proper name, and the former, a familiar one. But there is nothing to substantiate it. The name of the king on coins is Kācha and not Kāchagupta. The form *Kācha* occurs on gold coins alone, and on copper coins the name is invariably Rāmagupta. It is unthinkable that the same king issued coins in two different names, gold coins in the name of Kācha, and copper coins in the name of Rāmagupta

N N Dasgupta[55] points out that taking Rāma as a scribal error for Kācha 'is to run the risk of saying that the author of the MS must have also inadvertently written *Śakapati* for *Śarapati....*' He further states, 'It would be idle to conjecture that a MS with some scribal mistakes was destined to be the model of all other MSS, so that the mistakes of that particular scribe became accepted by all later scribes and readers of the work."[56] Significantly, the name of the king on the coins and in the three Durjanpur (Vidiśā) inscriptions, discussed below, is clearly Rāmagupta, which makes the suggestion of Bhandarkar completely untenable as it cannot be said that the engraver of the inscription also made the same mistake. However, in fairness to that scholar, it should be stated that till the time he expressed this view, neither coins, nor inscriptions of Rāmagupta were known. It may also be stated that he believed that

Kumāragupta I and Govindagupta (Chapter 8), and Skandagupta and Purugupta (Chapter 10) were one and the same, and perhaps in the same strain suggested that Kāchagupta and Rāmagupta were identical. Incidentally, now none of these identifications finds favour with scholars.

As regards the argument that Rāmagupta's coins are confined to Malwa region alone and have not been found in other areas of the Gupta empire, it has been stated that copper and silver coins in ancient India are mostly local in character. Generally, there is conservatism regarding the fabric and device of coins of a particular region, which in some cases did not change even with the change of the dynasty, as they were issued to meet local demand.[57] It was because of this consideration that Gupta rulers issued silver coins for the Surāshṭra region, in imitation of the coins of the Śaka rulers who ruled in that area for over three centuries before the Gupta emperor Chandragupta II uprooted them. In Magadha, where the Gupta capital, Pāṭaliputra, was located, only one silver coin of that king has been found.[58] Rāmagupta might not have issued gold coins for some reasons, like the one stated by K D Bajpai and cited above, as he was not in a position to do so.

Malwa was an important province of the Gupta empire. Its town Eran, which has been referred to as *sva-bhoga-nagara* of Samudragupta, lay on the route joining eastern Malwa with Vatsa kingdom *via* Vidiśā on the one hand, and with Avanti, on the other, and seems to have been chosen for occasional encampments, which might have turned it into a military out post.[59] This was the venue of a few battles in the Gupta period. It was because of its significance that it came to be placed under the charge of royal princes Rāmagupta, Govindagupta (No. 36), and Ghaṭotkachagupta (No. 19), during the reign of the Gupta kings Samudragupta, Chandragupta II and Kumāragupta I, respectively.

III

The Rāshṭrakūṭa epigraphs provide significant, though indirect, evidence for Rāmagupta's historicity and his being a king of the Gupta dynasty. In the Sanjan copperplates of Rāshṭrakūṭa Amoghavarsha, (No. 92), it has been stated: 'The despised donor of Kaliyuga of Gupta lineage, having killed his brother. . . seized his kingdom and also his wife', and recorded incorrectly in crores, the charity given in lakhs.[60] Significantly, the inscription mentions that the king belonged to the Gupta dynasty, though it neither gives the name of the ruler who killed his own brother, nor of the brother who was killed; also it does not mention the story relating to Chandragupta II's killing of the Śaka ruler. D R Bhandarkar[61] once suggested the identification of the Gupta king with Skandagupta, who, he supposed, might have killed a brother or brothers in a war for succession. There is, however, no definite evidence to show that Skandagupta killed his brother, and, certainly not even the slightest hint that he married his brother's widow. It may, however, be stated that when Bhandarkar made this suggestion, no significant evidence about Rāmagupta had come to light, and till then, of the Gupta kings, if any, it was Skandagupta, about whom some scholars had suggested the possibility of contesting for throne against his brothers.

Mirashi opines that the second part of the verse in the Sanjan copperplate tends to convey that the Gupta ruler used to get recorded his donations as lakh-crores, though actually made in lakhs.[62] U N Roy[63] states that in the Allahabad pillar inscription, Samudragupta is mentioned as a donor of one lakh cows, and in the Nālandā copperplate inscription (which is taken as reconstructed partly from the extant portion of a much damaged genuine plate and partly from the plate of one of his successors), he is mentioned as a donor of a crore cows. His view that this statement might have been added by Chandragupta II, is not acceptable, as the palaeography of the inscription is marked by the characteristics pertaining to a date later than the time of Chandragupta II, and there is no possibility of the scribe of Chandragupta II anticipating the form of letters characteristic of a period later than his time. Further, it is difficult to believe that the scribe of the Rāshṭrakūṭa plates knew the contents of the Nālandā copperplate inscription of Samudragupta, as the inscribed copper plate would have been handed over by the government officer to the donee to be kept by him in safe custody, to be shown as a proof of his being the grantee, if and when the need would arise. Even if it is conceded that access to the plate would have been managed, it would have been a problem to decipher the script. Roy[64] refers to K C Chattopadhyaya's view that while in the Allahabad pillar inscription, Samudragupta mentions his donation of one lakh cows, in the Mathurā pillar inscription of the time of his son, Chandragupta II, it is stated that he donated one crore cows, and that this could have been in the mind of the composer of the Sanjan copperplate inscription when he made the statement. But the territories of the Rāshṭrakūṭas lay away from Allahabad, and more so from Mathura, and their rule being much later in time from that of Samudragupta, it would have been not easy during their reign to decipher the text of the Allahabad pillar inscription and the Mathura pillar inscription, both written in early Gupta script. The Mathurā pillar inscription is not an official record, and was got written by a Pāśupata *āchārya*. It does not seem that the composer of the text of the Rāshṭrakūṭa plates knew the contents of that inscription, or even the existence of the pillar. The other alternate suggestion of U N Roy[65] that the term *alekhayat* in the Rāshṭrakūṭa plates, used in this context, may mean 'tore', indicating that the king tore off one lakh or one crore enemy in fight, a thing which was despised by the Rāshṭrakūṭa king Amoghavarsha (to whose reign the plates belong), who was a follower of Jainism, which lays much emphasis on *ahiṁsā*, is not convincing. Whether the king is a Jaina, a Buddhist or a follower of Brahmanical religion, he has to fight the enemies with all his might when there is a need for it, and obviously it would cause bloodshed.

The Cambay plates (No. 89) and Sangli plates (No. 90) of Govinda IV state that in making gifts and in valour, Govinda IV was like Gupta king, *Sāhasāṅka*, but unlike him, he did not behave cruelly with his brother, nor violate his brother's wife (*bandhu-strī-gamana*), nor did he resort to propitiation of vampire (*paiśāchya-vrata*), unmindful of whether it was a pious act or not.[66] The reference seems to be to Chandragupta II, who had the title *Vikramāṅka* (*Vikramāditya*) which means almost the same as *Sāhasāṅka*, and who, as the evidence of the extracts from the *Devī-Chandraguptam* and a few other texts suggests, killed his brother and married his widow and who is to be identified with Vikramāditya of the *Kathā-sarit-sāgara* and *Vaitāla-pañchaviṁśati*, which refer to him as propitiating vampire (*vetāla-sādhanā*).

Three undated inscriptions of Rāmagupta (No. 5) engraved on the pedestal of Jaina images, have been found in the village Durjanpur, about five kilometers from Besnagar (District Vidiśā, MP). The inscriptions are in the Gupta script of *c.* fourth century AD and the king bears the title *mahārājādhirāja*, which was the title borne by all the known Gupta kings Chandragupta I onwards. Each of the three epigraphs refers to the installation of the image of a Tīrthaṅkara (mentioned as an *arhat*). Of the three epigraphs, the first is well-preserved, while the second is considerably damaged, and the third is extremely mutilated. The first inscription records the installation of the image of *Arhat* Chandraprabha (the eighth Tīrthaṅkara) by *Mahārājādhirāja* Śrī-Rāmagupta as a result of the preachings of Kshapaṇaka Chella, son of Golakyānti, grand-disciple of *Pāṇipātrika* (i.e. one who uses his hand as bowl) *Āchārya* Kshapaṇaka Chandrakshamā, and disciple of *Āchārya* Sarpasena. The second inscription refers to the installation of the image of Pushpadanta, the ninth Tīrthaṅkara; the name of the Tīrthaṅkara in the third inscription is damaged, but most probably Padmaprabha the sixth Tīrthaṅkara was meant.[67]

The style of art in the images particularly in the depiction of the Tirthaṅkara figures and the halo, as also the absence of the *lāñchhana* on the Tīrthaṅkara images, which came to be introduced in *circa* fifth century AD, would favour placing the images in the fourth century AD.[68] D C Sircar[69] objects to Rāmagupta's being a Gupta ruler, on grounds that the homonym of the Vidiśā inscriptions was a Jaina, while the Gupta emperors were Vaishṇavas (*parama-bhāgavatas*). U N Roy[70] holds that Rāmagupta was a Gupta king who was earlier a Vaishṇava and later became a convert to Jainism. Significantly, Gupta ruler, Vainyagupta is mentioned as a Śaiva in the Gunaighar plate (No. 50), and a Vaishṇava (*parama-bhāgavata)* in his Nālandā seal (No. 51).[71] Rāmagupta has not been mentioned as a Jaina in the Durjanpur inscriptions; it is merely stated in them that he got the Jaina images installed, on the instructions of a Jaina monk, which he could have done because of his Jaina leanings, or even as a follower of brāhmanical faith with cosmopolitan religious outlook.

It may be mentioned in passing that in the Nālandā copperplate of Samudragupta (No. 3), Prince (*kumāra*) Chandragupta is mentioned, most probably, as the context indicates, as the *dūtaka* (officer-in-charge of the grant).[72] It may be argued that in the Gupta administration, there existed the office of *yuvarāja*, as the evidence of a few sealings of the Gupta period bearing the title of *yuvarāja* have been found (Chapter 8). If Chandragupta [II] was only a *kumāra* and not *yuvarāja*, then someone, else would have been holding the latter office; and it is quite possible that it was held by his elder brother, Rāmagupta.[73]

## IV

D C Sircar[74] opines that the script of the letters on the coins (and also in epigraphs) do not seem to be of the fourth century AD, but of the fifth or sixth century AD, and Rāmagupta of the coins and inscriptions could be an unknown king of the Later Gupta dynasty. It may be stated that

Ādityasena (seventh century AD) is the first among the Later Gupta rulers who took the title of *mahārājādhirāja*. It does not seem appropriate to ascribe Rāmagupta to the Later Gupta dynasty, as he is not known as a member of that dynasty and he ruled much earlier than Ādityasena. As to Sircar's placing Rāmagupta in the fifth instead of the fourth century, it may be stated that there is not much change in script within a short period. As pointed out by S R Goyal,[75] Sircar himself states that some letters of the Kushāṇa epigraphs resemble those of the Śakas of Mathurā who ruled before them, while some, those of the Gupta period. Taking Rāmagupta as an Imperial Gupta king, his rule is to be placed immediately after Samudragupta, and his date would be the end of the third quarter of the fourth century AD, which is not far away from fifth century AD, the date suggested by Sircar for him.[76] As stated above, there are several members of the Gupta family, such as Gupta, Ghaṭotkacha and Chandragupta I, whose epigraphs are not known, and also some whose coins have not been found, such as, Purugupta and Govindagupta and yet they are taken as Gupta kings. As regards the absence of the name of Rāmagupta in the genealogies met with on the Gupta epigraphs, they generally mention father-to-son succession leaving the collaterals, and in the case of Rāmagupta, his ignominiously agreeing to surrender his queen to the Śaka king would also have been a valid case for omission of his name. As Maity[77] states, Sircar's assumption that Rāmagupta was a local king, 'fails to explain the literary evidence as well as the traditional popularity of the episode'.

The *Devī-Chandraguptam* refers to Rāmagupta as king and to his younger brother Chandragupta as a *kumāra* (prince), and mentions that the former had a great affection for the latter. It is possible that after the death of Samudragupta, Rāmagupta succeeded to the Gupta throne as king of the whole empire. The title *mahārājādhirāja* for him would favour this view. The Śaka king, thinking that the mighty king Samudragupta was dead, attacked the Gupta territories. Rāmagupta, for purchasing peace agreed to surrender his wife to the Śaka king in lieu of his brother Chandragupta who was initially demanded by the invader. If the scene of war was in eastern Malwa, as opined by some scholars,[78] then it may be suggested that possibly shortly after his accession Rāmagupta went on an administrative-cum-pleasure trip to Eran, which has been referred to in the Eran inscription of Samudragupta (No. 2) as *sva-bhoga-nagara* (town as personal fief) of that king, and which on Rāmagupta's accession would have retained the same status in relation to him. He was accompanied by some officials, some family members which included his queen Dhruvadevī and his younger brother Chandragupta, and scanty force. It was then that the Śaka king attacked the Gupta king and forced him to accept the terms of treaty, referred to above. Chandragupta in the guise of the queen killed the Śaka king, and later also Rāmagupta, and married the latter's widow. An alternate possibility could be that the Śaka king of western India on the death of the mighty Samudragupta attacked the western territories of the Guptas, and Rāmagupta from his capital, Pāṭaliputra hurriedly marched with his family members and rather small army and suffered initial discomfiture at the hands of the invader. The killing of the Śaka king, etc., would be as in the first alternative.

If however Rāmagupta's encounter with the Śaka king took place in the Himalayan region, as the evidence of the *Kāvya-mīmāṁsā* would make us believe, then it is possible that the ruler of Kartṛipura who was of Khaśa or Śaka extraction, rebelled and Rāmagupta marched against him with a rather scanty force and accompanied by his queen Dhruvadevī and his younger brother, Chandragupta, and some ministers and officials. He and his men were besieged by the Śaka chief, who forced him to accept the above mentioned terms of peace. Chandragupta killed the Śaka king, as also Rāmagupta, and married Dhruvadevī. R K Mookerji,[79] opines that this episode actually relates to the Chandragupta II's conquest of the Śakas. S K Maity[80] takes this as the first blow of Chandragupta II against the Śakas. V C Pandey and Anup Pandey,[81] like K D Bajpai, believe that the conflict between Rāmagupta and the Śaka king took place in eastern Malwa and suggest that Rājaśekhara mistook Khaśas for Śakas, and as in his time the Khaśas dwelt in the Himalayan region (as they do even today), placed the scene of the conflict in that region. S R Goyal suggests that possibly the Śaka king attacked Rāmagupta and in the battle both of them were killed.[82]

Some scholars take *tatparigṛihīta* in the inscriptions (instead of the more usual expression *tatpādānudhyāta*), for Chandragupta in relation to his father Samudragupta to indicate that the former had been chosen as his successor by the latter. Rāmagupta, the elder brother, revolted against his younger brother, Chandragupta II, in the same way as Rāshṭrakūṭa Stambha, the elder brother of Dhruva, revolted when the latter was chosen successor by his father ignoring the law of primogeniture.[83] But *parigṛihīta* does not necessarily mean 'chosen.' Chandragupta II might have been an ambitious prince who without proper claim to succession captured the Gupta throne at Pāṭaliputra, and the elder brother Rāmagupta was left with no option but to declare himself as a king in the Malwa region, where he seems to have been posted as governor. Some scholars suggest that the expression *satputra,* (good son) for Chandragupta II in a Mathurā inscription (No. 6) is used in contrast to Rāmagupta who proved as a bad son.[84] R C Majumdar states that 'the inscriptions do not throw any light on the romantic elements of the story....'[85] But it is hardly expected that such stories would find mention in the inscriptions.

## V

The difference in the contents of various sources relating to Rāmagupta is somewhat baffling. One reason for the difference, as pointed out by scholars, could be that the author of a particular source referred only to that part of the story of this king that suited his context. For example, Bāṇa confines himself only to that part of it which shows how the carelessness in safety measures led to the killing of the king at the hands of the enemy, and says that Chandragupta, disguised as a female, killed the unguarded Śaka king, who coveted the other man's wife. Śaṅkarārya (twelfth century or later), a commentator on the *Harsha-charita*, specifies that Chandragupta II, in the guise of Dhruvasvāminī, killed the Śaka king who had coveted his brother's wife. In passing it may be mentioned that according to V A Smith,[86] Bāṇa's story that Chandragupta, in the guise of a woman killed the Śaka king is not 'genuine history.' The Rāshṭrakūṭa epigraphs refer to only those details of the story, which conveyed the idea that the ruler in question of that dynasty shared such qualities as bravery and charity with the Gupta king, but was devoid of his serious faults, such as killing his bother, taking his kingdom and marrying his widow, with a view to conveying that the Rāshṭrakūṭa king was much nobler and superior to the Gupta king. In none of the sources, is the name of the Śaka king mentioned.

Some parts of the story relating to Rāmagupta appear incredible, and some as against moral and ethical code. It contains such supernatural elements as propitiating the vampire *(vaitāla-sādhanā),* which robs it from some of its historical character. It apparently looks difficult to believe that the Śaka chief would reduce the immediate successor of the mighty king, Samudragupta, to such a state that he agreed to surrender his queen to him, and that Chandragupta could perform the ignominious act of slaying his brother and marrying his widow. Remarriage of widows was not disallowed. Nārada[87] allows a woman to marry her husband's younger brother on the death of her husband. But in practice this was not deemed proper and ethical, and would certainly be highly condemnable in the circumstances mentioned above, viz., when the younger brother was the slayer of her husband, which is also evident from the way it is mentioned in the Rāshṭrakūṭa inscriptions, discussed above. R C Majumdar states: 'The personal name of the queen, Dhruvasvāminī—one with fixed devotion to husband—also must have always been a bitter reproach to her life and conduct.'[88] But most of the personal names are auspicious and well-meaning, but a number of people with such names act in ways which is against what their name conveys. One can, to some extent, condone the killing of the brother and marrying his widow, if the evidence of *Mujmal-ut-Tawarikh* that Rawwal (i.e., Rāmagupta) had forcibly taken the maiden won in *svayaṁvara* by Barkamaris (i.e., Chandragupta II), and also on the ground that after Chandragupta saved the honour of Dhruvasvāminī by killing the Śaka king, Rāmagupta became jealous of him and was planning to eliminate him. U N Roy is of the view that since *svāmī*-ending names are common among the Śaka kings, *svāminī*-ending name in Dhruvasvāminī is indicative of her Śaka origin; and that perhaps she was one of those maidens who were offered by the Śaka ruler to the Gupta king or princes by way of *kany=opāyana-dāna* (No. 1) and that the Śaka king might have been in love with her and was keen to covet her. [89] The name of the Gupta queen was Dhruvasvāminī, as this is the form met with in her own seal. It was amended as Dhruvadevī (which is the form met with in all other Gupta inscriptions giving her name) with a view to bringing uniformity in the name-endings of all queens, and, if Roy's view is accepted, also for avoiding *svāminī*-ending, suggestive of her Śaka origin.[90]

Some scholars[91] suggest that it is possible that Rāmagupta was not as coward as he has been portrayed, and his decision to surrender his queen could as well have been a diplomatic move in extremely adverse circumstances when there was no hope for averting the defeat, and in the interest of the kingdom and the subjects, as they would have suffered much if peace was not purchased. May be Rāmagupta's ministers advised him to do so,[92] though that does not fully absolve him of this ignominious act, since being a king, the ultimate responsibility of taking decision was his.

While in history some kings are known to have been prepared to sacrifice their lives in saving the honour of their women, there were also others who not only failed to do so, but even consented to surrender their wives. For example, Ratnasena, a Rajput king, in adverse circumstances, is said to have agreed to offer his queen Padmāvatī to the invader, Alauddin Khalji.[93] Further, according to Kauṭilyan maxim, anything is fair if it is in the interest of the king and the State.[94] U N Roy[95] opines that Rāmagupta was a Jaina and having great faith in *ahiṁsā*, preferred to surrender his wife rather than fight a battle in which success was extremely doubtful, and which would have caused large-scale bloodshed. But the establishing of Jaina images by Rāmagupta does not necessarily prove that he was a follower of that religion, as he could have done that even as a liberal Vaishṇava. Even if he were a Jaina, as a king it was his utmost duty to defend his kingdom and subjects. Kings like Khāravela, who were devout Jainas, are known to have fought several wars, invading several regions, which must have ended in killings and wounding hundreds of people. Significantly, in the *Devī-Chandraguptam*, it is stated that Rāmagupta agreed to surrender his queen with a view to providing consolation to his subjects or ministers (*prakṛitīnāṁ śvāsanāya*), as *prakṛiti* may mean either of them. The text also mentions very cordial relations between Rāmagupta and his brother Chandragupta, and states that the former told that he considered his own queen insignificant in comparison to his brother (Chandragupta II).

S R Goyal,[96] in line with V S Pathak, opines that in biographical and some other works, the author, in order to paint his patron or hero as brave, kind, benevolent and just, portrays such persons as were harmed by their patron for no genuine reasons, in bad light, referring to them as wicked, cruel, coward and unjust. Bilhaṇa, in order to justify the claim of his patron, Vikramāditya, though a younger brother, to the throne bypassing the claims of the elder brother, says that Śiva pleased with King Someśvara I's devotion to him, made a prophecy that his second son, Vakramāditya, would be a *chakravartin*. The text also says that Vikramāditya declined the office of *yuvarāja* offered to him by his father, in favour of his elder brother (which is historically not true); and that when the latter, on becoming king, turned a cruel tyrant, Vikramāditya dethroned and killed him to save the subjects from his atrocities. Goyal[97] suggests that possibly Rāmagupta was portrayed as a coward who agreed to surrender his queen to the Śaka king, in order to justify Chandragupta's killing him and marrying his widow, and even suggests that possibly the *Devī-Chandraguptam* (of which only some fragments have been quoted by later writers), had, on the pattern of the later biographical works, contained the information that Chandragupta II had been selected by Samudragupta as his successor. He[98] opines that Viśākhadatta was probably patronized by Chandragupta II, and in order to justify the latter's killing of Rāmagupta, in the *Devī-Chandraguptam*, has portrayed the last-mentioned as a weak and coward king who agreed to surrender his queen to the invader, and the former as brave and one who would risk his life in saving the honour of the queen. U N Roy,[99] too, is of the opinion that Viśākhadatta was patronized by Chandragupta II and composed the work *Devī-Chandraguptam* to paint Rāmagupta in dark colour, and Chandragupta II in bright colour. However the contemporaneity of Chandragupta II and Viśākhadatta is very much doubtful (Chapter 1). It may also be stated that the Rāshṭrakūṭa king Dhruva dethroned his brother Govinda II, and in the epigraphs of Dhruva's successors, it is stated that he did not do that for his own sake, but for the sake of the Rāshṭrakūṭa family. They portray Govinda II as an extremely wicked person. In the same dynasty, Krishna III revolted against Govinda IV, and became king and the epigraphs relating to the former portrayed the latter as extremely vicious.

Till 1923 when Sylvan Levi first brought to light some fragments from Viśākhadatta's *Devī-Chandraguptam* quoted in the *Nāṭyadarpaṇa* of Guṇachandra and Rāmachandra, nothing was known about Rāmagupta. Thereafter there was a 'long array of corroborations' to the story based on this text. As a result of patiently and carefully piecing together the evidence, scattered here and there, by scholars, there was a gradual unfolding of the historicity of this Gupta king. Till Rāmagupta was known only from Indian literary sources, scholars were almost equally divided regarding his historicity, some accepting and others rejecting it. Then came the evidence of the Persian *Mujmal-ut-Tawarikh*, which considerably corroborated, and to some extent even supplemented what was known from the extracts from the *Devī-Chandraguptam*, a few more scholars accepted this view. The Rāshṭrakūṭa inscriptions corroborated the literary evidence regarding a Gupta king killing his brother and marrying his widow. It has been rightly argued[100] that in the grants of Rāshṭrakūṭa Amoghavarsha and Govinda IV, comparison between the Rāshṭrakūṭa monarchs and the Gupta king would not have been instituted if the matters relating to the latter, viz., his killing own brother, coveting his kingdom and marrying his widow, were not historical facts. The Gupta king is to be identified with Chandragupta II, and the brother who was killed, with Rāmagupta, and the latter's widow with Dhruvasvāminī. The find of the coins in fairly large number bearing the name of Rāmagupta in Gupta characters, added further weight to the historicity of that ruler. But since the coins were all in copper, and none in gold, whereas the Gupta coins are mostly in gold, and since the copper coins were found only in the Malwa region and did not bear any title, doubts were raised by a few scholars regarding the issuer of the coins being a king of the Gupta dynasty. But despite this, those who were quite hesitant in accepting the historicity of Rāmagupta agreed that the available evidence relating to him should not be 'dismissed off hand' as a 'figment of imagination'.[101] The discovery of three inscriptions in Gupta characters from Durjanpur near Vidiśā mentioning the name Rāmagupta with the title *mahārājādhirāja*, a title which was adopted by all the Imperial Gupta kings since the time of Chandragupta I, provided the most important and almost definite evidence in favour of identifying him as a Gupta king. Thus, as a result of piecing together the various bits of evidence—literary, epigraphic and numismatic—that came to light piecemeal within the span of almost half a century, it can be said that from doubtful historicity Rāmagupta has attained the status of an historical character, and a place among the kings of the Gupta dynasty.

## NOTES AND REFERENCES

1. Viśākhadatta is generally identified with the homonym who was the author of the *Mudrārākshasa* and is placed in the fourth century by some scholars (A S Altekar, *Journal of the Bihar and Orissa Research Society*, XIV, p. 242; XV, pp. 138ff.). U N Roy (*Gupta Rājavaṁśa tathā Usakā Yuga*, p. 216n) is of the view that *Pārthivaś-Chandraguptaḥ* met with in a manuscript of the *Mudrārākshasa* is the correct form, and *pārthivo Avantivarmā* and *pārthivo Dantivarmā* in others is a later adoption, and the reference to the *mlechchhas* conquered in the work should refer to the Śakas, rather than to the Hūṇas. He is of the view that *Devī-Chandraguptam* was composed at the behest of Chandragupta II. S R Goyal also considers him a contemporary of Chandragupta II (*The Imperial Guptas*, p. 262n). M Winternitz (in *Krishnaswami Aiyangar Commemoration Volume*, p. 360) is of the view that a play with such a damaging plot regarding the story of the Gupta king, could not have been written during the reign of Chandragupta II, and even that of his son, and that the non-mention of Viśākhadatta among great writers by Bāṇa (first half of the seventh century AD) would suggest that the

former flourished after the latter, perhaps in the second half of the seventh century AD, or thereafter.

2. *Journal Asiatique*, CCIII, pp. 193-218.
3. *Indian Antiquary*, LII, 1923, pp. 181ff.
4. These lectures were published later, in 1933, under the title *The Age of the Imperial Guptas*.
5. *Journal of the Benaras Hindu University*, II, pp. 23ff.
6. The verse has been cited by U N Roy (*Gupta Rājavaṁśa tathā Usakā Yuga*, p. 184).
7. *Harsha-charita* (N. S. Press) pp.199-200, *Aripure cha parakalatra-kāmukaṁ kāminī-veśa-guptaḥ Chandraguptaḥ Śakapatim=aśātayat*.
8. R N Dandekar (*A History of the Guptas*, p. 72) gives the date as AD 1713.
9. See, for example, U N Roy, *Gupta Rājavaṁśa tathā Usakā Yuga*, p.185.
10. *Ibid*.
11. *Kāvya-mīmāṁsā*, (Chowkhamba edn.), Chapter X, p. 132.
*Dattvā ruddha-gatiḥ Khaśādhipataye devīṁ Dhruva-svāminīṁ,*
*Yasmāt- khaṇḍita -sāhaso nivavṛite Śrī-Śarmagupto nṛipaḥ/*
*Tasminneva Himālaye guru-guhā-koṇa-kvaṇat-kinnare,*
*Gīyante tava Kārttikeya-nagara-strīṇāṁ gaṇaiḥ kīrtayaḥ. //*
U N Roy (*Gupta Rājavaṁśa tathā Usakā Yuga*, p. 180), places Khaśas in Nepal, and R B Singh (*Gupta Sāmrājya*, p. 86) in Himachal Pradesh. But they are very much there in Uttarakhand, within which Baijnath is located. It may be stated that N N Dasgupta (*Indian Culture*, IV, p. 220) connects Khaśas with Khasgar in south Kashmir.
12. D R Bhandarkar, *Corpus Inscriptionum Indicarum*, III, pp. 48ff.
13. D R Bhandarkar, *ibid*., p. 49, n. 2.
14. See A Cunningham, *Archaeological Survey Reports*, I, pp. 138-39.
15. *Vide* U N Roy, *Gupta Rājavaṁśa tathā Usakā Yuga*, p. 189.
16. A S Altekar, *Journal of the Bihar and Orissa Research Society*, XIV (ii), pp. 223-53.
17. D R Bhandarkar, *Corpus Inscriptionum Indicarum*, III, p. 48.
18. *Indian Antiquary*, LXII, 1933, pp. 201ff, at p. 205.
19. *Ibid*., pp. 201-202.
20. *Ibid*., pp. 204-205.
21. R K Mookerji (*Gupta Empire*, p. 64) does not take Aripura as the name of a city, and translates it as 'the city of enemy'. He is of the view that Khaśas were not powerful in the fourth century AD and therefore Śaka should be the reading, and by that term Kushāṇa sould be understood, as it were they who were then ruling in Punjab and Kabul.
22. *Journal of Indian History*, XXI, pp. 159ff.
23. *Ibid*., p. 167. He opines that with the exception of Bāṇa, all the sources referring to the king as Śaka are later than Rājaśekhara and there is a possibility that the verse quoted by him existed even before Bāṇa. (*ibid*.)
24. *Journal of the Bihar and Orissa Research Society*, XIV, pp. 223-53; XV, pp. 134-41.
25. Elliot and Dowson, *The History of India as Told by Its Historians*, I, pp. 110-12.

26. D R Bhandarkar, *Corpus Inscriptionum Indicarum*, III, pp. 46-47; R K Mookerji, *Gupta Empire*, p. 65.
27. D R Bhandarkar, *Corpus Inscriptionum Indicarum*, III, p. 47.
28. D R Bhandarkar, *ibid*., p. 50.
29. *Archaeological Survey of India—Annual Report*, 1913-14, p. 221, *vide* K D Bajpai, *Indian Numismatic Studies*, p. 201, n 13.
30. K D Bajpai, *Journal of the Numismatic Society of India*, XVIII, pp. 108-09; also in B Ch Chhabra *et al*. (ed.), *Reappraising Gupta History for S R Goyal*, pp. 196-201.
31. For nos. i to iv, see P L Gupta, *The Imperial Guptas*, p. 104; for nos. vi and vii, see K D Bajpai, in B Ch Chhabra *et al*. (ed.), *Reappraising Gupta History for S R Goyal*, p. 197.
32. K D Bajpai, in B Ch Chhabra *et al*. (ed.), *Reappraising Gupta History for S R Goyal*, p. 201.
33. *Ibid*., pp. 198-99.
34. P L Gupta, *The Imperial Guptas*, p. 104.
35. A H Dani, *Journal of the Numismatic Society of India*, XXVI, pp. 11ff.
36. In *Comprehensive History of India*, III(i), p. 49.
37. D C Sircar, *Journal of Ancient Indian History*, III (i-iv), p. 150.
38. D C Sircar, *ibid*., pp. 148-49.
39. S R Goyal, *The Imperial Guptas*, pp. 135-36.
40. D C Sircar, *Journal of Ancient Indian History*, pp. 148-49.
41. *Ibid*., pp. 149-50.
42. *Ibid*., pp. 148-49
43. Altekar, *The Coinage of the Gupta Empire*, p. 163. P L Gupta (*The Imperial Guptas*, p. 105) does not consider Rāmagupta's coins as based on the Mālava coins. He points out that the Mālavas were then in Jaipur region rather than in Malwa region, and that no Malwa coin has been found in the Vidiśā region, and no coin of Rāmagupta has been found in Rajasthan. Rāmagupta's coins are thicker than the Mālava coins, bear *garuḍa* or lion as device, and one or a few letters of the legend in their case is almost invariably out of flan (P L Gupta, *Gupta Sāmrājya*, p. 281). On Nāga coins, the device is mostly bull, and the legend is circular. On the coins of Rāmagupta, the bull figure is never represented. The legend on the Mālava coins is in incuse and complete.
44. A S Altekar, *The Coinage of the Gupta Empire*, p. 163.
45. P L Gupta, *The Imperial Guptas*, p. 293.
46. *Ibid*.
47. K D Bajpai, in B Ch Chhabra *et al*. (ed.), *Reappraising Gupta History for S R Goyal*, p. 200.
48. P L Gupta, *Gupta Sāmrājya*, p. 281: *Imperial Guptas*, p. 293.
49. P L Gupta, *ibid*.
50. *Malwa through the Ages*, p. 234.
51. K D Bajpai, in B Ch Chhabra *et al*. (ed.) *Reappraising Gupta History for S R Goyal*, p. 197.

52. *Malaviya Commemoration Volume*, p. 205.
53. *The Coinage of the Gupta Empire*, pp. 84-85. The name of king on coins is merely Kācha and not Kāchagupta just like the name of the second Gupta ruler was Ghaṭotkacha and not Ghaṭotkachagupta (the latter, was the form of the name of another king, a later one, of the Gupta dynasty who ruled for a short period in the second quarter of the fifth century AD).
54. *Journal of the Bihar and Orissa Research Society*, XVIII, p. 24.
55. *Indian Culture*, IV, p. 222.
56. *Ibid.*
57. See P L Gupta, *The Imperial Guptas*, p. 294.
58. *Ibid.*
59. K D Bajpai, in B Ch Chhabra *et al.* (ed.), *Reappraising Gupta History for S R Goyal*, p. 199.
60. *Epigraphia Indica*, XVIII, p. 248.
    *Hatvā bhrātarameva rājyam=aharddevīm cha dīnastato,*
    *Laksham̐ koṭim=alekhayatkila kalau dātā sa Guptānvayaḥ//*
61. *Epigraphia Indica*, XVIII, p. 242.
62. V V Mirashi, *Kālidāsa*, p. 19.
63. U N Roy, *Gupta Rājavaṁśa tathā Usakā Yuga*, p. 191.
64. *Ibid.*
65. *Ibid.*, p. 192, n.
66. *Sāmarthye sati ninditā pravihitā naivāgraje krūratā,*
    *bandhu-strī-gamanādibhiḥ kucharitair=āvarjjitaṁ nāyaśaḥ/*
    *śauchāśaucha-parāṅmukhaṁ na cha bhiyā paiśāchyam=aṅgīkṛitam*
    *tyāgen=āsama sāhasaiścha bhuvane yaḥ Sāhasāṅko'bhavat//*
67. S R Goyal, *Gupta Sāmrājya kā Itihāsa*, p. 192.
68. D R Bhandarkar, *Corpus Inscriptionum Indicarum*, III, p. 132. The epigraph was found after Bhandarkar had sent the manuscript for publication and has been added by the editors.
69. *Journal of Ancient Indian History*, III, p. 147.
70. U N Roy, *Gupta Rājavaṁśa tathā Usakā Yuga*, p. 208.
71. Most scholars consider the two as belonging to the same person. See Chapter 11, below.
72. D C Sircar, *Select Inscriptions*, I, p. 272, n. 10.
73. K K Thaplyal, in *Journal of Indological Studies* (Haryana Sahitya Academi), III, pp. 143-45.
74. *Journal of Indian History*, XL (iii), p. 535.
75. S R Goyal, *Gupta Sāmrājya kā Itihāsa*, pp. 193-94.
76. See S R Goyal, *ibid.*, p. 194.
77. *The Imperial Guptas and their Times*, p. 36.
78. For example, K D Bajpai, in B Ch Chhabra *et al.* (ed.), *Reappraising Gupta History for S R Goyal*, p. 200. In his opinion, the battle was fought either at Eran or at Vidiśā.

79. *Gupta Empire*, pp. 47-48.
80. *The Imperial Guptas and their Times*, p. 38.
81. *New History of Ancient India*, pp. 380-81.
82. S R Goyal, *Gupta Sāmrājya kā Itihāsa*, p. 199.
83. A S Altekar, *Rāshṭrakūṭas and Their Times*, pp. 59ff.
84. R C Majumdar, in *Comprehensive History of India*, III(i), p. 49.
85. *Ibid.*, p. 51.
86. V A Smith, *Early History of India*, p. 292.
87. *Nārada* (*Sacred Book of the East*, XXX), XII. 20, 97.
88. R C Majumdar, in *Comprehensive History of India*, III(i), pp. 50-51.
89. *Gupta Rājavaṁśa tathā Usakā Yuga*, p. 204.
90. For our view regarding the parentage of the Gupta queen, which is different from this, see Appendix VI.
91. S R Goyal, *The Imperial Guptas*, pp. 272-73; P L Gupta, *The Imperial Guptas*, p. 292; U N Roy, *Gupta Rājavaṁśa tathā Usakā Yuga*, pp. 208-09.
92. For example, suggested by U N Roy, *Gupta Rājavaṁśa tathā Usakā Yuga*, p. 208. Roy also feels that the Rashṭrakūṭa king Amoghavarsha being a Jaina had sympathies for Rāmagupta who too seems to have been a Jaina (*ibid.*, p. 207).
93. See also P L Gupta, *The Imperial Guptas*, p. 292.
94. *Ibid.*
95. U N Roy, *Gupta Rājavaṁśa tathā Usakā Yuga*, p. 208.
96. S R Goyal, *The Imperial Guptas*, pp. 266ff.
97. *Ibid.*, pp. 272ff.
98. *Ibid.*, p. 268.
99. U N Roy, *Gupta Rājavaṁśa tathā Usakā Yuga*, p. 208-09.
100. Ashvini Agrawal, *Rise and Fall of the Imperial Guptas*, p. 159.
101. R C Majumdar, in *The Vākāṭaka-Gupta Age*, p. 164.

# 7

# Chandragupta II: Further Expansion of the Empire

## I

Chandragupta II, son of Samudragupta begotten on Dattadevī, ascended the throne after eliminating his elder brother Rāmagupta. The Mathurā pillar inscription (No. 6) is the earliest dated record of his reign, in fact of the Gupta dynasty, and also the earliest one the date of which can be ascrribed to the Gupta era. It bears the date 61, and though the era is not named, it is to be taken as the Gupta era, the generally accepted initial date of which is AD 319. The date of the inscription would thus correspond to (319+61=) AD 380. It also bears the regnal year, which is partly mutilated but should better be reconstructed as *paṁchame*[1] (fifth), rather than *prathame*[2] (first), and accordingly his reign began in AD 376. The epigraph details the pious act of the *āchāryas* of the Lakulīśa Pāśupata sect. The Udaigiri inscription of his reign, dated GE 82 (No. 7), refers to the excavation of a Vaishṇava cave by his feudatory of the Sanakānīka family. An undated inscription from the same site (No. 11) refers to the excavation of a Śaiva cave by Chandragupta II's Minister of Peace and War, Vīrasena Śāba. He had come there accompanying the king who was intent upon making large scale conquests. A Sanchi inscription dated GE 93 (No. 9), mentions the pious act of his general Āmrakārddava in favour of the Buddhist *saṅgha*. An undated Mathurā inscription (No. 10) details the Gupta genealogy from the first Gupta king up to Chandragupta II.

King Chandra of the Mehrauli iron pillar inscription (No. 12), which refers to the Vaishṇava leanings of the king, to his victory over a confederacy of kings in Vaṅga, and to his successful campaign up to Vāhlīka region, is to be identified with Chandragupta II (Appendix III).

Chandragupta II issued gold, silver and copper coins.[3] His gold coin are of the following types: Archer, Standard, Lion-slayer, Horse-rider, King-and-Queen, Couch, *Chakra-vikrama* and *Chhatra*.[4] He issued silver coins for the newly conquered Śaka territories in Gujarat, in imitation of the silver coins of the Śaka rulers who had ruled there for nearly three centuries. The copper coins, though few in number, are of more than half a dozen types. Chandragupta II finds mention in some literary works which have been taken note of above in the context of the history of Rāmagupta (Chapter 6), and need not be repeated. Some scholars believe that certain conquests of Raghu mentioned in Kālidāsa's *Raghuvaṁśam* were inspired by the conquests of Chandragupta II and by those of his father, Samudragupta.[5]

The term *tatpādaparigṛihīta* for Chandragupta II in the Bhitari pillar inscription of Skandagupta (No.33), instead of *tatpādānudhyāta,* which is generally met with in the case of other Imperial Gupta kings in the context of mentioning succession, is taken by some scholars as indicative of his being selected as successor by his father. He has been referred to as *satputra* in his Mathurā stone pillar inscription (No. 6), which some consider as used to make a contrast with his ill-reputed brother Rāmagupta.[6] Some scholars suggest that Samudragupta selected Chandragupta as his successor, but Rāmagupta, elder son of Samudragupta and rightful claimant to the throne according to the law of primogeniture, on the death of his father, declared himself king, and it was after eliminating him that Chandragupta came to the throne.[7] However, as will be shown below, the term *tatpāda-parigṛihīta* need not necessarily be taken in the sense of being selected.

Chandragupta II had at least two queens; one of them is mentioned as Dhruvasvāminī in her own sealing (No. 13), and as Dhruvadevī in the Gupta epigraphs detailing genealogy. The possibility of the two being different persons, though not impossible, is extremely remote (Appendix VI). She was the mother of Govindagupta and Kumāragupta I. Her family is not mentioned in any source. Some suggestion has been offered about it in Appendix VI. The other queen of his was Kuberanāgā, a Nāga princess, and the mother of Prabhāvatīguptā who was married to the Vākāṭaka prince, Rudrasena II. One king, Kubera, is mentioned as a ruler of

Devarāshṭra in the Allahabad pillar inscription (No. 1) in the context of Samudragupta's south Indian campaign, and it is tempting to consider the Gupta queen Kuberanāgā as a sister of that king, on the basis of the similarity of their names. But since it is not known that the king was of Nāga lineage, it is better to take her as belonging to one of the Nāga families of the north India.[8] The recently found much mutilated Ramtek Prabhāvatī Memorial stone inscription (No. 85), according to the reading and interpretation of some scholars, seems to refer to at least three sons born of Kuberanāgā, though no details are known about them. The same inscription mentions Ghaṭotkachagupta, as the son of Chandragupta II, whose mother's name is not mentioned. He, it seems, was married to the daughter of his sister (or step-sister) Prabhāvatīguptā, the Vākāṭaka queen.

In the case of Chandragupta II, there is no such record which throws detailed light on his conquests and other achievements, and as such, information for the reconstruction of the history of his reign has to be culled from different literary, epigraphic and numismatic sources. His ascending the throne after killing his brother might have created enemies for him, and inspired some feudatories to raise their heads in revolt. His first task was to establish himself firmly, subdue the rebels and bring back to his dynasty the glory that had been lost during the reign of Rāmagupta. He was keen to expand the Gupta kingdom, and chose to do so at the expense of the Śaka territories. As seen in the preceding chapter, a Śaka king had the audacity to attack Rāmagupta and force him to agree to surrender his queen, and Chandragupta II would have been keen to avenge the great insult it caused to the Gupta dynasty, leading to the decline in its prestige. The Śaka territories of Gujarat and adjoining areas were like a thorn to the western provinces of the Gupta kingdom. According to Smith, '...differences of race, creed and manners supplied the Gupta monarch with special reasons for desiring to suppress the impure foreign rulers of the west'.[9] The desire to have control over Bharukachchha (Broach) and other ports of western India, which were important centres of profitable trade with western Asia would also have been an important motivating factor for launching an attack against the Śakas. Through the port of Bharukachchha passed not only indigenous goods, but also goods from China and Central Asia, because of political turmoil in the area through which the trade-route from China to West Asia passed. Though the peak period of India's trade with Western Asia and beyond had passed, it was still quite profitable for the Indians.[10]

## II

It is generally believed that Chandragupta II's own marriage with the Nāga princess Kuberanāgā, and later the marriage of his daughter Prabhāvatīguptā with Vākāṭaka prince, Rudrasena II, were meant to garner support of the Nāgas and the Vākāṭakas, respectively, in the campaign planned to be launched against the Śakas. Marriage alliances for political gain were not uncommon in Indian history.[11] As Smith states, the geographical position of the Vākāṭaka kingdom was such that in Gupta-Śaka conflict its king 'could be of much service or disservice' to the Guptas.[12] According to the same scholar, by marrying the Gupta princess to a Vākāṭaka prince, he secured subordinate alliance of the Vākāṭakas.[13] P L Gupta[14] is of the view that by this alliance the fear of a possible Vākāṭaka interference in the Gupta territory was avoided. Rudrasena II seems to have kept Chandragupta II in good stead in war against the Śakas. S K Maity,[15] too, holds that 'the marriage alliances of Chandragupta II were diplomatic prelude to his imperial expansion in western India'. S R Goyal,[16] however, opines that the marriage of the Gupta princess to the Vākāṭaka prince was not aimed at receiving their help against the Śakas, as, in his opinion, the Śakas were not so powerful that the Guptas would have needed the help of other powers to conquer them. But the Śakas who ruled for more than three centuries, and earlier during the reign of Rudradāman, as per his Junagarh Rock inscription,[17] defeated the Sātavāhanas and the Yaudheyas, were to be taken seriously, and not lightly. Had they been quite weak, the Vākāṭakas or the Nāgas, whose territories were in close proximity of theirs, would have conquered them earlier. One would expect that Samudragupta would have conquered them after he had defeated some Nāga rulers. But it may be argued that the Guptas wanted to crush the Śakas shortly after Chandragupta's marrying the Nāga princess Kuberanāgā during the reign of Samudragupta, but did not do so as they entered into a treaty with Samudragupta accepting him as paramount sovereign. However, soon after the death of Samudragupta, the Śaka ruler had the audacity of invading the Gupta ruler Rāmagupta and force him to agree to surrender his wife. Chandragupta II would have followed the maxim that the enemy should never be deemed weak, and as such tried his best to strengthen his position by matrimonial alliance with the Vākāṭakas. S R Goyal[18] is of the opinion that Prabhāvatīguptā was married to the Vākāṭaka prince

Rudrasena II, son of Pravarasena I in *c.* AD 380 and Chandragupta II's campaign against the Śakas took place in last years of the fourth or early years of the fifth century AD, and such a long term planning by the Guptas is rather difficult to envisage.[19] But the date for the Gupta-Śaka war suggested by Goyal, as shown below, is debatable. It has been surmised by some scholars[20] that Rudrasena II helped Chandragupta II in his Śaka campaign, and also that he died fighting for the Gupta emperor in that war.

Epigraphic and numismatic evidences throw some light on matters relating to Chandragupta II's Śaka conquest. An undated inscription from Udaigiri in Vidiśā district (No 11) states that Vīrasena *alias* Śāba, Minister of Peace and War, and a native of Pāṭaliputra, had come there along with his royal master, Chandragupta II, 'who had by prowess conquered the kingdoms and made kings his slaves' and who was seeking to conquer the 'whole world' (*kṛitsna-pṛithivī*). It appears almost certain that the official accompanied the king in his campaign against the Śakas. An inscription dated GE 82 from the same site (No. 7) records the gift of a *mahārāja* (i.e. feudatory) of Sanakānīka tribe owing allegiance to Chandragupta II. If the habitat of the Sanakānīkas was not far from Udaigiri, as many scholars believe, he could have visited the site any time at his convenience, got the cave excavated and the inscription recorded there. But if they are to be located in the north-west, as some scholars believe, then there is a greater possibility of his being summoned by Chandragupta II to participate in the campaign, may be to act as one of the commanders of the Gupta army.[21] The pious act of excavating a cave for Lord Vishṇu, it may be suggested, might have been undertaken by him with a view to seeking the blessings of the deity for victory in war against the Śakas. An inscription of GE 93 (= AD 412) of Chandragupta II's general Āmrakārddava, 'victorious in several battles', has been found at Sanchi, in the neighbourhood of Vidiśā (No. 9). If the Śaka conquest had been accomplished a couple of years earlier than that date, it can be presumed that either after the conquest the Gupta general stayed back to consolidate the gains of the victory, or he might have been sent there because of some administrative exigencies such as to quell a revolt, expected or actual, in that region.[22] The visit of a minister of foreign affairs, a general and a feudatory in the last phase of the fourth century AD and early years of the fifth century AD cannot be taken as a mere accident.[23] H C Raychaudhuri[24] categorically states that Chandragupta II assembled 'at or near

Vidiśā...many of his ministers, generals and feudatories' in connection with the campaign against the Śaka king. R K Mookerji opines: 'Eastern Malwa must have been the base of Chandragupta II's operations against the Śaka kingdom in western India'. In his view, the epigraphs suggest "successive steps in the advance of Gupta power towards west".[25] S R Goyal does not consider the epigraphic evidence as suggestive of either assembling of important officials in Vidiśā region, or that the war was a protracted one.[26]

The view of P L Gupta[27] that Vīrasena, the Sanakānīka *mahārāja* (No. 7), and Āmrakārddava (No. 9) and other officials had come there in the context of the Gupta king's visit to the Vākāṭaka capital to condole the death of Rudrasena II, and provide military and administrative help to the Vākāṭakas, does not seem to be convincing. On the one hand, there is no evidence of such a visit from any source, and on the other, the Udaigiri inscription of Chandragupta II (No. 11) clearly states that the king's journey was related to his desire of making conquests.

As stated above, the Vidiśā-Eran region, because of its strategic position had become a centre of military activities, and for that reason it had gained much political significance. The city of Eran had been a personal fiefdom of Samudragupta and royal princes, e.g. Rāmagupta, Govindagupta, and Ghaṭotkachagupta were appointed as governors of the region around it during the reign of different kings. The literary tradition[28] speaks of Chandragupta II as one who passed *kāvyakāra* examination at Ujjayinī, a provincial capital of the Guptas of great importance, perhaps as a prince holding some important administrative office there.[29]

According to P L Gupta,[30] the last dates met with on the coins of the hoards from Sarvania (Vidiśā disrict),[31] Sanchi,[32], and Godarmau (Bhopal district)[33] are 273 (Śaka = AD 351), 272 (Śaka = AD 350) and 270 (Śaka = AD 348), respectively, which indicate that in or shortly after Śaka 273, Śaka rule had ended in Rajasthan and Malwa. He[34] further states that the evidence of the two coin-hoards from the south of the Vindhyas suggests that the Śakas had hold over that area up to AD 379.

The details about the actual place of the battle and the strategy adopted by Chandragupta II in the warfare against the Śakas are not known. R C Majumdar[35] states that Bāṇa's reference to Chandragupta's killing the Śaka king in the guise of a female may actually refer to the strategy adopted by him in this war. He attacked, defeated, and perhaps killed the Śaka king, who in all probability was Rudrasiṁha III, and annexed his territories. With this ended 'lock stock and barrel' the Śaka rule of more than 300 years. Some centuries earlier, the Sātavāhanas had been responsible to roll back for some time 'the tide of the Scythian conquest', Chandragupta II finally stemmed it.[36] By his aggressive campaign, Chandragupta II carried the imperial policy of his father to its 'logical conclusion'.[37] The victory was cherished for its 'political, economic and sentimental' significance, and 'extinguishd the last vestiges of foreign rule in India'.[38] By his victory over the Śakas, he, like the legendary Vikramāditya, deserves the title *Śakāri.*

Possibly the war was long protracted, and Dandekar suggests that it may have involved more than one campaign.[39] The last date met with on Rudrasiṁha III's coins is 310+x (x=unit figure which is lost). This date, like all other dates of the rulers of this family, must be in the Śaka era, and would correspond to AD 388+x, which would mean any date between AD 388 and AD 397. For the convenience of the people of that territory, who were accustomed to the use of silver currency of the Śakas that had been in vogue there for well nigh three centuries, Chandragupta II issued coins in imitation of Śaka coins, as is evident from their metal, weight, shape, and style of the depiction of the king's head on them. However, to convey the message that thereafter the Guptas and not the Śakas were the rulers of the region, the hill symbol, so common on the coins of the Śakas, was replaced by the *garuḍa* figure, which was the insignia of the Vaishṇava Guptas, Śaka king's name and title, by Gupta king's name and title, and the date in Śaka era by that in the Gupta era. The earliest silver coins of Chandragupta II are dated [Gupta Era] 90 + x (the unit figure being lost),[40] i.e. AD 409+x. The end of Chandragupta II's reign took place any time between AD 412, his last known date, and AD 415—the first known date for his son Kumāragupta I, and in between these two dates is to be placed the rule of Govindagupta, whose history will be discussed below in Chapter 8. Therefore, Chandragupta II achieved success against the Śakas any time after AD 388 and before the end of his rule in *c.* AD 412. D R Bhandarkar[41] favours a date nearer to AD 388. In his view, Chandragupta II did not issue coins for the conquered territory for a fairly long period after its annexation, as a vast mass of Śaka coins being in circulation, there was no need of issuing fresh ones. A S Altekar,[42] however, places Chandragupta II's Śaka conquest near the end of his rule, on grounds that the silver coins of Chandragupta II are quite rare, which should not have been the case if he had conquered the Śakas much earlier than the date of issuing of these coins. The same is the view of S R Goyal, who takes the presence of Chandragupta II's general, Āmrakārddava, at Sanchi in AD 412 (No. 11) as related with this conquest.[43] He is of the view that the Tumain inscription of GE 116 (No. 19) takes cognizance of Chandragupta II's victory over the Śakas, as it mentions that Gupta monarch's rule extending over territories up to the sea (*medinīṁ sāgarāntām*).[44] This may be the case, although the phrase that the territory of a ruler extended up to the sea is used even in the case of feudatory kings, as for instance for *Mahārāja* Harivarman Maukhari in the seal inscriptions of his successors, though the sea was far off from his territory. Some scholars see a reflection of Chandragupta II's Śaka conquest in the famous Varāha image at Udaigiri, a place, as seen above, that had been visited by Chandragupta II. It is taken to convey, in symbolic form, that the Gupta king freed the territories from the Śaka rule as Varāha (incarnation of Vishṇu) rescued the Earth from Grāha. Incidentally, it has been pointed out that in the depiction of human figures on the back wall, which as per cannons of iconography related to Varāha *avatāra*, should represent the *ṛishis*, in the context of Chandragupta II, may depict the Śakas and other subordinate rulers as their dress and posture would suggest. [45]

As stated earlier, Goyal opines that the Śakas were an inferior power and the matrimonial alliances of the Guptas with the Nāgas and the Vākāṭakas was not meant for seeking their help against the Śakas. However, he[46] cites the view of Maity,[47] that one of the factors responsible for motivating Chandragupta II to conquer the Śakas was to safeguard his daughter's (Vākāṭaka) territories against the possible invasion from their side. This shows that Chandragupta II deemed the Śakas powerful enough to dare launch an attack on the Vākāṭakas, who were a power to be reckoned with. Further, as seen in Chapter 6, most of the scholars believe that the Śaka enemy of Rāmagupta was a Western Kshatrapa ruler who was bold enough to attack the Gupta king and achieve victory, at least initially, over him. Many scholars[48] believe that the war with the Śakas lasted for a long period, perhaps more than a decade, which would indicate that they provided a tough resistance to the Gupta invader. Goyal, however, is of the view that the war was not a protracted one.[49]

P L Gupta is of the opinion that after the Śaka rulers, kings of another dynasty, Śarva and his successors, ruled in Gujarat.[50] The issuing of silver coins by Chandragupta II after the conquest of the Śaka kingdom and other pieces of evidence, mentioned above, go against this view. It is also difficult to agree with his opinion that Chandragupta II had hold over eastern Malwa and Gujarat, but the area of western Malwa in between the two was not within his kingdom, and came to form a part of the Gupta territory only from the time of Kumāragupta I.[51] It would seem more reasonable that before he launched an attack on the Śakas ruling in Kathiawar and Gujarat, he would have secured hold over Western Malwa.

With the conquest of Gujarat, the boundaries of the Gupta empire extended up to the Arabian Sea. The Guptas came to have direct access to the ports on the western coast, and developed closer contact with traders who had contacts with the markets of the western Asia and beyond. The export of goods, particularly quality cloth and spices, to western Asia and Rome brought a good deal of wealth. Custom duties on goods would also have enriched the Gupta treasury. Ujjain upon which converged important trade routes from different directions became a great centre of trade. The inland trade and traffic increased as the whole area from Bengal to Gujarat came to form part of the Gupta empire.

### III

As stated earlier, like most scholars, we believe that Chandra of the Mehrauli pillar inscription is identical with Chandragupta II, and hence ascribe the achievements mentioned in that inscription to him. We concur with Fleet's view, which is accepted by most of the scholars, that the expression *visarjya gāṁ gām-āśrity=etarām* in the Mehrauli pillar inscription (No. 12) shows that the king had quit this world and has gone to the other world, i.e. was dead. A few scholars hold that the king was alive at the time. D R Bhandarkar[52] points out that the *Mahābhārata* mentions *tīrthas* in *pṛithivī* (i.e., plains) and *antariksha* (hilly region), and that in the same text, Naimisha is mentioned as *pṛithivī-tīrtha* and Pushkara (which Bhandarkar locates in the Himalayas, taking it as different from the one of this name in Ajmer) as *antariksha-tīrtha.* He believes that Vishṇupada, situated near the origin of Beas, which is on a higher plane, is an *antariksha-tīrtha*, where king Chandra was staying at the time of installing the pillar bearing the inscription at that place, from where, in a later period, it was transported to its present site Mehrauli.[53] S K Aiyangar[54] believes that the inscription was composed during the reign of Chandragupta I, but was recorded after his death. The use of the Gupta era in an inscription from

Shorkot (district Jhang) and the find of some Kushāṇa type of coins bearing the name Chandra from Punjab are taken by him as indicative of the Gupta king's influence in that region. D R Bhandarkar,[55] identifying Chandra of Mehrauli pillar inscription with Chandragupta II, suggests that he crossed western Rajasthan and made himself master of Sindh and Punjab and inflicted a defeat upon the Vāhlīkas. He points out that in the *Rāmāyaṇa*, in course of journey from Ayodhyā to Girivraja, capital of the kingdom of Kekaya (identified by Cunningham with Jalalpur in the Punjab, now in Pakistan), the messengers passed through the Bāhlika country to the Sudāmā hill and saw two rivers, Vipāśā and Śālmalī, as also Vishṇupada.[56] S K Aiyangar locates the Bahlikas in Sindh.[57] According to him, Vāhlīka is associated with Vishṇupada, and should be located not far from Beas where it joins Śālmalī. R C Majumdar,[58] however, points out that the Mehrauli pillar inscription does not in any way associate Vāhlīkas with Vishṇupada. Bhandarkar points out that the *Rāmāyaṇa*, at one place,[59] describes Vāhīkas living in the north of and distinct from the Kambojas, Yavanas and Śakas, and at another,[60] as located in the west and mentioned along with Saurāshṭra. From the *Kāśikā*,[61] it is known that the Vāhlīkas were fond of Sauvīra drink. According to D R Bhandarkar,[62] the combined evidence of the *Rāmāyaṇa* and the *Kāśikā*, shows that the Vāhlīkas occupied not only Sindhu and Sauvīra, but also parts of the Punjab. Allan[63] also does not believe that Chandragupta II reached Balkh, the route to which would not be the crossing of the mouth of the Indus. O Stein, too, locates Vāhīkas (=Vāhlīkas) in Punjab and Sindh.[64] Tarn opines that Vāhīka was used for foreign people in the north-west India, and so Vāhlīkas need not be taken to be people of Balkh (Bactria).[65]

Majumdar takes the *sapta-mukhas* (seven mouths) in the Mehrauli pillar inscription as seven feeders of the river Sindhu, viz., five rivers of the Punjab and the Kabul and the Kunar,[66] and the same is the view of Jayaswal.[67] V C Pandey,[68] who earlier agreed with this view, later changed his opinion, as he was in doubt if the last two rivers, which are seldom referred to in the post-Vedic literature, continued to form an entity of *Saptasindhu* as late as the Gupta period. On the basis of the *Mahābhārata* he identified the seven feeders of the sea (*sindhu*), viz., Gaṅgā, Yamunā, Sarasvatī, Rathasthā (Ramganga), Sarayū, Gomatī, and Gaṇḍakī, which the king crossed while marching from his capital Pāṭaliputra to Vāhlīka. This is not convincing, as it would be a queer way of referring to the seven mouths of the sea with reference to the march of the king to Vāhlīka, ignoring the rivers of Punjab.

Some scholars[69] take the seven mouths (*sapta-mukhāni*) of the Sindhu as seven mouths of the Indus when it falls into the sea, each of which has been mentioned by name by Ptolemy.[70] The *Raghuvaṁśam*[71] has the expression *nadīmukhen=aiva samudram=āviśata*, i.e. entered the sea through the mouth of the river. The king, it is believed by them, entered the Punjab through the Indus delta, which thus was the extension of the conquest of the Śaka territory by Chandragupta II.

R C Majumdar,[72] D C Sircar,[73] K A N Sastri[74] and many other scholars identify Vāhlīka with Bactria (Balkh). According to Sastri, Chandragupta II 'carried his arms beyond the Hindukush to Balkh'.[75] Some inscriptions from Chilas in Hunza district of Pak-occupied Kashmir mention Chandra, *Vikramāditya* and Harisheṇa. This seems to indicate that Chandragupta II had conquered that region, and this may be related to his victory over Balkh. The evidence of these inscriptions has been discussed in some detail in Appendix III—King Chandra of the Mehrauli Pillar. This victory of the Gupta king would have secured the north-western boundary and provided a deterrent to the foreign powers against invading the land.

## IV

In the Mathurā pillar inscription of [Gupta Era] 61 (No. 6), Chandragupta II has been referred to as *mahārāja* and *rājādhirāja*, which is based on the *mahārāja rājātirāja* title of the Kushāṇas, who had hold over the Mathurā region some time before it came under the Gupta rule. D R Bhandarkar[76] is of the opinion that Chandragupta II was the first Gupta king to conquer Mathurā. He does not consider Gaṇapatināga, a king of Āryāvarta defeated by Samdragupta, as ruler of Mathurā. Most scholars, in our view, rightly give credit of conquering that region to Samudragupta.

The Allahabad pillar inscription of Samudragupta mentions Samataṭa (south-eastern Bengal) as a frontier kingdom. The Mehrauli pillar inscription mentions King Chandra's defeating the rulers who had congregated against him in Vaṅga. R C Majumdar[77] considers Vaṅga same as Samataṭa, mentioned in the Allahabad pillar inscription as a border state of Samudragupta. It is possible that the ruler of Vaṅga became antagonistic to Chandragupta II when the latter ascended the throne after eliminating Rāmagupta. The view of K D Bajpai,[78] based on a solitary *śloka* of the *Mahābhārata* that Vaṅga stands for Makran in Baluchistan, is untenable.[79] Tāmralipti was an important centre of trade, inland, and overseas with the South-east Asian countries, and Gupta hold over it was conducive to a great economic gain. However, it is difficult to agree with the view[80] that it was because of Chandragupta II's hold over Tāmralipti that the Mehrauli pillar inscription mentions the scenting of the southern sea by the air of his prowess, since in literature, southern sea is differentiated from the eastern and western seas, and it has been suggested[81] that the expression is better explained in the light of the Gupta influence over the Vākāṭakas and the Kadambas.

There are pieces of evidence indicating political and other influences of the Guptas on the Vākāṭakas. The perceptions of the scholars regarding the evidence as also the extent of the influence, however, differ. The Poona (No. 82) and Rithpur (No. 84) plates of Prabhāvatīguptā, give her paternal (i.e. Gupta) genealogy,[82] and not that of the Vākāṭaka family to which her husband belonged, which shows her great reverence for paternal family. In all the Vākāṭaka records mentioning Prabhavatīguptā, her *gupta*-ending name is retained. In the above mentioned Rithpur and Poona plates, Prabhāvatīguptā has been referred to as of Dhāraṇa *gotra* which seems to be her paternal *gotra*, as her huband's *gotra* was Vishṇuvṛiddha.[83] Unlike his ancestors who were Śaivas, her husband, Rudrasena II Vākāṭaka, like the Gupta kings, was a Vaishṇava. The Poona copperplate inscription is in nail-headed script, characteristic of the Gupta alphabet, instead of the box-headed one, which is seen in most of the inscriptions of the Vākāṭakas, and as such is taken by some scholars as executed by the Gupta scribe present in the Vākāṭaka court.

The retaining of the *guptā*-ending name by Prabhāvatīguptā even after marriage may not necessarily be taken as intended to show that she belonged to the prestigious Gupta family. G*uptā* was used as a name-ending for the first time by Chandragupta I and all the successive kings of the Gupta dynasty followed him. It appears that it became part of the name not only of the Gupta princes, but also of the Gupta princesses. Mahāsenaguptā, the princess of the Later Gupta family, is known to have retained *guptā*-ending of her name even after she became Maukhari queen, probably because it was part of her name. To the best of our knowledge, from her *guptā*-ending name no scholar has drawn any inference regarding the political status of her paternal dynasty *vis-à-vis* her husband's family.

A S Altekar[84] suggests that Chandragupta II sent Kālidāsa for training the Vākāṭaka princes, and offered help in the administration of the Vākāṭaka kingdom by sending Gupta officials to their court. S R Goyal[85] says that there is no evidence for both these suggestions; he is critical of

Altekar's view[86] that the Gupta emperor sent officials of such low rank as scribes to the court of the Vākāṭakas. He[87] points out that at one place Altekar states that the Poona copperplates were drafted by Gupta officials deputed to the Vākāṭaka court,[88] and at another place, basing his evidence on their contents, opines that the drafters of the plates 'were bred up in the Deccan tradition'.[89] Generally the letters on the plates were written by persons, who were well versed in the language and the script, with such material as chalk, charcoal or ink, and then the engraver, who may or may not have been literate, engraved them following their outline; rarely the letters would have been directly copied from the draft on cloth or some other material by the engraver. In the Rithpur plate, the script is box-headed, while in the Poona copperplate it is the nail-headed Gupta script, yet both contain the Gupta genealogy with the same inaccuracies. The differences in the genealogy on these plates from that met with on the Gupta records are: it begins with king Ghaṭotkacha, instead of his father Gupta as is the case with the genealogy met with in the Gupta epigraphs (with the exception of the Supia pillar inscription of the time of Skandagupta, No. 32), the use of the title *mahārāja* for Chandragupta I and Samudragupta in the Rithpur inscription (No. 84) instead of their usual title *mahārājādhirāja*; and application of some epithets[90] to Chandragupta II, which in the Gupta epigraphs are mentioned for Samudragupta. If the matter of the Poona copperplate would have been drafted by an officer of the Guptas, as Altekar infers from the use of the nail-headed Gupta script, then inaccuracies relating to genealogy should not have been there. It may also be stated that some inscriptions, for example the Eran stone inscription of Samudragupta (No. 2), and the Vidiśā inscription of the time of Chandragupta II, dated year 82 (No. 7), are in box-headed characters, but no scholar has suggested in their case that the scribe was a Vākāṭaka official. Most of the Vākāṭaka scribes would have been versed in box-headed script in which most of the records of that dynasty are written; a few of them, however, would have been versed in the nail-headed script which was popular in north India. Vākāṭaka queen, Prabhāvatīguptā, being a Gupta princess, would have been more at home with the nail-headed script, and the use of this script in Poona copperplate during her regency is understandable. An important evidence in favour of Gupta influence on the Vākāṭakas is furnished by the Ramtek Prabhāvatī Memorial stone inscription (No. 85). It refers to Chandragupta II as 'bearing the burden of the great kingdom of the Vākāṭakas' and also as 'lord of the three seas' *(tri-samudra-nātha)* which suggests his great influence verging on 'political hegemony' over the Vākāṭakas in that period.[91] According to the view of some scholars, it provides the evidence that Ghaṭotkachagupta, a son of Chandragupta II, married a Vākāṭaka princess, who most probably was a daughter of Prabhāvatīguptā. This matrimonial alliance would have been arranged with a view to cementing the friendly relation between the two families.

Probably it was under the influence of the Vaishṇava Gupta ruler Chandragupta II and his daughter, Prabhāvatīguptā, that her husband, the Vākāṭaka king Rudrasena II, gave up his Śaiva faith which he had inherited from his ancestors, and became a Vaishṇava. On his death, which took place soon after his fifth regnal year (the date known from his Mandhal grant),[92] Prabhāvatīguptā acted as regent of her minor sons, Dāmodarasena and Pravarasena, for about twenty years, and during that period the Gupta influence on the Vākāṭaka administration would have increased.[93] After Pravarasena I who had the title *samrāṭ*, all the Vākāṭaka rulers bore the title *mahārāja*. The use of the higher title of *mahārājādhirāja* for some of the Gupta rulers, and of the lower title *mahārāja* for the Vākāṭaka rulers in the epigraphs of the latter is taken by some to indicate that the Vākāṭaka rulers had subordinate status in relation to the Guptas. R C Majumdar opines that the Vākāṭaka state for some period '... was an appendage to, if not vassal of, the Gupta empire'.[94]

A S Altekar[95] supposes that Chandragupta II visited the Vākāṭaka capital on the death of Rudrasena II to offer condolences to his bereaved daughter, advised her to act as regent of her minor son Divākarasena and assured her of his help, administrative as well as military. He also suggests that he made arrangement for the education of the Vākāṭaka princes and refers to the tradition according to which Pravarasena of Kuntala (identified by some with the homonym Vākāṭaka prince) composed the poem *Setu-bandha* under the guidance of Kālidāsa.[96] Similar is the view of P L Gupta[97] who adds that the Sanakānīka *mahārāja* of the Udaigiri inscription (No. 7) and Vīrasena Śāba of another inscription from the same site (No. 11) and Āmrakārddava of the Sanchi inscripion (No. 9) were deputed by Chandragupta II to the Vākāṭaka court and stayed there for some time to provide guidance and help to the minor Vākāṭaka princes. The Gupta king would have been much concerned about his daughter and grandsons, yet the presence of these officials in eastern Malwa, as stated above, is better explained in the context of Chandragupta II's campaign against the Śakas, which is well-documented. U N Roy[98] suggests that Chandragupta II perhaps saved Prabhāvatīguptā from committing *satī*, and brought her to Pāṭaliputra, just as Harsha saved his widowed sister Rājyaśrī from committing *satī* in the Vindhyan forest and took her with him. He further states that as the Pushpabhūti king Prabhākaravardhana brought the two sons of the Later Gupta king Mahāsenagupta to his capital, Chandragupta II brought to his capital the minor sons of Prabhāvatīguptā. This highly speculative reconstruction of history, is not supported by evidence.[99] There is no evidence to show that Prabhāvatīguptā wanted to commit *sati*. The news of the death of the Vākāṭaka king would have taken some days to reach Chandragupta II, and his journey to the Vākāṭaka capital, if it was at all made, would have taken a number of days. If Prabhāvatiguptā wanted to commit *satī* she would have done so, much before Chandragupta II could have reached the Vākāṭaka capital. As regards the minor sons of Prabhāvatīguptā, they stayed in the Vākāṭaka capital and ruled one after the other under the regency of Prabhāvatīguptā, and there is a tradition that Chandragupta II made arrangement for the education of the minor princes at the Vākāṭaka capital itself. It has been suggested that Rudrasena II Vākāṭaka fought the Śakas as an ally of his father-in-law, Chandragupta II and lost his life in the battle.[100] If this is accepted, though there is nothing to substantiate it, then one may suggest that the Gupta king could have visited the Vākāṭaka capital when the war was over, as it was located not far from the Śaka territory.

An inscription of Naravarman from Mandasor (No. 60) mentions the following Mālava rulers in genealogical and chronological order—Jayavarman, Siṁhavarman, and Naravarman. The Gangdhar inscription (No. 62) refers to Naravarman's son, Viśvavarman, and the latter is mentioned as the father of Bandhuvarman in the Mandasor inscription of the silk-weavers' guild (No. 38), bearing two dates in Mālava era—493 and 529. S R Goyal considers all the four kings as feudatories of the Guptas, and ruling from the middle of the fourth century to the middle of the fifth century AD. The expression *siṁha-vikrānta-gāmin* for Naravarman has been interpreted by Bhandarkar as follower of 'Siṁhavikrānta', whom he identifies with Chandragupta II, one of whose titles is *siṁhavikrama*.[101] But it has been pointed out that *gāmin* means 'gait', and not 'follower' for which *anugāmin* should have been used,[102] and that *Siṁha–vikrānta* and *siṁha-vikrama* do not mean the same. According to P L Gupta,[103] Bandhuvarman was the first Mālava ruler who accepted Gupta suzerainty. The use of the Mālava era, and not Gupta era, by these rulers is taken by some as an evidence in favour of their being independent rulers. However, this evidence does not necessarily lead to such a conclusion, as even Bandhuvarman, who, without doubt, was a Gupta feudatory, uses the Mālava era, and not the Gupta era.

The Talgunda inscription of the Kadamba Kākusthavarman (No. 91) mentions that the daughter of that king was married to a Gupta prince, and some scholars[104] identify the Kadamba princess and Gupta prince with Anantadevī and Kumāragupta I respectively. In the *Auchitya-vichāra-charchā* of Kshemendra,[105] it is stated that Vikramāditya sent Kālidāsa as a *dūta* to Kuntala, and in it a *śloka* has been cited from the *Kuntaleśvara-dautya* of Kālidāsa, which work is now not available. A verse from this work has been cited in the *Śṛiṅgāra-prakāśa* and *Sarasvatī-kaṇṭhābharaṇa* of Bhoja[106] and in the *Kāvya-mīmāṁsā* of Rājaśekhara,[107] which says that the Kuntala king, entrusting administration to Vikramāditya, indulged in luxuries and easy life, enjoying wine and women. Some scholars[108] believe that Chandragupta II sent Kālidāsa to the court of the Kadamba king, Bhagīratha (AD 380-420). U N Roy[109] holds that it is such a relationship with the Kadamba king that is responsible for the statement in the Mehrauli pillar inscription that the fame of Chandragupta II reached the southern seas.

Mirashi, on the basis of a legend, identifies Kuntaleśvara with the Rāshṭrakūṭa king, Devarāja of Mānapura.[110] According to the commentary *Rāmasetu-pradīpa* on the *Setubandha*, the work was revised by Kālidāsa at the instance of Vikramāditya. Altekar opines that Chandragupta II sent Kālidāsa to the Vākāṭaka court to train his daughter's sons, and Ramtek which was within the Vākāṭaka territory is identified by him with Rāmagiri mentioned in Kālidāsa's *Meghadūtam*.[111] S Krishnaswami Aiyangar is of the view that the marriage of Prabhāvatīguptā with Rudrasena II, not only brought the Vākāṭakas under the influence of the Guptas, but also under their administrative control.[112] He places Kuntala in the south-western portion of the former Nizam's dominions.[113] According to him, it was incorporated in the Vākāṭaka dominion by Pṛithvīsheṇa I, and since the region formed the most important part of the kingdom of Rudrasena II, he was called Kuntaleśa, and his son, Pravarasena II too came to be designated as such. Some scholars do not identify Kuntaleśa with Pravarasena II. They opine that according to the verse, Vikramāditya reacted to the Kuntala king's desire to enjoy life with wine and women by conveying to him that he may indulge in such acts of enjoyment, and he (the Gupta king) would take care of the administration of his kingdom, which he would not have done in case the ruler was his daughter's son, as he would not have liked his near and dear relative to be spoilt by women and wine. A few scholars[114] identify Pravarasena with the homonym of the Wasim branch of the Vākāṭakas. Ashvini Agrawal points out that the information in the Balaghat inscription of Pṛithivīsheṇa II Vākāṭaka that his father Narendrasena married the daughter of the lord of Kuntala, goes against identifying Kuntaleśvara with Vākāṭaka Pravarasena II.[115]

Some scholars take the statement in the Mehrauli pillar inscription that the southern seas were 'fragrant with the breeze of King Chandra's prowess' to mean that Chandragupta II made conquests in south India. Jagannath[116] considers the expression *kṛitsna-pṛithvī-jaya* in the Udaigiri inscription (No. 11) as 'undoubtedly synonymous with *digvijaya*', implying a military undertaking of a magnitude greater than the mere conquest of the Śakas. The *Vishṇu-purāṇa,* according to one manuscript, mentions Devarakshita[117] as one who extended his kingdom to Kosala (south Kosala), Oḍra, Puṇḍra, Tāmralipti and Purī. Devarakshita has been identified by some[118] with Chandragupta II who is referred to as Devarāja in his Sanchi inscription (No. 9) and Devagupta in a Vākāṭaka inscription (No. 83).[119] D R Bhandarkar,[120] too, believes that Chandragupta II made some conquests in south India. Ashvini Agrawal points out that the Kurud grant of King Narendra shows the Gupta suzerainty over Kosala.[121] Some scholars, however, doubt his making conquests in south India. According to one scholar, in contrast to the Allahabad pillar inscription of Samudragupta (No.1), which details the territories and the kings of Dakshiṇāpatha conquered by him, the expression 'southern seas were fragrant with the breeze of the king Chandra's (i.e. Chandragupta II's) valour' in the Mehrauli pillar inscription (No. 12) looks like a conventional hyperbolic tribute paid to the king.[122]

A Gutta (Gupta) family with a number of kings ruled for a fairly long period in Guttal, Dharwar district, Karnataka. The members of this family are referred to as descendants of the 'supreme lord of Ujjayinī, the best of towns' (*Ujjayinī-puravar=ādhīśvara*) and 'supreme lord of Pāṭali (i.e., Pāṭaliputra), the best of towns' (*Pāṭali-puravar=ādhīśvara*), and as descended through Vikramāditya, king of Ujjayinī.[123] Some scholars opine that Pāṭaliputra was situated too far eastwards of the Gupta empire to provide an adequate control over the vast Gupta empire, and so Ujjayinī, located in a relatively central place of the Gupta empire and being a centre of trade, religion and culture, was made a second Gupta capital.[124] There is a view that after about AD 402, Chandragupta II resided in Malwa, first at Vidiśā and later at Ujjain.[125]

The *Rāja-taraṅgiṇī*[126] refers to King Vikramāditya, with second name as Harsha, staying at Ujjayinī, who was a destroyer of the Śakas and who installed poet Mātṛigupta as king of Kashmir. After the death of his patron, Mātṛigupta is said to have abdicated in favour of Pravarasena II. It has been pointed out that in that work there is no mention of Kālidāsa, although Bhāravi, Vākpati and many other poets have been referred to in it. D R Bhandarkar,[127] following Bhau Daji, opines that it is Kālidāsa (literally 'servant of Kālī') who has been referred to as Mātṛigupta ('protected by Mother', i.e. Kālī). According to the same scholar,[128] Pravarasena Vākāṭaka's rule in Kashmir is supported by the find of coins bearing the name Pravarasena in 'Gupta' characters. The date of the coins and the identification of the king suggested by Bhandarkar, have not been accepted by scholars. The two works of Kālidāsa, *Vikram=orvaśīyam* and *Kumāra-sambhavam*, it has been suggested, may have been named after Chandragupta II Vikramāditya and Kumāragupta I, respectively. Some scholars consider Raghu's victory over the Hūṇas mentioned in the *Raghuvaṁśam* of Kālidāsa as reflecting the situation of the Gupta age. As stated above, some identify Kālidāsa with one who was sent by Vikramāditya as an ambassador to the court of Pravarasena Vākāṭaka, where he wrote *Kuntaleśvara-dautya*, and Pravarasena II composed *Setubandha* under his guidance.

V

The inscription on a stone horse found in a village Nagawa near Vārāṇasī, was read as *Chaṁdragu...*, and was taken as the Prākrit form of the name Chandragupta.[129] The horse, it was suggested, is a replica of the sacrificial horse of Chandragupta II. The reading however was found as faulty,[130] and as such its evidence not sufficient to conclude that Chandragupta II performed a horse-sacrifice. U N Roy[131] is a staunch believer that Chandragupta II performed a horse-sacrifice. He argues that if Pushyamitra Śuṅga, the conqueror of the Yavanas, could perform two horse-sacrifices, then Chandragupta II, who conquered the Kushāṇas (Roy identifies the Vāhlīkas of the Mehrauli inscription with them) and Śakas, must have performed at least one horse-sacrifice. The performance of the horse-sacrifice, by a monarch, however, is not necessarily related to the status of kings he defeated, or the number of conquests he made. Some great conquerors in ancient India are not known to have performed horse-sacrifice, while some kings who hardly made any significant conquests are known to have performed that sacrifice. Mādhavavarman of the Vishṇukuṇḍin dynasty was not a mighty king or a great conqueror, yet he is stated to have performed as many as eleven *aśvamedhas*.[132] So, it is not the capability of Chandragupta II's performing the horse-sacrifice that is in doubt, but the lack of evidence in this regard that goes against the view of Roy. Moreover it can be argued that if he would have performed horse-sacrifice, it being deemed as a significant achievement, would have found mention in his epigraphs as also in those of his successors detailing genealogy, as they mention such an achievement in the case of Samudragupta, and that like Samudragupta, he might have issued coins to commemorate the event. Altekar believes that Chandragupta II did not perform any horse-sacrifice. It is, however, difficult to agree with the reason he gives for his not performing *aśvamedha* despite his being a great conqueror, viz., that he was a devout Vaishṇava, and *ahiṁsā* is an important tenet of Vaishṇavism,[133] as Vaishṇava kings are known to have performed *aśvamedha* (Appendix II). Recently, some copper coins bearing the device of horse on one side, and *garuḍa* and the legend *Vikramaḥ* on the other, have been found in Bangladesh, which have been taken by some scholars as issued by Chandragupta II to mark his celebration of the horse-sacrifice.[134] But the fact that they are of copper, and not of gold, raises doubt about their genuineness: for all the Aśvamedha-type of coins of Samudragupta and Kumāragupta I are only in gold.

In the Poona (No. 62) and the Rithpur (No. 84) copperplate inscriptions of Prabhāvatīguptā, Chandragupta II has been given the appellations–*pṛithivyām=apratirathaḥ* ('one who has no rival on earth') and *sarva-rāj=ochchhettā* ('exterminator of all kings'). The Poona plates in addition have *chatur=udadhi-salil=āsvādita-yaśaḥ* ('whose fame has tasted the water of the four oceans'). These epithets are identical with those used for Samudragupta, as met with in his Nālandā copperplate inscription (No. 3), in one of the Mathurā pillar inscriptions of Chandragupta (No. 10) and in the Bilsad pillar inscription of Kumāragupta I (No. 14). Of these epithets, *sarva-rāj=ochchhettā* is also met with on the coins of Kācha, as seen above (Chapter 4). The above-mentioned two Vākāṭaka plates also refer to Chandragupta II as *aneka-go-hiraṇya-koṭi-sahasra-pradaḥ* (giver of thousands of crores of cows and gold [coins]), which is similar to *aneka-*

*go-hiraṇya-koṭi-pradaḥ* of the Allahabad pillar inscription (No. 1) mentioned with reference to Samudragupta. Either the epithets of Samudragupta were deliberately applied by the composers of the text of these plates to Chandragupta II with a view to glorifying the father of the Vākāṭaka queen, Prabhāvatīguptā, or it was the result of inadvertent carelessness on the part of the scribe.

In the *Raghuvaṁśam* of Kālidāsa,[135] amongst the kings present in the *svayṁvara* of Indumatī, the name of king of Magadha is mentioned first; and it is stated that "although there were kings by thousands, the earth was said to be under good rule through him alone".[136] The king of Magadha has been taken by some scholars as referring to Chandragupta II.[137] Certain officials of Chandragupta II find mention in the epigraphs. Vīrasena, who held the office of *sachiva* hereditarily (*anvaya-prāpta-sāchivya*) and was the Minister of Peace and War, is known from his undated inscription from Udaigiri (No. 11). S R Goyal,[138] on the basis of common name-ending, suggests that he probably was a son of Harisheṇa, a high official of Samudragupta (No. 1) and perhaps father of Anantasena, an officer of Kumāragupta I (No. 35). Śikharasvāmin, a brāhmaṇa of Aśvavājī *gotra*, is referred to in the Karamdanda inscription of Kumāragupta I (No. 20) as Chandragupta II's *mantrī* and *kumārāmātya*. Āmrakārddava was Chandragupta II's general (No. 9), *Mahārāja* Trikamala[139] was his feudatory in the Gaya region, and *Mahārāja* Viśvāmitrasvāmin[140] held the same status in the Besnagar region. A Sanakānīka *Mahārāja*, known from Udaigiri inscription of GE 82 (No. 7), owed allegiance to him. Svāmidāsa was a feudatory in Madhya Pradesh.[141] Chandragupta II's son, *Mahārāja* Govindagupta was his governor, probably at Vaiśālī (No. 13). A few *kumārāmātya* sealings have been found from Vaiśālī,[142] but they do not give any idea as to which kings' reign they belonged. Though himself a devout Vaishṇava, it appears that his Minister for Peace and War, Vīrasena, was a Śaiva (No. 11), his general Āmrakārddava, a Buddhist (No. 9), and his feudatory, the Sanakānīka *Mahārāja* (No. 7), a Vaishṇava, if the acts of charity and piety made by them were in favour of the divinity whom they worshipped.

The Chinese pilgrim, Fa-hien, came to India after crossing the Gobi desert, Khotan, the Pamir, Swat and Gandhāra, and stayed in this country between AD 400 and 410, when Chandragupta II was ruling, though he does not mention the name of the Gupta king. He visited several centres of Buddhism, and wrote about various aspects of the life of the people. He speaks of the people of Madhyadeśa as enjoying peace and prosperity.[143]

According to him, punishments were light, and there was no capital punishments, which provides a contrast to the administration of Chandragupta Maurya and Harsha in whose reign capital punishment for severe crimes was not uncommon.[144] While Hiuen-tsang, who stayed in India from *c* AD 629 to 645, is known to have faced dacoits twice, Fa-hien does not mention his ever facing them.

## VI

Chandragupta II has been referred to as *Śrīvikrama* on coins of the Archer and Couch types, *Siṁhavikrama, Narendrasiṁha, Siṁhachandra* and *Narendrachandra* on Lion-slayer type, *Ajitavikrama* on Horseman type, *Vikramāditya* ('puissant like the sun' or 'striding like the sun') on *Chhatra* type, on some silver coins of *Garuḍa* type and on copper coins, and *Vikramāṅka* on some silver coins of *Garuḍa* type.[145] The Udaigiri inscription of Vīrasena (No. 11) compares Chandragupta II with *arka,* which is a synonym of *āditya,* which forms the second half of the composite title of the Gupta rulers, such as *Vikramāditya* (Chandragupta II), *Mahendrāditya* (Kumāragupta I), *Kramāditya* (Skandagupta), *Bālāditya* (Narasiṁhagupta), etc. Chandragupta II is referred to as *Vikramāṅka* in the same way as Samudragupta is referred to as *Parākramāṅka*. Some scholars consider Chandragupta II as the originator of the *Vikramāditya* legend. Literary evidence for the title *Vikramāditya* is traced to the *Bṛihatkathā* of Guṇāḍhya (*c* first or second century AD), written in Paiśāchī, and Hāla's *Gāhāsattasaī* (*Gāthāsaptaśatī*) written in *c* first century BC.[146] The *Bṛihatkathā* has not been found but *Bṛhatkathāmañjarī* of Kshemendra (eleventh century AD) and *Kathā-saritsāgara* of Somadeva (eleventh century AD) are based on it, though they may also contain some matter which was not in the *Bṛihatkathā*.

The era known as the Vikrama era was founded in 57 BC. Taking *Vikramāditya* as an historical personality ruling in the first century BC, as has been done by some scholars,[147] has certain drawbacks. The purāṇas, which give accounts of the succession of different dynasties from King Parīkshita to the Gupta dynasty, do not mention any king with the name Vikramāditya. No king of the Kāṇva dynasty, which ruled from *c* 75 BC to c 30 BC, within which falls the date of the founding of the era known as Vikrama era, bears this title. The universal sovereignty (*chakravartī*) ascribed to Vikramāditya, could hardly have been enjoyed by the chief of the

Mālavas, who till about the third century AD, were still in the Rajasthan region, rather than in Malwa. No king is known to history as the uprooter of the Śakas in the first century BC. The Western Śakas ruled uninterruptedly from the *c* first century AD to *c* AD 400 when they were uprooted by Chandragupta II *Vikramāditya*. Of the nine luminaries, who according to tradition graced the court of Vikramāditya, Amarasiṁha and Kālidāsa, were most probably contemporary of Chandragupta II. Varāhamihira may be placed in the sixth century AD. Dhanvantari, Kshapaṇaka, Śaṅku, Vetālabhaṭṭa, Ghaṭakarapara and Vararuchi, cannot be dated; even their historicity is doubtful.

There are some similarities between what has been ascribed to Vikramāditya of the legend and Chandragupta II Vikramāditya. *Vikramāditya* of the legend was lord of Mālava, destroyer of the Śakas (Śakāri) and is known for *vetāla-sādhana* (propitiating vampires). Mālava formed an important part of the empire of Chandragupta II *Vikramāditya*;[148] he is known to have uprooted the Śakas, and there is literary and epigraphic reference to his resorting to the propitiation of vampires. The *Devī-Chandraguptam* mentions it, and the Sanjan copperplate of Rāshṭrakūṭa Amoghavarsha (No. 92) and Cambay copperplates of the Rāshṭrakūṭa king Govinda IV (No. 89) refer to it in relation to a Gupta ruler, who, as the context shows, is to be taken as identical with Chandragupta II. In an inscription of the Guttas (Guptas) from Guttal, Vikramāditya is mentioned as lord of Ujjayinī and Pāṭaliputra and as one who has mastered *ashṭa-siddhis* (eight great supernatural powers) and ruled over the *vetālas* (vampires). In the *Bṛihatkathāmañjarī*, Vikramāditya is said to have married a Nāga princess,[149] and one of the queens of Chandragupta II *Vikramāditya*, Kuberanāgā, was a Nāga princess. Vikramāditya of the legend is mentioned as avenger of insult to womanhood, and Chandragupta II is known to have avenged the insult to Dhruvasvāminī. The legendary Vikramāditya is said to have been a patron of art, literature and science, and all these thrived well in the time of Chandragupta II.

The *saṁvat* founded in 57 BC came to be known as Vikrama *saṁvat* from a late period and its earliest mention is in a ninth century epigraph.[150] From the fifth to the eighth century, it was known as the Mālava era, and before that as the Kṛita era. The first date that can be referred to the Gupta era is met with in the Chandragupta II's Mathurā stone pillar inscription (though in it the era has not been specified as Gupta era), and though most of the scholars give credit for the founding of the Gupta era to Chandragupta I, there are a few scholars who believe that it was Chandragupta II who founded that era, but counted the first year from AD 319—the date of accession of Chandragupta I (Appendix IV). Thus Chandragupta II 'has a better claim than any other sovereign to be regarded as the original of the mythical king Vikramāditya'.[151] Some scholars suggest that the Vikramāditya legend did not have its origin only in the achievements of Chandragupta II, but can be traced in the combined achievements of the Gupta kings,[152] more particularly Samudragupta, Chandragupta II and Skandagupta. Thus, Vikramāditya's influence on the islands (*dvīpas*) mentioned in the *Kathāsaritsāgara* and the *Bṛihatkathāmañjarī* reminds of Samudragupta's influence on them (*Saiṁhalak=ādibhiścha sarvvadvīpa-vāsibhiḥ* in the Allahabad pillar inscription). While the literature refers to the charitable quality of Vikramāditya, the Allahabad pillar inscription mentions the huge amount of gold and large number of cows offered by Samudragupta in charity. According to the *Kathā-saritsāgara*, Vikramāditya, son of Mahendrāditya, conquered the Hūṇas and the *mlechchhas*. Skandagupta, who had the title *Vikramāditya* (though his most common title was *Kramāditya*), and was the son of Kumāragupta I Mahendrāditya, is known to have conquered the Hūṇas (No. 33). R C Majumdar says that from such acts of the Gupta kings, 'developed slowly and gradually the complete cycle of legends out of which posterity built up the complete figure of a single Vikramāditya who was repository of all kingly power and virtues, conqueror of the Śakas, founder of an era, and patron of men of letters....'[153]

Chandragupta II's *Chhattra* type of coins may be taken as conveying his claim to the sovereignty; it emphasizes the high stature of the king by depicting the umbrella-bearer as quite short in size in his comparison to the figure of the king.[154] The Archer type was meant to convey that he was a skillful archer. The device and legend on the coins of Lion-slayer type reflects his personal valour, and perhaps were issued after his conquest of Gujarat, which till date is the most important habitat of lions in India.[155] The Couch type reflects his artistic temperament. The *Chakravikrama* type shows his receiving *prasāda* from Chakrapurusha, who, in certain works, is described as Vishṇu himself.[156] The three objects that he is shown receiving are taken as *mantra-śakti* (counselling), *utsāha-śakti* (energy), and *prabhu-śakti* (authority), as suggested by Altekar.[157] The coin may be interpreted as Chandragupta II, desirous of becoming a *chakravartī*, receiving blessings from Chakraprusha; the *Ahirbudhnya-saṁhitā* prescribes worship of Vishṇu in the form of *Chakra* by one who is desirous of becoming a *chakravartī.*[158] This interpretation is quite appropriate, yet there is another suggestion that the three objects symbolize *dama, tyāga* and *apramāda,* which in the Besnagar inscription of Bhāgavata (Vaishṇava) Heliodorus,[159] and also in the *Mahābhārata,*[160] have been mentioned as the three *amṛita-padas* (immortal steps) that lead to heaven, and hence appropriate for a *parama-bhāgavata* king to receive them from Chakrapurusha. Mention may also be made of the interpretation[161] that they represent the three worlds conferred on the king by Vishṇu (the allusion being to the Trivikrama form of Vishṇu).

The Udaigiri inscription (No. 11) significantly refers to Chandragupta II as *Rājarshi.* He has been identified with *Rājarshi* Devagupta of the Gupta family as mentioned in the *Kuvalayamālā* composed in Śaka 700 (= AD 778) by Udyotanasūri.[162] Devagupta also occurs as a name of Chandragupta II in the Chammak copperplate inscription of Pravarasena II Vākāṭaka (No. 83), of which the form Devarāja is met with in the Sanchi inscription of Chandragupta II (No 9), and *Deva-Śrī* of coins and Hunza inscriptions (Appendix III). *Deva* (god) may have been intended to suggest divinity of king. Chandragupta II's main title is *Vikramāditya* and *Vikrama* is also another name of Vishṇu. In the Standard type of coins of Chandragupta II, he has been referred to as conqueror of *tridiva* (three worlds).[163] Vishṇu's three steps have been referred to in the *Ṛigveda,*[164] and he is known for his three steps in his Vāmana incarnation, and the reference to the king as conqueror of *tridiva* might have been intended to project the Gupta king as Vishṇu.

Chandragupta II seems to have been a man of fine literary taste and his poetic talent, according to tradition, had been tested by an assembly of learned men at Ujjain.[165] According to the account of Fa-hien, who came to India during his reign, people were happy and prosperous. V A Smith opines that 'India has never been governed better 'after the oriental manner' than under Chandragupta II.[166] In the opinion of A L Basham,[167] in Chandragupta's reign people in India were more happy and civilized than anywhere in the world.[168]

## NOTES AND REFERENCES

1. As read by D C Sircar, *Select Inscriptions*, I, p. 277.
2. As read by D R Bhandarkar, *Corpus Inscriptionum Indicarum*, III, p. 240.

3. A S Altekar, *The Coinage of the Gupta Empire*, p. 90ff.
4. A few coins generally ascribed to Chandragupta II are taken by some scholars as issues of Chandragupta I, but nothing can be said with certainty in this regard (see above). A coin in Bamnala (Nimar district) hoard bears on the obverse an impression from Samudragupta's coin-die, and on the reverse from the Archer type of Chandragupta II with his usual epithet *Śrī-Vikramaḥ* (Diskalkar, *Journal of the Numismatic Society of India*, V(ii), p. 136; Altekar, *The Coinage of the Gupta Empire*, pp. 44-45; S R Goyal, *Journal of the Numismatic Society of India*, XXVII (ii), pp. 142-45). This appears due to the coin-manufacturer inadvertently using a obverse die of Samudragupta for the coin of Chandragupta II. It is less likely that Samudragupta adopted the title *Vikrama* along with *Parākrama*.
5. For example, S R Goyal, *The Imperial Guptas*, p. 254; Ashvini Agrawal, *Rise and Fall of the Imperial Guptas*, p. 35. From the fact that the work does not refer to Raghu's defeat of Śaka king, it has been inferred that Chandragupta II achieved this victory over the Śaka king after the composition of the work. In all probability, it is Chandragupta II who has been referred to as Vikramāditya and the Lord of Pāṭaliputra in the inscriptions of the Guttas of Dharwar (below).
6. D B Diskalkar, *Annals of the Bhandarkar Oriental Research Institute*, XVIII, p. 169.
7. P L Gupta, *The Imperial Guptas*, p. 298.
8. See also D R Bhandarkar, *Corpus Inscriptionum Indicarum*, III, p. 64.
9. V A Smith, *Early History of India*, p. 292.
10. S K Maity, *Economic Life of Northern India in the Gupta Period*, pp. 135ff.
11. For examples of such marriages, see R G Basak, *The History of North-Eastern India*, pp. 9-10.
12. V A Smith, *Journal of the Royal Asiatic Society of Great Britain and Ireland*, 1914, p. 325.
13. *Ibid.*, pp. 325-26.
14. P L Gupta, *The Imperial Guptas*, p. 302.
15. *The Imperial Guptas and their Times*, p. 38.
16. S R Goyal, *The Imperial Guptas*, pp. 274-75.
17. *Epigraphia Indica*, VIII, pp. 42ff.
18. S R Goyal, *The Imperial Guptas*, pp. 275-76.
19. The marriage of Chandragupta II with the Nāga princess would have been arranged by Samudragupta, who, it may be argued, was keen to conqueror the Śakas, but because of some circumstances was not able to do so. This assumption is based on the fact that Prabhāvatīguptā born of Kuberanāgā was marrired to the Vākāṭaka prince in *c.* AD 380, and at that time her age would have been about 18 years and her mother's marriage would have taken place in about AD 362, when Samudragupta was ruling. It is therefore difficult to agree with the view of P L Gupta (*Gupta Sāmrājya*, p. 296) that Chandragupta II's marriage with Kuberanāgā took place during his own reign.
20. For example, U N Roy, *Gupta Rājavaṁśa tathtā Usakā Yuga*, p. 662, n. 2.
21. U N Roy, *ibid.*, p. 226.

22. The possibility of his visiting Sanchi as a devout Buddhist on pilgrimage cannot be entirely ruled out, as he is known to have made donations there in favour of the Buddhist *saṅgha* (No. 9).
23. R C Majumdar, in *Comprehensive History of India*, III(i), p. 53.
24. H C Raychaudhuri, *Political History of Ancient India*, p. 490.
25. *Gupta Empire*, 47.
26. S R Goyal, *The Imperial Guptas*, p. 286.
27. P L Gupta, *The Imperial Guptas*, pp. 302-303.
28. *Kāvya-mīmāṁsā*, Chapter X, p. 143.
29. S R Goyal, *Imperial Guptas*, p. 260.
30. P L Gupta, *The Imperial Guptas*, p. 302.
31. *Archaeological Survey of India—Annual Report*, 1913-14, p. 245.
32. *Catalogue of Sanchi Archaeological Museum*, pp. 61ff.
33. *Indian Archaeology* 1954-55—*A Review*, p. 63.
34. P L Gupta, *The Imperial Guptas*, p. 308, n 34; *Gupta Sāmrājya*, p. 291, n. 34.
35. R C Majumdar, in *Comprehensive History of India*, III(i), p. 54.
36. H C Raychaudhari, *Political History of Ancient India*, p. 466.
37. R C Majumdar, in *Comprehensive History of India*, III(i), p. 54.
38. R C Majumdar (ed.), *The Classical Age*, Preface, p. xli.
39. R N Dandekar, *A History of the Guptas*, p. 85.
40. J Allan, *Catalogue of the Coins of the Gupta Dynasties, and of Śaśāṅka, the King of Gauḍa, in the British Museum, London*, pp. 49-50.
41. D R Bhandarkar, *Corpus Inscriptionum Indicarum*, III, p. 54.
42. A S Altekar, *The Coinage of the Gupta Empire*, p. 150.
43. S R Goyal, *The Imperial Guptas*, p. 286.
44. S R Goyal, *The Imperial Guptas*, p. 301.
45. Frederick M Asher, in *Essays on Gupta Culture*, ed. by Bardwell, L Smith, p. 56.
46. S R Goyal, *Gupta Sāmrājya kā Itihāsa*, p. 211.
47. S K Maity, *The Imperial Guptas and their Times*, p. 40.
48. R C Majumdar, in *The Vākāṭaka-Gupta Age*, p. 167.
49. S R Goyal, *The Imperial Guptas*, p. 286.
50. P L Gupta, *The Imperial Guptas*, p. 314, and 322n. He bases this on coins bearing the name Sarvabhaṭṭāraka. Earlier such coins had been ascribed by Cunningham to Bhaṭārka, king of the Maitraka dynasty.
51. S R Goyal (*The Imperial Guptas*, p. 261).also does not agree with Gupta.
52. D R Bhandarkar, *Corpus Inscriptionum Indicarum*, III, p. 58.
53. *Ibid.*
54. S K Aiyangar, *Ancient India and South Indian History and Culture*, I, p. 204.
55. R Bhandarkar, *ibid.*, p. 56.
56. *Ibid.*, p. 60.
57. S K Aiyangar, *Ancient India and South Indian History and Culture*, I, p. 195.
58. R C Majumdar, in *Comprehensive History of India*, III(i), p. 56.
59. *Rāmāyaṇa*, IV. 43. 12, as referred to by D R Bhandarkar, *Corpus Inscriptionum Indicarum*, III, p. 87.

60. *Rāmāyaṇa*, IV. 12. 6, as referred to by D R Bhandarkar, *Corpus Inscriptionum Indicarum*, III, p. 87.
61. On Pāṇini, VIII. 4. 9; see V S Agrawala, *Paṇinikālīna Bhāratavarsha*, p. 125.
62. D R Bhandarkar, *Corpus Inscriptionum Indicarum*, III, p. 57.
63. *Catalogue of the Coins of the Gupta Dynasties, and of Śaśāṅka, the King of Gauḍa, in the British Museum, London*, p. xxxvi.
64. *New Indian Antiquary*, I, p. 198.
65. W W Tarn, *The Greeks in Bactria and India*, p. 125.
66. R C Majumdar, *Journal of the Royal Asiatic Society of Great Britain and Ireland*, IX, pp. 179ff; in *Comprehensive History of India*, III(i), p. 55.
67. K P Jayaswal, *Journal of the Bihar and Orissa Research Society*, XVIII, p. 32.
68. V C Pandey, *Vishveshvaranand Indological Journal*, XII, p. 245.
69. Ashvini Agrawal, *Rise and Fall of the Imperial Guptas*, pp. 164-65.
70. J W McCrindle, *Ancient India as Described by Ptolemy*, p. 33.
71. *Raghuvaṁśam* of Kālidāsa, IV. 68.
72. R C Majumdar, *Journal of the Royal Asiatic Society of Bengal (L)*, IX, pp. 179, n. 6.
73. D C Sircar, in S M Katare and P K Gode (ed.), *A Volume of Studies in Indology, Presented to P V Kane*, pp. 469-71. He disagrees with the view that Vāhlika was in Punjab.
74. *Advanced History of India*, p. 190.
75. *Ibid.*
76. *Epigraphia Indica*, XXI, p. 3.
77. In *Comprehensive History of India*, III(i), p. 57.
78. *Dr Mirashi Felicitation Volume* (ed. G T Deshpande *et al*), pp. 355ff, on p. 358.
79. V C Pandey, *Vishveshvaranand Indological Journal*, XII, p. 241.
80. U N Roy, *Gupta Rājavaṁśa tathā Usakā Yuga*, p. 232.
81. See V C Pandey and Anup Pandey, *New History of Ancient India*, p. 390.
82. S R Goyal states "...the occurrence of the Gupta genealogy and *gotra* in the Vākāṭaka grants may easily be attributed to the custom current in the Vākāṭaka territory where queens usually introduced themselves with reference to their paternal family" (*The Imperial Guptas*, pp. 279-80).
83. Ashvini Agrawal (*Rise and Fall of the Imperial Guptas*, p. 83) interprets the text in the Vākāṭaka plates to indicate that Dhāraṇa was the *gotra* of Kuberanāgā, the mother of Prabhāvatī.
84. A S Altekar, in *The Vākāṭaka-Gupta Age*, pp. 111-12; *The Coinage of the Gupta Empire*, p. 5.
85. S R Goyal, *The Imperial Guptas*, p. 279.
86. A S Altekar, in *The Vākāṭaka-Gupta Age*, p. 112, n. 1.
87. S R Goyal, *The Imperial Guptas*, p. 279.
88. A S Altekar, in *The Vākāṭaka-Gupta Age*, p. 112, n. 1.
89. A S Altekar, in *ibid.*, p. 106.
90. For example, *nyāy=āgat=āneka–go-hiraṇya–koṭi-pradaḥ, sarva-rāj=ochchhettā, prithivyām= apratirathaḥ*, etc.

91. A M Shastri, *Vākāṭakas: Sources and History*, p. 128.
92. A M Shastri, *ibid.*, p. 43.
93. Earlier, Dāmodarasena and Pravarasena were considered by some scholars as two names of the same person, but the legend on the seal of recently found Moregaon (Bhandara district) plate (A M Shastri, *Vakāṭakas: Sources and History*, p. 70), mentioning Prabhāvatīguptā as mother of two kings, establishes that they were two different persons. She had a third son, Divākarasena who died as *yuvarāja*.]
94. R C Majumdar, *The Classical Age*, Preface, p. xliii. It is possible that Pravarasena I was called *samrāṭ* because among the Vākāṭaka kings, he alone had performed *vājapeya*, which according to the evidence of the scripture made one worthy of that title. Probably while the paramount sovereign in the Gupta dynasty came to be designated as *mahārājādhirāja*, in the Vākāṭaka dynasty, the rulers, even though independent, continued to be designated as *mahārāja*.
95. In *The Vākāṭaka-Gupta Age*, p. 111.
96. *Ibid.*, p. 112.
97. P L Gupta, *The Imperial Guptas*, p. 303.
98. U N Roy, *Gupta Rājavaṁśa tathā Usakā Yuga*, p. 662, n. 2.
99. For criticism of U N Roy's view, see S R Goyal, *The Imperial Guptas*, p. 276, n. 3.
100. U N Roy, *Gupta Rājavaṁśa tathā Usakā Yuga*, p. 66, n. 2.
101. D R Bhandarkar, *Corpus Inscriptionum Indicarum*, III, pp. 66-67. According to J P Singh (*History and Coinage of Skandagupta Kramāditya*, p. 13, n. 10), he would have taken part in Chandragupta II's conquest of the Śakas.
102. K C Jain, *Malwa through the Ages*, pp. 251-52; Ashvini Agrawal, *Rise and Fall of the Imperial Guptas*, p. 262n.
103. P L Gupta, *The Imperial Guptas*, p. 311.
104. U N Roy, *Gupta Rājavaṁśa tathā Usakā Yuga*, p. 221.
105. D R Bhandarkar, *Corpus Inscriptionum Indicarum*, p. 175.
106. D R Bhandarkar, *ibid.*, pp. 174-75.
107. *Ibid.*
108. For example, K A N Sastri, in *The Vākāṭaka-Gupta Age*, pp. 239-40.
109. U N Roy, *Gupta Rājavaṁśa tathā Usakā Yuga*, p. 223.
110. Mirashi, *Studies in Indology*, I, pp. 10-11.
111. A S Altekar, in *The Vākāṭaka-Gupta Age*, p. 112.
112. S K Aiyangar, *Ancient India and South Indian History and Culture*, I, p. 173.
113. S K Aiyangar, *ibid.*, I, p. 271; *Journal of Indian History*, VI, p. 54.
114. For example, S R Goyal, *Gupta Sāmrājya kā Itihāsa*, p. 210.
115. *Rise and Fall of the Imperial Guptas*, p. 170.
116. *Journal of Indian History*, XIX, p. 162.
117. F E Pargiter, *Dynasties of the Kali Age*, pp. 73-74. It mentions in plural (Devarakshitas) suggesting that people and not an individual is meant.
118. For example, Dasharatha Sharma, *Indian Historical Quarterly*, XXX, p. 377.

119. J P Singh (*History and Coinage of Skandagupta Kramāditya*, p. 12, n.6) rejects the identification for, he says, unlike the *Ārya-Mañjuśrī-mūlakalpa*, the purāṇas do not mention kings with pseudonames.
120. D R Bhandarkar, *Corpus Inscriptionum Indicarum*, III, p. 62.
121. *Rise and Fall of the Imperial Guptas*, p. 165.
122. V C Pandey, in B Ch Chhabra *et al.* (ed.), *Reappraising Gupta History for S R Goyal*, p. 162.
123. D R Bhandarkar, *Corpus Inscriptionum Indicarum*, III, pp. 61-62, and n. 2 on p. 51.
124. For example, D R Bhandarkar, *ibid*.
125. K C Jain, *Malwa through the Ages*, p. 236.
126. A. Stein's trans., intro. pp. 83-84.
127. D R Bhandarkar, *Corpus Inscriptionum Indicarum*, III, pp. 68-69.
128. D R Bhandarkar, *ibid*.
129. J Ratnakar, *Indian Historical Quarterly*, III, p. 719 ff.; see also R C Majumdar in *The Vākāṭaka-Gupta Age*, p. 169, n. 1; H C Raychaudhuri, *Political History of Ancient India*, p. 490, n 2.
130. R C Majumdar, *The Vākāṭaka-Gupta Age*, p. 169, n. 1.
131. U N Roy, *Gupta Rājavaṁśa tathā Usakā Yuga*, pp. 235-36.
132. *Vide* D R Bhandarkar, *Corpus Inscriptionum Indicarum*, III, p. 38; he gives references to the performance of the horse sacrifices by the feudatories in ancient and modern times (*ibid*., p. 39).
133. A S Altekar, *The Coinage of the Gupta Empire*, p. 90. R B Singh (*Gupta Sāmrājya*, p. 33), for the same reason, asserts that Kumāragupta I (even though he issued Aśvamedha type of coins), could not have performed the horse-sacrifice. If Chandragupta II could attack and conquer the Śakas which must have caused much bloodshed, then he could as well have performed horse-sacrifice, if he so desired. For the Vaishṇava king Bhāgavata Sarvatāta is mentioned in Ghosundi inscription (D C Sircar, *Select Inscriptions*, I, pp. 90-91) as the performer of the horse-sacrifice. Even kings like Khāravela, following Jaina faith, which lays great emphasis on *ahiṁsā*, are known to have fought several wars involving much bloodshed, and according to Jayaswal's reading and interpretation of a line in the Hathigumpha inscription (*ibid*., pp, 213ff) also performed horse-sacrifice. Moreover there is great possibility that Samudragupta too most probably was a Vaishṇava (though he has not been referred as *parama-bhāgavata* in epigraphs, except in the Nālandā and Gaya copperplates, which are not original ones), but there is no doubt that he performed horse-sacrifice.
134. Nicholos Rhodes and Ujjwal Saha, Two Copper Aśvamedha Coins of Chandra Gupta II (c AD 380-414), *Newsletter of the Indian Institute of Research in Numismatic Studies*, LI, p. 6.
135. *Raghuvaṁśam*, VI. 22.
136. D R Bhandarkar, *Corpus Inscriptionum Indicarum*, III, p. 70.
137. H C Raychaudhuri, *Political History of Ancient India*, p. 489; D R Bhandarkar, *Corpus Inscriptionum Indicarum*, III, p. 70.

138. S R Goyal, *Gupta Sāmrājya kā Itihāsa*, p. 220.
139. *Archaeological Survey of India—Annual Report*, 1922-23, p. 169.
140. *Archaeological Survey of India—Annual Report*, 1914-15, p. 81.
141. *Epigraphia Indica*, XV, p. 289.
142. K K Thaplyal, *Studies in Ancient Indian Seals*, pp. 103ff.
143. J H Legge, *Records of the Buddhist Kingdoms*, Chapter XVI.
144. U N Ghoshal, in *Classical Age*, p. 351.
145. See also H C Raychaudhuri, *Political History of Ancient India*, p. 491, n. 2.
146. *Vide* S R Goyal, *The Imperial Guptas*, p. 364.
147. For example, R B Pandey, *Vikramāditya of Ujjayinī*, Banaras, 1951. p. 1ff. Vikramāditya has also variously been identified with Gautamīputra Sātakarṇi, Kanishka and Yaśodharman. Kanishka founded the Śaka era in 78 AD, but he did not bear *Vikramāditya* title. Gautamīputra Sātakarṇi defeated Śaka king Nahapāna, and hence could be called Śakāri, but he ruled in the second century AD and neither founded any era nor bore the title *Vikramāditya*. Yaśodharman flourished in the first half of the sixth century; he defeated the Hūṇas, not the Śakas, founded no era, and did not bear the title *Vikramāditya*.
148. As seen above, some scholars opine that Chandragupta II made Ujjain his second capital.
149. *Vikramāditya Volume*, p. 175.
150. The Dhinki copperplate inscription of VS 794 (Bühler, *Indian Antiquary*, XII, pp. 155ff), which mentions the era, is regarded as spurious, and therefore the Dhaulpur inscription of Chāhamāna Chaṇḍa Mahāsena, dated VS 898, is the earliest epigraph dated in that era.
151. V A Smith, *Early History of India*, p. 290.
152. For example, S R Goyal, *The Imperial Guptas*, pp. 367ff; R C Majumdar, in *Comprehensive History of India*, III(i), pp. 54-55.
153. R C Majumdar, in *Comprehensive History of India*, III(i), p. 55. U P Shah (*Journal of the Oriental Institute*, IV, pp. 69ff) refers to the account of Mālavendra Śrī Vikramārka-nṛipa in the *Jyotividābharaṇa*, which mentions nine jewels, including Kālidāsa, in Vikramāditya's court and also his founding an era. The king is referred to as terror to Lāṭa, Gurjara, Dhāra, and Kamboja. Kamboja and Vāhlīkas have been used as *dvandva*-compound in the *Mahābhārata*, indicating their contiguity, and J C Vidyalankar identified Kamboja with Badakhshan and Pamir. Further, in this text, Vikramāditya is said to have conquered the Śaka ruler of Rummadeśa, and brought him to Ujjayinī. Rummadeśa is taken as Romā, i.e. Salt Range. There is, however, no reference in this work to the victory over the Western Kshatrapa Śaka king unless it is assumed that he fought jointly with and under the leadership of the king of Rummadeśa, which on its face does not seem to be the case. The evidence is a mixture of history and legend and cannot be relied for historical reconstruction.
154. R C Majumdar, in *The Classical Age*, p. 22.
155. R K Mookerji, *Gupta Empire*, p. 55.

156. C Sivaramamurti, *Journal of the Numismatic Society of India*, XIII, p. 182; A S Altekar, *The Coinage of the Gupta Empire*, 149.
157. A S Altekar, *The Coinage of the Gupta Empire*, p. 149.
158. See S R Goyal, *The Imperial Guptas*, p. 166.
159. D C Sircar, *Select Inscriptions*, I, pp. 88-89, at p. 89; See also Rajwant Rao, *Journal of the Numismatic Society of India*, LXIX, p. 109. H H Dwivedi is of the opinion that the three round objects symbolize the three *lokas* (see *ibid*.)
160. V. 43. 22, *vide* D C Sircar, *Select Inscriptions*, I, p. 89, n. 5.
161. V S Pathak and V B Rao, in M C Joshi and S K Gupta (ed.), *King Chandra and the Mehrauli Pillar*, p. 193.
162. A M Shastri, *Proceedings of the Indian History Congress*, 1965, pp. 110-11.
163. A S Altekar, *The Coinage of the Gupta Empire*, pp. 93ff.
164. *Ṛigveda*, I. 22. 17, *idaṁ Vishṇur=vichakrame tredhā-nidadhe padam*.
165. *Kāvya-mīmāṁsā* of Rajaśekhara, Chapter X, p. 143.
166. *Early History of India*, p. 298.
167. *The Wonder that was India*, p. 66.
168. S R Goyal (*Gupta Sāmrājya kā Itihāsa*, pp. 215ff) criticizes Chandragupta II for not pursuing the policy of vigorous conquests of his father. He holds that the fame of that Gupta king mainly rests on the growing of the legend around Vikramāditya which is his title. In his view, the exploits of King Chandra of the Mehrauli pillar inscription should be ascribed not to Chandragupta II, as is generally done, but to Samudragupta. This, as A M Shastri (in B Ch Chhabra *et al.* (ed.), *Reappraising Gupta History for S R Goyal*, p. 8.) points out, smacks of his partiality towards Samudragupta, and does not do justice to Chandragupta II.

# 8

# Govindagupta: Controversies Galore

Govindagupta is known from two sources—a Vaiśālī sealing (No. 29) and a Mandasor inscription (No. 36). The sealing bears the device of a segent lion and a four-line legend:

1. *Mahārājādhirāja-Śrī-Chandragupta-*
2. *patnī mahārāja-Śrī-Govindagupta-*
3. *mātā Mahādevī-Śrī-Dhruva-*
4. *svāminī.*[1]

The sealing belongs not to Govindagupta but to *Mahādevī* Dhruvasvāminī who has been referred to as 'wife of *Mahārājādhirāja* Chandragupta and mother of *Mahārāja* Govindagupta'. The Mandasor inscription dated Mālava era 524, i.e., AD 467 (No. 36), neither belongs to Govindagupta nor was meant for him. It refers to King Prabhākara's general, Dattabhaṭa, whose father Vāyurakshita had been a general of Govindagupta, son of *Mahārājādhirāja* Chandragupta II. The inscription eulogizes Chandragupta II and Govindagupta and refers to the latter as one of whom Indra was afraid, thinking that Govindagupta would attack him. S K Maity is not correct in stating that the information regarding Govindagupta is found in the Mandasor inscription of year AD 472.[2] Palaeographically, the Vaiśālī sealing and the Mandasor inscription are datable to the Gupta period and in both of these, Govindagupta has been mentioned as the son of Chandragupta, and therefore, Govindagupta of the two must refer to one and the same Gupta prince, and thus there is no room for Dandekar's statement in his *A History of the Guptas,*[3] that 'Govindagupta was *presumably* a scion of the Imperial Gupta dynasty...' (Italics for emphasis), In fact, in the same work he refers to the above mentioned Vaiśālī sealing of Dhruvasvāminī in which *Mahārājādhirāja* Chandragupta[II] and *Mahādevī* Dhruvasvāminī are mentioned as parents of *Mahārāja* Govindagupta.[4]

There is hardly any such enigmatic personality in Indian history as Govindagupta, about whose existence, career, status and date, there is much difference of opinion amongst scholars. As will be seen below, a few scholars[5] identified Govindagupta with Kumāragupta I, while most of the scholars rightly consider the two as different persons. Some scholars[6] take him to be the elder brother of Kumāragupta I, while others[7] consider him as the younger brother of that king. We concur with the former view and feel that in the Vaiśālī sealing, Dhruvasvāminī has been referred to as the 'mother of Govindagupta' as he was the eldest of her children. It is a fairly common practice in present times to refer to women as mother of the eldest child (after its name), and similar would have been the case in ancient times. Govindagupta has been mentioned as *mahārāja* in the Vaishali sealing, which title in the Gupta period generally denoted either a feudal lord or a governor, while the paramount sovereign had come to be designated as *mahārājādhirāja*. Since Govindagupta was not a feudatory but a prince, he should be taken as a governor at the time of the issuing of the seal, and since the sealing referring to him as *mahārāja* has been found at Vaiśāli, most of the scholars opine that he was the governor of Tīrabhukti with its headquarters at Vaiśālī. This may be the case, though the find of the sealing at Vaiśāli cannot be taken as a definite evidence for such a conclusion, as Dhruvasvāminī's sealed letter could as well have been dispatched to that city from outside, and addressed even to someone other than Govindagupta. It has been suggested that at the time of the seal Chandragupta II was alive, for if he would have been dead the Dhruvadevī would have been mentioned as mother of the ruling king (*rājamātā*).[8]

The evidence of the Mandasor inscription (No. 36) is taken by some scholars as indicative of Govindagupta's having served as a governor of the Malwa region. Some scholars hold that he was earlier governor of Vaiśālī, and later that of the Mandasor region,[9] and according to others,[10] it was *vice versa*. As regards his tenure as governor of Vaiśālī, it is argued that he held that office under his father, Chandragupta II. But regarding his governorship of Mandasor, some consider that he held that office under his father, while others, who believe that the assignment at Mandasor was later than that of Vaiśālī. hold that he served there as governor of his brother, Kumāragupta I.[11] However, his serving as a governor of Kumāragupta I is negated by the indirect evidence of the Mandasor inscription of Prabhākara, which eulogizes Chandragupta II and Govindagupta, but does not make even a passing reference to Kumāragupta I. If Kumāragupta I would have been the ruling king, and Govindagupta his governor, then the former would have been eulogized, at least mentioned, in that epigraph. According to S K Maity,[12] Govindagupta was a governor of Kumāragupta at Mandasor; he revolted and for sometime became king in that region, but was defeated and got replaced by Kumāragupta's son, Ghaṭotkachagupta. But the Vākāṭaka inscription from Ramtek (No. 85) clearly shows that Ghaṭotkachagupta was a brother, and not a son, of Kumāragupta I as was believed by Maity and some other scholars, and it was he, rather than Govindagupta who seems to have revolted against that Gupta king, as will be seen in Chapter 9.

The Mandasor inscription (No. 36) mentions Vivudhādhipa being suspicious of Govindagupta's power. Vivudhādhipa means Indra, and taking it as the same as Mahendra, which is the title of Kumāragupta I, it has been suggested that the intention was to convey that he was suspicious of Govindagupta's power.[13] References to kings as superior to Indra and other gods are not uncommon in literature and epigraphs. Vāyurakshita was the general of Govindagupta, It has been argued that from the inscriptions it is known that the Mālava region during the Gupta rule was administered by the local feudatory rulers, and Prabhākara, whom Dattabhaṭa served as general, himself was a local feudatory of the Guptas, there is hardly any place for Govindagupta's holding the office of governor.[14]

Some scholars are of the view that the eulogies of the type mentioned in the Mandasor inscription for Govindagupta do not apply to kings alone, but could as well be for one who was a governor or a feudal lord.[15] For instance, *Mahārāja* Harivarman Maukhari, though a feudatory, has been eulogized as one 'whose fame had crossed the four oceans',[16] and Bandhuvarman, a Gupta feudatory, too, is likewise highly praised in a

Mandasor inscription (No. 38). It has also been suggested that the expression *tatpād=ānudhyāta* used for Kumāragupta with reference to his father Chandragupta II, suggests that he was the immediate successor of his father. However, the expression does not necessarily convey that sense. Of those scholars who take Govindagupta as elder brother of Kumāragupta I, some suggest that he could not become king as he predeceased his father, while others, are of the view that he ruled as a king.

From the fact that Dhruvasvāminī in the Vaiśālī sealing has been referred to as *Govindagupta-mātā* (mother of Govindagupta), some scholars infer that the Gupta prince was a minor when he was serving as governor, and his mother acted as his regent. S K Aiyangar suggests that Govindagupta as a minor held that office during the absence of Kumāragupta I who was the heir-apparent and governor of Vaiśālī.[17] But it is difficult to accept the view that Govindagupta was then a minor, for if that would have been the case, then some high level experienced officer would have been deputed as regent to guide and help him in administration, rather than the queen mother Dhruvasvāminī. She would hardly have afforded being away from the capital for a long period, as her presence there in the capacity of chief queen would have been a must in performing religious ceremonies and rituals with her husband, and in formal royal functions. The sealing of Dhruvasvāminī, in our view, would have been affixed on some correspondence made by her from Pāṭaliputra, with someone at Vaiśālī, may be with Govindagupta himself, if he were, as he seems to have been, a governor with headquarters at Vaiśālī.

There are some scholars who doubt Govindagupta's ruling as king, and also some who feel that the evidence at hand is not sufficient enough to either accept or reject the view that he ruled as king.[18] Of the scholars who believe that Govindagupta ruled as king, some suggest that his accession to the throne might have been peaceful and also that he ruled over the whole of the Gupta territory, while others opine that he revolted and declared himself king in the Malwa region, while Kumāragupta I anointed himself king at Pāṭaliputra.

Those who take Govindagupta as one who ruled as king, hold different views regarding the date of his accession, and he has been variously placed as immediately after Chandragupta II in *c.* AD 412, or after Kumāragupta I in *c* AD 455, or after Skandagupta in *c* AD 467. No coin of Govindagupta has been found. While the Vaiśālī sealing and the Mandasor inscription refer to Govindagupta as son of Chandragupta II and Dhruvasvāminī, the Gupta epigraphs detailing genealogy mention Kumāragupta as son of

Chandragupta II and Dhruvadevī (= Dhruvasvāminī), and do not mention the name of Govindagupta. This, together with the absence of Govindagupta's coins, led some scholars to take Govindagupta and Kumāragupta I as identical. D R Bhandarkar[19] opines that the original name of the prince was Govindagupta, but after his great success in battles, he was identified with God Kumāra, and was named Kumāragupta after that deity. This, however, is proved wrong by the irrefutable evidence of the Mandasor inscription. This inscription, which is an official record, was engraved in AD 467, about 12 years after the death of Kumāragupta I in *c.* AD 455, and it gives the name of the Gupta prince as Govindagupta, and not as Kumāragupta, which should have been the case if the name had been changed from Govindagupta to Kumāragupta I. D R Bhandarkar[20] puts forth another ingenuous, though highly speculative interpretation of the numismatic evidence in favour of identifying Govindagupta and Kumāragupta I. He points out that the letters *ku* and *go* appear on some coins bearing the name Kumāragupta and the title *Kramāditya*, and should be taken as standing for Kumāragupta and Govindagupta respectively, and the two should be taken as one and the same person who issued such coins. The view, however, cannot be accepted for the following reasons: (i) On no coin of ancient India, the same king has been referred to by two names, (ii) The coin-type referred to by D R Bhandarkar actually belongs, not to Kumāragupta I, but to Kumāragupta II, and (iii) that the letter *go* also appears on the coins of some other kings,[21] and should therefore, not be taken as the initial of the secondary royal name.[22]

The absence of Govindagupta's name in the genealogies may be because they mostly mention father-to-son succession, and omit the names of collaterals.[23] The absence of coins of Govindagupta may be because he had a very short rule and, and as such, might not have issued any coins, or issued only a few ones, which have not been discovered so far. Purugupta's coins have not been found though there is no doubt that he ruled as a king. The explanation of R K Choudhury[24] for the absence of Govindagupta's coins, viz., that Kumāragupta I, because of his bitter relation with him recalled all the coins issued by that king, with a view to removing traces of his reign, is not acceptable. For the first, it is not known for certain that the relationship between the two brothers was extremely strained, and secondly, to recall all such coins would have been an extremely arduous task to be undertaken, particularly in those days when modern means of communication and transport were not available. There is no evidence in ancient India of any king recalling the coins of any predecessor.

II

From the reference in the Vaiśālī sealing to Dhruvasvāminī as wife of *Mahārājādhirāja* Chandragupta and the mother of *Mahārāja* Govindagupta, Bhandarkar[25] infers that Govindagupta held the office of *yuvarāja*. He writes: 'For in the seal of a queen, it is natural to expect the name of the husband, and her son, who is heir-apparent to the throne'.[26] The same is the view of Jagannath,[27] who opines that in the seal legend, the titles appear with a strict official accuracy, and in a formal tone, and Dhruvasvāminī mentioned herself as mother of Govindagupta because he was *yuvarāja*. He[28] rejects the possibility of that queen not giving the name of Kumāragupta I even though he was the elder son, either because of her greater affection for Govindagupta or because of her strained relation with Kumāragupta I, as she would not have liked to make such feelings public.

According to D R Bhandarkar,[29] Vaiśālī was deemed as a specially significant seat of administration, as it had been the capital of the Lichchhavi state before its amalgamation in the Gupta empire as a result of the marriage of Chandragupta I with the Lichchhavi princess Kumāradevī, which contributed immensely to the rise of his power. As such, it was placed under the administration of a *yuvarāja*, and during the rule of Chandragupta II, Govindagupta governed the province in that capacity. Bhandarkar first presumes that Govindagupta was a *yuvarāja*, and then, since he is given the title of *mahārāja* on the sealing, assumes that a *yuvarāja* had the status of a *mahārāja*.[30]

But there is difficulty in accepting the view that the evidence of the Vaiśālī sealing should be taken to mean that Govindagupta was a *yuvaṛāja*. The office of the *yuvarāja* was distinct and in a way more important than that of the *mahārāja* (feudatory or governor), and while in any given time, there would have been several *mahārājas* during the rule of a king of the Gupta dynasty, there could be only one *yuvarāja*, who normally would succeed the king. If Govindagupta had been a *yuvarāja*, he would have been referred to as such, as for example, the Vākāṭaka prince, Divākarasena, has been mentioned as *yuvarāja* in the seal attached to the Poona copperplate inscription (No. 82). Bhandarkar's opinion appears to be based on the fact that a few sealings bearing *yuvarāja* as part of the legend have been unearthed at Vaiśālī.[31] The legends on the sealings are: *yuvarāja-pādīya-kumārāmāty=ādhikaraṇasya*, i.e., 'office of the *kumārāmātya* attached to the *yuvarāja*', and *yuvarāja-bhaṭṭāraka-pādīya-kumārāmāty=ādhikaraṇasya*, 'office of the *kumārāmātya* attached to the *yuvarāja-bhaṭṭāraka*'.[32] Normally, the *yuvarāja* would have been stationed at the Gupta capital, Pāṭaliputra, where he was expected to help the king in administrative functions and discharging kingly duties when the king was absent from the capital on such business as leading military campaigns, or on long administrative tours, or when he fell seriously ill. In the view of this author, the seals referred to above found at Vaiśālī were affixed to the correspondence made by the office of *kumārāmātya* attached to the *yuvarāja* located at Pāṭaliputra and dispatched to some official located at Vaiśālī. A sealing unearthed at Vaiśālī belonged to the office of the *kumārāmātya* attached to the king,[33] which must have been affixed to a document dispatched by that official from the king's secretariat located at Pāṭaliputra. Thus the evidence provided by the contents of the legends on the seals found at Vaiśālī do not favour the view of D R Bhandarkar that all the seals originated in that city, and that the place where the seals (sealings) were found in large numbers was the factory office of the person who was solely entrusted with the manufacture of the seals.[34] That learned scholar also ignored the fact that some of the sealings bear string marks on their back side,[35] which provide definite proof of their having been affixed on letters and parcels, which had been dispatched to different offices, officials and private persons located at Vaiśālī. It may be stated that the *kumārāmātyas* were a class of *amātyas* who were granted certain privileges enjoyed by the royal princes (*kumāras*), and could variously be appointed as governors of provinces, heads of districts, or could be attached to kings, *yuvarājas*, or even high official like the one who was a *mahāśvapati-mahādaṇḍanāyaka*.[36] The Vaiśālī sealings referring to the *yuvarājas* are palaeographically datable to the Gupta period, but none of them bear the name of Govindagupta, for that matter of any prince; in fact, they do not bear any name. R K Mookerji states that on some Vaiśālī seals, Ghaṭotkachagupta has been referred to as a *kumārāmātya* and that the official would have been attached to Govindagupta, the governor of the Gupta province of Vaiśālī.[37] However, so far only one seal of Ghaṭotkachagupta is known, the one from Vaiśālī, and in the legend on it, he has not been designated as *kumārāmātya*; in fact, no official title has been attached to his name, only the honorific prefix *Śrī* is met with.

III

As regards the date for the rule of Govindagupta, there is no record of either Chandragupta II or Kumāragupta I for the period between AD 412—the last known date for Chandragupta II's rule from his Sanchi inscription (No. 9), and AD 415—the earliest date known for Kumāragupta I known from his Bilsad inscription (No. 14). Though it can be argued that Chandragupta II's rule could have continued to any time up to AD 415, or that Kumāragupta I's rule could have commenced any time in or after AD 412, yet with the evidence at hand, the rule of Govindgupta may very well be placed in between AD 412 and 415, as has been done by some scholars. We, however, do not agree with the argument put forth by R K Choudhury[38] to justify placing Govindagupta's rule within that period. He argues that unless we place Govindagupta in that period, viz. between 412 and 415, there would be a gap of three years in history, which would be inexplicable, as the throne could not have remained vacant. However, there are many such gaps in ancient Indian history, but that does not mean the throne remained vacant during such periods. In fact, there were hardly such gaps in history, but they appear so because of our lack of knowledge of the happenings relating to those periods. We prefer placing Govindagupta in that period, not only because there is a gap but also because with the evidence at hand, the rule of this Gupta prince fits in well in that gap.

Some scholars though believe that Govindagupta ruled as king, do not favour placing him between AD 412 and 415. R D Banerji[39] opines that Govindagupta asserted independence either immediately after the rule of Kumāragupta I or after the death of Skandagupta. According to R C Majumdar,[40] probably Govindagupta was a younger brother of Kumāragupta I, survived him, and rebelled against his nephew, Skandagupta, perhaps when the latter was fighting the Hūṇas, and might have declared himself king and ruled for a short period. This, in his opinion, would be in consonance with the repeated references to the threat to the family fortune (*vaṁśa-lakshmī*) in the Bhitari pillar inscription (No. 33) of Skandagupta. He argues that had Govindagupta ruled between AD 412 and 415, he would hardly have been remembered more than 50 years after his rule in AD 467 in the Mandasor inscription of Prabhākara (No. 36).[41] U N Roy[42] considers Govindagupta as ruling in AD 467 as he has been mentioned in the Mandasor inscription of that date. He argues that Govindagupta could not have been the eldest son of Chandragupta II, as then he would have been born within a couple of years after Chandragupta II's marriage with Dhruvasvāminī, the widow of Rāmagupta whom (the last-mentioned) he alienated in AD 376, and as such, it could be difficult to explain his acquiring the throne at the ripe old age of about 90. He further states that placing Govindagupta between AD 412 and 415 would mean two spells of his rule, which would be incongruous.[43] R N Dandekar[44] opines that the absence of the name of the ruling Gupta king in the Mandasor inscription of AD 467 suggests that Govindagupta severed his relations with the Imperial Guptas and 'immediately after the death of Skandagupta, ... refused to acknowledge the suzerainty of the Gupta emperor of Magadha'.

The above views of R D Banerji, R C Majumdar, R N Dandekar and U N Roy, as will be shown below, are not convincing. The Mandasor inscription eulogizes not only Govindagupta, but also his father Chandragupta II, and no scholar has inferred from this that the latter was ruling at that time. Govindagupta would very well have been born within a couple of years from AD 376 (the date of marriage of Chandragupta II and Dhruvasvāminī) and would have been about 35 years at the time of Chandragupta II's death in *c.* AD 412. Placing him after Kumāragupta I (*c* AD 455) would appear too late, as he would have been quite old at that time, almost an octogenarian, too loath to harbour a burning ambition to become the king by raising a banner of revolt against his relatively young, brave and dynamic nephew, Skandagupta. As even the date AD 455 is too late for the beginning of Govindagupta's rule, we need not discuss the above-mentioned view of scholars, according to which, his rule commenced after the end of the rule of Skandagupta in *c* AD 467. Much of the confusion regarding the date of Govindagupta's rule was because some scholars wrongly assumed that the Mandasor inscription of AD 467 (No. 36) refers to him as a reigning king. For example Dandekar labels that inscription as of 'Govindagupta and Prabhākara,'[45] which gives an impression as if Govindagupta was ruling in AD 467, and that would mean that his reign began after Skandagupta, whose last known is AD 467. R D Banerji[46] opines that Govindagupta was alive in AD 467, which is the date of the Mandasor inscription of Prabhākara, and either he did not acknowledge the suzerainty of Skandagupta, or the latter had died by then. But the inscription records the charitable acts of one Dattabhaṭa who mentions himself as a general of Prabhākara, and also informs that his father Vāyurakshita had been the general of Govindagupta. The 'use of the past perfect tense in narrating the happenings connected with Vāyurakshita, the general of Govindagupta, shows that both he and his master lived in the past'.[47] Thus, the evidence of the Mandasor inscription does not go against, and in fact indirectly favours Govindagupta's ruling between AD 412 and 415.

IV

Govindagupta's position as governor in the Mandasor region has to be reconciled with the rule of the local kings bearing *varman*-ending names, whose epigraphs have been found in Malwa. The rulers known are Jayavarman, Siṁhavarman, Naravarman (whose known date is ME 461, i.e., AD 404, as found in a Mandasor inscription (No. 60), Viśvavarman whose known date is ME 480, i.e., AD 423, as met with in the Gangadhar stone inscription (No. 62), and Bandhuvarman whose known date is ME 493, i.e., AD 436, as seen in a Mandasor inscription (No. 38). Bandhuvarman's overlord is mentioned as the Gupta king, Kumāragupta [I]. There is a difference of opinion as to whether other rulers were also feudatories of the Guptas, or they were independent. S R Goyal[48] opines that Chandragupta II had a hold over eastern Malwa, as is clear from his inscriptions at Sanchi (No. 9) and Udaigiri (Nos. 7, 11) and also on Gujarat region, as is evident from the numismatic evidence,[49] and so western Malwa, which lay in between these two regions, should also have been a part of his kingdom. P L Gupta[50] is of the opinion that the Varmans accepted the Gupta suzerainty sometime between AD 423—the date of the Gangdhar inscription of Viśvavarman (No. 62) which makes no mention of the then ruling Gupta king, and AD 436—the first of the two dates in the Mandasor inscription which mentions Bandhuvarman as a feudatory of his Gupta overlord. Jagannath[51] and P L Gupta[52] opine that there was no place for the viceroyalty of Govindagupta in the Mandasor region as it was ruled by the indigenous line of kings. D C Sircar,[53] however, points out that the Vākāṭaka kings are known to have appointed *senāpatis* in the capacity of viceroys over territories including *rājyas* under *rājās*. But the Gupta provinces were administered either by the governors or by the feudal lords; there is no evidence for joint administration of a prince and a feudal lord. Taking into consideration all the pieces of evidence and their interpretation for the reconstruction of the history of Govindagupta, the following possibilities may be suggested:

(i) Govindagupta was an elder brother of Kumāragupta I, and like him was born of the same mother, viz. Dhruvasvāminī (the form of name on her own sealing, but referred to as Dhruvadevī in Gupta epigraphs), and after the death of his father Chandragupta II, succeeded him in the natural course in AD 412 and ruled for a short period up to *c.* AD 415. He either died a natural death or was overthrown by Kumāragupta I.

(ii) Govindagupta might have been born of Rāmagupta (whose historicity is proved by literary, epigraphic and numismatic evidence, as seen in Chapter 6), and Dhruvasvāminī. The peculiar circumstances in which Chandragupta II-Dhruvasvāminī marriage took place have been detailed in Chapter 6, and need not be repeated. Chandragupta II, thus would be the stepfather of Govindagupta, and because of this relationship, Govindagupta is mentioned as the son of that king in the Mandasor inscription of AD 467. Govindagupta himself would have preferred to be called the son of Chandragupta II, rather than that of the discredited Rāmagupta.[54] Dhruvasvāminī would have possessed a charming and impressive personality, otherwise Chandragupta II would not have married her, the widow of his elder brother whom he had killed, as such a marriage would not have been deemed proper. She seems to have been an assertive and dominating lady, keen to preserve her separate identity as seen in her choice of lion as device for her seal, which, in all probability, was her paternal insignia, and certainly not the Imperial Gupta insignia which was *garuḍa*. Of all the queens of the Gupta dynasty, she is the only one whose seal has been found. She seems to have been the chief queen of Chandragupta II, although he had married Kuberanāgā many years before marrying her. Despite the fact that Kuberanāgā had at least three sons, most probably elder to those born of Dhruvadevī as per interpretation by some scholars of the evidence of the recently discovered Ramtek inscription (No. 85), yet it were sons born of the Dhruvasvāminī—Govindagupta and Kumāragupta,that succeeded as kings one after the other. S R Goyal[55] makes interesting comparison between Dhruvasvāminī, the Gupta queen, and Noorjahan, the Mughal queen. Noorjahan had great influence over Jahangir, who, because of his love for her, is said to have killed her husband and then married her. Dhruvasvāminī too seems to have exerted great influence over Chandragupta II, who had married her after killing her husband. In the Gupta epigraphs detailing genealogy, the chief-queen of Chandragupta II is invariably mentioned as Dhruvadevī, and not Dhruvasvāminī. We have the evidence of the queen of King Jayanātha of Uchchakalpa dynasty referred to as Muruṇḍasvāminī[56] and also as Muruṇḍadevī[57] in two different inscriptions. So Dhruvadevī and Dhruvasvāminī appear as identical, and one can suggest that the composers of the Gupta genealogies dropped *svāminī*-ending of the name and replaced it by *devī* as the names of all other queen ended in *devī*, and may be even because *svāminī*-ending smacks of Śaka type of name-ending (above, Chapter 7)

It seems that Dhruvasvāminī prevailed over Chandragupta II to grant Govindagupta all the privileges of a royal prince and as a result he was appointed governor (as can be inferred from his designation *mahārāja* in the Vaiśālī sealing), perhaps of the province with Vaiśālī as its headquarters. Kumāragupta I was born of Chandragupta II-Dhruvadevī/ Dhruvasvāminī wedlock, and projected himself as rightful claimant to the throne, for which he might have been supported by majority of ministers and other officials, and may be even by the king himself preferred him as his successor. Dattabhaṭa's inscription, referring to his father Vāyurakshita as general of Govindagupta, has been found at Mandasor, and it is quite likely that before becoming king, Govindagupta had been a governor of the Malwa region. Possibly, Kumāragupta I played some role in getting him transferred as a governor, from Vaiśālī to Mandasor. May be, he himself preferred to be away from the capital, Pāṭaliputra, to save himself from the cliques of Kumāragupta I and his supporters. Rāmagupta, most probably had been the governor of that region and had declared himself as king from there, as can be inferred from the fact that his coins, all in copper, have been found almost exclusively from that region. It appears that on the death of Chandragupta II, Kumāragupta I, who was staying at the capital, anointed himself as the king. The news of the death of Chandragupta II took some days to reach Govindagupta who was staying in Malwa. Envisaging that circumstances were not favourable in staking claims to the Gupta throne at Pāṭaliputra, Govindagupta declared himself as king in Malwa. The eulogy showered on him in the Mandasor inscription, referring to him as one to whose feet bowed the heads of several kings, and as one of whose power God Indra became suspicious, would go well in his capacity of a king.

But if it is accepted that western Malwa was under Varman rule, then Govindagupta might have been the governor of eastern Malwa, which, as seen above, was under the rule of the Guptas right from the time of Samudragupta. Rāmagupta's coins and a set of three epigraphs have come to light from that region. It appears that when Govindagupta declared himself independent in eastern Malwa, the then Varman ruler of western Malwa, whether independent or feudatory of the Guptas, being in close proximity of Govindagupta's territory, thought it wise to offer his allegiance to him. The eulogy of Govindagupta in the Mandasor inscription (western Malwa) would refer to that phase of his career when he was ruling as king. Govindagupta ruled for a short period (*c* AD 412-15) in the Malwa region, while Kumāragupta I ruled in the rest of the Gupta territory. Govindagupta either died a natural death, or was overthrown by Kumāragupta I. Jagannath[58] opines that the statement in the Tumain inscription (No. 19) referring to Kumāragupta I protecting the earth acquired by him by force as if she were his consort, is indicative of his dethroning Govindagupta forcibly. After the death of Govindagupta, the Varman ruler, either voluntarily or under force, shifted his allegiance to Kumāragupta I.[59]

The above reconstruction of history satisfactorily explains Dhruvasvāminī's being called 'mother of Govindagupta', Govindagupta being referred to as *mahārāja*, his status in relation to the Varman kings of Malwa, his being eulogized like a king in the Mandasor inscription, the paucity of his records, the absence of his coins, and the omission of his name in the Gupta genealogy.

## NOTES AND REFERENCES

1. T Bloch, *Archaeological Survey of India—Annual Report*, 1903-04, p. 107, pl. XLI.
2. S K Maity (*The Imperial Guptas and Their Times*, p. 51) states, 'A posthumous record of Mandasor of the year AD 472 (Mālava year 529) records that Indra was suspicious of the power of Govinda', i.e. Govindagupta. It is, however, stated in the Mandasor inscription of Prabhākara of AD 467 (Malava year 524), and not the Mandasor inscription of the year AD 472 which relates to the silk-weavers' guild. It may also be stated that there is no evidence to show that the Mandasor inscription of AD 472 is posthumous.
3. R N Dandekar, *A History of the Guptas*, p. 91. V S Agrawala (*Studies in Indian Art*, pp. 224-25) identifies this Gupta prince with Bhāgavata Govinda of a Deogarh inscription meaning "the gift of Bhāgavata Govinda at the holy feet of the lord

of Keśavapura". He refers to a fragmentary inscription of Chandragupta II from Katra Keshavadeva, Mathura, mentioning the construction of some temple by him, and suggests that Govindagupta got built a temple of Vishṇu after that Mathura temple. The mention of *bhāgavata* and not *parama-bhāgavata*, which is the designation used for the Gupta rulers, and the absence of any official title even that of the honorific *śrī*, makes the identification doubtful. Some scholars suggested that the identification of Govindagupta with Kṛishṇagupta of the Later Gupta dynasty. This is based mainly on the fact that the names Govinda and Kṛishṇa are synonymous and both are *gupta*-ending. It does not explain as to why in the Vaiśālī sealing and the Mandasor inscription he is referred to as Govindagupta and in the Later Gupta inscriptions as Kṛishṇagupta. More weighty reason for not accepting such identification is that there is much time lag between the Gupta prince and the scion of the Later Gupta dynasty; the former belonged to the first half of the fifth century and the latter to the first half of the sixth century AD.

4. R N Dandekar, *A History of the Guptas*, p. 91.
5. For example, D R Bhandarkar, *Corpus Inscriptionum Indicarum*, III, p. 72.
6. For example, Jagannath, *Indian Historical Quarterly*, XXII, p. 286; P L Gupta, *The Imperial Guptas*, p. 310.
7. For example, J Allan, *Catalogue of the Coins of the Gupta Dynasties, and of Śaśāṅka, the King of Gauḍa, in the British Museum, London*, p. xl; R C Majumdar, *Comprehensive History of India*, III (i), p. 64.
8. P L Gupta, *Imperial Guptas*, p. 313.
9. For example, S R Goyal, *Gupta Sāmrājya kā Itihāsa*, p. 251.
10. For example, D R Bhandarkar, *Corpus Inscriptionum Indicarum*, III, p. 79.
11. D C Sircar, *Select Inscriptions*, I, p. 407, n. 2; S R Goyal, *Gupta Sāmrājya kā Itihāsa*, p. 251. R C Majumdar, in *The Vākāṭaka-Gupta Age*, p. 174.
12. *The Imperial Guptas and their Times*, 51-52.
13. Jagannath, *Indian Historical Quarterly*, XXII, pp. 286ff.
14. *Proceedings of the Indian History Congress*, 1960, pp. 50ff.
15. D C Sircar, *Indian Historical Quarterly*, XXIV, p. 73.
16. K K Thaplyal, *Inscriptions of the Maukharis, Later Guptas, Puṣpabhūtis, and Yaśovarman of Kanauj*, pp. 147-50.
17. For example, S K Aiyangar, *Ancient India and South Indian History and Culture*, I, pp. 284-85; S R Goyal (*The Imperial Guptas*, p. 274) is of the view that Dhruvasvāminī meddled in the administration of Vaiśālī.
18. S R Goyal, *Gupta Sāmrājya*, pp. 151-52.
19. D R Bhandarkar, *Corpus Inscriptionum Indicarum*, III, p. 73.
20. *Ibid.*, p. 73.
21. J Allan, *Catalogue of the Coins of the Gupta Dynasties, and of Śaśāṅka, the King of Gauḍa, in the British Museum, London*, pp. 137-39; R C Majumdar, in *Comprehensive History of India*, III(i), p. 65.
22. *Indian Historical Quarterly*, XIX, p. 125.

23. To cite a well-known instance, Kumāragupta II's seal (No. 55) traces the genealogy from Kumāragupta I through Purugupta, omitting Skandagupta, whose rule is so well-attested by several epigraphs and coins pertaining to him.
24. *Journal of the Oriental Institute*, Baroda, XII, p. 375.
25. *Indian Antiquary*, 1912, p. 3.
26. *Ibid.*
27. *Indian Culture*, XII, p. 168.
28. *Ibid.*
29. *Corpus Inscriptionum Indicarum*, III, p. 72.
30. *Ibid.*, p. 254n.
31. D R Bhandarkar, *Corpus Inscriptionum Indicarum*, III, p. 72.
32. *Archaeological Survey of India—Annual Report*, 1903-04, p. 107.
33. The legend is *parama-bhaṭṭāraka-pādīya-kumārāmāty=ādhikaraṇasya* (*Archaeological Survey of India—Annual Report*, 1903-04, p. 108, no. 8).
34. D R Bhandarkar, *Indian Antiquary*, 1912, p. 3.
35. *Archaeological Survey of India—Annual Report*, 1903-04, p. 101.
36. For a detailed discussion on the status and functions of the *kumārāmātya*s, see K K Thaplyal, *Sudies in Ancient Indian Seals*, pp. 103ff. R K Mookerji's translation (*Gupta Empire*, p. 48) of *kumārāmātya* of the seal legends as 'Chief minister', and Maity's as 'prince of royal blood' (*The Imperial Guptas and their Times*, p. 15) do not hold good.
37. *Gupta Empire*, p. 12.
38. *Journal of the Oriental Institute*, Baroda, XII, pp. 374-75.
39. R D Banerji, *The Age of the Imperial Guptas*, p. 51.
40. R C Majumdar, in *Comprehensive History of India*, III(i), p. 66.
41. *Ibid.*
42. *Rajbali Pandey Smriti Grantha*, pp. 179-80.
43. *Ibid.*, p. 180.
44. R N Dandekar, *A History of the Guptas*, pp. 119-20.
45. *A History of the Guptas*, p. 120. However, earlier Dandekar correctly says that the inscription records the meritorious acts of Dattabhaṭṭa, who was a general of Prabhākara and also that Dattabhaṭṭa's father, Vāyurakshita had been a general of Govindagupta.
46. R D Banerji, *The Age of the Imperial Guptas*, p. 50. On p. 66 of the same work, however, he says, 'It is not clear from the wording of this inscription whether Govindagupta was alive in VS 524 = AD 467 or not'.
47. Jagannath, *Indian Historical Quarterly*, XXII, p. 288.
48. S R Goyal, *Gupta Sāmrājya kā Itihāsa*, p. 215.
49. Altekar, *The Coinage of the Gupta Empire*, pp. 150ff.
50. P L Gupta, *The Imperial Guptas*, pp. 310-11.
51. *Indian Historical Quarterly*, XXII, p. 287.
52. P L Gupta, *The Imperial Guptas*, I, p. 310.
53. *Indian Historical Quarterly*, XXIV, p. 73.

54. This suggestion was made by us in our article in *Indian Historical Review* (XXVII, pp. 41-60). S R Goyal (*The Imperial Guptas*, p. 311) finds this suggstion as 'fanciful.' He says that in the Mandasor inscription Govindagupta is called the son of Chandragupta II. This is not denied, and in fact this had been taken notice of. We had also suggested as to why Govindagupta could be called a son of Chandragupta II even though he would have been a son of Rāmagupta. It may be stated that we have not taken this as an established fact, but offered it as a suggestion, rather one of the suggestions.
55. S R Goyal, *Gupta Sāmrājya kā Itihāsa*, p. 226.
56. J F Fleet, *Corpus Inscriptionum Indicarum*, III, p. 136, *Muruṇḍa-svāminyām=utpanno Mahārāja-Śarvanāthaḥ.*
57. *Ibid.*, p. 137, *Muruṇḍadevyām=utpannaḥ Mahārāja – Śarvanāthaḥ.*
58. *Indian Historical Quarterly*, XXII, p. 289.
59. A third alternate suggestion, a remote one, may be that Dhruvasvāminī, who is mentioned as the mother of Govindagupta in a Vaiśālī sealing, was the widow of Rāmagupta and was different from Dhruvadevī, who is mentioned in the Gupta epigraphs detailing genealogy as mother of Kumāragupta I. The claim of Govindagupta, begotten on Dhruvasvāminī either by Rāmagupta or Chandragupta II, though elder, was challenged by Kumāragupta I, son of Chandragupta and Dhruvadevī. On Chandragupta II's death, Kumāragupta captured the throne at Pāṭaliputra. Govindagupta declared himself king in Malwa, where he was posted as governor. The reconstruction of history thereafter would be the same as suggested under the first alternative, above. However, the possibility of two queens of the same king with names Dhruvasvāminī and Dhruvadevi, is extremely rare. As mentioned above, there is an example of the queen of the Uchchalalpa king Jayanātha being referred to in one inscription as Muruṇḍadevī, and in another as Muruṇḍasvāminī.

# 9

# Kumāragupta I and Rebel Ghaṭotkachagupta

## I

A number of inscriptions, many of them dated, have been found for the reign of Kumāragupta I. Most of them refer to some religious or charitable acts related variously to Brahmanism, Buddhism and Jainism. The Bilsad (Etah district) inscription of GE 96 (No. 14) mentions the construction of a temple for Kārttikeya. The two Gaḍhwa (Allahabad district) stone inscriptions, one of GE 98 (No. 15), and another an undated one (No. 28), refer to donation of gold coins for the maintenance of a *sattra,* and for doling out alms, respectively. A Sanchi inscription of Gupta Era 131 informs of the permanent endowment of gold coins in favour of the Buddhist *saṁgha.* It does not mention the name of the king, but the date falls in the reign of Kumāragupta I.[1] An inscription from Udaigiri (Vidiśā district) of GE 106 (No. 16) refers to the installation of an image of Pārśvanātha, the Jaina Tīrthaṅkara. Three inscriptions are known from Mathurā, dated GE 107[2] (No. 17), GE 125 (No 23), and GE 135 (= AD 454).[3] The first one refers to the putting up of a Jina image by one Śyāmāḍhyā, and the second and the third, to the gift [of an image] each. The Mankuwar (Allahabad district) inscription of GE 109 (No. 27)[4] refers to the installing of a Buddha image by Buddhamitra,[5] and mentions Kumāragupta I as *mahārāja*, instead of *mahārājādhirāja*—his usual and appropriate title. The Kalaikuri-Sultanpur (Bogra district) copperplate inscription of GE 120 (No. 21), throws light on the administration of the *vīthi*, a subdivision of the district. The subdivisional officer was assisted by the *mahattaras*, Elders of the *vīthi*, and the *kuṭumbins*—the representatives of the householders, in carrying out administrative work. The Dhanaidaha (Rajshahi district, Bangladesh) copperplate of GE 113 (No. 18) is fragmentary, and though the name of the king is not preserved the date falls within the reign of Kumāragupta I. It records the gift of land in the Khādā(ṭa)pāra[6] *vishaya* to a brāhmaṇa. The two Damodarpur (Dinajpur district, Bangladesh) copperplates dated GE 124 (No. 22) and GE 128 (No. 24) respectively deal with the sale of land to a brāhmaṇa. The Baigram (Bogra district, Bangladesh) copperplate of GE 128 (No. 25) does not mention the name of the king, but the date falls within the reign of Kumāragupta I; it records the gift of land to a Vaishṇava temple (Govindasvāmī). The price of three *kulyavāpas* and two *droṇavāpas* of land is mentioned as six *dīnāras* and eight *rūpakas* respectively, at the rate of two *dīnāras* per *kulyavāpa*.[7] The Jagdishpur (Rajshahi district, Bangladesh) copperplate inscription (No. 26) is dated GE 128. The copperplate inscriptions, particularly those from Damodarpur, throw light on the administrative setup—the king in the centre of the administration, the *uparika* (governor) appointed by king as the head of the *bhukti* (province), and the *vishayapati* (head of district) appointed by the *uparika* in the *vishaya* (district), and also the presence and role of the advisory board in the district comprising representatives of the *kulikas* (artisans), *sārthavāhas* (caravan-merchants), *śreshṭhīs* (merchants-cum-bankers) and *kāyasthas* (scribes). These copperplate inscriptions throw light on the mode of sale and purchase of land as also the different rates of cultivable and fallow land. The application submitted for purchase of land was put up by the *pustapālas* before the representatives of the local bodies, and only after their approval was the sale allowed. The Tumain (Guna district, MP) inscription of GE 116 (No. 19) mentions the constructing of a Śaiva temple at Tumbavana (Tumain), and refers to prince Ghaṭotkachagupta administering the region. His relationship with Kumāragupta is not known from the epigraph because of its fragmentary nature, and hence some considered him as his son and others as his brother; but with the recently discovered Vākāṭaka record from Ramtek (No. 85) it is known for certain that the two were brothers. The Karamdanda (Faizabad district) inscription of GE 117 (No. 20) mentions the installation of a Śiva-*liṅga* of the name Pṛithvīśvara by one Pṛithvīsheṇa who was a *mantrī*, *kumārāmātya* and *balādhikṛita* of Kumāragupta I, and a son of *mantrī* and *kumārāmātya* Śikharasvāmī. The Mandasor (Mandasor district) inscription (No. 38) of the silk-weavers' guild bearing two dates, ME 493 (= 436) and ME 529 (= AD 472) shows that Bandhuvarman, a feudatory of Kumāragupta I, was administering the region around Mandasor in AD 436. It refers to the migration of the member of the silk-weavers' guild from Lāṭa to Mandasor, and the construction of a Sun temple by them, and later to its repair by the same guild in AD 472, in the reign of a later ruler, whose name is not mentioned.

Kumāragupta I issued the largest varieties (fourteen in number) of gold coins in the Gupta dynasty, and some of them are of great artistic merit. In the opinion of Dandekar, during his reign Gupta coinage 'reached the highest watermark in point of excellence and variety'.[8] His King-and-Queen type was issued after Chandragupta–Kumāradevī type, Tiger-slayer, *Aśvamedha* and *Vīṇāvādaka* (Lyrist) types after identical types of Samudragupta, and the Horse-rider, Archer, Lion-slayer and the *Chhatra* types after Chandragupta II. His original types are Swordsman, Elephant-rider, Elephant-rider-lion-slayer, Rhinoceros-slayer, Kārttikeya (or Peacock) and *Apratigha*. The repousse gold coins bearing the legend *Mahendrāditya* are considered by some scholars as issued by him;[9] others, however, do not agree with it.[10] He issued silver coins for western provinces in imitation of his father, Chandragupta II, who had based them on Śaka coins. Kumāragupta I was the first to introduce silver coins for the central provinces of the Gupta empire, which show the figure of a peacock, instead of *garuḍa* met with on the Imperial Gupta silver coins for the western province. His copper coins are extremely rare and some of them are silver-coated.[11]

Kumāragupta I is taken as identical with Mahendrāditya of the *Ārya-Mañjuśrī-mūlakalpa*, and Mahendrasena of the *Kathā-saritsāgara* and the *Chandra-garbha-paripṛichchhā*. The earliest date for Kumāragupta is AD 415, known from his Bilsad inscription (No. 14). The Eran inscription of Samudragupta (No. 2) refers to his sons and grandsons. Kumāragupta I and also Govindagupta, the grandsons of Samudragupta and sons of Chanadragupta II begotten on Dhruvadevī/Dhruvasvāminī, would not have been born during his reign, which must have ended a couple of years before AD 376, the date when Chandragupta II married Dhruvadevī after murdering Rāmagupta, his brother and her husband, who, as seen above, ruled for a short period. Chandragupta II, however, had by then children begotten on Kuberanāgā, whom he had married much earlier (Chapter 7). Kumāragupta I had at least two sons—Skandagupta, about whose mother's name there is controversy, as discussed in Chapter 10, and Purugupta, who was born of the chief-queen Anantadevī.[12] The Bihar stone inscription (No. 35), ascribed by different scholars variously to Skandagupta, Purugupta, Kumāragupta II and Budhagupta, refers to the marriage of Kumāragupta I with someone's sister, and mentions an officer by the name of Anantasena. On the basis of the similarity of name-ending, some scholars[13] suggest that Anantasena was a brother of Anantadevī. After the find of the Nālandā sealing of Budhagupta (No. 47), mentioning him as the son of Purugupta, the earlier view that he was the son of Kumāragupta I, no more stands. The view, it may be mentioned was based on Hiuen-tsang's statement that Buddhagupta (= Budhagupta) was a son of Śakrāditya, which means the same as Mahendrāditya—an *āditya* title of Kumāragupta I.[14] However, Kumāragupta I may be identical with Śakrāditya mentioned as the founder of one of the Nālandā *vihāras* in a Nālandā inscription.[15] The Ramtek inscription (No. 85) shows that Ghaṭotkachagupta (also known from the Tumain inscription, a Vaiśālī sealing and two gold coins) was a brother of Kumāragupta I, and not his son, as suggested earlier by some scholars. According to a bardic tradition, before becoming king, Kumāragupta had served as governor of Kathiawar.[16] On the basis of the title *rājādhirāja,* instead of his usual title *mahārājādhirāja*, on some silver coins of the western variety, Smith[17] considered them as issued by him in the capacity of a prince. However, this does not seem to be the case, as there is no evidence of a Gupta prince issuing coins, and the title *rājādhirāja,* is also known to have been used for King Chandragupta II in an Udaigiri inscription (No. 11).

## II

Though direct mention of the conquests of Kumāragupta I is not found in his epigraphs, some inferences regarding his conquests have been drawn from them and also from his coins. His giving prominence to Kārttikeya, the general of the gods, by depicting him on his gold coins, and replacing the device of *garuḍa*, the typical Gupta insignia, by peacock on some silver coins, and naming his son as Skanda (= Kārttikeya) may indicate his interest in military exploits. His *Aśvamedha* type of coins, if issued after performing the sacrifice and not merely in imitation of the coin-type of his grandfather, Samudragupta, also suggest that he might have made some conquests.

Kumāragupta I's rule over eastern Malwa is attested to by the Tumain inscription of AD 435 (No. 19), referring to prince Ghaṭotkachagupta as his governor. In western Malwa, with its capital at Daśapura, ruled the Aulikara (name or insignia of the family) ruler Bandhuvarmana. The genealogy of his family with all kings bearing *varman*-ending names, as known from inscriptions, runs as—Jayavarman, Siṁhavarman, Naravarman, Viśvavarman, and Bandhuvarman. There is no reference to any Gupta ruler or to Gupta suzerainty in the Aulikara epigraphs of kings preceding Bandhuvarman, who, as most scholars believe, was a feudatory of Kumāragupta I in AD 436, as per the evidence of a Mandasor inscription (No. 38). This has led some scholars to believe that it was Kumāragupta I who brought the Malwa region within the Gupta empire,[18] which, however, does not seem to be the case. During his rule a guild of silk-weavers which had migrated from Lāṭa to Daśapura (Mandasor) got built a Sun temple there in AD 436; the same guild repaired the temple in AD 472. The latter date seems to fall within the reign of Kumāragupta II, whose Sarnath inscription (No. 37) belongs to AD 473. Some scholars suggest that Bandhuvarman was ruling in AD 472 as well, otherwise it would be an unusual case of past ruler being eulogized, and the one then ruling not even mentioned.[19] But this seems to be negated by the fact that as per the evidence of an inscription from Mandasor (No. 36) Prabhākara was governing the Malwa region in AD 467.[20] Kumāragupta I is known to have ruled up to about AD 455, and was followed by Skandagupta (*c.* 455-67). Bhandarkar[21] considers all the above-mentioned Aulikara kings as Gupta feudatories, while Basak[22] is of the view that only Bandhuvarman and his father Viśvavarman had that status. It is not known that the Aulikara king or kings owed allegiance to the Guptas on being conquered, or were won over by diplomacy. It seems that though Bandhuvarman owed allegiance to the Gupta king, he enjoyed considerable autonomy in internal administration. The view[23] that even Bandhuvarman too was not subordinate of the Guptas and in the Mandasor inscription Kumāragupta I is referred to as his contemporary king and not as his overlord is difficult to accept, as it does not explain why a contemporary king should be praised without any valid reason. It should also be remembered that not only Kumāragupta I has been praised in glowing terms in the epigraph but an impressive description of his extensive territories has also been given. R C Majumdar[24] considers it probable that since Bandhuvarman is described as "a king more or less in the same terms which are applied to his father", he was an independent king in AD 436 when the temple was built but was a feudatory when Kumāragupta II was ruling, and that the annexation of Malwa by the Imperial Guptas would have taken place sometimes between AD 436 and 472, either during the reign of Kumāragupta I or shortly after his death. The inscription mentions that in between the construction (in AD 436) and the repair (in AD 472) of the Sun temple, many (at least three) kings, as indicated by the use of plural *pārthivaiḥ* (kings), ruled. Prabhākara is known as ruling most probably as a Gupta feudatory in Malwa in AD 467, as he refers to himself as fire to the enemies of the Guptas, and some scholars consider him as a son of Bandhuvarman, whose known date is AD 436 (No. 38).[25]

It is difficult to agree with the view[26] that the repair of the temple was neglected because the last days of Kumāragupta I's rule were full of troubles, which affected the state resources. The temple was got built by the guild of silk-weavers, and as such, its repair was also its responsibility, and not that of the king. In fact, the inscription clearly states that it was the guild which repaired it, and hence in doing that the economic resources of the guild, and not that of the king, would have mattered. Further, the repair of the temple was done about 17 years after the death of Kumāragupta I (*c.* AD 455), and most probably it was not damaged during his reign.

Kumāragupta I's silver coins of western variety provide evidence of his rule over Gujarat. According to D R Bhandarkar,[27] the Lion-slayer type of this king suggests his hunting exploits in the Gir forests of Kathiawar. However, the possibility of Kumāragupta I merely imitating Chandragupta II's identical coin-type cannot be ruled out.[28] From Gujarat, have been found coins bearing the legend *Rājño mahākshatrapa-mahāsāmanta- param=ādityabhakta-Sarvabhaṭṭārakasya*.[29] Earlier, Newton and Cunningham, reading the legend differently, had ascribed the coins to the Maitraka king, Bhaṭārka.[30] S R Goyal[31] rightly rejects P L Gupta's view[32] that Sarva of the coins ruled Gujarat after the Western Kshatrapas and before its conquest by the Guptas, as that would mean that Kumāragupta I, and not Chandragupta II, conquered the Gujarat region, whereas the issue of silver coins by Chandragupta II in imitation of the Śaka coins provides almost definite evidence of his conquest of that area. Goyal prefers Jai Prakash's view[33] that Sarva revolted and ruled for some time independently during the reign of Kumāragupta I. It is even possible that he ruled either during the last phase of the rule of Skandagupta, or shortly after it, when the Gupta hold over Gujarat became weak, or even ended. The similarity of some silver coins of Class III of Kumāragupta I, with the coins of the Traikūṭakas who ruled in south Gujarat in the middle of the fifth century AD, is taken by some as indicative of Kumāragupta I's victory over them,[34] and if Kumāragupta I performed *aśvamedha* after achieving victory, then this may be either sole victory, or one of the victories of that king.[35]

The Allahabad pillar inscription (No. 1) mentions Samataṭa as a border state of Samudragupta, and the Mehrauli inscription (No. 12) refers to the victory of king Chandra, whom, as stated above, like most scholars, we identify with Chandragupta II, over the confederation of his enemies, who had congregated against him in Bengal. The Damodarpur copperplates of the reign of Kumāragupta I, dated GE 124 (No. 22) and 128 (No. 24), the Dhanaidaha plate (No. 18) dated GE 113 (the portion bearing the name of the king is mutilated), the Kalaikuri-Sultanpur plate dated GE 120 (No. 21), and the Baigram plate, dated GE 128 (No. 26), clearly attest to the rule of this king over Bengal, and there is a view[36] that he was the first Gupta king to conquer that region. S R Goyal[37] however opines that the find of several copperplate grants of Kumāragupta I from Bengal gives an impression that this region had been part of the Gupta empire from earlier times. This seems to be reasonable, though some scholars opine that if Bengal would have been conquered by a Gupta king earlier than the reign of Kumāragupta I, then Gupta inscriptions of pre-Kumāragupta time should have been found there. In the Damodarpur grants, the governors have been referred to as *tatpādānudhyāta* in relation to Kumāragupta I. S R Goyal suggests that in this context, the term could mean 'favoured by' and not necessarily 'appointed by' and some of the governors appointed by Chandragupta II might have continued in office during the reign of Kumāragupta I. In fact, the evidence for Bengal, or at least part of it, being under the Gupta empire during Chandragupta II's reign is attested to by the Mehrauli pillar inscription, which mentions the victory of King Chandra (= Chandragupta II) over the confederation of enemy kings in Bengal (Appendix III, below). D R Bhandarkar[38] thinks that the Tiger-slayer type of coins of Kumāragupta I, which bear the legend *vyāghra-bala-parākrama* ('displaying the strength and prowess of a tiger') indicate his hunting exploits in Sundarban of Bengal, and R K Mookerji,[39] it may be pointed out, takes the evidence of the Tiger-slayer type of Samudragupta's coins as indicative of his conquest of the Ganga valley. According to H C Raychaudhuri, Kumāragupta I's coin-type suggests 'that he attempted to repeat the southern venture of his grandfather and penetrate into the tiger-infested territories beyond the Narmada'.[40] However, the type could as well be a mere imitation of the Tiger-slayer type of Samudragupta and may not be related to Kumāragupta I's conquests. J P Singh,[41] is of the view that the hunting scenes on the coins of the Gupta kings were meant to convey that the king was a skilful archer and should not be taken as evidence for the conquest made by him.

The Gupta-Vākāṭaka relations during Kumāragupta I's reign have been interpreted differently. Some scholars[42] suggest that the Pushyamitras mentioned in the purāṇas were under the Vākāṭakas, and became bold enough to attack the Guptas (*vide* No. 33) because of their support. The evidence of the Balaghat plates of Pṛithvīsheṇa II (No. 87) stating that the orders of his father Narendrasena were obeyed by Kosala, Mekala and Mālava, would suggest that he had brought some part of the Gupta territory under his rule. There is a view[43] that the praise for the achievements of Narendrasena in his son's Balaghat plate inscription (No. 87) should be taken as a conventional eulogy not based on facts. It is argued that the Guptas and the Vākāṭakas were bound by matrimonial alliance, and in normal course, the latter would not have liked to annoy the former, who were then the most important political power, and invite their wrath.[44] The hurdle in accepting the view that Narendrasena conquered some Gupta territory during Kumāragupta I's reign is that the two do not seem to have been contemporaries, as the great-grandfather of Narendrasena and the father of Kumāragupta I had been contemporaries.[45]

A new dimension in the Guptā-Vākāṭaka relations has been added by the Ramtek inscription (No. 85). According to its interpretation by some scholars, Ghaṭotkachagupta, a son of Chandragupta II, married the daughter of his sister (or step-sister) who is identified with Prabhāvatīguptā, the Vākāṭaka queen. This matrimonial alliance would have been contracted with a view to cementing the friendly relation between the two powers, already bound by such an alliance by the marriage of the Gupta princess Prabhāvatīguptā, with Vākāṭaka Rudrasena II. But the results were contrary to what was aimed at. Ghaṭotkachagupta, a governor of his brother Kumāragupta I in 435, as evidenced by the Tumain inscription (No. 19), in all probability raised the banner of revolt. He declared himself as king, as is attested by the find of a couple of his coins, discussed below in this Chapter, and by the reference to him as *rājarāja* in the Ramtek inscription (No. 85). It can be assumed that in his attempt at capturing the throne, he received inspiration and help from the Vākāṭakas. Probably, he lost his life in the battle against Kumāragupta I. That the Gupta–Vākāṭaka relations had turned sour can be inferred from the fact that from the Ramtek inscription, as interpreted by some scholars, Ghaṭotkachagupta's widow was forcibly brought to the Vākāṭaka capital by her brother (probably Pravarasena II).[46]

Ashvini Agrawal points out that the Balaghat and the Mahurjhari plates of Pṛithvīsheṇa II Vākāṭaka give him the credit for establishing the fortunes of the family[47] and also mention that his father Narendrasena's commands were honoured by the rulers of Kosala, Mekala and Mālava. Narendrasena was married to a Kuntala princess,[48] which would have made the two families friendly. The Vākāṭakas were distressed by the invasion of the Nala king, Bhavatta(=Bhavadatta)varman, who occupied the Vākāṭaka capital, Nandivardhana, and issued his Rithpur grant from there.[49] S R Goyal[50] feels that the Nalas were not so strong as to achieve of their own such a great success against the Vākāṭakas who were quite powerful, and it seems that they accepted the suzerainty of the Guptas[51] and received their help in their campaign against the Vākāṭakas. He[52] considers the *repousse* coins with legends *Śrī-Mahendrāditya* and *Śrī-Kamāditya*, which have been found in the area that was under the rule of the Nala dynasty, as issued by the kings of that dynasty in the names of their Gupta overlords.[53] This view seems to receive support from the fact that these coins are different from the other gold coins of the Guptas, and also that not a single such coin has ever been found in any hoard containing Gupta coins. S R Goyal[54] compares these coins with the Later Kushāṇa coins bearing the name either Samudra or Chandra, which suggests that they owed allegiance to the Gupta kings. Skandavarman, the Nala prince, seems to have been named after Skandagupta, a son of Kumāragupta I. Significantly, while Bhavatta(=Bhavadatta)varman was a worshipper of Śiva and Kārttikeya, Skandavarman was a devotee of Vishṇu, which seems to be due to the influence of the Vaishṇava Gupta kings.[55] The Rithpur grant mentions the gift made by the Nala king, Bhavatta(=Bhavadatta)varman, at Prayāga, which, it may be stated in passing, is taken by S R Goyal[56] as the capital of the early Gupta kings, a view with which some scholars do not concur. The grant was meant for the happiness in married life of the donor king. It has been inferred from this that the king married a daughter of the Gupta feudatory of Prayāga region,[57] or may be a Gupta princess. Ashvini Agrawal[58] does not take the reference to the Nala king and his wife as indicative of solemnizing their marriage at Prayāga, but to the ritual performed there by the couple, who had been married much earlier; for, he argues, if it would have been the case of marriage, and more particularly if the princess were of Gupta lineage, then it should have been mentioned specifically and prominently in that epigraph.

One of the two Indore copperplates of Pravarasena was issued from Tripurī (Tewar, six miles from Jabalpur), when that Vākāṭaka king was residing there. Mirashi[59] feels that the Vākāṭaka king moved across the Narmada towards the north and wrested some territory of the Guptas who were the lords of the north and that the reference to Skandagupta's passing night (or nights) on the bare earth in the Bhitari pillar inscription (No. 33) is related to his war against the Vākāṭakas. But some scholars doubt the Guptas ever having hold over the Jabalpur region.[60] The reference to the plight of Skandagupta in the Bhitari inscription should be taken with reference to the war against the Pushyamitras, the victory over whom is mentioned in that inscription immediately after it. It is suggested that Pravarasena might have been on tour to Tripurī and might have had a minor campaign against the then ruling king of the Uchchakalpa dynasty, since a later inscription, viz., the Karitalai (Jabalpur district) copperplate inscription (No. 69) of year (Gupta Era) 174 (= AD 493) belonging to Jayanātha of that dynasty suggests that the area was under his rule.[61]

## III

Some scholars, on the basis of the interpretation of purāṇic evidence, give Kumāragupta I the credit for the south Indian campaign. In the *Vishṇu-purāṇa*,[62] it is stated that Devarakshita will rule Kosala, Oḍra, Tāmralipti and Purī located on the sea shore, Mahendra will rule over Kaliṅga and Mahishaka and (these all areas) will be ruled by Guha *(Kośala-Oḍra-Tāmraliptān samudrataṭa-Purīṁ cha Devarakshito rakshishyati. Kaliṅgaṁ Māhishakaṁ Mahendraḥ bhūmau Guhaṁ bhokshyanti)*. The translation of the last part *bhūmau* etc, is based mainly on the parallel reading of the *Vāyu-puraṇa* which reads *etān janapadān sarvān pālayishyati vai Guhaḥ*. P L Gupta[63] opines that in this, the names of the kings have been mentioned in a rather peculiar way following the pattern of *Ārya-Mañjuśrī-mūlakalpa*, and so Devarakshita should be identified with Chandragupta II, who is known as Devarāja (No. 11) and Devagupta (No. 83), Mahendra for Kumāragupta I, whose title it was, and Guha (which is one of the names of Skanda) for Skandagupta. S R Goyal[64] points out that the purāṇas never refer to the kings in any other form than their proper names, and it is unthinkable that they give the extent of the Gupta empire when it was confined to the areas around Prayāga, Sāketa and Magadha, and thereafter mention its extension during the reign of Chandragupta II, Kumāragupta I and Skandagupta, but make no mention of the contribution made by Samudragupta in this direction, which had been the greatest. The conquest of Kaliṅga and Mahishaka by Kumāragupta I remain unsupported from any other source.[65] The *Vāyu-purāṇa* gives a somewhat different version, which has been translated as 'The Devarakshitas will enjoy the Kosalas, Andhras and the Pauṇḍras, the Tāmraliptas and coast-folk, and the charming city of Champā. Guha will protect all these territories, namely Kaliṅgas, Mahishas and the inhabitants of the Mahendra mountains'.[66]

Kumāragupta I devised a new silver currency for central India which, unlike his silver coins for Gujarat, was not in imitation of the Śaka coins. From the find of a hoard of 1395 silver coins from Samand (District Satara), and 13 coins from Elichpur (Berar),[67] it has been suggested that Kumāragupta I held sway over that region. This, however, is not certain as the coins could as well have reached there as a result of trade transactions.

Of the epithets used for Kumāragupta I, the most common is *Mahendra*, either alone or with some prefix or suffix. Thus, we have *Mahendra* in Archer type, *Mahendrāditya* (his *āditya* title) on *Chhatra* type gold coins (and also on silver coins), *Mahendra-siṁha, Siṁha-mahendra* on the Lion-slayer type, *Mahendra-kumāra* on the Kārttikeya type, *Ajita-mahendra* on the Horseman type, *Aśvamedha-mahendra* on the *Aśvamedha* type, *Mahendra-gaja* on the Elephant-rider type, and *Mahendra-khaḍga* on the Rhinoceros-slayer type. The epithet *Mahendra* was to Kumāragupta I, as *Vikrama* was to Chandragupta II and *Parākrama* to Samudragupta.[68] Besides, he has been referred to as *Vyāghra-bala-parākrama*, 'who was like tiger in power and prowess', on Tiger-slayer type, and *Apratigha*, ' who is of fixed determination' on *Apratigha* type. He has also been referred to as *Parama-daivata*, 'most divine', *Parama-bhaṭṭāraka*, 'most sacred', and *Parama-bhāgavata*, 'most devout worshipper of god (Vishṇu)'—an epithet which has been used practically for all the Gupta emperors from Chandragupta II onwards. His imperial title, like that of the other kings of the Gupta dynasty from Chandragupta I onwards, was *Mahārājādhirāja*. In the Mankuwar inscription (No. 27) and in the Supia inscription (No. 32), which (the latter) refers to him not by name but by the title *Mahendrāditya*, he has been referred to merely as *mahārāja*. This seems to be a scribal error, rather than indicative of decline in his status. Fleet[69], does not rule out the latter possibility. It may well be remembered that on one coin-type—the Tiger-slayer type—of Samudragupta, he has been referred to merely as *rājā*, not even as *mahārāja*.

Kumāragupta I issued *Aśvamedha* type of coins, and on its evidence some scholars credit him for the performance of that sacrifice. One may argue that Kumāragupta did not perform horse-sacrifice and merely imitated the *Aśvamedha* coin-type of his illustrious grandfather, Samudragupta. Allan[70] opines that Kumāragupta took the title *Mahendra* after performing horse-sacrifice. But this title is a short form of the *āditya* title, *Mahendrāditya* as *Vikrama* is the short form of Vikramāditya. Since such titles were not uncommon with the Gupta kings, it need not be related to *aśvamedha*. Some scholars believe that the bricks bearing the name Kumāragupta found at Bhitari would have been used for making sacrificial altar related to his *aśvamedha*.[71] There is no definite evidence that he made any significant conquest which normally and ideally forms an essential part of this sacrifice, though, in course of time, it no more remained its essential part.[72] It has been suggested that the Rhinoceros-slayer type of coins would have been issued by Kumāragupta I after the conquest of Assam, which has been the most common habitat of rhinoceroses till date,[73] though, no corroborative evidence is available, and there is a view that the hunting scenes on the coins were meant to convey that the king was a brave and skillful archer, and need not be interpreted as related to his conquests.[74] It would be worthwhile to refer to B N Mukherjee's reading of the three inscriptions in 'shell' script on a stone horse from Khairagarh, located in the State Museum, Lucknow, which has been discussed in Appendix II. According to it, the first inscription reads *Śrī-Mahendrāditya*, the second refers to 'powerful horse' and the third to 'a sacrificer'. He identifies the horse as a replica of the sacrificial horse of Kumāragupta I. This reading and interpretation is completely different from the earlier ones proposed by other scholars, some of whom considered the stone horse as related with the horse-sacrifice of Samudragupta (Appendix II). P L

Gupta[75] holds that since on the *Aśvamedha* type of coins of Kumāragupta I, the horse has been shown in two different ways, he would have performed two horse-sacrifices. But the evidence is not strong enough to lead to such a conclusion, and the two types of coins could as well have been issued relating to a single sacrifice. As stated above, the argument that since Kumāragupta I was a *parama-bhāgavata*, i.e., Vaishṇava, and since non-violence (*ahiṁsā*) is an important feature of Vaishṇava religion, therefore Kumāragupta I would not have performed the horse-sacrifice involving bloodshed, does not hold good. Some Vaishṇava kings are known to have performed that sacrifice. In one of his coin-types, Kārttikeya is shown riding his *vāhana*, peacock, which may suggest that the king was also a devotee of that deity, who is known as the general of the gods.

## V

It would be worthwhile to discuss here the evidence pertaining to Ghaṭotkachagupta, whose position as king for a short period has to be located within the reign period of Kumāragupta I. A sealing bearing the legend *Śrī-Ghaṭotkachaguptasya* in Gupta characters, was unearthed in the excavations at Vaiśālī (No. 21). Bloch, the excavator, identified him with the second Gupta ruler, Ghaṭotkacha.[76] Smith[77] too held the same opinion. The difference in name—the second Gupta king is invariably mentioned as Ghaṭotkacha and never as Ghaṭotkachagupta, and the chronological and other considerations, seem to rule out such an identification.[78] He should better be taken as a different member of the Imperial Gupta family, named after the second Gupta king, as it was not uncommon with the kings of that dynasty to be named after their ancestors. The absence of any title in the seal legend led Allan[79] to take him as a private individual. But at times, princes and officials are mentioned without titles, and as such, Ghaṭotkachagupta may as well be taken as a Gupta prince.[80] Vaiśālī, it may be mentioned, has also yielded the seal of Queen Dhruvasvāminī and a number of seals belonging to the *kumārāmātyas* and other officials, and hence there is a possibility of Ghaṭotkachagupta being an official or a prince.[81] It has been supposed by R K Mookerji,[82] that at Vaiśālī, Ghaṭotkachagupta served *Mahārāja* Govindagupta, who, he believes, was then the governor with provincial capital located in that city. He[83] also stated that Ghaṭotkachagupta is called *kumārāmātya* on some seals from Vaiśālī. However, only one seal (in fact a sealing) of Ghaṭotkachagupta has been found from that site and there is no mention of any office or title with his name; it has only *Śrī* prefixed to it, which has been taken by some scholars as indicative of his being a scion of the royal family.[84] The Tumain inscription (No. 19) dated GE 116 (= AD 435) of the reign of Kumāragupta I, eulogizes Chandragupta II in line 1, Kumāragupta I (and not Govindagupta, as stated by R D Banerji[85]) in line 2, and Ghaṭotkachagupta in line 3. The last mentioned is said to have won great fame by his own arms, which, according to some scholars, suggests that he was holding the office of governor during the reign of Kumāragupta I.[86]

Two gold coins of Ghaṭotkachagupta, both of the Archer type, are known. One, in St Petersburg Collection, weighing 141.22[87] grains, bears the legend *Ghaṭotkacha* beneath the king's left arm, and the marginal legend ending in *gupta*, indicating that the name of the king was Ghaṭotkachagupta. On the reverse is the title *Kramāditya*.[88] Another, a similar one, weighing 135.5 grains, is in Ajit Ghose's collection.[89] It may also be mentioned that P L Gupta[90] ascribes to Ghaṭotkachagupta a *Chhatra* type coin in the Bayana hoard with the legend *Kramāditya* on the reverse but with no name of the king, which is ascribed by Altekar to Skandagupta.[91] The two gold coins are unmistakable proof of Ghaṭotkachagupta's status as king. They closely resemble the coins of Skandagupta in device and weight, and hence, the rule of this Gupta king should be placed close to his reign. D R Bhandarkar[92] placed him immediately after Kumāragupta I, and before Skandagupta whom he took to be identical with Purugupta. It may, however, be mentioned that Allan,[93] on the grounds of style and weight, placed the coin of St Petersburg Collection (the only coin of this king known till then) to the end of the fifth century AD. He and D C Sircar[94] consider Ghaṭotkachagupta of coins as different from the homonym of the seal. Sircar places him at the end of the fifth or the beginning of the sixth century AD. However, in our view, Bhandarkar[95] rightly considers Ghaṭotkachagupta of the Vaiśālī seal, of the Tumain inscription and that of the two gold coins as identical. He[96] is of the opinion that Ghaṭotkachagupta was earlier governor at Erakiṇa under Kumāragupta I (*vide* No. 19), and thereafter, as *yuvarāja*, stationed at Vaiśālī where his seal has been found, and still later succeeded Kumāragupta I. R K Mookerji[97] holds that the Gupta prince first served Govindagupta who, according to him, was then a governor at Vaiśālī, and was later transferred as governor in Malwa. It may, however, be stated that whereas the Tumain inscription may be taken as almost a definite evidence of his serving as a governor in Malwa, the provenance of the sealing in itself cannot be taken as a definite proof of his serving at Vaiśālī, as it could as well have been affixed to some letter or parcel dispatched by Ghaṭotkachagupta from outside Vaiśālī. In the absence of the mention of the title *yuvarāja* in the Vaiśālī seal of Ghaṭotkachagupta, it is difficult to accept Bhandarkar's view that he held that office. It may be stated that his view is based on his presumption that the erstwhile territories of the Lichchhavis, with Vaiśālī as its capital, was a prestigious province within the Gupta administrative set-up, and, as such, was earmarked to be administered by a *yuvarāja*.[98] Bhandarkar considered Ghaṭotkachagupta as a son of Kumāragupta I[99] and suggested that he succeeded the latter but was killed in the revolt by the Nāga kings.[100] In the same work, at another place, Ghaṭotkachagupta, is stated to have been killed in the Hūṇa encounter who, we are made to believe, had Nāgas as allies.[101] But the newly discovered Ramtek inscription (No 85) clearly shows that Ghaṭotkachagupta was a brother, and not a son of Kumāragupta I as was believed by Bhandarkar and some other scholars, who also believed that on the death of Kumāragupta, he contested the throne against Skandagupta and other princes; though a few scholars included the possibility of his being a brother of Kumāragupta. Significantly, even earlier than the discovery of the Ramtek inscription (No. 85), P K Agrawala had pointed out that the comparison of Ghaṭotkachagupta with Chandra in line 3 of the Tumain inscription (No. 19) suggests his nearness to Chandragupta II, as his son.[102] Dandekar rightly inferred from the Tumain inscription that 'Ghaṭotkachagupta was then trying to be politically independent by severing all loyal connections, which he owed in the capacity of a provincial governor, to his sovereign in Magadha'.[103] The Ramtek inscription suggests that this Gupta prince revolted against Kumāragupta I, his brother or stepbrother. His father Chandragupta II died in *c* AD 412 as an old man. Ghaṭotkachagupta would have been a fairly grown up man in AD 435 when, as per the evidence of the Tumain inscription, he was serving as governor of Kumāragupta I and would have been quite an old man at the time of the death of Kumāragupta in AD 455, after a long reign of about 40 years, and hence at that age would hardly have fought for the throne against his nephew Skandagupta.

Significantly, the Ramtek inscription (No, 85) eulogizes Chandragupta II and also Ghaṭotkachagupta whom it calls *rājarāja* but does not make even a passing reference to Kumāragupta I. This omission of the name of the ruling king under whom Ghaṭotkachagupta had served as a governor and whom he had praised in the Tumain inscription, seems to be deliberate, and suggests that the relationship between the two had become strained. From the same epigraph, as per the interpretation of some scholars, it is known that Ghaṭotkachagupta was married to the Vākāṭaka princess, the daughter of his sister or stepsister, Prabhāvatīguptā. Being ambitious, he was not satisfied with the office of governor, and aspired for kingship, which could only be achieved by successful revolt against Kumāragupta I, the then ruling king. The territories of the Vākāṭakas were contiguous to those of the Guptas administered by him as governor, and hence, they could have been easily in touch with him, and were in a position to conveniently provide him help in men and material. They would have even been instrumental in instigating him to raise the banner of revolt, assuring him their support in that venture. It may be stated that even before the discovery of the Ramtek inscription, Jai Prakash Singh[104] had suggested that Ghaṭotkachagupta might have rebelled and contested the throne against Skandagupta, and taken shelter in the Vākāṭaka court, with a view to seek their support. It is another matter that the revolt did not take place after the death of Kumāragupta I, as suggested by him and some other scholars, but during his rule and against him. Kumāragupta I succeeded in crushing the revolt of Ghaṭotkachagupta. The strained Vākāṭaka-Gupta relationship during the time of Kumāragupta I is evidenced from the statement in the Ramtek inscription that Ghaṭotkachagupta's widow was brought to her paternal home by her brother, forcefully.

## VI

After discussing the brief rule of Ghaṭotkachagupta confined to the Malwa region, we resume the account of the reign of Kumāragupta I. The Mandasor inscription (No. 38) states that his suzerainty extended over the earth, which is 'decked with the four rolling seas as with rocking girdle' and with Sumeru and Kailāsa mountains as her large breasts, and smiling with the flowers of her forest glens.[105] R C Majumdar[106] opines that Kumāragupta I's reign has not been given as much importance as it deserves, because of his comparison with his two predecessors, Samudragupta and Chandragupta II, and his immediate successor, Skandagupta, all of whom are known for their great achievements. R D

Banerji[107] considers the earlier part of Kumāragupta's reign as 'by far the most prosperous in the total rule of the Gupta dynasty', when there was a good deal of influx of foreign gold due to overseas trade. He issued the largest number of coin-types in gold, some of which are the finest in the entire series of the Gupta coins. Because of the great artistic activities of his reign, he has been compared with Shahjahan of the Mughal dynasty.[108]

During his long reign, Kumāragupta I, ably kept intact the vast empire that he inherited, stretching from Bengal in the east to Gujarat in the west, and from the Himalayas in the north to the Narmada in the south. In the Tumain inscription (No. 19), he is said to have 'protected the earth having held her with the forehand of his valour'. He issued the largest variety of coins in the Gupta dynasty and the number of his inscriptions is also fairly large. Chirātadatta was the *uparika* (governor) of the province of Puṇḍravardhana (roughly Rajshahi division of Bangladesh). According to the Baigram grant (No. 25), *Kumārāmātya* Kulavṛiddhi was in charge of the administration of the district of Pañcha–nagarī (in the Bogra district of Bangladesh). Vaiśālī was an important Gupta province. In Daśapura (Mandasor) region, Bandhuvarman was his feudatory. In eastern Malwa, Prince Ghaṭotkachagupta was his governor for some time. From the western part of central India are known *Mahārājas* Svāmidāsa, Bhuluṇḍa and Rudradāsa, from their grants dated GE 106, 107 and 117, respectively.[109] Pṛithvīsheṇa was his general (No. 20). Some scholars opine that the king of Kyo-pi-li, who sent an embassy to China, should be identified with Kumāragupta I, but the other view is that he perhaps was a King of Kopili valley in Assam.[110] His reign for most part was peaceful. Ashvini Agrawal's[111] statement about Kumāragupta I that 'Neither did he meet with any military reverses during his lifetime, nor were there any invasions or internal rebellions so long as he occupied the throne', needs some amendment, as '...this moon among the Guptas seems to have suffered an eclipse in later years'[112] when there was invasion of the Pushyamitras, and according to some scholars, also that of the Hūṇas, which made the fortunes of the family unsteady (*vichalita*) and even overwhelmed (*vipluta*) for a short period.

Smith[113] read the date on a silver coin of Kumāragupta as [GE] 136 (AD 455), the latest known date for that Gupta king. This would mean that the king had a long reign of about 40 years (*c.* AD 415 to 455). The reading of date by Smith has been doubted by some scholars. A L Basham,[114] opines that the reading of the date does not seem to be correct, and even if it were correct, it might be a mint master's mistake, or the coin might have been issued posthumously,[115] and the king might have died about AD 450. P L Gupta[116] too holds a similar view and cites examples of the coins issued in the names of Akbar and Shahjahan posthumously. In his opinion, on the coin in question, the figures for 100 and 30 are clear, but the unit figure is lost. S R Goyal[117] says that his rule may have ended around AD 450 and certainly before AD 455, the latter being the first of the three dates in the Junagarh rock inscription of Skandagupta. There is, however, no difficulty in placing the end of his rule in AD 455.

A few scholars,[118] suggest that during the last days of Kumāragupta's rule, Prince Skandagupta was the *de facto* ruler. According to Somadeva's *Kathā-saritsāgara,* Mahendrāditya handed over the kingdom to Vikramāditya who had defeated the *mlechchhas*, and along with his wife, retired to Vārāṇasī.[119] In the *Chandra-garbha-paripṛichchhā*, we are told that Mahendrasena crowned Prince Duḥprasahahasta who had defeated the Yavanas, Pahlikas and Śakunas who had invaded the Gupta territories, and retired to religious life.[120] Mahendrasena and Mahendrāditya have been identified with Kumāragupta I, and Vikramāditya and Duḥprasahahasta with Skandagupta, and the *mlechchhas* with the Hūṇas,[121] who as per the evidence of the Bhitari pillar inscription (No. 33) were defeated by Skandagupta. A S Altekar[122] interprets the device and the legend on the *Apratigha* type of coins of Kumāragupta I as suggesting his firm decision to abdicate. However, it has been pertinently stated that the event of abdication, being an unpleasant one,[123] would not be a befitting theme for depiction on coins. Moreover, if Kumāragupta would have abdicated then he would have no authority to issue coins in his name, while the *Apratigha* type bears his name. If the *Apratigha* type of coins is taken as issued to commemorate the event by one of his successors, then the name of the commemorator should have been recorded on it.[124] The *Apratigha* coins range from 120 to 123 grains in weight[125] which, barring those of a few Archer type coins, is the lowest of Kumāragupta's coin-types. Since in the case of the Gupta gold coins, there was generally a tendency to increase the weight with the time, these being quite low in weight should be placed in the early years of his reign, and hence should not be taken as depicting the scene of abdication which would be the last event of the reign. In fact there is much difference of opinion amongst scholars regarding the interpretation of the device on the *Aprtigha* type of coins.[126] *Pitari sura-sakhitvaṁ prāpt=ātma-śaktyā* in the Junagarh inscription of Skandagupta (No. 30) has been translated by Fleet as 'when (his) father by his own power had attained the position of being a friend of the gods'[127] and taken to mean that Kumāragupta I committed suicide. But *prāptavat=ātma-śaktyā* should better be taken along with *avanim=avanat=ārir=yaḥ chakār=ātma-saṁsthāṁ* that precedes it, which would mean that Skandagupta brought the earth under him by conquering his enemies with his own power.[128] In the Bhitari inscription (No. 33) it is stated that after the death of his father he re-established the family fortune that had been convulsed. If his father would have abdicated and become monk, then there would not have been any reference to his death in the Bhitari pillar inscription (No. 33). Some scholars opine that he died a natural death, which took place when his son, Skandagupta, was fighting the enemies,[129] while others are of the view that he died fighting either the Pushyamitras or the Hūṇas, and Skandagupta, who had accompanied him to the battlefield, defeated the enemy, and returning from there conveyed the news of his victory to his mother, as per the evidence of the same inscription. A few scholars suggest that the battleground where he died was Bhitari, and it is because of this that at that site as per the evidence of the Bhitari pillar inscription, Skandagupta installed an image of God Vishṇu, granted a village in the name of that god, and raised a pillar (on which the inscription has been engraved) as a memorial for his father.[130]

## NOTES AND REFERENCES

1. S R Goyal, *Guptakālīna Abhilekha*, pp. 190ff.
2. This is the reading of D R Bhandarkar, *Corpus Inscriptionum Indicarum*, III, p. 272. Bühler had read the date as 113, which is also the reading of P K Agrawala, *Imperial Gupta Epigraphs*, p. 35.
3. S R Goyal, *Guptakālīna Abhilekha*, pp. 193ff.
4. As read by D C Sircar, *Journal of Ancient Indian History*, III, pp. 133-37; J F Fleet (*Corpus Inscriptionum Indicarum*, III, p. 46) had read it 129.
5. He is identified by K B Pathak (as cited by D R Bhandarkar, *Corpus Inscriptionum Indicarum*, III, p. 77) with the homonym, who was the teacher of the Buddhist scholar, Vasubandhu.
6. *Cf. Khādyāṭapākika*, in the Allahabad pillar inscription (No. 1).
7. Since one *kulyavāpa* is equal to eight *droṇavāpas*, so one *dīnāra* is equal to 16 *rūpakas*.
8. R N Dandekar, *A History of the Guptas*, p. 121.
9. J P Singh, *History and Coinage of Skandagupta Kramāditya*, p. 117.
10. S R Goyal, *The Imperial Guptas*, p. 320.
11. J Allan, *Catalogue of the Coins of the Gupta Dynasties, and of Śaśāṅka, the King of Gauḍa, in the British Museum, London*, p. xcvi.

12. According to some scholars (e.g. R N Dandekar, *A History of the Guptas*, p. 102), Queen Anantadevī was a Kadamba princess, and the Gupta-Kadamba matrimonial alliance, mentioned in the Talgunda inscription (No. 91), refers to her marriage with Kumāragupta I.
13. For example, P L Gupta, *The Imperial Guptas*, p. 172.
14. H C Raychaudhuri, *Political History of Ancient India*, p. 500 (text and n.)
15. *Memoirs of the Archaeological Survey of India*, 66, p. 38.
16. J B Watson, *Indian Antiquaqry*, II, 1873, p. 313, *vide* J F Fleet, *Corpus Inscriptionum Indicarum*, III, p. 49.
17. Smith, *Journal of the Royal Asiatic Society of Great Britain and Ireland*, 1889, p. 125.
18. See Ashvini Agrawal, *Rise and Fall of the Imperial Guptas*, p. 193.
19. R C Majumdar, *Comprehensive History of India*, III(i), p. 68.
20. No scholar accepts the view of R Shamasastry (*Annual Report of Mysore Archaeological Department*, 1923, p. 24) that even Kumāragupta of the first date, AD 436, should refer to the rule of Kumāragupta II; see also P L Gupta, *The Imperial Guptas*, p. 60, n. 122.
21. D R Bhandarkar, *Corpus Inscriptionum Indicarum*, III, pp. 66-67.
22. *The History of North-Eastern India*, p. 50.
23. V V Mirashi, *Journal of the Epigraphical Society of India*, IX, p. 51.
24. R C Majumdar, in *Comprehensive History of India*, III(i), p. 68.
25. For example, U N Roy, *Gupta Rājavaṁśa tathā Usakā Yuga*, p. 774.
26. B P Sinha, *Decline of the Kingdom of Magadha*, p. 70.
27. D R Bhandarkar, *Corpus Inscriptionum Indicarum*, III, pp. 66-67.
28. J P Singh (*History and coinage of Skandagupta Kramāditya*, p. 1) opines that the hunting (*mṛigayā*) scenes depicted on Gupta coins are not related to military exploits.
29. Mirashi, *Corpus Inscriptionum Indicarum*, IV, p. xxxvii.
30. For references, see V V Mirashi, *Journal of the Numismatic Society of India*, VI, pp. 14-15.
31. S R Goyal, *Gupta Sāmrājya kā Itihāsa*, pp. 254-55.
32. P L Gupta, *Gupta Sāmrājya*, p. 89, n. 2.
33. *History and Coinage of Skandagupta Kramāditya*, pp. 3ff.
34. J Allan, *Catalogue of the Coins of the Gupta Dynasties, and of Śaśāṅka, the King of Gauḍa, in the British Museum, London*, p. xcv; A S Altekar, *The Coinage of the Gupta Empire*, p. 223. His silver-plated coins with copper core are taken to have been minted for circulation in Valabhi area. Allan (*Catalogue of the Coins of the Gupta Dynasties, and of Śaśāṅka, the King of Gauḍa, in the British Museum, London*, p. xcvi) suggests that they were struck in a period of financial stringency.
35. H C Raychaudhuri, *Political History of Ancient India*, p. 500n.
36. S K Maity, *The Imperial Guptas and their Times*, p. 53.
37. S R Goyal, *The Imperial Guptas*, pp. 231-32.
38. D R Bhandarkar, *Corpus Inscriptionum Indicarum, III*, p. 78.
39. *Gupta Empire*, p. 35.

40. H C Raychaudhuri, *Political History of Ancient India*, p. 503.
41. J P Singh, *Journal of the Numismatic Society of India*, XXIV, pp. 152ff.
42. For example, S R Goyal, *The Imperial Guptas*, p. 348.
43. Ashvini Agrawal, *Rise and Fall of the Imperial Guptas*, p. 216.
44. A S Altekar, in *The Vākāṭaka-Gupta Age*, p. 117.
45. S R Goyal, (*Gupta Sāmrājya kā Itihāsa*, p. 295), however, says that the evidence based on generation for fixing the date is not foolproof, and the two could as well have been contemporaries.
46. She got erected a Vaishṇava temple in memory of her mother, Prabhāvatīguptā, who had by then died. The death took place after the 23rd regnal year of Pravarasena II, since she has been mentioned as living in his Tirodi grant of that date.
47. Ashvini Agrawal, *Rise and Fall of the Imperial Guptas*, pp. 196-97. S R Goyal (*Gupta Sāmrājya kā Itihāsa*, p. 258) gives credit for this to Narendrasena.
48. A S Altekar (in *The Vākāṭaka-Gupta Age*, p. 115) identifies her as a daughter of Kadamba king Kākusthavarman, who is known to have got his daughters married to the Gupta and other families (D C Sircar, *Select Inscriptions*, I, p. 478). Goyal (*The Imperial Guptas*, p. 318, n. 1) holds the same opinion.
49. *Epigraphia Indica*, XIX, pp. 100ff; A S Altekar, in *The Vākāṭaka-Gupta Age*, pp. 115-116.
50. S R Goyal, *The Imperial Guptas*, pp. 318-19.
51. J P Singh, *History and Coinage of Skandagupta Kramāditya*, p. 9) does not consider the Nala king as feudatory of the Guptas.
52. S R Goyal, *The Imperial Guptas*, p. 320.
53. S R Goyal, *ibid.*, pp. 319-20.
54. *Gupta Sāmrājya kā Itihāsa*, p. 259.
55. S R Goyal, *The Imperial Guptas*, p. 319.
56. S R Goyal, *ibid.*, p. 318.
57. D C Sircar, in *The Classical Age*, p. 188, n. 2.
58. Ashvini Agrawal, *Rise and Fall of the Imperial Guptas*, p. 198.
59. V V Mirashi, *Indological Research Papers*, I, pp. 65ff.
60. Ashvini Agrawal, *Rise and Fall of the Imperial Guptas*, pp. 198-99.
61. *Ibid.*, p. 199.
62. F E Pargiter, *Dynasties of the Kali Age*, pp. 73-74.
63. P L Gupta, *The Imperial Guptas*, p. 116.
64. S R Goyal, *Gupta Sāmrājya kā Itihāsa*, p. 253.This is also the view of J P Singh (*History and Coinage of Skandagupta Kramāditya*, p. 12, n. 6).
65. S R Goyal, *Gupta Sāmrājya kā Itihāsa*, p. 254)
66. F E Pargiter, *The Dynasties of the Kali Age*, pp. 73-74.
67. A S Altekar, *The Coinage of the Gupta Empire*, p. 217.
68. D R Bhandarkar, *Corpus Inscriptionum Indicarum*, III, p. 77.
69. J F Fleet, *Corpus Inscriptionum Indicarum*, III, p. 46.
70. J Allan, *Catalogue of the Coins of the Gupta Dynasties, and of Śaśāṅka, the King of Gauḍa, in the British Museum, London*, p. xliii.

71. D R Bhandarkar, *Corpus Inscriptionum Indicarum*, III, p. 83.
72. R G Basak (*The History of North-Eastern India*, p.58). P L Gupta (*Gupta Sāmrājya*, p. 304) and a few other scholars (below) believe that he made some conquests.
73. Y B Singh, *Journal of the Numismatic Society of India*, XLIII, pp. 67ff.
74. J P Singh, *Journal of the Numismatic Society of India* XXI, pp. 152ff.
75. P L Gupta, *Gupta Sāmrājya*, p. 304.
76. T Bloch, *Archaeological Survey of India—Annual Report*, 1903-04, p. 102.
77. *Journal of the Royal Asiatic Society of Great Britain and Ireland*, 1905, p. 153.
78. See also Allan, *Catalogue of the Coins of the Gupta Dynasties, and of Śaśāṅka, the King of Gauḍa, in the British Museum, London*, pp. xvi-xvii.
79. *Ibid.*, p. xvii.
80. Mattila of a sealing from Bulandshahr who has not been given any title (Chapter, 5, above), has been identified by some scholars with King Matila of the Allahabad pillar inscription, and Śrīgupta of a sealing is taken to be identical with the first homonym Gupta ruler.
81. P L Gupta (*The Imperial Guptas*, p. 327) is of the opinion that a coin with the *kramāditya* as *viruda* and without the name of the king found in the Bayana hoard should be ascribed to Ghaṭotkachagupta, rather than to Skandagupta as is generally done.
82. *Gupta Empire*, p. 73. This is also the view of a few other scholars.
83. *Ibid.*, p. 12.
84. *Ibid.*
85. R D Banerji, *The Age of the Imperial Guptas*, p. 50. However, in Appendix I on p. 66, which is based on the information received from M B Garde, Banerji rightly states that the Tumain inscription 'does not mention Govindagupta at all'.
86. R K Mookerji, *Gupta Empire*, p. 73.
87. *Vide* A S Altekar, *The Coinage of the Gupta Empire*, p. 354.
88. A S Altekar, *ibid.*, p. 264.
89. *Journal of the Numismatic Society of India*, XXII, pp. 260-61.
90. P L Gupta, *The Imperial Guptas*, p. 327.
91. A S Altekar, *The Coinage of the Gupta Empire*, p. 248.
92. *Corpus Inscriptionum Indicarum*, III, p. 81.
93. *Catalogue of the Coins of the Gupta Dynasties, and of Śaśāṅka, the King of Gauḍa, in the British Museum, London*, p. liv.
94. *Indian Historical Quarterly*, XXIV, pp. 71-72.
95. D R Bhandarkar, *Corpus Inscriptionum Indicarum*, III, pp. 79-80). It has been opined that the seal of Ghaṭotkachagupta is nearer in time to Chandragupta II, on palaeogaphic ground and also as it was found in the same archaeological context as the sealing of the Chief queen of Chandragupta II, whereas the coin should be placed some decades later. B P Sinha (*Decline of the Kingdom of Magadha*, p. 35) is of the view that the seal belongs to the early phase of the career of the prince while the coin to its later phase, when he became king, and that there was a fairly long gap between the two.

96. D R Bhandarkar, *Corpus Inscriptionum Indicarum*, III, p. 79.
97. *Gupta Empire*, p. 75.
98. *Corpus Inscriptionum Indicarum*, III, p. 79.
99. D R Bhandarkar, *ibid.*, p. 81.
100. *Ibid.*, pp. 80-81. The Nāgas had been conquered by Samudragupta, and their territories were merged in the Gupta kingdom. A scion of Nāga family, Skandanāga, was a governor of Antaravedī during the reign of Skandagupta. In the Junagarh rock inscription (No. 30), Skandagupta has been referred to as *garuḍa* in relation to other kings who have been referred as the *nāgas*, which is taken by some as indicating that he subdued the Nāga kings.
101. *Corpus Inscriptionum Indicarum*, III, p. 81.
102. P K Agrawala, *Imperial Gupta Epigraphs*, p. 39.
103. R N Dandekar, *A History of the Guptas*, p. 119.
104. *History and Coinage of Skandagupta Kramāditya*, p. 125.
105. H C Raychaudhuri, *Political History of Ancient India*, p. 501.
106. R C Majumdar, *The Classical Age*, p. 25.
107. *The Age of the Imperial Guptas*, pp. 36-37.
108. Johannah Gottfried Williams, *The Art of Gupta India*, p. 63.
109. D C Sircar, *Indian Historical Quarterly*, XXII, p. 64.
110. S R Goyal, *Gupta Sāmrājya kā Itihāsa*, p. 262.
111. Ashvini Agrawal, *Rise and Fall of the Imperial Guptas*, p. 199.
112. *Gupta Empire*, p. 75. H C Raychaudhuri (*Political History of Ancient India*, p. 502) holds that at least the invasion of the Pushyamitras took place in Kumāragupta I's reign, the Gupta king has been referred to in his coins as moon in the Gupta family—*Gupta-kula-vyoma-śaśi* (*The Coinage of the Gupta Empire*, p. 176), and *Gupta-kul=āmala-chandraḥ* (*ibid.*).
113. *Journal of the Asiatic Society of Bengal*, LXIII (i), 1894, p. 175.
114. *Bulletin of the School of Oriental and African Studies*, XVII (ii), pp. 366ff.
115. *Ibid.*, p. 367.
116. P L Gupta, *The Imperial Guptas*, pp. 185-86.
117. S R Goyal, *Gupta Sāmrājya kā Itihāsa*, p. 241.
118. For example, S R Goyal, *The Imperial Guptas*, p. 328.
119. *The Ocean of Story* (Tawney) edited by N M Penzer, IX, chapter XVIII, pp. 1ff, *vide* J Allan, *Catalogue of the Coins of the Gupta Dynasties, and of Śaśāṅka, the King of Gauḍa, in the British Museum, London*, p. xlix, n. 1.
120. For references, see B P Sinha, *Decline of the Kingdom of Magadha*, p. 2, n. 6.
121. K P Jayaswal, *Imperial History of India*, pp. 36-37; S K Maity, *The Imperial Guptas and their Times*, pp. 56-58; S R Goyal, *The Imperial Guptas*, p. 342.
122. A S Altekar, *The Coinage of the Gupta Empire*, pp. 209-10.
123. M C Joshi, *Journal of the Numismatic Society of India*, XXI, pp. 34-36.
124. Ashvini Agrawal, *Rise and Fall of the Imperial Guptas*, p. 200.
125. A S Altekar, *The Coinage of the Gupta Empire*, p. 210.
126. The device has variously been taken as depicting two women worshipping the central figure (Hoernle, *Journal of the Asiatic Society of Bengal*, 1883, p.144); king

and his two queens (Smith, *Journal of the Royal Asiatic Society of Great Britain and Ireland*, 1888, p. 107; also B P Sinha, *Journal of the Numismatic Society of India*, XVI, pp. 213-14); a device in imitation of non-Indian motif (J Allan, *Catalogue of the Coins of the Gupta Dynasties, and of Śaśāṅka, the King of Gauḍa, in the British Museum, London*, Intro, p. xcii); Śiva flanked by Nandi and Pārvatī and the name Mihirakula (R C Majumdar, *Journal of the Numismatic Society of India*, XII, pp. 72-73); a saint flanked by king and queen (V V Mirashi, *ibid*, pp. 68-71); king flanked by queen and prince or the general (A S Altekar, *The Coinage of the Gupta Empire*, p. 207ff). Sohoni first interpreted the device as Kārttikeya and his two wives (*S N Sinha Commemoration Volume*, 1943, pp. 177-78), then as God Kumāra with Kaśyapa and Aditi (*Journal of the Numismatic Society of India*, XVIII, pp. 56ff), and still later as King flanked by Śrī and Pratāpa (*Ibid.*, XXIII, pp. 345ff.). For these and other opinions, see S R Goyal, *The Imperial Guptas*, p. 341fn (continued on p. 342).

127. J F Fleet, *Corpus Inscriptionum Indicarum*, III, p. 62.
128. Even if it is taken in the context of Kumāragupta I, the intention could have been to convey that he gave up his life by his yogic power.
129. R N Dandekar, *A History of the Guptas*, p. 104.
130. R G Basak, *The History of North-Eastern India*, pp. 74-75.

# 10

# Skandagupta: Triumph over the Invaders

## I

The inscriptions and coin-types of belonging to the reign of Skandagupta are not many, which fact goes well with his relatively short reign (*c.* AD 455-67), in comparison to the reigns of his three illustrious predecessors, Kumāragupta I, Chandragupta II and Samudragupta. His Junagarh (district Junagarh) inscription (No. 30) bears three dates—GE 136, 137 and 138. It mentions the repair of Sudarśana lake that had burst due to excessive rains, and the construction of a temple of Vishṇu by Chakrapālita, who held the charge of the administration of Girinagara, and was the son of Parṇadatta, the governor of Surāshṭra. The inscription refers to Skandagupta's selection by Lakshmī as her lord, discarding other sons of king (or kings), and to his taking great pains and much caution in selecting a suitable governor for Surashṭra, till his choice fell on Parṇadatta. It is stated that he like *garuḍa* overpowered the snake-like kings (*narapati-bhujagas*), and won victory over the *mlechchhas* (i.e. the Hūṇas). The Supia (Rewa district) inscription of GE 141 (No. 32) gives the Gupta genealogy from Ghaṭotkacha, instead of Gupta as is the case in other Gupta inscriptions. The Poona (No. 82) and Rithpur (No. 84) copperplate inscriptions of the Vākāṭaka queen Prabhāvatīguptā also give the genealogy from Ghaṭotkacha. The Supia inscription does not mention

Chandragupta I, and refers to Chandragupta II and Kumāragupta I not by names but by their *virudas*—Vikramāditya and Mahendrāditya, respectively. Samudragupta, Mahendrāditya and Skandagupta have each been referred to as *mahārāja,* instead of their usual title *mahārājādhirāja.* Ghaṭotkacha, the second king of the dynasty, whose title was *mahārāja,* and Vikramāditya (i.e. Chandragupta II), whose usual title was *mahārājādhirāja,* are mentioned without any kingly titles. The Kahaum (Gorakhpur district, UP) inscription of Gupta era 141 (No. 31) records the installation of Jaina images 'in the peaceful year of Skandagupta' (*Skandaguptasya śānte varshe*).[1] The Indor (Bulandshahar district) copperplate inscription of GE 146, i.e. = AD 465 (No. 34), mentions Śarvanāga as a *vishayapati* of Antarvedī (the region between the Ganga and Yamuna) and refers to an endowment in favour of a Sun temple at Indrapura (modern Indor). A Gadhwa (Allahabad district) stone inscription bears the date GE 148, but does not mention the name of the king. This is also the last known date for Skandagupta as known from coins, and so the inscription may belong to his reign. It records the installation of a Vishṇu image and donation of land (or village) for its maintenance. A Mandasor (Mandsor district) inscription (No. 36) of ME 524 (= AD 467), which is also the last known date of Skandagupta, records the pious act of Dattabhaṭa, who was a general of Prabhākara, and the son of Vāyurakshita who (the latter) had been a general of Govindagupta. The most important epigraph for the political history of the reign of Skandagupta is the undated Bhitari (Ghazipur district) pillar inscription (No. 33). It gives the genealogy of Gupta kings from Gupta up to Skandagupta and highlights the great calamity that befell the Gupta dynasty due to the invasions of the Pushyamitras and the Hūṇas, and the success achieved by Skandagupta against them. The extremely mutilated Bihar (Patna district) pillar inscription (No. 35), which had been earlier ascribed to Skandagupta by Fleet,[2] is ascribed to Purugupta by some,[3] and to one of the sons of the latter, by others.[4]

The gold coins of Skandagupta show decrease in number and variety in comparison to those of his predecessors. His most common coin-type was the Archer type, followed by a coin-type labelled as King-and-Queen type by some[5] and King-and-Lakshmī type by others.[6] B P Sinha[7] takes it as issued to express his gratitude to goddess Lakshmī for favouring him for the kingship discarding other princes, as stated in the Junagarh inscription (No. 30). The *Chhatra* and the Horseman types known from one specimen each, and bearing not the name of the king but only the title *kramāditya* are generally ascribed by scholars to Skandagupta.[8] Some coins of Skandagupta are about 132 grains in weight, which is nearer to the weight followed in Kumāragupta's coins, while others are of higher weight of about 144 grains. Some scholars believe that he perhaps issued coins based on two weight standards. According to Altekar,[9] the weight was gradually increased with a view to attaining the *suvarṇa* standard of about 144 grains. But this, as pointed out by P L Gupta, is doubtful,[10] since the weight of the coins, even after attaining that mark, continued to increase in the reigns of his successors and reached 151 grains in the time of Vishṇugupta. B P Sinha[11] opines that there is nothing to substantiate the view generally held by scholars that the coins of higher weight belong to the later phase of his reign. Skandagupta's coins are more debased than those of his predecessors, yet because of their heavier weight, the gold content per coin was not less than that met with in their coins. Therefore, the debasement of coins need not be taken, as was done by some scholars, as reflecting poor economic condition caused by the invasions of the Hūṇas and the Pushyamitras.[12] Skandagupta issued *Garuḍa*, Bull and Altar types of silver coins for his western provinces; for Madhyadeśa he continued the 'Fan-tailed Peacock' type of coins which had been introduced by Kumāragupta I. Significantly, on one variety of his Altar type, instead of his usual title *kramāditya*, he has been given the title *Vikramāditya*, which is a title so special to Chandragupta II. It has been stated above that Smith read the date 136 on a silver coin of Kumāragupta I, now not traceable, that his reading of date on this coin and another coin as 135, has been doubted by some scholars, and that A L Basham and P L Gupta opine that even if the date has been read correctly, the coins could have been issued posthumously. Of the three dates in the Junagarh inscription, viz., GE 136, 137 and 138 (= AD 455, 456 and 457), the last mentioned one refers to the repairing of the dam, Sudarśana, during the reign of Skandagupta, and it is likely, though not certain, that the bursting of the dam, in AD 455, also took place during his rule. Some scholars[13] suggest that Kumāragupta I ruled up to *c* AD 455, and that after him there was a short rule of Purugupta, followed by that of Skandagupta. A few scholars[14] also included the brief rule of Ghaṭotkachagupta within this period, but this has to be given up in view of the evidence of the newly discovered Ramtek inscription (No. 85), from which it can be inferred that he rebelled against Kumāragupta I, his brother, declared himself king and ruled for a short period in Malwa and the adjoining regions, but lost his life, most probably in the battle against Kumāragupta.

The seventh verse of the Junagarh rock inscription (No. 30) mentions that Skandagupta after he had appointed governors in all other provinces (*sarveshu deśeshu)* made deep deliberations for the appointment of the governor of Surāshṭra, which before its conquest by Chandragupta II formed a major part of the Śaka kingdom. It is stated in the inscription that he carefully tested the probable candidates on the parameters of the qualifications, enumerated in the epigraph for an ideal governor, and appointed Parṇadatta, who, it is stated, fulfilled all of them. Before appointing governors, according to the inscription, he had made conquests—the expression is conquered the 'whole earth' (*pṛithvīṁ samagrām*). S R Goyal suggests that the accession of Skandagupta, his defeating enemies and rebel brothers, making conquests and appointing governors in different provinces, could not have been done in a short period, and therefore, it is better to consider that the invasion of the Pushyamitras and Hūṇas, and the war with his rival claimants contesting for the Gupta throne took place during the last days of the reign of his father, Kumāragupta.[15] However, in ancient India, most of the governors, as also many other officials, were allowed to retain their office, after the accession of a new king, in some cases even after the change of the dynasty, and only a few who were deemed corrupt, inefficient, physically handicapped, arrogant or disloyal would have been replaced by such ones as were considered free from such blemishes. Skandagupta, it can be assumed, would have also followed this pattern. It is possible that the governor of Surāshṭra had taken the side of Skandagupta's rival in the struggle for the throne, or rebelled and was on that account removed and replaced by Parṇadatta. Chakrapālita, who got the epigraph in question composed and engraved, has eulogised his father, ascribing to him all the qualities of a good governor.

## II

A F R Hoernle,[16] D R Bhandarkar,[17] K Deva[18] and a few other scholars identified Skandagupta with Purugupta. This identification would reduce one king from the four kings —Purugupta, Narasiṁhagupta, Kumāragupta [II] of the Sarnath inscription and Budhagupta, who, according to some scholars, are to be placed within a short period of nine years between 467—the last date known for Skandagupta, and 476—the first known date for Budhagupta. The name of the son of Kumāragupta I on the Bhitari seal of Kumāragupta [III] (No. 55) was earlier read as *Puragupta*, and it was suggested that Skandagupta was given this name 'in allusion to the resistance of his fortress to the Hūṇas'.[19] Later, the first part of the name on this seal was read by Cunningham[20] as *Puru*, and the above suggestion relating to Skandagupta being named as Puragupta was given up.[21] Since Puru means 'great', it was construed that Skandagupta was given the name Purugupta as he became great after his victory over the enemies. There was no change in this view even when on the Nālandā sealing of Narasiṁhagupta (No. 53) and also on the sealing of Vishṇugupta (No. 58), the name was read as *Pūru*, as it also means 'great'.[22] The last-mentioned form of the name also occurs on the Bihar pillar inscription (No. 35).

Some arguments put forth by scholar in favour of taking Skandagupta and Purugupta as one and the same person, together with counter arguments, may be stated:

1. Fleet[23] ascribed the authorship of the Bihar stone-pillar inscription (No. 35) to Skandagupta, and since the term *tat-pādānudhyāta*, which was taken by him in the sense of 'succeeded by', is applied to him in relation to his father, Kumāragupta I, while in the Bhitari seal and some Nālandā seals of the later Imperial Gupta kings, the epithet is used for Purugupta in relation to Kumāragupta I, and therefore Skandagupta and Purugupta should be taken to be the same person.

   But the name of the king in the Bihar stone inscription, with the help of better facsimile, has been read by R C Majumdar as *Pūrugupta*, instead of *Skandagupta*, and therefore the epithet *tatpādānudhyāta* applies to him.[24]

2. In the genealogy met with in the epigraphs of the later Imperial Gupta kings, Purugupta is mentioned as a king immediately after Kumāragupta I, and no mention is made of king Skandagupta who in his own inscriptions is mentioned as a successor of Kumāragupta, and the two should therefore be taken as identical.

   But the absence of the name of Skandagupta in the epigraphs detailing the genealogy seems to be because they do not strictly follow the chronological order of kings, and omit the names of collaterals. Budhagupta who ruled at least from AD 476 to AD 494, does not find mention in the genealogy met with on the seal of his brother, Narasiṁhagupta, and also on the seals of the latter's successors who ruled after him. The *Ārya-Mañjuśrī-mūlakalpa* seems to give a second name of Skandagupta as Devarāja, and not as Purugupta.

3. The last date on a coin of Kumāragupta I, as noted by Smith,[25] is GE 136, which is also the first date in the Junagarh rock inscription of Skandagupta and so hardly any place is left for the rule of a king named Purugupta.

   But most probably Purugupta did not precede but succeeded Skandagupta and ruled sometime between AD 467 and 473.

4. No coins and inscriptions of Purugupta have been found.[26]

   But this could be because of his very short reign period. It is unthinkable that the same person is mentioned in inscriptions and coins as Skandagupta, and in the genealogies on seals as Purugupta.

Thus the grounds for identifying Skandagupta with Purugupta are not strong enough, and they should better be taken as two different kings. It may be mentioned that till the reading of the name of the king on the coins had not been corrected from Purugupta to Budhagutpa,[27] it looked curious that the same king issued coins with two names—Skandagupta and Purugupta, there being no other instance of that type in the Gupta period, nay in the whole ancient history.[28] It was pointed out that Chandragupta II had another name, Devarāja (No. 9) and its variant Devagupta (No. 83) but he issued his coins only by the name Chandragupta and never by his other name.

## III

There is a difference of opinion regarding the order of succession after Kumāragupta I. Some scholars[29] suggest that on the death of Kumāragupta I, Purugupta, born of the chief-queen Mahādevī Anantadevī, and hence a rightful claimant to the throne, succeeded his father. As seen above, Purugupta on the seals of his successors, as also in the Bihar stone inscription (No. 35) has been mentioned as *pādānudhyāta* in relation to Kumāragupta I, which was taken by some scholars to indicate that he was the immediate successor of his father, and it was suggested that he was ousted by Skandagupta who though not born of the chief queen was more powerful and competent. It was also suggested that this act of his created animosity in the hearts of the descendents of Purugupta towards Skandagupta and because of that they did not mention his name in the genealogies detailed in their seal-inscriptions. But the omission of his name in the genealogies need not necessarily be explained in that way, as there are instances of not mentioning the name of collaterals in spite of cordial relationship, as also of mentioning even that of a rival collaterals.[30]

There is a greater possibility that Skandagupta was the immediate successor of Kumāragupta I and was followed by Purugupta, as that would make Purugupta and his descendants ruling in succession,[31] otherwise the order of succession would be Purugupta succeeded by Skandagupta, and the latter followed by the progenies of the former, which seems less probable. P L Gupta[32] argues in favour of the view that Skandagupta succeeded Kumāragupta I: "Had Skandagupta succeeded to the throne after a struggle with Purugupta, as a shrewd statesman, he would have *never* allowed him or his descendants to survive; who if alive, could not but be a constant danger to his life and throne." (Italics mine) Though this author prefers the view of P L Gupta that Skandagupta succeeded Kumāragupta and was in turn succeeded by Purugupta, yet like B P Sinha[33] does not consider the reason given by him in its favour as convincing.

The *Ārya-Mañjuśrī-mūlakalpa* which has the tendency of referring to the kings either by the initial letter of the name or a synonym of the name, has, at one place the following genealogy of the Gupta kings – Samudra, Vikrama, Mahendra and a name beginning with *sa* (*Sakārākhya*) and seems to refer to the last mentioned as Devarāja, who was succeeded by Bālāditya.[34] These kings are generally identified respectively with Samudragupta, Chandragupta II whose *viruda* was Vikramāditya, Kumāragupta I whose *viruda* was Mahendrāditya, and Skandagupta and Narasiṁhagupta Bālāditya. Skandagupta, like his grandfather, Chandragupta II, is known to have also borne the title *Vikramāditya*, and probably like him, also a second name, Devarāja. The use in this work of *ataḥ param* after Sakārākhya is taken by some scholars to suggest that Bālāditya was the immediate successor of Skandagupta.[35] According to Takakusu, Vikramāditya, mentioned by Paramārtha as one who sent his son Bālāditya and his queen for study to Vasubandhu, of whom he was the patron, should be identified with Skandagupta, and his crown-prince Bālāditya, with Narasiṁhagupta Bālāditya.[36] The Bhitari and the Nālandā seals (Nos. 53, 54, 55), however, clearly show that Narasiṁhagupta was the son of Purugupta. It may be stated that scholars have also identified Vikramāditya and his son variously with Chandragupta I and Samudragupta,[37] Chandragupta II and Kumāragupta I,[38] Chandragupta II and Govindagupta,[39] and Kumāragupta I and Purugupta.[40]

The term *pādānudhyāta*, which has been used for Purugupta in relation to his father, and not for Skandagupta in the same context, does not necessarily connote succession. It has been pointed out[41] that Mahendrapāla in Manahali grant is referred to as *Śrī-Rāmapāladeva pādānudhyāta*, although it is well known that he was not the immediate successor of that king—his father—as his brother preceded him. Besides being used in the context of royal succession, the term has also been used in the context of relationship of officials with their superior officials or with the king. Its various connotations in different contexts are 'favoured by', 'appointed by', 'attached to', or 'subordinate to',[42] In some cases, it could also be used for showing regard or loyalty to the high officer, prince or king.[43] In the religious context, it has been used to indicate that the person was a worshipper of god; for example, in the Gunaighar inscription (No. 50), Vainyagupta has been referred as *bhagavān-Mahādeva-pādānudhyāta.*[44] In the Bhitari pillar inscription (No. 33) *tat-pādānudhyāta* has been used for Kumāragupta I in relation to Chandragupta II, but not for Skandagupta in relation to Kumāragupta I. Some scholars[45] believe that this is because it was not Skandagupta but Purugupta who succeeded Kumāragupta I. Others,[46] however, point out that the epigraph refers to Skandagupta as one 'who subsisted (like a bee) on the wide-spreading water lilies which were the feet of (his) father',[47] which gives almost the same sense as *pādānudhyāta*, and is thus suggestive of his fidelity to his father. R K Mookerji[48] opines that because of his fidelity and competence, Skandagupta succeeded his father in a peaceful manner. D K Ganguly rightly states that in the seal of Kumāragupta III, each one of the kings – Kumaragupta I, Purugupta, Narasiṁhagupta and Kumāragupta III, are described as *pādānydhyāta* of their respective father, and if the term would have meant direct succession, there would be no place for the rule of Skandagupta and Budhagupta.[49] Some scholars believe that Skandagupta was the choice of his father for succession and interpret the coin-type *Apratigha* and the evidence of the *Kathā-saritsāgara* and *Chandra-garbha-pariprichchhā* to show that Kumāragupta I abdicated in his favour. But this is not acceptable for reasons given in Chapter 9. U N Roy opines that if Purugupta would have ruled in between Kumāragupta and Skandagupta then his name, despite his being collateral, would have been mentioned in the Supia inscription of the time of Skandagupta, as the epigraph was a private one, and not an official one.[50]

## IV

Fleet[51] believed that there was a division of the Gupta kingdom between Skandagupta and Purugupta. Allan[52] held the same view. He suggested that when Skandagupta was fighting the Hūṇas, Purugupta revolted against him and founded a new branch of the Gupta dynasty to which belonged Narasiṁhagupta and his son Kumāragupta II known from his Bhitari seal. Skandagupta remained king of the rest of the territory and to his branch belonged Prakāśāditya, Chandragupta III, and Ghaṭotkachagupta.[53] R G Basak[54] suggested that there was a peaceful division of the Gupta empire between Skandagupta and Purugupta, and kings of the latter's line 'were allowed by the former and his successors to enjoy a small kingdom, somewhere in the eastern portion of the Gupta empire, perhaps in south Bihar'. B P Sinha[55] disagrees with it, as in his opinion: 'It is hardly fair to postulate the continuous existence of a separate and independent kingdom under the three rather four successive sovereigns of four generations all claiming full imperial titles'. With the discovery of the Nālandā seal of Budhagupta (No. 47), it is known that he was the son of Purugupta, and not of Skandagupta, or of Kumāragupta II as was believed by some scholars, earlier. As regards Kumāragupta of Sarnath inscription (No. 37), whose parentage is not known, he could have been the son of Skandagupta or Purugupta or some other member of the Imperial Gupta family. The most decisive evidence against the theory of partition of the kingdom is that Skandagupta's inscriptions have been found from Bhitari in eastern Uttar Pradesh to Junagarh in Kathiawar, and that Budhagupta's inscriptions, ranging at least from AD 476 to AD 494, are known from various regions of northern India, from eastern Malwa to northern Bengal, as will be seen in Chapter 11. This does not leave space for another king ruling simultaneously. Further, a king, Chandragupta III Dvādaśāditya, was assumed by Allan on the basis of coins of much heavier weight than those known for Chandragupta II, and assigned by him to Skandagupta's branch. However, these coins have now been taken as issued by Vainyagupta, though there are a few scholars who believe that a few of such coins may be ascribed to Chandragupta III.[56]

## V

There is a good deal of controversy as to the name of the mother of Skandagupta, her family and also her social status. According to the Bhitari inscription (No. 33), Skandagupta, after his fathers death, betook himself to his mother who was with tears in her eyes, and broke the news of his victory over his enemies to her, in the same way as Kṛishṇa had announced his victory over his enemy to his mother Devakī.[57] It has been suggested by some scholars that the name of the mother of Kṛishṇa, Devakī, has been intentionally mentioned, as that was also the name of the mother of Skandagupta,[58] otherwise, comparison of Skandagupta with Kārttikeya, because of similarity of name (Skanda = Kārttikeya) and both being generals, one of the gods and another of men, would have been more appropriate, than with Kṛishṇa. But the choice of Kṛishṇa, an *avatāra* of Vishṇu, for comparison, would have been guided by the consideration that Skandagupta was a *parama-bhāgavata* (Vaishṇava) and also that the inscription records the installation of a Vishṇu image. It has also been pointed out that while Skandagupta's mother had become widow by the time he defeated his enemies, that was not the position of Devakī when Kṛishṇa killed Kaṁsa. The view that there is no point in comparing the mothers of the two, 'except on the basis that Skandagupta's mother happened to have the same name as Kṛishṇa's mother',[59] is not accepted by some scholars.

Since the enemy whom Kṛishṇa killed was his own maternal uncle (Kaṁsa), it has been surmised that the enemy of Skandagupta, who was responsible for the tottering of the fortunes of the Gupta family and whom Skandagupta defeated, was his maternal uncle (brother of his mother or that of his stepmother). D R Bhandarkar[60] suggests that his maternal uncle belonged to the Nāga dynasty. There is a view [61] that Anantasena, known from the Bihar inscription (No. 35), was a brother of Anantadevī, known from the seal inscriptions detailing the chronology as the queen of Kumāragupta I and mother of Purugupta, and that she belonged to the Nāga family. A few Nāga kings with *sena*-ending names are known, e.g. Nāgasena mentioned in the Allahabad pillar inscription (No. 1), and one Vīrasena known from his coins.[62] There is a view that the mother of Skandagupta was the same as that of Purugupta, viz., Anantadevī. Tarapada Bhattacharya[63] is of the opinion that in a Gadhwa inscription dicussed by Fleet[64] *Śrī Ku* should be taken as Śrī-Kumāragupta, and the name Anantaguptā should be taken to refer to his queen, and not to a private individual as Fleet (who was not aware of the existence of Anantadevī) had done. Another inscription of AD 467 (the last date known for Skandagupta) from the same site[65] refers to the establishment of a temple of Anantasvāmī, which seems to have been named after Anantadevī, who should be taken as the mother of Skandagupta. The view appears as good as any other, and has the merit that there is no doubt that Anantadevī was a queen of Kumāragupta I, and no other queen of his is known from any other source.

The Bhitari inscription mentions that when Skandagupta broke the news of the killing of the enemy to his mother, she was happy to hear it, which normally would not have been the case, if the enemy killed was her own brother, unless he was a cruel tyrant like Kaṁsa who for his self-interest would not spare even the life of his near relations. N N Dasgupta[66] considers the enemy, referred to in the inscription, as the head of the Pushyamitras. In the Gupta inscriptions detailing genealogy, along with the name of father of the ruling king, the name of his mother is also mentioned. In order to emphasize the point as to how important was the mention of the name of the mother was deemed, B P Sinha[67] refers to the evidence of a Vaiśālī sealing, and states: "Even the seal of Govinda Gupta mentions the name of his mother". The statement, however, is not correct. The seal in question does not belong to Govindagupta, but to Dhruvadevī and in the seal legend it is she who introduces herself as the "wife of *Mahārājādhirāja* Chandragupta and mother of *Mahārāja* Govindagupta" (Chapter 8). Since Skandagupta does not find mention in the genealogies inscribed on the seals, the question of the mention of his mother in them does not arise.

The Bhitari pillar inscription of Skandagupta (No. 33) mentions the names of the queens of Chandragupta I, Samudragupta, and Chandragupta II, but not that of Kumāragupta I, who was the reigning king's mother. Instead, Skandagupta is abruptly introduced as the son of his father. This, according to some scholars, could not be due to an accidental error of omission, but the result of deliberate choice.[68] Further, in the Gupta genealogy on seals of the later Imperial Gupta kings, it is Purugupta, born of *Mahādevī* Anantadevī, who is mentioned as the son and successor of Kumāragupta I. The non-mention of Skandagupta's name in these, according to one view, was because he was a collateral; the seals mention father- to-son succession of kings, rather than kings in chronological order. But according to another view, it may also be so because Skandagupta was not born of the chief queen, and for that reason had no natural claim to the throne. They also opine that it is for this reason that the name of Skandagupta's mother was deliberately omitted in the

Bhitari inscription. According to B P Sinha, the statement that Skandagupta got the throne by the strength of his own arms,[69] suggests that he had no legitimate claim to throne because of the low status of his mother.[70] Of the Gupta kings, he says, it is only Skandagupta who stresses the point of his belonging to the Gupta lineage, which, he would have done because he was not deemed the rightful claimant to the throne. Some scholars believe that there was struggle for succession between the rival princes—Skandagupta, Purugupta and others.[71]

H C Raychaudhuri[72] states that 'there was no rule prohibiting the mention of ordinary queens in inscriptions', and that Kuberanāgā, who was not the chief-queen, which position was held by Dhruvadevī, has been mentioned as *mahādevī* in the Poona copperplate of the Vākāṭaka queen Prabhāvatīguptā (No. 82). This, however, could be either due to inadvertence, or with the intention of glorifying the mother of the Vākāṭaka queen. It may be stated that this epithet has not been applied to Kuberanāgā in the Rithpur copperplate inscription (No. 84). Thus, the mention of a queen as *mahādevī* does not necessarily mean that she was the chief-queen, nor absence of it should be taken as a definite evidence of her not being the chief-queen. Even the name of the mother of the reigning king is sometimes omitted. In the Banskhera[73] and Madhuban[74] copperplates of Pushpabhūti king, Harsha, Yaśomatī is not mentioned as Harsha's mother, but in the Nālandā seal[75] and Sonpat seal,[76] she is mentioned as the mother of both Rājyavardhana and Harsha.[77] R C Majumdar,[78] however, opines that the reason for non-mention of her name in the two seals was because in them she had been mentioned as mother of the elder brother Rājyavardhana, and as such it was not deemed necessary to mention her name again as the mother of his younger brother Harsha, both being co-uterine. It has been pointed out that in one and the same inscription Yaśomatī is styled as merely *devī* while being mentioned as the mother of Rājyavardhana, who too like Harsha has been referred to as paramount sovereign (*parama-bhaṭṭāraka-mahārājādhirāja*), and *parama-bhaṭṭārikā-mahādevī* while mentioned as mother of Harsha. Such discrepancies suggest that from the non-mention of the name of Skandagupta's mother in the Bhitari inscription, it cannot definitely be concluded that she was not the chief queen.[79] H C Raychaudhuri[80] pleads that the evidence of the seals, which being royal are more accurate, should be differentiated from that of the ordinary *praśastis*, which at times omit the name of the mother of the reigning king, even though she may be the chief-queen,[81] and he gives the example from the Pāla epigraphs mentioning the names of *mahādevīs* in some and omitting them in others. Moreover, even in the Vākāṭaka records of Prabhāvatīguptā, of the same period, while the chief-queen of Chandragupta I, viz. Kumāradevī, has been mentioned in the context of stock phrases used for Samudragupta, in the Gupta epigraphs, viz., *Lichchhavi-dauhitrasya mahādevyāṁ Kumāradevyām=utpannasya*, the chief-queen of Samudragupta, namely Dattadevī, has not been mentioned, while Kuberanāgā—the queen of Chandragupta II—is mentioned because she was Prabhāvatīguptā's mother, and also because the records trace not the Vākāṭaka genealogy but that of Prabhāvatīguptā, through her parents. R K Mookerji[82] rightly observes: '...the epigraphic practice of mentioning mother of the ruling king is not uniform or conclusive'.

The text of the Bhitari pillar inscription (No. 33), up to the point where the last king, Kumāragupta I, is mentioned, is in prose, and thereafter in verse. The omission of the name of Skandagupta's mother and her title, according to some scholars, may be for consideration of metre. J Agrawal[83] opines that the poet who composed the Bhitari inscription was so keen for *vaṁśogāna* that he even forgot to mention name of the mother of Skandagupta. However, it may have been an inadvertent slip, which could be there even without over enthusiasm on the part of the author of the record.

According to P L Gupta,[84] Skandagupta's mother was not a chief-queen, not even a queen, but a woman of low origin, perhaps a keep or a female slave of the royal household and he was ashamed of calling himself as her son, and so the non-mention of her name in his epigraph is deliberate. Basham holds somewhat similar opinion.[85] He draws attention to the line in the Bhitari pillar inscription, as read by Fleet–*gītaiś=cha-stutibhiś=cha vandakaja(?)no(?) yaṁ prā(?)payaty=āryytām*,[86] and translated by that scholar as 'whom the bards raise to distinction with (their) songs and praises'.[87] Basham opines that it was the bards' (*vandakajanas'*) songs and praises that raised Skandagupta to the status of an *ārya*,[88] which otherwise he was not, as his mother, was an 'humble śūdrā concubine',[89] and that it is because of this that her name is not mentioned in his inscriptions. S K Maity asserts that 'there is *no doubt* that Skandagupta's mother did not possess the status of a queen'[90] (italic mine). J Agrawal[91] rejects Fleet's reading and translation, and inferences drawn from it by Gupta, Basham and some other scholars on the ground that the author of the *praśasti* would not have dared to include such a derogatory expression implying that it is only the eulogies of the bards, which made Skandagupta an *ārya*, otherwise he was an *anārya*. This portion of the inscription has been differently read by Fleet, D R Bhandarkar, J Agrawal, B Ch Chhabra, V C Pandey, and some other scholars.[92] It is difficult to make out the definite reading of the text, but this author is in agreement with J Agrawal's view that it would not have been meant to convey that Skandagupta was not an *ārya*,[93] and so far as the meaning is concerned, his reading—*vṛittakathane yaṁ hrepayaty=āryyatā*, meaning that Skandagupta blushed when his eulogy was recited, suits the context best, though the use of *hrepayati*, it has been pointed out, is rather unusual.

P L Gupta,[94] who accepts Fleet's reading and Basham's interpretation, sees nothing insulting in Skandagupta's being mentioned as of low origin from his mother's side. He opines that it was done with a view to showing that though born of a mother of low origin, by dint of his merit rose to the rank of king, and in support of his view he says that in modern times some men born in a family of low status but holding high position, take pride in telling that they have attained it by their own efforts.[95] This appears a case of superimposing a twentieth century idea in fifth century context. These days, people belonging to scheduled castes, enjoy certain privileges, whereas in ancient times, to be a śūdra was a disability. According to Gupta, even granting that the inscription mentions the name of Skandagupta's mother as Devakī, the indirect way of mentioning her name also creates doubt about her high social status. In his view, in the Bhitari inscription to indicate succession the lengthy expression *pitṛi-parigata-pāda-padma-vartī prathita-yaśāḥ*, instead of the generally used phrase, *tat-pādānudhyāta*, was chosen because he was not a rightful claimant to the throne.[96]

B P Sinha[97] and a few others believe that the use of such phrases as *sva-vaṁśa-ketu*, 'banner of his lineage' in line 25 of the Junagadh rock inscription (No. 30), *Gupta-vaṁś=aika-vīraḥ*, 'the most eminent hero of the Gupta dynasty' in line 4 of the Bhitari pillar inscription (No. 33), and *Guptānāṁ vaṁśajaḥ* 'born in the lineage of the Guptas' in line 2 of the Kahaum stone pillar inscription (No. 31) reflects Skandagupta's inferiority complex on account of his mother's low origin, and intended to convey that he should be accepted as a worthy member of the Gupta dynasty. But phrases like *Gupta-kula-vyoma-śaśi*, 'moon in the sky that is the Gupta dynasty'[98] and *Gupta-kul=āmala-chandra*, 'pure moon of the Gupta dynasty',[99] have been used for Kumāragupta I, which in his case have been taken to reflect his noble qualities, and the same may as well be the intention in using similar phrases for Skandagupta. It may be argued that it was his affection and regard for his mother that made him choose her as the first person to be conveyed the news of his victory over his enemies, and this was deemed so significant that in order to make this act to be known to people of his time and also to posterity, he got it recorded permanently on stone pillar. It has been pointed out that if Skandagupta's mother would have been a śūdrā, then, as per the testimony of Yājñavalkya, he would not have been recognized as a scion of the Gupta family.[100] and that it would not have mattered very much whether he was the son of the chief queen or a junior queen, as the Hindu law does not ordain that only the son of the chief queen should be king.[101]

The interpretations of the title *kramāditya* on Skandagupta's coins offered by some scholars may also be mentioned in this regard. Dasharatha Sharma[102] opines that it conveys that the kingdom he ruled had come to him in succession, and he had legitimate right on it. In contrast, P L Gupta[103] is of the view that the title conveys that Skandagupta got the throne by his own prowess, which he could not have got otherwise because of the low origin of his mother. But as will be seen later in Chapter 11, *kramāditya* is not a title borne exclusively by Skandagupta, but also by some other Gupta kings, and therefore need not be interpreted the way it has been in his context. In conclusion, it may be stated that there is nothing by way of evidence that can throw light on the status of the mother of Skandagupta. There is hardly anything to support the conjecture hazarded by Basham, P L Gupta and some other scholars that she was of low social status and therefore was not a legitimate queen. She might or might not have been the chief queen, she certainly was a queen.

## VI

From the statement in the Bhitari pillar inscription (No. 33), that when Skandagupta's father had gone to heaven (*pitari divamupete*) and there was convulsion (*vipluta*) of the family fortune (*vaṁśalakshmī*), it may be inferred that some enemies created trouble for the Gupta dynasty on the death of Kumāragupta I. Some scholars suggest that after the death of that king, there was a war of succession, and that Govindagupta, Purugupta, Ghaṭotkachagupta and a few other princes were involved in it. But if at all there was contest for throne then Ghaṭotkachagupta, whom Bhandarkar and a few other scholars considered as the main contestant,[104] and also Govindagupta have to be excluded from it. As seen in Chapter 9, from the Ramtek inscription (No. 85) it is known that Ghaṭotkachagupta was a son of Chandragupta II and rebelled against Kumāragupta I, whom, as per the evidence of the Tumain inscription (No. 19) he served as governor. As regards Govindagupta, whom R C Majumdar and a few other scholars consider as a contestant against Skandagupta, as stated earlier (Chapter 8), he would have been too old at the time of the death of Kumāragupta to be a contender for the throne against that Gupta prince, and there is evidence to suggest that he preceded, and not followed, Kumāragupta on the Gupta throne (*ibid.*).

In the Junagarh inscription of Skandagupta (No. 30), it is stated that he established himself as king by sheer dint of his prowess, which too is taken by some scholars to suggest that he became king after defeating his rivals. The statement in the Junagarh inscription that Lakshmī, after scanning the merits and demerits of the princes selected Skandagupta as her lord rejecting 'all sons of kings' (*vyapetya sarvān manuj=endra-putrāṁ=lLakshmī svayaṁ yaṁ varayāṁchakāra*), according to some scholars,[105] shows that the competition was between Skandagupta and the other Gupta princes. The same is inferred from a coin-type identified by some as King-and-Lakshmī type in which the king is shown as receiving something from the deity. According to others, this suggests that he was considered best fitted to be selected to rule because of his valiant and successful fight against the enemies of his family and the empire.[106] The expression used is *manuj=endra-putrān,* and is translated as 'sons of kings' by J F Fleet[107] and D R Bhandarkar.[108] The expression 'sons of kings' is at times also used for kings, which would mean the contestants were persons other than members of the Gupta family. But if it is translated as 'sons of king,' then the rivals could be his own brothers or stepbrothers. There are examples of kings who obtained kingship after defeating their rivals or enemies, being referred to as chosen by Lakshmī as her lord.[109] But in some cases, such a statement is used even though the prince did not face any contest in being installed as the king, as in the case with Śaka king Rudradāman.[110] The Junagarh inscription (No. 30) says, in exaggerated vein and in conventional phraseology, that Skandagupta brought the whole earth under his control by his own prowess, and also that he put down the 'serpent-like kings' who raised their heads in arrogance. Raychaudhuri[111] points out that in the *Harsha-charita*, the father of Harsha refers to him as one who has been accepted by Śrī of her own accord, though it is known that he was devoted to his elder brother who was then alive, and was the rightful claimant to the throne. An expression with similar meaning is met with, even for the *vishayapati* (district officer) Mātṛivishṇu in the Eran stone inscription of Budhagupta (No. 44). According to Raychaudhuri, the discarded kings in the Junagarh inscription should refer to the persons other than of the Gupta family, for, he points out, in a *svayaṁvara*, the princes invited are from outside the girl's family, and that it does not necessarily lead to fight, and even when it does, the contestants are from outside the family.[112]

Majumdar is of the view that in the expressions *vichalita-kula-lakshmī* (shaken fortune of the family) and *viplutāṁ-vaṁśa-lakshmī* (convulsed fortune of the family) in the Bhitari pillar inscription (No. 33), the words *vaṁśa* and *kula* have been chosen with care to indicate that there was great danger to the family, rather than to the empire,[113] and that if the intention had been to refer to foreign invasion, then, he says, the expression would better have been *rājya-lakshmī*.[114] H C Raychaudhuri,[115] on the other hand, opines that the use of the epithets like *amal=ātmā,* (pure soul), in the Bhitari pillar inscription and *para-hitakārī*, (benefactor of others) on coins[116] for Skandagupta do not warrant the conclusion that he shed the blood of his brothers.[117] But as against this, some scholars opine that such phraseology need not be taken literally, and point out that Govinda IV Rāshṭrakūṭa was responsible for killing his brother, yet he has been described as a noble person in his inscriptions, and even suggest that these epithets may have been used for Skandagupta to camouflage his killing of rival claimants to the throne. Raychaudhuri, on the other hand, categorically states: "There is not the slightest reference to fratricidal war".[118]

## VII

If Fleet's reading[119] of the text of the Bhitari pillar inscription (No. 33) as *Pushyamitrāṁś=cha* is correct, as to us it appears to be, then one of the enemies Skandagupta faced were the Pushyamitras. Divekar[120] reads it as *yuddhy=amitrāṁś=cha,* (enemies in war), which is taken to refer to rival princes, but in that case the expression *samudita-bala-kośa,* (whose power and wealth has risen), would not be appropriate for the Gupta princes as claimants to the throne,[121] who would have had access to resources accumulated for generations, and would instead refer to the enemy who had suddenly become powerful. P K Agrawala[122] reads the text as *samudita-*

*bala-kośābhyām=amttrāṁś=cha jitvā,* meaning that Skandagupta 'conquered his enemies with his augmented army and treasury', which is completely different from the readings offered by other scholars. In the Bhitari inscription, it is also stated that Skandagupta placed his left foot on the footstool that was the back of the king (*kshitipa-charaṇa-pīṭhe sthāpito vāma-pādaḥ*). The use of the singular favours reference to the chief of enemies, in all probability of the Pushyamitras, rather than to the different enemy kings. Bhandarkar took the expression to mean that Skandagupta put his foot on the king's stool, i.e. he occupied the throne.[123] V V Mirashi[124] rightly states that if this interpretation was intended then the words *kshitipa* and *vāma* would be redundant as a king would not put only his left foot on the footstool. The words have been used to show utter contempt for the enemy king. There is also a view that since the king was in the battlefield, and no footstool being available there, he made the enemy king's back as footstool. However, in that case the expression is to be taken as figuratively conveying that the king had been thoroughly subdued by Skandagupta, and not in the sense that he actually put his foot on the enemy king treating him as his footstool.

D R Bhandarkar rejects the reading of Fleet and accepts that of Divekar, as in his opinion, it is 'highly strange that such an insignificant clan as the Pushyamitras should all at once rise to such eminence as to dominate Gupta supremacy for a while, only to sink into perennial oblivion thereafter.'[125] Dandekar states that Divekar's objection against reading *Pushyamitrāṁścha,* as the 'tribe is not mentioned in the Allahabad Pillar Inscription of Samudragupta',[126] is not quite relevant. Ashvini Agrawal[127] counters Bhandarkar's argument by stating that if Bhavatta(=Bhavadatta)varman of a small Nala kingdom could defeat the Vākāṭakas who were masters of a fairly extensive kingdom, then the relatively insignificant Pushyamitras could as well have created serious trouble to the powerful Guptas by launching an offensive against them.

A number of scholars consider Divekar's reading *Yuddhyamitrāṁś=cha* as faulty,[128] and prefer *Pushyamitrāṁś=cha* as read by Fleet.[129] Attempts have been made to identify the Pushyamitras and the region inhabited by them. The mention of Pushyamitrika-*kula* in the Jaina *sūtras,*[130] and the seal with the legend *Pusamitasa* (which appears a personal name) in Kushāṇa characters from Bhita,[131] have hardly any bearing on the Pushyamitras in question. Smith[132] placed the Pushyamitras in the north. Hoernle[133] took them for the Maitrakas, which, however, does not hold good, since they appear to be subservient to the Guptas right from the time of Bhaṭārka, to that of Droṇasiṁha whose date AD 502 is known. N K Bhattasali considered the Pushyamitras as descendants of Pushyavarman, king of Kāmarūpa.[134] In his view, Mahendravarman, a descendant of Pushyavarman and performer of two horse-sacrifices, attacked Skandagupta. There is, however, no evidence to show that the descendants of Pushyavarman were called Pushyamitras. Moreover, it has been pointed out that Mahendravarman's date is much later than that of Skandagupta, and as such, he could not have been the invader.[135] S Chattopadhyaya takes *narapati-bhujagas* of the Junagarh inscription (No. 30) to stand for the Nāgas and identifies them with the Pushyamitras.[136] R D Banerji[137] identifies Pushyamitras with the Hūṇas. The identification may be rejected as the Hūṇas have been separately and categorically mentioned in the same inscription (No. 33). S R Goyal opines that they may be identified with the Varmans of Malwa.[138] K D Bajpai[139] identifies them with the scions of the Mitra dynasties of which the originator was Pushyamitra Śuṅga, and K C Jain considers them as progenies of the 'Śuṅga-Mitra chiefs of Ahichchhatrā, Mathurā, Ayodhyā and Kauśāmbī', who after being defeated at the hands of Samudragupta, took refuge in the forest region near the source of the river Narmada, and taking advantage of Hūṇa invasions and internal dissensions in the Gupta family, raised the banner of revolt.[140] However, it does not seem convincing that assorted people bearing *mitra*-ending names formed a powerful political group under the name of Pushyamitras, and became so strong as to challenge the Gupta king. The most convincing identification of the Pushyamitras, based on the testimony of the purāṇas, is that it was a tribe inhabiting Mekala (Amarkantak region) on the Narmada.[141] K A N Sastri[142] places them in the Vindhyan region, and considers them as of Iranian origin. The testimony of the Balaghat plates of Pṛithvīsheṇa Vākāṭaka (No. 87) shows that Mekala was a separate kingdom up to the fifth century AD. S R Goyal[143] believes that the Pushyamitras of Mekala, were assisted and abetted by the Vākāṭakas, in their attack on the Guptas when the latter were engaged in war with the Hūṇa invaders. This help from the Vākāṭakas, he believes, increased their military might, which makes the use of *samudita-bala-kośa* for them in the Bhitari inscription (No. 33) quite apt. He identifies king of the Pushyamitras with the Pāṇḍava ruler of Mekala who, he suggests, as a subordinate ally of Narendrasena Vākāṭaka attacked the Guptas.[144] A M Shastri points out that this was not possible as the beginning of the Pāṇḍuvaṁśī dynasty should be placed in c. AD 500.[145] The Bamnala (Nimar district, M P) hoard containing Gupta coins up to the time of Kumāragupta I and also a gold bar, which seems to be the result of the melting of ornaments—a practice generally followed by people in times of great insecurity—suggests that there was some political turmoil in the area in that period.[146]

In course of the fight against the Pushyamitras, Skandagupta had to undergo great hardship, and was forced to pass a whole night (or several nights)[147] sleeping on the bare ground (*kshiti-tala-śayanīye yena nītā triyāmā*), in the battlefield (No. 33). V C Pandey[148] suggests that it is not necessary to presume that Skandagupta spent the night sleeping on the bare ground because of the exigencies of the battle, and that possibly he had to fight the enemy on a day of mourning because of his father's death, and as part of the ritual, slept on the bare ground. The interpretation, though ingenuous, is not acceptable, in view of the fact that the inscription mentions that he had to undergo that ordeal with a view to making the family fortune stable. The defeating of the Pushyamitras during the last days of his father's reign might have made his father favour him as his successor.[149]

## VIII

Skandagupta's ordeal did not end with his victory over the Pushyamitras. He had to face an even more formidable enemy in the invading Hūṇas. That the invasion of the Hūṇas, followed that of the Pushyamitras can be inferred from the fact that the epigraph mentions the two invasions in that order, even though that of the Hūṇas was a more serious calamity. Goyal[150] suggests that the victory that he announced to his mother, refers not only to that won over the Pushyamitras, but also over other enemies whom, he might have fought simultaneously, and not necessarily in succession. B P Sinha[151] is of the opinion that Skandagupta defeated the Pushyamitras when he was a prince, and the Hūṇas after becoming king, as in the Bhitari inscription (No. 33), the latter victory is mentioned after it is stated that with his own arms he saved the tottering lineage and subjugated the earth.[152]

The Hūṇas—the nomadic horde from Central Asia, known for their skill in archery, and also for their ferocious and cruel nature—passed across the Oxus valley, conquered Gandhāra and advanced further south-east.

The battle between Skandagupta and the Hūṇas was terrific, and according to the Bhitari pillar inscription (No. 33), which is the only source of this war, it 'made the earth shake' (*dharā kampitā*). Skandagupta triumphed over the enemy, and thus saved the people from the scourge of the Hūṇas.

K P Jayaswal takes *ajayad Jato* (or *Gupto*) *Hūṇān*[153] in the *Chāndra-vyākaraṇa* to mean that the Gupta king, who is to be identified with Skandagupta defeated the Hūṇas. The Hūṇas fled to their country and did not invade this land for about half a century after that.[154] This conqueror of the Hūṇas bore the *āditya* title *Kramāditya* and, in only one coin-type as *Vikramāditya*, the latter being the most common title of his grandfather Chandagupta II, the conqueror of the Śakas.

The Junagarh rock inscription (No. 30, line 4) after mentioning the death of Skandagupta's father, says that eulogies of Skandagupta were sung in the *mlechchha* country by the defeated enemies, whose pride had been given a blow by him. The reference is to the foreign invasion, rather than to the internal rebellion, and, according to most scholars, by the *mlechchhas* the Hūṇas is meant.[155] In the Bhitari pillar inscription (No. 33), it is stated that his noble character and fame were praised 'in every region by happy men, even down to the children' *(ākumāraṁ manushyaiḥ).*[156] Since Kālidāsa mentions that the Hūṇas resided on the banks of river Vaṅkshu, some scholars opine that in the Gupta period, to which they ascribe the poet, the tribe was located in Bactria.[157] They conquered Gandhāra, and from there they moved south-eastwards.[158] They carried fire and sword, and laid into devastation villages, towns and cities. Internal troubles in the Gupta kingdom, and the invasion of the Pushyamitras would have provided them a suitable opportunity to launch an invasion against the Guptas. There is no evidence to support the view of D R Bhandarkar[159] that the Nāga ruler invited the Hūṇa chief to come to his succour. According to him the Nāgas and the Hūṇas were defeated, though the Gupta prince Ghaṭotkachagupta lost his life in this war. But the evidence of the Ramtek inscription (No. 85), as seen above (Chapter 9), the Gupta prince seems to have lost his life earlier, when he raised the banner of revolt against Kumāragupta I. Numismatic evidence in the form of two coins of this prince shows that he declared himself as king and issued coins. According to the *Kathā-saritsāgara,* Vikramāditya, son of Mahendrāditya, defeated the *mlechchhas*, among others, and scholars generally identify Mahendrāditya with Kumāragupta I, whose title it was, Vikramāditya with Skandagupta, and the *mlechchhas* with the Hūṇas.[160]

The Bayana hoard of Gupta gold coins contains coins of kings up to Kumāragupta I, with the exception of one coin bearing the legend *kramāditya*, which was the title of Ghaṭotkachagupta as well as Skandagupta. If the king is identified with Skandagupta, as we feel he should be,[161] then it can be said that the hoard was deposited at the beginning of his reign, when there was political turmoil.

The place where the battle between Skandagupta and the Hūṇas was fought has not been satisfactorily identified. Some scholars, following Fleet's reading *Gāṅga-dhvani* in the Bhitari pillar inscription, believe that the battle was fought on the banks of the Ganga. Others, however, believe that *Gāṅga-dhvani* has been used as a mere simile. Chhabra[162] and J Agrawal[163] instead read *śārṅga-dhvani* 'twang of the bow' and take it suggestive of some battle scene. The former compares it to *śārṅga-kūjita* in the *Raghuvaṁśa* of Kālidāsa in the context of the battle fought between Raghu and the Yavanas. J Agrawal rejects the reading *Gāṅga-dhvani*, as according to him, 'the Hūṇas never penetrated into any part of India near the Ganga'.[164] In contrast to this, there is a view that the Hūṇas overran the Gangetic plain up to Bhitari in the Ghazipur district,[165] which, for reasons detailed by this author elsewhere,[166] seems more plausible. Possibly Kumāragupta I died fighting at Bhitari, which place seems to be of much importance for the Guptas in general, and Kumāragupta I in particular. Bricks with the name of Kumāragupta have been found in the fields of Bhitari, near the pillar bearing the epigraph of Skandagupta.[167] In the light of *Aśvamedha* coins of Kumragupta I, it has been suggested that he performed horse-sacrifice (*aśvamedha*), and that the bricks with his name inscribed on them found at Bhitari were used for making the sacrificial altar related to it.[168] The installation of the image of Śārṅgin (Vishṇu) at this place, as evident from the inscription on the pillar located here, also testifies to the importance of the site.[169] Bhandarkar writes: "...the whole village of Bhitari is situated on the Gāṅgī-nadī, apparently a branch of the Ganges. That seems to be the reason Skandagupta erected this monument to his father on this holy spot. In fact, Bhitari is studded with so many large mounds that it is not impossible that it was the mausoleum or *pratimā-gṛiha* of the Gupta family." There is a view that the area around Bhitari was the original home of the Imperial Guptas, and that Bhitari was made the target of attack by the Hūṇas because of its great significance for the Imperial Guptas. J Agrawal[170] opines that the Hūṇa war was fought in Surāshṭra, the region for which Skandagupta is said to have deeply deliberated to find out a very competent official to govern (No. 30). S R

Goyal,[171] however, opines that there was no Hūṇa invasion of Surāshṭra during the reign of Skandagupta, and the serious deliberations regarding the appointment of governor there has nothing to do with the Hūṇa invasion.

Some scholars believe that there were more than one Hūṇa invasion. According to McGovern,[172] Skandagupta was defeated many times by the Hūṇas, and the Gupta empire almost tottered as a result of their successive invasions. R D Banerji[173] is of the view that Skandagupta died fighting the Hūṇas the third time. He suggests that during the Hūṇa invasion, Purugupta set himself as rival king and Skandagupta was defeated by the Hūṇas and died. According to Smith,[174] there were renewed Hūṇa invasions, and Skandagupta was unable to check them in the later part of his reign, as he had done in the earlier part of it, and succumbed to them. It appears that some scholars were so overwhelmed by the fighting skills of the Hūṇas as also the record of their success in battles fought outside India, that they took them as victorious against Skandagupta, despite the fact there is no evidence to substantiate it. The view that there were several Hūṇa invasions during the time of Skandagupta appears, to some extent, based on the presumption that there is debasement of the coins of that king, and that it was resorted to because of the poor economic condition caused by the Hūṇa invasions.[175] But the view of the debasement of coins was based on the chemical analysis of Skandagupta's coins as reported by Cunningham,[176] which is not fully reliable. Of the two classes of coins of Skandagupta, the coins of Class I are based on the weight standard of about 132 grains and as they are nearer to the weight of the coins of Kumāragupta I, they may be considered as earlier issues of that king. The coins of Class II weigh about 144 grains. The chemical analysis in the British Museum laboratory, which is more scientific than their earlier analysis referred to above, shows that despite more debasement seen in the heavy weight coins of Skandagupta, the quantity of pure gold in them is not less than that of the gold coins of his predecessors.[177] One is inclined to agree with the view that the defeat of the Hūṇas at the hands of Skandagupta was quite decisive and for about half a century they are not known to have caused depredations east of Gandhāra.[178] Incidentally, it may be stated that there is no evidence to substantiate the view that 'Purugupta had defeated the Hūṇas who had attacked his empire'.[179]

We may refer to the view, according to which there was Nāga-Hūṇa alliance against Skandagupta. The Junagadh inscription (No. 30) mentions

Skandagupta who like *garuḍa* (an insignia of the Gupta family and hence apt for that king) rendered such serpent-kings (*narapati-bhujagas*) devoid of poison as had uplifted their heads in pride and arrogance. D R Bhandarkar[180] opines that 'serpent kings' should refer to the Nāga rulers. He is of the view that after the death of Kumāragupta I 'the Nāgas raised the standard of revolt with such virulence and ruthlessness that the fortune of the Gupta dynasty sunk to the lowest level.' He holds that the Nāgas invited the Hūṇas to invade the Gupta empire.[181] His view that Ghaṭotkachagupta, whom he considered as the son and successor of Kumāragupta I, was probably killed in this war and was succeeded by Skandagupta,[182] has to be given up, as from the Ramtek inscription (No. 85) it is evident that the prince was the brother of Kumāragupta and as one who, it appears, rebelled against him. Though the 'serpent kings' referred to in the Junagarh inscription of Skandagupta (No. 30) would be apt for the Nāga kings, it is rather difficult to believe that the Nāgas would have been in a position to provide such a great challenge to the Gupta dynasty, as their kings ruling in Mathurā, Vidiśā, Padam-Pawaya and other regions had been uprooted by Samudragupta and their kingdoms merged in the Gupta empire. The Guptas and the Nāgas were bound by matrimonial alliance, as a Nāga princess, Kuberanāgā, had been married to Chandragupta II. At the same time, the possibility of the revolt of the Nāga chiefs cannot be entirely ruled out. S R Goyal opines that it is not impossible that 'serpent kings' is with reference to the Varmans of Malwa,[183] who, in his view, had by then shifted their allegiance to the Vākāṭakas.

## IX

R N Dandekar[184] and some other scholars, on the evidence of the Balaghat plate inscription (No. 87), suggest a military conflict between Skandagupta and the Vākāṭakas. He surmises that while Skandagupta was facing the invasion of the Hūṇas and Pushyamitras, during the last days of Kumāragupta I and early days of his own rule, Narendrasena Vākāṭaka attacked the Guptas but suffered a setback due to Skandagupta's success in the war; but later renewing hostilities during Skandagupta's last years and shortly after his death, Narendrasena, seems to have established his sovereignty in Kosala, Mekala and Mālava.[185] Goyal[186] speculates that Vākāṭakas and the Kadambas allied themselves against the Gupta-Nala combination towards the end of Kumāragupta I's rule. He suggests that the Pushyamitras were subordinate allies of Narendrasena Vākāṭaka, and it was because of the help and support of the Vākāṭakas to them that they dared attack the Guptas. He[187] opines that during the period of troubles for the Guptas, the Varmans of Daśapura shifted their allegiance from the Guptas to the Vākāṭakas. The Mandasor inscription of Prabhākara of AD 467 (No. 36), which is also the last known date for Skandagupta, mentions earlier Gupta kings Chandragupta II and Govindagupta and records that Prabhākara, presumably ruling over Daśapura, was like fire to the wood-like enemies of the Gupta dynasty, though it does not mention the name of the then ruling Gupta king. N P Chakravarti[188] considers Prabhākara as the successor, if not the son, of Bandhuvarman. But while Bandhuvarman and his ancestors bore *varman*-ending names and his family has been mentioned as Aulikara, the name-ending of Prabhākara differs and there is no evidence that he was an Aulikara; only the *kara*-ending is common between his name and the name of that family. Further, Ghaṭotkachagupta rebelled against Kumāragupta with the help of the Vākāṭakas, but suffered defeat. There is a view that Skandagupta appointed Prabhākara as governor in place of the Varman feudatory.[189] The non-mention of the name of Skandagupta in the record of Prabhākara, may be because by the time the record was engraved he had already died. Ashvini Agrawal[190] however, is of the view that there was no Gupta-Vākāṭaka conflict, for if it would have been so, it would have found mention in the Gupta inscriptions; and that since neither the inscriptions of Skandagupta nor the Mandasor inscription of the silk-weavers' guild composed in AD 472 (No. 38), make any such mention, the claims of Narendrasena's suzerainty over Malwa should be taken as a vain boast. It would perhaps not be justified to completely discard the evidence of the Vākāṭaka epigraph.

There is a view that while Parṇadatta was appointed as a civilian governor of Surāshṭra, Maitraka Bhaṭārka was stationed there as chief commander of the army, and that later he also held the office of the governor.[191] Some scholars, on the basis of the evidence of some inscriptions from Mandasor, suggest that in the administration of the Malwa region, side by side with the Varman rulers, Gupta governors such as Govindagupta, Ghaṭotkachagupta and Prabhākara, in succession, were also appointed.

Parṇadatta appointed his son, Chakrapālita, in-charge of the administration of Girinagara, after satisfying himself about his suitability for that office. The Sudarśana lake, as per the evidence of the Junagarh inscription of Rudradāman,[192]had been constructed during the reign of Chandragupta Maurya, and canals had been dug from it during the reign of Aśoka. It burst due to heavy rains and was got repaired by the governor of the Śaka king in AD 150. Skandagupta's inscription from the same site (No. 30) mentions that it burst in AD 455 due to heavy rains. Drained of waters, the inscription informs, Lake Sudarśana ('beautiful to look at') was turned into *durdarśana* ('ugly to look at'). Chakrapālita having concern for the welfare of the people and the king, got the badly damaged dam repaired in a short period of two months. The evidence of the two epigraphs testifies to the existence of the reservoir for more than 750 years. Chakrapālita got constructed a Vishṇu temple near the dam.[193]

Besides Parṇadatta, the governor of Surāshṭra, and his son, Chakrapālita, in charge of administration of the city of Girinagara, modern Girnar (No. 30), some other high officials of Skandagupta find mention in the epigraphs. Śarvanāga governed the region of Antarvedī, i.e., the *doab* between the Ganga and the Yamuna (No. 34),[194] and Bhīmavarman was governed the region around Kosam.[195] The find-spots of Skandagupta's inscriptions from Kahaum (Deoria district), Indor (Bulandshahr district), Gadhwa (Allahabad district), Supia (Rewa district), Bhitari (Ghazipur district) and Junagarh (Junagarh district), give a fairly good idea of the extent of his empire. The Kahaum inscription (No. 31) refers to 'heads of hundred kings falling at the feet by way of tendering homage to him' and compares him with Indra, while the Supia (Rewa district) inscription portrays him as a *chakravartī*. His *āditya* titles are *Kramāditya* and *Vikramāditya*, and, like many other Gupta kings, he has been referred to as *parama-bhāgavata*, i.e., Vaishṇava. To him are applied such epithets as *sucharita*, 'noble life', *amalātmā*, 'pure soul', and *vinīta*, 'humble'. The Junagarh rock inscription (No. 30), in a conventional hyperbole, states that within his kingdom there was no rogue, addict, irreligious, poor or afflicted.

There is no tangible evidence to show that Skandagupta conquered new regions and, as such, the use of the phrase conquering 'the whole earth' (*pṛithvīṁ samagrāṁ*), for him in the Junagarh inscription (No. 30) may be more a conventional eulogy than a statement of fact. He is, however, known for defeating the invaders like the Pushyamitras and the Hūṇas, and he might have also defeated the rival princes if there had been war of succession. B P Sinha,[196] on the basis of the *Kathā-saritsāgara* which states that Vikramāditya, with his mighty force, made a conquest of southern countries, Madhyadeśa, Surāshṭra, eastern regions of the Ganga, and Kashmir, considers the possibility of some of these regions being conquered by Skandagupta, whom he identifies with Vikramāditya. However, Surāshṭra was a part of the Gupta kingdom right from the time of Chandragupta II, and there is hardly any possibility of Skandagupta's conquering Kashmir, and some other areas mentioned in that text. The *Vāyu-purāṇa*[197] says, "The Devarakshitas will enjoy the Kosalas, the Andhras, and the Pauṇḍras, the Tāmraliptas and the coast-folk (coastal folk) and the charming city of Champā. Guha will protect all these territories, namely Kaliṅgas, Mahishkas and the inhabitant of the Mahendra mountains". The mention in plural, Devarakshitas, may be due to the text being faulty. The *Vishṇu-purāṇa* version is slightly different: "Devarakshita will extend his protection to Kosala, Oḍra, Tāmralipti and Puri on the sea, Mahendra to Kalinga and Mahisha, and Guha to (all this) area". The last part is better understood in the light of the *Vāyu-purāṇa*, referred to above. Some scholars identify Devarakshita with Chandragupta II, who, as per the evidence of the Chammak copperplate of Pravarasena II (No. 83), had another name, Devagupta, and that of an Udaigiri inscription (No. 11), as Devarāja.

Skandagupta has been hailed as a great hero of the Gupta dynasty (*Gupta-vaṁś=aika-vīraḥ*, No. 33). The Kahaum inscription (No.31) refers to GE 141 (= AD 460) as a peaceful year *(śānta-varsha)* of Skandagupta, which suggests that the early years of his reign were full of troubles, a fact which is confirmed by the Bhitari pillar inscription (No. 33) and the Junagarh rock inscription (No. 30). The statement, that he spent an entire night (or nights) lying on the bare ground (No. 33), shows that he actively participated in wars. Despite great internal pulls and serious external pushes which affected the vitality of the Gupta empire, Skandagupta was able to keep intact the territories he inherited, which extended from Bengal to Kathiawar and from the Himalayas to the Vindhyas. R K Mookerji[198] states, 'the decline and fall of the Gupta empire may be taken to date from the end of Skandagupta's reign....' The scarcity of silver coins with *garuḍa* on the reverse has led Allan[199] to opine that the western provinces of his empire were lost either in the last days of his reign or shortly thereafter. P L Gupta[200] opines that since no silver coins of Skandagupta of western fabric bearing imperial titles, and no inscription belonging to the later part of his reign, have been found in Surāshṭra, it appears that he lost that province. But it has been pointed out that his silver coins are not so scarce, and the relative chronology of his coins cannot be satisfactorily established.

No inscription of the time of his father or grandfather has been found in Surashtra, yet there is no doubt that the region formed a part of their territory. The non-mention of Skandagupta's name in the Mandasor inscription of Prabhākara of AD 467 (No. 36), which is also the last known date for Skandagupta, is perhaps because by then he had died, rather than he was bypassed. Earlier, Govindagupta and Ghaṭotkachagupta had been governors of Malwa, which region came to be turned into 'one of the most vulnerable spots of the body politic of the empire'. As mentioned above, according to some scholars, there was some turmoil in that region during the last days of Skandagupta's reign; Narendrasena Vākāṭaka, whose commands are said to have been obeyed by Kosala, Mekala and Mālava created problems either by invading that Gupta territory and/or by inciting local insurgency there.[201] However, the continuance of the Gupta rule over Kosala may be presumed on the evidence that Goparāja, the daughter's son of Śarabharāja, a ruler of that region, fought for the Guptas at Eran in AD 510 (No. 52) during the rule of Bhānugupta.[202] The purāṇic evidence, mentioned above, states that Guha, identified by some as Skandagupta, will rule Kaliṅga, Mahisha and Mahendra. The Sumaṇḍala plate suggests that the Gupta rule lasted in some areas of Kalinga at least upto AD 569,[203] but his rule over the other two is doubtful. The Shankarpur plate of the time of Budhagupta (No. 46) shows Gupta rule in Baghelkhand.

Skandagupta was the last in the 'glorious galaxy' of the great rulers of the Gupta dynasty.[204] In his reign are seen the 'last vestiges of the imperial structure.' He warded off the invasions of the Pushyamitras and the Hūṇas, subdued rebellious feudatories and perhaps also rival claimants to the throne, and appointed able administrators for governing the provinces. Though Skandagupta himself was a *parama-bhāgavata* (i.e. a Vaishṇava), Jaina images were set up during his reign (No. 31), and Nandī (Śiva's bull) is depiected on some of his silver coins. His most common *viruda* was *Kramāditya*, but on one variety of Altar type of silver coins it is *Vikramāditya*, and some scholars are of the view that along with Samudragupta and Chandragupta II, he also contributed to the growth of the Vikramāditya legend (Chapter 7, above). His last known date is AD 467, met with on his silver coins.[205] The next date known for a Gupta king is AD 473, met with in the Sarnath inscription of Kumāragupta II. According to the chronology followed by the author, Purugupta ascended the throne between these two dates. If Kumāragupta of the Sarnath inscription was not the son of Skandagupta, then the latter might not have had any son.[206] A coin-type of Skandagupta has been labelled as 'King-and-Queen' type by some scholars,[207] and as 'King-and-Lakshmī' by others.[208] He must have been a married man, as the performance of certain royal rituals and ceremonies required the presence of the queen. It is not known how his end came.

Dandekar states: 'His wise administration, his heroic wars, his patriotic ambitions—all these made Skandagupta one of the greatest of the Gupta emperors.'[209] Ashvini Agrawal,[220] however, considers him as "the greatest of all the Gupta rulers by all standards of judgment". Though the role played by Skandagupta in saving the fortunes of the Gupta dynasty deserves all praise, yet Samudragupta and Chandragupta II are no less, perhaps more deserving claimants for that position, and R C Majumdar rightly considers the former of the two as the greatest ruler of the dynasty.[211]

## NOTES AND REFERENCES

1. Bhagwanlal Indraji (*Indian Antiquary*, X, 1881, pp. 125-26) pointed out that J Prinsep and F E Hall (*Journal of the Asiatic Society of Bengal*, XXX, 1862, p. 3n.) were wrong in taking the expression to mean that Skandagupta was dead, and that Bhaudaji rightly translated *śānta* to mean 'peaceful'. According to one view the date refers to the extinct year of the era, *vide* R N Dandekar, *A History of the Guptas*, p. 110.
2. J F Fleet, *Corpus Inscriptionum Indicarum*, III, pp. 47ff.
3. D C Sircar, *Select Inscriptions*, I, pp. 325ff.
4. R C Majumdar, *Indian Culture*, X, pp. 175ff.; Budhagupta, according to D R Bhandarkar, *Corpus Inscriptionum Indicarum*, III, p. 347.
5. V A Smith, *Journal of the Royal Asiatic Society of Great Britain and Ireland*, 1889, p. 110.
6. J Allan, *Catalogue of the Coins of the Gupta Dynasties, and of Śaśāṅka, the King of Gauḍa, in the British Museum, London*, pp. xcviiff and 116ff; A S Altekar, *The Coinage of the Gupta Empire*, pp. 244-45.
7. *Decline of the Kingdom of Magadha*, p. 53. No scholar has accepted the view of B P Sinha (*Journal of the Numismatic Society of India*, XVI(ii), pp. 213-14) that the female figure on the coins of this type is *ekaveṇī* and should be identified with the widowed mother of Skandagupta shown as blessing him, or the view of Sohoni (*Journal of the Numismatic Society of India*, XXIII, pp. 263-65) that it depicts Skandagupta being greeted by his mother on his victory over the enemy.
8. The *Chhatra* type (Altekar, *The Coinage of the Gupta Empire*, pp. 247-49) weighs 130 grains, and it has been suggested that if the letter *vi* is missing and the title was *Vikramāditya*, then the coin may be ascribed to Chandragupta II. Smith

(*vide* Altekar, *The Coinage of the Gupta Empire*, p. 249) ascribed Horseman type to Chandragupta II, P L Gupta (*Journal of the Numismatic Society of India*, XIV, pp. 99ff) to Ghaṭotkachagupta and Nisar Ahmad (*Journal of the Numismatic Society of India*, XXX, pp. 84ff) to Govindagupta. Neither the coins of Govindagupta are known nor is it known that he bore the title *kramāditya*.

9. A S Altekar, *The Coinage of the Gupta Empire*, p. 240.
10. P L Gupta, *The Imperial Guptas*, pp. 69-70.
11. B P Sinha (*Decline of the Kingdom of Magadha*, p. 62) states that the report published by Cunningham is faulty and the chemical analysis done by the British Museum Laboratory shows that the coins of higher weight of about 144 grains contain as much pure gold as those of the lower weight of about 132 grains.
12. *Ibid*.
13. For example, S R Goyal, *The Imperial Guptas*, pp. 336ff.
14. For example, D R Bhandarkar, *Corpus Inscriptionum Indicarum*, III, pp. 79-80.
15. S R Goyal, *The Imperial Guptas*, p. 335.
16. *Journal of the Royal Asiatic Society of Great Britain and Ireland*, 1904, (no. 1), p. 129.
17. *Corpus Inscriptionum Indicarum*, III, p. 82. However, on p. 79 of the same work, Bhandarkar mentions the two as separate persons.
18. *Epigraphia Indica*, XXVI, p. 235fn.
19. A F R Hoernle, *Journal of the Royal Asiatic Society of Great Britain and Ireland*, 1909 (i), p. 129.
20. *Coins of Mediaeval India*, p. 13.
21. The reading is *Purugupta* in Kumāragupta III's Bhitari seal inscription and his Nālandā sealing.
22. Krishna Deva, *Epigraphia Indica*, XXVI, p. 236. See also B P Sinha, *Decline of the Kingdom of Magadha*, p. 3, n. 8 (continued on p. 4). P K Agrawala (*Imperial Gupta Epigraphs*) however invariably reads (or reconstructs, as the case may be) the name as *Pūru*. Puru is known as an ancestor of the Kauravas and the Pāṇḍavas. In 1893, Bühler had read the name as Sthiragupta, which the author of the Kaliyuga-rāja-vṛittānta of the *Bhavishyottara-purāṇa* included in its text. This showed that the work was a modern forgery.
23. J F Fleet, *Corpus Inscriptionum Indicarum*, III, No. 13, pp. 47ff.
24. *Indian Culture*, X, p. 171. R C Majumdar has also given reason to show that the inscription in fact belongs to the reign of one of the successors of Purugupta (*ibid*., pp. 171-72). D R Bhandarkar (*Corpus Inscriptionum Indicarum*, III, pp. 345ff.) has ascribed it to Budhagupta.
25. Though, as stated above, some scholars have doubted the reading of the date.
26. The coins ascribed to this king have been ascribed to Budhagupta after S K Saraswati corrected the reading *Pura* (as the first part of the name till then was read) as *Budha*. The Bihar stone pillar inscription seems to belong to one of the successors of Purugupta.
27. A few scholars believe that at least on some coins the name appears as Puru.
28. *Annals of the Bhandarkar Oriental Research Institute*, I, p. 73.

29. For example, B P Sinha, *Decline of the Kingdom of Magadha*, pp. 32-33.
30. Pulakeśin II's name is not mentioned in his brother's Satara grant. Bhoja Pratīhāra's name is not mentioned in the Pratapgarh inscription of his nephew, but it is mentioned in the inscription of his brother. Rarely, the names of rival uncle or brother find mention, for example, Maṅgaleśa—a Chālukya ruler, and Govinda—a ruler of the Rāshṭrakūṭa dynasty, in the inscriptions of their rivals and in the case of the latter also in those of his descendants. On the other hand, even an ancestor of a reigning king was sometimes omitted, e.g., Rudrasena II in an Ajanta inscription, and Dharapaṭa in his son's inscription (*vide* H C Raychaudhuri, *Political History of Ancient India*, p. 516, n. 2, also for references). Kings Budhagupta and his brother Vainyagupta do not find mention in the genealogy met with in the inscriptions of the Gupta kings ruling after them, as they were collaterals.
31. The genealogy as gleaned from different seals shows that Budhagupta, Narasiṁhagupta and Vainyagupta were the sons of Purugupta, and no son of Skandagupta finds mention in any source. The name of the mother of Purugupta was Anantadevī, but the name of the mother of Skandagupta is not known for certain.
32. P L Gupta, *The Imperial Guptas*, p. 346.
33. B P Sinha, *Decline of the Kingdom of Magadha*, p. 49.
34. K P Jayaswal, *Imperial History of India*, p. 35.
35. H C Raychaudhuri, *Indian Historical Quarterly*, VIII, p. 14. It is pointed out (e.g. S R Goyal, *The Imperial Guptas*, p. 338) that placing Purugupta before Skandagupta would go well with the statement of Hiuen-tsang that Sa-initialled king was succeeded by Bālādityā.
36. *Journal of the Royal Asiatic Society of Great Britain and Ireland*, 1905, pp. 33ff. Scholars have identified Vikramāditya and his son variously with Chandragupta I and Samudragupta (V A Smith, *Early History of India*, pp. 331, 334), Chandragupta II and Kumāragupta I (H P Sastri, *Journal of the Asiatic Society of Bengal*, I, NS, pp. 253-54), Chandragupta II and Govindagupta (D R Bhandarkar, *Indian Antiquary*, XLI, pp. 1ff), Kumāragupta I and Purugupta (Allan, *Catalogue of the Coins of the Gupta Dynasties, and of Śaśāṅka, the King of Gauḍa, in the British Museum, London*, pp. l-li).
37. V A Smith, *Early History of India*, pp. 331, 334.
38. H P Shastri, *Journal of the Asiaatic Society of Bengal*, I (NS), p. 253.
39. D R Bhandarkar, *Indian Antiquary*, XLI, pp. 1ff.
40. J Allan, *Catalogue of the Coins of the Gupta Dynasties, and of Śaśāṅka, the King of Gauḍa, in the British Museum, London*, pp. l-li.
41. H C Raychaudhuri, *Political History of Ancient India*, p. 516; R K Mookerji, *Gupta Empire*, p. 101.
42. See K K Thaplyal, *Studies in Ancient Indian Seals*, pp. 103ff.
43. J P Singh, *History and Coinage of Skandagupta Kramāditya*, p. 30.
44. K Chattopadhyaya (*Indian Historical Quarterly*, XVIII, pp. 63-64) says that grammatically, *pādānudhyāta* should mean 'meditated by the feet of'. However

from the context of its use, it means 'meditating on the feet of', and has been translated as such by all scholars.

45. For example, B P Sinha, *Decline of the Kingdom of Magadha*. p. 31ff; S R Goyal, *The Imperial Guptas*, p. 338.
46. R K Mookerji, *Gupta Empire*, 90; D K Ganguly, *The Imperial Guptas and Their Times*, p. 81.
47. J F Fleet, *Corpus Inscriptionum Indicarum*, III, p. 55.
48. *Gupta Empire*, p. 90.
49. D K Ganguly, *The Imperial Guptas and Their Times*, pp. 80-81.
50. U N Roy, *Gupta Rājavaṁśa tathā Usakā Yuga*, p. 307.
51. *Indian Antiquary*, XIX, p. 227.
52. *Catalogue of the Coins of the Gupta Dynasties, and of Śaśāṅka, the King of Gauḍa, in the British Museum, London*, liv- lv.
53. *Ibid*.
54. *History of North-Eastern India*, p. 77.
55. *Decline of the Kingdom of Magadha*, p. 6.
56. D C Ganguly, *Indian Historical Quarterly*, 1934, p. 195. Some scholars (e.g. P L Gupta, *The Imperial Guptas*, p. 195) believe that while on some coins Vainya is clear, on a few heavy weight coins the name Chandra is seen, and he should be identified as Chandragupta III. Ghaṭotkachagupta, known from Tumain inscription of AD 435 as governor of Kumāragupta I, did not rule later than Skandagupta, but was his uncle and as seen above, revolted during the rule of Kumāragupta I (*vide*, the Ramtek inscription, No. 85).
57. The tears could be of joy over Skandagupta's safe return from war after achieving victory, and also because she would be attaining the status of queen-mother (N N Dasgupta, *B C Law Volume*, I, p. 617). They could as well have been of sorrow, as her husband had died, and may be, like the mother of Kṛishṇa who was in prison, when he broke the news of his victory to her, she, too, had been confined to prison, and Skandagupta rescued her (R N Dandekar, *A History of the Guptas*, p. 105).
58. R Sewell, *The Historical Inscriptions of South India*, p. 349; H C Raychaudhuri, *Political History of Ancient India*, p. 506, n. 2.
59. R K Mookerji, *Gupta Empire*, p. 72. B P Sinha (*Decline of the Kingdom of Magadha*, p. 32, n. 2) on the evidence of *Kathā-saritsāgara* which refers to the mother of Vikramāditya as Saumyadarśanā, suggests that it was the name of the mother of Skandagupta, who has been referred to as Vikramāditya on one of his coins.
60. *Corpus Inscriptionum Indicarum*, III, p. 80.
61. S R Goyal, *Gupta Sāmrājya kā Itihāsa*, p. 286; Prashant Srivastava, in A K Sinha (ed.), *Perspectives in Indian History*, pp. 82-86.
62. See Prashant Srivastava, in A K Sinha (ed.), *Perspectives in Indian History*, pp. 82-86.
63. Tarapad Bhattacharya, *Journal of the Bihar Research Society*, XXXII(ii), 1946, pp. 182-63.

64. J F Fleet, *Corpus Inscriptionum Indicarum*, III, No. 64.
65. *Ibid.*, No. 66.
66. *B C Law Volume*, I, p. 617.
67. B P Sinha, *Decline of the Kingdom of Magadha*, p. 29.
68. R C Majumdar, in *Comprehensive History of India*, III(i), *p.* 71; B P Sinha, *Decline of the Kingdom of Magadha*, p. 31; P L Gupta, *The Imperial Guptas*, pp. 227ff.
69. *Decline of the Kingdom of Magadha*, p. 45.
70. *Ibid.*, p. 31.
71. D R Bhandarkar, *Corpus Inscriptionum Indicarum*, III, pp. 79ff.
72. H C Raychaudhuri, *Political History of Ancient India*, p. 505.
73. K K Thaplyal, *Inscriptions of the Maukharis, the Later Guptas, the Puṣpabhūtis and Yaśovarman of Kanauj*, pp. 177ff.
74. *Ibid.*, pp. 182ff.
75. *Ibid.*, p. 186ff.
76. *Ibid.*, p. 188.
77. See H C Raychaudhuri, *Political History of Ancient India*, pp. 505-06.
78. R C Majumdar, in *The Classical Age*, p. 26n.
79. J Agrawal, *Annals of the Bhandarkar Oriental Research Institute*, XLVIII-XLIX, p. 326.
80. H C Raychaudhuri, *Political History of Ancient India*, pp. 505-06.
81. It has also been pointed out that Skandagupta could very well have been the rightful claimant to the throne on merit, even if he was not born of the chief-queen or was not the eldest son.
82. *Gupta Empire*, p. 94.
83. J Agrawal, *Annals of the Bhandarkar Oriental Research Institute*, XLVIII-XLIX, pp. 325-27.
84. P L Gupta, *The Imperial Guptas*, p. 330.
85. A L Basham, *Bulletin of the School of Oriental and African Studies*, XVII, p. 367.
86. J F Fleet, *Corpus Inscriptionum Indicarum*, III, p. 54.
87. Fleet, be it stated, had indicated that the reading of some of the letters by him was not certain (*ibid.*, p. 56).
88. See also V C Pandey and Anup Pandey, *A New History of Ancient India*, p. 403, for similar view.
89. A L Basham, *Bulletin of the School of Oriental and African Studies*, XVII, p. 369.
90. S K Maity, *Imperial Guptas and Their Times*, p. 58.
91. *Annals of the Bhandarkar Oriental Research Institute*, XLVIII-XLIX, p. 326.
92. For different readings and translations, see V C Pandey, *Vishveshvaranand Indological Journal*, XVIII, 1980, pp. 435-38.
93. D K Ganguly (*The Imperial Guptas and Their Times*, p. 80) takes the text to convey, 'to whom respect was paid by the bards in the form of songs and panygyrics', which gives good sense.
94. P L Gupta, *Gupta Sāmrājya*, p. 319n.
95. *Ibid.*, p. 319, fn (continued on p. 320).

96. *Ibid.*, p. 321.
97. *Decline of The Kingdom of Magadha*, p. 44.
98. A S Altekar, *The Coinage of the Gupta Empire*, p. 180.
99. *Ibid.*, p. 181.
100. D K Ganguly, *The Imperial Guptas and Their Times*, p. 80.
101. Dasharatha Sharma, *Proceedings of the Indian History Congress*, 1956, p. 149.
102. *Journal of Indian History*, XLIII, p. 223.
103. P L Gupta, *Gupta Sāmrājya*, p. 322n.
104. One specimen of Archer type of coins (A S Altekar, *The Coinage of the Gupta Empire*, pp. 340-41) with the name Samudra, weighing 136 grains, of crude workmanship, and debased metal, if not forged, should be ascribed to Samudragupta II, and that he might also have been one of the contestants for throne (S R Goyal, *The Imperial Guptas*, p. 340) Altekar, however, considers it as a forged one.
105. For example, P L Gupta, *Gupta Sāmrājya*, p. 323; S R Goyal, *Gupta Sāmrājya kā Itihāsa*, p. 280.
106. H C Raychaudhuri, *Political History of Ancient India*, p. 508.
107. J F Fleet, *Corpus Inscriptionum Indicarum*, III, p. 62.
108. D R Bhandarkar, *Corpus Inscriptionum Indicarum*, III, p. 302.
109. S R Goyal, *Gupta Sāmrājya kā Itihāsa*, p. 280.
110. *Vide* his Junagarh inscription, D C Sircar, *Select Inscriptions*, I, pp. 175ff.
111. *Political History of Ancient India*, pp. 507-08.
112. *Ibid.*, p. 508.
113. R C Majumdar, in *Comprehensive History of India*, III(i), p. 70.
114. As against it, it has been stated that in ancient Indian polity, kingdom and the ruling dynasty are hardly distinguished. A coin-type of Skandagupta identified by some as King-and-Lakshmī (and as King-and-queen by others) has been interpreted as suggesting that the goddess of fortune had selected him as her lord. The expression that after his father's death, Skandagupta became king by his own prowess (*ātma-śaktyā*), has been taken by some to indicate that he defeated his rival claimants.
115. *Political History of Ancient India*, p. 509.
116. A S Altekar, *The Coinage of the Gupta Empire*, pp. 242-243. Allan, *Catalogue of the Coins of the Gupta Dynasties, and of Śaśāṅka, the King of Gauḍa, in the British Museum, London*, p. xx.
117. H C Raychaudhuri, *Political History of Ancient India*, p. 509.
118. *Ibid.*
119. J F Fleet, *Corpus Inscriptionum Indicarum*, III, p. 54. This was also the reading of Bhagwanlal Indraji (*Journal of the Bombay Branch of the Royal Asiatic Society*, XVI, p. 349, line 100).
120. *Annals of the Bhandarkar Oriental Research Institute*, I (1919-20), pp. 99ff.
121. H C Raychaudhuri, *Political History of Ancient India*, p. 507, n. 2.
122. *Imperial Gupta Epigraphs*, p. 71.

123. See also D R Bhandarkar, *Corpus Inscriptionum Indicarum*, III, p. 317, n. Dasharatha Sharma (*Proceedings of the Indian History Congress*, 1964, p. 141) also believes that *kshitipa charaṇa-pīṭhe* should be taken to mean royal stool and that the inscription refers to king's putting his foot on the royal stool, and not on the back of king. But in our view this would not be of such a significance to be mentioned in the epigraph. It is another matter that Skandagupta would not have put his feet on the back of the king, and the composer of the epigraph used this to impress upon the readers the might of the king who could reduce the enemy king to such a pitiable state.
124. V V Mirashi, *Journal of the Epigraphical Society of India*, VII, p. 88.
125. D R Bhandarkar, *Corpus Inscriptionum Indicarum*, III, p. 80. He says the ink impression of the epigraph shows that Divekar's reading is more reliable.
126. R N Dandekar, *A History of the Guptas*, p. 112.
127. Ashvini Agrawal, *Rise and Fall of the Imperial Guptas*, p. 211.
128. R D Banerji, *The Age of the Imperial Guptas*, p. 45; J Agrawal, *Indian Historical Quarterly*, XXII, p. 112ff.
129. U Thakur read it as *rāshṭra-mitrāṁścha labdhvā* (*Indian Historical Quarterly*, XXXVII, pp. 279-80).
130. *Sacred Books of the East*, XXII, p. 292.
131. *Archaeological Survey of India—Annual Report*, 1911-12, p. 56.
132. *Early History of India*, 3rd ed., p. 326.
133. *Journal of the Royal Asiatic Society of Great Britain and Ireland*, 1909, p. 126.
134. *Indian Historical Quarterly*, XXI, p. 24.
135. J Agrawal, *Researches in Indian Epigraphy and Numismatics*, pp. 44-46.
136. *Early History of North India*, p. 179.
137. R D Banerji, *The Age of the Imperial Guptas*, p. 46.
138. *The Imperial Guptas*, p. 359. In his opinion, after Bandhuvarman a feudatory of the Gupta king, Kumāragupta, the Varmans shifted their allegiance to the Vākāṭakas, and that the latter and their supporters joined hands against the Guptas.
139. K D Bajpai, in B Ch Chhabra *et al.* (ed.), *Reappraising Gupta History for S R Goyal*, p. 202.
140. K C Jain, *Malwa through the Ages*, p. 238.
141. F E Pargiter, *Dynasties of the Kali Age*, p. 51; H C Raychaudhuri, *Political History of Ancient India*, p. 502, n. 5.
142. *Advanced History of India*, p. 191.
143. S R Goyal, *The Imperial Guptas*, p. 348.
144. S R Goyal, *ibid*.
145. In B Ch Chhabra *et al.* (ed.), *Reappraising Gupta History for S R Goyal*, p. 7.
146. A S Altekar, *The Coinage of the Gupta Empire*, p. 356.
147. For translation as 'one night' see R D Banerji, *The Age of the Imperial Guptas*, p. 49; as 'several nights', D R Bhandarkar, *Corpus Inscriptionum Indicarum*, III, p. 316.
148. V C Pandey, *Vishveshvaranand Indological Journal*, XVI, p. 77.

149. R G Basak (*History of North-Eastern India*, p. 73) is of the view that prince Skandagupta had accompanied his father, Kumāragupta I in the battle against the Pushyamitras, and that the king died in the battlefield.
150. S R Goyal, *Imperial Guptas*, pp. 235-36.
151. B P Sinha, *Decline of the Kingdom of Magadha*, p. 2.
152. J Allan (*Catalogue of the Coins of the Gupta Dynasties, and of Śaśāṅka, the King of Gauḍa, in the British Museum, London*, p. xlvi) opines that the Hūṇa invasion took place in between AD 455 and 458.
153. If the version *Gupto* is accepted then it may refer to the victory of Skandagupta over the Hūṇas. Some scholars prefer the alternative –*jato* or *jarto* and take them to mean jat, and consider the Guptas as Jats (K P Jayaswal, *Journal of the Bihar and Orissa Research Society*, XIX, pp. 115-16).
154. R C Majumdar, in *The Vākāṭaka-Gupta Age*, p. 178.
155. J Allan, *Catalogue of the Coins of the Gupta Dynasties, and of Śaśāṅka, the King of Gauḍa, in the British Museum, London*, p. xlvi; D R Bhandarkar, *Corpus Inscriptionum Indicarum*, III, p. 81. They are the only foreign power who are known to have invaded the Gupta territory, and returned to their land after being defeated by Skandagupta. Acccording to the *Kathā-saritsāgara* of Somadeva, Vikramāditya, son of Mahendrāditya defeated the *mlechchhas* (R C Majumdar, in *Comprehensive History of India*, III(i), pp. 73-74). *Contra* B N Mukherjee, in H C Raychaudhuri, *Political History of Ancient India*, p. 781, who finds no reason for identifying the *mlechchhas* mentioned in the Junagarh inscription with the Hūṇas of the Bhitari pillar inscription. P L Gupta (*Gupta Sāmrājya*, p. 309) identifies the *mlechchhas* with the Kidāra-Kushāṇas, as according to him, the political situation across north-western India was such that the Hūṇas could not have invaded during the last phase of Kumāragupta I's and the early phase of Skandagupta's rule. B D Chattopadhyaya (*Journal of the Numismatic Society of India*, XXVII, pp. 39-40) identifies them with the Sassanians. R K Choudhary (*Journal of the Bihar Research Society*, XLIV, p. 117) says that since *mlechchhas* are mentioned separately in the Bhitari pillar inscription, they cannot be taken as Hūṇas. But in fact the *mlechchhas* are mentioned in the Junagarh inscription, and the Huṇas, in his Bhitari pillar inscription. According to Jai Prakash (*History and Coinage of Skandagupta Kramāditya*, pp. 54, 114), what has been read as *mlechchha*, should be read as *sarvva*; which is unlikely.
156. As translated by Fleet, *Corpus Inscriptionum Indicarum*, III, p. 55. Dasharatha Sharma (*Proceedings of the Indian History Congress*, 1956, p. 149) translates it as 'by men and even [king] Kumāragupta I', and believes that Kumāragupta I was alive at the time of Skandagupta's victory and praised him. But this does not sound convincing. One would expect that in the inscription of his son, King Skandagupta, the use of some suitable title, at least honorific prefix *Śrī* attached to the name of the king, which is not the case; even his full name is not given. It does not go well with a king singing in praise even though it may be of his own prince. A better interpretation is that by Chhabra (in G T Deshpande *et al.* (ed.),

*Felicitation Volume Presented to Mahamahopadhyaya Dr V V Mirashi*, pp. 362ff), who takes it to mean that praises were sung of his achievements, right from the days when he was a mere child, and compares it with Kālidāsa's praise of young Raghu. But to us, Fleet's translation, given above, which conveys the idea that his praises were sung by young and old alike, appears as the most acceptable one.

157. S R Goyal, *The Imperial Guptas*, p. 226.
158. J Agrawal is of the view that the Hūṇas marched through the Bolan Pass and first targeted Surāshṭra and Malwa (*vide*, Ashvini Agrawal, *Rise and Fall of the Imperial Guptas*, p. 214).
159. D R Bhandarkar, *Corpus Inscriptionum Indicarum*, III, p. 81.
160. J Allan, *Catalogue of the Coins of the Gupta Dynasties, and of Śaśāṅka, the King of Gauḍa, in the British Museum, London*, p. xlix, n. 1
161. P L Gupta (*The Imperial Guptas*, p. 93) takes it as a coin of Ghaṭotkachagupta.
162. In G T Deshpande *et al.* (ed.), *Felicitation Volume Presented to Mahamahopadhyaya, Dr VV Mirashi*, p. 369.
163. *Researches in Indian Epigraphy and Numismatics*, p. 29.
164. *Ibid.*
165. According to the the *Ārya-Mañjuśrī-mūlakalpa* (K P Jayaswal, *Imperial History of India*, p. 64) Hakārākhya (i.e. Hūṇa Toramāṇa) occupied the bank of the Gaṅgā up to Tīrtha, the city of the Gauḍas.
166. In 1972 (in *Studies in Ancient Indian Seals*, pp. 61-62) we pointed out that a Kauśāmbī sealing bearing two impressions—one from the seal of Toramāṇa and another from that of the Ghoshitārāma monastery, provides an unmistakable evidence for Toramāṇa's hold over Kauśāmbī region. We argued that the impression on the clay from both the seals were made at one and the same time, when the clay was still moist. Since there is unmistakable literary and epigraphic evidence that the Ghoshitārāma monastery was located at Kauśāmbī, the obvios conclusion would be that the impressions from the two seals on the clay lump were made there. The inference would be that Toramāṇa was present there and Kauśāmbī was under his rule (*ibid.*). It is possible that even earlier, during the last days of Kumāragupta I, the Hūṇas had reached upto Bhitari.
167. A Cunningham, *Archaeological Survey Reports*, I, p. 97, pl. XX.
168. D R Bhandarkar, *Corpus Inscriptionum Indicarum*, III, p. 83.
169. J Agrawal (*Researches in Indian Epigraphy and Numismatics*, p. 63) disagrees with the view of Raghvendra Vajpai (*Proceedings of the Indian History Congress*, 1983, pp. 70ff) that the image installed was that of Skandagupta, shown as bow-wielder, since the inscription clearly mentions the image as that of god (*bhagavato mūrtiḥ*).
170. *Proceedings of the Indian History Congress*, 1958, pp. 160-61.
171. *Gupta Sāmrājya kā Itihāsa*, pp. 299-300.
172. *The Early Empires of Central Asia*, p. 416.
173. *The Age of the Imperial Guptas*, p. 52.

174. *Early History of India*, 3rd ed., p. 310.
175. *Ibid.*, p. 311.
176. *Coins of Mediaeval India*, p. 16.
177. P L Gupta (*Gupta Sāmrājya*, p 328) says, the issue of higher weight coins could have aggrevated economic crisis rather than helped in solving it.
178. R C Majumdar, in *The Vākāṭaka-Gupta Age*, p. 178.
179. S K Maity, *Imperial Guptas and Their Times*, p. 48.
180. D R Bhandarkar, *Corpus Inscriptionum Indicarum*, III, p. 81.
181. *Ibid.*
182. *Ibid.*
183. S R Goyal, *Imperial Guptas*, p. 359.
184. *A History of the Guptas*, pp. 115, 117-18.
185. *Ibid.*, p. 118. P L Gupta (*Gupta Sāmrājya kā Itihāsa*, p. 305n) opines that Narendrasena could not have been a contemporary of Kumāragupta I, as the latter's father, Chandragupta II, was the maternal great-grandfather of the former. S R Goyal (*Gupta Sāmrājya*, p. 295), however, says that applying the standard of generations is not always safe for purpose of fixing the date.
186. S R Goyal, *The Imperial Guptas*, pp. 318-19.
187. *Ibid.*
188. *Epigraphia Indica*, XXVI, p. 131, n. 4 (editorial note).
189. S R Goyal, *The Imperial Guptas*, p. 359. He suggests that it were the heads of the Vākāṭakas, the Varmans and their allies who have been referred in the Junagarh inscriptionas so many serprnt-like kings lifting their hood who were crushed by Skandagupta (*ibid.*). Goyal opines that if Prabhākara belonged to the Varman family, he reestablished Gupta power in Malwa which has been eclipsed because of the invasion of the Vākāṭakas.
190. Ashvini Agrawal, *Rise and Fall of the Imperial Guptas*, pp. 215-16.
191. R N Dandekar, *A History of the Guptas*, p. 147.
192. D C Sircar, *Select Inscriptions*, I, pp. 175ff.
193. Some scholars have tried to locate the site of this dam but their conclusions differ. Bhagwanlal Indraji located Sudarśana lake to the east of Girnar hill (*Epigraphia Indica*, III, p. 257). Shambhu Prasad Desai places it away from Girnar hill near the meeting point of Palashini and Sonrekhi. R N Mehta is of the view that Sonrekha *nala*, in which meet several streams, was the source of its water, and that tradition says that it was a meeting point of rivers, perhaps of Palashini and Sonrekhā. He noticed traces of clay bund, which he identifies with the Sudarśana lake (*Journal of the Oriental Institute (Baroda)*, XVIII, pp. 20-28). For these and other identifications of the Sudarśana lake, together with references, seer R N Mehta, (*Journal of the Oriental Institute (Baroda)*, XVIII, pp. 20-28. See also P L Gupta, *Gupta Sāmrājya*, p. 325n (continued on p. 326).
194. D R Bhandarkar (*Corpus Inscriptionum Indicarum*, III, p. 83) would take it for the relatively small region around Kanauj.
195. *Vide* Kosam inscription dated Gupta era 139 = AD 458 (Fleet, *Corpus Inscriptionum Indicarum*, III, pp. 266-67).

196. *Decline of the Kingdom of Magadha*, p. 51.
197. F E Pargiter, *The Dynasties of the Kali Age*, pp. 73-74.
198. *Gupta Empire*, p. 102.
199. *Catalogue of the Coins of the Gupta Dynasties, and of Śaśāṅka, the King of Gauḍa, in the British Museum, London*, p. xlix.
200. P L Gupta, *The Imperial Guptas*, pp. 336-37.
201. R C Majumdar, in *Comprehensive History of India*, III(i), p. 77.
202. Ashvini Agrawal, *Rise and Fall of the Imperial Guptas*, p. 216.
203. *Epigraphia Indica*, XXVIII, pp. 79-85. 195.
204. R N Dandekar, *A History of the Guptas*, p. 121.
205. V A Smith, *Indian Antiquary*, 1902, p. 266.
206. See, e.g., J Allan, *Catalogue of the Coins of the Gupta Dynasties, and of Śaśāṅka, the King of Gauḍa, in the British Museum, London*, p. xlix.
207. V A Smith, *Journal of the Royal Asiatic Society of Great Britain and Ireland*, 1889, p. 110.
208. For example, J Allan, *Catalogue of the Coins of the Gupta Dynasties, and of Śaśāṅka, the King of Gauḍa, in the British Museum, London*, pp. xcviii-c; A S Altekar, *The Coinage of the Gupta Empire*, pp. 244-46.
209. R N Dandekar, *A History of the Guptas*, p. 121.
210. Ashvini Agrawal, *Rise and Fall of the Imperial Guptas*, p. 218.
211. In *The Classical Age*, p. 15; in *Comprehensive History of India*, III(i), p. 30ff.

# 11

# Successors of Skandagupta: Phase of Decline

## PURUGUPTA

The two forms of the name of the king, viz. Purugupta and Pūrugupta as found on different seals, and the earlier wrong reading of the name as Puragupta, which was for long accepted by scholars till it was read correctly, have been already discussed in Chapter 10. It has also been seen that the view that Skandagupta and Purugupta were one and the same person and also that there was a division of the Gupta kingdom between these two, do not hold good any more. Some scholars believe that after the death of Kumāragupta I, there was a war of succession among Gupta princes. A few scholars hold the view that Purugupta succeeded Kumāragupta I in *c* AD 455, and after a brief rule either died a natural death or was ousted by Skandagupta in the same year. In support of this view they point out that the evidence in the *Ārya-Mañjuśrī-mūlakalpa* that S-initialled (=Skandagupta) was succeeded by Bālāditya, who should be identified as Narasiṁhagupta Bālāditya (and not by Purugupta). Majority of scholars, however, do not give credence to the evidence of that Buddhist text, and hold that Purugupta followed Skandagupta, in or shortly after, AD 467, and his rule ended in or before AD 473, when Kumāragupta of the Sarnath inscription was ruling. But if Kumāragupta II was not the son of Purugupta, then the possibility of the latter ruling between AD 473 and AD 476—the first known date of

Budhagupta, cannot be ruled out. Basak, like Bhattasali, is of the opinion that Purugupta was a child of about four or five years at the time of the death of Kumāragupta I, and came to the throne not only after Skandagupta but also after Kumāragupta II, who seems to have died young and without a son.[1] Coins earlier attributed to Purugupta have been ascribed to Budhagupta, after S K Saraswati[2] read the name of the king on them as *Budha* for what earlier had been read as *Pura* (as the first part of the name of the king was till then known, which was later corrected to *Puru/Pūru)*.[3] Some scholars identify Purugupta with king Vikramāditya mentioned as king of Ayodhyā in Buddhist scholar Paramārtha's 'Life of Vasubandhu'.[4] He has invariably been given the title *mahārājādhirāja* in the Gupta seals detailing Gupta genealogy, and in the Bihar pillar inscription (No. 35). P L Gupta states: 'Purugupta may or may not have succeeded to the throne; yet he occupies a unique position in the Gupta genealogy'.[5] It is not understandable why, despite the imperial titles ascribed to him in the seals of his successors, his status as king has been doubted; and it is not made clear as to how his position is 'unique' in the Gupta genealogy. As per the evidence of the Bhitari (No. 55) and Nālandā (No. 54) seals of Kumāragupta, Purugupta's queen was Chandradevī.[6]

It would be worthwhile to discuss attribution of the *Prakāśāditya* type of coins. Some gold coins,[7] almost conforming to the *suvarṇa* standard (about 144 grains), bear on the obverse, the king riding a horse and attacking a lion with a sword, and a *garuḍa* standard. Under the horse, occurs the letter *u* or *ru* or *ma* and there is a circular legend, which cannot be read fully, but ends in *vijitya vasudhāṁ divaṁ jayati.* The reverse shows Lakshmī with her legs folded like a pillow, and the legend *Prakāśāditya*. Hoernle earlier identified Prakāśāditya with Purugupta[8] and later with Yaśodharman.[9] Smith[10] subscribed to the earlier view of Hoernle, and Allan[11] and Altekar[12] too accepted it. The main arguments in its favour were: (i) the Bharsar hoard contained coins of Samudragupta, Chandragupta II, Kumāragupta I, Skandagupta, and *Prakāśāditya*, and therefore the last mentioned one should have followed Skandagupta, (ii) the style of these coins is more degraded than those of Kumāragupta II; and (iii) these coins are finer than those of Narasiṁhagupta and his successors. Buit the evidence of the hoard should be taken with caution, as it would only suggests that Prakāśāditya ruled sometime later than Skandagupta, and not necessarily immediately after him.[13] Moreover, of about 160 coins of the hoard, only 32 could be recovered, and hence the possibility of the presence of the coins of intervening kings in the hoard cannot be ruled out.[14] Later, on some coins the name of the king was read by some scholars as *Pura*, and the title as *Vikramāditya*. Allan therefore opined that as Purugupta could not have been referred to both as *Prakāśāditya* and Vikramāditya,[15] Prakāśāditya should be identified with some unknown king ruling at the end of the fifth century AD.[16] Basak[17] identified him with Kumāragupta II, but his title, as known from coins, is *Kramāditya*, and not *Prakāśāditya*. K P Jayaswal[18] identified Prakāśāditya with Budhagupta. Dandekar held the same view. He states that since according to the *Ārya-Mañjuśrī-mūlakalpa*, Kumāragupta [II] was succeeded by Śrīmān U, and since the letter *u* occurs on Prakāśāditya's coins, it 'should conclusively prove that Śrīmān U, Prakāśāditya and Budhagupta are one and the same person'.[19] Since coins with the legend *Śrī Vikrama* which were ascribed to Purugupta have been taken as issued by Budhagupta, the theory fell, and instead the idea of identifying him with Purugupta was revived. Mookerji[20] in his work *Gupta Empire*, at one place identifies Prakāśāditya with Budhagupta, but in the same work he gives the heading of Chapter VIII as "Purugupta Vikrama/Prakāśāditya". *Prakāśāditya*, it seems was the title of Bhānugupta, as was once suggested by P L Gupta,[21] and supported by J W Curtis.[22] Later, K S Shukla read the name Bhānugupta on a *Prakāśāditya* coin.[23] It may be stated that P L Gupta, on the basis of the gold content (71%) and weight (average weight 145.4 grains) of the coins, the depiction of the folded legs of Lakshmī pooking like a pillow, and the presence of the individual letters, which are not found on the coins of Budhagupta and his predecessors, opined that he should be placed after that Gupta king and near about the time of Narasiṁhagupta.[24] This also favours his identification with Bhānugupta, who was the immediate predecessor of Narasiṁhagupta Bālāditya. Though P L Gupta later on identified *Prakāśāditya* with Tathāgatagupta,[25] we prefer his earlier suggestion of identifying the king with Bhānugupta. Goyal[26] is of the opinion that the combined testimony of coins, *Ārya-Mañjuśrī-mūlakalpa*, and Hiuen-tsang favours the possibility that Prakāśāditya should be placed in the period between Bhānugupta and Narasiṁhagupta. On the basis of the evidence of the *Ārya-Mañjuśrī-mūlakalpa*,[27] he takes Prakāśāditya as identical with Prakārākhya (*Pra*-initialled), son of Bhā, who was rescued from the prison and installed as king by Hakārākhya, who (the latter) is identified with the Hūṇa king Toramāṇa. H C Raychaudhuri[28] and K P Jayaswal[29] identified the Pra-initialled name with Prakaṭāditya of the Sarnath inscription (No. 97), wherein he has been stated as the son of Bālāditya, whom they identified with Bhānugupta, presuming that Bālāditya was his title. But whereas there is no evidence for Bālāditya being a title of Bhānugupta, there is unmistakable numismatic evidence to show that it was a title of Narasiṁhagupta, as it occurs on his coins along with his name, and therefore *Pra*-initialled king of the *Ārya-Mañjuśrī-mūlakalpa* should not be identified with Prakaṭāditya of the Sarnath inscription.[30] It may also be stated that some scholars place the Sarnath inscription in question in the post-Gupta period. From what has been stated above, there is hardly any possibility of identifying Prakāśāditya with Purugupta.

When Fleet[31] edited the Bihar pillar inscription (No. 35), Skandagupta was the only son of Kumāragupta I known, and it came in handy to him to restore the damaged first part of the partly mutilated name in line 23 as [Skanda]gupta. Cunningham,[32] too, for the same reason reconstructed the name in the same way. R C Majumdar,[33] who had access to a clearer lithograph of the inscription, read the name as [Pūru]gupta. He also pointed out that in the epigraph, the genealogy continued beyond line 23, and the king whose name is missing in line 25 could not be taken as the same as the one whose name, [Pū]rugupta, occurs in line 23.[34] According to him, it should be taken as giving the name of the son and successor of Purugupta,[35] who could be either Budhagupta, or Narasiṁhagupta, or Vainyagupta, or Kumāragupta II if he too was a son of Purugupta. According to R C Majumdar, what Fleet read as *Skandagupta-baṭa*, can as well be *[Chandra]gupta-baṭa* or *[Indra]gupta-baṭa*.[36] Purugupta had a short reign which is suggested by the absence of his coins.[37]

## KUMĀRAGUPTA II

Kumāragupta II's Sarnath inscription (No. 37), dated GE 154 (= AD 473),[38] is on the pedestal of a Buddha image installed by Buddhist monk Abhayamitra, who is to be identified with the homonym of the two identical Sarnath inscriptions of the time of Budhagupta (No. 39). The inscription does not mention Kumāragupta II's parentage, which has led scholars to make different speculations. In a Bhitari seal inscription (No. 55) and two Nālandā seal inscriptions (No. 54) of Kumāragupta, and in the Nālandā seal inscription of Vishṇugupta (No. 58), King Kumāragupta has been referred to as a son of Narasiṁhagupta. For determining the Gupta chronology for the post-Kumāragupta I period, it is vital to determine whether or not Kumāragupta of the Sarnath inscription is identical with the homonym of the Bhitari seal and the Nālandā seals. Some scholars consider the two as identical, while others take them as two different persons. Accepting the first view would mean accommodating Purugupta, Narasiṁhagupta, Kumāragupta and Vishṇugupta, between AD 467 (the last known date for Skandagupta) and AD 476 (the first date known for Budhagupta). The father of Kumāragupta of the Sarnath inscription has been variously identified with Skandagupta, or Purugupta, or some other member of the Imperial Gupta family.[39] A Ghosh[40] opines that if Kumāragupta of the Sarnath inscription was a son of Skandagupta, then Purugupta may have succeeded his nephew after AD 473, and was, in turn, followed by his son (as he believed him to be), Budhagupta, in AD 476.

S Chattopadhyaya[41] suggested that Kumāragupta II of the Sarnath inscription, who is not given any imperial title in that inscription, and is merely referred to as 'administering the earth' (*bhūmiṁ praśāsati*), was a governor and not king, and as such, Narasiṁhagupta and Kumāragupta of Bhitari seal inscription, which clearly mentions Kumāragupta as a king, need not be placed in the short period between AD 467 and 473. But the view was not accepted by scholars, as expressions similar to *bhūmiṁ praśāsati* is met with in the case of Budhagupta,[42] about whose kingly status, there was no doubt. A number of inscriptions of Budhagupta from different areas in northern India came to light, which refer to him as *mahārājādhirāja*, a title of independent king, and clearly show that he ruled over extensive territories.

A Mandasor inscription (No. 38) mentions Kumāragupta I as the king in whose reign the silk-weavers' guild erected a temple in AD 436. It does not mention the name of the king ruling in AD 472 when, as per the evidence of the same inscription, it was repaired by the same guild, after it got damaged. According to one view, there was a struggle for the Gupta throne in AD 472, and since there was confusion as to who was the king, the composer of the Mandasor inscription did not mention the name of the then ruling king. Most scholars believe that the king ruling at that time was Kumāragupta II. B P Sinha is of the view that since a king named Kumāragupta has been referred to in the context of the construction of the temple in AD 436, and a king of the same name was ruling in AD 472, the composer of the record, to avoid repetition, did not mention his name and thereby 'also introduced an element of intelligent imagination'.[43] If this view is accepted, it would mean that Kumāragupta II had come to the throne at least a year before AD 473—the date of his Sarnath inscription.

Before the find of the the Nalanda sealing of Budhagupta which shows that he was a son of Purugupta, there had been much speculation regarding the parentage of that king. Hiuen-tsang says that Buddhagupta (i.e. Budhagupta) succeeded Śakrāditya.[44] As Śakrāditya means the same as *Mahendrāditya*, which is a title of Kumāragupta I, some scholars had identified him with that king. P L Gupta rejected the identification as he believed that the monastic constructions at Nālandā did not take place as early as his reign period.[45] But the fact that a coin of Kumāragupta I has been found on the floor of a Nālandā monastery[46] and a sealing from Nālandā[47] refers to a monastery which was got built by Śakrāditya, which is taken as the same as *Mahendrāditya*, a title of Kumāragupta I, provide proof of the existence of such an establishment during his reign, and even before it. Since Kumāragupta II's known date is AD 473 and the earliest date known for Budhagupta is AD 476, it seems that the latter succeeded the former. R G Basak,[48] B P Sinha[49] and some other scholars believed that Kumāragupta of the Sarnath inscription was Budhagupta's father, presuming that he might have adopted the title of Kumāragupta I, his grandfather. However, there is no evidence of that king having borne that title, and numismatic evidence shows that his *viruda* was *kramāditya*. Basak suggests Kumāragupta [II] had an additional *āditya* title *Śakrāditya*. But the Gupta kings are not known to have borne two *āditya* titles. Skandagupta, no doubt, is known both as *Kramāditya* and *Vikramāditya*, but the latter title is an extension of the former. Sinha thinks it possible that the Chinese pilgrim was confused about the identity of the two kings of the name Kumāragupta and ascribed the title of the first king of that name to the second homonym king.[50] The Bharsar hoard contains coins of Samudragupta, Chandragupta II, Kumāragupta I, Skandagupta and Prakāśāditya. R G Basak[51] opines that Kumāragupta II, who is not far from Skandagupta in terms of time, should be identified with Prakāśāditya of coins. This does not seem to be convincing for reason that his *āditya* title was *kramāditya*. *Prakāśāditya*, as seen above, appears to be the title of Bhānugupta. P L Gupta[52] is of the view that Kumāragupta of Sarnath inscription may have been a son or a brother of Skandagupta, or a son of Purugupta or that of one of his brothers. However, the possibility of his being a brother of Skandagupta may be ruled out, as it would mean that both Kumāragupta I and his son bore the same name, which seems incredible.

The Mandasor inscription (No. 38), while referring to the repair of the Sun temple in AD 472, says that 'after the rule of other kings' (*anyaiścha pārthivaiḥ*), part of the Sun temple was damaged, but does not mention the name or the dynasty of the kings. Some scholars suggest that the kings ruling within 36 years, between AD 436 and 472,[53] should be taken in the context of the kings of the Gupta dynasty,[54] others take them as of the Hūṇa dynasty,[55] and still others, as local kings of Malwa.[56] If the last-mentioned view is accepted, one of them could have been Prabhākara, known from a Mandasor inscription of Mālava year 524, i.e. AD 467 (No. 36). Dasharatha Sharma[57] takes the relevant portion of the inscription to mean that the temple was damaged by other kings and infers that the Hūṇas were responsible for causing the damage. He opines that in that period, the dynasty of the Varmans had become extinct, and the Hūṇas had not fully settled, and the composer of the inscription did not like to give the name of the kings of the barbaric Hūṇas, who were detested by the people. This view, however, is not convincing. There is no definite evidence to show that the Hūṇas had occupied Malwa before Budhagupta (although such a possibility cannot be ruled out). The inscription refers to kings in plural, which, according to Sanskrit grammar, would mean at least three, and this does not fit in the context of the history of the Hūṇas. Further, from an inscription found at Eran (No. 75), it is known that a temple of Varāha (an *avatāra* of Vishṇu) was built at that place during the reign of Toramāṇa, and from an inscription located at Gwalior (No. 77), that a Sun temple was built at that place during the reign of Mihirakula, who himself was named after Mihira (Sun). Thus, the Hūṇa kings do not seem to have been destroyers of temples. Moreover, if they wanted to destroy the temple, then they could very well have razed it to the ground, rather than damaging it only partially, as stated in the inscription.[58] It is, therefore, more reasonable to believe that either there was some fault in the masonry or some natural factor, such as lightning, led to the damage of the temple.

Numismatic evidence[59] favours the existence of two kings of the name Kumāragupta other than Kumāragupta I, who was the son of Chandragupta II. Kumāragupta whose coins have been found in the Kalighat hoard along with the coins of Vainyagupta, Narasiṁhagupta and Vishṇugupta and classified as Class II, belong to Kumāragupta III, and those of the homonym known from other sources and classified as Class I, belong to Kumāragupta II. The coins of both these classes bear the legend *Mahārājādhirāja Śrī-Kumāragupta* on the obverse, but on the reverse, while the coins of Class I bear the legend *Kramāditya*, those of Class II bear *Śrī-kramāditya*. There is, however, difference in the style and purity of the metal between the two classes. Class I coins contain 70-80% gold, weigh less than 144 grains and are relatively better executed. Class II coins contain about 54% gold, weigh up to 148 grains and are inferior in execution. The letters on Class II coins show features which appear later than those on the Class I coins. Moreover, while there is presence of single letters like *jo, go,* or *ga,* on Class II coins, such letters are absent in Class I coins. Since such individual letters do not occur on Gupta coins till the time of Budhagupta, and are met with on those of Prakāśāditya, Narasiṁhagupta and Vishṇugupta, they should be placed later than the coins of Budhagupta.[60] Thus the numismatic evidence in the form of difference in style, execution, weight, purity of metal, title, palaeography of letters and presence or absence of individual letters, indicate that the coins of the two classes belong to two different kings. The king of Class I coins should be identified with Kumāragupta II, known from Sarnath inscription of AD 473 (No. 37), whose parentage is not mentioned in that epigraph, and that of Class II coins, with King Kumāragupta III, the son of Narasiṁhagupta Bālāditya who defeated Mihirakula in the first quarter of the sixth century AD.[61] The absence of silver coins of Kumāragupta II is taken by some as indicative of the loss of the Gujarat region to the Guptas.[62] The evidence of Bhamodra Mohota copperplate of Maitraka Droṇasiṁha of GE 183 = AD 502 (No. 96) suggests recognition of Gupta supremacy by the Maitrakas, even though nominal, in the area around Baroda, at least up to that date. The repair of the Sun temple in AD 472 by silk-weavers' guild in Mandasor, which in all probability took place in the reign of Kumāragupta II, shows his suzerainty over that region. His rule would have come to an end any time between AD 473 and 476, as on the latter date Budhagupta was on the throne.

## BUDHAGUPTA

A number of inscriptions have been found for the reign of Budhagupta: (i) two identical inscriptions dated Gupta year 157 (No. 39) on the pedestals of two Buddha images from Sarnath (Vārāṇasī district), (ii) Rajghat (Vārāṇasī district) pillar inscription dated GE 159 (No. 40), (iii) Paharpur

(Rajshahi district, Bangladesh) copperplate inscription dated GE 159 (No. 41), (iv) Mathurā Museum Buddhist image inscription dated GE 161 (No. 42), (v and vi) two Damodarpur (Dinajpur district) copperplate inscriptions, one (No. 43) dated GE 163, and another (No. 45) with the date mutilated, (vii) Eran (Sagar district) pillar inscription dated GE 165 (No. 44), (viii) Shankarpur (Sidhi district) copperplate inscription dated GE 168 (No. 46), (ix) Nandapur (Monghyr district) copperplate inscription dated Gupta era 169 (No. 48), (x) Nālandā (Nālandā district) sealing (No. 47) and (xi) an extremely fragmentary Bhitari (Ghazipur district) stone inscription of his time (*Budhaguptasya rājya-kāle*) found in course of excavations conducted under the auspices of the Department of A I H, C and Archaeology, Hindu University, Vārāṇasī (No. 56). Significantly, most of the epigraphs of Budhagupta bear dates, and all the dates, irrespective of whether the era is mentioned or not, are referable to the Gupta era.

Budhagupta's gold coins are quite rare. A few coins, which were earlier ascribed to Purugupta, have now been ascribed to him.[63] One coin of this ruler is in the Bharat Kala Bhawan (Vārāṇasī) collection,[64] one in the collection of the Arts Faculty (formerly College of Indology) of the Hindu University, Vārāṇasī,[65] and one in the collection of the State Museum, Lucknow.[66] About half a dozen of his coins in silver, all of Madhyadeśa type, and none of the Western variety, have also been found. One coin bears the date 175; the date read as 180 on another, is doubtful,[67] and the rest of the coins bear the date 174. All these dates are referable to the Gupta era. As stated above, the view that the coins bearing the legend *Prakāśāditya* should be ascribed to Budhagupta has to be given up as his title on coins is *Śrī Vikrama*.

Budhagupta became king either after the natural death of Kumāragupta of Sarnath inscription (No. 37), or, as the account of Hiuen-tsang[68] suggests, he forcibly occupied the throne.[69] He ruled from at least GE 157 (= AD 476—the date mentioned in his Sarnath inscription (No. 39) to at least GE 175 (= AD 494)—the date known from his silver coins, and if the reading of the date as Gupta Era 180[70] on one of his coins is taken as correct, then at least up to AD 499. In fact his rule could have begun anytime in or shortly after AD 473—the date known for Kumāragupta of Sarnath inscription—and could have ended in or any time before AD 507, the known date for Vainyagupta.

Basak[71] opines that Budhagupta could not have come on the throne after Narasiṁhagupta and his son Kumāragupta II, as held by Panna

Lall,[72] H C Raychaudhuri[73] and a few others, who take Kumāragupta of Sarnath inscription and the homonym who, as per the evidence of seals, was a son of Narasiṁhagupta, as identical. It looks abnormal, he argues, that in the brief span of nine years between GE 148 (= AD 467)—the last known date of Skandagupta, and GE 157 (= AD 476)—the first known date of Budhagupta, there should have been cramped the reigns of three kings – Purugupta, Narasiṁhagupta and Kumāragupta II; and to these should be added Vishṇugupta. A few scholars[74] do not consider Hiuen-tsang's account of Bālāditya's conquest of Mihirakula as historically correct, and opine that there is no need of finding a King Bālāditya as a contemporary of Mihirakula; majority of the scholars, however, consider his statement as fairly authentic.

When Fleet published *Corpus Inscriptionum Indicarum*, Volume III, dealing with the Gupta inscriptions, only Eran inscription (No. 44) was known for Budhagupta, and so he felt that his territories were confined to Malwa.[75] This was also the view of Smith[76] and Allan.[77] These scholars, however, did not take cognizance of the fact that the Eran epigraph refers to the territories that lay between Yamuna and Narmada as administered, not by Budhagupta, but by his provincial governor, Suraśmichandra, and assumed that the Gupta king's territories were confined to that region only.[78] In the absence of the imperial titles for Budhagupta, in the Sarnath inscription, which merely says 'Budhagupta ruling the earth' (*pṛithvīṁ Budhagupte praśāsatī).* In passing, it may be stated that B P Sinha is not right in stating that in that inscription he has been referred to as *mahārāja.*[79] N N Dasgupta[80] suggested that his status was that of a feudatory or governor, and not that of a king. When the Damodarpur copperplates of that ruler, dated GE 163 (= AD 482) (No. 43), referring to him as *mahārājādhirāja*, were discovered, the view of that scholar fell through. In the Rajghat (Vārāṇasī) pillar inscription of Budhagupta, dated GE 159 (No. 40), which was found later, he has been given the title *mahārājādhirāja*. No scholar accepted Dasgupta's later suggestion that from AD 476 (date of Sarnath inscription) to AD 482 (date of Damodarpur grant), Budhagupta was governor, and from AD 482 onwards, a king. In fact, the expression *pṛithvīṁ Budhagupte praśāsati* is in itself sufficient to indicate his kingly status. In a Mandasor inscription (No. 38), *pṛithvīṁ praśāsati* has been used for Kumāragupta I, and no imperial title has been used for him in that inscription, yet about his imperial status there is no doubt.

Before the discovery of the Nālandā seal of Budhagupta, from which it is known that he was a son of Purugupta, his paternity was not known, and scholars hazarded different guesses about it. As stated above, H C Raychaudhuri[81] suggested that he was the son of Kumāragupta I, since Hiuen-tsang mentions Buddhagupta (Budhagupta) as the son of Śakrāditya who is mostly identified with Kumāragupta I, whose title *Mahendrāditya* means the same as Śakrāditya. Gupte[82] was not sure whether he was the son of Kumāragupta of the Sarnath inscription of AD 473. P L Gupta[83] had suggested that Skandagupta, who has been compared with Śakra in the Kahaum inscription of that king (No. 31), could have been Śakrāditya, the father of Budhagupta. But comparisons of kings with Sakra (Indra) are not uncommon in ancient Indian inscriptions and literature, and cannot be taken as a substitute for the *āditya* title. In the Nālandā sealing of Budhagupta (No. 47), detailing the Gupta genealogy from *Mahārāja* Gupta to the owner of the seal, the missing portion in lines 7 and 8 is just sufficient to contain the name of his mother (Chandradevī), the usual attributes of Budhagupta, and therefore, there is no possibility of the mention of the name of any king intervening between Purugupta and Budhagupta.[84] With the find of that sealing, the above views regarding the identification of Budhagupta's father have proved wrong, as the sealing clearly mentions him as the son of Purugupta. R K Mookerji, in his *The Gupta Empire*, at one place,[85] basing on the evidence of Hiuen-tsang, takes Budhagupta as the son of Śakrāditya whom, like some other scholars, he identifies with Kumāragupta I *Mahendrāditya*, but at another place,[86] relying on the evidence of the Nālandā sealing of Budhagupta, rightly considers him as the son of Purugupta. The *Ārya-Mañjuśrī-mūlakalpa*[87] gives the genealogy as Deva, Chandra, and Dvādaśa, which are generally taken as identical with Budhagupta (Budha is taken the same as Buddha, who is Deva, i.e. god, for the Buddhists), Chandragupta III, and Vainyagupta Dvādaśāditya, respectively.[88] N N Dasgupta[89] suggested that Vishṇugupta followed Budhagupta, and A Ghosh,[90] too, made such a suggestion, which was based on the assumption that Kumāragupta of the Sarnath inscription and that of the Bhitari and Nālandā seals are identical. This, as will be seen below, does not seem to be the case.

A copperplate inscription (No. 46) from village Shankarpur (Sidhi district, MP), dated GE 168 (i.e. AD 487) mentions a dynasty whose founder was Sālaṇa, and in whose family ruled *Mahārāja* Gītavarman, his successor *Mahārāja* Vijayavarman, and the last mentioned one's son and successor

*Mahārāja* Harivarman, the issuer of the copperplate. B C Jain[91] identifies Harivarmā with the homonym Maukhari ruler, whose title was also *mahārāja* and from whom the inscriptions of the Maukhari rulers of Kanauj branch trace their ancestry. Since the date of the Haraha inscription (No. 94) of the fourth Maukhari king, Īśānavarman, is known as VS 611 (AD 554), Harivarmā can be placed in the last quarter of the fifth century AD and would be a contemporary of Budhagupta. This goes well with the evidence of the Shankarpur inscription. Gītavarman of that inscription would have been ruling in about the middle of the fifth century AD, and would thus have been a contemporary of Skandagupta, as suggested by Jain. S R Goyal[92] does not consider Harivarman of the inscription as identical with the Maukhari homonym, because his inscription has been found in the Baghelkhand region and in that inscription his three ancestors have been mentioned, while the Maukhari dynasty had its capital at Kanauj and in their inscriptions the genealogy begins with Harivarman. It, however, appears that Maukhari Harivarman was governor of Budhagupta in the area around the Sidhi district, Madhya Pradesh, and either he or his son and successor was transferred from there to Kanauj, where later the Maukhari kingdom came to be founded. An inscription from Narsinghgarh near Gwalior (Madhya Pradesh), datable to the beginning of the sixth century AD, shows the presence of the Maukharis in that region.[93] The non-mention of the three ancestors of Harivarman in the genealogy met with in the epigraphs of the kings of Kanauj branch of the Maukharis can be explained as below. The genealogy of the kings of that branch, first met with in the inscription of Īśānavarman, is mentioned as: Harivarman, Ādityavarman, Īśvaravarman and Īśānavarman. It appears that this was done as it was deemed proper to trace the pedigree of the ruling king to at least two or three generations, and so the earlier rulers, who probably were non-entities, were left out. Because of the same reason, in the epigraphs of Harivarman, three predecessors—his father *Mahārāja* Vijayavarman, his grandfather *Mahārāja* Gītavarman and another ancestor Sālaṇa—have been mentioned.

The two Damodarpur plates of Budhagupta's reign (Nos. 43, 45), one dated GE 163 (= AD 482), the date portion in the other being lost, refer to him as *parama-daivata-parama-bhaṭṭāraka-mahārājādhirāja*. Northern Bengal, where the province named Puṇḍravardhana was located, was administered by his governors, *uparika-mahārājas*, Brahmadatta and Jayadatta, respectively, one after the other. This may be contrasted with the governor being mentioned merely as *uparika* in the earlier Damodarpur copperplates of the time of Kumāragupta I (Nos 22, 24) and as *rājaputra-deva-bhaṭṭāraka,* a much elaborate one in the Damodarpur plate of a later date, belonging to the reign of Vishṇugupta (No. 57). From these copperplate inscriptions, we come to know that the district officer (*vishayapati*) was helped by the advisory council comprising *nagara-śreshṭhī* (head of city merchant-cum-bankers), *prathama-kulika* (head artisan), *sārthavāha* (caravan merchant) and *prathama-kāyastha* (chief scribe, who acted as chief secretary to the administrative council). The plates mention two different prices of land—one for agricultural land and another for fallow land, and also the procedure that was to be followed in the purchasing of land. In one of them it is mentioned that a *śreshṭhī* Ribhupāla had earlier applied for purchase of land for the two temples—Kokāmukhasvāmin and Śvetavarāhasvāmin, and wanted to purchase some more land for additional constructions relating to those temples.[94] The Eran inscription of the Gupta year 165 (= AD 484) mentions his provincial governor Suraśmichandra governing the region between Kālindī (Yamuna) and Narmadā, and Mātṛivishṇu as administering the district of Eran. A copperplate from Paharpur (Rajshahi district, Bangladesh), dated GE 159 i.e. AD 478 (No. 41), refers to the donation of a brāhmaṇa and his wife in favour of a Jaina *vihāra* and gives information about the district administration in the eastern part of Puṇḍravardhana province in which Paharpur is situated. The Sarnath inscriptions (No. 39) and the Rajghat (Vārāṇasī) pillar inscription (No. 40) indicate Budhagupta's rule over the regions around Vārāṇasī. The Mathurā inscription (No. 42) shows his hold over the region around that city. His seal from Nālandā may indicate his rule over that part, where there is also the evidence of the Buddhist monasteries being constructed and Buddhists patronized by him and some other Gupta rulers, including Narasiṁhagupta Bālāditya, one of his successors. The Nandapur copperplate inscription (No. 48) of GE 169 (= AD 488), mentioning the purchase of land after following the procedure in vogue there, shows that the region of Monghyr was under his rule. He, thus, ruled over an extensive empire.

The Parivrājaka *mahārājas* were ruling in the area which formed part of the former states of Nagod and Jessore, to the east of the territory governed by Budhagupta's governor Suraśmichandra. *Mahārāja* Hastin of this dynasty in his copperplates ranging in date from GE 156 (No. 63) to GE 198 (No. 66) i.e. from AD 475 to AD 517, is mentioned as 'enjoying territories under the Guptas' (*Gupta-nṛipa-rājya-bhukta*), but does not mention the name of the reigning Gupta king. This is taken by some scholars as indicative of the fact that he owed only nominal allegiance to the Guptas, and was more or less independent. Contiguous to the territories of the Parivrājakas was the kingdom of Uchchakalpa, known after the name of its capital. King Jayanātha of this dynasty issued land-grants in GE 174 (No. 69), and in GE 177 (No. 70).[95] There is no reference to the Gupta king or dynasty in them, which is taken by some scholars to suggest that the kings belonging to this dynasty ceased to owe allegiance to the Gupta kings.[96] Others opine that since the Parivrājaka kings whose territory lay to the south of that of the Uchchakalpa rulers owed allegiance to the Guptas, the latter would have also done the same.

The two land-grants of *Mahārāja* Lakshmaṇa, dated GE 158 (= AD 477) and found in Pali, near Kosam (Allahabad district),[97] suggest that he governed the region in the neighbourhood of Allahabad. There is no mention of Gupta sovereignty in these epigraphs, but since Budhagupta's inscriptions have been found at Vārāṇasī and Sarnath, Lakshmaṇa appears to have been his feudatory. No record of Budhagupta is known from the Kathiawar region, nor have his silver coins of western Indian variety been found. The Valabhī rulers of that region recognized *bhaṭṭāraka* as their overlord.[98] *Bhaṭṭāraka* has been taken by some scholars to refer to a Gupta king. It is not impossible, though much doubtful, that Budhagupta retained his hold over that region. *Mahārāja* Subandhu issued a grant in Gupta year 167 from Māhishmatī, without reference to the Gupta emperor. But this may not necessarily indicate his independent status, as in the Bhamodra Mohota coppeplate of Maitraka *Mahārāja* Droṇasiṁha of GE 186, i.e. AD 505 (No. 96), whose territories lay even beyond those of Subandhu, used the Gupta era, which may suggest that he owed allegiance, howsoever nominal, to the Guptas. In Malwa, *Mahārāja* Suraśmichandra (No. 44) was the governor of Budhagupta. The use of the Mālava era, and not the Gupta era, and the reference to the Mālava ruler as a vassal of Vākāṭaka Narendrasena, father of Pṛithvīsheṇa II in the Balaghat plate (No. 87), has been taken by some scholars to suggest that Malwa no more formed a part of the Gupta territory.[99]

According to Hiuen-tsang,[100] Buddha(Budha)gupta-rāja and Tathāgatagupta constructed a *saṅghārāma* each at Nālandā. Since Tathāgata and Buddha mean the same, they may refer to the same king,[101] and if so, it would mean that he erected two monasteries; but has been referred to in one case as Budhagupta and in another as Tathāgatagupta. However, the possibility of the two being separate kings cannot be ruled out.[102]

The Eran pillar inscription of Budhagupta, dated GE 165, i.e. AD 484 (No. 44), records the construction of a flagstaff for Vishṇu by *Vishayapati* (district officer), *Mahārāja* Mātṛivishṇu, and his younger brother Dhanyavishṇu. In another inscription from the same site—the stone Boar inscription of the time of Toramāṇa, year 1 (No. 75), Dhanyavishṇu is mentioned as the successor of his brother. It would mean that Toramāṇa had conquered the region around Eran from the Guptas after GE 165, either in the last days of Budhagupta's reign, or shortly after it. While Mātṛivishṇu has been referred to as *vishayapati* and *mahārāja*, Dhanyavishṇu, though holding the same office, has not been given even one of these designations. According to D C Sircar,[103] this indicates that till then, Dhanyavishṇu's appointment as *vishayapati* had not been confirmed by Toramāṇa. S R Goyal,[104] however, states: '...Dhanyavishṇu, a high official of the Guptas, had not hesitated to desert the emperor at this critical juncture and offer his services to the Hūṇa invader.' It, however, appears that Dhanyavishṇu succeeded his brother after the latter's death, in the normal course; and when the district passed from the hands of the Guptas to that of Toramāṇa, the Hūṇa king, following the common practice in ancient India, allowed Dhanyavishṇu to remain in office, after the latter offered allegiance to him. Toramāṇa in his Kura inscription[105] has been referred to as *rājādhirāja mahārāja shāhi javuvl.* Some of his coins bear year 52 as date, which is taken as the regnal year by some scholars, and as a date in the Hūṇa era by others.

Budhagupta is the last known Gupta king to have ruled over the vast Gupta empire extending from the Himalayas to the eastern Malwa and from eastern Punjab to Bengal. Mookerji states that his empire 'extended from Malwa to northern Bengal', and 'from the Kālindī (Yamunā) to Gaṅgā'.[106] Obviously 'Gaṅgā' is a slip for 'Narmadā;' In fact, the region administered by Budhagupta's governor has been stated in the Eran inscription of his time (No. 44) as lying between Kālindī and Narmadā. His governors of Bengal and Malwa bore the title *mahārāja*, and the feudatory Parivrājaka rulers vaguely referred to the Gupta sovereignty without mentioning the reigning Gupta king, which suggests the setting of the decline in the Gupta sovereignty. Centrifugal tendencies and internal bickering were growing. Local dynasties were gradually increasing their power, some at the cost of Imperial Gupta territories. D R Bhandarkar, at one place mentions that there is no proof that Budhagupta was defeated by Toramāṇa,[107] and at another, that the Hūṇa king overthrew him.[108] Some scholars identify Budhagupta with Deva[109] and Devarāja of the *Ārya-Mañjuśrī-mūlakalpa*,[110] whose last days are said to have been full of troubles, and who was surrounded and killed by his enemies. With the end of the rule of Budhagupta, the imperial status of the Guptas suffered a setback.

## VAINYAGUPTA

Vainyagupta is known from his Nālandā seal (No. 51), his Gunaighar (Comilla district) copperplate grant (No. 50) of Gupta Era 188 (= AD 507), —which is his only dated record so far available, and his gold coins bearing the device of *garuḍa*. Hiuen-tsang[111] mentions Tathāgatagupta between Buddhagupta (=Budhagupta) and Bālāditya. No coins or inscriptions of a king named Tathāgatagupta are known, nor does he find mention in the Gupta genealogy. May be Hiuen-tsang wrote Tathāgatagupta as a synonym for Buddhagupta (= Budhagupta),[112] although the possibility of the existence of two different kings cannot be ruled out.[113] Vainyagupta's date AD 507, known from his inscription (No. 50), suggests that he was a successor or a near successor of Budhagupta, whose last known date is AD 494 (or AD 499, if the reading of the date 180 on a coin of that king is accepted). Earlier, it was generally believed by scholars that Vainyagupta was the son of Budhagupta.[114] But, in the light of the evidence of his fragmentary Nālandā sealing (No. 51), discovered later than his Gunaighar grant, this view is no more held. In the seal inscription, the names of his ancestors are *gupta*-ending and he is mentioned as a grandson of Kumāragupta I. His father's name is however damaged, and of the letters before *gu* of the name-ending *gupta*, only *u*-medial is extant. Of the three kings whose names fulfil this condition—Purugupta, Bhānugupta (known date AD 510) and Vishṇugupta (known date 543)—the last two are ruled out as they are later in date than Vainyagupta (known date AD 507). The conclusion, therefore, follows that Purugupta was his father.[115] As D R Bhandarkar[116] states, the names of his parents 'can be restored more reasonably to Purugupta and Chandradevī than to the names of any other Gupta king and queen.' The evidence of seals provides a unique example of three sons of a king ruling, most probably one after the other. If Kumāragupta of the Sarnath inscription, whose parentage is not known, was also his son, then four of his sons ruled. S R Goyal[117] is of the view that in the inscription on seal, what is read as *u-mātrā*, can be taken as *ra* of *ndra*, and so the name of Vainyagupta's father could have been Chandragupta, who should be designated as Chandragupta III. This, he points out, is in consonance with the evidence of *Ārya-Mañjuśrī-mūlakalpa*,[118] as it places Dvādaśa (i.e., Vainyagupta *Dvādaśāditya*) after Chandra. In the Brāhmī script, both *u*-medial and subscript *ra* are added at the bottom of a letter. But a perusal of the letters in the illustration of the seal of Vainyagupta and other Gupta seals from the same site shows the distinction between *u*-medial, which is in the form of a slightly curved stroke towards the left, and subscript *r*, which is generally, and in the case of being attached to *d*, certainly, a straight stroke towards the left. Since in the case of the seal inscription in question the stroke is curved, it should be taken as *u-mātrā*, and not as *ra* subscript. Moreover, *ndra* being a conjoint of three letters, *ra* should have been written lower down, below the bottom alignment of the line, since the conjoint letters in the Brāhmī script are written vertically, and not horizontally, as is done in the case of most of the letters of the Devanāgarī script which has evolved from the Brāhmī script. We may state that according to some scholars, besides the evidence of the *Ārya-Mañjuśrī-mūlakalpa,* the possibility of the existence of a king Chandragupta other and later than Chandragupta II is suggested, by a few coins which are heavier than the coins of Chandragupta II.[119] However, the name on the seal is not Chandra.

The Gunaighar grant (No. 50) of Vainyagupta gives him the title *mahārāja*, which in the Gupta period generally denoted a governor or a feudatory, instead of *mahārājādhirāja*, which was the title of the Imperial Gupta kings Chandragupta I onwards. Further, in it he is referred to as *Bhagavān-Mahādeva-pādānudhyāta*, instead of *parama-bhāgavata* (i.e., Vaishṇava) which is the epithet generally used for the Imperial Guptas, and the device on the seal attached to the plate is bull—the *vāhana* of Śiva, and not *garuḍa*—the *vāhana* of Vishṇu. Normally, if *Mahārāja* Vainyagupta of the Gunaighar grant was a feudatory (or a governor), then the name of his overlord should have been mentioned, and if he were an independent king, then, according to the convention of his time, he should have been referred to as *mahārājādhirāja,* and not *mahārāja*. D R Bhandarkar considers *Mahārājādhirāja* Vainyagupta of the Nālandā seal, who was son of Purugupta and grandson of Kumāragupta I, and the homonym of the Gunaighar plate who is mentioned as *mahārāja,* as two different persons, as, in his opinion, the date AD 507 of the plate is too late for the Gupta king of that name.[120] He places Vainyagupta known from the seal immediately after Skandagupta, and the latter, is taken by him as identical with Purugupta. But there is a greater possibility of Vainyagupta of the Gunaighar grant and the Nālandā sealing being identical. It is possible that the reference to him as *mahārāja* instead of *mahārājādhirāja* is an inadvertent error. Basak[121] suggests that Vainyagupta might originally have been a governor (*mahārāja*) of an Imperial Gupta monarch, and though later became an independent ruler, retained the old title of *mahārāja* in the same way as Pushyamitra Śuṅga continued to be referred to as *senāpati* even after he had become king. P L Gupta[122] is of the opinion that Vainyagupta was an independent sovereign at the time of issuing the Nālandā seal which refers to him as *mahārājādhirāja*, but was reduced to the feudatory status due to Hūṇa inroads, when his Gunaighar grant was issued, which refers to him as *mahārāja*. In favour of the identification of Vainyagupta of the Nālandā seal and the Gunaighar grant, it has been stated that 'it is difficult to visualize two Gupta kings ruling within a short period, having the same name'.[123] more so when the name is not a common one. *Mahārāja* may be a scribal error for *mahārājādhirāja*. Such an error is also seen in the case of other kings too, for example Samudragupta in his Tiger-slayer type of coins, Kumāragupta I in the Mankunwar inscription (no. 27), Chandragupta I in the Poona copperplate inscription of Prabhāvatīguptā (No. 82), and Chandragupta I and Samudragupta in the Rithpur plate (No. 84) have been referred to as *mahārāja*, instead of *mahārājādhirāja*, which was their correct official title.[124]

The Gunaighar grant was made by Vainyagupta at the instance of *Mahārāja* Rudradatta, and the *dūtaka* was *Mahārāja* Vijayasena, who bore several other titles of distinction such as *mahāpratīhāra* (great chamberlain), *mahāpīlupati* (superintendent of royal stable for elephants), and *mahāsāmanta* (great feudatory). Since such high officials were serving under Vainyagupta, despite his title *mahārāja*, he should be taken as an independent king, more particularly since the Nālandā sealing refers to him as *mahārājādhirāja*.

As regards Vainyagupta's being referred to as a Śaiva in the Gunaighar grant and a Vaishṇava in the Nālandā sealing,[125] Ashvini Agrawal finds it strange that he 'professed devotion to Śiva in one part of the realm and to Vishṇu in another part.'[126] It is, however, possible that Vainyagupta might have been liberal in matters relating to religion and would have been a worshipper of both Śiva and Vishṇu. N N Dasgupta[127] points out that in the Kamauli inscription, Vaidyadeva of Kāmarūpa has been referred to both as *parama-māheśvara* and *parama-vaishṇava*. In view of this, the reference to Vainyagupta as Śaiva in his grant, and Vaishṇava in his seal, is not as incongruous as it appears at the first sight. It is equally possible that he was earlier a Vaishṇava, but later turned Śaiva.[128] Dandekar[129] opines that a king's religion need not be a criterion for determining his dynasty. It may, however, be stated that in the sixth century AD and afterwards Śaivism was quite popular with several kings and dynasties, for instance the Maukhari kings, Harsha Pushpabhūti, Gauḍa king Śaśāṅka, and the Hūṇa king Mihirakula were all Śaivas. B P Sinha rightly states that "the epithet *Parama-bhāgavata* had become almost a part and parcel of the official titles of the Gupta emperors"[130] and was continued to be used even when they shifted their allegiance to other religions. In support of this, the evidence relating to Narasiṁhagupta Bālāditya may be cited. His construction of Buddhist monuments, and his stopping of paying tribute to Mihirakula because of the latter's indulging in anti-Buddhist activities, Paramārtha's statement that *Bālāditya* was a pupil of Buddhist scholar Vasubandhu, and Yaśovarman's inscription of eighth century from Nālandā (No. 100) referring to a lofty Buddhist temple built by Bālāditya testify to his Buddhist affiliation, yet he has been referred to as *parama-bhāgavata* in his sealings.

According to P L Gupta,[131] Vainyagupta came to owe allegiance to the Hūṇa king, Mihirakula, who, as per the evidence of the Mandasor inscription of Yaśodharman (No. 80) and that of his own coins, was a staunch Śaiva, and it was under his influence that the Gupta king forsook his family faith, Vaishṇavism, and adopted Śaivism. But whereas the known date of Vainyagupta is AD 507, Mihirakula seems to have come to throne some years later, as can be inferred from the Risthal inscription of Prakāśadharmā of AD 515, which refers to his victory over the Hūṇa king Toramāṇa, and makes no mention of Mihirakula.

Coins earlier ascribed to Chandragupta III *Dvādaśāditya*, with corrected reading *Vainya* for *Chandra*, are now attributed to Vainyagupta *Dvādaśāditya*.[132] The shape, size, weight, device and legend of the coins, and the text of the seal inscription unmistakably show that Vainyagupta was a Gupta ruler. There are certain Archer-type gold coins bearing the legend *Chandra* on the obverse and the title *vikramaḥ* on the reverse, and much heavier than the coins of Chandragupta II (two of them weighing 141.8 and 145.8) have been ascribed by some scholars to Chandragupta

III.[133] Goyal,[134] basing on the evidence of the *Ārya-Mañjuśrī-mūlakalpa*[135] which mentions Deva (identified as Buddha = Budhagupta), Chandra and Dvādaśa, in that order, opines that Vainyagupta *Dvādaśāditya* was a son of Chandragupta III, who himself was the son of Budhagupta. However, scholars are not unanimous regarding the existence of a king Chandragupta III. Smith[136] considered the heavier weight coins of Chandra as of Chandragupta II, issued posthumously. Some scholars opine that Chandragupta II himself had issued some heavy weight coins,[137] though this does not go well with the general trend of weight in the Gupta coins, which generally increased with successive reigns. The *Ārya-Mañjuśrī-mūlakalpa* refers to a few of the later Imperial Gupta rulers as kings of Magadha and a few of them, including Dvādaśāditya (Vainyagupta), as of Gauḍa. This may suggest partition of the empire, with Vainyagupta ruling in the Gauḍa region.[138] The find of his copperplate from Gunaighar shows that Samataṭa, which was a border state during the reign of Samudragupta, had become a part of the Gupta empire, perhaps either in the reign of Chandragupta II or in that of Kumāragupta I.

R K Mookerji[139] identifies Vainya with Vajra mentioned by Hiuen-tsang, as Vainya is a patronymic from Veṇa, which is another name of Indra, the wielder of the *vajra.* But P L Gupta[140] points out that Vajra is mentioned by Hiuen-tsang as the successor of Bālāditya, whereas Vainya was his predecessor. Sinha[141] identifies Vainyagupta with Tathāgatarāja of Hiuen-tsang,[142] who according to him followed Buddha, i.e. Budha[gupta], in constructing monuments at Nālandā. This is also the view of S Chattopadhyaya.[143] According to the *Ārya-Mañjuśrī-mūlakalpa,* Deva (probably Budhagupta) and his two successors were killed after short reigns. B P Sinha,[144] is of the view that during the reign of Narasiṁhagupta, Vainyagupta ascended the throne with the help of the Hūṇa king, and because of it Narasiṁhagupta had to remain in wilderness for some years, till he regained the throne, overthrowing Vainyagupta. The view has rightly not found favour with scholars.

*Mahārāja* Vijayasena who finds prominent mention in the Gunaighar grant of Vainyagupta is identical with the homonym who issued Mallasarul copperplate[145] and was governing Vardhamāna-*bhukti* (Burdwan division of Bengal) in the third year of *Mahārājādhirāja* Gopachandra, In the Gunaighar plate, Vijayasena used the seal of Vainyagupta; but in the Mallasarul plate, he uses his own seal, which indicates a rise in his status, and also that the latter grant is later in date than the former. Either Gopachandra, who was king when the Mallasarul grant was issued, overthrew Vainyagupta or succeeded him in the normal course. Sinha,[146] like some other scholars, identifies Gopachandra with King Gopa of the *Ārya-Mañjuśrī-mūlakalpa*, who helped the Gupta king, Bālāditya (Narasiṁhagupta), in imprisoning Prakaṭāditya. Some scholars, however, identify Gopa with Goparāja, mentioned as an ally of Bhānugupta in an inscription from Eran (No. 52).

The reign of Vainyagupta shows signs of decline in the Imperial Gupta power. There is considerable difference in purity between the two classes of his coins; and the more alloyed ones may suggest that there was financial stringency. No coin or inscription of Vainyagupta has been found in the western provinces of the Gupta dominion, from which it can be inferred that he had no hold over them. The rise of a new ruling dynasty (or dynasties), represented by Dharmāditya, Gopachandra and Samāchāradeva in southern and western Bengal in the first half of the sixth century AD, possibly points to the extirpation of the Gupta rule from those areas. Puṇḍravardhana *bhukti* seems to have become the core of the Gupta kingdom. According to the *Ārya-Mañjuśrī-mūlakalpa* Dvādaśa (i.e. Vainyagupta Dvādaśāditya) had a short rule of a few months only and he, like his predecessors Chandra (taken as Chandragupta III by some scholars) and Deva (identified by some with Budhagupta), was murdered.[147]

## BHĀNUGUPTA

The parentage of Bhānugupta is not known. On the obverse of the coins of Vainyagupta, below the king's figure, the letter *bhā* is met with, which is taken by some as possibly an abbreviation of the name Bhānugupta, and it is surmised that the latter may have been a powerful relative of the former, and captured the throne after overthrowing him.[148] However, the fact that such individual letters also occur on the coins of other Gupta rulers who ruled after Budhagupta, makes the inference shaky. Ashvini Agrawal is of the view that Bhānugupta was a son of Purugupta.[149] But since at least three kings, Budhagupta, Narasiṁhagupta and Vainyagupta, are definitely known to have been the sons of that ruler, and there is a possibility that Kumāragupta of the Sarnath inscription, whose parentage is not known, was also his son, there is little likelihood of Bhānugupta also being his son. Barring the fact that the name Bhānugupta has been read on a Prakāśāditya coin by Shukla[150] (which has been doubted by some[151]), his coins are not known. He is known from the Eran inscription (No. 52). The purpose of the epigraph is to record the committing of *satī* (which incidentally is the first epigraphic reference to that practice in India) by the wife of Goparāja who died fighting as an ally of Bhānugupta. Most probably the battle was fought against the Hūṇas under their king Toramāṇa,[152] though the inscription neither mentions the name of that tribe nor of that king. The Mandasor inscription of Yaśodharman alias Vishṇuvardhana (AD 532) mentions Bhānuguptā as the wife of Ravikīrti, and grandmother of Dharmadosha—a minister of Yaśodharman and governor of Malwa. On the basis of similarity of the names, some scholars consider her as a sister of the Gupta king Bhānugupta.

According to the *Ārya-Mañjuśrī-mūlakalpa,* Pra-beginning name was a son of a Bha-beginning name. He was imprisoned by Gopa,[153] and was later anointed king by Hakārākhya.[154] Gopa has been identified with Goparāja[155] of the Eran pillar inscription (No. 52) by some and with Gopachandra[156] of the Mallasarul copperplate (No. 98), by others. Hakārākhya has been identified with Hūṇa king Toramāṇa.[157] It has been suggested by some scholars that *Pra*-beginning name may stand for Prakaṭāditya of a Sarnath inscription (No. 97), and *Bha*-beginning name for Bhānugupta.[158] Since the Sarnath inscription refers to Prakaṭāditya as the son of Bālāditya, some scholars suggest that Bhānugupta should be identified with Bālāditya.[159] One reason for doing so is that they believed that Narasiṁhagupta Bālāditya, son of Purugupta was the father of Kumāragupta of the Sarnath inscription, and ruled sometime between AD 467 and 473, whereas the known date of Bhānugupta is AD 510, which would make him a contemporary of Mihirakula. H C Raychaudhuri points out: '...the existence of several kings in the eastern part of the Madhyadeśa having the *viruda* Bālāditya is proved by the Sarnath inscription of Prakaṭāditya.'[160] But *Bālāditya* should better be identified with Narasiṁhagupta rather than with Bhānugupta, because it is only on his coins that the title *Bālāditya* occurs.[161] D R Bhandarkar considered Bhānugupta and Narasiṁhagupta as identical, and opined that the date, 510 known for the former is nearer to that of Mihirakula who according to Hiuen-tsang was defeated by *Bālāditya,* and it is only Narasiṁhagupta who is known to have borne the title Bālāditya, as evidenced by his coins.[162] But there is no evidence to substantiate this. As stated above, the name of king on a newly discovered[163] coin, with Horseman-lion-slayer device and the *viruda, Prakāśāditya,* has been read as Bhānugupta. The latter would not have borne, along with the *āditya* title *Prakāśāditya*, another *āditya* title, *Bālāditya,* and therefore, he should not be identified with the *Bālāditya* mentioned by Hiuen-tsang. P L Gupta[164] doubts Shukla's reading of the name of Bhānugupta on the coin, as, he states, the published photograph of the coin does not show the letters of the name of the king clearly. But even much before the publication of the coin in question, Gupta[165] himself had favoured the identification of Prakāśāditya with Bhānugupta, as, he states, 'Prakāśa (light) is the very essence of Bhānu (Sun)', and his view was accepted by J Curtis.[166] These and other views of different scholars regarding the identification of the king who issued the 'Prakāśāditya' coins have been discussed above.

S R Goyal interprets the pieces of evidence relating to Bhānugupta and other kings differently. According to him, Bhānugupta was unable to check the advance of Toramāṇa who had occupied the Ganga valley and had made Prakāśāditya, who should be identified with the *Pra*-initialled king of the *Ārya-Mañjuśrī-mūllakalpa*, his tributary. It was because of this that the latter's son Narasiṁhagupta *Bālāditya* came to be a tributary of Toramāṇa's son, Mihirakula.[167] He also states that the fact that *Prakāśāditya* coins have been found in western, and not in the eastern, Uttar Pradesh, suggests that he was under the influence of the Hūṇas.[168] Aware of the fact that *Prakāśāditya* is a title and not the name of the king, he states that in rare cases kings have been referred to by their titles.[169] However, as stated above, most probably *Prakāśāditya* was the title of Bhānugupta.

The absence of the title *mahārājādhirāja* for Bhānugupta in the Eran inscription (No. 52) has led some scholars to suggest that he was not a sovereign ruler, and fought the Hūṇas in the capacity of a governor of Malwa.[170] D K Ganguly[171] is of the view that Bhānugupta as a Gupta prince would have been sent from Pāṭaliputra to Malwa to combat the Hūṇas. But as the Eran inscription calls him a great king (*rājā mahān*) and compares him with Arjuna in great valour (*Pārtha-sama-ati-śūraḥ*), and since according to the same source, he had Goparāja, a son of king Mādhava and daughter's son of Śarabharāja, as his ally, it would be better to take him as a Gupta ruler.[172] The title *rājā,* instead of *mahārājādhirāja* usually borne by the Gupta kings, for Bhānugupta, may be an inadvertent error, which would be pardonable as the record is a private one. It has also been suggested that the use of *rājā* instead of *mahārāja* might have been due to the constraints of metre, the inscription being in verse.

The result of the battle against the enemy, to be identified as the Hūṇas, is not mentioned in the epigraph. It is also not known whether the battle was fought to defend the region around Eran against the invading Hūṇas, or to oust them from there, and recover the region from their possession.[173] The Eran pillar inscription of Budhagupta (No. 44) of GE 165 (= AD 484) shows that the area was under his rule. But another inscription from the same site, namely, the Eran Stone Boar Inscription of Hūṇa king, Toramāṇa (No. 75), shows that the territory around Eran had passed from the Guptas to the Hūṇas. While the inscription of Budhagupta Mātṛivishṇu is mentioned as *vishayapati*, in the inscription of Toramāṇa, his brother Dhanyavishṇu held the same office, which shows that this change took place shortly after AD 484. Sinha[174] believes that Bhānugupta was killed by the Hūṇas under the leadership of their king, Mihirakula. But the date of the Eran inscription is AD 510, and by that time Mihirakula does not seem to have become king. The Risthal inscription of AD 515 (No. 78) refers to the then reigning king Prakāśadharman's victory over the Hūṇa king Toramāṇa, and makes no mention of his son Mihirakula. R K Mookerji[175] is of the opinion that Bhānugupta lost the battle, and his defeat left the way clear for the further advance of the Hūṇas towards Magadha. D K Ganguly[176] is also of the view that the Guptas and their allies were routed by the Hūṇas. However, the fact that the inscription of the time of Bhānugupta has been recorded at Eran itself may suggest that the locality still formed part of the territories of the Guptas. In its support, it is pointed out that the Parivrājaka kings, whose territory was beyond, and not far from Eran district, seem to have acknowledged the sovereignty, at least nominal, of the Guptas up to GE 209 (No. 68). R C Majumdar[177] states that if Bhānugupta would have achieved victory, then it would have been described in glowing terms. However, he also includes the possibility of the victory being omitted because the inscription is a memorial one. The evidence seems more in favour of the Hūṇas being victorious.

The date for the end of Bhānugupta's rule, as for its beginning, is not known; it probably ended sometime about AD 515,[178] if he was not killed in the battle of AD 510. S R Goyal[179] takes *ā-Toramāṇa* in the Risthal inscription (No. 78) as meaning 'from Toramāṇa onwards,' and opines that probably Prakāśadharman defeated not only Toramāṇa, but also, Mihirakula. He also suggests that this was done under the leadership of prince Yaśodharman whose undated Mandasor inscription refers to his victory over that Hūṇa king. But this author is of the opinion that if the victory would have been achieved against Mihirakula, it being a great feat, should have found mention in the Risthal inscription.

The *Ārya-Mañjuśrī-mūlakalpa* states that 'after the death of Budhagupta, two kings in Gupta line were crowned, one in Magadha and another in Gauḍa'.[180] Because of the nearness of known dates of Vainyagupta, Bhānugupta and Narasiṁhagupta Bālāditya and also of the geographical areas they ruled, R C Majumdar suggested the possibility of the division of the empire—Bhānugupta ruling in Malwa, Vainyagupta in Bengal, and Narasiṁhagupta in Magadha,[181] though he considered it equally possible that the three—Vainyagupta, Bhānugupta and Narasiṁhagupta—reigned in that order.[182]

## NARASIṀHAGUPTA BĀLĀDITYA

Narasiṁhagupta Bālāditya is known from his two seal inscriptions from Nālandā (No. 53), the Bhitari seal inscription of Kumāragupta [III] (No. 55), discovered as early as 1889, two Nālandā seal inscriptions (No. 54) of the same ruler, and the Nālandā seal inscription of Vishṇugupta (No. 58). A Nālandā sealing refers to a *gandhakuṭī* named after Bālāditya,[183] who perhaps is identical with Narasiṁhagupta Bālāditya. He is to be identified with the Bālāditya mentioned in the Nālandā inscription of Yaśovarman as one who was of great valour and a great conqueror, and who got constructed a grand Buddhist temple at Nālandā. He also finds reference in the *Ārya-Mañjuśrī-mūlakalpa*. His coins have been found, which are all of the Archer type.[184] They bear the figure of a king holding a bow and the legend *Nara* is on the obverse, and the goddess and the legend *Bālāditya* on the reverse. The full name Narasiṁhagupta is preserved in the marginal legend of some better preserved coins.

The fixing of the date for his rule mainly depends on his synchronism with the Hūṇa king Mihirakula. If Narasiṁhagupta Bālāditya is taken as the father of Kumāragupta of the Sarnath inscription of AD 473, then he has to be placed before that date and one will have to find another Bālāditya, a contemporary of Mihirakula, ruling sometime in the second half of the first quarter of the sixth century AD. The date for Budhagupta (*c.* 476-94), Vainyagupta (known date 507) and Bhānugupta (known date 510) are known, and in the light of those dates, he should be placed after the last mentioned one.

Allan[185] classified the coins of Narasiṁhagupta Bālāditya into two classes. Class I are of purer metal with about 70% or more gold content, their execution is better, and on the obverse they bear a marginal legend and the letters *gre* and *gu* in between the king's feet. Class II coins are much debased, with only about 54.5 % of gold content, are rather crudely executed and do not bear a marginal legend, but like Class I coins bear individual letters. Altekar[186] suggested the possibility of two classes of Narasiṁhgupta's coins as belonging to two kings of the same name, in the same way as two classes of coins of Kumāragupta have been taken by most scholars as belonging to two kings of the same name, viz. Kumāragupta II and Kumāragupta III. S R Goyal,[187] however, considers it as certain that they belong to two different kings bearing the name Narasiṁhagupta. He suggests that Narasiṁhagupta I is to be taken as the the father of Kumāragupta of the Sarnath inscription, who is identified with the homonym of the Bhitari seal inscription and whose father's name was Purugupta. He reconstructs the considerably mutilated name of the father of Narasiṁhgupta in the Nālandā sealing as *Prakāśāditya*, instead of *Purugupta* as done by other scholars. Narasiṁhagupta of the Nālandā sealing is taken by him as Narasiṁhagupta II. Goyal suggests that the Buddhist text *Ārya-Mañjuśrī-mūlakalpa* has mixed up the history of the two Bālādityas. The statement in that work that Bālāditya was a Buddhist and a king of eastern direction is with reference to Bālāditya II, the conqueror of Mihirakula. In his opinion, it would be too late to place Narasiṁhagupta, the son of Purugupta (who, the latter, came to the throne either in AD 455 after Kumāragupta I, or in or shortly after AD 467 after Skandagupta), after Bhānugupta whose known date is AD 510.[188] In his view, the statement in the *Ārya-Mañjuśrī-mūlakalpa* that Bālāditya ruled peacefully without any rival and committed suicide at the age of thirty-six years and one month, is taken by him as pertaining to Bālāditya I. P L Gupta,[189] however, points out that those who believe in the theory of two kings bearing the name as Narasiṁhagupta do not explain how the coins of Narasiṁhagupta attributed to him 'as the father of Kumāragupta II are heavier in weight and more alloyed than the coins of his son, and those of his brothers Budhagupta and Vainyagupta', and that the letters 'in between his feet are seen only on his coins and reappear after a lapse of time in the reign of Vainyagupta and his successors.' Be it stated that while in the case of coins bearing the name Kumāragupta, the individual letters occur only on the coins of Class II, and are absent in Class I coins in the case of Narasiṁhagupta, they occur in both the classes. Besides, while a Kumāragupta is known independent of coins, from an epigraph of AD

473 from Sarnath (whose parentage is not known) who can be identified with the homonym of Class I coins; such evidence is not available for Narasiṁhagupta. Moreover, while there is difference in the *āditya* titles (*kramāditya* and *Śrī-kramāditya*) of two classes of coins of Kumāragupta, both classes of the coins of Narasiṁhagupta bear identical *āditya* titles, viz. *Bālāditya.*

As pointed out by Krishna Deva,[190] in the Nālandā sealing of Vishṇugupta (No. 58), of the name of the father of Narasiṁhagupta only traces of the subscript of the first two letters have been preserved, which in the first case is *ū*-medial, and in the second, *u*-medial, and that the only king whose name fulfils this condition is Pūrugupta. Goyal, however, opines that what has been taken as *u*-medial may be *ra* subscript, and reconstructs the name as Prakāśāditya.[191] He labels Narasiṁhagupta mentioned in the seal of Vishṇugupta as Narasiṁhagupta II, and differentiates him from the homonym known from the Bhitari seal whom he calls Narasiṁhagupta I. He considers the latter as identical with the first of the two Bālādityas mentioned in the Sarnath inscription of Prakaṭāditya (No. 97). He identifies Kumāragupta of the Bhitari seal, who is mentioned therein as a son of Narasiṁhagupta, with the homonym of the Sarnath inscription.

Although regarding the reading of letters in the broken part of the seal inscription Goyal's stand has remained the same throughout, yet one can see some change in the emphasis regarding it. He categorically stated that the view 'that Narasiṁhagupta of the Nālandā seal was the son of Purugupta is *not correct,*'[192] and that the 'name of Purugupta is *not in this epigraph at all,*'[193] (italics ours). He somewhat softens his stand and says that the 'so-called traces of *u-mātrā may equally* be taken as the remnants of the subscipt *ra* of the name Prakāśāditya',[194] that 'the reading of Krishna Deva is *not beyond doubt*',[195] and 'that the seal in question refers to Purugupta is *not an unquestionable fact*'[196] (italics added for emphasis).

A perusal of the illustration of the seal of Vishṇugupta shows that Goyal's reading is not acceptable. As D K Ganguly points out, Goyal 'does not take cognizance of the two strokes, one attached to the base, and the other by the downward elongation of the right vertical of the first letter',[197] which should be *ū*-medial, as also of 'the presence of the small hook at the bottom turned to the left showing the medial *u* in the second letter of king's name.'[198] Moreover, as stated by is author elsewhere,[199] *Prakāśāditya* is a title and not a name, and in the Imperial Gupta seals bearing genealogy, it is invariably the name of the king and never his *āditya* title (either alone or along with the name) that is mentioned. The existence of two sets of kings, father and son, bearing the names Narasiṁhagupta and Kumāragupta in the Gupta dynasty, as envisaged by Goyal, would appear rather unusual. The evidence at hand favours the view that there was only one king of the name of Narasiṁhagupta who was the son of Pūrugupta and father of Kumāragupta [III], and the last-mentioned one was different from Kumāragupta of the Sarnath inscription, whose parentage is not known.

In the Bhitari seal of Kumāragupta (No. 55), and in the two fragmentary sealings of Narasiṁhagupta from Nālandā, (No. 53), the name of the father and grandfather of Narasiṁhagupta are the same viz. Purugupta and Kumāragupta [I], and therefore, Narasiṁhagupta of the Bhitari and Nālandā seals should be taken as identical. Kumāragupta in his Bhitari seal, and his homonym in the Nālandā seal of Vishṇugupta too is mentioned as the son of Narasiṁhagupta, and should refer to one and the same person. He should be different from the homonym of the Sarnath inscription of year AD 473, whose parentage is not known as his father could not be that Narasiṁhagupta who was a contemporary of Mihirakula (second quarter of the first half of the sixth century AD).

The coins of Narasiṁhagupta with greater alloy may be taken as reflecting economic stringency during his reign. B P Sinha,[200] believes in the existence of a single king of that name, and considers the difference in the percentage of alloy as a result of the fluctuation in his political status caused mainly by the Hūṇa invasion. Vainyagupta (known date AD 507) revolted in the east, and Prakaṭāditya of Sarnath inscription (No. 97), son of [Narasiṁhagupta] Bālāditya, was anointed as the king of Magadha by Toramāṇa.[201] As a result of this, Narasiṁhagupta was in wilderness for about ten years, during which period he issued coins, which were more debased than those issued in the earlier part of his reign. Later he regained the throne and defeated Mihirakula.[202] The view of Sinha is not convincing. It is difficult to understand as to how Narasiṁhagupta could afford issuing coins even when he was living in wilderness.

According to the *Alaṅkārasūtra-vṛitti* of Vāmana, Vikramāditya sent his son Bālāditya, the *yuvarāja*, for learning to the Buddhist scholar Vasubandhu, and on becoming king, Bālāditya patronized that Buddhist scholar. As stated above, Narasiṁhagupta *Bālāditya,* whose sealings have been found at Nālandā is to be identified with Bālāditya who is referred to as 'of irresistible valour' and great conqueror and builder of a magnificent temple in an inscription of King Yaśovarman from the same site (No. 100). The reference to his being brave and also to his Buddhist leanings lends credence to the account of Hiuen-tsang relating to the victory of Bālāditya, a staunch Buddhist, over Mihirakula.[203] An inscription of Yaśodharman from Mandasor (No. 79) bears the date in Mālava era equivalent to AD 532, and an undated one, in duplicate, from the same site refers to his victory over Hūṇa king, Mihirakula. Most scholars believe that the victory was achieved before AD 532. R G Basak,[204] however, places it after AD 533-34. According to Hiuen-tsang,[205] Bālāditya was a vassal of Mihirakula. Knowing that the Hūṇa king was committing atrocities on the Buddhists, he refused to pay tribute to him, and in consequence the Hūṇa king invaded him. Bālāditya, fleeing with his ministers, family members and some other followers hid himself in an island. Mihirakula however was ambushed and taken prisoner.[206] He was set free on the interception of Bālāditya's mother who, unmindful of the 'political fall out' of such an act, was guided by religious belief that killing him would bring bad result.[207] Some scholars[208] doubt the authenticity of Hiuen-tsang's account. It has been pointed out[209] that the Chinese pilgrim mentions Gupta king's taking shelter in an island, the existence of which being within his kingdom is doubtful, and that he places Bālāditya some centuries before his own time, while there was a gap of about a century only between his coming to India (AD 629) and Narasiṁhagupta's rule (first half of the sixth century AD). From this it has been inferred that the account of the Chinese pilgrim is based on hearsay. But in favour of the authenticity of the account, it has been stated by B P Sinha[210] that in *Records*, Bālāditya is said to have taken refuge in an island of Bay of Bengal, and the time gap of 'some centuries' may be an exaggeration on the part of the Chinese pilgrim, and such exaggerations, are also met with in the accounts of some other Chinese travellers.[211]

Hiuen-tsang gives sole credit to Bālāditya for defeating Mihirakula and makes no mention of his defeat at the hands of Yaśodharman.[212] The Mandasor inscription of King Yaśodharman (No. 80) eulogizes him for defeating that Hūṇa king who had never been conquered before. The inscription refers to Yaśodharman's carrying victorious arms to regions which had not been conquered by the Guptas and where Mihirakula's commands failed to penetrate, and whose empire comprised territories right from the Lauhitya (Brahmaputra) to the Western Ocean, and from the Himalayas to Mahendragiri. It makes no reference to King Bālāditya's victory over that Hūṇa monarch. There is a difference of opinion among scholars whether Bālāditya and Yaśodharman defeated Mihirakula jointly or independently. Smith[213] opined that certain native princes under the leadership of Yaśodharman defeated the Hūṇa king, and was inclined to reject the statement of Hiuen-tsang giving the sole credit to King Bālāditya, as not based on fact. J Allan[214] rejected such a view as, in his opinion, it is contrary to the evidence of both Hiuen-tsang and the Mandasor inscription of Yaśodharman, and in his view, Bālāditya only defended against Mihirakula's attack, and it was Yaśodharman who routed the Hūṇa king. Fleet holds that Mihirakula was defeated by Yaśodharman in the west and Bālāditya in the east.[215] Hoernle[216] is of the opinion that Yaśodharman defeated Mihirakula as a feudatory of Narasiṁhagupta, but after becoming independent took the credit of victory over that Huṇa ruler, wihout making any reference to his overlord, while Hiuen-tsang gives the credit to Bālāditya who then was the paramount sovereign. It seems more plausible that Bālāditya and Yaśodharman defeated the Hūṇa king separately. Accepting this, the question arises as to who was defeated earlier, and when the two defeats took place. The defeat by Yaśodharman, probably took place sometime after Mālava year 572 (= AD 515), the date of the Risthal inscription of king Prakāśadharman, a predecessor of Yaśodharman, who refers to his defeating Toramāṇa, but makes no mention of Mihirakula. Yaśodharman's victory over Mihirakula finds mention in his undated inscription, in duplicate (No. 80), from Mandasor, a site from where another of his inscriptions, dated AD 532 (No. 79), has also been found. If the undated inscription is of the same date, or is earlier than the dated one, then the victory was attained in or before AD 532. Mihirakula's Gwalior inscription (No. 77) is dated in his 15th regnal year, so he should have ruled at least for fifteen years. The use of the epithets *janendra*, *rājādhirāja* and *parameśvara* for Yaśodharman in the dated inscription suggests that the victory had already been achieved. However, if the undated inscription is later than the dated one then it would as well have taken place after AD 532.[217] Altekar places this victory in AD 530.[218] B P Sinha[219] suggests that Bālāditya defeated Mihirakula in *c* AD 520 and Yaśodharman did the same after it and shortly before AD 532. H C Raychaudhuri[220] also believes that Mihirakula met his first defeat at the hands of Bālāditya, since according to the accounts of Hiuen-tsang, after being defeated by Bālāditya, Mihirakula went to Kashmir and captured the throne of the king ruling there and then conquered Gandhāra.[221] Dandekar believes that

Yaśodharman would have conquered the regions mentioned in his Mandasor inscription after the death of Bālāditya, as there would be no place for Bālāditya's empire during the rule of Yaśodharman.[222] Some scholars[223] hold that the defeat at the hands of Bālāditya was the second of the two defeats the Hūṇa king suffered. R C Majumdar[224] points out the drawbacks in both the views. He states that if Mihirakula had been already defeated by Bālāditya then the statement in the *praśasti* of Yaśodharman that he defeated the Hūṇa king who had never before submitted to any king would become redundant, and on the other hand, Hiuen-tsang states that Bālāditya was a tributary of Mihirakula, which could not have been his status if the Hūṇa king had already suffered defeat at the hands of Yaśodharman. Some inference regarding the date of Narasiṁhagupta may be drawn from another evidence. His father Purugupta died in or shortly before AD 473 (when Kumāragupta of the Sarnath inscription was ruling) and he would have been too old to have continued to rule beyond AD 532 when Yaśodharman was in full power.

Earlier it was believed that Yaśodharman rose like a meteor and dazzled the political horizon for a short while by his quick and extensive conquests, and fell like a meteor, and his empire ended with him.[225] But now, with the discovery of the Risthal inscription of AD 515 (No. 78), it is clear that at least his rise was not sudden, and several rulers of his family had preceded him, and also that his immediate predecessor, Prakāśadharman who perhaps was his father, had defeated the Hūṇa king Toramāṇa (No. 78). The view of S R Goyal,[226] that Prakāśadharman also defeated Mihirakula, and Yaśodharman took part in that campaign as a prince and later, on becoming king, claimed this victory as his own, is difficult to accept. For had that been the case it would have been mentioned in the Risthal inscription. R C Majumdar had suggested that probably Yaśodharman rose to power by freeing the region around Mandasor from the Hūṇa yoke.[227] But the region already formed a part of the kingdom of his predecessor Prakāśadharman, as the Risthal inscription refers to the construction of a temple at Daśapura (Mandasor) during his reign. It is not known for certain how the end of Yaśodharman came and who succeeded him.[228]

The two Nālandā sealings of Narasiṁhagupta (No. 53) bear *garuḍa* device, in one case partly damaged and in another considerably damaged, and refer to him as a *parama-bhāgavata* (i.e. Vaishṇava), in conformity with the traditional device and *viruda* of the Imperial Gupta kings.

However, there is evidence to show that he had Buddhist leanings. Hiuen-tsang states that Bālāditya built a *saṅghārāma* and a temple[229] and became a Buddhist recluse.[230] The *Ārya-Mañjuśrī-mūlakalpa*[231] informs that Bālāditya got constructed a large number of Buddhist *vihāras, ārāmas* and *maṇḍapas* throughout the country. He is to be identified with Bālāditya of the eighth century Nālandā stone inscription of Yaśovarman (No. 100), which refers to him as of irresistible valour and conqueror of all the enemies, and one who got built a high and magnificent Buddhist temple at Nālandā; the temple seems to be the one seen by Hiuen-tsang.[232] A Nālandā sealing mentions Bālāditya Gandhakuṭī named after him. On the complaint of Bālāditya, according to the accounts of Hiuen-tsang,[233] the *saṅgha* made a rule that those members of Buddhist establishments who have not been fully ordained should be ranked according to their age.

The find of Narasiṁhagupta's coins from Bengal[234] and Oudh[235] and of his sealings from Nālandā, and the donation by him of a village located within Nagara-*bhukti* in Shahabad district, Bihar, as mentioned in an inscription of the Later Gupta dynasty,[236] suggest his rule over parts of Bengal, Bihar and Uttar Pradesh.

The Parivrājaka inscriptions, dated GE 191, i.e. AD 510 (No. 71) and GE 198, i.e. AD 517 (No. 66), use the expression meaning 'in the enjoyment of the sovereignty of the Guptas', though they do not mention the then ruling Gupta monarch. The first date belongs to the reign of Bhānugupta and the second, in all probability, to that of Narasiṁhagupta. Droṇasiṁha, a Maitraka ruler, is said to have been anointed as king by his paramount sovereign, 'the lord of the circumference of the whole world' (*akhila-bhuvana-maṇḍala–svāmī)* in his own records and in those of his successors. The overlord of the Maitraka ruler is taken by most scholars as a Gupta king, and some scholars identify him with Narasiṁhagupta.[237] R C Majumdar opines that the allegiance is referred to in conventional phraseology which seems appropriate for a reputed dynasty rather than for a new conqueror.[238] The Maitrakas issued grants of land independently between AD 502 and AD 526, without making reference to the Gupta kings.[239] B P Sinha opines that perhaps it was in the reign of Narasiṁhagupta Bālāditya that an embassy was sent from India to China in AD 502.[240] In the scheme of chronology followed by us, Narasiṁhagupta would not have come to the throne before AD 510, the known date of Bhānugupta, and if a Gupta king is to be credited for sending the embassy to China, then it should be Budhagupta, as suggested by Cunningham.[241] Hiuen-tsang[242] mentions Bālāditya as a successor of Tathāgatagupta, and the father and predecessor of Vajra, whereas Narasiṁhagupta according to the evidence of seals was the son of Purugupta, and father of Kumāragupta [III]. The title *Bālāditya* occurs only on coins bearing the name Narasiṁhagupta. It has been suggested[243] that the anomaly between Hiuen-tsang's account and other sources is because the Chinese pilgrim speaks only about those Gupta kings who were donors to the monastic establishment at Nālandā, and often do not mention the mutual relationship of the rulers, or the chronological order of their succession to the Gupta throne. Since Narasiṁhagupta's father Purugupta would have died in *c.* AD 473 (the date known for Kumāragupta of the Sarnath inscription), and if the former might have ruled up to *c.* AD 530, he must have been an old man at the end of his rule. He probably died before the victorious march of Yaśodharman up to the Brahmaputra. In later years he seems to have become involved in constructional and other activities related to Buddhism. According to Hiuen-tsang, Bālāditya gave up the throne and became a monk,[244] which finds some corroboration from the *Ārya-Mañjuśrī-mūlakalpa*, in which it is stated that he committed suicide through *dhyāna*.[245]

## KUMĀRAGUPTA III

According to the evidence of seals, Narasiṁhagupta was succeeded by his son Kumāragupta. This appears to be supported by the *Ārya-Mañjuśrī-mūlakalpa* which says that Bāla (i.e. *Bālāditya*, a title of Narasiṁhagupta) was succeeded by Kumāra. There are some coins bearing the name Kumāragupta, which have been classified as Class I and Class II.[246] In comparison to coins of Class I, those of class II are cruder in fabric, contain more alloy, bear the reverse legend *Śrī-Kramāditya* instead of *Kramāditya* of Class I, and show the letter *go* between king's feet, a feature which is not met with on the coins of Class I. In passing, it may be stated that D R Bhandarkar[247] ascribed these coins to Kumāragupta I, and took *go* to stand for Govindagupta and since the legend gave the name of Kumāragupta, he considered this as an evidence in support of his theory that Govindagupta and Kumāragupta I were two names of one and the same person, which, as seen above (Chapters 8 and 9), is not correct and, as such has not been accepted by scholars. Because of the differences in the coins of the two classes, those of Class I are ascribed to Kumāragupta, who is taken as identical with the homonym of the Sarnath inscription, and those of Class II, to Kumāragupta known from the Bhitari and Nālandā seals. The former should be designated as Kumāragupta II, and the latter, as Kumāragupta III.[248] Some scholars[249] identify Kumāragupta III with Vajra who is mentioned by Hiuen-tsang after King Bālāditya, presuming that Vajra was an abbreviation of the *āditya* title *Vajrāditya*. But this view is not acceptable as the *āditya* title of Kumāragupta III was *Śrī-kramāditya*. P L Gupta[250] suggests that Vajra was either Vishṇugupta or his successor. However, if Vajra is taken as an abbreviation of the title *Vajrāditya*, then his identification with Vishṇugupta is negated by the fact that his *āditya* title was *Chandrāditya*.

The Bhitari seal of Kumāragupta III (No. 55) would have been attached to the copperplate recording the grant to a brāhmaṇa or brāhmaṇas or to some temple, may be the one that, as per the evidence of the Bhitari pillar inscription of Skandagupta (No. 33), was got constructed by Skandagupta. To whomsoever the grant was made, it lends support to the view that Bhitari was a place of great importance for the Guptas, and also that the area around it continued to be within the Gupta kingdom during the rule of Kumāragupta III, if the grantee was, as it seems to be, located at the place where the copperplate has been found.

According to some scholars, Kumāragupta III was the Gupta king who suffered defeat at the hands of Yaśodharman who, as per the testimony of his Mandasor inscription (No. 80), in the course of his campaign marched up to the Brahmaputra and conquered territories which even the Gupta kings could not bring under their sway. The view of Mirashi[251] that the epigraph intends to convey that Yaśodharman protected his territories, which had not been conquered by the Hūṇas or the Guptas is not acceptable, as that would not reflect the greatness of Yaśodharman, and instead could even lead to the inference that he lost some of his territories to the Hūṇas and the Guptas, which certainly is not expected to be mentioned in the inscription containing his *praśasti*.

Despite the serious damage caused to the Gupta empire by the invasion of Yaśodharman, there is evidence for the continuity of some of the features of political and administrative system, though with some modification, within the Gupta territories, as can be inferred from a comparison of the evidence of the Damodarpur copperplates of the time of Kumāragupta I and Budhagupta with the plate belonging to the reign of Vishṇugupta (below). The Parivrājaka kings were acknowledging Gupta suzerainty, however nominal it might have been.[252] Vishṇugupta was ruling in AD 543, and his gold coins have been found in fairly large number. Some scholars consider the statement in the Mandasor inscription that Yaśodharman conquered territories up to the Brahmaputra, as a highly exaggerated one.[253] However, it would be reasonable to believe that there would have been some basis for such a claim.[254] In the inscription of the Maitraka kings, ranging between AD 525 and 545, homage has been paid to their overlord, by referring to themselves as *parama-bhaṭṭāraka pādānudhyāta*. It has been suggested that the *parama-bhaṭṭāraka* most probably refers to the Gupta king, as in the inscriptions with reference to the overlord, the old phraseology, without any change, has been retained. If there would have been change of the dynasty, it is opined, the name of the new dynasty and even the name of the king, his overlord, would have been mentioned.[255] Coins of Kumāragupta III have been found in fairly large numbers. S R Goyal[256] suggests that he might have been the king during whose rule a Chinese embassy visited India in AD 539, and the Indian king (name not mentioned) sent Paramārtha with it to China.[257] His rule would have ended some time before 543 when, as will be seen below, Vishṇugupta was on the throne. The circumstances of his death are not known. B P Sinha[258] suggests that he died fighting Yaśodharman.

## VISHṆUGUPTA

Vishṇugupta, the son and successor of Kumāragupta III, is known from his coins, his sealing from Nālandā (No. 58) and from the fifth Damodarpur copperplate of GE 224 (No. 57) of his reign. A fragmentary stone inscription of the [Gupta] year 221 from Bhitari (No. 56) referring to a person bearing the titles *mahādaṇḍanāyaka* and *mahārāja,* might have belonged to his reign. His coins, all of Archer type, are known since 1783 with the find of the Kalighat hoard,[259] which practically is the sole source of his coins. The coins bear on their obverse a king holding a bow and the legend *Vishṇu*, and the letter *u* between the feet of the king, and on the reverse, the figure of the goddess and the legend *Chandrāditya*. They range in weight from 147.4 to 152 grains,[260] and their gold content is about 43%. As stated above, some stray single letters are also found on these coins which are also met with on those of some other later Imperial Gupta kings who ruled after Budhagupta. J Allan[261] on the basis of the shape, size, device, weight and gold content dated such coins between *c.* AD 540 and 560, which date was later, to a large extent, corroborated by the find of the fifth Damodarpur plate of AD 543 (No. 57) belonging to the reign of that ruler. It may in passing be mentioned that R K Mookerji,[262] reconstructs the mutilated name of the king on the fifth Damodarpur copperplate as Kumāragupta stating that the letter *ku* has been preserved. But as stated above, of the name of the king, only *gupta*, and *u* medial preceding it, have been preserved. Though Mookerji refers to the evidence of the Nālandā sealing of Vishṇugupta, which mentions him as the son of Kumāragupta and grandson of Narasiṁhagupta, yet the learned scholar writes not a word about Vishṇugupta, and ends the account of the Gupta history abruptly with his father Kumāragupta [III].[263]

V A Smith[264] had identified Vishṇugupta of the coins with the homonym of the Later Gupta dynasty and placed him in *c* AD 700. His view has not been accepted as the Later Gupta kings are not known to have issued coins and the date suggested for him is too late, on palaeographic grounds, as the letters on the coins show features of mid-sixth century AD. Further, the individual letters that are seen on his coins are found on the coins of the kings of the Imperial Gupta dynasty ruling after Budhagupta. Hoernle[265] had identified the issuer of the coins bearing the name Vishṇu with Yaśodharman-Vishṇuvardhana[266] of the Mandasor inscription (No. 79). He preferred to take the reverse legend as *Dharmāditya*, since, according to him, *Chandrāditya* is 'an impossible Sanskrit compound'. The presence of the letter *u* on these coins, he explained as indicative of the fact that the coins had been issued from the Ujjain mint.[267] Allan[268] rightly rejected this view and ascribed them to a King Vishṇugupta, whom on the basis of their style and form he considered as issued by a king of the Imperial Gupta dynasty. He also pointed out that *Chandrāditya* of the legend is a correct Sanskrit word.[269] The absence of the letters *gupta* in the end part of the name does not create any problem in ascribing the king to the Imperial Gupta dynasty, as this is also the feature of coins of some other Gupta kings; for example on Narasiṁhagupta's coins generally the name is only as Nara.[270] It has been opined that according to the *Ārya-Mañjuśrī-mūlakalpa*, Kumāra was followed by *U-kārākhya*,[271] and the presence of the letter *u* on the coins may be explained in the light of this statement in that text. The Buddhist text also speaks of disunion and disruption after this king, which suits well in the context of Vishṇugupta, as no name of any Imperial Gupta king after him is known. Most of the coins of Vishṇugupta are slightly higher in weight[272] and more debased[273] than the coins of Kumāragupta

III, which features suggest that they should be placed later than those of the latter.[274] Rapson[275] also came to the same conclusion on typological grounds. The relative chronology of these two kings is clearly established by a fragmentary sealing of Vishṇugupta from Nālandā on which the name of his father is Kumāragupta, and that of his grandfather, Narasiṁhagupta. As seen above, of the name of his great-grandfather only subscripts of the first two letters have been preserved, which can be identified as *ū*-medial and *u*-medial respectively, from which it can be inferred that the name was Pūrugupta, as of the Gupta kings this feature is seen only in his name.

Though it has been mentioned above that the date of the fifth Damodarpur plate is 224 GE and also that the plate belongs to Vishṇugupta, it must be stated that the reading of the date and the restoration of the name of the king on the plate has been a matter of debate. Basak,[276] who edited the inscription, read the date as 214, which was corrected by K N Dikshit[277] as 224, and the corrected date has been accepted by almost all scholars, including Basak.[278] R K Mookerji[279] gives the date as 214—the same as the earlier reading by Basak—though he is aware of its correction as 224 by K N Dikshit. He does not assign any reason for his preference for the reading which was discarded by Basak himself. D R Bhandarkar at one place[280] rejects both the readings, 214 as well as 224, and opines that it should be read as 211, and, curiously, at another place in the same work, he gives the date as 224.[281]

As regards the name of the king on the plate, its first part is damaged, and completely lost and only the second part *gupta* has survived. The king to whose reign the plate belonged to has variously been taken as belonging to the Imperial Gupta dynasty, or Later Gupta dynasty, or some other dynasty. The name has been reconstructed variously as Kumāragupta, who has been identified with Kumāragupta III of the Imperial Gupta dynasty,[282] or with the homonym of the Later Gupta dynasty;[283] Bhānugupta of the Imperial Gupta dynasty;[284] Vishṇugupta of the Imperial Gupta dynasty,[285] or the homonym of the Later Gupta dynasty; and Dāmodaragupta of the Later Gupta dynasty.[286] H C Raychaudhuri[287] suggested that the name could be Kṛishṇagupta, Harshagupta or Jīvitagupta, all kings of the Later Gupta dynasty, though he did not rule out the possibility of the king belonging to the Imperial Gupta dynasty or even some other dynasty. It must be stated that some of the identifications mentioned above were suggested when the Nālandā sealing of Vishṇugupta had not come to light. One reason for taking the king of the fifth Damodarpur plate as of Later Gupta dynasty was the belief of some scholars that Kumāragupta of the Sarnath inscription (No. 37), whose known date is AD 473 and whose parentage has not been mentioned in that inscription, and the homonym of the Bhitari seal inscription (No. 55) should be taken as identical. This would mean that Kumāragupta's grandfather Purugupta, his father Narasiṁhagupta, he himself, and his son Vishṇugupta should be placed in between AD 467 and AD 476, the former being the last date for Skandagupta, and the latter, the first known date for Budhagupta. It was at that time unthinkable that a scion of the Imperial Gupta family was ruling as late as AD 543.

The king in the plate has been given the titles *parama-daivata, parama-bhaṭṭāraka* and *mahārājādhirāja*. No king of the Later Gupta dynasty is known to have borne such high sounding titles. On the other hand, these precisely are the titles, which were borne by the kings of the Imperial Gupta dynasty. The text of the copperplate inscription in question closely resembles that of the copperplate inscriptions of the Imperial Gupta kings Kumāragupta I (Nos. 22, 24) and Budhagupta (Nos. 43, 45) from the same site, viz. Damodarpur, and the era used should refer to the Gupta era. Therefore the king of the fifth Damodarpur plate should be taken as an Imperial Gupta ruler. As regards the reconstruction of the damaged part of the name on the plate as Damodara, it is ruled out as the space on the seal which contained the name was not enough to accommodate such a long name; it seems just enough for accomoddating two letters. B P Sinha[288] rejects the possibility of the name being Damodara also on chronological grounds, which however is not based on the correct evidence. He argues that as per the evidence of the Haraha Inscription of AD 554 of Iśānavarman, the Maukhari ruler and Kumāragupta of the Later Gupta dynasty were contemporaries, and therefore it is unlikely that Kumāragupta's son Damodaragupta was ruling in AD 543. It is, however, not the Haraha inscription of Iśānavarman Maukhari, but the Aphsad inscription of the Later Gupta king Ādityasena[289] which mentions the victory of (his ancestor) Kumāragupta, over the Maukhari king, Īśānavarman. It may be stated that of the kings of the Imperial Gupta dynasty who can be placed in the sixth century AD, the names of only two fulfil the condition of comprising two letters (before *gupta*), viz. Bhānu and Vishṇu. Bhānugupta is known as ruling in AD 510 from an Eran pillar inscription (No. 52), and it does not seem that his rule continued up to as late as AD 543, particularly when Narasiṁhagupta Bālāditya and his son Kumāragupta III are known to have ruled after that king. Hence it is almost certain that the name of the king who issued the fifth Damodarpur plate was Vishṇugupta.[290]

According to the *Ārya-Mañjuśrī-mūlakalpa*, Kumāra, generally identified with Kumāragupta III, was followed by *Ukārākhya* (i.e. *u*-initialled name). On the coins of Vishṇugupta Chandrāditya, the letter *u* occurs between the feet of the king.[291] H C Raychaudhuri[292] points out that *Ukārākhya* may stand either for Upagupta or Upendra, and in the latter case, it being a synonym of Vishṇu would refer to Vishṇugupta. In the former case, the person may be a brother of Queen Upaguptā, mother of the Maukhari king Īśānavarman, as per the evidence of the Asirgarh seal[293] and the Nālandā seals of his son, Śarvavarman.[294] The suggestion is based on the fact that in some cases, brothers and sisters were given the same name, the difference generally being that in the former case the names being male are either *akārānta* or *ikārānta*, and in the latter case the names being female, *ākāranta* or *īkārānt*. There are however other suggestions regarding the identification.[295]

Although there was an interval of 60 years between the Damodarpur copperplates of Budhagupta dated AD 483 (No. 43) and the Damodarpur plate of Vishṇugupta dated AD 543 (No. 57), in both of them there is much similarity in the administrative machinery at the district level and also in the procedure of sale and purchase of the land. Significantly, the combined evidence of the Damodarpur copperplates of the time of Budhagupta and Vishṇugupta shows that one *nagara-śreshṭhī*, Ribhupāla, who was a member of the district advisory board during the reign of Budhagupta, continued to serve in the same capacity even some 60 years later, during the rule of Vishṇugupta. However, some change is noticeable in the status of the governor. In the two Damodarpur copperplate inscriptions of Kumāragupta I (No. 22, 24), the governor has been mentioned simply as *uparika*, in the two plates of the time of Budhagupta (Nos. 43, 45) from the same site, as *uparika mahārāja*, and in the Damodarpur plate of Vishṇugupta (No. 57), as *mahārājaputra-deva-bhaṭṭāraka*. The last-mentioned expression shows that the king's son was appointed to that office,[296] which would have been done because of some special reason (Chapter 12). All the *uparikas* mentioned in the plates of Kumāragupta and Budhagupta bear *datta*-ending names indicating that they belonged to one and the same family, testifying to the hereditary nature of the office. The practice came to an end with the appointment of the prince as *uparika* in the reign of Vishṇugupta. May be that the victorious campaign of

Yaśodharman was responsible for the end of the viceregal family of the governors with *datta*-ending names. It may also be mentioned that according to the Jaina tradition Harigupta was the preceptor of Toramāṇa and also that of prince Devagupta of the royal house of the Guptas. It is difficult to say if Deva-bhaṭṭāraka of the plate is identical with that of Devagupta.[297] The invasion of Yaśodharman took place probably in the reign of Vishṇugupta's father Kumāragupta III. Yaśodharman campaigned up to River Brahmaputra, passing through the Gupta territories, overwhelming them. Although his campaigns did not lead to the end of the Gupta rule, nor even to permanent occupation of all the Gupta territories which he subdued, yet it gave a great blow to the prestige and resources of the Gupta empire and, contributed even more than the Hūṇa invasions to its downfall. The Damodarpur copperplate inscription of Vishṇugupta shows his authority over north Bengal, while the Nālandā seals may indicate his hold over some parts of Magadha.[298] In view of the fact that the Gupta rule survived in these areas, some scholars consider the statement in the Mandasor inscription (No. 80) regarding Yaśodharman's large-scale conquests as much exaggerated The issue of gold coins by Vishṇugupta, which have been found in fairly large number, the title *mahārādhirāja* used for him both in the Nālandā seal and the Damodarpur plate, and the nominal allegiance paid by the Maitraka rulers to the Gupta overlords till AD 545 would, according to some scholars, suggest that perhaps some semblance of imperial fabric still existed during his reign. R G Basak,[299] however, is of the view that Vishṇugupta 'acknowledged the authority of Yaśodharman.'

The Amauna (Gaya district) grant of *Mahārāja* Nandana of AD 551 (No. 99) instead of mentioning the name of the then reigning Gupta king as his overlord, refers to Nandana's *guru*, suggesting that he did not deem the Gupta ruler worthy of mention. This shows that the Guptas had ceased to exercise effective control over greater part of Magadha, though Nandana's titles *mahārāja* and *kumārāmātya* show that he was hesitant to declare himself as an independent ruler. In parts of Bengal, there is evidence for the rule of three kings—Gopachandra, Dharmāditya and Samāchāradeva—none of whom belong to the Gupta dynasty.[300] As per the evidence of the Haraha inscription (No. 94) dated [VS] 611 (= AD 554) Īśānavarman Maukhari, with his capital at Kanauj, in contrast to his three predecessors who bore the title *mahārāja*, has been designated as *mahārājādhirāja*, suggesting his stature of a paramount sovereign. His contemporary and rival, the Later Gupta king of Magadha, Kumāragupta, contested the imperial status of the Maukhari king and as per the testimony of the Aphsad inscription (No. 95) defeated him. In the western Uttar Pradesh and eastern Punjab ruled the early Pushpabhūti rulers, bearing the title *mahārāja*. The *Harivaṁśa* of Jinasena[301] informs that the Gupta rule lasted 231 years, and counting from AD 319, which is the date of the beginning of the independent Gupta rule as well as the founding of the Gupta era,[302] the date would be AD 550. The Sumandal plates from Ganjam district of Orissa dated GE 250 (= AD 569), however, refers to the Gupta rule in that region. Vishṇugupta's coins have been found in fairly large numbers, from which it has been inferred that he had a long reign. R C Majumdar suggests that his rule ended in about AD 550;[303] his earlier view was that Vishṇugupta perhaps was the last ruler of the dynasty and might have ruled from *c*. AD 540 to *c*. AD 570.[304] There is a possibility of the existence of a successor or a few successors of Vishṇugupta, though no definite evidence is available for that. Some scholars suggest that Deva in the expression *Rājaputra-Deva-bhaṭṭāraka* of the fifth Damodarpur plate is the name of a prince,[305] a son of the ruling king Vishṇugupta, and he might have succeeded his father as king. The *Ārya-Mañjuśrī-mūlakalpa*, it may be stated, also mentions a king named Deva, though his chronological position is uncertain.

## NOTES AND REFERENCES

1. R G Basak, *History of North-Eastern India*, p. 93.
2. *Indian Culture*, I, pp. 692-93.
3. While some scholars, e.g. Krishna Deva (*Epigraphia Indica*, XXVI, pp. 235ff), D C Sircar (*Select Inscriptions*, I, p. 330, n. 2) and R C Majumdar in *The Vākāṭaka-Gupta Age*, p. 186, n. 1), P L Gupta (*Indian Historical Quarterly*, XXVI, p. 255n), A K Narain (*Journal of the Numismatic Society of India*, xii, pp. 112-115), and A S Altekar, (*The Coinage of the Gupta Empire*, 263ff and 275ff) are inclined to accept Saraswati's reading on some coins, others, e.g., Burn (*Annual Bibliography of Indian Archaeology*, X, for the year 1935-37, p. 11), Jagannath (*All India Oriental Conference*, Nagpur, 13th Session, 1946, Section IX, p. 135), and N N Dasgupta (*B C Law Volume*, I, p. 618) doubt it. See also B P Sinha, *Decline of the Kingdom of Magadha*, p. 1, and S R Goyal, *The Imperial Guptas*, p. 339, n. 1.
4. *Journal of the Royal Asiatic Society of Great Britain and Ireland*, 1905, p. 49.
5. P L Gupta, *The Imperial Guptas*, p. 349.
6. As the name has been read by N P Chakravarty (*Archaeological Survey of India—Annual Report*, 1934-35, p. 65). Earlier Hoernle (*Journal of the Asiatic Society of*

*Bengal*, LVIII, p. 89) had read the name as Vatsadevī, and H N Sastri (*Memoirs of the Archaeological Survey of India*, 66, p. 65) as Vainyadevī.

7. J Allan, *Catalogue of the Coins of the Gupta Dynasties, and of Śaśāṅka, the King of Gauḍa, in the British Museum, London*, pp. 135-36; Altekar, *The Coinage of the Gupta Empire*, pp. 285-86.
8. *Journal of the Asiatic Society of Bengal*, LVIII, 1889, pp. 93-94.
9. *Journal of the Royal Asiatic Society of Great Britain and Ireland*, 1905, pp. 135.
10. *Indian Museum Catalogue*, I, p. 119.
11. *Catalogue of the Coins of the Gupta Dynasties, and of Śaśāṅka, the King of Gauḍa, in the British Museum, London*, p. 135.
12. A S Altekar, *The Coinage of the Gupta Empire*, p. 284.
13. A Ghosh, *Indian Historical Quarterly*, IX, p. 122, n. 4.
14. A S Altekar, *The Coinage of the Gupta Empire*, p. 306; J Allan, *Catalogue of the Coins of the Gupta Dynasties, and of Śaśāṅka, the King of Gauḍa, in the British Museum, London*, p. li. Allan says that only two-thirds of coins were available for examination (*ibid.*).
15. J Allan, *Catalogue of the Coins of the Gupta Dynasties, and of Śaśāṅka, the King of Gauḍa, in the British Museum, London*, p. lii. There is a suggestion (H C Raychaudhuri, *Political History of Ancient India*, p. 518) that Purugupta might have borne two *āditya* titles as Skandagupta bore the titles *Vikramāditya* and *Kramāditya*, and a king of the Maitraka dynasty, both *Dharmāditya* and *Śīlāditya*. But the titles of Skandagupta should be taken, not as two different ones, but as two forms of the same, one full and the other abbreviated, and both meaning the same. S R Goyal (*The Imperial Guptas*, p. 452) suggests that what looks as a title may, in fact be a name.
16. *Catalogue of the Coins of the Gupta Dynasties, and of Śaśāṅka, the King of Gauḍa, in the British Museum, London*, Introduction, p. lii.
17. R G Basak, *History of North-Eastern India*, p. 90. D K Ganguly prefers to identify Prakāśaditya either with Purugupta or Kumāragupta II (*The Imperial Guptas and Their Times*, p. 92).
18. K P Jayaswal, *History of India*, p. 38.
19. R N Dandekar *A History of the Guptas*, p. 139.
20. *Gupta Empire*, p. 118.
21. P L Gupta, *Journal of the Numismatic Society of India*, XII, pp. 34-35.
22. J W Curtis (*Journal of the Numismatic Society of India*, XX, pp. 73ff) supports this view.
23. K S Shukla, *Journal of the Numismatic Society of India*, XLII, pp. 120ff. Shukla, however considers Bhānugupta and Prakāśāditya as two different kings.
24. P L Gupta, *The Imperial Guptas*, p. 358.
25. P L Gupta, *Gupta Sāmrājya*, pp. 346-47.
26. S R Goyal, *The Imperial Guptas*, p. 449.
27. For the evidence of the *Ārya-Mañjuśrī-mūlakalpa*, see K P Jayaswal, *Imperial History of India*, pp. 53ff. and p. 63.

28. H C Raychaudhuri, *Political History of Ancient India*, p. 524. This is the view of some other scholars.
29. K P Jayaswal, *Imperial History of India*, p. 54.
30. S R Goyal, *The Imperial Guptas*, p. 452, n. 1.
31. J F Fleet, *Corpus Inscriptionum Indicarum*, III, pp. 47ff.
32. A Cunningham, *Archaeological Survey Reports*, I, pp. 37-38.
33. *Indian Culture*, X(iv), pp. 170ff.
34. J F Fleet suggested the reading *Skandagupta* in both the lines (*Corpus Inscriptionum Indicarum*, III, pp. 49 and 50).
35. R C Majumdar, *Indian Culture*, X, p. 172.
36. I Kartikeya Sarma (*Journal of the Oriental Institute, Baroda*) XVII, 1967-68, pp. 267ff.), however, agrees with Fleet's reading *Skandagupta* and *Skandagupta-baṭa*, and disagrees with the reading of R C Majumdar. According to him, the nature of writing, the placing of the text on the inscription, and the palaeography favour that there are two separate records –the first belonging to Kumāragupta I, and the second to Skandagupta. S R Goyal (*Journal of the Epigraphic Society of India*, VII, pp. 49ff), too, takes it as two separate records, but, ascribes them to Kumāragupta I and Purugupta, respectively.
37. There are a few scholars who do not agree with the reading Budha, for *Pura* (*Puru*), and some of these opine that apart from these coins, there are a few other ones on which *Puru* can be read. For references, see S R Goyal, *The Imperial Guptas*, p. 339.
38. The expression in the inscription—*varsha-śate Guptānāṁ sa-chatuḥ-pañchāshad=uttare*—should be compared with *Guptānāṁ samati-krānte shad-pañchāshad=uttare* of the two identical Sarnath inscriptions of Budhagupta (No. 39), and is to be taken to mean that 'in the year hundred together with four and exceeded by fifty of the [era of the] Guptas'. In Budhagupta's inscription, *uttare* has the same meaning, i.e. exceeded by. See J Agrawal, *Vishveshvaranand Indological Journal*, XV, 1977, pp. 121-22. It should not be taken to mean 'after Guptas had passed away', i.e., when the Gupta dynasty had ended, as was, done by N P Joshi (*Vishveshvaranand Indological Journal*, XIV, pp. 245ff.).
39. B P Sinha (*Decline of the Kingdom of Magadha*, p. 64) is of the view that it is better to take Kumāragupta as son of Skandagupta than that of Purugupta, as in the latter case it would be an abnormal situation of two sons of Purugupta, viz. Kumāragupta and Budhagupta dying childless. However, the fact that there is no reference to the existence of the son (or child) of a king does not necssarily mean that the king was childless.
40. *Indian Historical Quarterly*, XIX, p. 122, n. 9.
41. S Chattopadhyaya, *Early History of North India*, p. 224.
42. The Sarnath inscription of Budhagupta (No. 39) has *pṛithivīṁ Budhagupte praśāsati*.
43. B P Sinha, *Decline of the Kingdom of Magadha*, p. 70.
44. *On Yuan Chwang's Travels in India*, II, p. 164.
45. P L Gupta, *The Imperial Guptas*, p. 188.

46. See S R Goyal, *The Coinage of Ancient India*, p. 4.
47. *Memoirs of the Archaeological Survey of India*, 66, p. 38.
48. R G Basak, *History of North-Eastern India*, p. 90.
49. B P Sinha, *Decline of the Kingdom of Magadha*, p. 69.
50. *Ibid*.
51. R G Basak, *History of North-Eastern India*, p. 90.
52. P L Gupta, *The Imperial Guptas*, pp. 181-82.
53. K Rama Pisharoti (*Indian Historical Quarterly*, IV, p. 111) took the text of the inscription to mean that the temple was renovated 529 years after its construction in AD 436, i.e. in AD 965. However, the script of the epigraph is not of the tenth century but of the Gupta period. The view was rightly not accepted by any scholar. See also R M Shastri, *Indian Historical Quarterly*, IV, p. 361.
54. R N Dandekar (*A History of the Guptas*, p. 129) is of the opinion that Skandagupta, Purugupta, Narasiṁhagupta and Kumāragupta II ruled between the construction of the temple (AD 436) and its repair (AD 472).
55. Dasharatha Sharma, *Indian Culture*, IV, pp. 262-63.
56. R K Mookerji, *Gupta Empire*, p. 71.
57. *Indian Culture*, III, p. 380.
58. See also R M Shastri, *Indian Historical Quarterly*, IV, pp. 361-63.
59. *Journal of the Numismatic Society of India*, XII, pp. 31-33.
60. B P Sinha, *Decline of the Kingdom of Magadha*, pp. 67-68.
61. D K Ganguly (*The Imperial Guptas and Their Times*, pp. 88-89) opines that the difference in the legend is marginal and the presence of isolated letters could denote time lag and not necessarily the existence of two kings, and the coins of both the classes should be ascribed to one and the same king, Kumāragupta II or Kumāragupta III, though their greater correspondence with the coins of Vishṇugupta would favour the latter.
62. B P Sinha, *Journal of the Bihar Rsearch Society*, XXXIV, pp. 18-26.
63. S K Saraswati, *Indian Culture*, I, p. 692.
64. A S Altekar, *The Coinage of the Gupta Empire*, p. 275.
65. A S Altekar, *ibid*.
66. P L Gupta, *The Imperial Guptas*, p. 354.
67. A S Altekar, *The Coinage of the Gupta Empire*, p. 279.
68. *The Life of Hiuen Tsiang*, p. 110.
69. Some scholars (e.g. R K Mookerji, *Gupta Empire*, 105) suggest that Budhagupta either ruled before Narasiṁhagupta or after his grandson Vishṇugupta, otherwise there would be irregular succession, which is unlikely.
70. A Cunningham, *Archaeological Survey Reports*, I, p. 25n.
71. R G Basak, *History of North-Eastern India*, p. 97.
72. Panna Lall, *Journal of the Bihar and Orissa Research Society*, IV, pp. 412ff.
73. H C Raychaudhuri, *Political History of Ancient India*, pp. 516ff.
74. V V Mirashi, *Journal of the Epigraphical Society of India*, IX, p. 53; Ashvini Agrawal, *Rise and Fall of the Imperial Guptas*, p. 236.

75. J F Fleet, *Corpus Inscriptionum Indicarum*, III, Introduction, p. 46, n. 2 (continued on p. 47). He considered Budhagupta of Eran inscription (the only inscription of the king then known) as different from Buddhagupta of Hiuen-tsang (S Beal, *Buddhist Records of the Western World*, II, pp. 168). H C Raychaudhuri (*Political History of Ancient India*, p. 518, n. 6) states that such corrupt forms as *Skandha* for *Skanda* are not unknown in the Purāṇas.
76. *Journal of the Royal Asiatic Society of Great Britain and Ireland*, 1889, p. 135.
77. *Catalogue of the Coins of the Gupta Dynasties, and of Śaśāṅka, the King of Gauḍa, in the British Museum, London*, Intro., p. lxii.
78. See also R G Basak, *History of North-Eastern India*, pp. 105-06.
79. B P Sinha, *Decline of the Kingdom of Magadha*, p. 19.
80. *B C Law Volume*, I, p. 621.
81. H C Raychaudhuri, *Political History of Ancient India*, p. 504.
82. *Vide Archaeological Survey of India—Annual Report*, 1914-15, p. 126.
83. P L Gupta, *The Imperial Guptas*, p. 335.
84. A Ghosh, *Indian Historical Quarterly*, XIX, p. 120; D C Sircar, *Indian Historical Quarterly*, XIX, p. 274.
85. R K Mookerji, *Gupta Empire*, p. 72.
86. *Ibid.*, p. 104.
87. Verses 676-78, cited in P L Gupta, *The Imperial Guptas*, p. 123.
88. See S R Goyal, *Gupta Sāmrājya*, p. 338; P L Gupta, *The Imperial Guptas*, p. 124.
89. *B C Law Volume*, I, p. 621.
90. *Indian Historical Quarterly*, XIX, p. 120.
91. *Journal of the Epigraphical Society of India*, IV, p. 63.
92. S R Goyal, *Gupta Sāmrājya kā Itihāsa*, p. 332.
93. K D Bajpai, B Ch Chhabra *et al.* (ed.), *Reappraising Gupta History for S R Goyal*, p. 205. A Maukhari family was ruling in the Gaya district in the fifth century (K K Thaplyal, *Inscriptions of the Maukharis, the Later Guptas, the Puṣpabhūtis, and Yaśovarman of Kanauj*, pp. 133ff).
94. R K Mookerji (*Gupta Empire*, p. 113) is of the opinion that Ribhupāla made a pilgrimage to Varāha (Kokāmukha) *kshetra* of Nepal, and thereafter out of devotion for that deity, constructed two shrines at his native place, Damodarpur, installing the images of Śvetavarāha and Kokāmukha in imitation of the icons in the shrine at Nepal. D R Bhandarkar (*Corpus Inscriptionum Indicarum*, III, p. 343) is of the view that the shrines were constructed somewhere near Darjeeling and Sikkim districts, to which area extended the limits of Koṭivarsha *vishaya*.
95. F Kielhorn (*Epigraphia Indica*, V, Appendix, p. 55) and D R Bhandarkar (*Epigraphia Indica*, XIX, Appendix, p. 159, n. 5) take the date to refer to Kalachuri era, and Ojha and Haldar (*Epigraphia Indica*, XIX, p. 127), K N Dikshit (*Epigraphia Indica*, XXI, pp. 127ff) and V V Mirashi (*Epigraphia Indica*, XXIII, pp. 177ff) as Gupta era. See also B P Sinha, *Decline of the Kingdom of Magadha*, p. 75, n. 3.
96. R C Majumdar, in *The Vākāṭaka-Gupta Age*, p. 89.
97. *Epigraphia Indica*, II, p. 364.
98. For example, Bhamodra Mohotta copperplate inscription (No. 96).

99. K C Jain, *Malwa through the Ages*, p. 245.
100. T Watters, *On Yuan Chwang's Travels in India*, II, p. 164.
101. S R Goyal, *Gupta Sāmrājya kā Itihāsa*, p. 333.
102. R N Dandekar (*A History of the Guptas*, p. 140) believes that Budhagupta was succeeded by Tathāgatagupta. P L Gupta does not exclude the possibility of Budhagupta and Tathāgatagupta being identical, though he considers their separate identities more probable, and prefers to identify the latter with Prakāśāditya of the coins, and names a separate chapter as 'Tathāgatagupta (?) – Prakāśāditya'.
103. *Select Inscriptions*, I, p. 421, n. 6.
104. S R Goyal, *The Imperial Guptas*, p. 412.
105. D C Sircar, *Select Inscriptions*, I, p. 421.
106. R K Mookerji, *Gupta Empire*, p. 118.
107. D R Bhandarkar, *Corpus Inscriptionum Indicarum*, III, p. 86.
108. *Ibid.*, p. 87.
109. *Ārya-Mañjuśrī-mūlakalpa*, verse 676, as cited by P L Gupta, *The Imperial Guptas*, p. 123.
110. *Ārya-Mañjuśrī-mūlakalpa*, verse 647, as cited by P L Gupta, *The Imperial Guptas*, p. 122.
111. T Watters, *On Yuan Chwang's Travels in India*, II, p. 164.
112. P L Gupta, *The Imperial Guptas*, p. 358.
113. *Ibid.*
114. Once suggested by R C Majumdar, in *The Vākāṭaka-Gupta Age*, p. 190.
115. R C Majumdar, *Indian Historical Quarterly*, XXIV, (i), p. 68.
116. D R Bhandarkar, *Corpus Inscriptionum Indicarum*, III, p. 85.
117. S R Goyal, *The Imperial Guptas*, p. 447.
118. *Ārya-Mañjuśrī-mūlakalpa*, verses 676-78, as quoted in P L Gupta, *The Imperial Guptas*, p. 123.
119. P L Gupta, *The Imperial Guptas*, p. 356.
120. D R Bhandarkar, *Corpus Inscriptionum Indicarum*, III, p. 85. He is of the view that Vainyagupta, Kumāragupta II and Budhagupta were brothers who ruled in that order and were killed in the Hūṇa encounter (*Ibid.*, p. 85).
121. *History of North-Eastern India*, p. 224.
122. P L Gupta, *The Imperial Guptas*, p. 362.
123. Ashvini Agrawal, *Rise and Fall of the Imperial Guptas*, p. 233.
124. R N Dandekar (*A History of the Guptas*, p. 142), too, considers *mahārāja* as a mistake for *mahārājādhirāja*.
125. The upper portion of the sealing which contained the device is missing, but in all probability, as in case with other Imperial Gupta seals, it bore the figure of *garuḍa*, the vehicle (*vāhana*) of Vishṇu, which goes well with the epithet *parama-bhāgavata* used for him.
126. Ashvini Agrawal, *Rise and Fall of the Imperial Guptas*, pp. 233-34.
127. *Indian Culture*, V, p. 297.

128. D K Ganguly (*The Imperial Guptas and Their Times,* p. 95) states that the Gupta seals do not invariably show the *garuḍa* device, and, the one attached to the fifth Damodarpur plate, for example, shows the device of trident. But the seal in question belongs to the office of the district of Koṭivarsha (the legend being *Koṭivarshsh= ādhishṭhān=ādhikaraṇasya*), and not to the Gupta king.
129. R N Dandekar, *A History of the Guptas,* p. 141.
130. *Decline of the Kingdom of Magadha*, p. 84.
131. P L Gupta, *The Imperial Guptas,* p. 362.
132. E J Rapson (*Numismatic Chronicle*, 1891, p. 51) tentatively read the legend as *Chandra*. Allan (*Catalogue of the Coins of the Gupta Dynasties, and of Śaśāṅka, the King of Gauḍa, in the British Museum, London*, p. liv) was not sure of this reading. With the find of the Gunaighar grant of Vainyagupta, D C Ganguly (*Indian Historical Quarterly*, IX, p. 784) suggested the reading *Vainya* for *Chandra*, which was accepted by scholars.
133. B P Sinha, *Decline of the Kingdom of Magadha*, pp. 38-39; P L Gupta, *The Imperial Guptas,* p. 195; S R Goyal, *The Imperial Guptas,* pp. 145-46. B P Sinha (*Decline of the Kingdom of Magadha*, pp. 38-39) considers him as one of the contestants for throne after Kumāragupta I. P L Gupta ascribes to him seven coins in the British Museum, which are lesser in weight than the coin just referred to, but showing a *maṇḍapa*-like device between king's head and the standard, a device not met with on the coins of Chandragupta II.
134. S R Goyal, *The Imperial Guptas,* pp. 446-47.
135. Stanzas 676-78, K P Jayaswal, *Imperial History of India,* text, p. 50.
136. V A Smith, *Indian Museum Catalogue,* I, p. 106, n. 1
137. R C Kar, *Journal of the Numismatic Society of India,* VII, pp. 15-16.
138. R G Basak, *History of North-Eastern India,* pp. 224-25. See also R K Mookerji, *Gupta Empire,* p. 106.
139. *Gupta Empire,* p. 106.
140. P L Gupta, *The Imperial Guptas,* p. 188.
141. *Decline of the Kingdom of Magadha*, p. 100.
142. *The Life of Hiuen-Tsiang,* p. 110.
143. *Early History of North India,* p. 191.
144. *Decline of the Kingdom of Magadha*, p. 101.
145. D C Sircar, *Select Inscriptions,* I, p. 372ff
146. *Decline of the Kingdom of Magadha*, p. 102.
147. *Vide* S R Goyal, *Gupta Sāmrājya kā Itihāsa*, p. 341.
148. A S Altekar, *The Coinage of the Gupta Empire,* p. 282; S R Goyal, *The Imperial Guptas*, p. 448.
149. Ashvini Agrawal, *Rise and Fall of the Imperial Guptas*, p. 234.
150. K S Shukla, *Journal of the Numismatic Society of India,* XLII, pp. 120ff; T P Verma (*Journal of the Numismatic Society of India,* XLII, pp. 122ff, Editor's Note) agrees with Shukla's reading.
151. P L Gupta, (*Gupta Sāmrājya*, pp. 36-37) and Nisar Ahmad (*Journal of the Numismatic Society of India,* L, p. 91) doubt the reading of the legend as *Bhānugupta*.

152. According to D R Bhandarkar (*Corpus Inscriptionum Indicarum*, III, p. 87), the fight was against the Maitras.
153. *Ārya-Mañjuśrī-mūlakalpa*, verses 759-62, as quoted in P L Gupta, *The Imperial Guptas*, p. 125.
154. *Ibid.*, verses 763-64 and 768, as quoted in P L Gupta, *The Imperial Guptas*, p. 126.
155. S R Goyal, *The Imperial Guptas*, pp. 412-13.
156. H C Raychaudhuri, *Political History of Ancient India*, p. 557, n. 6; B P Sinha, *Decline of the Kingdom of Magadha*, p. 102.
157. S R Goyal, *The Imperial Guptas*, p. 413. The *Ārya-Mañjuśrī-mūlakalpa* mentions the preceptor of Toramāṇa as of Gupta lineage who, it has been suggested, may be identified with Harigupta of copper coins found in northern Pañchāla, which closely resemble those of Chandragupta II and Kumāragupta I, and one datable on palaeograhic grounds to the end of the fifth or the beginning of the sixth century AD (Allan, *Catalogue of the Coins of the Gupta Dynasties, and of Śaśāṅka, the King of Gauḍa, in the British Museum, London*, p. 152; Altekar, *The Coinage of the Gupta Empire*, p. 318). D C Sircar (*Epigraphia Indica*, XXXIII, p. 95) identifies this king with Harirāja of the Gupta family known from a bronze image inscription from Ichchhawar in Banda district.
158. *Ibid.*, p. 451.
159. H C Raychaudhuri, *Political History of Ancient India*, p. 524. K P Jayaswal, *Imperial History of India*, pp. 47, 53.
160. H C Raychaudhuri, *Political History of Ancient India*, p. 519.
161. J Allan, *Catalogue of the Coins of the Gupta Dynasties, and of Śaśāṅka, the King of Gauḍa, in the British Museum, London*, p. 137, nos. 558 and 560.
162. D R Bhandarkar, *Corpus Inscriptionum Indicarum*, III, p. 87.
163. K S Shukla, *Journal of the Numismatic Society of India*, XLII, pp. 120f.
164. P L Gupta, *Gupta Sāmrājya*, pp. 37-38.
165. P L Gupta, *Journal of the Numismatic Society of India*, XII, pp. 34-35. Later, because of the absence of Prakāśāditya coins in the Bharsar hoard, which contained coins of Vainyagupta, Narasiṁhagupta and his successors, and because *Prakāśāditya* coins have more gold content than Vainyagupta's coins, and almost the same as Budhagupta's coins, he did not favour Bhānugupta as the author of the Prakāśāditya coins, and preferred to ascribe their authorship to Tathāgatagupta, if he was different from Budhagupta.
166. J W Curtis, *Journal of the Numismatic Society of India*, XX, pp. 75-76. D K Ganguly (*The Imperial Guptas and Their Times*, pp. 90-91) doubts this identification mainly on the ground that *Prakāśāditya* coins have been found at various places in Uttar Pradesh but never in Malwa 'the area of Bhānugupta's activity'. But the fact that Bhānugupta finds mention in the Eran inscription only does not mean that his rule was confined to that region alone.
167. S R Goyal, *The Imperial Guptas*, pp. 417, 453.
168. *Ibid.*, p. 452.
169. *Ibid.*, pp. 452-53.

170. For example, R K Mookerji, *Gupta Empire*, p. 120. B P Sinha (*Decline of the Kingdom of Magadha*, p.95, n.) does not favour taking Bhānugupta as a Gupta ruler.
171. D K Ganguly, *The Imperial Guptas and Their Times*, p. 119.
172. D K Ganguly (*ibid.*) states that Goparāja has been referred to as *rajeti viśrutaḥ*, i.e. a king. But in fact this is not stated for him, but with reference to his grandfather. His father has also been mentioned as *rājā*. See the text in D C Sircar, *Select Inscriptions*, I, pp. 345-46.
173. R C Majumdar, in *The Vākāṭaka-Gupta Age*, p. 191; in *Classical Age*, p. 34.
174. *Decline of the Kingdom of Magadha*, pp. 102-03.
175. *Gupta Empire*, p. 120.
176. D K Ganguly, *The Imperial Guptas and Their Times*, p. 118.
177. R C Majumdar, in *Comprehensive History of India*, III(i), p. 89.
178. A S Altekar (*The Coinage of the Gupta Empire*, p. 267) places his rule between AD 510 and AD 518.
179. S R Goyal, *The Imperial Guptas*, pp. 415-16.
180. R K Mookerji, *Gupta Empire*, p. 120.
181. In *The Vākāṭaka-Gupta Age*, p. 192.
182. *Ibid.*
183. See *Memoirs of the Archaeological Survey of India*, 66, p. 38.
184. J Allan, *Catalogue of the Coins of the Gupta Dynasties, and of Śaśāṅka, the King of Gauḍa, in the British Museum, London*, pp.137-39; A S Altekar, *The Coinage of the Gupta Empire*, pp. 270-71.
185. J Allan, *Catalogue of the Coins of the Gupta Dynasties, and of Śaśāṅka, the King of Gauḍa, in the British Museum, London*, pp. 137-39.
186. *The Coinage of the Gupta Empire*, pp. 267ff.
187. S R Goyal, *The Imperial Guptas*, pp. 397-99.
188. It may be stated that N K Bhattasali, with a view to showing Narasiṁhagupta Bālāditya, son of Purugupta, as a contemporary of Mihirakula, suggested that Purugupta was about four years old at the time of the death of his father, and so Skandagupta came on the throne and was followed by Kumāragupta II, Budhagupta, Bhānugupta and Purugupta in that order. But since from the Nālandā sealing, discovered thereafter, Budhagupta is known as a son of Purugupta, the theory became untenable.
189. P L Gupta, *The Imperial Guptas*, p. 201n.
190. Krishna Deva, *Epigraphia Indica*, XXVI, p. 236.
191. S R Goyal, *The Imperial Guptas*, p. 398.
192. *Ibid.*
193. *Ibid.*
194. *Ibid.*
195. *Ibid.*
196. *Ibid.*
197. *The Imperial Guptas and Their Times*, p. 86.
198. *Ibid.*
199. K K Thaplyal, *Journal of the Numismatic Society of India*, XXXV, pp. 166-70.

200. *Decline of the Kingdom of Magadha*, pp. 99-100.
201. *Ibid*.
202. B P Sinha, *Decline of the Kingdom of Magadha*, pp. 99-100.
203. S Beal, *Si-yu-ki, Buddhist Records of the Western World*, p. 169.
204. *History of North-Eastern India*, p. 116.
205. S Beal, *Si-yu-ki, Buddhist Records of the Western World*, I, p. 168; T Watters, *On Yuan Chwang's Travels in India*, I, pp. 288-89.
206. T Watters, *On Yuan Chwang's Travels in India*, I, pp. 288-89.
207. S Beal, *Si-yu-ki, Buddhist Records of the Western World*, I, pp. 170-71.
208. For example, Ashvini Agrawal, *Rise and Fall of the Imperial Guptas*, p. 236.
209. *Ibid*., p. 236.
210. B P Sinha, *Decline of the Kingdom of Magadha*, p. 106.
211. For example, I-tsing, who stayed in India in the last quarter of the seventh century AD, places Śrīgupta 500 years before him, whereas the Gupta king ruled much later. See Chapter 3.
212. The dated Mandasor inscription of Yaśodharman (No. 79), mentions Yaśodharman and Vishṇuvardhana. Janendra Yaśodharman has been referred to as *samrāṭ* and *narādhipa*, and Vishṇuvardhana as *rājādhirāja* and *parameśvara*. The undated inscription from the same site (No. 80) mentions Yaśodharman only. Some scholars consider Yaśodharman and Vishṇuvardhana as two different persons, but most scholars rightly take them as identical. The non-mention of any relationship between the two and the mention of *sa eva* (i.e. the same) immediately after Vishṇuvardhana makes the identity almost certain. See also D R Bhandarkar, *Corpus Inscriptionum Indicarum*, III, p. 18, and R C Majumdar, in *Comprehensive History of India*, III (i), pp. 93ff.
213. *Early History of India*, 3rd ed., pp. 320, n. 1.
214. *Catalogue of the Coins of the Gupta Dynasties, and of Śaśāṅka, the King of Gauḍa, in the British Museum, London*, p. lix.
215. *Indian Antiquary*, 1889, p. 228.
216. *Journal of the Royal Asiatic Society of Great Britain and Ireland*, LVIII, p. 96.
217. D R Bhandarkar (*Corpus Inscriptionum Indicarum*, III, p. 88) holds that Mihirakula was defeated by Yaśodharman fairly long after his defeat at the hands of Bālāditya in AD 510. He takes Bālāditya as a title of Bhānugupta, whom he identifies with Narasiṁhagupta Bālāditya.
218. A S Altekar, *The Coinage of the Gupta Empire*, p. 10.
219. *Decline of the Kingdom of Magadha*, p. 110.
220. H C Raychaudhuri, *Political History of Ancient India*, pp. 524-25. He considers *Bālāditya* as a *viruda* of Bhānugupta.
221. Beal, *Buddhist Records of the Western World*, I, p. 171.
222. R N Dandekar, *A History of the Guptas*, pp. 157-58.
223. For example, Heras, *Indian Historical Quarterly*, III, p. 18.
224. R C Majumdar, in *Comprehensive History of India*, III(i), p. 92.
225. R C Majumdar, in *The Classical Age*, 40. S R Goyal (*The Imperial Guptas*, p. 414) says, '*...even a scholar like R C Majumdar* had opined that Yaśodharman rose and

fell like a meteor' (italics for emphasis). But with the evidence then available, this had to be, and was, the opinion of all scholars.

226. S R Goyal, *The Imperial Guptas*, pp. 415-16.
227. In *The Vākāṭaka-Gupta Age*, p. 204.
228. There is no evidence to support the view of K P Jayaswal (*Imperial History of India*, p. 41) that Yaśodharman was a predecessor of Pushpabhūti king Harsha.
229. S Beal, *The Life of Hiuen-Tsiang*, p. 111.
230. *Ibid.*
231. K P Jayaswal, *Imperial History of India, ślokas* 648-50, on p. 48.
232. *Si-yu-ki, Buddhist Records of the Western World*, I, p. 74.
233. S Beal, *Si-yu-ki, Buddhist Records of the Western World*, II, p. 169.
234. J Allan, *Catalogue of the Coins of the Gupta Dynasties, and of Śaśāṅka, the King of Gauḍa, in the British Museum, London*, p. 138n.
235. *Journal of the Royal Asiatic Society of Bengal, Letters*, VII, p. 135.
236. Deo-baranark inscription of Jivitagupta II. See Fleet, *Corpus Inscriptionum Indicarum*, III, No. 46, pp. 213ff.
237. B P Sinha, *Decline of the Kingdom of Magadha*, p. 90. Other identifications proposed with the Gupta kings are: Budhagupta, Vainyagupta (R N Dandekar, *A History of the Guptas*, pp. 144-47). Some scholars identify the overlord with kings of a dynasty other than the Gupta. Fleet (*Indian Antiquary*, XV, p. 187 and Goyal (*The Imperial Guptas*, pp. 433-34) identify him with Yaśodharman Aulikara. Goyal points out (*ibid.*, p. 434) that in the first half of the sixth century AD the Aulikara and the Hūṇa kingdoms intervened between those of the Maitrakas and the Guptas and as such it is difficult to believe that the Guptas exercised suzerainty over the Maitrakas. He has also been identified with the Hūṇa king Toramāṇa (Smith, *Early History of India*, p. 316), and Harisheṇa Vākāṭaka of Vatsagulma branch (K K Virji, *Early History of Surashṭra*, pp. 27-29). See S R Goyal, *The Imperial Guptas*, pp. 433-34.
238. R C Majumdar, in *Comprehensive History of India*, III(i), p. 96.
239. R N Dandelar, *A History of the Guptas*, p. 149.
240. B P Sinha, *Decline of the Kingdom of Magadha*, p. 91.
241. A Cunningham, *Bhilsa Topes*, p. 162.
242. *Si-yu-ki, Buddhist Records of the Western World*, II, pp. 168, 170.
243. B P Sinha, *Decline of the Kingdom of Magadha*, p. 100.
244. T Watters, *On Yuan Chwang's Travels in India*, II, p. 164.
245. See K P Jayaswal, *Imperial History of India*, p. 33.
246. J Allan, *Catalogue of the Coins of the Gupta Dynasties, and of Śaśāṅka, the King of Gauḍa, in the British Museum, London*, pp. 137-39.
247. D R Bhandarkar, *Corpus Inscriptionum Indicarum*, III, p. 73.
248. Some scholars identify Kumāragupta of the Sarnath inscription with the homonym of the Bhitari and Nālandā seal-inscriptions and believe in the existence of only one Kumāragupta other than Kumāragupta I.
249. For example, R G Basak, *History of North-Eastern India*, p. 75. He, however, identifies Kumāragupta as Kumāragupta II. See also B P Sinha, *Decline of the Kingdom of Magadha*, p. 113.

250. P L Gupta, *The Imperial Guptas*, p. 189.
251. V V Mirashi, *Journal of the Epigraphical Society of India*, IX, p. 53. He says that the word used in the inscription is *bhunakati* which should be taken to mean 'protected'.
252. The Navagram grant of *Mahārāja* Hastin of Gupta Era 198 (No. 66) and Betul plate of Saṁkshobha of Gupta Era 199 (No.67) and his Khoh plate of Gupta Era 209 (No. 68).
253. R C Majumdar, in *The Vākāṭaka-Gupta Age*, p. 203; D C Sircar, *Studies in Geography of Ancient and Mediaeval India*, p. 10; P L Gupta, *The Imperial Guptas*, p. 368.
254. R C Majumdar, in *The Vākāṭaka-Gupta Age*, p. 203; in *Classical Age*, p. 40. *Contra* the view of Ashvini Agrawal (*Rise and Fall of the Imperial Guptas*, p. 4): "There is no room for being sceptic about the limits of the empire of Yaśodharman, when the author has so specifically mentioned its boundaries from east to west and from north to south."
255. R C Majumdar, in *Comprehensive History of India*, III(i), p. 96.
256. *Gupta Sāmrājya kā Itihāsa*, p. 371.
257. V A Smith, *Early History of India*, p. 313.
258. *Decline of the Kingdom of Magadha*, p. 120.
259. J Allan, *Catalogue of the Coins of the Gupta Dynasties, and of Śaśāṅka, the King of Gauḍa, in the British Museum, London*, pp. cxxiv-cxxvi.
260. J Allan, *ibid.*, pp 145-46.
261. J Allan, *ibid.*, p. xxxvii.
262. *The Gupta Empire*, p. 124.
263. *Ibid.*, Chapter XIV.
264. *Coins of Ancient India: Catalogue of Coins in Indian Museum Calcutta*, I, p. 121.
265. *Journal of the Royal Asiatic Society of Great Britain and Ireland*, 1903, p. 552.
266. It must be said that when Hoernle expressed his view the Nālanda sealing of Vishṇugupta had not been discovered.
267. *Journal of the Royal Asiatic Society of Great Britain and Ireland*, 1903, p. 552.
268. *Catalogue of the Coins of the Gupta Dynasties, and of Śaśāṅka, the King of Gauḍa, in the British Museum, London*, p. lxi.
269. *Ibid.*
270. J Allan, *Catalogue of the Coins of the Gupta Dynasties, and of Śaśāṅka, the King of Gauḍa, in the British Museum, London*, pp. 137-39.
271. K P Jayswal, *Imperial History of India*, p. 33.
272. J Allan, *Catalogue of the Coins of the Gupta Dynasties, and of Śaśāṅka, the King of Gauḍa, in the British Museum, London*, pp. 140-43.
273. A S Altekar, *The Coinage of the Gupta Empire*, p. 300.
274. B P Sinha, *Decline of the Kingdom of Magadha*, p. 123.
275. *Indian Coins*, p. 26.
276. *Epigraphia Indica*, XV, p. 142.
277. *Epigraphia Indica*, XVII, p. 193.
278. *History of North-Eastern India*, pp. 92-93.
279. R K Mookerji, *Gupta Empire*, p. 124.

280. *Corpus Inscriptionum Indicarum*, III, p. 88.
281. D R Bhandarkar, *ibid.*, p. 89.
282. R K Mookerji, *Gupta Empire*, p. 124; A S Altekar, *The Coinage of the Gupta Empire*, pp. 267-68.
283. R N Dandekar, *A History of the Guptas*, p. 171.
284. R G Basak, *History of North-Eastern India*, p. 109; R D Banerji, *The Age of the Imperial Guptas*, p. 61.
285. D R Bhandarkar, *Corpus Inscriptionum Indicarum*, III, p. 361; R C Majumdar, in *Comprehensive History of India*, III (i), p. 98.
286. B C Sen, *Some Historical Aspects of the Inscriptions of Bengal*, p. 239.
287. *Political History of Ancient India*, p. 527.
288. B P Sinha, *Decline of the Kingdom of Magadha*, p. 125.
289. J F Fleet, *Corpus Inscriptionum Indicarum*, III, p. 203.
290. D R Bhandarkar, *Corpus Inscriptionum Indicarum*, III, p. 361.
291. J Allan, *Catalogue of the Coins of the Gupta Dynasties, and of Śaśāṅka, the King of Gauḍa, in the British Museum, London*, pp. 145-46.
292. H C Raychaudhuri, *Political History of Ancient India*, p. 521, n. 1.
293. K K Thaplyal, *Inscriptions of the Maukharis, the Later Guptas, the Puṣpabhūtis, and Yaśovarman of Kanauj*, pp. 147ff.
294. *Ibid.*, p. 189. For some examples of brother and sister having similar names, see. H C Raychaudhuri, *Political History of Ancient India*, p. 521, n. 1.
295. K P Jayaswal's (*Imperial History of India*, p. 55) opines that his identification with Budhagupta is not convincing.
296. B P Sinha, *Decline of the Kingdom of Magadha*, p. 127n. He does not rule out the possibility of *Deva* being the name of the prince (*ibid.*).
297. R C Majumdar, in *Comprehensive History of India*, III(i), p. 102.
298. It can be argued that Nālandā being a great monastic centre kings of various dynasties would correspond with letters in sealed covers, and hence the find-spot of seal or seals need not necessarily be taken as an evidence of the rule over that area.
299. *History of North-Eastern India*, pp. 119-20.
300. Five copperplate grants found in the Faridpur district of Bengal and one at Mallasarul in Burdwan district of West Bengal, show that three kings—Gopachandra, Dharmāditya and Samāchāradeva bearing the title *mahārājādhirāja* ruled either in different parts of Bengal, or were probably related to one another and formed a dynasty. H C Raychaudhari (*Political History of Ancient India*, p. 557) suggests the possibility of identifiying Dharmāditya with Dhakārākhya of the *Ārya-Mañjuśrī-mūlakalpa* and younger brother of Vakārākhya (i.e. Vajra), and Pakārākhya with Prakaṭāditya. For grant of Gopachandra, year 3, see *Epigraphia Indica*, XXIII, p. 155 and *Epigraphia Indica*, XXX, pp. 161-63; for his second grant of year 18, and for Dharmāditya's two grants (one dated year 3, and the other undated), *Indian Antiquary*, XXXIX, 1910, pp. 193-216. The grant of Samāchāradeva, year 7, is unpublished, and for the second grant of Samāchāradeva, see *Journal of the Asiatic Society of Bengal, NS*, VI, pp. 429ff; *ibid., NS*, VII, p. 426; *Epigraphia Indica*, XVIII, pp. 74f. A seal of Samāchāradeva was

found at Nālandā and his coins are also known. According to N K Bhattasali (*Epigraphia Indica,* XVIII, p. 84) the three kings ruled in whole of eastern India, while in Basak's opinion (*History of North-Eastern India,* p. 160) their rule was confined to Samataṭa, Karṇasuvarṇa and adjoining region. Vijayasena is mentioned in the Gunaighar grant of Vainyagupta and also in the Mallasarul plate of Gopachandra dated 18th or 19th year (*Epigraphia Indica,* XXIII, pp. 155ff). Since Vijayasena has higher status in the latter inscription, he being called *mahārāja* and *mahāsāmanta,* the inference would be that Gopachandra followed Vainyagupta; the succession was either peaceful, or the former overthrew the latter. It may be stated that a few scholars identified Gopachandra with Gopa of the *Ārya-Mañjuśrī-mūlakalpa* who is mentioned therein as one who put Pakārākhya, whom some take to be identical with Prakaṭāditya of Sarnath inscription (No. 97), into prison. Others identify him with Goparāja of the Eran inscription of Bhānugupta, in which case the event took place before AD 510, as by then, as per the evidence of that inscription he was dead. R C Majumdar (in *Comprehensive History of India,* III(i), p. 202) places these three rulers in the last three quarters of the sixth century AD. It is difficult to accept Hoernle's view (*Indian Antiquary,* 1910, p. 208) that Dharmāditya should be identified with Yaśodharman and Gopachandra with prince Govi (Gopi) who according to Tāranātha was a grandson of Bālāditya and son of Kumāragupta [III] whom, he believes, Yaśodharman displaced. The three kings do not seem to be related to the Imperial Guptas (Basak, *History of North-Eastern India,* p. 232). N K Bhattasali (*Journal of the Asiatic Society of Bengal,* NS, 1923, pp. 54-56) suggests that Samāchāradeva was a predecessor of Saśāṅka, probably his father. One Nāgadeva is mentioned as *Mahāpratihāra, kumārāmātya* and *uparika* in a grant of Gopachandra and also in a grant of Samāchāradeva, both from Faridpur. Nayasena is mentioned as *jyeshṭha-kāyastha* in the records of Gopachandra and Dharmāditya. Vijayasena, as seen above, is met with in the Gunaighar grant of Vainyagupta and the Mallasarul plates of Gopachandra. The sena-ending names of the officials suggest that the offices were hereditary. The *Ārya-Mañjuśrī-mūlakalpa* mentions Gopākhya *nṛipati* as a king of the *Prāchya janapada,* who may be indentified with Gopachandra (Basak, *History of North-Eastern India,* p. 234). Pargiter (*Indian Antiquary,* 1910, pp. 206ff) opines that Dharmāditya was succeeded by Gopachandra, who according to *Ārya-Mañjuśrī-mūlakalpa* helped Narasiṁhagupta in imprisoning Pakārākhya (or Prakaṭāditya). Basak (*History of North-Eastern India,* p. 234) says it was *vice versa.*

301. See Chapter 12, below. *Harivaṁśa-purāṇa,* ed. by Hiralal and A N Upadhye, *gāthā* 1503. See P L Gupta, *The Imperial Guptas,* pp. 129ff. It may be stated that the Jain tradition assigns a period of 242 years of rule to ths Śakas counting from the beginning of the Śaka era in AD 78. (*ibid.*).
302. For example, R C Majumdar, in *Comprehensive History of India,* III(i), p. 102-03.
303. *Ibid.,* p. 104.
304. R C Majumdar, in *Classical Age,* p. 45.
305. R C Majumdar, in *Comprehensive History of India,* III(i), p. 99.

# 12

# Factors Leading to the Decline and Fall of the Gupta Empire

The Gupta rule had a humble beginning with its first two kings, Gupta (*c* AD 275-300) and Ghaṭotkacha (*c* AD 300-319), as feudatories and bearing the title of *mahārāja*. There was extension of the Gupta kingdom during the reign of the first *mahārājādhirāja*, Chandragupta I (*c* 319-44), particularly due to the amalgamation of the Lichchhavi territories in it, which he got as a result of matrimonial alliance with the Lichchhavis (Chapter 3). Then followed a period of rapid expansion of the empire due to extensive conquests by Samudragupta (*c* AD 344-74) in the north as well in south India. Chandragupta II carried on the expansion of the empire, conquering the Śakas in western India and marching as far as Balkh in the north-western direction. He also won a victory over the enemies congregated in Vaṅga. Kumāragupta I might or might not have added any new territory to the already extensive empire, he certainly was able to keep the Gupta empire intact. Some scholars think that the issuing of silver-plated copper coins by Kumāragupta I reflects economic stringency, as a result of the invasions; others however opine that this was resorted to by the king as due to tribal movement in north-western India there was decline in the supply of silver.[1] There were external invasions and internal troubles in the beginning of Skandagupta's reign, but he emerged victorious.

Symptoms of decline of the Gupta rule are noticeable after the end of Skandagupta's reign. He was the last Imperial Gupta ruler whose coins have been found in Surāshṭra region.[2] His successors proved unequal to the task of holding the empire intact; there is no definite evidence that Saurashtra formed a part of the Gupta empire after him. The gold coins of Skandagupta, though not scant, are of four types only, in contrast to those of his father which have been found in large numbers and comprise as many as fourteen types. The coins of the successors Skandagupta are fewer in number and lack variety. They are almost confined to the Archer type only. This suggests some decline in the economy and also in the political power of the Guptas. P L Gupta is of the opinion that since no inscription of Skandagupta belonging to the later phase of his reign has been found in western province of the Guptas and of his coins of western fabric none bearing imperial titles are known, and since the Mandasor inscription of Prabhākara, of AD 467 (No. 36) does not make any mention of him, he might have lost his western provinces.[3] This, however, does not seem to be the case for reasons given above. Buddhagupta, though ruled over an extensive empire, does not seem to have had hold over the western provinces of the empire as can be inferred from the absence of his silver coins of the western variety; and either during the last days of his rule or shortly after it (*c* AD 500) the region of Eran came to be occupied by the Hūṇas.

Till the end of the reign of Samudragupta there is no evidence of any power attacking the Gupta kingdom. There was an invasion of a Śaka ruler during the rule of his son and successor, Rāmagupta. This invasion does not seem to have been of great magnitude, and would not have put much strain on the economy of the state, but it did affect considerably the prestige of the Gupta dynasty, particularly as for purchasing peace Rāmagupta agreed to surrender his queen to the Śaka king. During the last days of the rule of Kumāragupta, the Pushyamitras, with their military and economic power augmented (*samudita-bala-kośa*), attacked the Gupta kingdom and it was with great effort that prince Skandagupta could defeat them (No. 33). There was an invasion of more formidable and powerful enemy, the Hūṇas. The battle fought between the Guptas and the Hūṇas was fierce, which 'made the earth tremble.' Skandagupta, 'the unique hero of the Gupta dynasty' (*Gupta-vaṁś=aik-vīraḥ)* was able to defeat them. This victory must have been achieved at the cost of a great toll of men and material, which in turn must have had an adverse effect on the economy of the Gupta empire. D R Bhandarkar[4] and some other scholars opine that some royal princes lost their lives in fighting the Hūṇas. The kings of the Gupta dynasty do not seem to have made any attempt to check the invaders from the north-west at the entry points on the boundaries of their empire, and there were inroads from that direction from time to time. Hūṇa rulers, Toramāṇa and his son, Mihirakula, were able to carve out sizable territories for themselves, partly at the cost of the Gupta empire. Some scholars suggest that a few high officials and disgruntled princes like Harigupta and Prakārākhya of the *Ārya-Mañjuśrī-mūlakalpa* joined hands with the invaders against the ruling Gupta king.[5] The Eran inscription of the time of Bhānugupta (No. 44) refers to the death of his ally, Goparāja, while fighting the enemy, in all probability the Hūṇas. It is not known for certain whether in this conflict the Guptas or the Hūṇas were victorious, though there is greater possibility of the success of the latter. Malwa formed a gateway between the North and the South, and in it converged trade routes from different directions. The safety of Malwa region was of utmost importance for the safety of the Gupta kingdom.[6] It however did not receive due attention, and Eran, one of its cities, became 'a troubled spot' of the Gupta empire.

The rise of the Aulikara family played a great role in the decline of the Gupta empire. The Risthal inscription of AD 515 (No. 78) gives the following genealogy of the Aulikara dynasty: Drapa(Druma?)varddhana Jayavarddhana, Ajitavarddhana, Vibhīshaṇavarddhana, Rājyavarddhana and Prakāśadharman. In the conflict between the Guptas and the Hūṇas the latter under their king Toramāṇa were successful in wresting Eran and its neighbouring region from the Guptas, either during the last days of Budhagupta or shortly thereafter. He was able to occupy the region around Kauśāmbī as is clear from the evidence of his seal impressed on the clay lump also bearing the impression of the seal of the Ghoshitārāma monastery (located at that site) obtained in the course of excavations at Kauśāmbī. As discussed by us elsewhere, the impressions from the seal of Toramāṇa and that of the monastery must have been made almost simultaneously, when the clay lump was moist, which would show Toramāṇa's presence at Kauśāmbī, and also his control over that region.[7] The Risthal epigraph (No. 78) mentions that Prakāśadharman inflicted a crushing defeat on the Hūṇa king, Toramāṇa.[8] Mihirakula, the son of Toramāṇa was defeated by Yaśodharman, as mentioned in his undated inscription (of which there are two copies) from Mandasor (No. 80). It says that his feet were worshipped by that Hūṇa king (*Mihirakula-nṛipeṇa architaṁ pādayugmam*) and also of his victorious march up to Brahmaputra, which could have been possible only by passing through the Gupta territories. He is said to have conquered territories which had not been conquered either by the Guptas or the Hūṇa king Mihirakula. The campaign though successful, does not seem to have led to a permanent occupation of all the conquered Gupta territories, for the Gupta rule continued, though restricted to some parts of Bengal and Orissa, and may be also some areas of Bihar. It, however gave a severe blow to the power and prestige of the Guptas. The pressure of the Hūṇas and Yaśodharman from the west forced the Guptas to confine themselves to their eastern territories, which is also reflected in the *Ārya-Mañjuśrī-mūlakalpa* which mentions Bālāditya as 'Eastern,' and Kumāra (i.e. Kumāragupta III) as king of Gauḍa.[9]

There does not seem to have been a fixed law of succession in the Gupta dynasty. It is not known as to what extent the law of primogeniture was followed, or what weight being a son of the chief queen carried in the matter of accession to the throne. Samudragupta was selected as successor by his father, in all probability, bypassing the law of primogeniture, and that his accession did not go uncontested. There was internal bickering in Imperial Gupta family in successive generations, and some scholars variously suggest that there was struggle for throne between Kācha and Samudragupta, between Rāmagupta and Chandragupta II, between Govindagupta and Kumāragupta I, between Kumāragupta I and Ghaṭotkachagupta, and between Skandagupta and Purugupta, though this cannot be proved in all the cases. The theory of the division of empire between Skandagupta and Purugupta is not acceptable for reasons given above (Chapter 10), but the suggestion of Majumdar that perhaps after Budhagupta, the following ruled simultaneously—Bhānugupta in eastern Malwa, Vainyagupta in Bengal, and Narasiṁhagupta in Magadha, cannot be entirely ruled out. S Chattopadhyaya at one time held the view that Bhānugupta and Vainyagupta ruled contemporaneously, and placed Tathāgatagupta in the central part of the kingdom.[10] There was a unique case of at least three brothers, all sons of Purugupta, viz. Budhagupta, Vainyagupta and Narasiṁhagupta (and may be also Kumāragupta II of Sarnath inscription, whose parentage is not known) ruling as kings. This brother-to-brother succession, denying the throne to the eldest son, would have caused bickering amongst the princes who were aspirants for the throne.

Samudragupta had conquered several south Indian kings and reinstated them after they accepted his suzerainty and agreed to pay him tributes. There were other categories of powers which had entered into alliance with him with a view to keeping him pleased by their actions and obedience. There are references to a number of feudatories in the epigraphs of his successors. Maitraka Bhaṭārka was a *senāpati* (commander) who according to one view was also assigned the civil administration of Surashṭra region after the end of the governorship of Parṇadatta. The Maitraka rulers, with Valabhī as their capital, trace their genealogy from him. While Bhaṭārka's eldest son Dharasena I, like him, was satisfied with the title *senāpati*, the latter's successor, Droṇasiṁha, was anointed *mahārāja* (king) by his overlord. This led to the rise of the power of the feudatory Maitrakas and encouraged the feudatories of other regions to increase their power. Up to the reign of Dharasena, whose last date is AD 545, the Maitraka rulers used the phrase *parama-bhaṭṭāraka–pādānudhyāta,* suggesting that they paid at least nominal allegiance to their overlord, who most probably was a Gupta ruler. The phrase does not occur in the Grant of King Guhasena, whose earliest date is AD 557. The loss of direct hold on the western province, deprived the Guptas of their profit in the oversea trade with western Asia.

To the east of the Gupta province bounded by Kālindī and Narmadā was the kingdom of the Parivrājakas, roughly comprising the area from near Allahabad to Malhar.[11] Of this dynasty, inscriptions of only two kings –Hastin and Saṁkshobha have been found, although three predecessors of Hastin are known. In the inscriptions of Hastin, of AD 510 (No. 65) and AD 517 (No. 66), and in those of his son Saṁkshobha of AD 518 (No. 67) and AD 528 (No. 68), the suzerainty of the Guptas is mentioned in a general way, without mentioning the name of the reigning king. The copperplate grants of the Uchchakalpa King Śarvanātha, whose territories adjoined the Parivrājika kingdom, range in date between 193 (No. 72) and 214 (No. 74), which should be referred to the Gupta era, and would be equal to AD 512 and 533 respectively. The epigraphs do not mention the name of the then ruling Gupta kings, not even the Gupta dynasty. Some scholars believe that the kings of the Parivrājaka dynasty were getting slack in their allegiance to the reigning Gupta kings, while the kings of the Uchchakalpa dynasty had ceased to owe allegiance to them. The Bhumra stone inscription refers to the understanding between the Parivrājaka king Hastin and the Uchchakalpa king Śarvanātha that the dispute regarding the boundary of their kingdoms would be arbitrated by the Imperial Gupta sovereign, without mentioning his name.[12]

The Gupta kingdom gradually came to be fragmented into small territories under kings of different dynasties. In the Gunaighar copperplate inscription of AD 507 (No. 50) of the Gupta king Vainyagupta, *Mahārāja* Vijayasena is mentioned as a high official of that Gupta king. From the Mallasarul copperplate inscription it is known that this very official was serving king Gopachandra of another dynasty. The shifting of the allegiance by this Gupta official reflects the weakening of the Gupta hold over its feudatories, who increased their power at the cost of the Gupta empire. After Gopachandra, Dharmāditya and Samāchāradeva are known as ruling, most probably one after the other, rather than simultaneously in different parts of Bengal. In the Amauna (Gaya district) copperplate of Nandana (No. 99) dated [GE] 232 (= AD 551), he has been referred to as *deva-guru-pād=ānudhyāta*, 'meditating on the feet of god and preceptor'. There is no mention of the then ruling Gupta king, which suggests that Gupta rule in Magadha had virtually ended by that time.

The inscriptions of one family of the Maukharis have been found in the Barabar hill (Gaya district)[13] in the very heart of the Gupta kingdom. They mention three rulers – Yajñavarman, his son Śārdūlavarman and the latter's son Anantavarman, who are designated as *mahārājas* (i.e. feudatories); they do not mention the ruling Gupta sovereign or even Gupta dynasty, as if they were *de facto* independent rulers. However, it was another branch of the Maukharis, with its seat at Kanauj, that was destined to play an important role in the political history of that age and posed a great threat to the Gupta empire. The inscriptions of this dynasty have been found from Jaunpur (No. 93) in the district of the same name, Haraha in Barabanki district (No. 94), and a few other places and their seals have been found at Nālandā and other places.[14] The evidence of this epigraphical material shows that some of the areas which once formed a part of the Gupta empire came under the rule of the Maukharis. The first three kings of this dynasty, viz. Harivarman, Ādityavarman and Īśvaravarman', were mere *mahārājas*, the first two most probably were feudatories of the Guptas.[15] S R Goyal interprets the evidence of the Jaunpur inscription of Īśvaravarman (No. 93) to convey that when the Maukhari ruler defied the Aulikara overlord, Yaśodharman, the latter sent a force against him from his base at Dhārā.[16] The Haraha inscription (No. 94) mentions Īśānavarman's victories over the Andhras, the Śūlikas and the Gauḍas. These victories would have been responsible for raising his status from *mahārāja* to *mahārājādhirāja*. He is also known to have issued coins. He had become a formidable power in Uttar Pradesh by the middle of the sixth century, and has been credited with the victory over the Hūṇas in the Aphsad inscription of the Later Gupta king, Ādityasena (No. 95, and not in the Haraha inscription of Īśānavarman Maukhari as stated by Dandekar[17]). This victory must have been achieved by him after he had made the conquests of the powers mentioned in the Haraha inscription of AD 554, as it does not find mention in that inscription. It must have been deemed an extremely significant achievement, as of so many victories to his credit, this one over the barbarous Hūṇas alone has been mentioned in the inscription of that Later Gupta king. With the rise of the Maukharis, the political gravity shifted from Pāṭaliputra, which had been the capital of several dynasties like the Nandas, the Mauryas, the Śuṅgas and the Guptas, to Kanauj, and continued to be there for many centuries that followed, under the rule of the Maukharis, Harsha Pushpabhūti, Yaśovarman, and the kings of the Pratīhāra and the Gāhaḍvāla dynasties.

The Later Guptas also played an important role in the decline of the Imperial Gupta power.[18] They steadily grew in power, since the time of Kṛishṇagupta, the founder of the dynasty. The inscriptions of this dynasty, all belonging to post-Harsha period have been found in Bihar. The evidence of *Harshacharita* indicates that Malwa was their earlier home. The first two kings, with the title *mahārāja* in all probability were feudatories of the Guptas. The Aphsad inscription (No. 95) mentions the campaigns of the third ruler, *Mahārāja* Jīvitagupta, in the Himalayan region and on the sea-shore, which were under the Gupta king,[19] or under the Aulikara king Yaśodharman, as has been suggested by S R Goyal.[20] The fourth ruler of the Later Gupta dynasty, viz. Kumāragupta, was quite powerful and an independent king. With a view to establishing his supremacy, he challenged Īśānavarman, the first *mahārājādhrāja* of the Maukhari dynasty, who, as seen above, was credited with significant conquests, and defeated him. The Hūṇas and the Aulikaras, who were powers to be reckoned with, were soon out of race for supremacy at the cost of the Imperial Guptas, and instead the Maukharis and the Later Guptas became prominent contenders for it. While the Maukharis brought to its end the Imperial Gupta rule in Uttar Pradesh, the Later Guptas did the same in parts of Bihar.

Of the Aulikaras of the family of Bandhuvarman, in father–to-son relationship, the following kings are known: Jayavarman, Siṁhavarman, Naravarman, Viśvavarman and Bandhuvarman. The testimony of the Mandasor inscription of the silk-weavers' guild (No. 38) which describes the boundaries of the extensive territories and the eminence of Kumāragupa I is in favour of Bandhuvarman's being a feudatory in AD 436; and there is a possibility of other members of the family, at least some of them, also having the same status with reference to other Gupta kings, though a few scholars hold different opinion. However, Prabhākara, whose known date from a Mandasor inscription is AD 467 (No. 36) was a feudatory of the Guptas, since he claims to have vanquished their enemies. The non-mention of the name of the Gupta king in his epigraph has led some scholars to suggest that he did not owe allegiance to the Guptas. There was another branch of the Aulikaras known from one inscription from Mandasor and one from Chhoti Sadri in the Chittorgarh district. The Mandasor inscription mentions one Ādityavardhana who seems to have been the sovereign ruler who after defeating his enemies set up his rule at Daśapura (Mandasor). It also mentions Gaurī, who seems to have been his feudatory. Ādityavardhana was probably related to *Mahārājādhirāja* Dravya-vardhana of Avanti from whom Varāhamihira the author of *Bṛihatsaṁhitā* (6th century AD) is said to have learnt lessons of astrology. Neither the relationship of this family with, nor its chronological positioning in regard to, the Aulikara family to which Yaśodharman belonged is known. Though the family was not a formidable one, it carved out a territory for itself from the Gupta territory in western Malwa.

The Vākaṭakas who were friendly with the Guptas till the time of Chandragupta II, whose daughter Prabhāvatīguptā was married to Vākāṭaka Rudrasena II. The relations became sour during the reign of Kumāragupta I. The Vākāṭakas seem to have sided with the Gupta prince Ghaṭotkachagupta, when he rebelled against his brother Kumāragupta I, the then Gupta ruler. The rebellion, however, did not meet with success. The Vākāṭakas became quite formidable under the leadership of King Narendrasena (No. 87) and there is a view that Vyāghra, a Gupta feudatory, shifted his allegiance to him (No. 88). Narendrasena has been referred to as lord of Kosala, Mekala and Malwa, which is taken as a true statement by some scholars and a vain boast by others.

The Kahaum inscription of Skandagupta (No. 31), speaks, though in an exaggerated form, the presence of hundreds of feudatory kings in his

Assembly. In two copperplates, one from Allahabad district and another from former Rewa state, both dated [Gupta era] 158 (= AD 477), *Mahārāja* Lakshmaṇa,[21] makes no reference either to Budhagupta, the then ruling Gupta king, or to the Gupta dynasty; nor does Subandhu do so in his grant of [Gupta era] 167 issued from Mahishmatī.[22] Though their geographical position would suggest that they perhaps paid at least nominal allegiance to the Guptas, yet the non-mention of the king and dynasty shows that they were asserting themselves as a political power.

There was gradual rise in the status of the governors and the feudatories who were adopting high-sounding titles. According to an inscription (No.34) during the reign of Skandagupta Śarvanāga, who governed the region of Antarvedī, i.e. the land between Ganga and Yamuna, is referred to merely as *vishayapati.* During the reign of Budhagupta as per the testimony of the Eran inscription of that king (No. 44), Suraśmichandra, who governed the region between Kālindī (Yamuna) and Narmadā, is referred to as *mahārāja,* and even Matṛivishṇu who was an officer under him administering the region around Eran as *vishayapati* (district officer), too, is called a *mahārāja*. Significantly the latter is also referred to as one who was selected by Rājyalakshmī, and whose fame had reached four oceans, which epithets have been generally used for kings.

The feudatories collected taxes from people who considered them, rather than the king, as their masters. Under strong kings the feudatories remained loyal, obedient and helpful carrying out their obligations properly; but during the reign of weak kings they showed scant respect towards their overlord, became slack in performing their duties, and lax in sending regular tributes to the king, and in some cases even stopped doing so, and thereby posing threat to his authority and causing loss to the royal exchequer. The more powerful feudatories harboured ambitions to become independent.

The governor of the Puṇḍravardhana *bhukti* during the reign of Kumāragupta (*vide* Nos. 22 and 24) was designated *uparika*, and in Budhagupta's reign (Nos. 43 and 45) as *uparika mahāraja*. During the rule of Vishṇugupta, as per the evidence of the fifth Damodar copperplate of GE 224 (No. 57), the office was held by king's son who has been referred to as *uparika-mahārāja–rājaputra-Deva-bhaṭṭāraka*. In the description of the governor is added *hast=yaśva-jana*, 'elephants, cavalry and infantry,'which is not met with in earlier Damodarpur plates, and indicates increase in the importance of the governor. The reason for change from appointing a governor hereditarily to the appointing of a prince on that post could be either because the governor proved disloyal, or the last governor had no son, or the king wanted to have closer control on the *bhukti* as he had greater faith in the loyalty of the prince than in that of the hereditary governor.[23]

There are examples of a number of high government officials holding the office hereditarily. Harisheṇa the *sāndhivigrahika, mahādaṇḍnāyaka* and *kumārāmātya* of Samudragupta was a son of *mahādaṇḍanāyaka* Dhruvabhūti. (No.1). Vīrasena Śāba, holding the portfolio of Minister of Peace and War under Chandragupta II, was a minister hereditarily (*anvayaprāpta sāchivya,* No. 11). Pṛithvīsheṇa, a *mantrī, kumārāmātya* and *mahābalādhikṛita* of Kumāragupta I was son of Śikharasvāmī, a *mantrī* and *kumārāmātya* of Chandragupta II (No. 20). S R Goyal considers the possibility of Harisheṇa, Vīrasena, Pṛithvīsheṇa and also Anantasena—the first an officer of Samudragupta, the second, of Chandragupta II, and the last two, of Kumāragupta, being members of one and the same family.[24] Chirātadatta was an *uparika* (governor) of Puṇḍravardhana *bhukti* during the reign of Kumāragupta I as per the evidence of the first and second Damodarpur copperplates (Nos. 22, 24). He, as the common *datta* name-ending suggests, in all probability, was the ancestor of *Uparika* Brahmadatta and *Uparika* Jayadatta who administered the same *bhukti* in succession during the reign of Budhagupta, as per the evidence of the third and fourth Damodarpur copperplates (No. 43 and No. 45) respectively. This is not the case with the governor of the time of Vishṇugupta, when a prince was appointed to that office, as per the evidence of his Damodarpur copperplate of Gupta Era 543 (No. 57). It has been suggested that perhaps the change was brought in course of the campaigns of Yaśodharman up to Brahmaputra river, passing through Gupta territories.

The early Gupta kings not only followed aggressive policy but also cultivated friendly relations with some of the contemporary powers by contracting matrimonial alliances. Chandagupta I married the Lichchhavi princess Kumāradevī and this marriage played a great role in increasing the power and prestige of the Guptas. Chandragupta II married Nāga princess Kuberanāgā and got married his daughter Prabhāvatī to the Vākāṭaka prince Rudrasena II. His son Ghaṭotkachagupta was married to the Vākāṭaka princess who was probably the daughter of Prabhāvatīguptā. The daughter of the Kadamba king Kākusthavarman was married to a Gupta prince. There is no definite evidence of kings after the reign of Kumāragupta I winning the friendship and cooperation of contemporary political powers by following the policy of contracting matrimonial alliance with them. On the other hand, there is evidence of matrimonial alliance between the Later Guptas and the Maukharis. Maukhari king Ādityavarman's queen Harshaguptā was most probably a sister of the Later Gupta king Harshagupta, and Maukhari king Īśanavarman's mother Upaguptā too seems to have been a Later Gupta princess.

Samudragupta is said to have performed horse-sacrifice in full detail and quite elaborately (Appendix II). He has been mentioned in the Vākāṭaka records as one who performed several horse sacrifices, which may be either an exaggeration, or the king might have actually performed many sacrifices, or, though less likely, paid *dakshiṇā* few times more than was to be paid in performing a single *aśvamedha*, and by doing so was known as performer of more than one (*aneka*) horse sacrifice (Appendix II). Kumāragupta's *aśvamedha* type of coins, unless issued merely in imitation of Samudragupta, suggests that he, too, performed a horse-sacrifice. These rituals no doubt raised the prestige of the Gupta dynasty and created an impact on the contemporary kings and tribal republican states, but this was achieved at the cost of heavy expenditure, causing a burden on the exchequer. The granting of the revenue of villages or land to the brāhmaṇas or to the Buddhist *saṁghas* would have deprived the exchequer of the money that it earned earlier by way of revenue from such land or villages. Some kings and officials are referred to in inscriptions and literature as to have erected large-sized religious edifices. According to Hiuen-tsang, a number of kings – Śakrāditya (Kumāragupta I), Buddhagupta (Budhagupta), Tathāgatagupta and Vajra got built Buddhist monuments, and the *Ārya-Mañjuśrī-mūlakalpa* informs that [Narasiṁhagupta] Bālāditya got a large number of Buddhist monuments constructed in eastern India 'up to the sea'.[25] Such constructions must have caused heavy loss to the state exchequer.

The weakening of the fabric of the empire is evident from coins of the later Imperial Gupta kings. While some coins of Narasiṁhagupta contain 70% of gold, others, contain only 54% of it. It is assumed that the former were issued before the Hūṇa invasion and the latter after it,[26] though this may partly be the result of his lavishly spending in the erection of Buddhist monuments. Chinese Buddhist pilgrim Fa-hien, who came to India during the reign of Chandragupta II describes Nālandā as a village.[27] Within a short period some Gupta monarchs are said to have got constructed sizable Buddhist monuments at that site. The testimony of Hiuen-tsang shows that during his time (in the second quarter of the seventh century AD). Nālandā had acquired the status of the largest and most developed Buddhist centre of religion and learning,[28] and that it received lavish grants from successive kings.

Some scholars suggest that Buddhist leanings of later Imperial Gupta rulers had an adverse effect on their military power.[29] There is a view that the *Apratigha* type of coins of Kumāragupta I shows him in the guise of Buddhist monk and the legend *Apratigha* (one who is above anger) indicates that following the tenets of Buddhism he had become monk.[30] Paramārtha, a Buddhist scholar, generally taken as belonging to the Gupta period, states that King Vikramāditya sent his crown-prince, Bālāditya and his queen for study under the Buddhist scholar Vasubandhu. The identification of the king and the prince has been a matter of controversy, but it does show the influence of Buddhism on the royal household. Bālāditya as per the evidence of the *Ārya-Mañjuśrī-mūlakalpa* and Hiuen-tsang was a great champion of Buddhism, while Mihirakula was a staunch Śaiva, as is evident from the Mandasor inscription of Yaśodharman which says he did not bow to anyone except Sthāṇu (Śiva), and also from his coins showing Śaiva devices. S R Goyal[31] is of the view that while Śaiva Mihirakula showed aggressiveness, Bālāditya under the Buddhist influence had become a pacifist. Whereas Chandragupta II is known to have led campaign against the Śakas and Skandagupta gave a crushing defeat to the invading Hūṇas, Bālāditya on being attacked by Hūṇa king Mihirakula, instead of facing him in the battlefield, hid himself in an island.[32] He had been a tributary of Mihirakula but stopped paying him tributes as that Hūṇa king was anti-Buddhist and was known for hurling atrocities on Buddhists. The Gupta king did not envisage that the consequences of his act would invite the wrath of and invasion by the Hūṇa ruler, for facing which he was not prepared. And when, contrary to expectation, somehow Mihirakula was ambushed and captured,[33] Bālāditya, instead of punishing him set him free at the interception of his mother who believed that by doing so she and her son would earn religious merit.[34] This 'misplaced clemency' of the Gupta king towards the invading tyrant was a political folly. According to the *Ārya-Mañjuśrī-mūlakalpa*,[35] Balāditya a staunch Buddhist gave up his life while sitting in *dhyāna*. There is ample evidence to show that in the sixth century Śaivism had gradually emerged as the most popular religion of both masses and classes, and kings belonging to the Nāga, the Maukhari, the Aulikara and the Hūṇa dynasties also Śaśāṅka king of Gauḍa and Harsha Pushpabhūti were Śaivas. Religious difference might also have been to some extent responsible for some of the political powers not being friendly towards the Guptas who were mostly Vaishṇavas, but some later kings of the dynasty had developed Buddhist leanings. If there is truth in the story of Hiuen-tsang,[36] then the Buddhist *saṅgha* was also responsible for Mihirakula's hurling atrocities on the Buddhists. It is said that on the Hūṇa king's request for sending a learned Buddhist monk to teach him the tenets of Buddhism, the *saṅgha* sent a monk who had been a servant of the royal family. Annoyed at this, he vowed to harm Buddhism and caused destruction of a number of Buddhists and Buddhist monuments.[37]

The gravity of the Gupta supremacy during its last phase, under pressure of powers from western and north-western direction, gradually shifted to eastern India. The fertile Gangetic valley had been an attraction for the invaders from the north-west from very early times and the invasion of the Hūṇās was from that direction. Hiuen-tsang[38] calls Bālāditya as the king of Magadha and the *Ārya-Mañjuśrī-mūlakalpa*[39] refers to Bāla (i.e. Bālāditya) as the king who decorated the earth with *chaityas* in the East up to the sea, Kumāra[gupta] [III] as the king of Gauḍa, and Bhakārākhya (Bhānugupta) as the king of the East. Most of the coins of Kumāragupta III and Vishṇugupta are found in the Kalighat hoard. Close to the last phase of the Gupta rule the kingdom was confined to some parts of Magadha, Bengal and Orissa, and in the last phase, to the last two regions only. The Gupta kings lost parts of Uttar Pradesh to the Maukharis, and parts of Magadha to the Later Guptas, and parts of Bengal, to the Gauḍas. Towards the end of the Gupta rule there was pressure from Kāmarūpa, which had been a subordinate frontier state of Samudragupta in the east. The Badganga Rock inscription[40] refers to King Bhūtivarman (*c* AD 518-42) of Kāmarūpa as a performer of an *aśvamedha* sacrifice. From this it can be inferred that he made some conquests, which could have been at the cost of the Gupta empire.

According to the *Harivaṁśa-purāṇa* (composed in AD 783), the Guptas ruled for 231 years, that is up to (319+ 231=) AD 550.[41] The *Tiloyapaṇṇati*, in one stanza,[42] gives the same figure for the total Gupta rule, but in another stanza, gives the figure for the same as 255 years, i.e. ending in (319+255=) AD 574, which goes well with the evidence of the Sumaṇḍala copperplate inscription of Pṛithivīvigraha of GE 250[43] (= AD 569) which speaks of that king as ruling in the dominion of the Guptas. This shows that 'the last flicker' of the lamp of the Gupta rule lingered in the Ganjam area till AD 569. The non-mention of Gupta sovereignty in the Soro copperplate of Śambhuyaśas of G E 260 (= AD 579)[44] shows that the Gupta rule had come to an end by that time. D C Sircar[45] holds that the tradition of 231 years of Gupta rule refers to that phase when Gupta power was wrapped from U.P., Bihar and Bengal, by *c* AD 550, and that of 255 years, to that phase when the Guptas were overthrown in Orissa, to which area their kingdom had by then become confined. Like the beginning of the Gupta rule, its end was not abrupt but gradual. It took about half a century for the kings of the Gupta dynasty to emerge from the feudatory (*mahārāja*) status to an independent one (*mahārājādhirāja*), which status they enjoyed both in spirit and letter till the end of the rule of Budhagupta. After that there was gradual loss in their power, though they continued to be designated as *mahārājādhirāja,* and in slightly more than half a century thereafter the rule of the Gupta dynasty came to an end.

## NOTES AND REFERENCES

1. D K Ganguly, *The Imperial Guptas and Their Times,* p. 108.
2. Skandagupta discontinued issuing silver coin after Class II and Class III coins of Kumāragupta I, and instead introduced 'Bull and Altar' coin type (A S Altekar, *The Coinage of the Gupta Empire,* p. 250).
3. P L Gupta, *The Imperial Guptas,* pp. 336-37.
4. *Corpus Inscriptionum Indicarum,* III, p. 81.
5. S R Goyal (*Imperial Guptas,* p. 412) opines that Dhanyavishṇu, who succeeded his deceased brother as district officer of Eran, changed his allegiance from the Guptas to Toramāṇa. But it seems this he did after Toramaṇa had conquered that region (Chapter 11).
6. D K Ganguly, *The Imperial Guptas and Their Times,* pp. 128-29.
7. K K Thaplyal, *Journal of the Numismatic Society of India,* XXXI(ii), pp. 184-85.
8. We do not agree with S R Goyal for reason given above, that he also defeated Mihirakula.
9. See K P Jayaswal, *Imperial History of India,* p. 33.
10. *Indian Historical Quarterly,* XXIX, pp. 158-59. Later on, he identified Vainyagupta with Tathāgatagupta and considered Bhānugupta as mere governor, and not as king.
11. R N Dandekar, *A History of the Guptas,* p. 149.
12. *Ibid.,* p. 150.

13. K K Thaplyal, *Inscriptions of the Maukharis, the Later Guptas, the Puṣpabhūtis, and Yaśovarman of Kanauj*, pp. 133-36.
14. For these and other Maukhari inscriptions, see K K Thaplyal, *Inscriptions of the Maukharis, the Later Guptas, the Puṣpabhūtis, and Yaśovarman of Kanauj*, pp. 139 ff.
15. S R Goyal (*The Imperial Guptas*, p. 42) considers Īśvaravarman as a feudatory of Yaśodharman. In his view, the victories over the Andhras, Gauḍas and the Śūlikas mentioned in the Haraha inscription of Īśānavarman (AD 554) were achieved by him as a prince during the rule of his father Īśvaravarman, who was a feudatory of Yaśodharman.
16. S R Goyal, *The Imperial Guptas*, pp. 440-41.
17. R N Dandekar, *A History of the Guptas*, p. 159.
18. Despite the *gupta* name-ending of the kings, some names of kings being common, and the fact that some area was under the rule of kings of both the dynasties, the rulers of the Imperrial Gupta dynasty and those of the Later Gupta dynasty do not seem to have been related by blood.
19. R C Majumdar, in *The Classical Age*, p. 72.
20. S R Goyal, *The Imperial Guptas*, pp. 438-39.
21. *Epigraphia Indica*, II, p. 364.
22. *Epigraphia Indica*, XIX, pp. 261ff.
23. R C Majumdar, in *Comprehensive History of India*, III (i), p. 99.
24. S R Goyal, *The Imperial Guptas*, pp. 385-86. He has been forcefully pleading for multidisciplinary approach in writing history. He rightly infers the possibility of such family relationship on the basis of identical or near identical name-endings. However, regarding the inferences drawn by us on the basis of 'identical name-endings, devices, provenance of source materrial' etc., he writes: 'the entire evidence... cited is *extremely thin and takes much for granted*' (italics ours). This is likely to give an impression that it would not have been so if we, like him, would have drawn the inferences from identical name–endings only. See Goyal's comments (*The Imperial Guptas*, p 386n) on K K Thaplyal, 'Scions of the Hitherto Unknown House of Kauśāmbī, *vis-à-vis* Their Gupta Overlords', *Indian Historical Review*, No. XXI(ii), pp. 1-8.
25. K P Jayaswal, *Imperial History of India*, p. 33.
26. P L Gupta, *Imperial Guptas*, p. 365; S R Goyal (*The Imperial Guptas*, p. 398), however, takes them as issues of two kings bearing the same name.
27. H A Giles, *Travels of Fa-hien*, p. 49.
28. S Beal, *The Life of Hiuen-Tsiang*, p. 112.
29. S R Goyal (*The Imperial Guptas*, pp. 377ff) lays much emphasis on it.
30. S R Goyal, *ibid*.
31. *Ibid*. pp. 420-21.
32. S Beal, *Si-yu-ki, Buddhist Records of the Western World*, I, p. 168.
33. S R Goyal (*The Imperial Guptas*, pp. 421-22) is of the view that the victory was achieved by Bālāditya with the help of the Maukharis, who were the Gupta

feudatories, and whose king Īśānavarman has been given the credit of defeating the Hūṇas in an inscription of the Later Gupta dynasty (No. 95).

34. S Beal, *Si-yu-ki, Buddhist Records of the Western World*, I, p. 168.
35. K P Jayaswal, *Imperial History of India*, p. 33.
36. T Watters, *On Yuan Chwang's Travels in India*, I, p. 288.
37. Mihirakula is said to have destroyed 1600 Buddhist monuments and nine *koṭis* of Buddhists (Watters, *On Yuan Chwang's Travels in India*, I, p. 289). However, the Kura inscription of the reign of Toramāṇa refers to the construction of Buddhist monastery during his rule, and the evidence of the *Kuvalayamālā* shows his leanings towards Jainism (S R Goyal, *The Imperial Guptas*, p. 417).
38. T Watters, *On Yuan Chwang's Travels in India*, I, pp. 288-89.
39. *Ārya-Mañjuśrī-mūlakalpa*, verses 648, 674 and 760, respectively.
40. D C Sircar, *Select Inscriptions*, I, pp. 384-85.
41. *Harivaṁśa-purāṇa*, as cited by D C Sircar, in H R Gupta (ed.), *Sir Jadunath Sarkar Commemoration Volume*, II, pp. 343ff.
42. *Tiloyapaṇṇati* of Jadi Vāsaha (Yati Vṛishabha), as dicussed by D C Sircar, in H R Gupta (ed.), *Sir Jadunath Sarkar Commemoration Volume*, II, p. 346.
43. D C Sircar, Sumandala plates of the Time of Pṛithivīvigraha-bhaṭṭāraka, Gupta Year 250, *Epigraphia Indica*, XXVIII, pp. 79ff.
44. *Epigraphia Indica*, XXIII, pp. 197ff.
45. D C Sircar, in H R Gupta (ed.), *Sir Jadunath Sarkar Commemoration Volume*, II, p. 346; see also R C Majumdar, in *Comprehensive History of India*, III(i), pp. 103-05.

# Appendix I

## Chandragupta I-Kumāradevī Type of Coins

Chandragupta I-Kumāradevī' type (also known as King-and-Queen type) of coins,[1] shows on the obverse the king (Chandragupta I) standing to left, wearing trousers, a close-fitting coat and a head-dress, and holding a crescent-topped standard in the left hand. He is shown offering something, identified on different coins variously as a ring, a *sindūradānī* and a bracelet, to Kumāradevī wearing sārī, an upper garment and a head-dress, and decked with various ornaments. The legend giving the names of the king and the queen reads *Chandragupta* and *Śrī-Kumāradevī* (or *Kumāradevī-śrī).* The reverse shows a female figure riding a lion and wearing sārī, a bodice and an upper garment and necklace and other ornaments, holding a noose in her right hand and a cornucopiae in her left hand, and bears the legend *Lichchhavayaḥ.* The female figure has been identified variously as Durgā,[2] Lakshmī,[3] Rājalakshmī,[4] Vaishṇavī Mahālakshmī,[5] and Dattadevī—the chief queen of Samudragupta.[6] The very fact that the female figure is shown riding a lion, excludes the possibility of her identification with the queen. Further, the ascription of the authorship of the coin-type to Samudragupta, as suggested by some scholars, is not acceptable for reasons given below, and therefore the question of identification of the female figure on the reverse with his queen does not arise. The cornucopiae in the Indian context indicates horn as a symbol of plenty.[7] According to Chhabra,[8] the *pāśa* in one hand and the horn (cornucopiae) in the other hand of the goddess, and the *rājadaṇḍa* in one hand and gift in the other hand of the king, represent, in each case, *nigraha* (punishment) and *anugraha* (reward) respectively.

The coins of this type have been found at Mathurā, Ayodhyā, Lucknow, Sitapur, Tanda, Ghazipur and Vārāṇasī, all in Uttar Pradesh, Ropar in Punjab, Bayana in Rajasthan, Hajipur in Bihar, and Chandraketugarh in West Bengal.[9] In the whole range of the Gupta numismatics, Chandragupta I-Kumāradevī type of coins have the following special characteristics: (i) they bear the name of the queen with *Śrī* prefixed or suffixed to it. (ii) They bear the name of her clansmen, the Lichchhavis. (iii) They do not bear a circular legend, which is generally met with on other Gupta coins. The authorship of this much-discussed coin-type has been a subject of great controversy, some scholars ascribe it to Chandragupta I, others to Samudragupta, and still others to the Lichchhavis.

Allan[10] and some other scholars[11] opine that Samudragupta was the author of this type of coins. The main arguments in favour of this view, most of them first stated by Allan, are:

(i) The Chandragupta-Kumāradevī type is more evolved than Samudragupta's Standard type which is a slavish imitation of the Later Kushaṇa money. If Chandragupta I would have issued coins of this type, which shows much originality, then it is not understandable why Samudragupta, instead of following this innovative type, copied Kushāṇa coin-types. Therefore, on typological grounds, Chandragupta-Kumāradevī type of coins should be placed after the Standard-type of Samudragupta.

(ii) If Chandragupta I would have issued these coins, then in his fairly long reign (as Allan and most of the scholars believe, he had) he would not have confined himself to this type only, particularly as the type is considered by some scholars as a commemorative one, and would have issued other types as well.

(iii) The Chandragupta-Kumāradevī type of coins would have been issued later than a few other coin-types which are nearer to the coin-types of the Kushāṇa, as no model was available for it in the Kushāṇa coins. It is difficult to believe the introduction of a series of coins beginning with such an evolved type showing the king and the queen on the obverse together with their names and substituting the throne with lion as a seat for the goddess on the reverse, during the reign of Chandragupta I.

(iv) The Guptas would have issued coins only after they came in contact with the Kushāṇa territories, which first took place during Samudragupta's time, and not in that of Chandragupta I.

(v) It can be argued that the Standard type of Samudragupta's coins, which are nearer to the Kushāṇa type in style, has the legend referring to Samudragupta as victorious in '100 battles' (*samara-śata*), suggesting that the type was issued in the later part of his reign after he had made major conquests, and after which he came in contact with the Kushāṇas. If Chandragupta I-Kumāradevī type of coins is taken as issued by Chandragupta I in the early phase of his reign when the Gupta territories were confined to eastern Uttar Pradesh and Bihar, then there should not have been such a gap between this type and the Standard type of Samudragupta.

(vi) The representation of the goddess on the Chandragupta I-Kumāradevī type of coins is akin to the goddess on the Lion-slayer type of Chandragupta II, and so the two should be nearer to each other in date.

(vii) It is not necessary that since Chandragupta I was a *mahārājādhirāja*, he must have issued coins, as many powerful independent kings did not issue any coins, and therefore it would be more proper to take such coins as issued by Samudragupta.

Smith,[12] Altekar,[13] R C Majumdar,[14] and a number of other scholars consider Chandragupta I as the author of the coin-type in question. Altekar[15] points out that Kushāṇa money would have been in circulation beyond the boundaries of the later Kushāṇa kingdom, and as such there is nothing against the Kushāṇa coins being available to the Guptas even before the time of Samudragupta. As regards the argument that if Chandragupta I issued Chandragupta I-Kumāradevī type of coins then why he in his fairly long reign did not issue any other type, it has been pointed out by Altekar that such coins might have been issued by that king in the last phase of his reign, when Chandragupta was formally consecrated *mahārājādhirāja*, and hence, it remains his only coin-type.[16] The same scholar[17] suggests that political pressure from the Lichchhavis would have desisted him from issuing any other coin-type. As against this, Sohoni[18] says there is nothing to show that Chandragupta formally consecrated himself *mahārājādhirāja* in the last phase of his reign. Chandragupta I's issuing only one type is not so strong an argument, against that king being the author of the coin-type, as a number of Gupta kings are known to have issued only one coin-type. There is no doubt that, for their political ascendancy, the Guptas were indebted to the Lichchhavis which is reflected in the persistent reference to Samudragupta as *Lichchhavi-dauhitra,* 'son of the daughter of the (chief) of the Lichchhavis', in his and his successors' records. It is however difficult to believe that the Guptas could have been pressurized by the Lichchhavis to include not only the figure and name of Kumāradevī, but also the name of their tribe.

P L Gupta[19] points out that not only Samudragupta's Standard type, but even some other types of Gupta coins, such as the Archer type coins of Chandragupta II and Kumāragupta I, are very much based on Kushāṇa coin-types, that Chandragupta I-Kumāradevī type is not as original as it is considered to be by some scholars, and also that while the Standard type of Samudragupta's coins is a close copy of the Kushāṇa prototype, his *Aśvamedha* type of coins is more Indianized than most of the coin-types of his successors. It was political exigency that made it necessary to issue Chandragupta I-Kumāradevī type of coins with the name of the Lichchhavis; and as such it was somewhat apart from the series marking regular development of Gupta coin-types. The dress of the king—long coat and trousers on Chandragupta I–Kumāradevī type of the coins is in imitation of the king's dress on Kushāṇa coins. As regards the representation of goddess on lion, and not on throne, it may be stated that the goddess is similarly depicted on some coins of Huvishka and Kanishka III. May be Durgā was the family deity (*kuladevī*) of the Lichchhavis and as such was chosen as coin-device.[20] According to S K Aiyangar, the 'legend *Lichchhavayaḥ* seems rather to indicate that the goddess is personified representation of Lichchhavi people' and the lion is perhaps their totemic representation.[21] Some scholars,[22] following Allan, attribute the authorship of this type to Samudragupta, yet, unlike him, place it earlier than the 'Standard type' of that ruler. They argue that (i) the Chandragupta I-Kumāradevī coins are confined to a small area, and therefore should belong to the earlier phase of the Gupta empire, while the standard type has been found from places located in a much larger area; and that (ii) majority of Samudragupta's coin-types including the Standard type of coins bear metrical legends and therefore should be placed later than Chandrgupta I-Kumāradevī type which does not bear metrical legends.[23]

In the context of the Gupta coins, it is believed that generally the earlier the coins, greater will be the influence of the Kushāṇa coins; in other words, the more the coin bears Kushāṇa influence the earlier it should be in date. However, as Altekar rightly states, "...the relative closeness to the prototype does not necessarily prove that the type in question is chronologically earlier than another, which shows lesser imitation of the original."[24] Therefore Gupta coins which are close imitation of the Kushāṇa coins should not invariably be taken as earlier in date, and for establishing relative chronology other factors should also be taken into consideration. At times, in issuing coins, an old model has been preferred as against a new one. For example, Kumāragupta I issued King-and-Queen type in imitation of Chandragupta I-Kumāradevī type, and not on the model of King-and-Queen type of his father, Chandragupta II, which was nearer to him in terms of time. Thus, apart from the models available, factors like temperament of the king, the training, skill, imagination and even whims of the mint master and the die-cutter, the political circumstances and compulsions would also have been responsible for the creation of a particular coin-type.[25] For King-and-Queen type there was no Kushāṇa model, and no such model is available in the entire indigenous numismatics of pre-Gupta phase. Therefore for king's figure Kushāṇa model was imitated by the mint master. Since no numismatic model was available for the queen, the die-cutter followed the model of the graceful female figure available in the sculptural art of the period. S R Goyal opines that Chandragupta I could not have issued such coins as he could have the services only of the indigenous artists, and could not have direct access to the services of the Kushāṇa die-cutters, which advantage would have been there for Samudragupta the boundaries of whose empire came close to that of the Kushāṇas, who entered into a subordinate alliance with him. However, even Chandragupta I could very well have employed Kushāṇa artists if he so desired.

In passing reference may be made to the theory according to which, generally speaking, the percentage of gold content in the Gupta coins decreased in successive generations.[26] Judging by this standard, the Chandragupta I-Kumāradevī type, with more percentage of gold content than any other type of Gupta gold coins, should be considered as the earliest coin-type.[27]

One strong argument against the ascription of this coin-type to Samudragupta is that in that case it should be taken as a commemorative one, issued by him,[28] and as such, the coins should have borne his name as the commemorator, which however is not the case. In the case of the commemorative coins issued by the Indo-Greek kings, Antimachus, Agathocles,[29] Eukratides, etc, the name of the king as commemorator is invariably mentioned along with the name of the king commemorated. The revealing of the identity of the commemorator as different from the one commemorated was deemed so important that in the Indo-Greek commemorative coins the name of the king commemorated is given in nominative, and that of the issuer of the coin in the genitive to make it clear that the coin is his, i.e. has been issued by him. Nisar Ahmad[30] opines that the comparison with the Indo-Greek coins is not apt as because of considerable gap between the rule of the Indo-Greek kings and Gupta kings, there was no continuity of tradition between the two. But the logic of the mention of the name of the commemorator on commemorarive coins stands by itself independently, and the reference to the Indo-Greek kings is by way of citing an example in its support. Altekar[31] points out that if Samudragupta would have been the commemorator then the legend on the reverse would have been *mātā-pitṛi-bhaktaḥ Samudraguptaḥ*. One expects that if not the name at least his main *viruda,* namely, *parākrama,* should have been there, as it is in the case of his *Aśvamedha* type of coins bearing the legend *Aśvamdha-parākramaḥ*. It is difficult to agree with the view that Samudragupta did not inscribe his name 'out of sheer humility and modesty'.[32]

Smith,[33] and some other scholars consider Chandragupta I-Kumāradevī type of coins as jointly issued by the Guptas and the Lichchhavis. However, the coins bear the name of the Lichchhavis, but not of the Guptas, which one feels should have been there if it were a joint issue of these two ruling families.

Some scholars[34] are of the view that these are joint coins of Chandrgupta and Kumāradevī, the former as heir to the Gupta throne and the latter as heiress to the Lichchhavi throne. It is argued that the mention of the Lichchhavis in the legend was done with a view to showing the indebtedness of the Guptas to the Lichchhavis who exercised considerable authority and who would have insisted that on coins along with the figure and the name of the Gupta prince not only the name and figure of their princess but the name of her tribe should also appear. The status of Chandragupta and Kumāradevī, Altekar[35] suggests, is comparable to William III and Mary in the British history. In accordance with the

British law, Mary, daughter of King James II of England, was made joint ruler with her husband William of Orange. Her status was not merely that of a queen consort but also of queen reigning, and on coins her portrait appeared by her husband's side. But, as seen above, in the case of Chandragupta I-Kumāradevī type of coins the peculiar thing is the name of the Lichchhavi tribe along with the figures and names of Chandragupta and Kumāradevī. Nisar Ahmad[36] opines that on the analogy of William and Mary, Chandragupta I would have been invited to Vaiśālī and offered the right to rule over the Lichchhavi territory. A H Dani[37] points out that "there is no instance of a 'joint rule' of king and queen in Indian history nor is it conceived of in any political theory of ancient India. We know of sons or younger brothers being associated with the father or elder brother in administration, but no instance of queen having equal legal right with the husband." Had it been a joint issue of of Chandragupta I and Kumāradevī then one would expect mention of the Guptas alongside the Lichchhavis on the reverse side, as on the obverse occur the names and figures of Chandragupta and Kumāradevī representing the Gupta and Lichchhavi houses. Sohoni[38] states that that it is 'unlikely that a clan, said to have a republican organisation should have entered into an arrangement of joint administration with an emperor,' and even if joint rule would have been there, then it should have been that of Chandragupta I and his father-in-law, or brother-in-law.

V S Pathak,[39] in line with Allan and some other scholars, considers Chandragupta I-Kumāradevī type of coins as issues of Samudragupta. Like Allan, he opines that if the coin-type is to be ascribed to Chandragupta I then it is difficult to explain as to why he confined himself only to that type and also that typologically the type should be placed later than the 'Standard type' of Samudragupta. According to him, Samudragupta as a *dvāmushyāyaṇa*, i.e. a successor to his father (in the Gupta family) and to his maternal grandfather (in the Lichchhavi family) struck these coins to commemorate the marriage of his parents – Chandragupta and Kumāradevī and the consequent amalgamation of the Gupta and Lichchhavi territories. He points out that Kumāradevī has been represented on the right of Chandragupta I, and not on his left side which is the place of a wife in relation to her husband. In his view the depiction of the marriage scene was intended, as according to some ancient texts in marriage ceremony, before its completion, the bride is placed on the right of the bridegroom, and such depiction is seen in the *vaivāhika* or

*Kalyāṇasundara* icons of Śiva.[40] But Altekar,[41] has described the king and the queen as facing each other, and this seems to be the intention of the coin-maker, rather than showing the queen on the right of the king.[42] If, however, the queen is taken as on the right of the king then such is also the representation of the queen in relation to the king on the King-and-Queen type of Kumāragupta I,[43] but no scholar has interpreted the coin-device as representing a marriage scene.[44] Aware of the fact that the commemorative coins must show the identity of the issuer, Pathak seeks to infer the identity of the commemorator in the coin-legend. He ingenuously suggests that the names of Chandragupta, Kumāradevī and of the Lichchhavi tribe on them, are meant to convey *Chandraguptasya putrasya Kumāradevyām=utpannasya Lichchhavidauhitrasya,* which is the way Samudragupta is mentioned in his and his successors' inscriptions, and infers from it that Samudragupta was the commemorator.[45] However, we feel that if that would have been the intention, then the coin-legend should not have been *Lichchhavayaḥ,* but *Lichchhavi-dauhitrasya,* an epithet used for him in his and his successors' records, and which could have been accommodated as legend on the coin-type and would mean as '(coin) of the Lichchhavi *dauhitra*'

S V Sohoni[46] also ascribes the issue of this coin-type to Samudragupta, as according to him the names Chandragupta, Kumāradevī and Lichchhavis 'were intended as unmistakable pointer not towards Chandragupta I but somebody else in whose career alone could be found an occasion for expressing gratitude to all these three'. But as D K Ganguly[47] pertinently points out, '... ancient Indian numismatics hardly furnishes us with a parallel instance where a king has disclosed his identity merely by referring to his parentage'...

One argument against the view of Pathak that the Chandragupta I-Kumāradevī type of coins commemorate the marriage of Chandragupta I and Kumāradevī is that in the Indian tradition, commemoration of parents' marriage would not be deemed proper and rather considered as out of etiquette, and against the Indian ethos, as was pointed out by K P Jayaswal.[48] S R Goyal[49] accepts the view of Pathak that the coins depict marriage scene. He also concurs with the view of Jayaswal that the depiction of parent's marriage would be out of etiquette, and therefore suggests that it is because of this consideration that Samudragupta did not give his own name, and instead gave the name of the Lichchhavis as commemorators. But it is difficult to explain as to why Samudragupta should at all have chosen to portray the scene of the marriage of his parents if it was not deemed proper for a son to do so.

Sohoni[50] is of the view that the obverse of Chandragupta I-Kumāradevī type of coins shows the king taking leave of the queen before proceeding on a military campaign. According to him, Chandragupta holds in his hand a bracelet meant to be worn at the time of proceeding on a campaign. But the identification of the object as a bracelet is doubtful as also the view that it was put by the king to ward off impending danger on the eve of the military operation. It may be mentioned that Sohoni himself had identified the object on some coins as a ring. Further, it has been pointed out that the king seems to be already wearing a bracelet. Moreover, if the scene would have been related to warfare, the legend on the coin-type would have been related to the scene.[51] The identification of the object as a ring would suit well if the depiction is of a marriage scene, as opined by V S Pathak, but there is little possibility of representing such a scene. It has also been pointed out that the posture of the queen is such as to give an impression that she is an observer and not a recepient.[52]

There is a view[53] that the Chandragupta I-Kumāradevī type of coins might have been issued by Samudragupta to impress upon the people that he was not only the successor to the throne of the Guptas, but as a *Lichchhavi-dauhitra*, also to that of the Lichchhavis. However, it is difficult to understand as to why he did not give his name or his characteristic and specific title on these coins, without which it would have been difficult for the people to identify their author, and consequently would not serve such a purpose.

The presence of the legend *Lichchhavayaḥ*, according to V S Agrawala[54] and a few others,[55] may be taken to indicate that the Lichchhavis were the authors of this type of coins. Though we also believe that the coin-type was issued by the Lichchhavis, yet we find it difficult to agree with V S Agrawala that the legend *Lichchhavayaḥ* is meant for *Lichchhavayaḥ jayanti*, which in his opinion 'is tantamount to saying that they are the power associated with the using of money.' If *jayanti* was intended then it could have very well been inscribed, as much larger legends are found on the Gupta coins. There was numismatic tradition of using the expression *jaya* as part of the legend. On the Mālava coins occurs such legend as *Mālavānāṁ jayaḥ* and on the Yaudheya coins, *Yaudheyānāṁ jayaḥ*. Like Allan, Agrawala too believes on typological consideration that the coin-type was issued not during the reign of Chandragupta I but that of

Samudragupta, when, in his opinion, the amalgamation of the territories of the Guptas and the Lichchhavis took place. But, as stated above, typology has its limitations, and also that the recording of the name of the Lichchhavis would appear more appropriate till they had separate identity than after their territory had been amalgamated with that of the Guptas.[56] R K Mookerji, following Allan, states that Chandragupta I-Kumāradevī type of coins were issued by Samudragupta and discusses these coins in his *Gupta Empire* under the Chapter 'Samudragupta Parākramāṅka'. He opines that they 'were in circulation in Lichchhavi territory which now passed into the possession of Chandragupta I as one of the results of his Lichchhavi alliance.'[57] However, at one place,[58] in the same work, he takes this coin-type as issued by the Lichchhavis. A L Srivastava[59] who, like V S Agrawala, ascribes their authorship to the Lichchhavis, opines that they were meant for exclusive circulation in the Lichchhavi territory. But the view of these scholars is negated by the fact that almost all the sites (and there are a number of them as mentioned above), where coins of this type have been found are outside the region which formed part of the Lichchhavi territories. Goyal[60] has taken care of this evidence of the distribution of coins and used it in support of his view that Samudragupta was the author of these coins. He opines that Samudragupta issued these coins for circulation in the Gupta territory (within which they have been found) where there were chances of his rival or rivals garnering support for themselves, and not for circulation in the Lichchhavi territories where by virtue of his being the son of the Lichchhavi princess the support of the people for him was taken for granted. B B Singh,[61] who considers such coins as issued by the Lichchhavis, likewise, realizing that they have not been found in their territory, suggests that they were issued for circulation in the Gupta territory with a view to conveying the message that Samudragupta being born of the Lichchhavi princess should be the rightful choice for the Gupta throne.

A L Srivastava[62] opines that these coins were issued by the Lichchhavis from a Gupta mint. But since, in our view, no Gupta coins earlier than those belonging to this coin-type are known, so no mint of the Guptas existed before that, and thus both the Guptas and the Lichchhavis, till the issuing of the Chandragupta-Kumāradevī type lacked the experience in respect of issuing coins. If the Lichchhavis were to issue coins then they would have established their own mint for the manufacture of the coins rather than requested the Guptas to establish a mint for minting coins for them. Moreover, if these are taken as Lichchhavi coins issued from the Gupta mint, then it would look curious that the Guptas issued coins for the Lichchhavis from their mint, but refrained from issuing their own coins from the same.[63] According to Pathak,[64] pieces of such numismatic evidence as find-spots of coins, legends, devices, conventions followed, sequence of coins, etc. clearly shows that the Chandragupta I-Kumāradevī coins were issued by the Guptas and not by the Lichchhavis. But their being issued by the Lichchhavis does not go against such numismatic evidence. The Lichchhavis issued the coins in the context of the Guptas, and with the amalgamation of Lichchhavi territories into the Gupta kingdom, the Lichchhavi mint would have become a Gupta mint. It is but natural that coins issued from this mint as also from other Gupta mints that would have been established later, should fit in well with the Gupta numismatic series issued by the successive kings of that dynasty, there being no more coin-type issued by the Lichchhavis, who lost their political identity. This would also meet the query of D K Ganguly as to why "...no coins which should be classed Lichchhavi issues have been discovered as yet."[65] In passing, we may state that though we believe that the coin-type was issued by the Lichchhavis, we do not agree with the view of Ganguly that the ascription of these coins to Chandragupta I 'would involve a violation of all numismatic rules and conventions'.

Ashvini Agrawal[66] thinks that after negotiations culminating into Chandragupta I-Kumāradevī marriage, there was no political authority left with the Lichchhavis, and hence, they could not have been the issuers of the coins. But the prefixing or suffixing of *Śrī* to the name of Kumāradevī, and not to the name of Chandragupta, and the place given in the coin-legend to the members of her tribe—the Lichchhavis, and not his family—the Guptas, shows that at the time of the issue of the coin-type they had political authority. R K Mookerji, as stated above, in his work, *The Gupta Empire*,[67] ascribes these coins to Samudragupta, but at one place in the same work, to the Lichchhavis. In the latter case, his perception of the status of the tribe at the time of issuing this coin is that though the 'Lichchhavi republic perhaps became part of the Gupta empire, it did not affect the local autonomy of the Lichchhavis who thus exercised the right to issue their own coins.'[68] To us, it seems more likely that the Lichchhavis issued these coins before their territory became a part of the Gupta empire, rather than after it.

D R Bhandarkar[69] is of the view that Chandragupta, by marrying the Lichchhavi princess, became the joint ruler of the territory of the Lichchhavis, who are referred to on the reverse of the coin-type. This view of Bhandarkar explains the mention of the name of the tribe on the coin type better than some other suggestions offered by various scholars, referred to above. But while Bhandarkar takes the coin-type as issued by Chandragupta I, we consider it as issued by the Lichchhavis.

As seen above, there is no sufficient justification for ascribing the coin-type to Samudragupta. D R Bhandarkar emphatically says: 'No historian or even numismatist will now subscribe to the view that Gupta coinage originated with Samudragupta....'[70] With the elimination of Samudragupta as the author of this coin-type, we are left with two choices, viz. either Chandragupta I issued these coins, or the Lichchhavis. For reasons given below, despite the fact that a large number of scholars favouring the view that they were issued by the former, we prefer to take them as issued by the latter. The addition of *Śrī* to the name of Kumāradevī, and not to that of Chandragupta, indicates that more importance has been given to the former than to the latter. This was done as she was the heiress to the Lichchhavi throne, and as legally not Chandragupta, but a son born of this union would be the successor to the Lichchhavi throne. It is also possible that Chandragupta was a mere prince, and not a king at the time of his marriage, when the Chandragupta-Kumāradevī type of coins were issued by the Lichchhavis. The mention of the Lichchhavis, and not of the Guptas, on such coins, provides a strong evidence in its favour.

The Lichchhavi state in the Gupta period, in the pattern of earlier times seem to have been governed by a council comprising representatives of the Lichchhavis, and was presided over by their chief, called *rājā*.[71] The office of the Lichchhavi chief, according to most scholars, had become hereditary. Kumāradevī, in all probability, was the only child of her parents and so one who would marry her was expected to inherit the office of the chief of the *gaṇa*. For this reason as for other considerations, several Lichchhavi chiefs would have been keen to marry her. The *Vinayapiṭaka*[72] mentions that the Lichchhavi chiefs desirous of getting married could ask the Corporation of the Lichchhavis to get them proper brides. Some of the chiefs while making such a request might have indicated their choice for Kumāradevī.

We hazard a conjecture regarding the circumstances of marriage of Kumāradevī with Chandragupta. With their many good qualities, and their charming features, for which Buddha compared them with the Tāvatiṁśa gods,[73] the Lichchhavis were rather haughty and egoistic. Earlier, in the fifth century BC, King Ajātaśatru's ministers, playing on these weaknesses of the Lichchhavi chiefs, were able to create dissension amongst them, and each of them claimed that he was the *rājā* of the *gaṇa*.[74] Marrying Kumāradevī to anyone chief would antagonize other chiefs, who, to attain their objective of marrying Kumāradevī could resort to fights leading to civil war and consequent bloodshed. The Lichchhavi councillors would also have been apprehensive of Kumāradevī's meeting the fate of Āmrapālī whom because of her enchanting beauty and talent a number of Lichchhavi chiefs were keen to marry, and to avoid possible infight and bloodshed, the Council decided that she be given the status of *nagaravadhū* of Vaiśalī, and by which she would not be the property of one man but of the whole community. It seems some of the sane Lichchhavi councillors, particularly those who because of their old age, or for some other reason were not in the race for Kumaradevī's hand in marriage, realizing that marrying Kumāradevī to a Lichchhavi chief was fraught with dangerous consequences for the whole clan, resolved to get her married outside the clan, to Prince Chandragupta of the rising dynasty of the Guptas whose territory was contiguous to that of the Lichchhavis. This led to the formation of a union of the territories of the Lichchhavis and the Guptas. The Lichchhavis, with a view to safeguarding their own interest, reached an understanding with the Guptas that the son born of the Chandragupta I-Kumāradevī union would inherit the amalgamated territories of the Guptas and the Lichchhavis. The Allahabad pillar inscription shows that Chandragupta I honoured this condition by declaring in the Gupta assembly that Samudragupta was his heir.

The Lichchhavis hailed this marriage as of extraordinary significance, as it averted the impending civil war and also ensured the succession of the son of their princess to the would be amalgamated Gupta-Lichchhavi territories. To commemorate the marriage they issued the coin-type in question, depicting the figures of Chandragupta I and Kumāradevī, together with their names, with a *Śrī* prefixed or suffixed with the name of the latter on the obverse, and representing a goddess-on-lion device and name of their clan in plural (*Lichchhavayaḥ*) as issuer of the coin-type, on the reverse. As to why such coins have been found in areas, which before the amalgamation of the two territories formed part of the Gupta territory, and not in those which formed part of the Lichchhavi territory, it may be suggested that the coins which served as commemorative medals, were presented as souvenir to the members of the bridegroom's marriage party who carried them to their homes. As stated above, after the amalgamation of the two territories, Lichchhavi mint became the Gupta mint, which would explain as to how this coin-type, though issued by the Lichchhavis, fits in well with the Gupta coin series as regards 'findspot, device, metallurgy, convention and sequence'.

## NOTES AND REFERENCES

1. A S Altekar, *The Coinage of the Gupta Empire*, pp. 26ff.
2. *Ibid.*, p. 28.
3. J Allan,*Catalogue of the Coins of the Gupta Dynasties, and of Śaśāṅka, the King of Gauḍa, in the British Museum, London*, p. 8.
4. B Ch Chhabra, *Journal of the Numismatic Society of India*, XI (i), p. 28; in *Catalogue of the Gupta Gold Coins of the Bayana Hoard in the National Museum*, p. 3, he mentions the deity as 'Ambikā (?)'.
5. R K Dikshit, *Journal of the Numismatic Society of India*, XXVI, p. 104; S N Misra, *Journal of the Numismatic Society of India*, XXX (i), p. 83.
6. B S Sitholey, *Journal of the Numismatic Society of India*, X, p. 69.
7. Motichandra as referred to in D R Bhandarkar, *Corpus Inscriptionum Indicarum*, III, p. 41.
8. *Catalogue of the Gupta Gold Coins of the Bayana Hoard in the National Museum*, p. xxiii.
9. A S Altekar, *The Coinage of the Gupta Empire*, p. 26; S R Goyal, *Gupta Sāmrājya kā Itihāsa*, p. 46; Ashvini Agrawal, *Rise and Fall of the Imperial Guptas*, p. 90; R K Mookerji, *Gupta Empire*, p. 15.
10. *Catalogue of the Coins of the Gupta Dynasties, and of Śaśāṅka, the King of Gauḍa, in the British Museum, London*, Introduction, pp. lxiv-lxviii.
11. V S Pathak, *Journal of the Numismatic Society of India*, XIX, pp. 140-41; A H Dani, *ibid.*, XX, p. 8.
12. V A Smith, *The Early History of India*, 3rd edn., p. 280.
13. A S Altekar, *The Coinage of the Gupta Empire*, pp. 28-32.
14. R C Majumdar, *The Vākāṭaka-Gupta Age*, p. 128.
15. *The Coinage of the Gupta Empire*, p. 29.
16. As stated above, a variety of the *Chhatra* type of coins with legend *Vikrama* or *Vikramāditya*, and a unique coin of Standard type ascribed by most scholars to Chandragupta II, are ascribed by some to Chandragupta I.
17. *The Coinage of the Gupta Empire*, p. 31.
18. S V Sohoni, *Journal of the Numismatic Society of India*, XIX, p. 147.
19. P L Gupta, *Gupta Sāmrājya*, p. 239n.

20. A S Altekar, *The Coinage of the Gupta Empire*, p. 28.
21. S K Aiyanger, *Ancient India and South Indian History and Culture*, pp. 184-85.
22. For example, S R Goyal, *The Imperial Guptas*, pp. 139 ff.
23. S R Goyal, *The Imperial Guptas*, p. 135.
24. A S Altekar, *The Coinage of the Gupta Empire*, p. 130.
25. See also Goyal, *The Imperial Guptas*, p. 137.
26. S K Maity, *Early Indian Coins and the Currency System*, pp. 98-100.
27. However, in establishing chronology, like typology, consideration of gold content present in coins has pitfalls, and we do not press this point any further.
28. T P Verma (*Journal of the Numismatic Society of India*, LIII, p. 121) states that coins of his type were issued by Samudragupta at the time of his performing the *aśvamedha*.
29. Not Agathoclea, as stated in *Journal of the Numismatic Society of India*, XII, p. 79.
30. Nisar Ahmad, *Journal of the Numismatic Society of India*, LIII, p. 107.
31. A S Altekar, *The Coinage of the Gupta Empire*, p. 28.
32. V C Pandey and Anup Pandey, *A New History of the Indian People*, p. 355.
33. V A Smith, *Indian Museum Catalogue*, I, pp. 95, 99-100.
34. For example, A S Altekar, *The Coinage of the Gupta Empire*, pp. 30-31.
35. *Ibid.*
36. Nisar Ahmad, *Journal of the Numismatic Society of India*, LIII, p. 102.
37. A H Dani, *Journal of the Numismatic Society of India*, XX, pp. 7-8.
38. S V Sohoni, *Journal of the Numismatic Society of India*, XIX, p. 147.
39. V S Pathak, *Journal of the Numismatic Society of India*, XIX, pp. 135ff.
40. *Ibid.*, p. 136.
41. A S Altekar, *The Coinage of the Gupta Empire*, p. 32.
42. S V Sohoni, *Journal of the Numismatic Society of India*, XIX, p. 145.
43. A S Altekar, *The Coinage of the Gupta Empire*, p. 138 and pl. IX, 6.
44. A H Dani (*Journal of the Numismatic Society of India*, XIX, pp. 5-6), too, has shown his disagreement with the view that the icon represents marriage scene.
45. V S Pathak, *Journal of the Numismatic Society of India*, XIX, p. 141.
46. S V Sohoni, *Journal of the Numismatic Society of India*, XVI, p. 9.
47. D K Ganguli, *The Imperial Guptas and Their Times*, p. 41.
48. *Journal of the Bihar and Orissa Research Society*, XIX, p. 91; *Imperial History of India*, p. 91n.
49. S R Goyal, *The Imperial Guptas*, p. 138.
50. S V Sohoni, *Journal of the Numismatic Society of India*, XIX, p. 151.
51. Ashvini Agrawal, *Rise and Fall of the Imperial Guptas*, p. 94.
52. D K Ganguly, *The Imperial Guptas and Their Times*, p. 48.
53. V S Pathak, *Journal of the Numismatic Society of India*, XIX, p. 141; S R Goyal, *The Imperial Guptas*, p. 140.
54. V S Agrawala, *Journal of the Numismatic Society of India*, XVII, pp. 117-19.
55. J S Negi, as referred to by S R Goyal, *The Imperial Guptas*, p. 139; A L Srivastava, *Journal of the Numismatic Society of India*, XXXVI, pp. 57ff; K K Thaplyal, *Purātattva*, XII, pp. 152-54.

56. D K Ganguly, *The Imperial Guptas and Their Times*, p. 42.
57. *Gupta Empire*, pp. 14-15.
58. Under 'Addenda' on p. 158, Mookerji opines that the legend *Lichchhavayaḥ* on the reverse of the Chandragupta-Kumāradevī coins 'should be interpreted to mean that the coin in question was issued by the republican community'.
59. *Journal of the Numismatic Society of India*, XXXVI, pp. 57ff.
60. S R Goyal, *The Imperial Guptas*, p. 140.
61. *Journal of the Numismatic Society of India*, XLI, pp. 78ff.
62. A L Srivastava, *Journal of the Numismatic Society of India*, XXXVI, pp. 57-61.
63. See also A M Shastri, *Journal of the Numismatic Society of India*, XIX, p. 61 (Editorial note).
64. *Journal of the Numismatic Society of India*, XIX, p. 139.
65. D K Ganguly, *The Imperial Guptas and Their Times*, p. 42.
66. Ashvini Agrawal, *Rise and Fall of the Imperial Guptas*, p. 94.
67. *Gupta Empire*, pp. 32ff.
68. *Ibid.*, p. 158.
69. D R Bhandarkar, *Corpus Inscriptionum Indicarum*, III, p. 4.
70. *Ibid.*, p. 5.
71. H C Raychaudhuri, *Political History of Ancient India*, p. 112.
72. See B B Singh, *Journal of the Numismatic Society of India*, XLI, pp. 78-81.
73. *Vide* H C Raychaudhuri, *Political History of Ancient India*, p. 111.
74. *Ibid.*

# Appendix II

# Reappraisal of the Evidence Relating to the *Aśvamedha* of Samudragupta

I

That Samudragupta performed *aśvamedha* admits of no doubt as there is definite evidence in its favour. Samudragupta was a great conqueror as is evident from his large-scale conquests, both in northern and southern India mentioned in the Allahabad pillar inscription (No. 1), and, according to strict śāstric injunctions, conquest is a pre-requisite for the performance of that sacrifice. He was a follower of brahmanical religion, which prescribes performance of an *aśvamedha* for a king who is keen for obtaining the status of *samrāṭ* (paramount sovereign).[1] His successors refer to him as performer of horse-sacrifice. In the Poona copperplate inscription (No. 82) of the Vākāṭaka queen, Prabhāvatīgupta, daughter of the Imperial Gupta king Chandragupta II, Samudragupta has been referred to as performer of many horse-sacrifices. He issued *Aśvamedha* type of coins,[2] which show on the obverse, in front of a *yūpa*, the sacrificial horse – the most important item relating to this sacrifice, and bear the legend *rājādhirājaḥ pṛithivīṁ vijitya divaṁ jayaty=āhṛita-vājimedhaḥ* (king of kings after conquering the earth, conquers heaven); a few coins bear *pṛithivim=avitvā* (protecting the earth) instead of *pṛithivīṁ vijitya*. On the reverse is shown a female figure identified by most scholars as chief-queen,[3] who plays a significant role in this ritual, holding a *chowrie*, and the legend *aśvamedha–parākramaḥ*, i.e. whose valour is established by (the performance of) the horse-sacrifice. He gifed a large number of cows and a huge amount of gold, as mentioned in the Gupta epigraphs (Nos. 1, 3, 4, 14), which is also an important feature of *aśvamedha*. A sealing of unknown provenance in the British Museum Collection shows a horse with a *yūpa* and the legend *parākramaḥ*.[4] *Parākrama* is a title of Samudragupta, and the sealing belongs to him, and the presence of the horse before *yūpa* shows that it is related with his *aśvamedha*. D R Bhandarkar is of the view that the sealing 'must have been originally attached to some document dispatched from Samudragupta's Sacrificial Hall'.[5] It does not seem to have been an official seal as the official seals of the Imperial Guptas invariably bear the *garuḍa* insignia.

## II

As no model of *aśvamedha* type of coins was available to Samudragupta, the type being first introduced by him, it cannot be said that he copied an earlier type, and as such there should not be any doubt that he issued such coins to celebrate his performing the *aśvamedha*. The epigraphs of his successors categorically mention him as performer of horse-sacrifice. Kumāragupta I also issued *Aśvamedha* type of. coins,[6] but in his case, while there is a possibility that he issued such coins on performing the *aśvamedha*,[7] it is possible to suggest that such coins were issued by him merely in imitation of the coin-type of his illustrious grandfather, Samudragupta, without himself performing that sacrifice.[8] B N Mukherjee's reading of the inscriptions on the stone horse from Khairagarh in the Lucknow Museum provides evidence of Kumāragupta's performing a horse-sacrifice.

It is a matter of debate whether the *aśvamedha* type of coins were issued as tokens for distribution as *dakshiṇā* (gift) to the brāhmaṇas participating as priests in the horse-sacrifice,[9] or formed part of regular coinage. Since there is more than one variety of *aśvamedha* coins, some scholars suggest that these were produced in different mints, and opine that they would not have been meant for offering *dakshiṇā* to the priests, for if they were meant for that purpose then they should have been produced from one and the same mint. This could be so; but it would have been the number of the coins to be minted as also some other factors that would have been responsible for the use of one mint or more than one mint, rather than the consideration whether they were tokens meant for *dakshiṇā* or coins to be used for economic transactions. The possibility of issuing two varieties of coins from a single mint cannot be ruled out.

The Allahabad pillar inscription, at least the preserved part of it, does not mention Samudragupta's horse-sacrifice. It is generally agreed upon by scholars that if his horse-sacrifice had been performed before the engraving of the said inscription, then, being a very important achievement, it must have been recorded in it, as it has been done in the inscriptions of his successors. This suggests, as most scholars also believe, that the sacrifice was performed after the recording of this inscription; it seems unlikely that it was recorded in the mutilated portion of the text of that epigraph.

Most probably, Samudragupta performed the *aśvamedha* after completing his conquest of northern and southern India.[10] D R Bhandarkar is of the opinion that after the conquest in south India, on his journey back to Pāṭaliputra, he along with the sacrificial steed halted for some time at Kauśāmbī, the meeting point of the great 'arteries of communication in India' and it was then that the panegyrics were recorded on the Aśokan pillar (which was long after shifted to Allahabad where it now stands) so that his fame may long endure. From there, Bhandarkar adds, the Gupta ruler proceeded to Pāṭaliputra, where, the final rituals relating to *aśvamedha* were performed.[11] However, if Samudragupta marched through eastern coast and, after reaching Kāñchī, returned through the same route, as is the most probable and most accepted view, then Kauśāmbī would not have been on his route to Pāṭaliputra, unless he made a change in the route of his return journey from that of his forward journey. Bhandarkar assumes that Samudragupta had been marching with the sacrificial steed from Pāṭaliputra throughout his campaign in south India, and brought it back with him to Pāṭaliputra after his victorious march.

S R Goyal opines that the Allahabad pillar inscription was engraved when the *aśvamedha* was in progress, as, according to the *śāstras*, on the occasion of *aśvamedha*, the description of battles was necessary; he even labels the pillar bearing the inscription as *śobhā-yūpa*.[12] P L Gupta states that from a line in the Allahabad pillar inscription, it can be said that Samudragupta was planning to perform *aśvamedha*.[13] Ashvini Agrawal opines that the Prayāga *praśasti* was composed to be sung at the time of the *aśvamedha*.[14] But the inscription is partly in verse and partly in prose. If it were meant to be sung, then the whole inscription could have been composed in verse, particularly as Harisheṇa, the composer of the *praśasti,* as evinced by the verses in the epigraph, was a highly talented poet.

V C Pandey and Anup Pandey[15] are of the view that Samudragupta had performed the horse-sacrifice before the engraving of the Allahabad pillar inscription, and its performance was mentioned in the beginning lines of the inscription, which are mutilated. They believe that the gifting of hundreds of thousands of cows mentioned in the Allahabad Pillar Inscription is related to this sacrifice. Further, they find a reference to the *dīkshā* ritual in *mantra-dīkshā* in line 26 of the epigraph, and refer to *Āpastamba*, according to which the performer of this sacrifice was to undergo such a ritual. They also suggest that in the inscription (as per their reading) there occurs *pravitata* which seems to refer to the *govitata* sacrifice—a kind of *aśvamedha* sacrifice, which, being much cumbersome, was very rarely preformed, and as such has been referred to in the epigraph as one that was long in abeyance. However, as pointed out by Ashvini Agrawal, there is hardly any possibility of reading *pravitata* in the inscription.[16]

M K Dhavalikar[17] suggests that since the coins of *Aśvamedha* type do not bear the name of Samudragupta who performed the sacrifice and instead bear the legend *aśvamedha-parākramaḥ,* they should be taken as coins issued not by him, but by Chandragupta II to commemorate the *aśvamedha* performed by Samudragupta. This, however, is not acceptable, as the coins bear the title *parākrama,* which was so peculiar to Samudragupta that there cannot be any possibility of misunderstanding about the authorship of these coins. Moreover, if they would have been issued by Chandragupta II with a view to commemorating the performance of the *aśvamedha* by his father, then as a commemorator, his name, or at least his *āditya* title *Vikramāditya,* should have been recorded. We may state that despite the fact that a large number of scholars consider Chandragupta-Kumāradevī type of coins as issued by Samudragupta to commemorate his parents, we do not agree with that view mainly because neither the name of that Gupta ruler, nor his typical *viruda* as commemorator occurs on such coins (Appendix I). It would be unfair to deprive Samudragupta of the authorship of the coin-type as it bears the device and legend pertaining to his performance of *aśvamedha,* about which there is no doubt, and also as it gives his typical title, *parākrama,* and take it as issued by Chandragupta II, neither whose name nor whose title occurs on the coins.

## III

The epithet *chir=otsann=āśvamedh=āharttā* occurs on Samudragupta's Nālandā (No. 3) and Gaya (No. 4) plates, which are not original ones but, in all probability, partly copied from the damaged original plates and partly restored with the help of the copperplate inscriptions of one of his successors. It is also met with in the Bilsad inscription of Kumāragupta I (No. 14), and in the Bihar pillar inscription (No. 35), variously ascribed to Skandagupta or Purugupta or to one of the successors of the latter (Chapter 11). The expression has been taken by some scholars to mean as 'performer of horse-sacrifice which had been long in abeyance'.[18] This translation is not acceptable as it is not historically correct to say that horse-sacrifice had been long in abeyance. As H C Raychaudhuri points out, '... the *aśvamedha* was celebrated by several kings during the interval which elapsed from the time of Pushyamitra Śuṅga to that of Samudragupta, e.g., Pārāśarīputra Sarvatāta, Sātakarṇi the husband of Nāyanikā, Vāsishṭhīputra Ikshvāku Śrī-Chāṁtamūla, Devavarman Śālaṅkāyana, Pravarasena I Vākāṭaka, Śiva-Skandavarman Pallava, and the Nāga kings of the House of Bhāraśivas'.[19] Of these, Pushyamitra is known to have performed two horse-sacrifices,[20] Pravarasena I,[21] four, and the Bhāraśivas, ten.[22] Raychaudhuri further states, 'It is probable, however, that the court poets of the Guptas knew little about these monarchs.'[23] We, like some other scholars, however, feel that they must have known at least about some, if not all, of those rulers, particularly about the ones who were their near contemporaries. No king known to Indian history has better claims to the title of *aśvamedha-yājī* than Samudragupta,[24] and one could argue that the epithet, though not historically correct, was ascribed to the Gupta emperor with a view to glorifying him. But a more suitable interpretation of *chir=otsann=āśvamedh =āharttā* met with in the Gupta epigraphs than the one given above can be offered. But before it is discussed in the next paragraph, another interpretation proposed by some scholars may be mentioned. V S Pathak[25] and J Agrawal[26] take *chir=otsanna* to mean not as 'long in abeyance', but as 'long protracted', i.e. which lasted for a long period of time. It is true that this is a feature of the *aśvamedha* sacrifice, yet it is difficult to agree with this translation in the present context, as the fact that *aśvamedha* is a long lasting ritual must have been well known to the people, and so there was no need to state the obvious; beside stating this would not add to the glory of the king.

D R Bhandarkar points out[27] that in the *Śatapatha Brāhmaṇa*,[28] there is a mention of *utsanna-yajña*. In it is stated: *utsanna-yajña iva vā esha yad=aśvamedhaḥ kiṁ vā hyetasya kkriyate kiṁ vā na*, 'Verily what is (called) *aśvamedha* is, as it were, a decayed sacrifice, because something thereof is performed and something not.' In the *Taittirīya-saṁhitā*,[29] it is stated: *utsanna-yajño vai esha yad=aśvamedhaḥ*. Sāyaṇa explains that *aśvamedha* is called *utsanna-yajña* because some parts (*avayava*) of it were either utterly lost (*vinashṭa*) or completely forgotten (*ativismṛita*).[30] Bhandarkar, accepting Sāyaṇa's commentary, attempts to explains as to how Samudragupta was in a position to perform *aśvamedha* in its full detail. According to him, perhaps, Vedic lore was better preserved in south India than in the north India, and Samudragupta, in the course of his south Indian expedition, was able to recover from there such elements of sacrifice as had been forgotten in north India.[31] It is difficult to agree with this view. Even if it is accepted that vedic rituals were better preserved in south India during the Gupta period, Samudragupta could very well have invited vedic scholars from there, as from other places, honouring them in various ways and offering them the lure of sumptuous *dakshiṇā*, and with their guidance, got collected all the details regarding the rituals relating to the sacrifice. Moreover, before Samudragupta, some south Indian kings, as stated above, are known to have performed *aśvamedha*, and if full details regarding the performance of the sacrifice were available in south India, then they would have performed the sacrifice in accordance with all the details, and therefore the use of the epithet *chir=otsann=āśvamedh=āharttā* in that sense would not be quite appropriate for Samudragupta.

The evidence of *Śatapatha Brāhmaṇa* mentioned above shows that even in the period when it was composed while some *aśvamedhas* were performed strictly following śāstric injunctions in all their details, others, due to certain reasons, such as constraint of time and resources, could not be performed in that manner. As stated above, the *Taittirīya-saṁhitā* mentions a type of *aśvamedha* as *utsanna-yajña*; it, however, does not state why it is so designated. It is the commentator, Sāyaṇa, who lived in the second half of the fourteenth century AD,[32] more than two millennia after the composition of that text, who explains the term *utsanna-yajña* as one regarding which some parts of śāstric injunctions are utterly lost or completely forgotten. This, in our view, reflects the situation that existed during the time of the commentator rather than in the time of the composition of the *Taittirīya-saṁhitā*. We are of the opinion that some kings performed the *aśvamedha* following śāstric injunctions in their full details, while others did not or could not perform it in that way. The latter type was known as *utsanna-yajña*. The reason for not performing sacrifices with complete details was not because some of the injunctions had been lost or forgotten, but because of certain constraints such as of time and resources. But by the time of Sāyaṇa, so far as his knowledge went, some of the details regarding the performance of the sacrifice had been either lost or forgotten and therefore he interpreted the expression in that sense. J Agrawal[33] points out that in the *Taittirīya-saṁhitā*, the term *utsanna* has been applied not only to the *aśvamedha* but also to *agnichayana* ritual, and in the *Śatapatha–brāhmaṇa* for *chāturmāsya* (ii. v. 2. 48) and for *aśvamedha* (XII. 3. 3. 6). In the *Kāṭhaka* and *Maitrāyiṇī-saṁhitās*, he points out, the word *utsanna* has been used for *vājapeya*. Agrawal rightly observes that it is impossible to believe that Vedic rites of such outstanding importance as the *aśvamedha, vājapeya* and *chāturmāsya* had gone into disuse at that point of time when these works were composed.[34]

We are of the view that the expression *chir=otsann=āśmedh=āharttā* in the context of Samudragupta is meant to convey that he performed *aśvamedha* sacrifice in full details meticulously, and that before him, for a long time (*chira*) the sacrifices had not been performed in that way. This interpretation would absolve the Gupta panegyrists of the charge of being ignorant of the *aśvamedha* sacrifice performed by near contemporary and earlier kings.

## IV

In earlier texts like the brāhmaṇas[35] and the śrauta-sūtras,[36] the paramount sovereign alone was entitled to perform *aśvamedha*, but later, even feudatories are known to have done so,[37] and the *aśvamedha* came to be associated with a variety of purposes, such as 'attainment of a son' (*putra-prāpti*)[38] and washing away of sins.[39] Despite this, *aśvamedha* remained a royal privilege; other people, howsoever prosperous or powerful they might have been, were not entitled to perform this sacrifice.[40] However, in the case of Samudragupta, the representation of a horse on *Aśvamedha* type of coins and the legend *aśvamedha-parākramaḥ*, i.e., 'who performed *aśvamedha* through his valour', and the circular legend stating that he performed the sacrifice after conquering the earth, would show that the horse was actually let loose and the sacrifice was performed in accordance with the śāstric injunctions and in the capacity of a paramount sovereign.[41]

Some scholars relate Samudragupta's Lyrist (*Vīṇā-vādaka*) type of coins[42] with his *aśvamedha* sacrifice. According to the śāstric injunction, in that sacrifice lute-players who sang to the lute, included *rājanya*. It has been suggested[43] that Samudragupta himself performed that act in his own *aśvamedha*. In the *aśvamedha* the *rājanya* sings to the lute verses composed by him and it is opined that some verses in the Prayāga *praśasti* were meant for that purpose.[44] However, if he had done so, and if the horse sacrifice had been performed before the engraving of the Allahabad Pillar Inscription then, as stated above, this would have been mentioned in that inscription; a proper place for the mention of his performing the act of *vīṇā-vādaka* in his horse-sacrifice in the inscription would have been where it has been stated that in musical skill, he surpassed Nārada and Tumburu.

V

In the Poona copperplate of Prabhāvatīguptā (No. 82), the widowed queen of the Vākāṭaka king Rudrasena II, and the daughter of Gupta emperor Chandragupta II, Samudragupta, her grandfather, is mentioned as performer of 'more than one' horse-sacrifice (*anek=āśvamedha-yājī*). As seen above, some other kings, who were much inferior to Samudragupta, are said to have performed many *aśvamedhas*, and one such king, Mādhavavarman of Vishṇukuṇḍin dynasty, is credited with the performance of as many as eleven *aśvamedhas*.[45] *Aśvamedha* sacrifice, in its original form, is long protracted, involving huge expenditure, requiring mighty forces and great resources, entailing large-scale campaigns and warfare, and as such, performing of eleven horse-sacrifices by Mādhavavarman, who is not known to have been a very powerful king, seems incredible. Bhandarkar, significantly, cited evidence from the *Mahābhārata* where Vyāsa is stated to have said to Yudhishṭhira that by increasing *dakshiṇā* threefold,[46] the sacrifice would become threefold. It would seem that the Vishṇukuṇḍin king paid eleven times the *dakshiṇā* that he chose to pay as fee for one sacrifice, and thereby claimed to have performed eleven sacrifices. V V Mirashi[47] does not agree with the view of Bhandarkar that the Vishṇukuṇḍin king was not so powerful and resourceful as to have actually performed eleven sacrifices, and as such in most cases merely paid some *dakshiṇā* to the priests in the name of horse-sacrifice. He argues that if merely by paying *dakshiṇā* in the name of horse-sacrifice one would become entitled to be called as 'one who has performed horse-sacrifice' then 'there would have been many more instances of multiple *aśvamedhas*... [and] people would not have attached any value to such fictitious *aśvamedhas*'.[48] But, as stated above, in course of time, even in the ancient period, *aśvamedha* had lost its original importance, and besides being performed for establishing the status of a paramount sovereign, it also came to be performed for such purposes as attainment of a son or washing away sins.

D R Bhandarkar tries to justify the statement *anek=āśvamedha=yājī* for Samudragupta in the Vākāṭaka inscriptions by suggesting that Samudragupta performed only one horse-sacrifice solemnly, but distributed *dakshiṇā* many times more than he doled out for one sacrifice.[49] We have seen above, while describing the *aśvamedha* type of coins, that the legend on some coins has *avitvā* ('after protecting') and on others *vijitya* ('after conquering'). Some scholars consider that the coins bearing two different legends should be taken as issued from two different mints and on two different occasions, as indicative of more than one sacrifice performed by him. Since neither Samudragupta's own records, nor those of his descendants mention him as performer of many (more than one) horse-sacrifices, and merely refer to him as one who performed horse-sacrifice, we feel that Samudragupta performed only one horse-sacrifice, and that the statement in the Vākāṭaka records need not be taken as a historical fact. As regards the difference in the legend on *Aśvamedha* type of coins, there would not have been any bar in issuing coins with two different legends as related to one and the same horse-sacrifice, either from the same mint or from two different mints. Ashvini Agrawal,[50] who also does not believe that Samudragupta performed many sacrifices, feels that in mentioning him as performer of many horse sacrifices, the Vākāṭaka records either exaggerate his achievements, or such statement is the result of scribal error. Since the Vākāṭaka records, which refer to Samudragupta as a performer of more than one horse-sacrifice, make glaring mistakes in detailing the Gupta genealogy and ascribe many epithets typical of Samudragupta, to Chandragupta II, their evidence in this respect cannot be relied upon. It cannot be considered as a scribal error, as the scribe normally would not, of his own, have added *aneka* in the epigraph. It appears that since Pravarasena I Vākāṭaka has been mentioned in the

Vākāṭaka records as one who performed four horse-sacrifices, Prabhāvatīguptā did not like to portray her grandfather, Samudragupta, who certainly was mightier than that Vākāṭaka king, in lesser light than him. She felt that ascribing him less than four sacrifices would place him in a lower position than the Vākāṭaka king, and giving a figure more than four would be a great exaggeration and would not go well with the people, and so the word *aneka* (more than one) was deliberately chosen. If Samudragupta had performed many horse-sacrifices, then his successors, who mention him as *chir=otsann=āśvamedh=āharttā*, would have also called him *anek=āśvamedh=āharttā,* as in our view, the latter title would reflect no less, nay even more, significant achievement than the former. Incidentally, we may recollect that a descendant of Pushyamitra āuṅga, in his epigraph, proudly refers to that ruler as *dvir=aśvamedha-yājī*, 'who had performed two horse-sacrifices'.[51] S R Goyal[52] is of the opinion that Samudragupta performed a few *aśvamedhas* of abbreviated type, followed by an elaborate one after he had made extensive conquests, and that while his successors took pride in his performing elaborate *aśvamedha*, Prabhāvatīguptā laid emphasis on his performing several *aśvamedhas*, particularly as Pravarasena Vākāṭaka has been referred to as a performer of four *aśvamedhas*.

An almost life-size stone horse, discovered near Khairagarh in Kheri district, bears an inscription in Gupta characters which was read as *...ddaguttassa deyadhamma*,[53] (i.e., 'religious benefactions of *...dragupta*'). Bhandarkar, like some other scholars, restored the missing letters at the beginning of the inscription as *Samu*, and took the horse as a representation of the sacrificial horse of Samudragupta, in stone. He also opined that after performing the horse-sacrifice, representations of sacrificial horse 'were put up by Samudragupta at important places in his empire as souvenirs of this celebration'.[54] It is difficult to agree with the view of the learned scholar. Firstly, Khairagarh, where the stone horse has been found, does not seem to have been a place of much political or religious significance in the Gupta period. Secondly, no such representation of the horse has been found in such important cities as Pāṭaliputra and Ujjayinī, and therefore it is too much to conclude from a single representation of a horse sculptured in stone that such ones were put at different places of importance. The missing letters at the beginning of the inscription on the stone horse, it has been suggested, could as well be restored as *Chaṁ or Iṁ*, and the name could as well have been Chandragupta or Indragupta, who could very well have been a private individual and not necessarily a king. Had the horse been related to *aśvamedha* of Samudragupta, then some indication of it would have been given in the inscription on it, by inscribing something like *aśvamedha-parākramaḥ*, which occurs on the *aśvamedha* type of coins of that ruler, rather than merely the words *deya-dhamma* (pious gift). Thirdly, the language of the inscription, as read by Bhandarkar and some other scholars is Prakrit, and not Sanskrit. Bhandarkar says that the use of Prakrit language need not be a hurdle in its being ascribed to the Gupta king, as even in the Gupta period, that language continued to be the language of the masses.[55] But the inscriptions of the Imperial Gupta kings, and the legends on their coins and seals are in Sanskrit, and not in Prakrit. If the inscription in question belonged to the Gupta emperor Samudragupta, then it is not understandable as to why Sanskrit has not been used for it, more so when it is related to horse-sacrifice, a typical Brahmanical ritual of vedic origin, in the performance of which all the *mantras* to be recited are in Sanskrit.

A new dimension has been added to the identification of the king and the purpose for which the stone horse, referred to above, was stalled, by the reading of the inscriptions on the stone horse by B N Mukherjee.[56] According to him, there are three inscriptions—one on the neck in the Gupta Brāhmī, and two in the *Śaṅkha-lipi* on the back and the buttock respectively. The Brāhmī inscription which was read by most of the scholars as *...dda Guttasa deyadhamma* is read by Mukherjee as *Aśvarasa yajño*, which refers to horse-sacrifice. Each of the two other inscriptions in the '*Śaṅkha-lipi*' is read by him as *Mahendrādityaḥ*. He takes the stone horse as a replica of the sacrificial horse of Kumāragupta I whose title was *Mahendrāditya*. This reading has the merit that it refers to the *aśvamedha*, it gives the title of the king who performed the sacrifice, and also that the language used is Sanskrit. But this does not explain why *Śaṅkha-lipi* was used for the two inscriptions, instead of the Brāhmī, which has been used in all inscriptions of the Guptas. It is still not clear why Khairagarh was chosen for installing the stone horse. It may be suggested that it was originally installed at Naimisha, an important religious centre located in the neighbourhood of Khairagarh, and transported to Khairagarh from there at a later period. Mukherjee's reading is accepted, it would provide an unflinching evidence regarding the performance of horse-sacrifice by Kumāragupta I, and the inscribed horse would no more be taken as an evidence related to Samudragupta's *aśvamedha*.

## NOTES AND REFERENCES

1. *Śatapatha-brāhmaṇa*, as referred to by H C Raychaudhuri, *Political History of Ancient India*, p. 53.
2. A S Altekar, *Coinage of the Gupta Empire*, p. 67ff.
3. C D Chatterjee (*Journal of the Numismatic Society of India*, XXXVII, pp. 86-87) does not agree with the view that the female figure stands for the queen on the grounds that: (i) In the śrauta-sūtras there is no mention of a queen holding *chaurie* in her right hand and *pāśa* in the left, (ii) the object before the female figure is like *śakti* and not *sūchī* as is mentioned in the works detailing horse-sacrifice, and (iii) in the *aśvamedha* the role of the Chief queen is hateful and vulgar and her husband would not have liked to portray her in that context. P L Gupta (*Gupta Sāmrājya*, p. 31) agrees with Chatterjee and accepts his suggestion that the *chowrie*-bearing female figure should be identified as a goddess and not a queen. However, Altekar opines that the important role the queen played in the ritual relating to horse sacrifice justifies the identification of the female figure with her and the identification suggested by him is generally followed by scholars.
4. E J Rapson, *Journal of the Royal Asiatic Society of Great Britain and Ireland*, 1901, p. 102.
5. D R Bhandarkar, *Corpus Inscriptionum Indicarum*, III, p. 41.
6. A S Altekar, *The Coinage of the Gupta Empire*, pp. 200ff.
7. A S Altekar is emphatic about Kumāragupta's having performed at least one horse-sacrifice (*The Coinage of the Gupta Empire*, p. 200). The ascription of the performance to Chandragupta II, on the basis of the wrong reading of the inscription by J Ratnakar on a stone horse found in a village near Vārāṇasī (*Indian Historical Quarterly*, III, pp. 719ff) has rightly been rejected by scholars. See, e.g., R C Majumdar, *The Vākāṭaka-Gupta Age*, p. 169, n. 1.
8. Kumāragupta I also issued Lyrist type of coins (Altekar, *The Coinage of the Gupta Empire*, pp. 211ff). It is difficult to say whether he was a skilled musician or merely imitated the coin-type of Samudragupta.
9. V A Smith, *Journal of the Royal Asiatic Soceity of Great Britain and Ireland*, 1889, p. 67; J Allan, *Catalogue of the Coins of the Gupta Dynasties and of Śaśāṅka, King of Gauḍa, in the British Museum, London*, p. xxxi.
10. D R Bhandarkar, *Corpus Inscriptionum Indicarum*, III, p. 35; Ashvini Agrawal, *Rise and Fall of the Imperial Guptas*, p. 125.
11. D R Bhandarkar, *Corpus Inscriptionum Indicarum*, III, p. 35.
12. S R Goyal, *Gupta Sāmrājya kā Itihāsa*, p. 159.
13. P L Gupta, *Gupta Sāmrājya*, p. 274. He, however, does not specify the line.
14. Ashvini Agrawal, *Rise and Fall of the Imperial Guptas*, p. 127.
15. V C Pandey and Anup Pandey, *A New History of Ancient India*, 1998, p. 371.
16. Ashvini Agrawal, *Rise and Fall of the Imperial Guptas*, p. 127.
17. *Journal of the Numismatic Society of India*, XX (ii), p. 175-77.
18. J F Fleet, *Corpus Inscriptionum Indicarum*, III, pp. 44, 54; R G Basak, *History of North-Eastern India*, 2nd ed., 1967, p. 36.

19. H C Raychaudhuri, *Political History of Ancient India*, p. 484.
20. The Ayodhyā Stone Inscription of Dhanadeva, D C Sircar, *Select Inscriptions*, I, pp. 94-95.
21. Basim Copperplate Inscription of Vindhyaśakti II, D C Sircar, *Select Inscriptions*, I, pp. 430ff.
22. D R Bhandarkar, *Corpus Inscriptionum* Indicarum, III, p. 37. To these may be added a king named Śīlavarman, ruling in the area around Kalsi in Dehradun district, Uttarakhand in the third century AD who is said to have performed at least four horse-sacrifices. The inscription on bricks used for the construction of the sacrificial altar reads—*chaturthasy=āśvamedhasya chityo'yaṁ Śīlavarmaṇaḥ* (T N Ramchandran, *Journal of Indian History*, XXII, p. 100).
23. H C Raychaudhuri, *Political History of Ancient India*, p. 484.
24. R C Majumdar, in *Comprehensive History of India*, III (i), p. 32.
25. V S Pathak, *Journal of the Numismatic Society of India*, XIX, pp. 14ff.
26. J Agrawal, as referred to by Ashvini Agrawal, *Rise and Fall of the Imperial Guptas*, pp. 95, 127.
27. D R Bhandarkar, *Corpus Inscriptionum Indicarum*, III, p. 38.
28. *Kāṇḍa* XIII, *vide* D R Bhandarkar, *Corpus Inscriptionum Indicarum*, III, p. 38.
29. *Taittirīya-saṁhitā*, V. 4. 12. 3 *vide* D R Bhandarkar, *Corpus Inscriptionum Indicarum*, III, p. 38.
30. As referred to by D R Bhandarkar, *Corpus Inscriptionum Indicarum*, III, p. 38.
31. *Ibid.*
32. K A N Sastri, *A History of South India*, 3rd ed., Oxford, 1966, p. 266.
33. H R Gupta (ed.), *Sir Jadunath Sarkar Commemmoration Volume*, II, pp. 10-13.
34. *Ibid.*, p. 13.
35. For example, *Śatapatha-brāhmaṇa*, XIII. 1. 6. 3; *vide* D R Bhandarkar, *Corpus Inscriptionum Indicarum*, III, p. 35.
36. *Baudhāyana-śrauta-sūtra*, XV. 1. 1; *Āpastamba-śrauta-sūtra*, XX. 1. 1, as referred to by D R Bhandarkar, *Corpus Inscriptionum Indicarum*, III, p. 36.
37. D R Bhandarkar, *Corpus Inscriptionum Indicarum*, III, p. 39.
38. For example, *Rāmāyaṇa*, 1. 12. 3, 9, 12, as referred to by D R Bhandarkar, *Corpus Inscriptionum Indicarum*, III, p. 36n.
39. *Mahābhārata*, XIV. 18. 16, as referred to by D R Bhandarkar, *Corpus Inscriptionum Indicarum*, III, p. 36.
40. D C Sircar, *Indian Historical Quarterly*, IV, pp. 272-73.
41. R C Majumdar, in *Comprehensive History of India*, III(i), p. 33.
42. A S Altekar, *The Coinage of the Gupta Empire*, pp. 73ff.
43. Ashvini Agrawal, *Rise and Fall of the Imperial Guptas*, pp. 127ff.
44. *Ibid.*, p. 127.
45. E Hultzsch, Ramtirtham Plates of Indravarman, *Epigraphia Indica*, XI, pp. 133ff, at p. 134, line 3.
46. *Mahābhārata*, XIV. 88. 13-15, *vide* D R Bhandarkar, *Corpus Inscriptionum Indicarum*, III, p. 40.

47. *Journal of the Epigraphical Society of India,* IX, p. 50.
48. *Ibid.*
49. D R Bhandarkar, *Corpus Inscriptionum Indicarum,* III, p. 40.
50. Ashvini Agrawal, *Rise and Fall of the Imperial Guptas,* p. 126.
51. D C Sircar, *Select Inscriptions,* I, pp. 94-95.
52. S R Goyal, *The Imperial Guptas,* p. 241.
53. V A Smith, *Journal of the Royal Asiatic Society of Great Britain and Ireland,* 1893, p. 98; D R Bhandarkar, *Corpus Inscriptionum Indicarum,* III, p. 41. Allan (*Catalogue of the Coins of the Gupta Dynasties and of Śaśāṅka, King of Gauḍa, in the British Museum,* London, p. xxxi) reads the legend as ... *adaguttasa deyadhamma* and he, like Bhandarkar, suggests that it refers to Samudragupta's horse-sacrifice.
54. D R Bhandarkar, *Corpus Inscriptionum Indicarum,* III, p. 41.
55. *Ibid.*
56. See 'Decipherment of the Shell Script', *Saṅgrahālaya Purātattva Patrikā,* No. 31, pp. 1-46 and plates.

# Appendix III

## King Chandra of the Mehrauli Pillar Inscription

The achievements of King Chandra have been recorded in Brāhmī script of the Gupta period on an iron pillar (No. 12), 7.21 m in height and about six tonnes in weight, standing near village Mehrauli on the southern outskirts of Delhi. The text, from its first reading, as also its interpretation have undergone several modifications. The epigraph does not give the genealogy of King Chandra, nor does it mention the name of his father, which makes the problem of the identification of the king difficult and controversial. In identifying the king with a known ruler, it should be examined as to whom the achievements mentioned in the inscription about the king apply the best, and the evidence of the script of the inscription, which is undoubtedly of the Gupta period, should also be taken into consideration.[1] The following information is available from the epigraph about the king:

(i) His name was Chandra.

(ii) He was dead when the inscription was engraved, as is clear from the expression that his bodily form does not exist, only his fame remains.[2]

(iii) He acquired sovereignty by the prowess of his own arms.

(iv) He ruled for a fairly long time.

(v) He defeated a confederacy of enemy kings in Vaṅga.

(vi) He conquered the Bāhlikas, crossing the seven mouths of the Sindhu.
(vii) The southern sea was perfumed by his prowess.
(viii) He was a Vaishṇava and raised a flag-staff for Vishṇu on the Vishṇupada hill.[3]

Scholars have suggested identification of King Chandra variously with Chandragupta Maurya, Chandra-Kanishka, one of the two Nāga kings – Sadāchandra and Chandrāṁśa, one of the three Gupta kings—Chandragupta I, Samudragupta and Chandragupta II, Chandravarman of the Susunia inscription, younger brother of Mihirakula, and Devarakshita of the Khaḍga family. One scholar considers it impossible to identify him.[4] The various identifications of King Chandra suggested by the scholars, will be discussed below one by one, highlighting the main arguments put forth by them in support of their views as also their merits and demerits.

## CHANDRAGUPTA MAURYA

B Prasad[5] (the same as B P Sinha) and H C Seth[6] pointed out that Chandragupta Maurya fulfils what the Mehrauli pillar inscription states about the achievements of King Chandra. The Maurya emperor made extensive conquests. His empire extended as far south as Mysore, and by defeating Seleucus, he acquired territories even beyond Afghanistan in the north-west. He had a fairly long reign (*c*. 324-299 BC) and he is mentioned as Chandra in the *Mudrārākshasa*. But the script of the Mehrauli pillar inscription is not of the Mauryan period, but that of the Gupta. Prasad suggested that Chandragupta II, the destroyer of the Śakas, got this *praśasti* engraved out of respect for Chandragupta Maurya, who had overthrown the Yavana rule in north-western India, and defeated the Yavana invader, Seleucus. H C Seth[7] opines that the pillar with the *praśasti* engraved on it was erected by Chandragupta Maurya, in whose reign, as the evidence of the *Arthaśāstra* shows, metallurgy was highly advanced. In course of time, the epigraph got effaced, and was again recorded by Samudragupta out of admiration for that Maurya king, in the script of his own time, i.e. Gupta Brāhmī. It is, however, unbelievable that a Gupta king, separated from Chandragupta of the Maurya dynasty by about 700 years, and unconnected with him by any family relationship, would have got engraved the *praśasti* for him with a view to perpetuating his memory.

Besides, Chandragupta Maurya is known as a Jaina who died penancing as a devout Jain, whereas King Chandra of the Mehrauli pillar inscription was a Vaishṇava. B Prasad's argument that Chandragupta Maurya would have been a Vaishṇava, who later became a Jaina, does not hold good as the *praśasti*, posthumous as it is, is expected to refer to the religion to which the king had leanings during the last days of his life.

## KANISHKA

R C Majumdar[8] pointed out that a Khotanese manuscript states that Chandra Kanishka in the kingdom of Bāhlika, was the 'King of Jambudvīpa'. Tradition speaks of Kanishka's attack on Pāṭaliputra and carrying off Aśvaghosha from there. His coins have been found as far as Orissa and Bengal, and there is a possibility that he might have conquered these territories. Kanishka's date may be later than the generally accepted view of the first century AD, and the posthumous inscription would have been engraved much after his death. Majumdar also stated that a type of Kushāṇa alphabet resemble early Gupta alphabets, and though Kanishka is known as a Buddhist, he has shown eclecticism in depicting the figures of deities belonging to different religious pantheons on his coins, and, as such, could have erected a flag-staff for Vishṇu.

As pointed out by G R Sharma,[9] the question of Kanishka's conquest of Balkh does not arise as he was the king of that region from the very beginning of his rule and the find of Kushāṇa coins in Bengal could be the result of trade contacts rather than the region being within his kingdom on account of his conquest of it. In the name Chandra-Kanishka met with in the Khotanese manuscript, Kanishka is the primary name, and Chandra a secondary epithet prefixed to it, whereas Chandra in the Mehrauli pillar inscription is the main and sole name. Chandra of the Mehrauli pillar inscription marched from the east to the north-west, while Kanishka's march of conquest was from the north-west to the south-east. Though Kanishka's coins depict deities of different pantheons, he is known as a devout Buddhist, while King Chandra is clearly mentioned as devoted to Vishṇu. Palaeographically the epigraph belongs not to the Kushāṇa but to the Gupta period. Later, Majumdar himself gave up the view of identifying King Chandra with Kanishka, in favour of his identification with Chandragupta II.[10]

## CHANDRAGUPTA I

J F Fleet,[11] R G Basak[12] and S K Aiyangar[13] identify King Chandra of the Mehrauli pillar inscription with Chandragupta I, the first *mahārājādhirāja* of the Gupta dynasty, who, in their view, could have achieved what is ascribed to King Chandra in the inscription.[14] His lineage, it is argued, was not given in the epigraph since his father and grandfather were feudatories (*mahārājas*). S K Aiyangar[15] believes that Chandragupta I marched across Malwa, Rajputana, Sindh and crossing seven mouths of Sindhu, defeated the Vāhlīkas and that he must have been a man of far greater achievements than ascribed to him by scholars who generally base their conclusion on the evidence of rarity (or absence, according to one view) of his coins and absence of his inscriptions.

But Chandragupta I's kingdom seems to have been confined to Prayāga on Gaṅgā, Sāketa and Magadha – the Gupta territory described in most of the Purāṇas (Chapter 3) to which the territory of the Lichchhavis was added as a result of his marriage with the Lichchhavi princess, Kumāradevī. The extensive conquests of Samudragupta in northern and southern India (No. 1) clearly show that his father's kingdom must have been quite small in comparison to that of King Chandra of the Mehrauli pillar inscription. Chandragupta I could hardly have been in a position to undertake campaigns of such magnitude as are mentioned in that inscription, and carve out an extensive territory for himself.

## CHANDRAVARMAN OF SUSUNIA INSCRIPTION

Some scholars[16] identify King Chandra with Chandravarman of Susunia (Bankura district) inscription (No. 59), wherein he is mentioned as son of Siṁhavarman, 'lord of Pushkaraṇa', as 'chief of the servants of Vishṇu' and as one who dedicated a *chakra* (wheel) to Chakrasvāmin (Vishṇu), while Chandra of the Mehrauli pillar inscription erected a flagstaff for Vishṇu (Vishṇu-*dhvaja*). A Mandasor inscription (No. 60) mentions Naravarman as a powerful and valiant ruler of Pushkaraṇa and as a son of Siṁhavarman and brother of Chandravarman. On the basis of the fact that both Susunia and Mandasor inscriptions mention Siṁhavarman as father of Chandravarman and both also mention Pushkaraṇa, King Chandravarman of the two inscriptions is taken by some scholars as referring to one and the same person. But the identification being highly conjectural is not acceptable. Neither of these inscriptions mentions any conquest made by Chandravarman. The panegyric of the Mehrauli pillar inscription giving Chandra the credit for the conquest of Vaṅga and Vāhlīkas cannot even remotely apply to him who was a mere chief with the title *mahārāja*,[17] whereas king Chandra of the Mehrauli pillar inscription has been mentioned as 'sole monarch', which seems to be a substitute for *mahārājādhirāja* for metrical exigencies. Pushkaraṇa of the Susunia inscription should be identified not with Pokurna (Pokharan in Jodhpur district) but with Pokaran, about 25 miles from Susunia.[18] King Chandravarman of the Susunia inscription seems to be identical with the homonym Āryāvarta ruler who, as per the Allahabad pillar inscription, was defeated by Samudragupta. Unlike the inscriptions of the Varman rulers, the Mehrauli pillar inscription does not provide the lineage of the ruling king; even the name of his father has not been mentioned in it.[19]

## SADĀCHANDRA OR CHANDRĀṀŚA

According to the purāṇas, there were Nāga dynasties ruling in the Yamuna valley and central India in the fourth century AD. The *Vishṇu-purāṇa*[20] refers to Nāga dynasties at Padmāvatī, Mathurā and probably also at Vidiśā. Two prominent Nāga kings Sadāchandra and Chandrāṁśa have Chandra as part of their names. According to H C Raychaudhuri,[21] either of the two, preferably the latter, and according to A V Venkatarama Aiyar,[22] the former should be identified with the Chandra of the Mehrauli pillar inscription. The kings, no doubt, belong to the early Gupta period and have Chandra as part of their name, but it does not seem that either of them was powerful enough to defeat the confederation of kings in Vaṅga and conquer the land of the Vāhlīkas. We have no idea whether or not they ruled for a long time and if they had won territories by the prowess of their own arms. Besides, the Nāgas were Śaivas while Chandra was a Vaishṇava. As seen above, Raychaudhuri criticizes H P Sastri's identification of King Chandra with Chandravarman of the Susunia inscription on the ground that a local ruler cannot be identified with the great conqueror of the Mehrauli pillar inscription. But this argument can very well be applied to his own suggestion that King Chandra should be identified either with Sadāchandra or with Chandrāṁśa.

## BROTHER OF MIHIRAKULA

Fleet,[23] though identified King Chandra with Chandragupta I yet also made an alternate suggestion that he may be identified with the unnamed brother of Mihirakula, who has been mentioned by Hiuen-tsang.[24] This identification is mainly based on the supposition that the name Mehrauli is derived from Mihirapurī, and that the town was named after Mihirakula. It is not known from any source that Mihirakula's brother was named Chandra, nor hat the made any of the conquests attributed to King Chandra.

## DEVARAKSHITA

B C Sen[25] points out that according to the Purāṇas, kings of the Devarakshita dynasty had hold over Puṇḍra (northern Bengal), Kosala, Oḍra and Tāmralipti, and also over sea-coasts. Sen interprets *tīrtvā sapta-mukhāni ena samare Sindhorjitā Vāhlīkā* in the Mehrauli pillar inscription to mean that King Chandra defeated the Vāhlīkas, who had crossed the seven mouths of the Indus.[26] Following Pargiter's view that Rakshita kings ruled after the Vindhyakas, Sen suggests that one of the Devarakshita rulers might have encountered the Vāhlīkas in the Vindhya region. This suggestion of Sen has hardly anything to commend, and has not been accepted by scholars. It may also be stated in passing that some purāṇas mention Devarakshita as a name and that he has been identified by some scholars with Chandragupta II who has been referred to as Devagupta in Vākāṭaka inscriptions (No. 83), and Devarāja in a Sanchi inscription of his general (No. 9).

## SAMUDRAGUPTA

The popular view, as will be shown below, has been that King Chandra of the Mehrauli pillar inscription should be identified with Chandragupta II. Allan,[27] however, pointed out the following difficulties in accepting this view:

(i) Unlike Gupta inscriptions, the Mehrauli pillar inscription does not detail any genealogy.

(ii) It is doubtful if the name of the king was Chandra.

(iii) Though the inscription refers to the erection of a Vishṇu-*dhvaja*, it does not give the king the title *parama-bhāgavata*, which is mentioned with the names of the Gupta kings in epigraphs and on coins.

(iv) The reference to 'the breeze of his prowess perfuming the southern seas' is more appropriate for Samudragupta than to Chandragupta II, and that

(v) It is doubtful if the script of the epigraph is of the fifth century AD, or even that the inscription belongs to a king of the Gupta dynasty.

As against Allan's arguments, it may be, and has been, said that the non-mention of genealogy and also that of the epithet *parama-bhāgavata* may be because of the consideration of metre, the epigraph being in verse. The Junagarh rock inscription of Skandagupta is also in verse and does not detail genealogy, or refer to him as *parama-bhāgavata*. Other arguments of Allan, too, are not incontrovertible, as will be shown below. While Allan merely suggested some similarities between the achievements of Samudragupta and King Chandra of the Mehrauli pillar inscription, Goyal turns the suggestion of Allan into a theory that Chandra of the Mehrauli inscription was Samudragupta, and forcefully supports it. According to him, the achievements of King Chandra mentioned in the Mehrauli pillar inscription suit Samudragupta more than any other king. He concludes that '... *all the facts* about the king mentioned in the Mehrauli inscription coincide with what we know about Samudragupta, *neatly, squarely and most justifiably*'[28] (italics ours). Goyal argues, '...it is not necessary to presume that the king mentioned in the inscription should be known to us by the name 'Chandra',[29] and in identifying the king more than the name 'Chandra', the facts mentioned about him in the inscription should be the basis of the identification'.[30] We, like many other scholars, are of the opinion that the foremost criterion for the identification of a king in history should be his name. Basham[31] observes: '... this is a memorial inscription, and as such one would expect a clear mention of the king commemorated'. The very purpose of recording a *praśasti* is to make lasting the name and fame of the king and if the name is not clearly stated, the very purpose of the *praśasti* is lost.[32] One comes to know the achievements of a king by his name, and not *vice versa*.[33] Moreover, 'the scribe may omit, magnify, emphasize or deemphasize the exploits of a king, but he could hardly ever alter his name beyond understandable limits, and that neither any inscription nor coin of the ruler, nor those of his successors speak of Samudragupta as Chandra'.[34] It is difficult to explain why the same king is called Chandra in the Mehrauli pillar inscription and Samudragupta in all other epigraphs. The method of finding out a known king whom the exploits mentioned in the Mehrauli pillar inscription can be attributed, ignoring his name, does not seem to be the right approach.[35] To this author so important is name for the identification of a king, that despite Allan's forceful arguments in favour of ascribing coins of the

Chandragupta I-Kumāradevī type to Samudragupta on typological grounds, he would not accept the view because they bear the names of Chandragupta, Kumāradevī and the Lichchhavi tribe, but not the name of Samudragupta.

Fleet translated the text to indicate that the name of the king was Chandra, but stated that an alternate translation of the passage *Chandrāhvena* etc could also be: '(and) who, carrying a beauty of countenance like (the beauty of) the full moon, had (in consequence) the name of Chandra'.[36] From this, Goyal[37] infers that the king's name would not have been Chandra, and the king was merely compared with Chandra, i.e. the moon, for the beauty of his face. Allan[38] too had thought of such a possibility. But the translation appears to be a forced one,[39] and as J Agrawal[40] points out, there is no word in the original inscription for 'in consequence', and if it is removed, as it should be, since there is no need for adding anything to make the translation intelligible, Chandra becomes a name. Comparing the countenance of a person, particularly a king with the moon is not uncommon in ancient literature and epigraphs. For example, in a Nasik inscription,[41] Gautamīputra Sātakarṇi's countenance is compared with the full moon. Kumāragupta I, in his coin-legends,[42] is compared with the moon. The word *āhva* (= name) suffixed to Chandra in the Mehrauli pillar inscription clearly shows that Chandra is the name of the king. The Mandasor inscription of Mālava Era 524, i.e. AD 467 (No. 36) refers to Chandragupta II as 'the very moon in the sky' and also one who was pleasant to look at like the new moon, and this would go well with the 'beauty of the full moon' used for him in the Mehrauli pillar inscription.[43] In the Lion-slayer type of Chandragupta II, he is called *Narendrachandra*, 'moon among kings'.[44] Another evidence put forth by Goyal in favour of Chandra not being the name of the king is Prinsep's reading[45] *dhāvena* in line 6 of the inscription and his suggestion that Dhāva (and not Chandra) could be the name of the king.[46] Allan[47] and D C Sircar[48] have shown that the first letter in what was read as *dhāvena* is quite different from the letter *dha*, which occurs six times in this very epigraph, and clearly resembles the letter *bha*, and the reading *bhāvena* very much suits the meaning of the text. With this reading, the existence of a king bearing name the Dhāva ceases to exist. It may also be stated that Dandekar[49] prefers to read it as *devena* and takes it to refer to Chandragupta II, who is known as Devarāja (No. 9) and Devagupta (No. 83).

In support of his view that Chandra was also another name of Samudragupta, Goyal[50] refers to Vāmana's *Kāvyālaṁkāra-sūtra-vṛitti*, according to which one Chandraprakāśa was a son of Chandragupta and had Vasubandhu as his minister. He, like some other scholars, identifies King Chandra with Chandragupta I, and Chandraprakāśa with Samudragupta, taking it as his second name. However, many scholars doubt this identification, and some outright reject it. Several distinguished monks with the name Vasubandhu are known, including one who took part in the Fourth Buddhist Council during the reign of Kanishka.[51] Some scholars[52] identify Chandragupta with Chandragupta II, and Chandraprakāśa with Kumāragupta I, who in the coin legends is referred to as *Guptakul=āmalachandra,*[53] 'the spotless moon in the firmament of the Gupta dynasty', and *Guptakula-vyomaśaśi*, 'moon in the sky of the Gupta family'.[54] Incidentally, Paramārtha mentions Vikramāditya as a king of Ayodhyā, and refers to his successor Bālāditya, who, on coming to the throne, patronized Vasubandhu. Some scholars identify Vikramāditya with Chandragupta II.[55] Allan[56] identifies Bālāditya with Narasiṁhagupta Bālāditya, and Vikramāditya with Purugupta.

Goyal makes a suggestion that Chandra could be a second name of Samudragupta, as Devarāja was of Chandragupta II. But it would be difficult to explain as to why in all the epigraphs, coins and seals, the name is Samudragupta, and only in the Mehrauli pillar inscription, which is an official record, as Chandra. It may be noted that Devarāja has never been used as a substitute for Chandragupta II in Gupta official record. If Chandra is taken as another name of Samudragupta, it would mean three Gupta kings of three successive generations—he, his father and his son, were named Chandra, which would be extremely unusual and create confusion in the minds of the people as to which of the three Chandras the achievements recorded in this inscription should be ascribed. It may be mentioned that ancient texts[57] prescribe that a child may be named after the name of his grandfather or a remote ancestor, but not after that of his father.

R S Misra[58] holds that the Mehrauli pillar inscription details Samudragupta's achievements, and that it was composed in his reign, but was engraved during the reign of Chandragupta II, whose officials retained the text of the *praśasti* as it was, but unscrupulously replaced the name of Samudragupta with that of Chandra (i.e. Chandragupta II). This is hardly possible. The Mehrauli pillar inscription is posthumous, and therefore in a *praśasti* of Samudragupta, written during his lifetime, he could not have been mentioned as dead. Besides, there was no need for Chandragupta II to put his name in the *praśasti* of his father, as he could very well have got composed a *praśasti* for himself, ascribing to him real as well as imaginary achievements of his choice.

It is difficult to accept the statement of S R Goyal that the Mehrauli pillar inscription 'merely describes *mutatis mutandis* in three brief verses what the Allahabad *praśasti* says in 33 long lines'.[59] The Mehrauli pillar inscription, for example, does not refer to the king as a poet, or a musician, or a conqueror of nine north Indian and twelve south Indian kings or the acceptance of his suzerainty by the tribal republics and the bordering states and political powers of foreign origin. Instead of the battle scarred body of Samudragupta mentioned in the Allahabad pillar inscription, the Mehrauli pillar inscription refers to the full moon like face of the king. The former does not refer to him as a Vaishṇava while the latter mentions his erecting a *Vishṇudhvaja*. The non-mention in the inscription, which is posthumous, of the performance of the horse-sacrifice, an event of great political significance and to commemorate which he issued the *Aśvamedha* type of coins and for which he has been eulogized by his successors (See Appendix II), does not support the view of Goyal. V C Pandey[60] pertinently observes: "None of his two *praśastis*, two copper plates, and six types of coins contains the slightest suggestion that he had assumed 'Chandra' as his other name. Neither in the records of his successors nor in those of contemporary dynasties is he referred to as 'Chandra'."

## CHANDRAGUPTA II

Basak[61] states that there is no literary or epigraphic evidence to show that any family of kings other than that of the Guptas made an attempt to assume imperial power and dignity by conquering distant countries in the fourth-fifth centuries AD, and as such, King Chandra should be identified with the homonym king of that dynasty. Since we have seen above that the evidence at hand does not favour the identification of King Chandra of the Mehrauli pillar inscription with Chandragupta I, it would be worthwhile to discuss the possibility of identifying him with Chandragupta II. According to Goyal,[62] Chandragupta II could not claim establishing the empire by his own arms, which the Mehrauli pillar inscription ascribes to Chandra, while Samudragupta fulfils this condition by his large-scale conquests. But as Chandragupta II came on the throne after killing his discredited brother Rāmagupta (Chapter 6), it has been suggested that he may be referred to as one who attained kingship by the force of his arms.[63] J Agrawal[64] considers the possibility of revolts in some provinces after Chandragupta II killed Rāmagupta, and his successfully curbing them. The Udaigiri inscription (No. 11) refers to Chandragupta II as acquiring territories by his own prowess, and as one who was intent on conquering the whole world (*kṛitsna-pṛithvī-jaya*). In passing, it may be mentioned, though it cannot be taken as established fact, that K C Chattopadhyaya,[65] on the basis of the style of composition, holds that Vīrasena Śāba, the author of the Udaigiri inscription was also the author of the Mehrauli pillar inscription. The Mandasor inscription of AD 467 (No. 36) refers to Chandragupta II as snatching away territories of the kings by the dent of his intellect and valour.[66] The erecting of flagstaff for God Vishṇu by King Chandra in the Mehrauli pillar inscription shows that he was a Vaishṇava. Samudragupta's choice of *garuḍa* device on coins may as well be due to his Vaishṇava leanings, but it may as well indicate that he was like a *garuḍa* for the serpent-like Nāga kings. The Gupta inscriptions refer to kings from Chandragupta II onwards as *parama-bhāgavatas*, and do not mention that epithet for Samudragupta (except in the Nālandā and Gaya copperplates of Samudragupta, which are not original), and on a coin-type of Chandragupta II, he is shown as receiving *prasāda* from Chakrapurusha, an *āyudha* of Vishṇu represented in human form,[67] which goes well with the erection of Vishṇu-*dhvaja* by him.

According to the Mehrauli pillar inscription, King Chandra defeated the kings who had congregated in Vaṅga. In the Allahabad pillar inscription, Samataṭa has been referred to as a bordering state of Samudragupta's kingdom, and he had conquered the region of Bankura district where Chandravarman of the Susunia inscription ruled. Vaṅga seems to have been conquered by Chandragupta II by defeating the congregation of kings there.[68] S R Goyal[69] opines that the evidence of Dhanaidaha and Damodarpur copperplates of Kumāragupta I indicate a firmly established administrative machinery in Bengal, which suggests that the region had become part of the Gupta kingdom earlier than his reign. Goyal gives credit of its conquest to Samudragupta, but as stated above, it is more probable that it was conquered by Chandragupta II. Even if the region had been conquered by Samudragupta, it is possible that some rebellious kings might have confederated against Chandragupta II and he defeated them.

King Chandra is said to have conquered the Vāhlīkas after crossing the seven mouths (*sapta-mukhāni*) of the Indus (Sindhu). Some[70] identify seven mouths with the five rivers of the Punjab and Kabul and Kunar in Afghanistan. Others identify them with the seven points where the river Indus joins the sea, and their names have been given by Ptolemy[71] and the expression *nadī-mukhena samudram=āviśata*, 'entering the ocean through the mouth of the river' in Kālidāsa's work,[72] also favours the view. J Agrawal, like some other scholars, places Vāhlīkas in Bactria, situated on the Oxus in Afghanistan,[73] which according to the *Amarakośa* was famous for its saffron, and should be considered as different from Vāhīka, which was part of Punjab where saffron does not grow.[74]

The *Pāda-tāḍitakam* of Śyāmilaka, it has been pointed out by J C Joshi,[75] refers to *Mahāpratīhāra* Bhadrāyudha, who was the chief of the region occupied by the Vāhlīkas and the Kārūśa-Maladas and maintained the glory of the house of Magadha. He refers to the view of T Burrow that Bhadrāyudha ruled in the Vāhlīka region as a feudatory of Chandragupta II who is to be identified with King Chandra of the Mehrauli pillar inscription, credited with the conquest of the Vāhlīkas.

The inscriptions from Chilas in Hunza, Gilgit district, Kashmir,[76] discovered in 1979 mention Śrī-Chandra, Devaśrī-Chandra, Śrīdeva-Chandra, Śrī-Chandradeva, Chandraśrī-deva, Vikramāditya, etc., in Gupta characters and in some of them, the date 143 also occurs. Devaśrī of the inscription reminds of Devaśrī (the legend being *Devaśrī-mahārājādhirāja-śrī-Chandragupta)* on Chandragupta II's coins,[77] Devarāja of Sanchi inscription (No. 9) and Devagupta of the Vākāṭaka record (No. 83), used for Chandragupta II. The absence of *gupta* suffix to the name Chandra in the Mehrauli pillar inscription is considered by some scholars as a hurdle in identifying the king with Chandragupta II. It may, however, be stated that on the copper coins of Chandragupta II, he has been mentioned as *Chandra* only. In some inscriptions from Chilas, the name of Harisheṇa also occurs. An officer of that name is known as holding the offices of Minister of Peace-and-War, *kumārāmātya* and General in Samudragupta's reign who was the author of the Allahabad pillar inscription (No. 1). He, it appears, continued to hold high offices in the reign of his son and successor, Chandragupta II. His religious leanings are not clearly stated. Goyal objects to the above-mentioned identification as the Hunza inscription refers to Harisheṇa's establishing a Buddhist *dharmachakra*, though, in his view, he, like his Gupta overlord, would have been a Vaishṇava. But even as a liberal Vaishṇava he could very well have shown favour to the Buddhists. Āmrakārddava—a general of *Parama-bhāgavata* Chandragupta II (No. 9) is known to have made a grant in favour of the Buddhist. It is also possible that Harisheṇa (as also Āmrakārddava) would have been a Buddhist. The absence of any royal title as also of *gupta* name-ending in the name Chandra, in the Chilas inscriptions, while some persons have been referred to as *mahārajas*, led T P Verma[78] to suggest that Chandra of these epigraphs does not seem to be a paramount sovereign and hence should not be identified with Chandragupta II. The date read by some scholars as 143, if referred to in Vikrama or Śaka or Gupta era, does not fall in the reign of Chandragupta II, but referring it to the Kalachuri era, the date would be (248+143 =) AD 391, when Chandragupta II was ruling. However, the use of Kalachuri, and not Gupta era in the context of the Gupta king seems curious. The earliest date that can be referredd to the Gupta era is 61, met with in the Mathurā pillar inscription of Chandragupta II, and it is possible that till that date the Gupta era had not become popular, particularly in a far-flung area like Chilas. T P Verma ascribes the date 143 of these epigraphs to the Gupta era, which would be equivalent to AD 462, when Skandagupta was ruling, and opines that the epigraphs were engraved during his reign to commemorate the visit of Chandragupta II who had passed through this place in his expedition against the Vāhlīkas. But in that case, one would expect that the name of Skandagupta, the then ruling king, should have also been recorded, which, however is not the case. A H Dani[79] opines that the date 143 is in the Harsha era, which would be equivalent to (606 + 143 =) AD 749, and that Vikramāditya of the inscription should be identified with a king of local Patola Sahi dynasty bearing that title. According to him, the Gupta form of letters continued to be in use in this remote area for a long time after the Gupta rule had come to an end. S R Goyal[80] rightly points out that the script cannot remain static for such a long period. In his view the date should be taken in the Gupta era which accords well with the script. He is of the opinion that Deva-śrī-Chandragupta Vikramāditya would have been a local ruler of Gilgit probably related to Patola Shāhī dynasty.[81] It is difficult to agree to this view as there is more satisfactory evidence in favour of identifying the king with Chandragupta II. B N Mukherjee[82] reads the date as 103 [Gupta Era=AD 422] and takes these epigraphs as non-official records, got written by the travellers and traders, to commemorate the visit of Chandragupta

II and Harisheṇa to that place in connection with the punishing of a local chief Siṁha, whose name is found in these epigraphs. The inscriptions more probably were written shortly after Chandragupta II's success in that area either by the members of his party or local people, rather than traders and travellers a decade after the death of Chandragupta II (*c.* AD 412).

The Hunza rock also bears epigraphs of the Kushāṇas, from which it has been inferred that it was located on an established route between Bactria and India, which would have been followed by Chandragupta II in his expedition against the Vāhlīkas in Bactria.[83] Pathak and Rao[84] refer to some Brāhmī and Kharoshṭhī inscriptions found in Kara Tepe at Tarmez near ancient Bactria on the Oxus. One Brāhmī inscription reads *Māheśvara-dharmasya* and shows prevalence of Śaiva religion in that area. The device of trident and Brāhmī letters occur on coins of Sassanian king Yazdgird (accession AD 399), which suggests Indian influence of political significance. A Sassanian seal shows a deity holding one round object in each of his hands, and a person holding a round object in his hand, facing the deity. The device, according to Pathak and Rao, seems to bear the influence of the motif represented on the *Chakravikrama* type of coins of Chandragupta II.[85] They believe that Chandragupta II defeated the Hūṇas in Bactria, and this seems to have been the source of Raghu's defeating the Hūṇas on the banks of the Oxus,[86] as mentioned in the *Raghuvaṁśam* of Kālidāsa. S R Goyal,[87] however, considers the presence of Śaiva inscriptions at Kara Tepe as a result of religious exchange and the influence of the *Chakravikrama* motif as a result of trade. But the cumulative evidence of the Brāhmī inscription at Tarmez, *triśūla* device and Brāhmī letters on Sassanian coins, the device on the Sassanian seal resembling that on the *Chakravikrama* type of coin, the Hunza inscriptions giving the name Chandra and title *Vikramāditya* and the name Harisheṇa, would favour the suggestion that Chandragupta II won victory over that region.

The Mehrauli pillar inscription refers to the breeze of the prowess of King Chandra perfuming the southern ocean. Samudragupta's conquering the regions in the south at least up to Kañchī, is known from the Allahabad pillar inscription. No definite evidence of Chandragupta II's conquest in southern India is available. D R Bhandarkar,[88] however, gives credit to Chandragupta II for some conquests in south India, though does not cite any substantial evidence. Some scholars opine that he might have taken a leading role in the successful southern campaign of his father as a prince, and after becoming king, claimed share in the victories,[89] while others suggest that the expression in the inscription may refer, not to the conquest by Chandragupta II, but to his political influence in south India.[90] Chandragupta II's daughter, the Vākāṭaka queen, Prabhāvatīguptā's retention of her Gupta-ending name and paternal *gotra* and inserting of her paternal genealogy in her inscriptions written in nail-headed Gupta Brāhmī, are taken as indicative of the Gupta influence on the Vākāṭaka court. A recently discovered Vākāṭaka inscription from Ramtek (No. 85), according to the reading and interpretation offered by some scholars, seems to indicate that Chandragupta II's son, Ghaṭotkachagupta, was married to the daughter of Prabhāvatīguptā, and Chandragupta II has definitely and significantly been referred to in that epigraph as 'lord of three seas', reminding us of similar expression for the Sātavāhana king Gautamīputra Sātakarṇi in a Nasik epigraph.[91] As seen above (Chapter 7), the Gupta rulers of Vanavāsī trace their origin to Vikramāditya who was the lord of the cities of Pāṭaliputra and Ujjayanī (i.e., Chandragupta II). A Kadamba king, Kākusthavarman, married his daughter to a Gupta prince (No. 91), perhaps to Kumāragupta I. Literary tradition speaks of the work of Pravarasena, identified with homonym Vākāṭaka ruler, revised by Kālidāsa. It is said that *Kuntaleśvara-dautya* was written by Kālidāsa when he was an ambassador in the court of Kuntala. Some scholars are of the opinion that the Kadambas and the Vākāṭakas acknowledged the suzerainty of the Guptas. According to Goyal these references to Chandragupta II's influence on powers of the Deccan and South are not sufficient to warrant that the southern seas were perfumed with the breeze of his prowess. T P Verma[92] suggests that southern seas may refer to western sea in relation to the northern empire of Chandragupta II. But the Arabian Sea has been referred to as 'Western Sea' (*paśchima-payodhi*) in the Mandasor inscription of Yaśodharman (No. 80), and the region of Saurashtra as Pratīchī (western region) in the Junagarh rock inscription of Skandagupta (No. 30). Spreading of fame to south India, mentioned in the epigraph, may as well be a conventional phraseology. The Maukhari ruler, *Mahārāja* Harivarman, and the Pushpabhūti king, Prabhākaravardhana, have been referred to as one whose fame had gone across the four oceans,[93] though the boundary of neither of these two kings extended up to the sea. We may, in passing, mention that Ashvini Agrawal[94] opines that the mention of Kosala, Oḍra, Puṇḍra and Tāmralipti in the *Vishṇu-purāṇa* as under Chandragupta II (whom like some scholars, he identifies with Devarakshita of the purāṇas) suggests that he might have conquered these areas. It may, however, be stated that this purāṇic evidence has also been interpreted differently.

One can argue against Chandragupta II's identification with King Chandra of the Mehrauli pillar inscription on grounds that the epigraph, although posthumous, does not mention his greatest achievement, namely, the victory over the Śakas. But it can also be said that the identification with Samudragupta has a great hurdle as it does not refer to the *aśvamedha* performed by that king, which was of utmost political significance. Further, the conquest of the Vāhlīkas, crossing the seven mouths of the Indus presupposes conquest of the Western Śaka territories. It has been pointed out that Samudragupta cannot be credited with the victory of the area as the *Daivaputrashāhi-Shāhānushāhi* on the north-western boundary of his kingdom had not been conquered by him.[95] The Mehrauli pillar inscription, it seems, does not detail all the conquests of the king, but of only some extreme parts of the boundaries of the empire. D C Sircar[96] points out that the boundaries in the north, east, south and the west are Bactria, Vaṅga, southern sea and seven mouths of the Indus falling in the Arabian sea, respectively which resembles the boundaries of King Raghu who is said to have conquered Vaṅga in the east and the Hūṇas on the banks of the Oxus in Bactria. It is likely that the intention of the Mehrauli pillar inscription was to portray the king as a *digvijayī*,[97] though Goyal considers the epigraph as a factual eulogy.[98]

The palaeography, name, religious leanings and conquests of King Chandra favour his identification with Chandragupta II. D R Bhandarkar[99] says that the boundary of King Chandra tallies with that of Samudragupta's, only it extended much beyond in the north-west, and therefore, Chandragupta II is best suited for the identification of this king. The identification of King Chandra with Chandragupta II is far more convincing than with any other king, as it 'accords with all the known facts of Indian history'.[100] No other king named Chandra would claim even the semblance of the achievements described in the record.[101] K A N Sastri[102] favours this identification 'for none of the other suggestions offered is half as good as this'.

## NOTES AND REFERENCES

1. J F Fleet (*Corpus Inscriptionum Indicarum*, III p. 140) preferred fourth century as its date, though he also made an alternate suggestion (*ibid*., Introduction, pp. 12-

13) of placing him during the reign of Mihirakula (first half of the 6th century AD). Hoernle (*Indian Antiquary*, XXI, 1872, p. 43), D C Sircar (*Select Inscriptions*, p. 283), etc., place it in the fifth century AD.

2. This is the view of most of the scholars (J F Fleet, *Corpus Inscriptionum Indicarum*, III, p. 140; J Allan, *Catalogue of the Coins of the Gupta Dynasties, and of Śaśāṅka, the King of Gauḍa, in the British Museum, London*, Introduction, p. xxxvii). D R Bhandarkar (*Corpus Inscriptionum Indicarum*, III, pp. 57ff) opines that King Chandra was alive though not ruling. He opines that since no one can go to the other world in bodily form (as the inscription has *mūrttyā...gatavataḥ*), the king was not dead, but had gone to another place, viz. Vishṇupada. Dasharatha Sharma (*Indian Culture*, V, pp. 207-08), too, does not consider the inscription as posthumous.
3. Some scholars identify Vishṇupada hill with the hillock where the pillar stands (Fleet, *Corpus Inscriptionum Indicarum*, III, p. 141; S K Aiyangar (Studies in Gupta History, *Journal of Indian History*, VI, p. 16). Smith (*Journal of the Royal Asiatic Society of Great Britain and Ireland*, 1897, p. 16) felt that Mehrauli cannot be the place as it is not a hilly area. However, the same objection can be raised to his view that it stands for the Katra mound, Mathura, where Keshavdev Temple stands. Other scholars locate the original place where the pillar was established variously near Kurukshetra (D C Sircar, *Select Inscriptions*, I, p. 285, n. 4); Siwalik in the Solasingi range, near Beas (J C Vidyalankar, *Journal of the Oriental Society, Madras*, XX, pp. 97-100); in Ambala district (Dasharatha Sharma, *Journal of Indian History*, XVI, p.13); near Hardwar (K P Jayaswal, *Journal of the Bihar and Orissa Research Society*, XVIII, p. 31); and Gaya (B P Sinha, in M C Joshi and S K Gupta (ed.).*King Chandra and the Mehrauli Pillar*, p. 255). It may, however, be stated that in the Nasik inscription of the time of Vāsishṭhīputra Pulumāvi (D C Sircar, *Select Inscriptions*, I, p. 205), the Tirhuṇa (Triraśmi) hillock has been compared with the Kailāsa mountain. So it is possible that even a slightly raised area has been referred to as a hill in the inscription.
4. Stein, *New Indian Antiquary*, I, p. 198.
5. *Proceedings of the Indian History Congress*, 1943, pp. 124-27.
6. *Journal of Indian History*, XXVI, 1931, pp. 117ff.
7. *Ibid.*, p. 129.
8. *Journal of the Royal Asiatic Society of Bengal, Letters*, IX, 1943, pp. 179ff, cited in M C Joshi and S K Gupta (ed.), *King Chandra and the Mehrauli Pillar*, p. 254, n.1.
9. *Indian Historical Quarterly*, XXI, pp. 202-12.
10. *Ancient India*, 5th edn, 1968, p. 234.
11. *Corpus Inscriptionum Indicarum*, III p. 140, n. 1.
12. *History of North-Eastern India*, pp. 14ff.
13. Studies in Gupta History, *Journal of Indian History*, VI(ii), pp. 22f.
14. For a criticism of identifying Chandragupta I with Chandra of the Mehrauli pillar inscription, see R D Banerji, *Epigraphia Indica*, XIV, pp. 367ff.
15. Studies in Gupta History, *Journal of Indian History*, VI(ii), pp. 16-17.

16. For example, H P Sastri, *Epigraphia Indica*, XII, pp. 317-18; R D Banerji, *The Age of the Imperial Guptas*, pp. 10-11.
17. H C Raychaudhuri, *Political History of Ancient India*, p. 472n; R K Mookerji, *Gupta Empire*, p. 67.
18. K N Dikshit, *vide* D R Bhandarkar, *Corpus Inscriptionum Indicarum*, III, p. 55.
19. H C Raychaudhuri, *Political History of Ancient India*, p. 472n.
20. F E Pargiter, *Dynasties of the Kali Age*, p. 49.
21. *Political History of Ancient India*, p. 472n.
22. As referred to by D R Bhandarkar, *Corpus Inscriptionum Indicarum*, III, p. 55n.
23. *Corpus Inscriptionum Indicarum*, III, p. 140, n. 1; also Introduction, pp. 12-13.
24. *Ibid.*, Introduction, pp. 12-13.
25. *Some Historical Aspects of the Inscriptions of Bengal*, pp. 205-07.
26. *Ibid.*, p. 206.
27. J Allan, *Catalogue of the Coins of the Gupta Dynasties, and of Śaśāṅka, the King of Gauḍa, in the British Museum, London*, pp. xxxvii-xxxviii.
28. S R Goyal, in M C Joshi and S K Gupta (ed.), *King Chandra and the Mehrauli Pillar*, p. 81.
29. *Ibid.*, p. 76.
30. *Ibid.*, p. 77.
31. *Ibid.*, p. 199.
32. T P Verma, *ibid.*, p. 180.
33. Sushmita Pande, *ibid.*, p. 170.
34. V C Pandey, in B Ch Chhabra *et al.* (ed.), *Reappraising Gupta History for S R Goyal*, p. 155.
35. L Gopal and K K Gopal, in M C Joshi and S K Gupta (ed.), *King Chandra and the Mehrauli Pillar*, p. 126.
36. J F Fleet, *Corpus Inscriptionum Indicarum*, III, p. 142, n. 2
37. M C Joshi and S K Gupta (ed.), *King Chandra and the Mehrauli Pillar*, pp. 76-77.
38. *Catalogue of the Coins of the Gupta Dynasties, and of Śaśāṅka, the King of Gauḍa, in the British Museum, London*, Introduction, pp. xxxvi-xxxvii.
39. A M Sastri, in M C Joshi and S K Gupta (ed.), *King Chandra and the Mehrauli Pillar*, p. 86.
40. In *ibid.*, p. 98.
41. D C Sircar, *Select Inscriptions*, I, p. 207.
42. A S Altekar, *The Coinage of the Gupta Empire*, p. 176.
43. J Agrawal, in M C Joshi and S K Gupta (ed.), *King Chandra and the Mehrauli Pillar*, p. 103.
44. A S Altekar, *The Coinage of the Gupta Empire*, p. 106.
45. *Vide*, M C Joshi and S K Gupta (ed.), *King Chandra and the Mehrauli Pillar*, pp. 76-77.
46. S K Aiyangar (Studies in the Gupta History, *Journal of Indian History*, VI, p. 14) prefers *Dhāvena*, meaning 'pure'
47. J Allan, *Catalogue of the Coins of the Gupta Dynasties, and of Śaśāṅka, the King of Gauḍa, in the British Museum, London*, p. xxxvi.

48. *Select Inscriptions*, I, p. 285, n. 2.
49. *A History of the Guptas*, p. 28.
50. S R Goyal, *The Imperial Guptas*, p. 234.
51. U Thakur, in M C Joshi and S K Gupta (ed.), *King Chandra and the Mehrauli Pillar*, p. 189.
52. For example, J Agrawal, in M C Joshi and S K Gupta (ed.), *King Chandra and the Mehrauli Pillar*, p. 100; U Thakur, in *ibid.*, p. 189.
53. A S Altekar, *The Coinage of the Gupta Empire*, p. 176.
54. *Ibid.*, p. 176.
55. U Thakur, in M C Joshi and S K Gupta (ed.), *King Chandra and the Mehrauli Pillar*, pp. 188-89.
56. *Catalogue of the Coins of the Gupta Dynasties, and of Śaśāṅka, the King of Gauḍa, in the British Museum, London*, Introduction, p. 1.
57. For example, *Baudhāyana-gṛihya-sūtra*, II, 1. 24; *Mānava-gṛhya-sūtra*, I, 18. 2. Goyal cites a few examples of father and son bearing the same name. His ascribing to us the statement that in ancient India, a son was *never* named after his father, is not correct.
58. In M C Joshi and S K Gupta (ed.), *King Chandra and the Mehrauli Pillar*, pp. 147-48.
59. *Ibid.*, p. 237.
60. B Ch Chhabra *et al.* (ed.), *Reappraising Gupta History for S R Goyal*, p. 155.
61. R G Basak, *Early History of North India*, p. 18.
62. M C Joshi and S K Gupta (ed.), *King Chandra and the Mehrauli Pillar*, p. 218.
63. S Pandey, in *King Chandra and the Mehrauli Pillar*, p. 168. S R Goyal (*The Imperial Guptas*, p. 231) however says that by killing his brother he would be called a fratricide, rather than empire builder.
64. In M C Joshi and S K Gupta (ed.), *King Chandra and the Mehrauli Pillar*, p. 103.
65. Quoted by S Pande in *ibid.*, p. 169.
66. J Agrawal, in *ibid.*, pp. 102-03.
67. A S Altekar, *The Coinage of the Gupta Empire*, p. 145ff.
68. K D Bajpai (in M C Joshi and S K Gupta (ed.), *King Chandra and the Mehrauli Pillar*, p. 106), on the basis of a single *śloka* in the *Mahābhārata*, places Vaṅga in the west on the Makran coast, which however, is not acceptable.
69. In M C Joshi and S K Gupta (ed.), *King Chandra and the Mehrauli Pillar*, p. 79.
70. For example, K P Jayaswal, *Journal of the Bihar and Orissa Research Society*, XVIII, pp. 31ff; R C Majumdar, *Journal of the Royal Asiatic Society of Bengal, Letters*, IX, 1943, pp. 179.
71. J W McCrindle, *Ancient India as Described by* Ptolemy, p. 33.
72. J Agrawal in M C Joshi and S K Gupta (ed.), *King Chandra and the Mehrauli Pillar*, pp. 96-97.
73. *Ibid.*, p. 97.
74. *Ibid.*
75. J C Joshi, *ibid.*, p. 260.

76. A H Dani, 'The Sacred Rock of Hunza', *Journal of Central Asia*, VIII (ii), December 1985, pp. 34ff; B N Mukherjee, 'The Hunza Valley and the Imperial Guptas', *Journal of the Bihar Research Society*, LXVII-LXVIII (i-iv) p. 561; Commentary on H C Raychaudhari, *Political History of Ancient India*, p. 768.
77. Altekar, *The Coinage of the Gupta Empire*, p. 93.
78. T P Verma in M C Joshi and S K Gupta (ed.), *King Chandra and the Mehrauli Pillar*, pp. 184-85.
79. A H Dani, as quoted by T P Verma, in M C Joshi and S K Gupta (ed.), *King Chandra and the Mehrauli Pillar*, pp. 184-85.
80. S R Goyal, *The Imperial Guptas*, p. 290.
81. S R Goyal, *ibid.*, p. 291; also in M C Joshi and S K Gupta (ed.), *King Chandra and the Mehrauli Pillar*, p. 225.
82. Commentary on H C Raychaudhuri, *Political History of Ancient India*, p. 768.
83. T P Verma in M C Joshi and S K Gupta (ed.), *King Chandra and the Mehrauli Pillar*, p. 185; *contra* S R Goyal (*The Imperial Guptas*, p. 289) who is of the view that Hunza area does not lie *en route* from Punjab to Bactria.
84. In M C Joshi and S K Gupta (ed.), *King Chandra and the Mehrauli Pillar*, pp. 190-91.
85. Pathak and Rao, *ibid.*, p. 193.
86. *Ibid.*, pp. 193-94.
87. S R Goyal, *ibid.*, pp. 225-26.
88. D R Bhandarkar, *Corpus Inscriptionum Indicarum*, III, p. 56.
89. For example, S S Rana, in M C Joshi and S K Gupta (ed.), *King Chandra and the Mehrauli Pillar*, p. 202.
90. A M Shastri, in *ibid.*, pp. 88-89.
91. D C Sircar, *Select Inscriptions*, I, pp. 203ff.
92. In M C Joshi and S K Gupta (ed.), *King Chandra and the Mehrauli Pillar*, p. 186.
93. *Chatussamudrātikrāntakīrti*, K K Thaplyal, *Inscriptions of the Maukharis, the Later Guptas, the Puṣpabhūtis, and Yaśovarman of Kanauj*, pp. 147, 152.
94. Ashvini Agrawal, *Rise and Fall of the Imperial Guptas*, p. 162.
95. T P Verma, in M C Joshi and S K Gupta (ed.), *King Chandra and the Mehrauli Pillar*, p. 184.
96. *Journal of the Royal Asiatic Society of Bengal, Letters*, V, 1939, p. 412-13.
97. A L Basham in M C Joshi and S K Gupta (ed.), *King Chandra and the Mehrauli Pillar*, p. 199.
98. S R Goyal, in *ibid.*, p. 219.
99. *Corpus Inscriptionum Indicarum*, III, p. 55.
100. G R Sharma, in M C Joshi and S K Gupta (ed.), *King Chandra and the Mehrauli Pillar*, p. 258.
101. K G Krishnan, in *ibid.*, p. 112.
102. *Advanced History of India*, p. 190.

# Appendix IV
# The Gupta Era

The dates in the inscriptions of the Gupta kings, from year 61, met with in the Mathurā pillar inscription of Chandragupta II (No. 6) to year 224 as seen in the fifth Damodarpur plate of Vishṇugupta (No. 57), are in succession, and hence should belong to some era. The expressions used in the context of date are variously as *saṁvatsara, rājya-saṁvatsara, vijaya-rājya-saṁvatsara, kāla, abda* and *varsha,* at times along with 'of the Guptas' or 'during the reign of the Guptas' in the epigraphs of the Gupta dynasty, as well as in those of other dynasties some of which continued to use it even when the Gupta rule had come to an end, as late as the year 300 (= AD 619)—the date met with in the Ganjam plate of Śaśāṅka.[1] Examples of dates in the Gupta era may be cited:

1. *Kālānuvartamāna-saṁvatsara* is met with in the Mathurā inscription of Chandragupta II year 61 (No. 6). D R Bhandarkar[2] restores the missing portion of the inscriptions as *Gupta-nṛipa-rājya* and translates it as 'in the year 61 according to the era of the Gupta kings'. In this inscription along with the date in the era, there is another date, which is mutilated and has been restored as *prathame* by D R Bhandarkar[3] and as *paṁchame* by D C Sircar.[4] This obviously refers to the regnal year; Dating in regnal was a common practice in ancient epigraphs. As stated above (Chapter 5), the years 5 in the Nālandā copperplate inscription (No. 3), and year 9 in the Gaya copperplate (No. 4) of Samudragupta appear to be regnal years, rather than the date in the Gupta era.

2. *Guptānvayānāṁ nṛipa-sattamānāṁ rājye kulasy=ābhi-varddhamāne shaḍbhir=yyukte varsha-śate,* 'In the augmenting reign of the family of the best of the kings, belonging to the Gupta lineage, in a century of years, coupled with six....'[5] in Udaigiri inscription of the time of Kumāragupta I GE 106 (No. 16).
3. *Gupt=ānvayanāṁ vasudh=eśvarāṇāṁ samā-śate shoḍaśa-varsha-yukte,* 'one hundred sixteen years of the [era] of the family of the Guptas, rulers of the earth' in Tumain inscription of the time of Kumāragupta I, GE 116 (No. 19).
4. *Gupta-prakāle gaṇanāṁ vidhāya,* 'calculating as per Gupta era' in the Junagarh rock inscription of Skandagupta (No. 30).
5. *Guptānāṁ-kāla-krama-gaṇite,* 'counting as per Gupta era' in the Junagarh rock inscription of Skandagupta (No. 30).
6. *Varsha-śate-Guptānāṁ-sachatuḥ-pañchāśaduttare,* 'when one hundred and fifty-four years of the Gupta era have passed', in the Sarnath inscription of Kumāragupta II, GE 154 (No. 37).
7. *Guptānāṁ samatikkrānte śapta-pañchāśaduttare śate samānāṁ,* 'one hundred and fifty-seven years of the (era) of the Guptas had passed', in the Sarnath inscription of Budhagupta, GE 157 (No. 39).[6]
8. *Gupta-nṛipa-rājya-bhuktau,* 'when Guptas enjoyed the earth', occurs along with the year, in the inscriptions of the Parivrājaka kings (Nos. 63, 68).
9. *Gupta-rājye varsha-śata-dvaye pañchāśaduttare,* 'in the dominion of the Guptas, year two hundred and fifty', in the Sumaṇḍala copperplate of Pṛithvīvigraha.[7]
10. *Gaupta-kāla saṁvatsare āśīty-uttara-śatadvaye* 'in the year two hundred and eighty of the Gupta era', in the Kanas copperplate of Lokavigraha.[8]
11. *Guptānāṁ-saṁvatsara-śate 200 80 2,* ' In the year of the Guptas in hundreds 282', in the Arang copperplate of Bhīmasena II.[9]
12. *Gauptābde varsha-śata-traye,* 'in the year three hundred of the Gupta era' in the Ganjam copperplate of Śaśāṅka.[10]

Some of the epigraphs mentioned above were brought to light after Fleet's *Corpus* was published. But he did not consider such expressions as *Gupta prakāle* in the Junagarh inscription as sufficient evidence to prove that the era was founded by the Guptas. The main basis of determining the date of the foundation of the Gupta era is the statement of Alberuni[11] that the Gupta era is separated from the Śaka era by an interval of 241 years. Since the date of the beginning of the Śaka era, which is still in use, is definitely known as AD 78, the date of commencement of the Gupta era would be 78 + 241 = AD 319.[12] He also states that the Gupta era was also called the Valabhī era,[13] which would have been so called because the Valabhī rulers used it extensively, as it was the era of the Guptas, who were their overlords. According to Fleet,[14] the Gupta era was basically the era founded by the Lichchhavi king Jayadeva of Nepal, from whom it was taken by Chandragupta I, who, in his opinion, married a Lichchhavi princess of that country. There is, however, no tangible evidence to show that the era belongs to the Lichchhavis as also that the Lichchhavi princess married by Chandragupta was from Nepal. Fleet's main argument against ascribing the era to a Gupta king was that placing the accession of Chandragupta I in AD 319 would give a total of 129 years, with an average of 32.25 years rule for Gupta rulers Chandragupta I, Samudragupta, Chandragupta II and Kumāragupta I, belonging to four successive generations, which appears to be quite long a period. But this objection is not sustainable. For the first, the average cannot be considered very high. Secondly, the rule of Kācha between Chandragupta I and Samudragupta, of Rāmagupta in between Samudragupta and Chandragupta II, and of Govindagupta in between Chandragupta II and Kumāragupta, even though brief ones, have to be accommodated within this period. As seen above, the epigraphic evidence (some of which, it may be mentioned, was not available to Fleet) clearly refers the era as the Gupta era.

Fleet was the first to firmly establish the date of the beginning of the Gupta era, which he did with the help of the evidence provided by the Mālava era. He pointed out that the Mandasor inscription (No. 38) shows that Kumāragupta I was ruling in the Mālava year 493. The dates known till then for this king from other sources, ranged between GE 96 known from the Bilsad inscription (No. 14) and 129 known from his Mankuwar inscription (No. 27). Fleet presuming that Mālava year 493 fell in the middle of these two dates, i.e. in (96 + 129 = 225÷2 =) GE 112.5, say 113, calculated that 113 + 78 (the beginning of the Śaka era) + 241 (the difference between the Śaka era and the Gupta era, as per the statement of Alberuni) and arrived at the figure AD 432 and concluded that AD 432 was equivalent to 493 of the Mālava era mentioned in the Mandasor inscription. The beginning of the Mālava era would be about 493 – 432 = 61 BC. Since the equation Mālava era 493 = GE 113 is only approximate, he concluded that Mālava era is the same as the Vikrama era, which began in 57 BC.

This was corroborated by the evidence of three dated epigraphs of the Chāhamāna dynasty.[15] An inscription, of Pṛithvīrāja II Chāhamāna's is dated in 1226 of the Vikrama era, and one, of his uncle who preceded him, in the Vikrama era 1220, while an inscription of his another uncle, who succeeded him is dated in 1226 of Mālava era. Since these three dates belonging to the reigns of the kings of the same dynasty are very close in time, they should refer to the same era, and therefore the Mālava era and Vikrama era must be taken as identical.

The date year 493 of Mālava era for Kumāragupta I known from Mandasor inscription would be equal to (493 – 57 =) AD 436, which falls in between the date of Bilsad inscription of (319—the date arrived at on the statement of Alberuni that Gupta ear begins 241 years after Śaka era, which began in 78 AD, + 96 =) AD 415 and that of the Mankunwar inscription of (319 + 129 =) AD 448 of that ruler. Thus the validity of Alberuni's statement that Gupta era begins 241 years after the Śaka era was established.

The date of the beginning of the Gupta era is also corroborated by the Ganjam copperplate inscription of Śaśaṅka. This gives the date Gupta year 300 (= 300 + 319) = AD 619, which fits in well with the known history, as Śaśāṅka was a contemporary of Harsha who ruled between AD 606 and 648.

Another piece of evidence in support may be cited. Chandragupta II conquered the Śakas and issued silver coins in imitation of Śaka coins. The last date known for Chandragupta II is Gupta era 93, and the last known date of the Śaka dynasty is Śaka era 31x (the value of x is any figure between 1 and 9, which has been lost), i.e., any date between AD 388 and 397. Only by taking the beginning of the Gupta era as founded in AD 319, and of Śaka era, founded in AD 78, the contemporaneity of Chandragupta II with the last Śaka ruler Rudrasiṁha III, whom he overthrew, can be established.

The credit of founding the Gupta era has been given variously to Gupta (the first ruler of the dynasty), Chandragupta I, Samudragupta, and Chandragupta II. The view that ascribes the founding of the era to Gupta,[16] has nothing to commend itself[17] as there is hardly any possibility of a feudatory (*mahārāja*), founding an era, and also as AD 319 would be too late a date for the beginning of his rule, as it would mean placing his reign period together with those of Ghaṭotkacha, Chandragupta I, Kācha, Samudragupta and Rāmagupta, some of whom, as their achievements indicate, should have ruled for a fairly long period, between AD 319 and 376.

If Chandragupta I, the first *mahārājādhirāja* of the Gupta dynasty, founded the Gupta era in AD 319, it should be taken to mark the date of his accession. If the accession of Chandragupta I is placed in AD 319, then Samudragupta's Nālandā copperplate bearing the year 5 and Gaya copperplate bearing the year 9, if taken as dated in the Gupta era, would appear spurious, as that would mean that Chandragupta I ruled for a very short period, less than five years, which, does not seem to be the case. Chandragupta I's assuming the higher title *mahārājādhirāja* in contradistinction to that of his two predecessors who were mere *mahārājas*, would favour the view that his rule was not short. Apart from accession, the most important event known in the life of Chandragupta I, which has a significant bearing on the Gupta history, is his marriage with Kumāradevī, the Lichchhavi princess, as it led to the amalgamation of the Lichchhavi territories with those of the Guptas, and augmented considerably the power and prestige of that dynasty. One of the factors in the selection of Samudragupta by his father Chandragupta I as his successor would have been his being born of the Lichchhavi princess. One may suggest that the era was founded to mark the event of Chandragupta I's marriage. But if the Nālandā and Gaya plates of Samudragupta are genuine copies of the original ones, then the founding of the era in AD 319 could not be related to his marriage, as it would be unbelievable that Samudragupta, at less than five years of age, was nominated on merit by Chandragupta I as his successor. Smith placed Chandragupta I's accession and marriage in AD 308 and the formal coronation in AD 319. It is, however, not known from any source that there was a gap, and that too of as many as eleven years, between the accession and coronation of that king. Since Samudragupta's reign ended a couple of years earlier than AD 376 when Chandragupta II came on the throne after a short reign of Rāmagupta in between Samudragupta and Chandragupta II, he should have come on the throne in about AD 344 as his extensive conquests, both in the north and the south, indicate that he had a fairly long reign, say of about thirty years.

If Samudragupta is considered as the founder of the Gupta era, as suggested by some,[18] then referring year 5 of the Nālandā copperplate to that era, its date would be (319 + 5 =) AD 324. In the inscription, Chandragupta [II] is mentioned, in all probability, as a *dūtaka*.[19] Taking him to be of about 20 years of age to perform the responsible task of a *dūtaka*, his date of birth would be *c*. AD 304. Since he ruled at least up to AD 412, at the time of his death, he would have been about 108 years old, which appears incredible. Some scholars consider the Nālandā plate, dated year 5 (and also the Gaya plate, dated year 9) as spurious. But if the date potion of the Nālandā plate is a genuine copy of the original plate that got partly damaged, then the date 5 should not taken not in the Gupta era, but as regnal year of Samudragupta. Besides, if Samudragupta is taken as the founder of the Gupta era, then he has to be assigned an unusually long reign of about 55 years—from AD 319 to *c* AD 374.

Since the earliest definite date that can be referred to the Gupta era is year 61, met with in the Mathurā pillar inscription of Chandragupta II, some scholars[20] believe that it was he who founded the Gupta era, but counted the date, not from the time of his accession, but from AD 319, which was important in the Gupta history as it marked the accession of Chandragupta I, the first *mahārājādhirāja* of the dynasty. It is well known that some eras like the Buddha era, were founded much later than the period they were reckoned from.[21] In the Mathurā inscription of Chandragupta II, regnal year 5, is also mentioned along with the date 61 in the (Gupta) era. Since in the dated Gupta records, afterr year 61 referrable to the Gupta era, regnal year is not mentioned, some scholars suggest that till Gupta Era 61, the Gupta inscriptions were dated only in regnal years, and since Chandragupta II was the first ruler to use the Gupta era, he should also be given the credit of founding the same. According to this view, the date year 5 in the Nālandā plate would be regnal year of Samudragupta. S R Goyal[22] also believed in this theory. However he felt that the date 30 in the Mandargiri cave inscription,[23] as also in the Mundesvari inscription,[24] should be referred to the Gupta era as they are palaeographically datable to the Gupta period. Their date, which in Christian era would be (319 + 30 =) AD 349, is much earlier than the accession of Chandragupta II in AD 376.[25] But the dates in these two inscriptions may very well be regnal years. In one of his latest works, *The Imperial Guptas*, Goyal prefers to give credit for founding the Gupta era to Chandraguptra II, who counted the date from the accession of Chandragupta I. However, the most accepted view is that the Gupta era was founded in AD 319 by Chandragupta I, to mark his accession and, in contrast to the title *mahārāja* of his father and grandfather denoting their feudal status, took the grandiloquent title of *mahārājādhirāja*, which by then had become the hallmark of an independent sovereign ruler.

## NOTES AND REFERENCES

1. *Epigraphia Indica*, VI, p. 144.
2. *Corpus Inscriptionum Indicarum*, III, p. 240.
3. *Ibid.*
4. D C Sircar, *Select Inscriptions*, I, p. 277.
5. J F Fleet, *Corpus Inscriptionum Indicarum*, III, p. 259.
6. As J Agrawal (*Vishveshvaranand Indological Journal*, XV, pp. 121-22) points out, N P Joshi's translation '154 years after the Gupta dynasty had ended' is wrong. It would be incongruous with the fact that the inscription belongs to the Gupta king. In fact *Samatikkrānte* (expired) qualifies *śate.*
7. *Select Inscriptions*, I, p. 490.
8. *Epigraphia Indica,* XXVIII, p. 331.
9. *Epigraphia Indica,* IX, p. 345.
10. *Epigraphia Indica,* VI, p. 144.
11. Translated by M Rein, *vide* J F Fleet, *Corpus Inscriptionum Indicarum,* III, Introduction, p. 24.
12. Calculations by scholars show that the Gupta era commenced either on February 23, AD 320 or on December 30, AD 318. We have taken the middle date – AD 319 for its commencement, throughout this work.
13. Curiously, he also says that the Guptas were wicked and the era began when the rule of the Gupta dynasty had come to an end. See Sachau's translation of Alberuni's work as referred to by Fleet, *Corpus Inscriptionum Indicarum*, III, Introduction, p. 24.
14. *Corpus Inscriptionum Indicarum*, III, Introduction, p. 136.
15. For references, see P L Gupta, *The Imperial Guptas,* pp. 212-13.
16. *Indian Historical Quarterly*, 1942, p. 273n.
17. H C Raychaudhuri, *Political History of Ancient India,* p. 530.
18. R C Majumdar, in *Comprehensive History of India,* III(i), p. 15, n. 44, and p. 36.
19. D C Sircar, *Select Inscriptions*, I, p. 272, n. 10. If the plate is a forged one them the forger might have added the name of Chandragupta. *Dūtaka* may be an honorary title like Prince of Wales (R C Majumdar, *Comprehensive History of India*, III (i), p. 15, n. 44) which could have been borne even as a child by Chandragupta.
20. For example, P L Gupta, *The Imperial Guptas*, p. 208.
21. See *ibid.*, p. 209.
22. *Gupta Sāmrājya kā Itihāsa*, pp. 6f.
23. *Epigraphia Indica*, XXXV, p. 304.
24. *Indian Antiquary*, 1920, pp. 21ff.
25. S R Goyal, *Gupta Sāmrājya kā Itihāsa*, pp. 7-8.

# Appendix V

## Genealogy and Chronology of the Imperial Gupta Kings

There is great controversy regarding the genealogical and chronological position of several kings of the Gupta dynasty. It is relatively less complicated up to the reign of Kumāragupta I, but after him it becomes a knotty problem. The earliest definitely known date for the Gupta king is [Gupta Era] 61, i.e., AD 380 in an inscription from Mathurā (No. 6). Since the inscription was recorded in the fifth regnal year of Chandragupta II (Chapter 7, above), his accession took place in AD 376. This, incidentally, makes Chandragupta II as the only Gupta ruler whose date of accession is known for certain. Rāmagupta, elder brother of Chandragupta II, whose reign appears to have been quite short may tentatively be placed between AD 374 and AD 376. Samudragupta, who made extensive conquests, must have ruled for a fairly long period. But for reasons given below, he may be assigned a reign period of say 30 years only and his rule may be placed between AD 344 and AD 374. According to the chronology followed in this work, Samudragupta was preceded by Kācha, known from a few coins only (Chapter 4), who may be assigned the rule of only about a year (AD 343-344). Chandragupta I's rule may be placed between 319 (the date for the commencement of the Gupta era, in all probability to mark his accession),[1] and AD 343, and assigning a reign of 25 years each to the two preceding kings, his father, Ghaṭotkacha, may have ruled from c. AD 294 to *c* AD 319, and the latter's father, Gupta, from *c* AD 269 to *c* AD 294. Chandragupta II would have ruled for at least 36 years, from AD 376 to least AD 412, and Govindagupta, between AD 412 and AD 415—the last known date of Chandragupta II and first known date of Kumāragupta I, respectively. Kumāragupta I had a long reign of 40 years, from AD 415 to 455, the two dates known from the Bilsad inscription (No. 14) and his coins, respectively. During his region Ghaṭotkachagupta rebelled and ruled as king in Malwa regin for a short period.

The genealogy from Gupta, the first Gupta king, to Kumāragupta I may be traced as below:

1. *Mahārāja* Gupta
|
2. *Mahārāja* Ghaṭotkacha
|
3. *Mahārājādhirāja* Chandragupta I = Kumāradevī
(accession AD 319)
|
4. Kācha — 5. *Mahārājādhirāja* Samudragupta=Dattadevī
|
6. *Mahārājādhirāja* Rāmagupta =Dhruvadevī — 7. *Mahārājādhirāja* Chandragupta II = Dhruvadevī
|
8. Govindagupta (title not known) — *Mahārājādhirāja* Kumāragupta I=Anantadevī — 9. Ghaṭotkachagupta

The difficulty in determining the chronology of the Gupta kings, particularly after Kumāragupta I, is that the Gupta epigraphs detailing genealogy give father-to-son succession and do not mention collaterals. In post-Kumāragupta I period a fairly large number of kings have to be accommodated within about a century. Their position has to be determined within the framework of the following known dates (as converted from Gupta era to the Christian era):

1. The date for Ghaṭotkachagupta, AD 435, known from Tumain inscription (No. 19).
2. Last date of Kumāragupta I, AD 455, based on the date on his coins as read by some scholars.
3. First known date for Skandagupta, AD 455 (No. 30).
4. Last date known for Skandagupta, 467, as known from a variety of silver coins[2].
5. The Mandasor inscription of the time of Prabhākara, AD 467 (No. 36).
6. Date of Kumāragupta of Sarnath inscription, AD 473 (No. 37). If he is the king (name not mentioned) in whose reign the silk-weavers' guild repaired the Sun temple at Mandasor in AD 472 (No. 38), then that would be the first known date for that king (See Chapter 11, under Kumāragupta II).
7. The earliest known date of Budhagupta, AD 476 (No. 39).
8. The latest known date of Budhagupta, 494 as known from his coin (The date AD 499, based on the evidence of another coin is doubtful).
9. Known date of Vainyagupta, AD 507 (No. 50).
10. Known date of Bhānugupta, AD 510 (No. 52).
11. Date of defeat of Toramāṇa by Prakāśadharman, before AD 515 as it finds mention in the Risthal inscription of that date (No. 78).
12. Yaśodharman's conquest of the Hūṇa king Mihirakula, before AD 532, presuming that the date of the undated inscription (No. 80) of Yaśodharman from Mandasor, mentioning his victory over Mihirakula, is the same as that of his another inscription dated AD 532 from the same site (No. 79).
13. Date of Vishṇugupta, AD 543 (No. 57).

The most important evidence for the Gupta genealogy of the post-Kumāragupta I period is provided by the sealings of the kings of the Gupta dynasty, which have been mentioned under the Sources (Chapter 1) and also while dealing with the history of the later Imperial Gupta kings (Chapter 11) but may briefly be referred to here again. The Nālandā sealing of Budhagupta traces the genealogy from the first king, Gupta, to himself and mentions him as the grandson of Kumāragupta I and the son of Purugupta. The Nālandā sealing of Narasiṁhagupta mentions him as the son of Purugupta. The Bhitari metal seal of Kumāragupta, which is complete, gives the genealogy from the first king, Gupta, to the owner of the seal, who is mentioned as the son of Narasiṁhagupta and the grandson of Purugupta. The extant portion of the Nālandā sealing of Vainyagupta has the following genealogy: Chandragupta II, Kumāragupta I, Purugupta, and Vainyagupta. S R Goyal[3] takes what R C Majumdar took as traces of *u-mātrā* as subscript *ra* of *ndra,* and reconstructs the name of the father of Vainyagupta, as Chandra, and labels him as Chandragupta III. This, he opines, would be in consonance with the evidence of the *Ārya-Mañjuśrī-mūlakalpa* according to which Dvādaśāditya (= Vainyagupta *dvādaśāditya*) was a son of Chandra, and that the last-mentioned might have been a son of Budhagupta. But in the Gupta script in conjoint *ndra, n, d* and *ra,* are written vertically, one below the other, and hence *ra* would have been written lower down the alignment of the line, which however is not the case.

The Nālandā seal of Vishṇugupta mentions him as the son of Kumāragupta, grandson of Narasiṁhagupta and great-grandson of a king whose name is mutilated but can be restored as Purugupta. S R Goyal[4] is of the view that in the name of the father of Narasiṁhagupta, what has been taken as traces of the *ū mātrā* attached to the letter *p* by Krishna Dev, are remnants of the subscript *ra* and the name might have been Prakāśāditya, a king known from the Horseman-lion-slayer type of coins, rather than Pūrugupta. The view, however, is not acceptable for reasons given above (Chapter 11). The name of the king, the first part of whose name is missing, in the fifth Damodarpur plate, on grounds specified above (Chapter 11), should be restored as Vishṇugupta.

As the last known date of Skandagupta is AD 467 and the first known date for Budhagupta, AD 476, long back Panna Lall, with the evidence then available to him,[5] suggested following chronology for the Gupta kings:

1. Kumāragupta I

2. Skandagupta I (AD 455-467) 3. Purugupta (467- )

4. Narasiṁhagupta 6. Budhagupta (AD 476-94)

5. Kumāragupta [II] (AD 473)

To this should be added Vainyagupta (AD 507), Bhānugupta (AD 510) and Vishṇugupta known from his Nalanda sealing (No. 58), who were not known when Panna Lall wrote. Vishṇugupta, son of Kumāragupta, according to his scheme would have preceded Budhagupta. This would place, four kings of four successive generations—Purugupta, Narasiṁhagupta, Kumāragupta and Vishṇugupta, between AD 467 and 476. H C Raychaudhuri[6] points out that six Kashmiri kings are known to have ruled for six years and three Chālukya kings, belonging to three generations ruled for less than eight years. According to this view, Vishṇugupta, the great-grandson of Purugupta (who did not rule before AD 455, and more probably not before Skandagupta whose last known date is AD 467), must have been a mere stripling at the time of his accession.[7]

If Narasiṁhagupta, the only Gupta king whose coins bear the title *Bālāditya*, is placed in between AD 467 and 473, he could not be Bālāditya whom Hiuen-tsang gives the credit of defeating Mihirakula in the first half of the sixth century AD. A few scholars consider Hiuen-tsang's account as untrustworthy;[8] But if the Chinese pilgrim is to be believed, and most scholars do so, then Bālāditya has to be placed in the first quarter of the sixth century AD. There is no tangible evidence to support the speculation of K P Jayaswal[9] and H C Raychaudhuri[10] that Bhānugupta bore the title *Bālāditya* and was the king who defeated Mihirakula. Some scholars even deny Bhānugupta the status of a king, as no imperial title like *mahārājādhirāja* is known for him, and his name does not figure in the Gupta genealogy. However, there is greater possibility of his having ruled as a king for reasons stated in Chapter 11, above.

To avoid the rule of four kings running into four generations within a very short period of nine years (AD 467-76), an alternate suggestion is that Narasiṁhagupta succeeded his father Purugupta. He was succeeded by his son Kumāragupta [II] (known date AD 473), and the latter was succeeded by his uncle Budhagupta (first known date AD 476). The last-mentioned was succeeded by his brother Vainyagupta (known date AD 507), and he in turn was succeeded by Bhānugupta (known date AD 510), whose relationship with any Gupta king is not known. Bhānugupta was followed by Vishṇugupta son of Kumāragupta [II], who should be identified with the king of the fifth Damodarpur copperplate, dated AD 543 (No. 57). The order of succession may be shown in tabular form as below:

- 1. Kumāragupta I
  - 2. Skandagupta (AD 455-467)
  - 3. Purugupta (467- )
    - 4. Narasiṁhagupta
      - 5. Kumāragupta [II] (AD 473)
        - 9. Vishṇugupta (AD 543)
    - 6. Budhagupta (AD 476-94)
    - 7. Vainyagupta (AD 507)
      - 8. Bhānugupta (AD 510)

But this too does not make [Narasiṁhagupta] Bālāditya contemporary of Mihirakula. Numismatic evidence favours the existence of two Kumāraguptas other than Kumāragupta I. If Kumāragupta of the Sarnath inscription of Gupta era 154 (AD 473) whose parentage is not known, is different from Kumāragupta of the Bhitari and Nālandā seals, who was a son of Narasiṁhagupta and grandson of Purugupta, then the former may be taken as Kumāragupta II and the latter as Kumāragupta III, and the genealogy and chronology would be as below:

- 1. Kumāragupta I
  - 2. Skandagupta (AD 455-467)
  - 3. Purugupta (c. 467-473)
    - ? 4. Kumāragupta II (AD 473)
    - 5. Budhagupta (AD 476-95)
    - 6. Vainyagupta (AD 507)
      - ? 7. Bhānugupta (510)
    - 8. Narasiṁhagupta
      - 9. Kumāragupta III
        - 10. Vishṇugupta (AD 543)

The position of Vishṇugupta as the last known ruler is supported by the numismatic evidence, as amongst the Gupta rulers, his coins are the heaviest, and most debased, and also by the fifth Damodarpur copperplate of AD 543 (No. 57) of that king. By taking Kumāragupta of the Bhitari and that of Nālandā seals as different from the homonym of the Sarnath inscription, there would not be the problem of extremely short reigns for four successive kings belonging to four generations. Further, the merit of this scheme is that Narasiṁhagupta *Bālāditya* becomes contemporary of Mihirakula.

While Altekar[11] suggested the possibility of the existence of two kings bearing the name of Narasiṁhagupta, S R Goyal[12] considers it as certain. He takes Kumāragupta of the Sarnath inscription (No. 37) as identical with the homonym of the Bhitari seal (No. 55) who is therein stated as son of Narasiṁhagupta and grandson of Purugupta, and considers Narasiṁhagupta and Kumāragupta of the Nālandā sealing of Vishṇugupta (No. 58) as different from them, as he restores the name of the father of Narasiṁhagupta and grandfather of Kumāragupta on the Nālandā sealing of Vishṇugupta, not as Purugupta as done by Krishna Dev and some other scholars, but as Prakāśāditya. He restores the name of the father of Vainyagupta on his sealing (No. 51) as Chandragupta, instead of Purugupta as done by others. On the basis of the evidence of the *Ārya-Mañjuśrī-mūlakalpa*, he considers Chandra as son of Budhagupta and father of Dvādaśa, i.e. Vainyagupta *Dvādśāditya*. He believes that Purugupta succeeded Kumāragupta I and was followed by Skandagupta. The genealogy would be as below:

1. Kumāragupta I

2. Purugupta 3. Skandagupta

4. Narasiṁhagupta 6. Budhagupta

5. Kumāragupta II 7. Chandragupta III

8. Vainyagupta

?

9. Bhānugupta

?

10. Prakāśāditya

11. Narasiṁhagupta II

12. Kumāragupta III

13. Vishṇugupta

But while the numismatic evidence for two kings bearing the name Kumāragupta, other than Kumāragupta I, is quite clear, it is not so for two kings bearing the name Narasiṁhagupta. The name of the father of Narasiṁhagupta on the Nālandā sealing (No. 53), as on the Bhitari seal (No. 55), should be read as Purugupta, rather than Prakāśāditya, which (the latter) is not a name but an *āditya* title, and as pointed by us elsewhere, in the Gupta genealogies, it is invariably the name of the king that finds mention, and never his title.[13] Also, the existence in the Gupta dynasty, of two sets of each of two kings—Narasiṁhagupta-Kumāragupta with father and son relationship within a relatively short period, seems unlikely.

Hiuen-tsang[14] mentions kings who got constructed Buddhist monuments at Nālandā, namely, Śakrāditya, Budhaguptarāja, Tathāgatagupta, Bālāditya and Vajra. It is, however, not known for certain whether the kings are mentioned in chronological order, or there was father-son relationship between successive kings in all cases. It is generally believed that they all belonged to the Gupta dynasty. The views regarding the identification of the kings mentioned by Hiuen-tsang, with the exception of Vajra, have been referred to above, while discussing their history (Chapter 11) and need not be repeated. As regards Vajra, R K Mookerji,[15] identifies him with Vainyagupta, who was a predecessor of Bālāditya who, according to Hiuen-tsang, conquered Mihirakula. Basak's view[16] that Vajra may be an abbreviation of an *āditya* title (*ajrāditya*), and that it may be ascribed to Kumāragupta III, stands refuted, as the title on his coins is *Śrī-Kramāditya*. H C Raychaudhuri[17] takes Vajra as identical with the Gupta ruler who was defeated by Yaśodharman, and as a son of Bhānugupta—whom he identifies with Bālāditya of Hiuen-tsang, Vakārākhya of *Ārya-Mañjuśrī-mūlakalpa*, and younger brother of Prakaṭāditya of the Sarnath inscription. P L Gupta[18] is of the view that Vajra was either Vishṇugupta or his successor, who was the Gupta king ruling when the Sumandala plate[19] was engraved. But if *Vajrāditya* is taken as a title, then the identification with Vishṇugupta is negated, as the title on his coins is *Chandrāditya*. Of the kings mentioned in the *Ārya-Mañjuśī-mūlakalpa*, Jayaswal identifies Deva with Devagupta, a Later Gupta king, son of Ādityasena, Dvādaśa with Vainyagupta, and Chandra with Vishṇugupta, father of The Later Gupta king Jīvitagupta. But Vainyagupta and Vishṇugupta Chandrāditya are definitely Imperial Gupta rulers, and Deva should also be taken as belonging to the same dynasty.[20] P L Gupta suggests that Deva of Hiuen-tsang and Devarāja of the *Ārya-Mañjuśī-mūlakalpa* could be identical with Budhagupta, as, Budha (= Buddha) is a *deva* (god) for the Buddhists, and that he was succeeded by Chandra of coins, and was in turn, succeeded by Vainyagupta *Dvadaśāditya*.[21] The *Ārya-Mañjuśī-mūlakalpa*[22] mentions Bāla (i.e., Bālāditya) after Devarāja. Kumāra and U-initialed king mentioned in that Buddhist text as Bāla's successors, should be identified with Kumāragupta III and Vishṇugupta.[23] K P Jayaswal,[24] however, identified Kumāra with Kumāragupta II, and *u*-initialed king as Budhagupta, and the latter he identified with Prakāśāditya, whose coins bear the letter u. But the reading of the name Bhānugupta on a recently discovered Prakāśāditya coin goes against it.[25] All said, the genealogy and chronology of the Gupta kings after Kumāragupta I still remains a matter of controversy.

## NOTES AND REFERENCES

1. The view that Gupta era beginning in *c.* AD 319 was founded by Samudragupta does not hold good for reasons stated in Appendix IV.
2. A S Altekar, *The Coinage of the Gupta Empire*, p. 258.
3. *The Imperial Guptas*, p. 447.
4. *The Imperial Guptas*, pp. 453-54.
5. *Journal of the Bihar and Orissa Research Society*, IV(iv), 1918, pp. 412ff.
6. *Political History of Ancient India*, pp. 491-92.
7. A Ghosh, *Indian Historical Quarterly*, XIX, pp. 120-21.
8. V V Mirashi, *Journal of the Epigraphical Society of India*, IX, p. 53; Ashvini Agrawal, *Rise and Fall of the Imperial Guptas*, pp. 236, 245.
9. K P Jayaswal, *Imperial History of India*, pp. 47-53.
10. *Political History of Ancient India*, p. 524.
11. *The Coinage of the Gupta Empire*, pp. 266ff.
12. S R Goyal, *The Imperial Guptas*, pp. 393ff.
13. K K Thaplyal, *Journal of the Numismatic Society of India*, XXXV, p. 169.
14. T Watters, *On Yuan Chwang's Travels in India*, II, pp. 164-65.
15. *Gupta Empire*, p. 106.
16. *History of North-Eastern India*, p. 94.
17. *Political History of Ancient India*, p. 525, text, and n. 2.
18. *The Imperial Guptas*, p. 189.
19. *Select Inscriptions*, I, p. 490.
20. P L Gupta, *The Imperial Guptas*, p. 190.
21. *Ibid.*
22. K P Jayaswal, *Imperial History of India*, pp. 37-38.
23. P L Gupta, *The Imperial Guptas*, p. 190.
24. *Imperial History of India*, p. 38.
25. K S Shukla, *Journal of the Numismatic Society of India*, XLII, pp. 120ff.

# Appendix VI

## Imperial Gupta Kings *vis-à-vis* Scions of the Feudal Family of Kauśāmbī

The Appendix attempts at identifying certain high officials as belonging to the feudatory family of Kauśāmbī,[1] reconstructing their genealogy and chronology, and establishing their contemporaneity with the different rulers of the Gupta dynasty. This has been done by piecing together evidence of different nature such as palaeographic considerations (all epigraphs are datable to the Gupta period on palaeographic grounds), similarity in names, identical name-endings, similarity of device and the same provenance of the source material (sealings and inscriptions), and fitting such evidence within the already known historical framework. These pieces of evidence taken singly may well be treated as accidental, but when taken together they seem to provide some outline of connected history. The Appendix evolved out of the new evidence brought forth in our three articles dealing with (i) a sealing of Tilabhaṭṭa from Kauśāmbī,[2] (ii) a seal-die of the office of *kumārāmātya* attached to *mahāsenāpati* and *mahādaṇḍanāyaka* Vishṇurakshita from the same site,[3] and (iii) the nativity and parentage of Dhruvasvāminī, the chief-queen of Chandragupta II.[4]

The Kauśāmbī sealing of early Gupta period belonging to *Mahārāja* Tilabhaṭṭa refers to him as serving under[5] the king, his overlord.[6] *Mahārāja*

Tilabhaṭṭa of the sealing is to be identified with Tilabhaṭṭaka of Samudragupta's Allahabad pillar inscription (No. 1) wherein he has been referred to as a *mahādaṇḍanāyaka* of that ruler. There are examples of the same person being referred to by two names, quite similar to each other. For example, Achyu of the coins found in and around Ahichchhatrā[7] and king Achyuta mentioned in the Allahabad Pillar Inscription are taken as identical; Chandragupta II has been referred to as Devarāja in the Sanchi inscription (No. 9) and Devagupta in a Vākāṭaka inscription (No. 83). Two forms of the name of the chief-queen of Chandragupta II, namely, Dhruvadevī and Dhruvasvāminī, are known—the first in the genealogical portion of the epigraphs of the successors of Chandragupta II (nos. 14, 55) while the second, in her own sealing from Vaiśālī (No. 13), in the same way as Muruṇḍasvāminī and Muruṇḍadevī are the two forms of the same name,[8] and Pṛithvīsheṇa and Pṛithvīrāja refer to the same Vākāṭaka king in the epigraphs of that dynasty.[9] It is worthwhile to note that earlier the emendation of the name Tilabhaṭṭaka in the Allahabad Pillar Inscription into Tilakabhaṭṭa was suggested.[10] But the name as it was to be engraved on the sealing would have been conveyed to the seal-maker in writing by the person for whom the seal was to be made or by his close associate, and therefore the form Tilabhaṭṭa met with on the seal, and not Tilabhaṭṭaka mentioned in the Allahabad pillar inscription, should be taken as the correct form of the name. The suffix *ka* denotes smallness and it may be presumed that the form *Tilabhaṭṭa* was deliberately amended to *Tilabhaṭṭaka* in the Allahabad pillar inscription by the official himself to show his humbleness in relation, to the his overelord, King Samudragupta, whose *praśasti* the inscription records, and the engraving of which (*praśasti*), as per the evidence of that epigraph, was done under his direct supervision (*anushṭhitaṁ Tilabhaṭṭakena*).

Tilabhaṭṭa has been referred to as *mahārāja* in the Kauśāmbī sealing and *mahādaṇḍanāyaka* in the Allahabad Pillar Inscription. In the Gupta period, the former epithet denoted a 'subordinate king', or a 'feudal lord' or a 'governor';[11] and the latter, which means a 'general' or a 'judge' or even a 'police officer', was also a title, which at times was also conferred on the feudatories. The reference to Tilabhaṭṭa as *mahārāja* in the sealing and *mahādaṇḍanāyaka* in the inscription needs explanation. Tilabhaṭṭa, a scion of the royal family of Kauśāmbī, used the designation *mahārāja* in the correspondence he made in the capacity of feudal chief, while in the Allahabad pillar inscription, which is a royal record detailing the achievements of his Gupta overload, Samudragupta, he has been referred to by his official designation of *mahādaṇḍanāyaka*, which office he owed to the king. It would be appropriate in this context to mention the evidence of the Amauna copperplate inscription (No. 99), which has the titles *mahārāja* and *kumārāmātya* for the issuer of the grant, namely, Nandana. An explanation given for the use of the two titles is that Nandana is mentioned as a *kumārāmātya*, an official designation, which he owed to his overlord; however, his presence in his own territory at the time of making the grant prompted him to mention with a sense of pride his titular position, *mahārāja*.[12]

Identity of device,[13] even of style of smiling,[14] has been taken as an evidence of family relationship and, as such, the device of a "lion facing a *chakra* sideways", seen on the Vaiśālī sealing of Dhruvasvāminī (Dhruvadevī)—chief-queen of *Mahārājādhirāja* Chandragupta II and mother of *Mahārāja* Govindagupta (No. 13)—and also on the Kauśāmbī sealing of *Mahārāja* Tilabhaṭṭa, is significant.[15] It is striking that the device is not just a lion and a wheel which separately are quite common devices on ancient Indian seals (and also coins), but in both the cases the two are depicted as positioned in a way which is specific and peculiar and hence of a greater import as an evidence to suggest that Tilabhaṭṭa and Dhruvadevī belonged to the same family. This inference can also be made by arguing that since Dhruvadevī did not use the device of *garuḍa* – the insignia of the Imperial Gupta house[16] to which her illustrious husband, Chandragupta II, belonged[17] – it would be pertinent to assume that the device of lion facing a *chakra* used by her was that of her paternal family. Perhaps this was done with a view to conveying that from her paternal side too she belonged to a family of high status. Besides, this would also indicated her separate identity amongst the co-wives, the ancient kings generally being polygamous.[18] The assumption that Tilabhaṭṭa and Dhruvasvāminī belonged to the same family is the main plank on which rest the identifications of the members of the feudal family of Kauśāmbī, and the determining of their genealogy and chronology *vis-à-vis* their Gupta overlords.

Tilabhaṭṭa, as per the evidence of the Allahabad pillar inscription, was responsible for the execution[19] of the epigraph detailing Samudragupta's *praśasti* on the pillar at Kauśāmbī where it was originally located; it was later, perhaps during the reign of Akbar or Jahangir, that it was shifted to Allahabad where it now stands. The sealing of Tilabhaṭṭa has been found at Kauśāmbī, and though the find-spot of the sealing, in contrast to the findspot of the seal-die, is not a definite proof of the owner of the seal-die being stationed at that place, yet there is much possibility for that. One of the reasons for Tilabhaṭṭaka (= Tilabhaṭṭa) himself taking up the task of the execution of the said epigraph could be that as an official he was stationed at Kauśāmbī. Normally the execution of an epigraph did not require the services of such a high-ranking officer as *mahādaṇḍanāyaka*. It would seem that Tilabhaṭṭaka (Tilabhaṭṭa) of his own accord took this task upon himself because of his close family relationship with Samudragpta. Significantly, there is another piece of evidence, an independent one, to indicate Dhruvadevī's association with Kauśāmbī. According to the *Chandragarbha-paripṛichchhā*, King Mahendrasena (=Mahendrāditya, a title of Kumāragupta I, a son of Chandragupta [II] begotten on Dhruvadevī) was born at Kauśāmbī.[20] The practice of females going to their parents' house for the delivery of child, was there since hoary antiquity and continues even to this day. It is well known that Buddha's mother Mayādevī was on way to her paternal house to deliver her child, but gave birth to him in Lumbini grove where she had stopped to rest for a while. It may be presumed that in accordance with this practice, Dhruvadevī delivered her child, Kumāragupta I, at her parental place, Kauśāmbī.

It would be worthwhile to ascertain when the Kauśāmbī kingdom became part of the Gupta empire and who was the king of that region at that time. The first two Gupta rulers—Gupta and Ghaṭotkacha—are known as *mahārājas*, which seems to indicate their feudatory status. The purāṇic evidence referring to the extent of Gupta empire as comprising regions of Prayāga (Allahabad), Sāketa (Faizabad) and Magadha pertains to a period before the conquests of Samudragupta as a result of which the Gupta empire became quite extensive. Therefore, the purāṇic evidence regarding the extent of the Gupta kingdom should better be taken as belonging to the reign of his father, Chandragupta I (Chapter 3). It appears that the ruler of Kauśāmbī accepted the suzerainty of Chandragupta I whose original kingdom was probably in Magadha, either after being defeated, or even without giving a fight and was allowed to rule as his feudatory. He probably was a predecessor of Tilabhaṭṭa rather than Tilabhaṭṭa himself. After inferring that Tilabhaṭṭa was a feudal lord of a region with its headquarters at Kauśāmbī and that Dhruvadevī's paternal place was also the same, we may try to determine the relationship between

Tilabhaṭṭa and Dhruvadevī. The Allahabad pillar inscription belongs to the late phase of Samudragupta's rule as it was, no doubt, engraved after he had made all the conquests mentioned in that inscription, and as Tilabhaṭṭa is mentioned in that epigraph as *mahādaṇḍanāyaka* of that Gupta ruler, the king and his general, it may be suggested, would have been of about the same age. Since Chandragupta II was a son of Samudragupta, his wife Dhruvadevī, it may be suggested, was perhaps the daughter of Tilabhaṭṭa (Tilabhaṭṭaka).

We may discuss the evidence of certain sealings, ten in number, unearthed at Bhita in course of excavations conducted by Marshall at that site,[21] and a seal-die from Kauśāmbī published by us in the *Epigraphia Indica*.[22] All the sealings and the seal-die bear an identical legend[23] which clearly shows that they belonged to the office (*adhikaraṇa*) of *kumārāmātya* attached to *Mahāśvapati* ('great cavalry leader') and *Mahādaṇḍanāyaka* Vishṇurakshita. The evidence of the find of the seal-die from Kauśāmbī is significant for, in contrast to sealings, which are affixed to letters and parcels that might be dispatched to places both far and near, seal-dies would remain with the persons at the issuing end and, hence, should almost invariably be found at places where their owners were stationed. Hence, in all probability, like Tilabhaṭṭa, *Mahāśvapati-mahādaṇḍanāyaka* Vishṇurakshita was stationed at Kauśāmbī. There is hardly any possibility of two *daṇḍanāyakas* serving at Kauśāmbī simultaneously. It would seem that Viśṇurakshita held that office after Tilabhaṭṭa as his successor.

There is no incongruity in a *kumārāmātya* being attached to a person holding the office of *mahāśvapati* and *mahādaṇḍanāyaka* since this class of officials, as pointed out by us elsewhere,[24] enjoyed certain privileges exclusive to princes (*kumāras*) and could be assigned different tasks variously at the level of district, province and Centre, or entrusted special tasks, or attached to very high officials. Both Bhita and Kauśāmbī, it may be stated, form part of the present-day district of Allahabad. It appears during those days, Kauśāmbī was the capital of a Gupta province comprising Vatsa region, and at the time of the issue of the seals it was administered by *Mahāśvapati-mahādaṇḍanāyaka* Vishṇurakshita. The sealings found at Bhita must have been affixed to letters and other documents dispatched by the office of *kumārāmātya* who was attached to *Mahāśvapati-mahādaṇḍanāyaka* Vishṇurakshita with headquarters located in that city. Bhita would have been an important town within the province, may be a district headquarter, and sealed letters from provincial capital, Kausāmbī, were dispatched to some official or officials located there.

There is evidence to show that high officials in the Gupta period were often hereditary,[25] probably more so in the case of feudal chiefs. It seems that *Mahāśvapati-mahādaṇḍanāyaka* Vishṇurakshita of the Kauśāmbī seal-die (and Bhita sealings) was a feudal chief of Kauśāmbī under the Imperial Guptas which, as suggested above, was also the status of Tilabhaṭṭa. One gets the impression that Vishṇurakshita was a son of Tilabhaṭṭa and succeeded him as a feudal chief of the Kauśāmbī region. Further, as per the testimony of the Allahabad pillar inscription, Tilabhaṭṭaka (=Tilabhaṭṭa) was the *mahādaṇḍanāyaka* of Samudragupta. Vishṇurakshita too is referred to as the *mahādaṇḍanāyaka* (together with *mahāśvapati*), as per the evidence of the seal-die and sealings. The latter, it appears, held this office during the reign of Chandragupta II son and successor of Samudragupta. It seems that Vishṇurakshita, like Tilabhaṭṭa, was also entitled to use the designation of *mahārāja* by virtue of being the scion of the old ruling house. But since the seal and sealings referring to him belonged not to him but to the office of *kumārāmātya* attached to him, they mention only his official designations *mahāśvapati* and *mahādaṇḍanāyaka*, and not his family status of *mahārāja*.

An inscription from Mandasor (No. 36) dated in the Mālava year 524 (= AD 467) mentions one Dattabhaṭṭa whose father Vāyurakshita was a *senāpati* (general) of Govindagupta. The last mentioned is highly eulogized in that inscription which refers to him as the son of the Gupta king Chandragupta [II]. In the Vaiśālī sealing, he is mentioned as *mahārāja* and son of *Mahārājādhirāja* Chandragupta and Dhruvasvāminī. Since Govindagupta was a prince, the title *mahārāja* in his context cannot be taken to mean feudal lord and should denote a governor. The Mandasor inscription mentions two persons—Vāyurakshita, the father, and Dattabhaṭṭa, the son—with names ending in *rakshita* and *bhaṭṭa* respectively, and the former has been referred to as the general of Govindagupta. Likewise, in the context of Kauśāmbī, the family of the feudal lords of the Imperial Guptas, there were two persons, namely, Tilabhaṭṭa and Vishṇurakshita, father and son, whose names end with *bhaṭṭa* and *rakshita* respectively. On the basis of these name-endings, it could be argued that Vāyurakshita and Dattabhaṭṭa too belonged to the feudal family of Kauśāmbī. Most likely, Vāyurakshita, the *senāpati* of Govindagupta, was a son of Vishṇurakshita who (the latter) appears to have been a brother of Dhruvasvāminī, the mother of Govindagupta. This would mean that Vāyurakshita, the general of Govindagupta, was also his maternal cousin. The choice of the members of old royal house of

Kauśāmbī for the important office of general of Govindagupta was perhaps guided by the consideration that members of that family had at least for two successive generations served as *mahādaṇḍanāyakas* of the Gupta rulers and also as they were deemed loyal and trustworthy on account of their family relationship with the Gupta house.

The Mālava province, at least the area around Eran, after Budhagupta, or may be even during the last days of his reign (AD 476-94), came under the Hūṇas. One Mātṛivishṇu, as head of a district (*vishayapati*), was administering the region around Eran under Budhagupta as per the evidence of the Eran Pillar Inscription of that King (No. 44). But shortly thereafter, Mātṛivishṇu is referred to as deceased, and his brother Dhanyavishṇu as owing allegiance to Toramāṇa as per the evidence of Eran Stone Inscription of that Hūṇa King (No. 75). The Hūṇa invasion referred in the Bhitari Pillar Inscription (No. 33) of Skandagupta might have taken place, during the last days of his father's reign or the beginning of his own reign. May be the Hūṇa hordes had started pouring in even before that in the Malwa region. If the reference in the Mandasor inscription to Govindagupta belongs to the phase when he was governor then it can be said that for counteracting Hūṇa menace and other problems appointment of trustworthy governor and general for the Mālava region were the need of the time, and that for the governorship the choice fell on the royal prince, Govindagupta,[26] and for generalship, on Vāyurakshita, the scion of the old royal house of Kauśāmbī which had provided two successive generals (*mahādaṇḍanāyakas*) to the Gupta royal house, namely, Tilabhaṭṭa and Vishṇurakshita. It is also likely that the evidence of the Mandasor inscription of Prabhākara refers to Vāyurakshita as general of Govindagupta as a king, and not as prince-governor, which seems to receive some support from the fact that in the Mandasor inscription it has been stated that Indra was afraid of Govindagupta's power, which statement suits him better as a king.

It is significant that the names Vishṇurakshita and Govindagupta carry the same meaning. Vishṇu and Govinda being two names of the same deity, and both *rakshita* and *gupta* mean 'protected'. It may further be noted that the meaning of Rāmagupta ('protected by Rāma') elder brother of Chandragupta II and the first husband of Dhruvasvāminī (Dhruvadevī), is also the same as that of Vishṇurakshita and Govindagupta. This similarity of the meaning of the names also favours the view that the two families were related by matrimonial alliance. Possibly,

Rāmagupta was elder to Vishṇurakshita, and the latter being a member of the feudatory family was named after the Gupta prince. The practice of naming the son of a feudatory after that of the member of the overlord imperial family is known. For example, Samudravarman of the Bhauma-Naraka dynasty of Kāmarūpa, which was subordinate to the Imperial Gupta family, has been taken by scholars as a case of naming the prince after Gupta emperor Samudragupta and his queen Dattadevī after the queen of that ruler.[27] The Kauśāmbī feudatory family, however, instead of giving a name identical to that of the Gupta prince, preferred to give a name, which had the same meaning. Incidentally, the names Vishṇurakshita, Rāmagupta and Govindagupta are Vaishṇava, which is befitting for the Vaishṇava Gupta rulers and their feudatories. That the Imperial Gupta kings were Vaishṇavas is clear from the title *parama-bhāgavata* used for most of them, and from their royal insignia of *garuḍa*, the vehicle of Vishṇu. It is not known whether the members of the ruling family of Kauśāmbī were also Vaishṇava, or they became converts to Vaishṇavism under the influence of their Gupta overlord, after the family became feudatory of the Guptas. It is known that the Vākāṭakas were originally Śaivas but under the influence of the Guptas, Rudrasena II, the son-in-law of Chandragupta II became a Vaishṇava (No. 83). From what has been stated above, it appears that the Imperial Gupta family was matrimonially related to the family whose members were scions of the old royal house of Kauśāmbī, and in the Gupta administration, the latter enjoyed the status of feudal lords, and held important high offices in successive generations under successive Gupta kings.

The above is an attempt to reconstruct, with a little bit of conjecture, of the family relationship of the Imperial Gupta family with the feudal family of Kauśāmbī, establish the genealogy and chronology of the latter family, and point out the contemporaneity between the scions of the two families in successive generations and also the official relationship that existed between them. The same is presented in a tabular form:

**A. Members of the feudatory Family of Kauśāmbī**

**B. Members of the Gupta Family**

Father of Tilabhaṭṭa (name not known) — Chandragupta I

Tilabhaṭṭa (referred to as *Mahārāja* Tilabhaṭṭa in the Kauśāmbī sealing and *Mahādaṇḍanāyaka*, Tilabhaṭṭaka in the Allahabad pillar inscription of Samudragupta) — Samudragupta

Vishṇurakshita (referred to as *Mahāśvapati* and *Mahādaṇḍanāyaka* in a Kauśāmbī seal-die and in the sealings from Bhita.)

Dhruvadevī (first married to Rāmagupta and later to Chandragupta II) — Rāmagupta; Chandragupta II

Vāyurakshita (General of Govindagupta as per the evidence of the Mandasor Inscription of AD 467) — Govindagupta

Kumāragupta I

Dattabhaṭa (General of Prabhākara as mentioned in the Mandasor Inscription of AD 467) — Skandagupta

## NOTES AND REFERENCES

1. Vatsa *janapada* with its capital at Kausāmbī was one of the most important states among the sixteen *mahājanapadas* in northern India in the sixth-fifth century BC. In the fourth century BC it came to be incorporated in the Magadhan kingdom. With the downfall of the Maurya empire, barring the rule of the Kushāṇa kings Kanishka and Huvishka, the region around Kausāmbī came under the rule of a number of local kings known from inscriptions, coins and seals, till it came to be incorporated in the Gupta empire in the first half of the fourth century AD.

2. K K Thaplyal, *Prāgdhārā*, No. 1, pp. 123-25.
3. K K Thaplyal, *Epigraphia Indica*, XLII, pp. 158-60; and plates.
4. K K Thaplyal, in J P Joshi (ed.), *Facets of Indian Civilization—Recent Perspectives* (*Essays in Honour of Prof B B Lal*), pp. 884-89.
5. The expression used for him is *pādānudhyāta*, which literally means "meditating on the feet". But it also indicates the sense of "serving under", "appointed by", "attached to", or "favoured by".
6. The term used is *bhaṭṭāraka* (literally "worshipful one"). A common designation of king in the Gupta and post-Gupta periods is *parama-bhaṭṭāraka*.
7. E J Rapson, *Journal of the Royal Asiatic Society of Great Britain and Ireland*, 1897, p. 420; V A Smith, *Indian Museum Catalogue*, I, pp. 185ff; J Allan, *Catalogue of the Coins of the Gupta Dynasties, and of Śaśāṅka, King of Gauḍa, in the British Museum, London*, p. xxiii.
8. J F Fleet, *Corpus Inscriptionum Indicarum*, III, p. 136 (Muruṇḍasvāminī), and *ibid.*, p. 137 (Muruṇḍadevī).
9. V V Mirashi, *Vākāṭaka Rājavaṁśa kā Itihāsa tathā Abhilekha*, pp. 206-07.
10. D R Bhandarkar, *Corpus Inscriptionum Indicarum*, III, p. 35. However, in the text of the inscription (*ibid.*, p. 215) the name has been correctly given as Tilabhaṭṭaka. But the editors—B Ch Chhabra and G S Gai—have, in their editorial note (*ibid.*, p. 230, n. 6) suggested the possibility of the name being Tilakabhaṭṭa.
11. D R Bhandarkar (*Corpus Inscriptionum Indicarum*, III, p. 95) considers it similar to "Duke", "Earl" and "Viscount".
12. D R Bhandarkar, *Corpus Inscriptionum Indicarum*, III, p. 92.
13. On the basis of the types of helmet that Eukratides and Seleukos I are shown wearing, they are considered as belonging to the same family (W W Tarn, *The Greeks in Bactria and India*, Cambridge, 1951, p. 196.)
14. On the basis of the style of smiling Antimachos has been identified as a son of Euthydemos and younger brother of Demetrios (*ibid.*, p. 75).
15. K K Thaplyal, *Prāgdhārā*, No. I, pp. 123ff.
16. For *garuḍa* as insignia of the Imperial Gupta family, see A S Altekar, *The Coinage of the Gupta Empire*, p. 151.
17. Dhruvasvāminī (=Dhruvadevī) as per śāstric injuction became member of the Gupta house after her marrige, and should have adopted its *gotra* and, one expected, also its insignia, but such is not the case.
18. At least one more queen of Chandragupta II, namely, Kuberanāgā, is known from the records of the Vākāṭakas, the royal family in which her daughter, Prabhāvatīguptā, was married.
19. D R Bhandarkar, *Corpus Inscriptionum Indicarum*, III, p. 220. The original Sanskrit expression is *anusṭhitam*.
20. R C Majumdar, in *The Classical Age*, p. 26, fn. 1.
21. *Archaeological Survey of India—Annual Report*, 1911-12, pp. 52-53.
22. *Epigraphia Indica*, XLII, pp. 158-60, and plates.
23. Only one shows the complete legend as *Mahāśvapati Mahādaṇḍanāyaka Vishṇurakshita pādānudhyāta kumārāmaty=ādhikaraṇasya.* See J H Marshall, in

*Archaeological Survey of India—Annual Report*, 1911-12, p. XVIII, No. 32. In other cases the legend is partly out of flan.

24. K K Thaplyal, *Studies on Ancient Indian Seals*, p. 113.
25. The Allahabad Pillar Inscription (No. 1) mentions Harisheṇa, the *sāndhivigrahika*, *kumārāmātya* and *mahādaṇḍanāyaka* of Samudragupta, as a son of *Mahādaṇḍanāyaka* Dhruvabhuti, while the Karamdanda Inscription of Kumaragupta I (No. 20) refers to *Mantrī, Kumārāmātya and Mahābalādhikṛita* Pṛithvīsheṇa as son of *Mantrī* and *Kumārāmātya* Śikharasvāmī.
26. Another possibility is that Prince Govindagupta rebelled against Kumāragupta I and declared himself independent on the death of his father Chandragupta II. The view that he rebelled against Skandagupta is not acceptable (Chapter 8).
27. *Vide* Nidhanpur copperplate inscription, *Epigraphia Indica*, XII, p. 65.

# Plates

**Plate I**

1. Samudragupta: Standard type

2. Samudragupta: Archer type

3. Samudragupta: Battle-axe type

4. Samudragupta: Lyrist type

5. Chandragupta II: Archer type

**Plate II**

1. Chandragupta II: Lion-slayer type

2. Chandragupta II: *Chhatra* type

3. Kumāragupta I: Archer type

4. Kumāragupta I: Horseman type

5. Kumāragupta I: Lion-slayer type

## Plate III

1. Kumāragupta I: *Aśvamedha* type

2. Kumāragupta I: Kārttikeya type

3. Kumāragupta I: *Apratigha* type

4. Skandagupta: Archer type

5. Skandagupta: King-and-Queen or King-and-Lakshmī type

## Plate IV

1. Budhagupta: Archer type

2. Prakāśāditya: Horse-rider-Lion-slayer type

3. Narasiṁhagupta: Archer type

4. Vishṇugupta: Archer type

**Plate V**

1. Chandragupta I: Chandragupta I-Kumāradevī type

2. Samudragupta: Tiger-slayer type

3. Samudragupta: *Aśvamedha* type

4. Chandragupta II: Horseman type

5. Chandragupta II: Couch type

6. Chandragupta II: *Chakravikrama* type

## Plate VI

1. Kācha: Kācha type

2. Kumāragupta I: Swordsman type

3. Kumāragupta I: *Chhatra* type

4. Kumāragupta I: Tiger-slayer type

5. Kumāragupta I: Elephant-rider-Lion-slayer type

6. Kumāragupta I: Rhinoceros-slayer type

**Plate VII**

1. Kumāragupta I: Elephant-rider type

2. Kumāragupta I: Lyrist type

3. Kumāragupta I: King-and-Queen type

4. Skandagupta: *Chhatra* type

5. Kumāragupta II: Archer type

6. Vainyagupta: Archer type

Plate VIII

Kahaum Pillar Inscription of Skandagupta

# Bibliography

## A. LIST OF INSCRIPTIONS


1. Allahabad Stone Pillar Inscription of Samudragupta (D R Bhandarkar, *Corpus Inscriptionum Indicarum*, III, p. 203, pl. I).
2. Eran Stone Inscription of Samudragupta (D R Bhandarkar, *Corpus Inscriptionum Indicarum*, III, p. 220, pl. II).
3. Nalanda copper-plate Inscription of Samudragupta, year 5 (D R Bhandarkar, *Corpus Inscriptionum Indicarum*, III, p. 224, pl. III).
4. Gaya copper-plate Inscription of Samudragupta, year 9 (D R Bhandarkar, *Corpus Inscriptionum Indicarum*, III, p. 228, pl. IV).
5. Vidisha Stone Image Inscription of Rāmagupta (D R Bhandarkar, *Corpus Inscriptionum Indicarum*, III, p. 231, pl. V).
6. Mathura Pilaster Inscription of Chandragupta II, year 61 (D R Bhandarkar, *Corpus Inscriptionum Indicarum*, III, p. 234, pl. VI).
7. Udaigiri Cave Inscription of Chandragupta II, year 82 (D R Bhandarkar, *Corpus Inscriptionum Indicarum*, III, p. 242, pl. VII).
8. Gadhwa Stone Inscription of Chandragupta II, year 88 (D R Bhandarkar, *Corpus Inscriptionum Indicarum*, III, p. 244, pl. VIII).
9. Sanchi Stone Inscription of Chandragupta II, year 93 (D R Bhandarkar, *Corpus Inscriptionum Indicarum*, III, p. 247, pl. X).
10. Mathura Stone Inscription of Chandragupta II (D R Bhandarkar, *Corpus Inscriptionum Indicarum*, III, p. 252, pl. X).
11. Udaigiri Cave Inscription of Chandragupta II (D R Bhandarkar, *Corpus Inscriptionum Indicarum*, III, p. 255, pl. XI).
12. Mehrauli Iron Pillar Inscription of Chandra (D R Bhandarkar, *Corpus Inscriptionum Indicarum*, III, p. 257, pl. XII).

13. Basarh Clay Seal Inscription of Dhruvasvāminī (D R Bhandarkar, *Corpus Inscriptionum Indicarum*, III, p. 260, pl. XIII).
14. Bilsad Stone Pillar Inscription of Kumāragupta I, year 96 (D R Bhandarkar, *Corpus Inscriptionum Indicarum*, III, p. 267, pl. XVI).
15. Gadhwa Stone Inscription of Kumāragupta I, year 98 (D R Bhandarkar, *Corpus Inscriptionum Indicarum*, III, p. 270, pl. XVII).
16. Udaigiri Cave Inscription of Kumāragupta I, year 106 (J F Fleet, *Corpus Inscriptionum Indicarum*, III, 258).
17. Mathura Image Inscription of Kumāragupta I, year 107 (D R Bhandarkar, *Corpus Inscriptionum Indicarum*, III, p. 272, pl. XVIII).
18. Dhanaidaha copper-plate Inscription of Kumāragupta I, year 113 (D R Bhandarkar, *Corpus Inscriptionum Indicarum*, III, p. 273, pl. XIX).
19. Tumain Inscription of Kumāragupta I, year 116 (D R Bhandarkar, *Corpus Inscriptionum Indicarum*, III, p. 276, pl. XX).
20. Karamdanda Stone Inscription of Kumāragupta I, year 117 (D R Bhandarkar, *Corpus Inscriptionum Indicarum*, III, p. 280, pl. XXI).
21. Kulaikuri copper-plate Inscription, year 120 (D C Sircar, Kalaikuri Copper-plate Inscription of the Gupta Year 120, *Indian Historical Quarterly*, XIX, pp. 12-26).
22. Damodarpur copper-plate Inscription of Kumāragupta I, year 124 (D R Bhandarkar, *Corpus Inscriptionum Indicarum*, III, p. 282, pl. XXII).
23. Mathura Image Inscription of Kumāragupta I, year 125 (D R Bhandarkar, *Corpus Inscriptionum Indicarum*, III, p. 287, pl. XXIII).
24. Damodarpur copper-plate Inscription of Kumāragupta I, year 128 (D R Bhandarkar, *Corpus Inscriptionum Indicarum*, III, p. 288, pl. XXIV).
25. Baigram copper-plate Inscription of Kumāragupta I, year 128 (R G Basak, Baigram Copper-plate Inscription of the [Gupta] Year 128, *Epigraphia Indica*, XXI, p. 78).
26. Jagdishpur copper-plate Inscription of the Time of Kumāragupta I, year 128 (D C Sircar, *Epigraphic Discoveries in East Pakistan*, Sanskrit College, Calcutta, 1973, pp. 8-14, 61-63; P K Agrawal, *Imperial Gupta Epigraphs*, pp. 51-54).
27. Mankuwar Stone Inscription of Kumāragupta I, year 129 (D R Bhandarkar, *Corpus Inscriptionum Indicarum*, III, p. 291, pl. XXV).
28. Gadhwa Stone Inscription of Kumāragupta I (D R Bhandarkar, *Corpus Inscriptionum Indicarum*, III, p. 293, pl. XXVI).
29. Basarh Clay Seal Inscription of Ghaṭotkachagupta (D R Bhandarkar, *Corpus Inscriptionum Indicarum*, III, p. 294, pl. XXVII).
30. Junagarh Rock Inscription of Skandagupta, years 136, 137, 138 (D R Bhandarkar, *Corpus Inscriptionum Indicarum*, III, p. 296, pl. XXVIII).
31. Kahaum Stone Pillar Inscription of Skandagupta, year 141 (D R Bhandarkar, *Corpus Inscriptionum Indicarum*, III, p. 305, pl. XXIX).
32. Supia Pillar Inscription of the time of Skandagupta, year 141 (D R Bhandarkar, *Corpus Inscriptionum Indicarum*, III, p. 317, pl. XXXII).

33. Bhitari Stone Pillar Inscription of Skandagupta (D R Bhandarkar, *Corpus Inscriptionum Indicarum*, III, p. 312, pl. XXXI).
34. Indore copper-plate Inscription of Skandagupta, year 146 (D R Bhandarkar, *Corpus Inscriptionum Indicarum*, III, p. 308, pl. XXX).
35. Bihar Stone Pillar Inscription of Purugupta (?) (D C Sircar, *Select Inscriptions*, I, p. 325). The same as D R Bhandarkar, *Corpus Inscriptionum Indicarum*, III, No. 41, p. 345, pl XLI, who tentatively assigns the epigraph to Budhagupta.
36. Mandasor Stone Inscription of the time of Prabhākara, (Mālava Year) 524 (D C Sircar, *Select Inscriptions*, I, p. 406).
37. Sarnath Stone Inscription of Kumāragupta II, year 154 (D R Bhandarkar, *Corpus Inscriptionum Indicarum*, III, p. 321, pl. XXXIV).
38. Mandasor Inscription of Kumāragupta I and Bandhuvarman, (VS) 493, 529 (D R Bhandarkar, *Corpus Inscriptionum Indicarum*, III, p. 322, pl. XXXV).
39. Sarnath Stone Inscriptions of Budhagupta, year 157 (D R Bhandarkar, *Corpus Inscriptionum Indicarum*, III, p. 332, pl. XXXVI).
40. Rajghat (Vārāṇasī) Stone Pillar Inscription of Budhagupta, year 159 (D R Bhandarkar, *Corpus Inscriptionum Indicarum*, III, p. 334, pl. XXXVII).
41. Paharpur copper-plate Inscription of Budhagupta, year 159 (K N Dikshit, Paharpur Copper-plate Grant of the [Gupta] Year 159, *Epigraphia Indica*, XX, p. 59; D C Sircar, *Select Inscriptions*, I, p. 395).
42. Mathura Stone Image Inscription of Budhagupta, year 161 (K K Thaplyal and A K Srivastava, Mathura Stone Pedestal Inscription of the Time of Budhagupta, Gupta Year 161, *Journal of the Epigraphical Society of India*, IX, pp. 6-11).
43. Damodarpur copper-plate Inscription of Budhagupta, year 163 (D R Bhandarkar, *Corpus Inscriptionum Indicarum*, III, p. 335, pl. XXXVIII).
44. Eran Stone Pillar Inscription of Budhagupta, year 165 (D R Bhandarkar, *Corpus Inscriptionum Indicarum*, III, p. 339, pl. XXXIX).
45. Damodarpur copper-plate Inscription of Budhagupta (D R Bhandarkar, *Corpus Inscriptionum Indicarum*, III, p. 342, pl. XL).
46. Shankarpur copper-plate Inscription of Budhagupta, year 168 (B C Jain, Shankarpur Copper-plate of Budhagupta and Harivarman: Gupta Year 166, *Journal of the Epigraphical Society of India*, IV, 1977, pp. 62-66).
47. Nalanda Clay Seal of Budhagupta (D R Bhandarkar, *Corpus Inscriptionum Indicarum*, III, p. 350, pl. XLII).
48. Nandapur copper-plate Inscription, year 169 (N G Majumdar, Nandapur Copper-plate of the Gupta Year 169, *Epigraphia Indica*, XXIII, pp. 52ff).
49. Bhitari Stone Inscription of the time of Budhagupta, year 170 (P K Agrawal, *Imperial Gupta Epigraphs*, pp. 111-112).
50. Gunaighar copper-plate Inscription of Vainyagupta, year 188 (D C Bhattacharya, A Newly Discovered Copper-plate from Tippera, *Indian Historical Quarterly*, VI, p. 45-60; D C Sircar, *Select Inscriptions*, I, p. 340).
51. Nalanda Clay Seal of Vainyagupta (D R Bhandarkar, *Corpus Inscriptionum Indicarum*, III, p. 319, pl. XXXIII).

52. Eran Stone Inscription of Bhānugupta, year 191 (D R Bhandarkar, *Corpus Inscriptionum Indicarum*, III, p. 352, pl. XLIII).
53. Nalanda Clay Seals of Narasiṁhagupta (D R Bhandarkar, *Corpus Inscriptionum Indicarum*, III, p. 354, pl. XLIV).
54. Nalanda Clay Seals of Kumāragupta III (D R Bhandarkar, *Corpus Inscriptionum Indicarum*, III, p. 355, pl. XLV).
55. Bhitari Copper-Silver Seal of Kumāragupta III (D R Bhandarkar, *Corpus Inscriptionum Indicarum*, III, p. 358, pl. XLVI).
56. Bhitari Fragmentary Stone inscription, Gupta year 221 (P K Agrawala, *Imperial Gupta Epigraphs*, p. 122).
57. Damodarpur copper-plate Inscription of Vishṇugupta, year 224 (D R Bhandarkar, *Corpus Inscriptionum Indicarum*, III, p. 360, pl. XLVII).
58. Nalanda Clay Seal of Vishṇugupta (D R Bhandarkar, *Corpus Inscriptionum Indicarum*, III, p. 364, pl. XLVIII).
59. Susunia inscription of Chandravarman (D C Sircar, *Select Inscriptions*, I, pp. 351-352).
60. Mandasor Inscription of Naravarman, (VS) 461 (D R Bhandarkar, *Corpus Inscriptionum Indicarum*, III, p. 261, pl. XIV).
61. Bihar Kotra Inscription of Naravarman, (VS) 474 (D R Bhandarkar, *Corpus Inscriptionum Indicarum*, III, p. 266, pl. XV).
62. Gangdhar Stone Inscription of Viśvavarman, (VS) 480 (J F Fleet, *Corpus Inscriptionum Indicarum*, III, p. 72, pl. X; D C Sircar, *Select Inscriptions*, I, p. 399).
63. Khoh copper-plate Inscription of Hastin, year 156 (J F Fleet, *Corpus Inscriptionum Indicarum*, III, p. 93).
64. Khoh copper-plate Inscription of Hastin, year 163 (J F Fleet, *Corpus Inscriptionum Indicarum*, III, p. 100).
65. Majhgawan copper-plate Inscription of Hastin, year 191 (J F Fleet, *Corpus Inscriptionum Indicarum*, III, p. 106).
66. Navagrama copper-plate Inscription of Hastin, year 198 (K N Dikshit, Navagrama Grant of the Mahārāja Hastin (G E 198), *Epigraphia Indica*, XXI, p. 124).
67. Betul copper-plate Inscription of Saṁkshobha, year 199 (Hira Lal, Betul Plates of Saṁkshobha, The Gupta Year 199, *Epigraphia Indica*, VIII, p. 284).
68. Khoh copper-plate Inscription of Saṁkshobha, year 209 (J F Fleet, *Corpus Inscriptionum Indicarum*, III, p. 112).
69. Karitalai copper-plate Inscription of Jayanātha, year 174 (J F Fleet, *Corpus Inscriptionum Indicarum*, III, p. 117).
70. Khoh copper-plate Inscription of Jayanātha, year 177 (J F Fleet, *Corpus Inscriptionum Indicarum*, III, p. 121).
71. Sohawal copper-plate Inscription of Śarvanātha, year 191 (R R Halder, The Sohawal Copper-plate Inscription of Mahārāja Śarvanātha—The Year 191, *Epigraphia Indica*, XIX, p. 127).
72. Khoh copper-plate Inscription of Śarvanātha, year 193 (J F Fleet, *Corpus Inscriptionum Indicarum*, III, p. 123).

73. Khoh copper-plate Inscription of Śarvanātha, year 197 (J F Fleet, *Corpus Inscriptionum Indicarum*, III, p. 132).
74. Khoh copper-plate Inscription of Śarvanātha, year 214 (J F Fleet, *Corpus Inscriptionum Indicarum*, III, p. 133).
75. Eran Stone Inscription of Toramāṇa, regnal year 1 (J F Fleet, *Corpus Inscriptionum Indicarum*, III, p. 139).
76. Sanjeli copper-plate Inscriptions (R N Mehta and M S Thakkar, M S University Copper Plates of the time of Toramāṇa, *M S University, Baroda, Archaeological Series*, No. 14, 1978).
77. Gwalior Stone Inscription of Mihirakula, regnal year 15 (J F Fleet, *Corpus Inscriptionum Indicarum*, III, p. 162).
78. Risthal Inscription of Prakāśadharman (S R Goyal, *Ancient Indian Inscriptions: Recent Finds and New Interpretations*, pp. 176ff).
79. Mandasor Stone Inscription of Yaśodharman *alias* Vishṇuvardhana, [VS] 589 (J F Fleet, *Corpus Inscriptionum Indicarum*, III, p. 152; *Indian Antiquary*, XVIII, p. 220; XX, p. 188; D C Sircar, *Select Inscriptions*, I, p. 411).
80. Mandasor Stone Pillar Inscription of Yaśodharman (J F Fleet, *Corpus Inscriptionum Indicarum*, III, p. 146; *Indian Antiquary*, XVIII, p. 219; XX, p. 188; D C Sircar, *Select Inscriptions*, I, p. 418).
81. Nachna-ki-talai Stone Inscriptions of the Mahārāja Pṛithivīsheṇa (J F Fleet, *Corpus Inscriptionum Indicarum*, III, pp. 233 ff.).
82. Poona copper-plate Inscription of Prabhāvatīguptā, regnal year 13 (D C Sircar, *Select Inscriptions*, I, p. 435).
83. Chammak copper-plate Inscription of Pravarasena II, regnal year 18 (D C Sircar, *Select Inscriptions*, I, p. 442).
84. Rithpur copper-plate Inscription (of Prabhāvatīguptā) of the time of Pravarasena II, regnal year 19 (D C Sircar, *Select Inscriptions*, I, p. 439).
85. Ramtek Prabhāvatīguptā Memorial Stone Inscription (A M Shastri, *Early History of the Deccan: Problems and Perspectives*, Chapter V; *Vākāṭaka: Sources and History*, New Delhi, 1997, pp. 125-135.
86. Ajanta Cave Inscription of the time of Harisheṇa (D C Sircar, *Select Inscriptions*, I, p. 449).
87. Balaghat Plates of Pṛithvīsheṇa II, (F Keilhorn, Balaghat Plates of Pṛithivīsheṇa II, *Epigraphia Indica*, IX, pp. 267ff).
88. Ganj Inscription [of Vyāghra] of the time of Pṛithvīsheṇa II (D C Sircar, *Select Inscriptions*, I, p. 456).
89. Cambay copper-plate of Govinda IV (D R Bhandarkar, Cambay Plates of Govinda IV: Śaka-*Saṁvat* 852, *Epigraphia Indica*, VII, pp. 26ff).
90. Sangli Plate of Govinda IV (J F Fleet, *Indian Antiquary*, XII, pp. 250ff).
91. Talgunda Pillar Inscription of Kākusthavarman (F Kielhorn, *Epigraphia Indica*, VIII, pp. 24ff.
92. Sanjan copper-plate of Amoghavarsha I (D R Bhandarkar, Sanjan Plates of Amoghavarsha I: Śaka-*Saṁvat* 793, *Epigraphia Indica*, XVIII, pp. 235ff).

93. Jaunpur Stone Inscription of Īśvaravarman (J F Fleet, *Corpus Inscriptionum Indicarum*, III, pp. 228ff).
94. Haraha Stone Inscription of Īśānavarman, [VS] 611 (D C Sircar, *Select Inscriptions*, I, pp. 385ff).
95. Aphsad Stone Inscription of Ādityasena (J F Fleet, *Corpus Inscriptionum Indicarum*, III, pp. 200ff).
96. Bhamodara-Mohota copper-plate Inscription of Droṇasiṁha, year 183 (D C Sircar, *Select Inscriptions*, I, pp. 426ff).
97. Sarnath Inscription of Prakaṭāditya, (J F Fleet, *Corpus Inscriptionum Indicarum*, III, No. 79, pp. 284ff.)
98. Mallasarul copper-plate Inscription [of Vijayasena] of the time of Gopachandra—Regnal Year 33 (D C Sircar, *Select Inscriptions*, I, pp. 373ff.).
99. Amauna copper-plate Inscription of *Mahārāja* Nandana (T Bloch, *Epigraphia Indica*, pp. 49f).
100. Nalanda Stone Inscription of Yaśovarman (K K Thaplyal, *Inscriptions of the Maukharis, Later Guptas, Pushpabhūtis and Yaśovarman of Kanauj*, pp. 191ff).

## B. SELECT BOOKS AND ARTICLES

Agrawal, Ashvini (1988), A Note on the Identity of Kācha of the Gupta Gold Coins, *Journal of the Numismatic Society of India*, L, pp. 79-81.

—— (1989), *The Rise and Fall of the Imperial Guptas*, Delhi.

Agrawal, Jagannath (1946), The Pushyamitras of the Bhitari Inscription, *Indian Historical Quarterly*, XXII, No. 2, pp. 112-17.

—— (1946), The Location of T-china Temple and the Original Home of the Imperial Guptas, *Indian Historical Quarterly*, XXII, No. 1, pp. 28-33.

—— (1958), Samudragupta's Performance of Aśvamedha Sacrifice, in Hariram Gupta (ed.), *Sir Jadunath Sarkar Commemoration Volume, II, Essays Presented to Sir Jadunath Sarkar*, pp. 10-13.

—— (1965), A Rare Clay Sealing from Sunet, *Journal of the Numismatic Society of India*, XXVII (i), pp. 98-99.

—— (1968), The Status of Skandagupta's Mother, *Annals of the Bhandarkar Oriental Research Institute*, XLV-XLIX, pp. 325-327.

—— (1969-70), The Status of Govindagupta, *Journal of Ancient Indian History*, III, pp. 101-107.

—— (1986), *Researches in Indian Epigraphy and Numismatics*, Delhi.

—— (1989), Comments and Observations on the Lead Paper of S R Goyal in M C Joshi and S K Gupta (ed.), *King Chandra and the Mehrauli Pillar*, pp. 95-104.

Agrawala, P K (ed.) (1983), *Imperial Gupta Epigraphs*, Varanasi.

Agrawala, V S (1954), An Explanation of the Chakravikrama Type Coin of Chandragupta II, *Journal of the Numismatic Society of India*, XVI (i), pp. 97-101.

—— (1956), Review of *Catalogue of the Gupta Gold Coins in the Bayana Hoard* by Dr. A S Altekar, in *Journal of the Numismatic Society of India*, XVII, pp. 114-123.

—— (1963), *Matsya Purāṇa—A Study*, Varanasi.

Ahmad, Nisar (1962), On the Historicity of Rāmagupta, *Indian Historical Quarterly*, XXXVIII, No. 4, pp. 283-91.

—— (1971), On Some Repousse Coins, *Journal of the Numismatic Society of India*, XXXIII (ii), pp. 115-17.

—— (1988), The Coins of Prakāśāditya: A Study, *Journal of the Numismatic Society of India*, L, pp. 89-96.

—— (1991), Chandragupta-Kumāradevī Type of Gupta Coinage: Examination of Arguments of Allan and Altekar on the Question of its Issuer, *Journal of the Numismatic Society of India*, LIII, pp. 100-113.

Aiyangar, S Krishnaswami (1927), Studies in Gupta History, *Journal of Indian History*, VI (ii), pp. 1-61.

—— (1941), *Ancient India and South Indian History and Culture*, I, Poona.

Allan, John (1914), *Catalogue of the Coins of the Gupta Dynasties, and of Śaśāṅka, King of Gauḍa*, London.

Altekar, A S (1928), A New Gupta king, *Journal of the Bihar and Orissa Research Society*, XIV, pp. 223-53.

—— (1929), Further Discussion about Rāmagupta, *Journal of the Bihar and Orissa Research Society*, XV, pp. 134-41.

—— (1947), Identity of Kāchagupta, *Journal of the Numismatic Society of India*, IX (ii), pp. 131-36.

—— (1954), *Catalogue of the Gupta Gold Coins in the Bayana Hoard*, Bombay.

—— (1957), *The Coinage of the Gupta Empire and its Imitations*, Varanasi.

—— (1959), A Note on the Apratigha Type, *Journal of the Numismatic Society of India*, XXI (i), pp. 71-72.

—— (1959), Lyrist Type of Samudragupta in Silver, *Journal of the Numismatic Society of India*, XXI, pp. 191-92.

Bajpai, K D (1961), Rāmagupta, A Gupta King, *Journal of the Numismatic Society of India*, XXIII, pp. 340-44.

—— (1962), Fresh Light on the Problem of Rāmagupta, *Indian Historical Quarterly*, XXXVIII, No. 1, pp. 80-85.

—— (1964), Identification of Rāmagupta, *Journal of Indian History*, XLII (ii), pp. 389-93.

—— (1967), The Problem of Pushyamitras, *Bulletin of Ancient Indian History and Archaeology*, No. 1, pp. 13-19.

—— (1969), A Note on Svabhoganagara in the Eran Inscription of Samudragupta, *Bulletin of Ancient Indian History and Archaeology*, I, pp. 69-70.

—— (1976), *Indian Numismatic Studies*, New Delhi.

Banerjea, J N (1955), Gupta Gold Coins in the Bayana Hoard, *Journal of the Numismatic Society of India*, pp. 210-16.

Banerji, R D (1933), *The Age of the Imperial Guptas*, Benaras.

Basak, Radhagovinda (1919-20), The Five Damodarpur Copper-plate Inscriptions of the Gupta Period, *Epigraphia Indica*, XV, pp. 113-45.

—— (1967), *The History of North-eastern India*, Revised edn, Calcutta.

Basham, A L (1955), The Date of the End of the Reign of Kumāragupta I and the Succession after his Death, *Bulletin of the School of Oriental and African Studies*, XVII (ii), pp. 366-69.

—— (1983), The Mandasor Inscription of the Silk-weavers, in Bardwell L Smith (ed.), *Essays on Gupta Culture*, Delhi, pp. 93-105.

Beal, Samuel (1906), *Si-yu-ki, Buddhist Records of the Western World*, 2 vols. London.

—— (2003), *The Life of Hiuen-Tsiang*, reprint (first published 1911), Delhi.

Bhandarkar, D R (1932), New Light on the Early Gupta History, in *Malaviya Commemoration Volume*, Varanasi, pp. 189-211.

—— (1981), *Corpus Inscriptionum Indicarum*, III, edited by B Ch Chhabra and G S Gai, New Delhi.

Bhattacharya, B (1944), New Light on the History of the Imperial Gupta Dynasty, *Journal of the Bihar Research Society*, XXX (i), pp. 1-46.

Bhattacharya, D C (1930), A Newly Discovered Copper-plate from Tippera, *Indian Historical Quarterly*, VI, No. 1, pp. 45-60.

Bhattacharya, Sibesh (1992) Ghaṭotkacha the King Kācha of Coins, B Ch Chhabra, *et al.* (ed.), *Reappraising Gupta History for S R Goyal*, pp. 77-82.

Bhattacharya, Tarapada (1946), Was Anantadevī Mother of Skandagupta?, *Journal of the Bihar Research Society*, XXXII, pp. 182-83.

Brown, C J (1920),*Catalogue of the Coins of the Guptas, Maukharis, etc., in the Provincial Museum, Lucknow.*

—— (1973), *Coins of India*, (reprint), Varanasi.

Buddha Prakash (1957), *Daivaputra-shāhi-shāhānushāhi* in the Allahabad pillar inscription of Samudragupta, *Indian Historical Quarterly*, XXXIII, No. 2, pp. 119-28.

—— (1965), *Aspects of Indian History and Civilization*, Agra.

—— (1971), Samudragupta's Southern Expedition: A New Interpretation, in *Prof K A Nilakanta Sastri Felicitation Volume*, Madras, pp. 15-31.

Chakravarty, D K, (1989), Study on Gupta Kings from Anthropological Point of View, *Journal of the Numismatic Society of India*, LI, pp. 60-61.

Chakraborti, Haripada (1978), *India as Reflected in the Inscriptions of the Gupta Period*, New Delhi.

Chatterjee, C D (1975), Gold Coins of the Standard Type (Class I) of Chandragupta II, *Journal of the Numismatic Society of India*, XXXVII, pp. 85-99.

Chattopadhyay, Aparna (1972), A Note on the Kācha Problem of Gupta History, *Journal of the Oriental Institute* (Baroda) XXII, Nos. 1-2, pp. 64-67.

Chattopadhyaya, Sudhakar (1953), The Later Imperial Guptas, *Indian Historical Quarterly*, XXIX, No 2, pp. 156-61.

—— (1958), *Early History of North India, from the Fall of the Mauryas to the Death of Harsha, c 200* BC – AD *650*, Calcutta.

Chhabra, B Ch (1947), Chandragupta's Abdication, *Indian Culture*, XIV, No. 4, pp. 141-50.

—— (1947), Coin-legends of the Gupta Emperors and the Vishṇu-sahasranāma, *Journal of the Numismatic Society of India*, IX (ii), pp. 137-45.

—— (1948), Allahabad Inscription of Samudragupta is not Posthumous, *Indian Historical Quarterly*, XXIV, No. 2, pp. 104-13.

—— (1963), Some Observations on the Bhitari Inscription of Skandagupta, *Journal of Indian History*, XLI (ii), pp. 543-49.

—— (1965), Beauties of the Bhitari Inscription of Skandagupta in G T Deshpande, *et al.* (ed.), *Felicitation Volume Presented to Mahamahopadhyaya Dr V V Mirashi*, Nagpur, pp. 362-71.

—— (1986), *Catalogue of the Gupta Gold Coins of the Bayana Hoard in the National Museum*, New Delhi.

Chhabra, B Ch, P K Agrawala, Ashvini Agrawal and Shankar Goyal (ed.) (1972), *Reappraising Gupta History for S R Goyal*, New Delhi.

Choudhary, Radha Krishna (1962-1963), Govindagupta of Vaiśālī Seal and Mandasor Inscription (A Gupta Emperor between G E 93 and 96), *Journal of the Oriental Institute* (Baroda), XII, No. 4, pp. 370-76.

—— (1964), A Critical Study of the So-called *Apratigha* Coin Type of Kumāragupta I, *Journal of the Numismatic Society of India*, XXVI (i), pp. 15-26.

—— (1964), A Rare Gupta Terracotta Seal of Samudragupta from Naulagarh, *Indian History Congress Proceedings*, Session XXVI, pt. I, pp. 137-40.

Curtis, J W (1958), Bhānugupta Prakāśāditya: Aspect of his Reign in the Light of a New Suvarṇa Variety, *Journal of the Numismatic Society of India*, XX, pp. 73-76.

Dandekar, R N (1941), *A History of the Guptas*, Poona.

—— (1982), *The Age of the Guptas and Other Essays*, Delhi.

Dani, A H (1958), Chandragupta I-Kumāradevī Coin Type, *Journal of the Numismatic Society of India*, XX, pp. 4-8.

—— (1964), Rāmagupta Problem – A New Solution, *Journal of the Numismatic Society of India*, XXVI (i), pp. 11-14.

Dasgupta, N N (1938), Rāmagupta, *Indian Culture*, IV, No. 2, pp. 216-22.

—— (1944), The Kācha Problem, *Indian Historical Quarterly*, XX, No. 4, pp. 351-52.

Dhavalikar, M K (1958), On the Attribution of the Aśvamedha Type of Samudragupta, *Journal of the Numismatic Society of India*, XX, pp. 175-77.

Dikshit, K N (1923), A Note on the Dates of the Gupta Copper-plates from Damodarpur, *Epigraphia Indica*, XVII, p. 193.

Dikshit, S K (1939), Chandragupta II, Sāhasāṅka alias Vikramāditya and the Nine Jewels, *Indian Culture*, VI, No. 2, pp. 191-210.

Dikshitar, V R R (1993), *The Gupta Polity*, (reprint), Delhi.

Diwakar, R R (1959), *Bihar Through the Ages*, Bombay.

Diwekar, H R (1919-20), Pushyamitras in the Gupta Period, *Annals of the Bhandarkar Oriental Research Institute*, I (ii), pp. 99-103.

Fleet, J F (1888), *Inscriptions of the Early Gupta Kings and their Successors, Corpus Inscriptionum Indicarum*, III, Calcutta.

—— (1890), Bhitari Seal of Kumāragupta II, *Indian Antiquary*, XIX, pp. 224-28.

Gai, G S (1969-70), Three Inscriptions of Rāmagupta, *Epigraphia Indica*, XXXVIII, pp. 46-49.The same article in *Journal of the Oriental Institute*, (Baroda), XVIII, pp. 247-251.

Ganguly, D C (1938), The Early Home of the Imperial Guptas, *Indian Historical Quarterly*, XIV(iii), pp. 532-35.
—— (1952), The Original Home of the Imperial Guptas, *Indian Historical Quarterly*, XXVIII, No. 4, pp. 386-91.
Ganguly, D K (1973-74), A Study of the Aśvamedha Coin Type of Samudragupta, *Visvabharati Quarterly*, XXXIX, Nos. 3-4, pp. 280-87.
—— (1981), The Rāmagupta Problem, *Journal of the Numismatic Society of India*, XLIII (ii), pp. 97-113.
—— (1987), *The Imperial Guptas and Their Times*, New Delhi.
Ghose, Ajit (1960), Discovery of a Second Gold Coin of Ghaṭotkachagupta, *Journal of the Numismatic Society of India*, XXII, pp. 260-61.
Ghosh, A (1939-40), Nalanda Plate of Samudragupta: The Year 5, *Epigraphia Indica*, XXV, pp. 50-53.
—— (1943), Nalanda Seals of Budhagupta and Vishṇugupta, *Indian Historical Quarterly*, XIX, pp. 119-25.
Giles, H A (1923), *The Travels of Fa-hsien*, London.
Gokhale, B G (1952), The Origin of the Imperial Guptas, *Journal of the Bombay Branch of the Royal Asiatic Society, New Series*, XXVII, Supplement, pp. 275-78.
—— (1962), *Samudragupta: Life and Times*, Bombay.
Gopal, Lallanji and Krishna Kanti Gopal (1989), Comments and Observations on the Lead Paper of S R Goyal, in M C Joshi and S K Gupta (ed.), *King Chandra and the Mehrauli Pillar*, Meerut, pp. 124-34.
Goyal, S R (1966), Nalanda and Gaya Records of Samudragupta, *Journal of the Bihar Research Society*, LII, pp. 52-55.
—— (1966), Attribution of the Coins of Prakāśāditya, *Journal of the Numismatic Society of India*, XXVIII (i), pp. 17-20.
—— (1967), *A History of the Imperial Guptas*, Allahabad.
—— (1980), Bihar Stone Pillar Inscriptions of the Imperial Guptas, *Journal of the Epigraphical Society of India*, VII, pp.49-53.
—— (1984), *Gupta Kālīna Abhilekha*, Meerut.
—— (1987), *Gupta Sāmrājya kā Itihāsa*, Meerut.
—— (1989), Re-appraisal of the problem of the identification of King Chandra, in M C Joshi and S K Gupta (ed.), *King Chandra and the Mehrauli Pillar*, pp. 107-37.
—— (1989), The Inscription of King Chandra: Text and Translation, in M C Joshi and S K Gupta (ed.), *King Chandra and the Mehrauli Pillar*, pp. 69-70.
—— (1994), *An Introduction to Gupta Numismatics*, Jodhpur.
—— (2005), *The Imperial Guptas*, Jodhpur.
Gupta, P L (1950), The Attribution of the Coins of Prakāśāditya, *Journal of the Numismatic Society of India*, XII(i), pp. 34-35.
—— (1950), Place of Kāchagupta in the Gupta Chronology, *Journal of the Numismatic Society of India*, XII(i), pp. 36-37.
—— (1950), The Coins of Rāmagupta, *Journal of the Numismatic Society of India*, XII(ii), pp. 103-11.

—— (1952), Place of Ghaṭotkachagupta in the Gupta Chronology, *Journal of the Numismatic Society of India*, XIV, pp. 99-102.

—— (1991), *Gupta Sāmrājya*, 2nd ed., Varanasi.

—— (1998), *The Imperial Guptas*, I, Varanasi.

Gupta, P L and Sarojini Srivastava (1981), *Gupta Gold Coins*, Varanasi.

Handa, Devendra (1971), A Clay Sealing from Sunet, *Vishveshvaranand Indological Journal*, IX (i), pp. 119-20.

Heras, H (1948), Kāchagupta and Rāmagupta, *Journal of the Bihar Research Society*, XXXIV (i-ii), pp. 19-27.

Hoernle, A F R (1889), Remarks on the above (Inscribed Seal of Kumāragupta II), *Journal of the Asiatic Society of Bengal*, LVIII, pp. 88-103, under the article 'Some Problems in Ancient Indian History'.

Indraji, Bhagwanlal (1881), The Kahaum Inscription of Skandagupta, *Indian Antiquary*, X, pp. 125-26.

Jagannath (1946), Are Skandagupta and Purugupta Identical? *All India Oriental Conference Proceedings*, Session 13, Part II, pp. 126-29.

Jain, B C (1977), Shankarpur Plate of Budhagupta and Harivarman: Gupta Year 166, *Journal of the Epigraphical Society of India*, IV, pp. 62-66.

Jain, K C (1972), *Malwa Through the Ages (from the Earliest Times to 1305 AD)*, Delhi.

Jaiswal, S K (1993), Can Kācha be Ghaṭotkacha, *Journal of the Numismatic Society of India*, LV, pp. 114-15.

Jayaswal, K P (1933), *History of India*, c. 150 AD to 350 AD (Nāga-Vākāṭaka Imperial Period), Lahore. The same as *in Journal of the Bihar and Orissa Research Society*, XIX (i & ii), 1933, pp. 1-222.

—— (1934), *An Imperial History of India in a Sanskrit Text (c. 700 BC – c. 770 AD) with a Special Commentary on the later Gupta period*, Lahore.

Jayaswal, P K (1966), On the Attribution of the Coins of Prakāśāditya, *Journal of the Numismatic Society of India*, XXVIII (i), pp. 65-68.

Joshi, M C (1959), Apratigha Type: A Study, *Journal of the Numismatic Society of India*, XXI, pp. 34-36.

Joshi, M C and S K Gupta (ed.) (1989), *King Chandra and the Mehrauli Pillar*, Meerut.

Jouveau-Dubreuil, G (1920), *Ancient History of Dekhan*, Pondicherry.

Kar, R C (1950), King Chandra of the Mehrauli Iron Pillar Inscription, *Indian Historical Quarterly*, XXVI, No. 3, pp. 184-92.

Kielhorn, F (1905-06), Talgunda Pillar Inscription of Kākusthavarman, *Epigraphia Indica*, VIII, pp. 24-36.

Krishna Dev (1941-42), Nalanda Seal of Vishṇugupta, *Epigraphia Indica*, XXVI, pp. 235-39.

Krishnarao, B V (1942), A *History of the Early Dynasties of Andhradesa, Madras.*

Legge, J H (1886), *Record of the Buddhistic Kingdoms*, Oxford.

Maity, S K (1961), Metrological Study of the Gold Coins of Early India, *Journal of the Numismatic Society of India*, XXIII, pp. 259-66.

—— (1975), *The Imperial Guptas and Their Times*, New Delhi.

Majumdar, R.C (1933), Literary Reference to Samudragupta, *Indian Historical Quarterly*, IX, No. 4, pp. 930-33.

—— (1943), King Chandra of Mehrauli Iron Pillar Inscription, *Journal of the Royal Asiatic Society of Bengal, Letters*, XIX, pp. 179-83.

—— (1944), A Forged Purāṇa Text on the Imperial Guptas, *Indian Historical Quarterly*, XX, pp. 345-50.

—— (1944), Bihar Stone Inscription of Skandagupta, *Indian Culture*, X, No. 4, pp. 170-73.

—— (1945), The Gaya and Nalanda Plates of Samudragupta, *Indian Culture*, XI, No. 4, pp. 225-30.

—— (1948), The Seal of Vainyagupta, *Indian Historical Quarterly*, XXXIV (i), pp. 67-68.

—— (1952), The Original Home of the Imperial Guptas, *Journal of the Bihar Research Society*, XXXVIII (iii-iv), pp. 410-18.

—— (1971), *History of Ancient Bengal*, Calcutta.

Majumdar, R C, and A S Altekar (ed.) (1946), *A New History of the Indian People, Vol. VI: The Vākāṭaka-Gupta Age (circa 200-500 AD)*, Lahore.

Majumdar, R C, and K K Dasgupta (ed.) (1981-82), *A Comprehensive History of India*, III, (part 1), New Delhi.

Majumdar, R C, and A D Pusalker (ed.) (1954), *History and Culture of the Indian People, III: The Classical Age*, Bombay.

McCrindle, J W (2000), *Ancient India as Described in Ptolemy*, reprint (first published 1927). New Delhi.

Mehta, R N and A M Thakkar (1978), *M S University Copper Plates of the time of Toramāṇa*, Baroda.

Mirashi, V V (1963), *Corpus Inscriptionum Indicarum*, V, *Inscriptions of the Vākāṭakas*, Ootacamund.

—— (1964) *Vākāṭaka Rājavaṁśa kā Itihāsa tathā Abhilekha*, Varanasi.

—— (1967), *Kālidāsa* (in Hindi), Bombay.

—— (1968), *Studies in Indology*, 3 vols., Nagpur.

—— (1980), Bhitari Stone Inscription of Skandagupta, *Journal of the Epigraphical Society of India*, VII, pp. 86-92.

—— (1982), *Indological Research Papers*, I, Nagpur.

—— (1982), Notes on D R Bandarkar's Inscriptions of the Early Gupta Kings, *Journal of the Epigraphical Society of India*, IX, pp. 48-57.

Mishra, R S (1989), Comments and Observations on the Lead Paper of S R Goyal, in M C Joshi and S K Gupta (ed.), *King Chandra and the Mehrauli Pillar Inscription*, pp. 143-48.

Mookerji, R K (1942-43), Character of Samudragupta from his Inscriptions and Coins, *Indian Culture*, IX, pp. 177-79.

—— (1948), Chandragupta II Vikramāditya (*c.* 376-414 AD), in *Vikrama Volume*, Gwalior, pp. 323-59.

—— (1997), *The Gupta Empire*, reprint, Delhi.

Mukherjee, B N (1981-82), The Hunza Valley and the Imperial Guptas, *Journal of the Bihar Research Society*, LXVII-LXVIII, p. 561-66.

—— (1983), Decipherment of the Shell Script, *Bulletin of Museums and Archaeology in UP*, No. 31, pp. 1-46, and plates.

—— (1992), *Coins and Currency System of Gupta Bengal*, New Delhi.

Mukherjee, B N, and T N Raychaudhuri (1990), *The Indian Gold, An Introduction to the Cabinet of the Gold Coins in the Indian Museum, Calcutta*, Calcutta.

Narayanan, M G S (1983), A Reappraisal of Samudragupta's *Digvijaya*, in B N Mukherjee *et al.* (ed.), *Sri Dineśacandrikā: Studies in Indology: Sri D C Sircar Festschrift*, Delhi, pp. 283-93.

Negi, J S (1966), *Some Indological Studies*, I, Allahabad.

Nilakanta Sastri, K A and G Srinivasachari (1970), *Advanced History of India*, Bombay.

Ojha, K C (1950), Was Kācha a Brother of Samudragupta?, *Journal of the Numismatic Society of India*, XII (ii), pp. 170-75.

—— (1951), An Analysis of the Rāmagupta Tradition, *Journal of the Bihar Research Society*, XXXVII (i & ii), pp. 39-47.

Pandey, Sushmita (1989), Comments and Observations on the Lead Paper of S R Goyal, in M C Joshi and S K Gupta (ed.), *King Chandra and the Mehrauli Pillar*, pp. 167-70.

Pandey, V C (1972), Samudragupta's Aśvamedha—A Reappraisal, *Annals of the Bhandarkar Oriental Research Institute*, LIII, pp. 228-32.

—— (1974), Vaṅgas and the Vāhlīkas of the Mehrauli Pillar Inscription, *Vishveshvaranand Indological Journal*, XII, pp. 241-45.

—— (1978), Bhitari Pillar Inscription: Some Observations, *Vishveshvaranand Indological Journal*, XVI (i), pp. 74-78.

Pandey, V C and A Pandey (1998), *A New History of Ancient India*, Jalandhar.

Panna Lall (1918), Some Problems of Gupta Chronology, *Journal of Bihar and Orissa Research Society*, IV (iv), pp. 412-17.

Pargiter, F E (1913), *The Purāṇa Text of the Dynasties of the Kali Age*, London.

Pathak, V S (1957), Notes on the Gupta Coinage: Chandragupta-Kumāradevī Type, *Journal of the Numismatic Society of India*, XIX (ii) pp. 135-44.

Pathak, V S and V B Rao (1989), Comments and Observations on the Lead Paper of S R Goyal, in M C Joshi and S K Gupta (ed.), *King Chandra and the Mehrauli Pillar*, pp. 190-96.

Raghavan, V (1947), The Allahabad Pillar Inscription, verses 3 and 8, *Journal of Oriental Research*, Madras, XVI (iii), pp. 159-62.

Rājaśekhara, *Kāvyamīmaṁsā* (Gaekwad Oriental Series, Baroda, No. 1 (1964).

Ramdas, G (1925), Kingdoms of the Deccan (mentioned in the Allahabad pillar inscription of Samudragupta), *Indian Historical Quarterly*, I, No. 4, pp. 679-89.

Rana, S S (1989), Some Observations on the Theory of S R Goyal, in M C Joshi and S K Gupta (ed.), *King Chandra and the Mehrauli Pillar*, p. 202.

Rapson, E J (1897), *Indian Coins*, Strassburg.

Ramesh, K V and S P Tiwari (1983), Risthal Inscription of Aulikara Prakāśadharmā (Vikrama) year 572, *Journal of the Epigraphical Society of India*, X, 96ff.

Raychaudhuri, H C (1989), Extracts from Some Earlier Suggestions on the Problem, in M C Joshi and S K Gupta (ed.), *King Chandra and the Mehrauli Pillar*, pp. 245-46.

—— (2004), *Political History of Ancient India* (with a commentary by B N Mukherjee), 7th ed., Oxford.

Roy, U N (1976), Govindagupta kā eka Abhinava Mūlyāṅkana, in S R Chaturvedi *et al.* (ed.), *Dr Raj Bali Pande Smriti Grantha*, Deoria, pp. 176-88.

—— (1981), A Fresh Investigation of the Imperial Gupta Capital, in J S Jha (ed.), *K P Jayaswal Commemoration Volume*, Patna, pp. 361-72.

—— (1996), *Gupta Rājavaṁśa tathā usakā Yuga*, 4th ed., Allahabad.

Sachau, E C (1914), *Kitab-ul-Hind*, English translation as *Alberni's India*, London.

Saraswati, S K (1935), A Gold Coin of Budhagupta, *Indian Culture*, I (iv), pp. 691-92.

Sarma, I K (1968), Bihar Stone Pillar Inscription–A Revised Study, *Journal of the Oriental Institute*, XVII, No. 3, pp. 267-74.

Sastri, H P (1913), King Chandra of the Mehrauli Pillar Inscription, *Indian Antiquary*, XLII, pp. 217-19.

Sastri, Hirananda (1942), *Nalanda and its Epigraphic Material*, (*Memoir of the Archaeological Survey of India*, No. 66), Delhi.

Sastri, Sakuntala Rao (1943), The Nalanda and Gaya Plates of Samudragupta, *Indian Culture*, X, No. 2, pp. 77-78.

—— (ed.), (1952), *Kaumudī-mahotsava*, Bombay.

Sen, B C (1942), *Some Historical Aspects of the Inscriptions of Bengal*, Calcutta.

—— (1989), Extracts from Some Earlier Suggestions on the Problem, in M C Joshi and S K Gupta (ed.), *King Chandra and the Mehrauli Pillar*, p. 263.

Seth, H C, Extracts from Some Earlier Suggestions on the Problem, in M C Joshi and S K Gupta (ed.), *King Chandra and the Mehrauli Pillar* (1989), pp. 250-51 (from *Journal of Indian History*, 1937, pp. 129f).

Shah, U P (1969), Some Aspects of the Rāmagupta Problem–A Reply to Mm Mirashi, *Journal of the Oriental Institute* (Baroda), XIX, Nos. 1-2, pp. 152-56.

Sharma, Dasharatha (1939), The Śaka Rival of Rāmagupta, *Indian Culture*, V, pp. 228-30.

—— (1953), The Origin and Original Home of the Imperial Guptas, *Journal of the Bihar Research Society*, XXXIX (iii), pp. 265-68.

—— (1956), The Interpretation of "*ā-kumāram manushyaiḥ*" of Skandagupta's Bhitari Inscription and Connected Problems, *Indian History Congress Proceedings*, Session XIX, pp. 148-50.

—— (1965), Some New Light from the Skandapurāṇa on the Dhāraṇa *gotra* of the Guptas, *Purāṇa*, VII, No. 1, pp. 183-85.

—— (1965), The Legitimacy of Skandagupta's Succession, *Journal of Indian History*, XLIII (i), pp. 219-25.

Sharma, G R (1945), Chandra of the Mehrauli Pillar Inscription, *Indian Historical Quarterly*, XXI, No. 3, pp. 202-12.

Sharma, M J (1974), The Identification of Kācha – A Fresh Study, *Journal of the Epigraphical Society of India*, I, pp. 75-84.

Sharma, T R (1978), *Personal and Geographical Names in the Gupta Inscriptions*, Delhi.

Shastri, A M (1979), *Kauśāmbī Hoard of Magha Coins*, Nagpur.

—— (1987), *Early History of the Deccan, Problems and Prospects*, Delhi.

—— (1989), Comments and Observations on the Lead Paper of S R Goyal, in M C Joshi and S K Gupta (ed.), *King Chandra and the Mehrauli Pillar*, pp. 85-89.

—— (1997) *Vākāṭakas: Sources and History*, Delhi.

—— (ed.) (1992), *The Age of the Vākāṭakas*, Delhi.

Shastri, R M (19), Mandasor Inscription of Vatsabhaṭṭi, *Indian Historical Quarterly*, IV, pp. 361-63.

Shukla, K S (1980), A Unique Gold Coin of Bhānugupta and Prakāśāditya, *Journal of the Numismatic Society of India*, XLII, pp. 120-26. (article on pp. 120-22, and Editor's note, pp. 122-26)

Singh, Jai Prakash (1976), *History and Coinage of Skandagupta Kramāditya*, Varanasi.

Sinha, B P (1954), *Decline of the Kingdom of Magadha* (circa 455-1000 AD), Delhi.

—— (1977), *Dynastic History of Magadha*, New Delhi.

—— (1989), Comments and Observations on the Lead Paper of S R Goyal, in M C Joshi and S K Gupta (ed.), *King Chandra and the Mehrauli Pillar*, pp. 93-94.

—— (1989), Extracts from Some Earlier Suggestions on the Problem, in M C Joshi and S K Gupta (ed.), *King Chandra and the Mehrauli Pillar* (1989), p. 255.

—— (1993), *Twilight of the Imperial Guptas*, Delhi.

—— (ed.), (1974), *Comprehensive History of Bihar*, I (ii), Patna.

Sircar, D C (1934), Samudragupta's Aśvamedha Sacrifice, *Journal of Indian History*, XIII (i), pp. 35-40.

—— (1938-39), A Note on the Damodarpur Grant of the time of Budhagupta and Jayadatta, *Indian Culture*, V, pp. 432-33.

—— (1939), Digvijaya of King Chandra of the Mehrauli Pillar Inscription, *Journal of the Royal Asiatic Society of Bengal, Letters*, V, pp. 407-15.

—— (1941), The Vāhlīkas of the Mehrauli Pillar Inscription, in S M Katre and P K Gode (ed.), *A Volume of Studies in Indology Presented to Prof P V Kane on his Sixty-first Birthday*, Poona, pp. 469-71.

—— (1941-42), Spuriousness of the Nalanda Plate of Samudragupta, *Epigraphia Indica*, XXVI, pp. 135-36.

—— (1943), Evidence of Nalanda Seals, *Indian Historical Quarterly*, XIX, pp. 272-281.

—— (1944), The *Bhavishyottarapurāṇa* and the Early Gupta History, *Journal of the Numismatic Society of India*, VI, pp. 34-36.

—— (1948), Govindagupta, *Indian Historical Quarterly*, XXIV, No. 1, pp. 72-75.

—— (1949-50), Sumaṇḍala Plates of the Time of Pṛithivīvigraha Bhaṭṭāraka: Gupta year 250, *Epigraphia Indica*, XXVIII, pp. 79ff.

—— (1950), Gupta Rule in Orissa, *Indian Historical Quartely*, XXVI, pp. 75-79.

—— (1958), End of the Gupta Empire, in H R Gupta (ed.), *Sir Jadunath Sarkar Commemoration Volume: Essays Presented to Sir Jadunath Sarkar*, II, pp. 343-47.

—— (1965), *Select Inscriptions Bearing on Indian History and Civilization*, I, 2nd ed., Calcutta.

—— (1968), *Studies in Indian Coins*, Delhi.
—— (1969), *Ancient Indian Malwa and Vikramāditya Tradition*, Delhi.
—— (1969-70), Vidiśā Jain Image Inscriptions of the Time of Rāmagupta, *Journal of Ancient Indian History, III*, pp. 145-51 (note 7 under Indological Notes).
—— (1987), Kumāragupta I and his Feudatory Bandhuvarman, in B Sahai (ed.), *History and Culture: B P Sinha Felicitation Volume*, New Delhi, pp. 212-14.
Sitholey, B S (1950), Was Kācha a Gupta Monarch, *Journal of the Numismatic Society of India*, XII, pp. 38-40.
Sivaramamurti, C (1951), Chakravikrama Type, *Journal of the Numismatic Society of India*, XIII, pp. 180-82.
Smith, Bardwell L (ed.), (1983), *Essays on Gupta Culture*, Delhi.
Smith, V A (1897), The Conquest of Samudragupta, *Journal of the Royal Asiatic Society of Great Britain and Ireland*, pp. 859-910.
—— (1897), The Iron Pillar of Delhi (Mehrauli) and the Emperor Chandra, *Journal of the Royal Asiatic Society of Great Britain and Ireland*, pp. 1-18.
—— (1906), *Coins of Ancient India: Catalogue of Coins in Indian Museum, Calcutta*, I, Oxford.
—— (1989), Extracts from Some Earlier Suggestions on the Problem, in M C Joshi and S K Gupta (ed.), *King Chandra and the Mehrauli Pillar*, pp. 241 and 247.
—— (1999), *The Early History of India*, 3rd edn, reprint, New Delhi.
Sohoni, S V (1957), Chandragupta I-Kumāradevī Coin Type: A Reexamination, *Journal of the Numismatic Society of India*, XIX (ii), pp. 145-54.
—— (1976), Govindagupta, *Journal of the Ganganath Jha Kendriya Sanskrit Vidyalaya*, XXXII, pp. 1-10.
Srivastava, A L (1974), Political Significance of the Legend *Lichchhavayaḥ*, *Journal of the Numismatic Society of India*, XXXVI, pp. 57-61.
Srivastava, Prashant (1996), *Aspects of Ancient Indian Numismatics*, Delhi.
—— (2004), Skandagupta and the Nāgas, in A K Sinha (ed.), *Perspectives in Indian History*, New Delhi, pp. 82-86.
Takakusu, J A (1896), *Records of the Buddhist Religion as Practised in India and the Malay Archipelago by I-tsing*, Oxford.
Thakur, Upendra (1961), Skandagupta and Hūṇas, *Journal of the Bihar Research Society*, XLVII, pp. 72-88.
Thakur, Vijay Kumar (1977), The Place of Kācha in Gupta Chronology, *Journal of the Numismatic Society of India*, XXXIX, pp. 108-113.
Thaplyal, K K (1969), Did Toramāṇa Conquer Gangetic Valley—Evidence of a Sealing Re-examined, *Journal of the Numismatic Society of India*, XXXI, pp. 184-85.
—— (1968-71), *Kumārāmātya* – A Review, *Bharati*, Nos 12-14, pp. 307-19.
—— (1971), Imperial Gupta Seals –A Review, *Journal of the Numismatic Society of India*, XXXIII (i), pp. 49-60.
—— (1972), *Kumārāmātya*—A Reappraisal, in B Ch Chhabra, P K Agrawal, Ashvini Agrawal and Shankar Goyal (ed.), *Reappraising Gupta History for S R Goyal*, New Delhi, pp. 224-31.
—— (1972), *Studies in Ancient Indian Seals*, Lucknow.

—— (1973), The Nalanda Seal of Vishṇugupta—Some Problems, *Journal of the Numismatic Society of India*, XXXV, pp. 166-70.

—— (1977-78), Observations on a Seal-die Bearing Incomplete Legend, *Epigraphia Indica*, XLII, pp. 158-60.

—— (1980-81), Chandragupta-Kumāradevī Commemorative Medals, *Purātattva*, No. 12, New Delhi, pp. 152-53.

—— (1985), *Inscriptions of the Maukharis, Later Guptas, Puöpabhūtis, and Yaśovarman of Kanauj*, Delhi.

—— (1989), Comments and Observations on the Lead Paper of S R Goyal, in M C Joshi and S K Gupta (ed.), *King Chandra and the Mehrauli Pillar*, pp. 117-21.

—— (1990-91), Kauśāmbī Sealing of *Mahārāja* Tilabhaṭṭa, *Prāgadhārā*, No. 1, pp. 123-25.

—— (1995), Scions of the Hitherto Unknown House of Kauśāmbī *vis-à-vis* Their Gupta Overlords, *Indian Historical Review*, XXI (ii) pp. 1-8.

—— (1997), Critique of the Views on the Identification of King Chandra of Mehrauli Pillar Inscription, in B M Khanduri and Vinod Nautiyal (ed.) *Hima Kanti—Archaeology, Art and History (Prof. K P Nautiyal Felicitation Volume)*, Delhi, pp. 189-203.

—— (1997), Parentage and Nativity of Dhruvasvāminī, Chief Queen of Chandragupta II, in J P Joshi (ed.), *Facets of Indian Civilization–Recent Perspectives (Essays in Honour of Prof. B B Lal)*, III, New Delhi, pp. 884-89.

—— (2000), Situating Govindagupta in History, *Indian Historical Review*, XXVII, pp. 41-60.

—— (2003), Gupta Inscriptions from Mathura, in Jitendra Kumar, (ed.) *Gupta Yugīna Mathura*, New Delhi, pp. 158-64.

—— (2006-07), Reappraisal of the Evidence Relating to the Horse Sacrifice of Samudragupta, *Jñāna- pravāha*, No. 10, pp. 37-48.

—— (2007), Kācha Coins: A Reappraisal, *Journal of the Numismatic Society of India*, LXIX, pp. 91-106.

—— (2010), Reappraisal of the Evidence Relating to the Historicity of Rāmagupta, in *Bulletin of Museums and Archaeology in UP*, Nos. 57-58, pp. 23-46.

—— (2010), Name, Status and Date of the First King of the Imperial Gupta Dynasty in S D Trivedi (ed.), *The Glorious Heritage of India* (in Memory of. Prof. R C Sharma), Delhi, pp. 329-36.

—— Observations on the Theory of two Narasiṁhaguptas in the Gupta History in S Bandyopadhyaya Felicitation Volume (in press).

—— (2012) Chandragupta I—the First *Mahārājādhirāja* of the Imperial Gupta Dynasty: an Historical Reconstruct, in Srinivas V Padigar and B Shivananda (ed.), Pratnakīrti: Recent Studies in Epigraphy, History, Archaeology and Art, in honour of Prof. Srinivas Ritti, Vol. II, Delhi, pp. 309-20.

Thaplyal, K K, and A K Srivastava (1982), Mathura Stone Inscription of the time of Budhagupta, Gupta Year 161, *Journal of the Epigraphical Society of India*, IX, pp. 6-11.

Trautmann, Thomas R (1972), Lichchhavidauhitra, *Journal of the Royal Asiatic Society of Great Britain and Ireland*, pp. 2-15.

Upadhyaya, Vasudeva (1971), Prayāga–The Capital of the Guptas, *Journal of the Bihar Research Society*, LVII, pp. 11-20.

—— (1974), *Gupta Abhilekha*, Patna.

Verma, T P (1989), Comments and Observations on the Lead Paper of S R Goyal, in M C Joshi and S K Gupta (ed.), *King Chandra and the Mehrauli Pillar*, pp. 180-186.

—— (1992), Samudragupta: the Founder of the Gupta Dynasty, in B Ch, Chhabra *et al.* (ed.), *Reappraising Gupta History for S R Goyal*, New Delhi.

—— (2006-07), The Nalanda and the Gaya Copperplate Grants of Samudragupta, *Prāgadhāra*, No.17, pp. 113ff.

Watters, T (1961). *On Yuan Chwang's Travels in India* (I and II in one volume), reprint, Delhi.

# Index